CW00672027

NORTHAMPTON TOWN F.C.
THE OFFICIAL
CENTENARY HISTORY

By:
Frank Grande

Published by:
Yore Publications
12 The Furrows, Harefield,
Middx. UB9 6AT

© Frank Grande 1997

....

All rights reserved
No part of this publication may be reproduced or copied in any manner
without the prior permission in writing of the copyright holders

British Library Cataloguing-in-Publication Data
A catalogue record for this book
is available from the British Library

ISBN 1 874427 67 4

YORE PUBLICATIONS specialise in football books, normally of an historic nature...
Club histories, Who's Who books, etc. plus non-League football.
Three free Newsletters are issued per year, for your first copy,
please send a S.A.E. to the address above.

Printed and bound by The Bath Press

Foreword by Barry Stonhill
(Vice-Chairman Northampton Town F.C.)

When I was first approached to write this forward I was somewhat taken aback bearing in mind that I can only reflect on a small section of The Cobblers centenary of action. I also felt greatly honoured and I only hope that in the bicentenary publication people will feel that during my involvement with the Club progress was made.

It is only when you are involved in the "inner circle" that you fully realise the difficulties of running a professional football club like Northampton and I take my hat off to people like Nev Ronson who kept the club afloat at no little cost to himself during the seventies.

I arrived in Northampton in the early seventies but didn't really become involved with the Cobblers until the early eighties when the club was playing at the dilapidated County Ground with a gate of under 1 000 and permanently marooned towards the foot of the then fourth division. My wife Jacqui worked for the club on matchdays and had been a Cobblers fanatic since birth (you should see our loft full of programmes). She urged me to do something about it and at that time a late great friend of mine Charles Barham and I formed the "Friends of the Cobblers" which coincided with the arrival of Derek Banks. The money raised by this organisation purchased Richard Hill and Trevor Morley. Charlie and Mark Deane joined the board and I followed a year later.

During my time with the club I have worked with 4 Chairmen - Derek Banks, Richard Underwood, Michael McRitchie (albeit for 2 months) and Barry Ward. Certainly Derek and Richard had good intentions for the club and enjoyed limited success but the problem always seemed to be the well documented difficulties surrounding the County Ground, which meant the club just got deeper and deeper in debt. I have also worked with 5 managers - Graham Carr, Theo Foley, Phil Chard, John Barnwell and Ian Atkins and one day I will write a book on my experiences with all these various gentlemen which I can assure you would make more than interesting reading to any Cobblers fan.

It was always my ambition to relocate the club and this dream became reality in 1994 when the Cobblers arrived at Sixfields. I can assure you the club owes a great debt to people like Alwyn Hargrave, Les Patterson and Geoff Howes for their foresight and support and Sixfields is the catalyst for the progress of Northampton Town F.C. The Cobblers are no longer a joke with the Football League and the foundations for the future are well in place both on and off the field.

Another highlight was of course WEMBLEY 1997. Who on earth could ever forget the scenes of this most famous of stadiums before and after the match. Surely one of the best days in the life of all Cobblers fans and I just wonder what a second visit to the twin towers would be like? Here's hoping we find out before the next 100 years.

Obviously I have mentioned various names in this foreword but I have saved the best to last. The real unsung heroes of Northampton Town over the last 10 years or so are people like David Kerr, Barry Hancock, Martin Church and Bob Church who I can assure you have kept the club alive. These people do not receive the recognition their actions deserve and without them Northampton Town would have "died" during the early Nineties and that's a fact! Barry Ward and latterly Chris Smith have also been great servants of the club and all the directors of Northampton Town F.C. are fans of the club and chants of "sack the board" do hurt when all anyone is trying to do is what is best for the cobblers.

Thank you for taking the time to read my notes and raise a glass to the next 1 00 years of Northampton Town F.C. - The Cobblers.

THE COBBLERS

- 1897 - 1997 -

Acknowledgements:

To 'The Chronicle and Echo' for their assistance, and for permission to use the Wembley photograph on the dust-jacket, and to Simon Atkins, the photographer.

To John Harley for his constant checking and updating.

To Dave Walden for the use of his collection of old photographs.

To Pete Norton, club photographer, for the use of his modern team photographs.

To my wife Tina, who checks my spelling, corrects my grammar, and gave me 100% backing on this project.

To Sean & Helen O'Callaghan, Will Townley, and Dave Twydell for the use of additional illustrations and photographs.

Unfortunately original photograph copies of a number of illustrations within the book could not be traced, and therefore the quality of reproduction on these is not to as a high a standard as desired. However, it was felt that the inclusion of these would be appreciated, if only for record purposes, rather than to omit them.

Every effort has been taken to trace the source of photographs and illustrations, and accordingly acknowledged above, but this has not always been possible, and therefore apologies are offered should copyright have inadvertently been infringed.

CONTENTS

CHAPTER ONE
1897-1907

1897-98

When Albert Joseph Darnell accepted an invitation to accompany the Northampton Town boys to watch them play Leicester boys as a curtain raiser to a Leicester Fosse v Notts County Second Division match on September the 12th 1896, little did anyone realise this would be the conception of Northampton Town Football Club. Darnell was a well respected Solicitor in the town. He was also well known as a lover of sport, already secretary of the cricket club, an ex-Rugby player, and he was now to pioneer the town into professional football. He watched the boys game, but it was the league game that followed that 'hooked' Darnell - a 3-2 win for Notts County. From that moment on he made energetic enquiries about all aspects of professional football.

It could well be that the people who invited Darnell, who was known as 'Pat', may well have had something like this in mind, for they were schoolteachers who, only a season before, had set up a schools League. Many had come from outside the area and were somewhat surprised that the County town had no professional football club, while many of the smaller teams in the area had been playing professional football for some time. Arthur 'Dado' Jones was one of the teachers, he was a Welshman who had recently taken a post at Military Road school, after moving from Wellingborough, and was surprised that the town had shown no interest in a professional football club. It took some time but, on the 6th March 1897, a meeting was held at the Princess Royal on the Wellingborough Road, and from that gathering Northampton Town F.C. was born.

A committee was formed; Darnell became President, Jones, the Secretary, and the host of the Public House, Charlie Gyde, elected treasurer. L.Swain, and W. Westmorland - headmaster at St.Matthews boys school - were also enthusiastic members, as was Dave Stanton, master tailor, and later landlord of the 'Cock Hotel'. The County Ground was obtained, with the proviso that the games did not start until September 1st, and ended by May 1st. At this stage it was just a pitch, for everything else had to be added later as money became available.

"The Southern League match between Crystal Palace and New Brompton will decide which club is nearly as bad as Northampton Town"

'The Referee' 1907

Application was made, and accepted, to join the Northants League (later and currently known as the United Counties League), and the first professional was signed on a part-time basis, Frank 'Waff' Howard, a centre-half from St.Giles Rovers, a cabinet maker by trade. He was followed by Albert Dunkley, a left-winger from Rushden, plus Charlie Baker, a centre-forward from the same area, who earned his living as a cooper. The rest of the players were made up of enthusiastic Amateurs.

Before a ball was kicked, the club encountered its first problem. The club formed itself as *'Northampton Football Club'*, but the Rugby club protested that this was their name. Mr.Roland Hill made a protest to the football Association, and a meeting was set up in London, when a compromise was reached that the soccer club was to be called *'Northampton Town Football Club'*.

The new team kicked off with a friendly versus the 48th Regiment at Wootton Barracks, and won 7-1. The club's debut at the County Ground followed, against Earls Barton. Barton had lost their trainer the week before, and all the players wore black arm bands. Northampton won 4-1, with Albert Dunkley scoring two of the goals..... against his brother in the Barton goal.

There were only Eight teams in the Northants League, which gave a fixture list of just 14 games, so the club 'padded' out its season with friendlies, and also entered the Junior Cup and Wellingborough Charity Cup.

The first league gamed ended in a 2-0 defeat at Desborough, and the second a 4-1 reverse to Rushden Reserves; it was a shame that the first goal registered to the club was to be an own goal. However, the first league match at home gave the club its first victory, with Maurice Jones - believed to be a relative of Arthur - netting twice in a 3-1 victory.

It is interesting to note that the newspaper report of the day stated around 500 people watched the match, although later it was revealed that the takings were

9/4½d (47p), either an over-estimation by the reporter, or a lot of free entrants!

George Thompson had the honour of taking the club's first penalty, versus Finedon reserves, and missed, but made amends with his second attempt against Wellingborough Reserves. He was later to play for England..... at cricket! George was the County's first international, was also assistant secretary at the cricket club, and it seemed was 'available' to fill in on occasions.

The club signed T.Minney a half-back from Rushden in early December, and he bolstered the side who were not doing too badly in their first season. Local lad, J.Litchfield, was taken on in a friendly v Wolverton reserves, and scored one of the three

A.J.Darnell

goals. He was on the scoresheet again versus Raunds, in the league this time, and netted a hat-trick, but never scored again. The Raunds game made history, a 6-3 win for Northampton at the County Ground, but the Town forward Baker, and the visitors defender Bailey were both booked and then sent off - although later both agreed that they were continuing a personal feud that had gone on for some years. Full back W.Liddell was a commercial traveller, and was not always in a position to assist, but he was to have a bearing on the club's history in future years.

Leicester agreed to send a team if the club would pay them a 'guarantee', which they did, but only Eight players turned up, and most of these were reserves. Northampton lent them three men, some kit, and then thrashed the visitors 8-1!

It seemed that disinterest was setting in when, in the last game of the season at Kettering, the club had to 'borrow' two town league players, and played several more out of position, in an attempt to put 11 men on the field. Even then one missed the train and did not arrive until half-time, hence the 5-1 thrashing by Kettering reserves.

Northampton town finished fourth in the league and lost £54 on the season, but overall not a bad start.

1898/99

The 1898/99 season was one to remember, for the Northants League was won with 28 out of a possible 32 points. Only one game was lost and maximum points were obtained at home. Everard Lawrence, a forward, signed from Wellingborough and netted 30 goals in as many games, including friendlies. Full-back Byles scored with nine of the twelve penalties awarded, while new winger, Billy Brawn, a man who lived up to his name at six feet and weighing thirteen stone, supplied many of the goals.

The club also reached the finals of the Northants Senior Cup and the Wellingborough Junior Cup, falling at the last hurdle in both cases over a five day period, however any joy was soured in the F.A.Cup. After beating Hinckley in the first qualifier, they drew Wellingborough, who they beat 2-0. However, their opponents complained that Northampton should not have played Spencer as there was some problem with his registration. The F.A. deemed the match should be replayed, this time without Spencer, and Welling-borough won 6-1.

Another incident took place, away at Kettering Reserves. Northampton took a 1-0 lead in a match that was played in a snowstorm, and Kettering asked for the game to be abandoned. The referee refused and the home players walked off 15 minutes from time, but the League ruled the 1-0 result to Northampton should stand.

The end of the season saw the first player 'sold', when Frank Howard was sold to Derby for £50. A solid centre-half with a quick temper, who once smashed up his parents' grandfather clock, thinking it was an intruder! He never made it at Derby and was to return some years later, via Wellingborough, and in the 30's became a gateman at the County Ground. He always maintained he never got his 5% of the transfer sum.

1899/00

It was decided to join the Midland League for the 1899/1900 season, with a higher standard of play, and the club had a healthy balance sheet, making over £200 profit on the previous season. The club put their faith in that season's players, signing only goalkeeper Leo Bullimer, and forward Bill Miller, the only two with any experience.

The season started at Wellingborough, and was the first ever game at the Dog and Duck. The game was held up due to a torrential rainstorm two minutes before half-time and the referee took the players off early, brought them back, played two minutes the same way, then turned straight around; the game ended 2-2. A South African team, the Kaffirs, were touring the Country and stopped off at the County Ground - the first foreign football team to do so - and provided entertaining opponents in Northampton's 7-4 victory .

Letter to Frank Howard from his new club - Derby.
He was the first player be transferred.

Reads: " Dear Sir, Enclosed please find cheque for £4-0-0 for wages due to you to this date. The Directors have decided that training for next season shall commence on Wednesday August 2nd after which date no further leave of absence can be allowed . I shall therefore be glad if you will make your arrangements accordingly and report yourself at the Baseball Ground at 2.30 p.m. on the day named.
Yours truly,

J.H.R.Richardson Secretary.

The club was progressing well in its new league, but were finding plenty of teething problems, like the time that Burton Wanderers arrived late, and the game finished in darkness. In one match, both 'keepers were injured, but luckily it was only a friendly v Burwell, and the club borrowed Thraves, from Leicester, who had played in that Leicester Fosse/Notts County game that had captured Darnell's imagination.

A home match v Doncaster Rovers saw the referee fail to appear, and Arthur Jones took up the whistle, and while playing Burton at their new ground near the River Trent, three footballs were used. The first two were kicked into the river and were carried away by the current.

Alex Stewart joined the club in October. He was a much travelled forward, in the veteran stages, but his foresight and knowledge played a large part in showing combination forward play. On January the 23rd, Billy Brawn joined Sheffield United for a 'nominal fee' plus a game. Ironically it was not United, but his next club - Aston Villa - where he would find fame, and go on to play for England.

Third position, was achieved, in the team's first Midland League season, producing support around 2-3,000 for home games, and money was also raised from a two day bazaar at the corn exchange.

1900/01

Interest was being shown in the new club, and better quality players were joining. Six new faces appeared at the County Ground, including Jimmy Frost, a right-winger from Wolverton, Tom Scrivens a much travelled forward, and Dick Murrell who came from Wellingborough. Murrell was to have a long relationship with the club, and was a great favourite with the crowd because of his 100% effort. An example was the game at Ilkeston, where he had to be helped off the field but came back and scored the winner from 25 yards. Tom Scrivens was finding the net regularly, and helped himself to four goals in a 7-0 win at home to Coalville, it could have been more as two efforts were disallowed. F.A.Cup winners Bury came to the County Ground in October to play an exhibition match, when 3,000 supporters watched the League side win 4-0, but went away happy having seen one of the best games of football ever played.

The clubs venture into the F.A.Cup this season, away to Hinckley, was doomed from the start, for first team 'keeper Bullimer was injured, and the reserve goalie, Whiting, was ineligible, so the third choice, Clarke, had to play. The bad luck continued when free-scoring Scrivens broke his leg, much to the annoyance of the referee who insisted he was despatched to the dressing room as swiftly as possible, as he wanted to get on with the game. Still in pain, Scrivens was carried to the Station on a stretcher after the game and brought home, where he was taken to hospital; he never played football again. It seemed of little interest that the game had ended in a 0-3 defeat.

If that was not enough, the two clubs were to meet at the County Ground the following Saturday, in a Midland League match, but only five Hinckley players turned up, the rest had missed their connection, and when it became obvious that the rest were not going to appear, the club had to refund the gate money.

Bill Miller who played for the club the previous season, but had decided to retire, signed again, as a replacement for Scrivens, and no sooner had he put pen to paper then it was discovered Jimmy Frost was ill and would not play for some time, so the club coaxed Albert Dunkley back to Northampton. Dunkley had joined Leicester in the hope of playing League football, but had lost his place and was happy to return to Northampton. He did leave again at the end of the season and played for New Brompton, Bristol Rovers - where he won a Southern League championship medal - Blackburn and Blackpool, before two knee operations ended his professional career. He returned to Northampton taking over the 'Old house at Home' in the Wellingborough road, and often turned out for the reserves between 1908-1912. He remained at the public house until his death in the late 1940's.

Sheffield United Reserves had ran away with the Midland League title, but Northampton had made a comfortable third position, hence the club applied to join the Southern League, only one league away from the Football League itself, a great achievement considering they were just four years old.

1901/02

It was also decided to upgrade the reserves, who until now were all Amateurs playing in the town league, for now they were to join the Northants League, and allow the fringe professionals to play. With the exception of Jimmy Frost, who was now fully fit, a complete new forward line was signed; Herbert Chapman from Worksop, John Coleman from Kettering, Arthur Saxon from Bedminster and Joe Farrell from New Brighton.

Fred Cooke a goalkeeper from Wellingborough also joined the club. Despite losing the first Southern League game, away to Reading by 3-1, the club made great strides and a 3-1 victory over Tottenham brought great praise from the national press.

Another old face returned, in the shape of Everard Lawrence - the prolific scorer in the 1898/99 season. He found goals a little bit harder to come by in this league, but having converted to a left winger, he put in some stirring performances.

It was fair to say the league was an unknown quantity, as far as the opposition was concerned, for an 11-0 defeat at Southampton was followed by two 1-0 victories at New Brompton and West Ham, and then a 5-1 defeat at Portsmouth was followed by an 8-0 home win over Swindon. The defeat at Southampton, the worst ever in the club's history, was put down to the fact that the train they caught from Waterloo stopped at every station, and they arrived just minutes before kick-off. Then it was discovered they only had boots for a hard pitch, and the ground was like a quagmire, and of course, Southampton were a far better team.

Eleventh out of Sixteen teams was not a bad result for the club's first season in this league. Once again lady luck played a hand in the season, both good and bad. On one occasion the team kit got lost in changing connections on the railway, amazingly the game was only at Kettering, then being 2-0 down at Wellingborough and losing Chapman with a broken collar bone, but luck changed sides for Northampton ran out 4-2 winners. While playing at Millwall, the home side scored and the ball was kicked out of the ground; minutes later, with a new ball, Millwall 'scored' again, but as they did so the original ball came back on the pitch and the referee disallowed the claimed goal!

The F.A.Cup brought the most interest that season. It started at Gresley, who were offered money to switch the fixture, but refused and Northampton won 2-0. Then Burton were offered the same deal, they too refused and were despatched at the third attempt, after an abandonment and a draw. Kettering were next to go, after a replay, which saw a train derailment and several players and the referee arrive late. After Darwen fell 4-1 in the next round, for the first time ever, Northampton were in the F.A.Cup proper, with a home tie versus Sheffield United.

United offered Northampton £50, and half the gate, to switch the fixture, but the Southern League side were having none of it, and set their stall out for a record crowd of 15,000, with the gates being closed before the game started when the match receipts totalled £399. United won the tie 2-0, but it gave the Northampton public the chance to see 'Fatty' Foulkes and 'Nudger' Needham, two of football's great characters.

There was a mass clear out during the close season, but the club had no say in it and did not receive a penny. Almost as the clock struck 12 midnight on the day their contracts expired, the players were approached by representatives of League teams; Coleman and Lawrence joined Arsenal, Chapman went to Sheffield United - who offered him the chance to continue his mining exams - Farrell joined West Ham, and Pell went to Glossop. In Arsenal's defence, they did offer the Cobblers, as they were now known, a friendly match later in the season.

Again the character of Darnell shone through, many would have said 'enough is enough', realising quality players were going to be snapped up for nothing, but he just got on with the job; it was easy to see why the Southern League were so keen to have him on their management committee. Herbert Dainty, a Kettering based centre-half, and Len Benbow a centre-forward from Stoke, were the new acquisitions.

The club had made a profit of over £1,000 in their first Southern League season and were going some way to clearing their debts.

1902/03
There was an indifferent start to the season, but on the 18th of October, the club made the national newspapers, when they beat Portsmouth 1-0, at Fratton Park, through a Len Benbow goal. Nothing too startling in that, but it was Portsmouth's first ever defeat at Fratton Park, in 66 games, and the day also turned out to be one of their longest journeys, leaving Northampton at 8.48 am on the Saturday, and arriving home 1.30 am on Sunday morning. It was about this time that the rail services realised Northampton had a football team, and Midland Railway ran an excursion to Burton for the F.A.Cup match for just 3/3d (17p), however the cup run was to be short-lived, as Burton won 2-0.

Two home matches were abandoned that season, the first against Reading when the referee arrived late, then stopped the game eight minutes from time with Reading winning; however

James Frost who was a player with the club for seven years, from 1900

the Berkshire team had the last laugh, for they won the re-match 2-0. The second game was against Q.P.R., when Leo Bullimer was asked to replace Cooke in goal as the management committee felt the usual 'keeper needed to be 'rested'. But Bullimer refused because of the 'stick' he was receiving from a section of the home crowd, and Cooke played after all; but the game only lasted 45 minutes before bad weather intervened! Leo Bullimer was christened Bouillimier, and was of French extraction. A colourful character, he had played in goal for Brighton - where he had saved a man from drowning - and Lincoln, before coming to Northampton. When the club joined the Southern League, he stepped down from the number one spot and ran the reserves, and later took up the whistle becoming a first class referee, before casting his attentions to the other side of the County Ground. He became the cricket club scorer, and raised much needed money for them during the 1930's.

During a Southern League match at Kettering, a home forward, Wally Smith, shoulder-charged Cooke - in the accepted manner of the day - and nothing more was thought of it until he was taken ill in the dressing rooms, helped home, and a doctor called. Smith was despatched to hospital and for some time it was felt his life was in danger, his illness due to internal injuries, however he recovered and later played for the Cobblers,

Who could have realised that when a meeting was set up at the Exeter rooms in March 1903, in an attempt to raise money for summer wages and new players, it would be repeated some 90 years later. However, the £500 needed was no where near the figure quoted in 1992.

Len Benbow finished the season, not only as the club's top scorer, with 22 Southern League goals, but also the top scorer in the League; he also beat Everard Lawrence's club record of 18 goals. On a lighter note, thieves broke into the County Ground, and emptied the contents of the penny in the slot gas meter, not knowing it had been emptied the day before; they got away with one shilling (5p)!

1903/04
Once again many of the better players were snapped up by League clubs, Herbert Dainty agreed to sign for another season, but when Notts County offered him better terms he left, five of last seasons regular first team moved on and it was a case of seeing what was available.

Murray, a winger, came from Sunderland and McIntyre, a forward, was signed from Walsall - but the biggest coup was the signing of William Perkins, a goalkeeper, who had helped Liverpool to the League championship only a few seasons earlier. It was not a good start to the season, in fact it was the fourth game before they picked up their first win, 2-1 over Bristol Rovers. Local lad Harry Brown scored both, and he hit another brace in the 4-0 victory over Brighton.

The F.A.Cup saw an exit at the first hurdle at Wellingborough, on a pitch that was so bad there were no markings, and in some places was ankle deep in water. Despite protests from the Cobblers, the referee insisted the game went on, and Wellingborough won 2-0. Arthur Jones returned to Northampton and wrote a letter to the F.A. but the result stood. This showed some of the character of Arthur Jones, who was a schoolteacher, with the general attitude of the victorian schoolteacher, he demanded attention and respect, and was to some - bombastic - but he was 100% a Northampton Town man. One old-time supporter related a story about Jones, recalling when he walked into the ground one day to pay for his season ticket, and Jones was giving a lecture to the players. *"What do you want?"*, he enquired of the supporter: *"I want to pay for my season ticket,"* the supporter replied. *"I'm busy, you will have to come back"* Jones retorted. *"Either you take it now, or not at all; I am not coming back"*, the supporter snapped, unhappy at the Secretary's attitude, and at being made to look small in front of the players. There was a few moments silence, and then Jones spoke calmly, *"Then give me your address, sir, I will come to you."* and he did!

By October Harry Brown had joined West Bromwich Albion, together with Fred Cooke. No one wanted to see Brown go, but at least the club were getting a fee for him, unlike the players who were spirited away when their contracts expired. Harry Brown was only 19, and he gave good service to West Brom., Southampton, Bradford City, Fulham and Newcastle, the latter with whom he won a League Championship medal. He retired in 1913 and became a publican, but contracted diabetes, which led to blindness and his premature death in 1934.

Problems with the trains caused Northampton to arrive late for a league match versus Southampton, and the game kicked off at 3.15, before being abandoned at half-time due to bad light. It was decided it would be more economic to stay in Southampton and play the game the following Monday. Unfortunately Ralph Howe, the left-half, was taken ill over the weekend, but because they only had the 11 players, he had to play, and

Southampton won 5-1. A Boxing Day game with Luton was full of incident. First Clarke, the Cobbler's full-back missed his train, and arrived 10 minutes after the start, then the referee went off injured, and a linesman took over. It was one of the worst seasons to date, and only Kettering's poor form kept the club from bottom spot. They ended 15th out of 18 clubs, but the reserves were on a roll.

On the fifth of April the first team, without a fixture, played a Northants League game with Kettering that won the point that gave them the Northants League championship, while the reserves themselves beat Wellingborough in the Wellingborough Charity Cup. Four days later, the second eleven beat Desborough to win the Northants. Junior Cup.

1904/05
Ex-England International centre-half, Arthur Chadwick signed for the club from Portsmouth, having won three Southern League championship medals with Southampton, and another with the Fratton Park club. Bill Marriot, a left-winger, came from Aston Villa, and another old face returned, Herbert Chapman. He had by now joined Notts County, but was in dispute with the club, and although still on their books joined Northampton. Many players who 'fell out' with their League clubs, signed for Southern League teams, as the latter were not bound by rules of the former.

After two games the Cobblers topped the Southern League but came down with a bang, in a 0-3 defeat at Portsmouth, which saw both Chadwick and Benbow having to leave the field, injured. A home game versus Brentford saw the Cobblers change at half-time as their claret stripes, clashed with the 'Bees' red and white stripes. Northampton Town had the smallest wage bill in the Southern League, having only 15 professionals, the rest of the squad being made up of willing amateurs, but attendances were averaging just over 4,000.

The F.A.Cup threw up some interesting facts, and stories. In the first qualifying round that season, the Cobblers were drawn away to Burton United, and they offered them £25 plus half the gate to switch the fixture. The United refused, only to find their share of their home gate was just £23, and they lost into the bargain. Next round, was an away game at Kettering, which resulted in another victory for the Cobblers, but an unusual incident occurred during the game when the referee twice spoke to a linesman, and then dispensed with his services; the game continued with one linesman!

Leicester Fosse were next but by the time the game came round the bad weather had set in, and 50 of the town's unemployed were used to clear ice and snow off the pitch. It could well have been the inclement weather that kept the crowd down to 4,000 for this match against local league opposition, for the week before 6,000 had watched the club lose, 3-0 to Southampton. The cup match ended 2-2, when Len Benbow returned and scored the goals, but for the replay he was forced to play left-back and the forward power went, allowing Leicester a 2-0 victory.

Back to the Southern League, and the customary fixture at Luton saw five penalties awarded, three to Luton, all converted, and two to Northampton, who scored with one one and missed the second, in the 2-4 defeat.

Two pieces of club history were made in a four day period in January. A friendly with Port Vale saw Len Benbow injured again, and both clubs agreed to allow Herbert Chapman on as his substitute - the first case of a Northampton player being substituted - while four days later, in a league match versus Norwich, Jimmy Frost scored direct from a corner, the first time this was achieved by the club. Then some bombshells were dropped. With Len Benbow still injured, and his situation looking bad, he was sent to Manchester to see a knee specialist; Notts County, called back Herbert Chapman, and sold him to Tottenham for £250; the remaining 13 league games realised just eight goals, and one of those was via an opponents boot.

Len Benbow made a one match comeback versus Southampton, at centre-half, and he scored the Cobbler's goal in a 1-1 draw, significant in the fact it was the first point won against the Saints. For the away match at Watford, the railway company ran a special excursion for the game, but with a total crowd of 2,500 it seemed that not many bothered to take it up.

Twelfth position was not bad considering the upheavals of the season.

1905/06
The AGM revealed that the club had made a profit of £436 in the 1904/05 season, and the working loss was down to £1,618.

Again the club tried to sign experienced players. Drennan joined the club from Aston Villa, replacing Dillon Clarke who had moved to Southampton. From Arsenal came the experienced Gooing, at centre-forward; Turner, an outside-left came from Southampton, to replace Marriott who had moved in the other direction; Platt (Portsmouth), Tirrell (Kettering) and Cole (Wellingborough), were also engaged.

Three defeats in the first three league games, and 12 goals conceded was not the start the club were looking for, however, there was a bright spot when they entertained A.C.Parisian in a friendly, which was won 9-0, and a penalty was missed. A 2-1 home defeat by Southampton was made worse when another penalty was missed, and amateur Springthorpe, failed to appear. It was the 6th league game, home to Reading, that the team recorded their first win, Jack Platt scoring the only goal of the game, then the Cobblers strung a six match undefeated run together, lifting themselves off the bottom of the league.

It took two matches to dispose of West Stanley in the F.A.Cup but the club fell at the next hurdle, away to New Brompton. It was interesting to read the description of the West Stanley ground, prior to the cup-tie, being described thus; 'take the worst part of Cow Meadow, the worse piece of the racecourse, put on a slope as bad as the Kettering Grounds, cover it with pools of water and as much mud as you like, and you have the West Stanley ground'.

Jimmy Frost missed the replay with West Stanley and was replaced by his brother George, a Wolverton Amateur, who also appeared in the league game which followed, versus Queens Park Rangers. In December Arsenal offered £350 for James Frost but it was turned down, the club did not want to lose one of their biggest assets, while Frost himself was not keen to leave. Despite all the problems on and off the field, the club never lost sight of its commitments, for both Jimmy Frost and Ralph Howe were awarded testimonials, and a game was played at Kettering to help the club who were struggling to survive.

Back on the field things went from bad to worse. An away game versus Bristol Rovers saw four players injured, two more were injured in the next game, then Springthorpe an Amateur, announced he would not be able to accompany the side to Southampton, so, with six reserves in the side, the Saints won 9-1.

Benbow had just 15 minutes training before his knee gave way, and it looked like the end of his playing career, while Dilks the winger was injured in a cycling accident. Despite finishing bottom of the league, there were a couple of highlights, for amateurs A. Vann, B. Vann, Denton and Springthorpe were picked to tour Europe with the top Amateur side, the Pilgrims, and the penultimate home game, with Luton, attracted a crowd of 9,000, with receipts of £222. One interesting fact emerged, for while the club finished bottom of the Southern League, their reserve side were third in the United Counties League.

George Cooch, a goalkeeper from Wellingborough, replaced Perkins, and Mark Watkins, an ex-Welsh international centre-forward came in for Gooing who had retired. The season kicked off on the 1st of September, and it was recorded as the hottest day ever for a start to the season. So intense was the heat, that all games started at 4.00 p.m.

One win and four points from their last eight games was all the club could muster, then a 1-1 draw at home to Brighton ended with the visiting full-backs, Turner and Gregory, complaining that they were assaulted on their way back to the dressing rooms. This resulted in a F.A. enquiry, and Northampton were told they must build a walkway between the pitch and dressing room; extra expense at a time when they could not afford it.

Of the 29 players used only 13 were professionals, which showed the club's dependence on Amateurs, who were in most cases as good as their professional counterparts, but lacked the commitment, for many had jobs that included working Saturday mornings, which made it hard for away travel. Harry Springthorpe was one example, for he was a bank Clerk, and his job later took him to Grimsby, whom he assisted, but he was tragically killed while serving with the Lincolnshire regiment on the 3rd of November 1915. The ship he was travelling on, the SS Mercian, was torpedoed, by a German submarine. The Vann boys, Albert and Bernard, were both amateurs, and both had a profession, Bernard was a schoolteacher and later a chaplain, and he also lost his life in the first World War. He won the military cross, and bar, the Croix de Guerre with Palm, and the Victoria Cross.

Bernard Vann was an ordained Deacon, and assistant master at Wellingborough School, and on the outbreak of the War he applied for an Army chaplaincy, but impatience got the better of him and he joined the Sherwood Foresters. Within Three years he had made the rank of Lieutenant-Colonel. His awards came from acts of bravery, for while leading his battalion at Bellenglise, he came under heavy fire from both flanks, but realising the only way was forward, he led the charge himself, under heavy fire from machine, and field guns. With his contempt for danger, the whole situation changed, and the Army captured the camp, Bernard Vann himself taking out a machine-gun, complete with its three operators. Throughout the war he was wounded eight times, but continued to lead his men, until October the 3rd 1918, when he was killed at Ramicourt.

Bernard Vann had been married less than a year to his Canadian wife, and never saw his son Bernard who was born in June 1919. He is believed to be the most decorated ex-footballer in the Country.

Fred Dunkley, cousin of Albert, who was in that first team of 1897, was asked to come out of retirement, which he did, and assisted the club. He had an Inn at Earls Barton where he displayed his England Amateur caps. A solid and reliable half-back, it was said that he was the star player in this 'poor' cobbler's side; not bad considering he was 34 years of age.

A game between Crystal Palace and new Brompton was described as *"The match to see which side is nearly as bad as Northampton"*. To cap a disaster of a season, goalkeeper Cooch broke his collarbone in the win over 'Spurs, and for the second season running, the club finished bottom.

Only five victories, and 24 defeats; just 29 goals compared to the 88 conceded and a meagre 19 points - the worst season on record. It was suggested in some national sporting papers that Northampton should be relegated to the Southern League Second Division, but they remained in the First, as one paper put it, *"Thanks to the silvery tongue of Darnell"*.

Lesser men would have thrown in the towel by now, for here was a club relying on amateurs and 'lower division' professionals; they were in debt, renting their ground, and bottom of the league. The gates were around 4,500, and the club seemed to be going nowhere. 'Pat' Darnell was made of sterner stuff, for he sat down with the committee before the season ended and they decided the only way forward was to appoint a manager who would be responsible for bringing the right kind of players to Northampton, and selecting the team.

Their first choice was Sam Ashworth, the ex-Stoke, Manchester City, Everton and Port Vale half-back. He was an amateur throughout his career, and at 30, they hoped he would give the club a couple of years as player/manager, but all to no avail when terms could not be agreed.

Walter Bull, was next, he was the Spurs centre-half and he said he would give it some thought. Legend has it, that after a vigorous match versus Q.P.R., Bull was sitting in the bath, and told Chapman that he was going to have another season at 'Spurs, and suggested that Chapman himself apply for the job as he had played for Northampton twice before.

Although there is no reason to disbelieve the latter part of the tale, the match in question took place on the 27th of April, and Chapman was appointed manager on the 1st May, therefore if this was fact, then things moved very quickly considering the pace of the day. Chapman discussed the idea with his wife, a schoolteacher, about moving to Northampton, as many County's did not allow married female schoolteachers. He then sat down and wrote the letter, applying for the job, and it was believed that one sentence clinched it for him... *"Pay me what you like."*

Herbert Chapman was a footballing nomad, he left school and got a job in a ticket printers, but soon got fed up. He then applied for a job in the mines, on the engineering side, but while halfway through his exams, he was given the opportunity to play professional football, and his career saw him move around the Country to Worksop, Rochdale, Swindon, Sheppey, and of course Northampton. An inside-forward, he found his best form in his first spell at Northampton, and moved to Sheffield United when they offered him the chance to finish his exams, the rest is history.

Chapman came to Northampton, surveyed the scene, and got to work with vengeance. Of the Amateurs, only Dunkley and Springthorpe remained, with professionals full-back Tom Drennan, wing-half Pat Tirrell, and forwards Jack Platt and 'Neddy' Freeman together with goalkeeper George Cooch. The latter caused a lot of interest, for after breaking his collarbone he disappeared! Chapman made great efforts to find him and reward him with a contract, but his digs had been empty for some time, and suddenly the local newspaper was full of 'I spotted Cooch' letters, one person had even written an eight verse poem about the missing 'keeper. Some said he was disillusioned with the last season, others said he had taken the well trodden path to Scotland where many ex-professionals were going, but he was eventually found, and accepted the offered terms.

Edwin Lloyd-Davies
He was soon to become
an influential player at
Northampton Town

1907/08

Dave McCartney, who had skippered Watford to the Southern League Second Division title, was Chapman's first signature. The player had gone to Chelsea but found it hard to find a place in their first team; he was to be the centre-half and captain. He was quickly followed by two of Chapman's old team-mates, George Badenoch, a winger, from Watford, and Fred McDiarmid from 'Spurs, plus a double-signing from Stoke, Fred Lessons, and Harry Benson, a centre-forward and a full-back respectively; Charlie Brittan came from Portsmouth,

Five debutants took the field at home to Plymouth, plus Chapman himself, but it was to be no fairy tale start - a 0-1 home defeat. But the crowd was pleased with the standard of football played, and it was obvious that for the first time in three seasons the club was not going to struggle.

"Wee Willie Walden Works Wonders"

Exeter local Newspaper Sports headlines after Walden had starred in their 4-0 defeat.
April 1913

After that defeat, Northampton were to go Eight more league games before they were to lose again, and by that time they were third in the table. A bizarre incident in the match with Portsmouth saw the opposition open the scoring with a goal via the side netting, and despite the protests of the Cobbler players the goal was allowed to stand. But Northampton fought back and won the game 3-2. Fred Lessons was proving to be a worthy find, he netted six times in a six match spell.

Bradford (Park Avenue) had joined the Southern League, and being so far away it was decided to travel on a Friday night. Unfortunately, winger George Badenoch was taken ill with a heavy cold and early in the morning Pat Darnell received a telegram asking him to send reserve winger Fred Didymus up on the train. Darnell got him to the station and giving him his connection times, he arrived with little time to spare, only to find Badenoch had recovered, and was well enough to play.

With things looking brighter, it did not take long for something to go wrong. Fred McDiarmid, who had been putting in some excellent performances at left-half, picked up a knee injury, and was sent to the same specialist that Len Benbow went to some years earlier, however, McDiarmid's injury was a short term thing, and he was back playing within a month.

Due to public demand the club agreed to allow supporters to bring in their bicycles at 2d (1p) a time, but with the cycles of the day all looking the same, it would have been an interesting sight watching the supporter trying to find his particular machine! November the 23rd, was a day to remember, for the first team without Chapman, went to New Brompton. When they arrived they were met by their manager, who introduced them to their new left-back, Edwin Lloyd Davies, the ex-Welsh international. Chapman had done the unthinkable, for he had asked the committee for money. He knew Stoke were in financial disarray, and reckoned they would part with the Welshman for a fee. Again this shows the kind of person Darnell was, for without a doubt part of the money, if not all, came from his pocket. It was the first time the club had paid a fee for a player, a not inconsiderable £400. Lloyd Davies played against New Brompton and helped his side to a 1-0 win.

While all this was going on, history was being made at the County Ground, for in the morning Northampton boys entertained the Newark boys and won 11-0, while in the afternoon the Reserves beat Peterborough Loco 11-0, making 22 goals in one day, more than the first team had scored at home all last season!

It was not until the F.A.Cup match, that the home fans got to see the new defender, who had cost so much money. He was only 5 feet 6 inches tall and had a very military stance; his muttonchop sideburns and drooping moustache giving him an authoritarian look, and supporters were later to find out what a professional Lloyd Davies was. Sutton Town were the opponents in the Cup, when Lessons had to cry off injured and Harry Lowe, an amateur, replaced him, but it was to be a match he would remember. Chapman opened the scoring after two minutes, and the Sutton team held out until five minutes from half-time when the Cobbler's scored two quick goals. The second-half saw the floodgates open when seven more goals went in; Badenoch and Platt both scored hat-tricks, and Chapman was the unlikeliest on the score sheet, netting two and having three more disallowed. There were four more goals cleared off the line, and the only shot Cooch had to save was a penalty, which went well wide. Badenoch's three goals were an achievement, because in his 34 league games, he had failed to score. The following week the club earned their first piece of silverware for some time, when the Reserves won the Senior Cup beating Rushden 2-1. Bristol Rovers ended the clubs run in the F.A.Cup, and in January, it was reported that Jack Platt was seriously ill with a kidney infection. He was out for six weeks, and as soon as he was match-fit he had to drop out due to the death of his father.

Other highlights of the season were the visit of Bradford, sporting shirts of scarlet, gold, black and white; the visit of New Brompton, where full-back Harvey struck a spectator as he left the field; the Reserves being fined 12/6d (63p) for fielding an unregistered player, and Charlie Brittan's injury versus Brighton that saw him leave the field in the first minute. Finishing eighth in the Southern League, the club was no longer the joke team of the division.

It is worth mentioning one of the players who moved on, wing-half Pat Tirrell. He went to West Ham, but returned to the area playing for clubs in the Peterborough area - Peterborough City, Peterborough Brotherhood and Fletton United - where he reverted to goalkeeper and became player/manager. While there he was quoted as saying he was going to build a 'Posh team'; it is believed that was how the Peterborough United of today got their nickname, ironically from an ex-Cobbler player.

1908-09
Dick Murrell was now the clubs trainer, and he fitted in well with Chapman's plans - Murrell got them fit, Chapman coached them. Robert Bonthron was signed from Sunderland to replace Drennan who had joined Coventry. Robert Walker came from 'Spurs, and Jock Manning, a wing-half, joined. Manning had found it hard to break into the Blackburn side, having arrived from Scotland, and jumped at the chance of first team football.

Albert Lewis was the 'coup', a free-scoring forward from Coventry. Again we rely on legend, but it is said that Chapman invited him into his office, locked the door, and hid the key, stating: *"You wont get out of here until you have signed."* He signed, and formed a formidable partnership with Lessons. The season started on a Wednesday, and Northampton had to travel to New Brompton, leaving Castle Station at 11.20 a.m. that day, and arriving home at 2.30

Albert Lewis

a.m. the next. An incident in the away match at Norwich made the news, for the Cobblers were 1-0 down when the referee ended the game. Chapman insisted the game had ended five minutes early, the referee said it had not, but Chapman stood his ground and the referee called the players back to play the last five minutes. By then the ground was only one third full, and there was no addition to the score.

Like Bradford, of the previous season, clubs seemed keen to parade in the most colourful shirts, like Reading who came up in purple and white, and Swindon who played in scarlet, each time sending the Cobblers back into the dressing room to change into their all white strip, one that Chapman favoured, as opposed to the Claret and White stripes.

On Boxing Day, a crowd of 15,000 packed into the County Ground for the match with Southend. It could well have been more, for a gate was broken at the Wellingborough Road end and several hundred got in free. After beating New Brompton 7-0, they allowed the celebration to continue into the next day, when George Badenoch got married; it must have been a well publicised event, for he wed the daughter of the Towncrier.

The F.A.Cup brought Derby County to the County Ground, and the match resulted in a 1-1 draw, in front of 14,798, whilst the replay at Derby only attracted 11,250, but ended in a 4-2 win for the League side. The three days the Cobblers spent in Matlock 'acclimatising' did not seem to do the trick.

Mid-January saw an injury crisis, Lewis, Walker, Badenoch and Dunkley were all out, Then Bonthron had to leave the field in the game with Watford, feeling unwell, and did not even train again for some weeks. Cooch was injured in the cup-tie, he was replaced by Bill Bailiff, a Welshman who had played for a host of Welsh clubs, but had little experience at Southern League level. He had made two earlier appearances, playing in Dick Murrell's testimonial match versus Leicester that ended 2-0 and again v Crystal Palace, which produced a 3-2 win. However, he was out of his depth in this game at Watford, and the Cobblers went down 4-1. Bailiff was not retained at the end of the season but went back into Welsh football and later played for Wales. The third choice keeper was Haywood, who was also the Northamptonshire County Cricket, wicket-keeper. He appeared in the 2-1 defeat by

Norwich, and conceded one of the goals as he thought it was offside, no doubt he was later advised of the old cliche, 'Play to the Whistle'.

With everyone back to full fitness the club's form moved upwards, and in the penultimate game of the season, they drew 1-1 at Queens Park Rangers. Every effort was made to find out the result of the Swindon v Luton match, for the Wiltshire club was the only one who could catch the Cobblers. As the team travelled back on the train from London they enquired at every station until they arrived home at Castle Station, then they saw the hundreds of people on the platform waving and cheering. Then they knew they had won the Southern League championship. Sadly Chapman did not join in the celebrations, he instead he continued up North to see his seriously ill father.

After beating Plymouth 2-1 in the last game of the season, Northampton Town were invited to meet Newcastle, at Stamford Bridge, to compete for the Charity Cup; in those days the match was competed for by the Football League Champions and the Southern League Champions. Newcastle won 2-0 in an exiting match that attracted 7,000. That was not the last game of the season, for Wolverton had asked for a friendly and it could have been easy to send a strong reserve side, but Darnell insisted on as many of the first team play as possible. A thankyou to Wolverton for their assistance when Northampton were a struggling club. Lloyd Davies was capped for Wales, and Dunkley was selected for the England Amateur side again - not bad for a 35 year-old.

1909-10
George Cooch moved on to Norwich, where he was to have a short stay before returning to the Northampton area and played for a few of the Northants League sides, while taking a pub and also becoming a lay preacher. Tommy Thorpe, his replacement, had seen service with Doncaster and Barnsley. Winger Beadling was signed from Grimsby and Codling a wing-half from Swindon, as well as Whittaker from Exeter, another winger. The season did not get off to a flying start, with defeats at Leyton and Coventry. But these set-backs were followed by a 5-1 win in the first home game versus Plymouth, that started a run of victories, including a 10-0 thrashing of Croydon Common, whose first team 'keeper was out, and the reserve replacement limped off near the end.

In the Southern League Charity Cup, a young inside-forward was drafted in for the home match with Watford. Although the visitors won 2-1, the youngster gave a creditable performance and kept his place for the league match at home to Luton. Northampton

supporters must have wondered what could this little man of 5 feet 2 inches do against these heavy defenders. They soon found out, for he scored a hat-trick in the 6-1 win; his name was Fred Ingram Walden, affectionately known as 'Fanny', and he was to become, not only a big name at Northampton but also nationwide.

On the 30th of December the club recorded their biggest ever win 11-0 versus Southend, when Lewis hit four goals and Walden three in this emphatic victory, in front of 10,000. But it was back to reality for the following match - away to Watford - when the train arrived late and the players had to change in the compartment, which could have had some bearing on their 2-0 defeat.

The F.A.Cup had a bitter-sweet taste this season, for the club only scored once in four games, but the goal dismissed Sheffield Wednesday from the competition. 60,000 in total watched the games, but on the down-side Manning was sent off versus Nottingham Forest. Chapman was well ahead of his time, for he had ideas that were laughed at at the time, but later were incorporated.... floodlights, European competitions, and the numbering of players shirts. He showed another side to his many talents, when 800 Norwich supporters arrived early, and he quickly arranged a tour of the town that ended at the Northants Brewery owned by the club Chairman, Pickering Phipps. This was a clever way of avoiding what could have been a troublesome situation! Second place, five points behind Swindon was the best the club could muster, but both Lloyd Davies (Wales) and Lewis (Southern League representative side), were honoured.

One incident in a reserve match, is worth mentioning, when the reserves were playing Peterborough Loco in a Senior Cup match, and the score was 0-0. In the dying minutes the Loco keeper made a grand save, and as the players ran upfield, with the referee about to blow for full time, the 'keeper kicked the ball out, whereupon it hit one of his defenders in the back, and entered the net: Northampton Reserves 1 Peterborough Loco 0!

1910-11
There were three new faces for the start of the season in Frank Bradshaw, a forward from Sheffield Wednesday and an ex-England International. Bradshaw had become disillusioned with League football - he had played once for his country and scored three goals in an 11-1 win over Austria, but was never capped again, and now he was struggling to hold down a place in the Wednesday, first team. He joined Northampton for £250. John Hampson, a wing-half came from Welsh side Oswestry, and Fred Clipstone, a full-back, who was born in Geddington, arrived from Portsmouth.

The season started with a 2-0 win over Watford, and 'keeper Tommy Thorpe converted a penalty, making him the first Northampton Town goalkeeper to score, the next was to be 65 years later. This season saw the start of the Hospital Cup, a one-off match against a First Division side, with all proceeds going to the Northampton Hospital. In this inaugural season, they entertained Nottingham Forest and beat them 1-0 thanks to a Fred McDiarmid goal. Seven thousand watched the game, bringing in £200 for the hospital.

A league match v Coventry caused some special unrest. The midland side did not leave home until 2.00 p.m., thinking they had plenty of time, but a hold up at Watford gap meant they did not arrive until 4.55 p.m. and kicking-off five minutes later. Fifty-five minutes on, the game was abandoned due to bad light, and as the game had started supporters could not have their money back. The crowd were annoyed to say the least, and for several days after the newspapers were full or letters from irate fans. This prompted Chapman to take a leaf out of Darnell's book, for he wrote a letter to the newspapers, apologising on behalf of both Northampton and Coventry, explaining his hands were tied, and used the occasion to promote his idea of floodlight football.

It was about this time that the first 'sponsorship deal' was made public, when Stewarts - a tailor of Gold Street - offered an overcoat to both the player and a friend, to any team member who scored two goals in a Southern

League match at home. This was a national sponsorship for any town that had a Stewart's shop. It is not known if messrs. Bradshaw, Whittaker, Lessons, Lewis and Walden received their overcoats, or what goalkeeper Tommy Thorpe thought about the deal!

Some things never change in football, and even as far back as 1910 referees came under fire. A match at Luton, on November the fifth, really did produce some fireworks in Northampton's 3-1 victory. First it was claimed that Walden handled the ball as he set up the first goal, then Lewis was the only player in the Luton half, except for the Luton keeper, when he received the ball and scored. It could almost be seen as an act of 'balancing' things out when the referee disallowed the Cobbler's goal, then awarded Luton a 'dodgy' penalty. Three weeks later, at Brighton, the home side won 5-0, but their first goal was hotly disputed, it took the referee a full seven minutes to decide the goal would stand.

Any supporter who was at the Coventry game, that never took place, would not be to happy with the re-match, played on December the first, for it was played in pouring rain and in a high wind that killed good football. Cobblers won 4-1, and the following Monday they entertained Kettering in a friendly that was so one-sided that at half-time goalkeeper, Thorpe, swapped places with Whitaker. Cobblers won 8-3, with seven different players scoring, including all five forwards.

PLAY UP NORTHAMPTON !

2 OVERCOATS FOR EVERY 2 GOALS.

OUR OFFER IS THIS :—We will present one of our Famous Sovereign Overcoats to any Northampton Player who scores 2 goals in a Southern League Match played at home. In Addition, we will give AN EXTRA COAT TO ANY SPECTATOR THE SUCCESSFUL PLAYER BRINGS ALONG WITH HIM.

The local Stewart's shop giving details of its special offer - the first 'sponsorship'.

The F.A.Cup was the highlight of the season, away to the mighty Newcastle United, of Division One.

Special trains were arranged and many supporters were to travel up to watch the game. Lloyd-Davies, who was centre-half, stated how much he was going to enjoy his tussle with Shepherd, the Newcastle forward. The two had met many times in the past, and Davies claimed he always had the upper hand, but Shepherd did not play - his infant son died suddenly - and he pulled out.

The game ended 1-1 thanks to a Bradshaw goal, and the 42,023 crowd brought the Cobbler's share of the gate to £675-13s, the biggest cheque the club had ever received. Many of the fans who were travelling back to Northampton were talking eagerly about the coming replay, but little did they know that at 8.00 p.m., an agreement was signed for Newcastle to buy the ground rights for £900. All hell broke loose at Northampton, for the fickle supporters, who not long ago were singing the praise of Chapman, were now asking whether he had the clubs supporters thoughts at heart; once again the newspapers were full of angry letters to this end.

Of course it was nothing to do with Chapman, the decision was made by the committee, although without doubt Chapman would have been consulted. Darnell, never a man to shirk his duties, explained in a newspaper article that the money would keep the club solvent for sometime without having to sell key players. The balance sheet at the end of the season actually showed a £149 deficit, that would have been over £1,000 had it not been for the money received from selling the ground rights.

The replay took place on the following Wednesday, and Newcastle won 1-0. Jack Shepherd had returned for the replay, and converted a penalty against Tommy Thorpe, who on the morning of the match went down with an outbreak of boils, but insisted on playing. The penalty was awarded against Charlie Brittan for 'hands', although he insisted he never touched it. Only two games in the F.A.Cup, but £1,748 made from it, nearly 75% of the total money the league games brought in, and over five times that made by the reserve matches throughout the season!

The home gates did drop for a time, but it did not last long, and the clubs winning ways brought back the supporters. 4,000 watched the next home game versus New Brompton, but 7,000 came to the Q.P.R match, and 6,000 for Luton. The club arrived for an away match at Millwall only to find that the referee, a Mr.Dommett, had wired the club to say he was too ill to travel, but a Mr.Clarke, County secretary of the Essex F.A. was at the game and agreed to take the middle.

There was another scare when the club arrived at Exeter, and found Bradshaw had missed his train. A telegram was sent to League headquarters and Chapman obtained permission to play, but as he started to get changed Bradshaw walked in.

Second place, five points behind Swindon, was the final outcome at the end of the season, and still a force in the league. A special mention for goalkeeper Tommy Thorpe should be given, for he took four penalties, scoring twice, missing one, and having one saved. On the other side he faced six and conceded four - when one was missed and one saved.

1911-12

The only new face was forward Harry King, a man with League experience but who had dropped into non-League football. Gone was Fred McDiarmid who had moved to Ireland and played for Distillery. Albert Lewis missed the start of the season with a throat infection and was allowed to recover in Blackpool, hence he missed playing against his old club, Coventry, in the opening game that saw Northampton win 2-1.

A slip-up by the League saw a Norwich referee appointed to the Norwich v Northampton clash, a sharp-eyed Arthur Jones spotted this and made his complaints. Mr.Plastow of Grimsby was appointed in his place, but Norwich still won. Newcastle did eventually play at the County Ground, nine months after the F.A.Cup match that caused such a stir, for they came for the Hospital Cup match, and won 2-1.

After drawing 1-1 with Palace, the club lost both their full-backs for the next game versus Southampton, for Brittan was representing the Southern League, and Clipstone reported ill. This meant Lloyd Davies was moved back to left-back and Eric Tomkins came in to the side; the Rushden lad had joined the club from Rushden Windmill and was captain of the very first England Schoolboy team. Tomkins had made his Cobblers debut earlier, against his old club, in a friendly to raise money for their secretary who had his leg amputated.

October the 21st saw a double transfer, with Charlie Brittan joining Tottenham, and Walter Tull, the first coloured player to wear a Northampton shirt, coming the other way. As a makeweight, Britton was to have a long career with both Spurs and Cardiff, before retiring in the mid-twenties and setting up in business in Birmingham. Much has been written about Tull, who had a West Indian father and an English mother. Unfortunately both were to die while he and his brother were both infants, which led to them being put into an orphanage.

Walter was offered a job as a printer and at the same time played amateur football for Clapton, with whom he won an Amateur Cup winners medal.

Tottenham signed him on as a professional and took him on their tour of South America. Three seasons at Spurs realised him just ten games and two goals, hence his decision to move to Northampton. A transfer had been arranged to Heanor some months earlier but for some unknown reason did not take place. Basically the player left 'Spurs for first team football, which he hoped to get at Northampton.

Less than three weeks later the club lost another key player, Harry Bradshaw, who wanted another bite at League football. He put in a transfer request and joined Everton for £2,000, where he was to give them three seasons, before joining Arsenal for the next five and winning a London Challenge Cup winners medal. His last official visit to the County ground was in the 1923-24 season as manager of Aberdare.

Walter Tull
Northampton's first coloured player

of his long legs. Darlington were next, and after a 1-1 draw at Feethams, they came back to the County Ground, and the Cobblers finished as 2-0 winners.

However Fulham, away, proved to be the stumbling block, and in front of 32,035 the London side won 2-0.

One problem came in the shape of a rail strike, and so for the away game at Exeter, it was decided to travel down on Friday, and stay overnight, which cost the club an extra £10.

So short were the club for uninjured players, that they had to play Lloyd Davies, who was not fully fit, against Bristol Rovers. But the Cobbler's ran out 5-0 winners with Walter Tull scoring four of the goals.

Third place, just two points behind the leaders, and 82 goals scored - the most in the division; three players in the Southern League representative side, and an average crowd of 7,500, was the final outcome of the season.

Injuries to key players in December, badly reduced a dwindling playing staff. Walden was carried off in the game versus Swindon, while at Luton, goalkeeper Thorpe was carried off after a kick on the head. John Hampson went into goal, but Thorpe returned before the end.

The game itself, which ended 3-3 was full of incident. The Luton forward, Johnson, charged Hampson over the goal-line for one of the goals, as was the practise of the day, but as they both fell over the line, Johnson fell awkwardly, and it was discovered he had broken his leg and spent Christmas in hospital.

Two home games over Christmas, versus Brighton and Coventry, brought an aggregate attendance of 24,006, and four points; the former match had the gates opening at 1.55 p.m. to allow the swelling crowds in. The F.A. Cup saw a home tie v Bristol City, which was won 1-0 thanks to a goal from 'Spider' Lewis, so named because

But still the club were short of money. Despite this factor, it was always ready to help others and played Kettering in a game to raise money for the titanic disaster fund. Just over £59 was realised, but little could be made of the result - 4-1 to Kettering - as only Clipstone, Lessons and Freeman were first team regulars

1912-13

Herbert Chapman, left Northampton Town. There was no ill feeling, but Chapman had ambition, and he could not see Northampton getting any further than he had taken them. A job came up at Leeds City, and he went for it, Darnell announced that he and the committee were sad at losing such a manager, but would not stand in his way, Chapman was to have some success with Leeds, but unfortunately was caught up in the web of underhanded dealing that saw the club expelled from the football League. Although Chapman claimed his innocence, he along with all the directors and administration staff, were suspended.

Herbert Chapman was not a man to let the grass grow under his feet, for he then took a job in a munitions factory, and before long was running it, so much part of the set-up that he had living quarters built at the factory.

When his suspension was lifted, he became coach to Huddersfield Town and then manager, taking them to two Division One League championships. While they were on course for a third, he left Leeds Road for Arsenal. In his time at Arsenal, he did it again, winning the championship twice, and was on course for a third, when he went out on a scouting mission and returned home with a heavy cold. He went straight to bed, but he never got up again, for he died on the 6th of January 1934, and ironically he was to have made a speech to the Northampton sportsman's club the next day; he always had a great affection for Northampton.

Herbert Chapman was a disciplinarian, but always believed in treating people like human beings. He transferred a player within 24 hours of him kicking an opponent on the field, he sacked a trainer for shouting and swearing at the players, but at the same time he insisted everyone in the office said goodnight to him. Of course no one would have dared go in until after finishing their training. He must still rate as one of the games top managers, and at the time he was head and shoulders above the rest.

Chapman's replacement, when he left Northampton, was Walter Bull, his old 'Spurs team-mate, who was approached to take the job five years earlier. After he finished playing, Bull moved to South America where he coached several clubs, before deciding to return home. Bull had also played in that Leicester Fosse/Notts County game that was to be the starting point of Northampton Town F.C.

The only notable addition to the squad was Harry King, a centre-forward, who had played for Birmingham City for three seasons and then moved on to Crewe. Fred McDiarmid, no longer considered a first-teamer, joined Distillery in Ireland,

Bull's first job was to appoint assistant trainer, Harry Burrows, to head trainer, as Dick Murrell had joined Chapman at Leeds. Burrows had been with the club since it was formed, first as a bill poster and odd job man, then as trainer to the reserves when they joined the Northants League.

The first five games of the season saw five different players take the centre-half spot. John Hampson started, away to Southampton, but he was injured and in the second game Walter Tull was tried.

Although the Cobbler's won the match with Gillingham, Tull struggled in that position. Walter Bull put himself in for the home match with Southampton, but he was well past his 'sell-by-date' and played a large part in the 'Saints' victory. Fred Lessons moved back to centre-half, something he had done regularly in the past, but it left a void up front, where he was needed to hold the forward line together. John Rawlings, the reserve centre-half, eventually got the job and kept it until Hampson was fit again.

Tull, who was in and out of the side, was tried at wing-half, a position more suited to his style of play for he was a little too slow for a forward. He adapted well, so well that the club signed another inside-forward, Wallace Smith, who was the same player who was seriously injured while playing for Kettering against the Cobbler's some years earlier.

In October of 1912, the club made a newspaper appeal for money, explaining the club's finances, and set up a 'shilling fund', to which people - from businessmen to schoolboys - made donations of a shilling (5p), or as many shillings as they were able, and were rewarded with their names printed in the paper. The fund went well, and by its closing date the club had the money they needed to survive.

A classic example of the problems the club were encountering was brought to light in the home match with Merthyr, when only 3,500 watched the game, with takings of £81. The club needed £150 to break even, which meant an average gate of 6-7,000, and this season it was just over 5,000.

A training ground 'incident', resulted in some of the players being disciplined, although there is no record of who, and at the same time, Walter Bull parted company with the club. It was not reported if this departure had any bearing on the training ground problem, but Bull never seemed to enjoy the success that Chapman had in his short time at the County Ground, and the club had stated they felt they would like a player-manager. The two appearances the ex-'Spurs man had made in the first team gave a good indication that he would not have held down a regular spot.

The management committee set itself up again and picked the team until the end of the season, with some interesting results. Stoke City were beaten 9-0, in the first Saturday of 1913, 'Fanny' Walden hitting Four goals, and Harry King netted another three in a game when rain fell throughout, and the attendance was just 2,500.

A fortnight later, the same 11 players travelled to First Division Blackburn for an F.A. Cup-tie, and lost 7-2, which at the time was the biggest defeat in the competition suffered by the club.

Part of the crowd at the Exeter v. Northampton match in 1913

reaction, so promptly put the ball over the line. The referee consulted the linesman, and awarded a free kick to the Cobblers. This prompted a Plymouth supporter to jump the fence and approach the linesman, but before he reached him he felt 'the long arm of the law' and was evicted from the ground. However, Plymouth won the game 2-0, and the Southern League by two points.

The team had a settled look about it, for Thorpe kept goal, with Fred Clipstone and captain, Edwin Lloyd Davies, at full-backs; Walter Tull, 'Jock' Manning and Eric Tomkins made up the half-back line, and Walden and local boy Freeman made up the right wing, with Hughes and Smith on the left; free-scoring Harry King was at centre-forward.

March brought some interesting games, including a 4-0 win at home to Exeter, which saw 'Fanny' Walden do a single-handed destruction job on the Devon club, laying on all four goals for his fellow forwards.

This feat prompted the Exeter paper to print the sports headlines; *'Wee Willie Walden, Works Wonders'.* Exeter on the other hand said that on the way to the ground they passed a funeral, and it was a superstition at the time that any team that passed one always lost! The away match at West Ham was delayed until 4.00p.m., as King George was travelling through London earlier, and a game at Coventry, saw the Cobbler's four goals down at half-time. But they pulled them all back, and by full time, Harry King had achieved a hat trick.

Earlier in the season the club had announced that had it not been for the 'Shilling Fund', which raised £647-2s, they would have had to allow Walden to move to Leeds City, who had made an attractive offer. But thanks to the money received they did not have to release him....but let him go to Tottenham instead! No one had bothered to ask Walden, who was keen to play in a higher grade of football, and when the London club came in for him, he wanted away. Chapman was not too disappointed, for he captured John Hampson from Northampton, and later signed Walden as a guest during World War One.

The last day of the season saw Northampton at Plymouth, who needed to win the game to win the championship. During the game a Plymouth player shot at goal, but the ball stuck in the mud; he looked up at the linesman, saw no

1913-14
The club decided to offer the manager's job to Lloyd-Davies , but he had business interests in Wales, and a family, hence he declined the offer, so it was then offered to another seasoned professional, Fred Lessons, who accepted. David Brown an inside-forward was signed from Morton, and Tom Birtles a winger came from Rotherham, although he had seen League experience with Barnsley. Albert Lewis had left the club, having joined West Bromwich Albion, ironically the club he had left to join Coventry nine years earlier.

The first 'incident' came in October, when Fulham agreed to send a team to play in the annual Hospital Cup match, however it appeared to clash with one of their London cup-ties, and they sent their reserves. This did not go down well, especially as 10,000 people had turned up to watch the game, but the Cobbler's annoyance turned to embarrassment when Fulham's 'Stiffs' won 2-1.

Just prior to a home match versus Millwall on the 18th of October, Lloyd-Davies received a telegram from Wales informing him that his infant son had died. The management gave him permission to drop out, but in true professional style he played the game. For the same match Eric Tomkins was dropped, for the first time in 80 consecutive appearances. Fred Lessons had taken over the centre-half spot, allowing 'Jock' Manning to revert to wing-half, and with Tull on the other wing, there was no place for Tomkins

The club did well under Lessons, he made few changes, but midway through the season he brought in two new faces, Ben Bellamy, an inside-forward who was also a Northants County cricketer, and insisted to everyone he was christened Ben, not Benjamin.

The other newcomer was Archie Rawlings, a winger from the Leicester area, who was an electrician in a colliery, but decided that he had a future as a professional footballer. He came to Northampton and it was to be the start of an 18 years playing career, that took in Preston, Liverpool, and Bradford, as well as his winning an F.A.Cup runners up medal in 1922.

Travel seemed to be the biggest bugbear of the day, as it was invariably by train, and everything relied on timing connections; more time was spent on the train than on terra-firma. One example was the time the club travelled to Exeter, leaving Castle Station at 8.45 a.m. and arriving at Exeter 30 minutes before kick-off, or when Southampton arrived a few minutes late for their game at the County Ground and the referee made the clubs change straight round at half-time, claiming the light was fading fast.

When Norwich came to play their league match on 27th of December, it ended one all, Wilson scoring for Norwich, and King replying for the Cobbler's. This was the first goal seen at the County ground since the 15th of November, and the first scored by an opponent since November the 1st. During the home match against Portsmouth, Dexter, the Pompey full-back, was sent off for kicking Harry King in the penalty area. King took the penalty-kick himself but saw it saved, and the game ended scoreless.

The season ended with Northampton in third place, three points behind the champions, Swindon. Harry King netted 22 league goals, of the 50 scored, but made it clear he would not sign a new contract as he felt he could play in a higher grade of football. In an effort to cut their losses, they released him rather than pay his summer wages. Highlight of the season was the Benefit match for Lloyd-Davies against a Welsh select side, that included Billy Meredith who played the whole game chewing on a tooth pick; this was not recommended considering the physical contact allowed at this time!

The Welshmen won 5-0, giving an excellent display of football to the 5,000 crowd. The game also saw the debut in the Cobbler's side of George Whitworth, a name that would later be on many supporters lips.

1914-15

Bill Lockett, a centre-forward from Wolves, took over from King, having failed to break into the Wolves side on a regular basis. He was a team-mate of Eric Tomkins in the first ever England schoolboy match. Syd Dawson, an inside-forward, also signed from Kilnhurst. Another familiar face, Len Benbow, returned to the County Ground, but as the financial secretary. He had by now set up his own accountancy firm, Benbow and Ayres, and was to control the clubs purse strings.

A strange fixture list saw the Cobbler's play just one home match in September, and their next, in October, at home to Croydon Common, was packed with incident, for both Hughes and Lloyd-Davies were taken off injured, and Fred Clipstone scored a goal - for both sides - in the 3-2 victory for Northampton.

With the storm clouds of the first world war gathering, all matches were attended by magistrates or recruiting officers looking for volunteers to join the British Army, and several games had such a recruiting drive either before or after the game. A good run around Christmas, plus a territorial base being set up in the town, saw attendances rise, and a home game with Bristol Rovers realised a crowd of 10,000; of this number 8,000 were soldiers.

Fred Lesson's appearances were becoming less and less, a knee injury had kept him out for most of the season, but he was hoping to play in the cup-tie versus Grimsby. Lesson played, although his knee gave way, but the side managed a 3-0 win, and went out in the next round to Grimsby's neighbours Hull where the cobbler's were led onto the field by their new Mascot, a bull-dog. Animal mascots were not new, for when the club won the Southern League championship they were presented with a goat. However, Chapman was not happy, and promptly gave it away.

By Easter, there was a still a chance of the championship but the club were having a see-saw run in. The home match versus Watford ended 1-1, when Freeman missed a penalty and Clipstone put through his own net, but in the home match against Portsmouth, Tommy Thorpe saved a penalty, which if successful would have given Portsmouth a share of the points. With three games left, the Cobblers were just a point behind the leaders, but there was no fairytale ending, for 5-2 defeats at Southampton and at home to Cardiff, put paid to any chance of the championship, and it was an 'After the Lord Mayor's show' game, that saw the team beat Millwall 5-0, with nothing but pride to play for.

It was the London club who created somewhat amusing interest in their programme notes, after beating Northampton 2-1 way back in October, which read thus; *"Mr. Lutwyche of Birmingham was in the unfortunate position of not witnessing many infringements which crept into the game, and also erred in the judgement on several occasions, when palpably illegal methods were indulged in by several players. The scoring of Northampton's goal was easily traceable to one of his bad decisions, in as much as he ignored the appeal for a corner kick made by our players, with the result that half the team appeared to be discussing the oversight, when Northampton, very luckily, scored that goal.*

To caution a player on no less than three occasions for rough play, then allow him to proceed with his illegal tactics, show great weakness on part of the official. Mr. Lutwyche it is regrettable to say, allowed this condition of affairs to prevail".

The club finished in 5th place, and despite a small squad, wages outweighed gate receipts by £228.

1915-19

League Football was suspended during world war one, but the club allowed a band of willing Amateurs to play under their name, and at the County Ground, in an effort to raise money for the War effort, and to entertain the wounded soldiers, after they returned from the front. Football was frowned upon during the war, the question being asked why were these people playing sports, while fellow country men were dying in France? In fact many of the players who played in these matches were soldiers either in training, or waiting to be shipped out to serve, and some were convalescing after being wounded. Throughout the season many of the ex-professionals made appearances for the team - George Whitworth, Eric Tomkins, Neddy Freeman, Fred Clipstone, Jock Manning, and Edwin-Lloyd Davies. Guests also played, while in the area, the likes of Fanny Walden, Corporal Satterwaitte (of Gillingham), Private Martin of Raith, Seargent Beech of Manchester City, and Private Upex of Croyden Common.

Added to these were several willing, and good Amateur, footballers. One who stands out was a young inside-forward, who later became a referee, before moving into local football and holding several posts with the Northants League before stepping up to become a director and later chairman of Northampton Town F.C. He was Ted Buller, to date the only chairman, who ever played for the club.

The games were obviously all friendlies, against local teams or against Army elevens who were in the area. Many of these teams had ex-professionals in their sides, so some of the games were of a high quality and very entertaining. One particularly interesting result came over a Christmas period. On Christmas day, the 'team' travelled to Luton and lost 2-9; four days later, they entertained Luton with such a patched-up side that goalkeeper Newman was forced to play wing-half, but they won 8-2!

As far as the war was concerned, the worst ever conflict for casualties, the club lost several players, and ex-players. Walter Tull, lost his life in France; he was the first 'Cobbler' to sign for the 17th Middlesex regiment, and was on his second spell in France with the 23rd battalion (he had been sent home wounded the first time he was shot while advancing on the enemy). Despite the efforts of his colleague, Private Billingham, who tried to carry his body back for a decent burial, he was left on the battlefield near Favreuil. Tull had risen to the rank of Second Lieutenant, the first black soldier to do so, and received the British War and Victory Medal, and was recommended for a Military Cross. He was the only first team player to lose his life, although there was talk that had war not broken out, he was going to join his brother in Glasgow and sign for the Rangers, as his wing-half position, at Northampton, was in jeopardy.

Frank Norman, a reserve left-back and amateur player was also killed in action. Amateurs Bernard Vann and Harry Springthorpe also died, as did George Badenoch - who had emigrated to Canada, but returned with a Canadian battalion to fight; Lancelot Driffield Grimley, another amateur full-back from Kingsthorpe who had played for the club in its early days, was also a casualty.

1919-20

After the conflict was over, the club rolled up its sleeves and set out to find as many of its old players as possible in an effort to continue in the Southern League. They were lucky in one respect, as the band of amateurs that had played under the name 'The Northampton War Team' had agreed to be the club's reserve side, and without these there was grave doubt that the club could have continued.

The nucleus of the pre-War side returned, and only three new faces appeared when the club kicked off its season at Crystal Palace. Forscutt a full-back, Facer a winger, and Rushton an inside-forward. The game ended 2-2, with Rushton and Whitworth scoring. Once again the club found that the problem with amateurs was commitment, for many of them worked on Saturday mornings, and were not available for away games.

Another problem was the train strike; a game at Merthyr kicked off at 5.00p.m. the team stayed until Monday, and then, after playing a game in Mid-Rhondda, returned home by Charabanc. But spare a thought for Plymouth, who left home on Thursday, and did not expect to arrive home until the following Thursday!

It was around this time that the ex-Cobblers trainer Dick Murrell contacted his friend, and former trainer Harry Burrows, and told him about a young right-winger who could do Northampton 'a good turn'. Arrangements were made for the player to come to Northampton by train, and Burrows was to meet him at Wellingborough station. Unfortunately the train was very late and when the player arrived all public transport had closed, so the two men walked to Northampton in the early hours of the morning, yet still the player gave such a creditable performance the next day, that he was signed on. His name was Billy Pease, and he was to become part of Northampton, folklore.

To win at Southampton was an achievement in itself, but to win 6-2 was even amazing. Both Whitworth and Dickens scored hat-tricks, and a special mention for Parker of Southampton should be given, since he missed a penalty for the 'Saints', then had to go in goal when their 'keeper was injured, and saved a shot from the 'spot'.

By Christmas the club had won three games, two of these away, and were close to the bottom of the Southern League. There was little cheer in the F.A. Cup. A home tie versus Bristol Rovers raised some eyebrows when the opponents revealed they had to use their third team 'keeper. However, the game ended 2-2, with all four goals coming in the last 15 minutes, and Rovers won the replay 3-2. A December 5-1 home victory over Newport was followed by a defeat by the same score, also at home, to Brighton!

Things seemed to go from bad to worse, for 'keeper Tommy Thorpe broke a rib, and the reserve, Smith, was injured. An Amateur named Faulkner made his debut, but in four games, he picked the ball out of the back of the net 15 times; Tomkins was out with an ankle injury, and a home match versus Merthyr was badly affected by the Saints rugby match.

The committee had decided not to appoint a manager for this season, and they made themselves responsible for team selection. Darnell once again showed what he was made of when pressured to appoint a manager, for he simply replied, *"we will finish the job we started"*, and as if by magic the club hit some kind of form, winning six of its last seven home games. One of these matches, a 3-1 victory over Southampton, saw the referee stop the game, and refuse to start it again until a rowdy spectator was removed! The last home match was a 3-2 win over Millwall, and was used as a benefit match for Manning and Thorpe.

Nineteenth position was achieved, and re-election was avoided by three points. Lockett and Whitworth scored 43 goals between them, more than two-thirds the total, while the defence shipped in 103, a club record,

32 players were used during the season, 11 of them amateurs, and several of the professionals were at the veteran stage.

The committee had achieved what they set out to do - rebuild a side that was good enough to compete in the Southern League, who were to move 'on bloc' to become the Third Division South the following season. Another feather in the cap for Darnell, Jones and Co.

Edwin Lloyd-Davies retired, he was offered a job with the club but turned it down preferring to return to his native Wales and run the shop he had set up many years before.

He did go through a bad spell when he was almost made bankrupt, but he pulled himself round, and ran the shop for many years. One of his sons played for Manchester United during the second world war. Fred Clipstone never got over the Malaria he caught while away on active duty, he played just three games for the club but was a shell of his former self. He retired in April, and died the following June. Jock Manning, another at the veteran stage retired and settled in the town with his family. Joe Smith, a reserve winger was rushed into hospital and died of peritonitis during the season.

So the club's Southern League days come to an end, and their Football League career was about to start.

THE COBBLERS BRING A SHIP TO PORT

Despite this victory over Southampton, It was not going to be all plain sailing in the Football League.

CHAPTER THREE
1920-21

1920-21

Bob Hewison was the club's new player/Manager. A utility player, he started his career with Newcastle, giving them five seasons before World War One. During the hostilities he assisted Leeds City, and was recovering from a broken leg when the club were fined and disbanded for irregularities. He was given the job of Secretary for clearing up the club's paperwork. Hewison returned to Newcastle in 1919, but found he was only considered a reserve, so when the Northampton job came up he applied for it, although there is the possibility that Herbert Chapman, by this time working in his munitions factory, may have had some influence.

"I Would rather Loasby score six goals than to see him carried off, as he was."

Williams, the Brighton, 'keeper, after his clash with Harry Loasby resulted in a broken leg for the Northampton man.

December 1927

Hewison brought with him three new faces in John McKechnie, a Scotsman from Newcastle reserves, Willie Watson, from the Carlisle area - a full-back - and the experienced George Jobey, at centre-half. Newcastle-born Jobey was 35, and was considering an offer to become player-manager of non-League Ebbw Vale, but jumped at the chance of continuing his League career. He twice entered the record books, being the first player ever to score at Highbury, while he was an Arsenal player, and his first ever F.A. Cup appearance for Newcastle, was in the 1911 final versus Bradford City.

The first home game. In the photo. - although now worn with age - Lockett can be seen scoring the second goal (the player marked with an 'x').

So the Northampton team that kicked-off the 1920/21 season, the club's first in the League, away to Grimsby, read; Tommy Thorpe in goal (the long serving 'keeper; McKechnie and Sproston at full-back, the latter assisting the 'war team' during the war; Hewison took the right-half position, ex-Schoolboy international Eric Tomkins, at left-half, and Jobey in the middle; Billy Pease was the right-winger, with George Whitworth, a more complete forward since his spell with Crystal Palace during the war, alongside; the long-serving Eddie Freeman and Bill Thomas took up the left, and free scoring Bill Lockett played at centre-forward.

Season tickets were sold at £1-11-6d (£1.57p) plus 4/- (20p), while ladies had the advantage of buying their ticket for £1-4-0d (£1.20p) plus 2/6 (12p) tax.

All the club came away with from Grimsby was the box of fish - given to the opponents as a gift in those days - the 'Mariners' winning 2-0, but five days later, the club beat Queens Park Rangers 2-1 on their own ground, and followed this up with a 4-1 win in the return match with Grimsby.

In the early days of the Division 3, teams played their opponents in consecutive matches, or as near to as possible, which produced some topsy-turvy results. After beating Q.P.R in London, the Cobblers lost to the same side, 3-0 at home, lost a close encounter at home to Watford 1-0, which may have produced a different result

had Whitworth converted a penalty, then seven days later, the Hertfordshire club, beat Northampton 7-1. It was obvious that Sproston and McKechnie were not up to standard and were dropped, with Watson and Hewison himself falling back to the full-back positions. This allowed Fred Grendon into the side, another ex-War team player.

Northampton must have been held in some esteem, during this period, for Swansea player Jack Williams used the 'Swans' home game with the Cobblers as his testimonial; Beneficiaries were allowed to choose which game they wanted, and 12,000 watched the match. Games against Plymouth always seemed full of incident, and in the home match in November, the two centre-halves scored in the 1-1 draw, and both were headers from corners.

Mid-table was the best the Cobblers were going to get, from a string of indifferent results. At Exeter, the club were 1-3 down with 20 minutes to go, before pulling back to 3-3. The club then beat Gillingham three times in a nine day period, twice in the League and once in the F.A. Cup, but the Cup dream came to an end at Southampton, after a scoreless draw at the County Ground. This match attracted 16,000 spectators, the crowds gathering outside the ground at 10.30a.m. for a 2.30p.m. kick-off. When the players entered the field, the Cobblers carried their new mascot - a black cat - who once it heard the noise, jumped out of its carrier's arms and ran away. Some said it was the luck running out..... they were right!

Several incidents during the season are worth mentioning. After beating Reading 1-0 at home, the team travelled to the Berkshire club, who reshuffled their forward line, and extracted revenge with a 4-0 win. Swindon did the double over Northampton in the Easter programme, but Jefferson, the Swindon player, will remember it for the wrong reasons, for he missed a penalty in the first game, and was then carried off in the second. The away match at Norwich made history when the players were ferried to the game in a fleet of motor cars.

Fourteenth in their Division was not a bad start. George Whitworth ended the season with 28 goals, joint top-scorer in the Division. McKechnie and Sproston were not retained, although McKechnie moved on to Exeter, but was released after a year. He was to appear for 2nd Division Clapton Orient for three seasons. Both Freeman and Thorpe retired, Freeman being the last playing link with Herbert Chapman's Southern League winning side. Thorpe returned home but was coaxed back into playing for his old club Barnsley, whom he gave another season - not bad for a man of 40.

1921-22

Three new faces arrived; William Williams, a spindly wing-half or full-back with amazing stamina, he joined from Cardiff. Arthur Seabrook came from Luton Clarence, where he was a prolific scorer, and a winger, Joe Harron, arrived from Hull.

On the field, things did not start well, for within the first three games the club had failed to convert two penalties, and an away match at Bristol Rovers failed to produce one shot on goal from the Cobblers, resulting in a 0-2 defeat.

Joe Harron

It was hoped that Seabrook would replace Thomas, who had joined Millwall, but he was not yet ready for League football, and Hewison took his place. Billy Williams also had an indifferent start at left-back, and found himself out of the first team, but he came back a few weeks later, taking Hewison's vacated left-half position, and made it his own. This allowed in amateur Tommy Jeffs, from Rugby.

Things were still not going right, and a 7-0 defeat by Brighton, saw Doran scores five, Brighton lose a man injured, and Jobey cautioned. At Southampton, in a Christmas Eve game, the Saints won 8-0, but it is fair to say Northampton had lost Watson, and George Jobey was missing.

The F.A.Cup saw an away win at Lincoln thanks to the winner coming via Lockett, with the last the kick of the game. Lancaster went out in the next game, via a George Jobey goal, then Bill Lockett netted a hat-trick versus Reading in the first round proper, to go with the two he scored against them in the League. Then came Stoke City. With Willie Watson injured, the club had to play Len Hawtin in his place, this meant both the full-backs were amateurs, the first time this situation had occurred for Northampton in the F.A.Cup. The game ended 2-2 with 16,532 watching, but Stoke won the replay 2-0.

While the club were drawing 2-2 at Swansea, in front of 3,000 supporters, 7,500 were at the County Ground, watching Northampton Nomads playing South Bank in the F.A.Amateur Cup, the record attendance at the County Ground for an Amateur game.

The home match with Portsmouth, a 0-0 draw, was used as a benefit game for Arthur Jones, and it was also the last game that George Whitworth played for the club, for he then moved on to Crystal Palace for an undisclosed fee. He later played for Hull, Sheffield Wednesday, Peterborough and South Shield, eventually settling in that

The Directors: (Back) C.Yarde, J.J.Martin
(Front) T.S.James, F.C.Parker, G.Gyde, R.P.Seal

town where he ran a fish and chip shop. George was often nicknamed 'Twitty', and was something of a deep character who did not suffer fools easily, and was once restrained from throwing a team-mate out of a moving train after a heated argument! Whitworth was replaced by Billy Graham from Lancaster. When the two clubs met in the F.A.Cup, he was a star player, and Hewison remembered him.

Hewison himself, hit a hat-trick against Norwich, albeit two of the goals came from the penalty spot, however he too caught the 'penalty missing disease', and his failure versus Leicester saw them take the Hospital Cup back to Filbert Street.

Seventeenth in the League was a backwards step, but with no money to strengthen the side, all manager Bob Hewison could do, was to try and pick up decent amateurs, or quality free transfer players. George Jobey retired to take the manager's job at Wolves, Joe Harron, returned North to York City, but he was later to return to League football with Sheffield Wednesday.

1922-23

The club became a Public Company in 1922, when they allowed 8,000 shares at £1.00 each to be released. Supporters could purchase these by paying 2/6 (12½p)

on application, 7/6 (37½p) on allotment, and the remaining 10/- (50p) a month after the date of agreement. The prospectus revealed many things, such as the rent which was £350 a year, with the 'landlords' having the option to 'determine' the figure at the end of seven and 14 years.

The first set of directors were; Charles Parker, chairman and bookmaker; builder John Martin; boot manufacturer Tom Sears; Tom James the provision's merchant; Charles Gyde the owner of the Princess Royal; Russell Seal, cycle access-ories; John Covington, cin-ema proprietor; Tom Gillett, the farmer from Wilby; and Cyril Yarde, the nurseryman. Barclays were the club's Bankers, Darnell and Price the solicitors, with Benbow and Ayres as accountant, and Swannell and Brown as brokers.

On the field, Bob Hewison had brought in Frank Newton, a defender from Bradford City to replace Jobey, William Brown a forward from South Inch, Colin Myers, a nomadic inside-forward from Aberdare, and Louis Page, a left-winger from Stoke. The latter was something of a coup, as he had business interests in the Liverpool area and had arrangements with all his previous clubs to train in Liverpool. But Northampton was too far away, however, the lure of regular League football was enough to win him over.

The club started in familiar fashion, missing penalties versus Gillingham and Swindon, and the latter would have given the club a well needed point. Good news was to follow, for a 3-0 win at Gillingham gave the club its first away win in the League since Christmas 1920, and that was against..... Gillingham! A friendly for the financially struggling Wellingborough Town helped them to raise £56, thanks to a crowd of 1,700. It was at this point that the club released the details of their practise matches. The total of £141-4-3d was raised and divided among the General Hospital, British Legion,

Crippled Children, Good Samaritans, N.F.A.Benevolent Fund, The National F.A. Benevolent Fund and Nazareth house.

Back on the field, Louis Page would well remember the 1-0 defeat at Norwich, for he had a goal disallowed, was knocked out, came back, and carried off injured again, and when the two clubs met again the following week, he failed to complete 90 minutes, being helped off yet again. The attendance for the 5-2 victory over Southend in November was swelled by a number of unemployed who were marching through the town, on their way to London. They were given free tickets.

The club were going through a good spell before they lost 1-0 to Plymouth on Christmas day, having gone nine games without defeat. But good news came on Boxing Day, when they beat the Devon side 1-0, in front of 18,123, a new record at the County ground for a League game. It was also the first time that gate takings exceeded £1,000.

Lady luck deserted the club during February, in the home match versus Swansea. Two visiting players were taken off injured in the first-half, yet still the Welshmen won 3-1, and against Newport, Colin Myers received a broken nose, but returned to the field of play, only to get his marching orders.

Edmund Wood was signed from Redditch in March, and took over the centre-half mantle, which gave the club some stability, but at this stage of the season a respectable place in the Division was all they could aim for. This they achieved with eighth. One interesting point to note concerned the crowds against Charlton, for when Northampton lost 2-0 to the Athletic in the F.A.Cup only 5,000 watched, yet the corresponding League fixture, with nothing at stake, brought in 8,000.

1923-24
The season started with two new faces in the first team, Frank Brett, a full back from Aston Villa, and Willie Wood a winger from Parkgate. The club had also raised £5,000 to build a stand, with a tunnel underneath.

The County Ground was going through something of a re-vamp, as supporters at the hotel end were getting a better view thanks to the newly installed terracing.

Colin Myers was the focal point of the two matches versus Swansea. He was taken ill prior to the away match, and manager Bob Hewison took his place, for what was to be his last ever game for the club, as a player. The home match saw Myers score both goals, to inflict Swansea's first defeat of the season.

A 2-0 victory over Gillingham proved to be the start of a curse on the centre-half position that season. Edmund Wood was taken to hospital with a broken ankle, and this won a reprieve for 'Ginger' Bedford, but after 15 League and cup games he also joined the injury list.

Albert Facer, the local lad, was given a run, but he lasted just two games before being carried off. This resulted in the signing of Ernest Needham, a nephew of the famous 'Nudger' Needham, to fill the central defender's role. Northampton's 100th league game was low keyed, and only 7,000 watched the 3-0 victory over Newport, the poor crowd being mainly due to the visit of Lloyd George to the town.

The highlights of the season were the opening of the stand, prior to the match with Norwich, when the flag was raised for the first time, and the F.A. Cup run. Lincoln were beaten 5-1 in the first round of the Cup, and Wigan Borough had six goals put past them at Springfield Park, the most goals ever scored away from home by the Cobblers. Round three brought Halifax to the County ground. Adam Thompson, a Halifax supporter with a partly disabled leg, walked from Halifax to Northampton to watch the game as he could not afford the travel costs. After the game was drawn, he started his return journey, hoping to make the replay. There is no record to say that he made the second replay at Sheffield United's ground, which Halifax won 4-2.

Eighth place in the League, and over £1,000 profit from the Cup run were the end results of the season.

1924-25
John Cook, an inside-forward from Notts County arrived together with Billy Poyntz from Leeds, the latter having scored a hat-trick three hours after getting married in his early days at Leeds. One point from the first two games gave the club a poor start to the season, made worse by the fact Louis Page had yet again missed a penalty, in the scoreless draw at Charlton. However, it all came good in the first home match of the season, versus Aberdare, for the Cobblers won 5-0, and Billy Lockett scored four goals, to prove there was still life in the old dog yet. A South African touring team arrived at the County Ground in September and beat the Cobblers 2-1.

Frank Brett was tried at centre-forward with some success, but Bob Hewison reverted to the old guard, when entertaining Swansea in the League. The referee for the game, a Mr.Attwood, arrived 20 minutes late, and linesman Horne took over with Dado Jones running the line - and this was a man in his 50's. It was around this time that the club announced they had turned down an attractive offer from Leicester City for Louis Page, and the previous season Sunderland made a five figure offer for both Page and Pease, and that too was turned down. One player who did leave was Colin Myers, when the nomadic forward joined his sixth club in seven seasons, joining Q.P.R. Richard Oxley moved in the opposite direction.

Lockett was out injured, and with neither Cook or Poyntz fitting in well, Hewison signed two forwards from Luton, Ernest Cockle and Ralph Hoten. Cockle had been a reserve player for both Arsenal and Luton, having come into the game late, while Hoten had assisted Portsmouth and Notts County, and was a first team regular at Luton, until this season.

Chairman F.C.Parker - who upset the supporters!

Bob Hewison took over the mantle of penalty taker again and converted one, to give his team both points against Brighton, but he failed to convert another against Brentford, and the points were lost. Lockett took a penalty against Millwall and missed, whilst Page stepped up again and failed, in the home match with Watford.

The F.A. Cup run of 1924/25 lasted one game, but 32,718 watched the Tottenham team beat the Cobblers 3-0, in a game when fog slowly descended, and due to this weather there was no half-time interval.

In February Bob Hewison announced he was leaving the club, with no ill-feelings on either side. He moved to Q.P.R., while the Cobbler's stated they were looking for a player-manager. Hewison was to give Q.P.R. six seasons, before parting company with them, when he returned to Northampton as he had a confectionary shop in Kingsthorpe. He trained the Nomads until he moved to Bristol, as City's manager in 1931, where he stayed until after the Second World War.

He later managed Guildford and Bath, and finished his days as a scout for Bristol Rovers. He would well remember his last game in charge at Northampton, it was at Swansea, and with five minutes to go, Northampton had a single goal lead, but the Swans netted twice in the remaining five minutes. The directors continued to run the club, until a replacement was found.

In the meantime, Pease, Page, Lockett and Cockle all missed penalties, bringing the seasons total to eight. It was agreed that Charlie Evans, recently arrived from Cardiff, would take the spot-kicks, and even if he missed the first one, he would continue.

The supporters club was formed on the 31st May 1924 at the Whitworth Road Conservative Club, the club that Darnell had built for the 'blue collared' Tories. The supporters set to work raising money for their parent club, through events and by building up their number. By February 1925, the supporters had 342 members, and enough money to make their first donation to the club. With this in mind, they set up a meeting with the club chairman, Charles Parker, never dreaming of what was to take place.

Parker was also the president of the supporters club, and at the meeting he was handed the money, with a proviso that it should be spent on players, and nothing else. On this instruction, Parker, gave them back their money, and resigned from the presidentship of the supporters club, and told the players not to have any contact with any member of the supporters club. (how the players, were to know who was a member and who was not is unknown!) The supporters held an emergency meeting and discussed disbanding only nine months after they started, but once again the club's saviour stepped into the unholy row and poured oil over troubled waters. 'Pat' Darnell addressed the supporters, accepted the post of president, and even invited their chairman, W.Liddell, onto the management committee of the club. Liddell was a player in the club's first season and he was later to be invited on to the board.

Around this time, the club announced that Page and Lockett were up for sale, although regarding the latter it was rather tongue in cheek, for Lockett had lost his first team place, to Cockle, and at 32 would hardly fetch a large fee, but there was no doubt, that Page would be much sought after, and he made it clear he would like to return North to keep an eye on his business interests.

In the 1-0, home win over Q.P.R., a presentation was made by the Cobblers to the London club's manager, Bob Hewison, in recognition of all his hard work. The following week, after a 1-1 draw at home to Norwich in which Page missed the 9th penalty of the season (8 League, 1 F.A.Cup), the Kingsthorpe Grove School played St.James' School in the School Cup Final, the Kingsthorpe team winning 6-0.

Ninth place was one place lower than last season, but if each one of those missed penalties had earned a point, the club would have come third. Penalty-taker Charles Evans joined Grimsby, Poyntz returned North with Bradford City, and Cook retired. There was speculation that Fanny Walden would return as player-manager, he had been released by Spurs, and he applied for the vacant manager's job. But when a deal was made with Burnley that they would sign Page in exchange for Tresadern and a fee, then Walden withdrew his request, for Tresadern, the ex-England international, was also to become the club's new player-manager.

Page was to give Burnley Seven seasons, in which he won seven England Caps, not only at football, but also baseball. He later assisted Manchester United and Port Vale, before turning his hand to management, with Yeovil, Newport, Glentoran, Swindon and Chester, before later scouting for Leicester.

1925-26

The season had not started before the first piece of sad news came, when Burrows, the trainer, died. He had been with the club since its formation and held down several jobs in the 28 years he was with them. His replacement was Joe Webster from Watford.

John (Jack) Tresadern had spent 12 seasons at West Ham, winning two England caps and an F.A.Cup winners medal. He had always been part-time with the Londoners, never giving up his job as a shipping clerk, however, when the company he worked for transferred, so did he, and moved to Burnley. But he was keen to enter management, and Northampton offered him the chance, although his playing career was going to be limited since he was 35, but little did he know it was the start of a 38 year management career. Percy Allen of Lincoln was signed to replace Evans, being an old team mate of Tresadern's at West Ham, and he was followed by Leslie Robinson, also from West Ham, a prolific

scoring forward. Then came the club's first foreign transaction, William Shaw who was signed from Barcelona, the ex-Scarborough man had scored 31 goals in 38 games for the Spanish club.

The club could not have had a better start, a 4-3 win at Brentford, with Ernie Cockle netting all four goals, and this was followed by a 4-0 win against Crystal Palace. After a 1-1 draw away to Bristol City, two victories followed in two home games, 3-2 against Aberdare, and 2-1 against Plymouth, the Devonians first defeat since March, when they were beaten by.... Northampton! However, the bubble burst at Aberdare, when the Welsh club won 1-0, and if that was not convincing, then Southend made sure with a 6-1 victory; Allen missed a penalty - it seemed that happened when you put on a Northampton shirt.

Things did not get better, and from top place the club sank down the League, although they did pull three goals back, when five goals down to Merthyr. By the time the F.A.Cup had come round in November, 18 players had been used. Barnsley at home was the first tie, and Northampton had a convincing 3-1 win, although it could have been more had Cockle not missed a penalty. Newport County were beaten in round two, by three clear goals, thanks to a Robinson hat-trick, while the third round saw old rivals Crystal Palace at the County Ground.

Bill Lockett was recalled for that one, and scored his 100th goal for the club, with Robinson netting two more, to give the club a 3-0 lead. This was the state of play with 11 minutes to go, then Palace scored three in the closing stages, took the Cobblers back to London, and won 2-1.

Plymouth took the brunt of the club's revenge. Northampton having been the first club to beat them in the League this season, they now became the first club to beat them at Home Park. A 4-1 victory over Merthyr was hard fought, and at one stage the referee was going to send Robinson off the field, but a word from skipper Billy Pease and another with a linesman convinced him to change his mind.

After a great start, mid-table was a poor finish. Twenty players were used, and the bulk of the goals came from Robinson and Cockle. Fred Ferrari, who despite his name was born in Stafford, was signed in mid-season, and looked a bright prospect, but he was tempted away to Sheffield Wednesday. There, he lost his way, and it was some time later before he reappeared at Norwich, but he never realised his full potential.

Bill Lockett was released, another great servant, he scored in his last game for the club, away to Q.P.R., and threw in his lot with Kidderminster, and then settled in Market Harborough. Billy Pease also moved on, he joined Middlesborough, and like the tale of how he arrived at Northampton, there was another tale on how he left.

Middlesborough were interested in him, and the manager suggested to the chairman that they travel down to Northampton and watch him play. Together with two other directors, they travelled by car, only to break down at Peterborough. Finding that the repair would take some time they tried to find a car hire firm, and when they were at last successful, they carried on to Northampton, in haste. Arriving at half-time, they settled into their seats for the second period..... only to find Pease was not playing! Billy Pease went on to make one international appearance, versus Wales in 1927, in the same match that Louis Page made his England bow. In the early thirties it was thought that Pease might return to Northampton, but he chose Luton, giving them one season before he retired.

1926-27

Tom Adey came from Swindon, and Evan Edwards from Swansea. There was also an old face that returned, Fanny Walden, who had relented and decided on a comeback with the town, where he filled the void left by Pease.

Another good start to the season, a 3-0 win at Coventry, against a side with ten debutants, the only former player, Houndley, scoring an own goal. The first home match, versus Brentford, saw the new Spion Kop open, but still under construction. It held 4 to 5,000, but when complete there would be room for another 2,000. The supporters club had paid the £650 for the Spoin Kop, and officially handed it over to the club. So short of fit players, Tresadern played himself, although not 100% fit, against Millwall, in the 4-2 defeat, and against Swindon, Jones became the 6th player to have been tried at outside-right. On the credit side the supporters club ran a three day bazaar at the Town Hall, in an effort to raise more money, but things were just not right on the field.

The away match at Luton was stopped 18 minutes from time, and both teams lectured on their physical play. At Norwich, the home side took a 6-1 lead, then netted a seventh, only for the referee to claim he blew his whistle before it crossed the line. While travelling to Swindon, the players missed their connection at Paddington, lunched on the train to Didcot, then hired a charabanc to Swindon, arriving just seven minutes before kick-off.

The F.A.Cup draw had decreed Northampton play away to Boston, and in view of this town's position they did not risk the train, instead using a Charabanc. The game ended 1-1, and in the replay Boston's train broke down, with the players arriving by Taxi. The Cobblers won 2-1, but went out in the next round to Exeter.

Allon and Maloney were signed from Peterborough, for a joint fee of £1,000, whilst William Oxley came from Merthyr, having played against the Cobblers earlier, and Fraser arrived from East Stirling. But the club's fortunes never changed. Full-backs, Brett and Yorke, were tried in the forward line against Gillingham. Brett netted both goals, in the 2-1 win, but in the next home game, with Brighton, player-manager Tresadern broke his leg in a clash with Williams the Brighton keeper. Complications set in, and it was two months before he even returned to managing the club.

The Cobblers finished three points off a re-election place, 31 players were used - only Brett and Hammond were ever-present - and Ernie Cockle was the only goalscorer to reach double figures. Robinson moved on to Norwich in an exchange deal that brought Aitken and Price to Northampton. Also gone was Fanny Walden, he was only a shell of his former self, injuries having got the better of him. He gave the cricket club a few more seasons, and then became an umpire. He took several pubs in the area, including the Dog and Duck at Wellingborough, and also served behind the bar at the Peacock on the Market Square.

1927-28

There was a great influx of players for the start of this season. George O'Dell, from St Albans, a wing-half, winger Joe Daley, Tom Smith - who two seasons earlier had been in Manchester United's first team (he cost Northampton £250). Harry Loasby had a great scoring record with Wellingborough, 66 goals the previous season, and now he was given the chance to show what he could do in the Football League. Aitken and Price had come from Norwich in exchange for Robinson, and full-back George Russell, arrived from Watford. Added to this list, there was winger Tommy Wells who had signed during the latter part of the last season from Arsenal.

When the team kicked off the season at Millwall, only goalkeeper Hammond, full-backs Watson and Jeffs, and Ralph Hoten remained from Hewison's team. Tom Smith captained the side, and in true Northampton tradition missed a penalty in the opening match versus Millwall, but with a 5-2 scoreline it did not matter too much. Defeats followed at Brentford and Crystal Palace, at the latter's ground there was a pitch invasion, when the referee turned down a penalty appeal for Palace.

The sad news of two deaths rocked the club, first it was Alf Cockerill, who had given the County Ground to sport. He had arrived in the town with his mother, and while working for a butcher, grew some vegetables on a piece of land he bought. He first sold these from a barrow, then a shop, then bought a farm at the Eastern part of the town, The County Ground being part of it. But before his death he gave the ground to the Northants County Cricket club, with an agreement that Football should be allowed to be played there. The other loss was that of Joe Webster, the trainer, who died during an Appendix operation. He was soon replaced by the giant Ernie Mellors from Derby.

On the field, things got better, and a five match spell in September brought five wins and 20 goals, Harry Loasby having scored eight and Tommy Wells four. November the 5th, really did bring a fireworks display, of goals, with Loasby, Smith and Wells each scoring a hat-trick, in a 10-0 thrashing of Walsall, in the first ever League encounter between the two clubs. Loasby had scored 18 goals in sixteen League games, plus another three in one F.A.Cup game, when tragedy struck.

Brighton were the second round opponents, in front of 16,000 at the County Ground. A one-on-one situation between Loasby and the Brighton 'keeper Williams, ended with the latter diving bravely at Loasby's feet, but in the clash, Loasby broke his leg, in what was a carbon copy of manager Tresadern's injury.

The manager's injury was against the same team, and the same goalkeeper. Williams was visibly shaken by the incident, and later said, *"I would rather Loasby score six goals, than to see him carried off as he was'*. Complications set in with Loasby's injury and he had to have the leg broken and reset. It was 14 months before he played again.

It was at this time that the programme notes stated that rumours of pending transfers and discipline action against certain players were unfounded. But with 23 players competing for 11 places, there was sure to be a certain amount of friction.

Christmas, was a traditional football time, but it snowed, and snowed heavily, and the club decided not to travel to Luton by train for their festive clash, but took to the road instead, They got stuck at Wendover, and ended up pushing the bus out of a snowdrift. Meanwhile their supporters and Luton waited patiently only to be told, 'the games off'.

The following day, the return match at the County Ground caused a stir, for Luton raced into a 5-1 half-time lead. Whatever was said to the Cobbler's team is unknown, but they scored five goals in the second half, to win 6-5. Unhappiest man was Luton's Jimmy Reid, for he netted four goals, yet finished on the losing side.

So annoyed were Luton, over the Cobblers non-appearance and that defeat, that every time Northampton made a compensation offer over the Christmas game, Luton rejected it, and the matter ended up in the hands of the League management committee.

The third round of the cup brought an away match at Roker Park against Sunderland, and as expected the home team took a commanding (3-1) lead, but the Cobblers pulled two goals back. Not only did they bring them back to Northampton, but made £577 from the tie. The replay attracted 21,148, a new ground record, but no fairy tale, for the Cobblers lost 0-3.

Amazing incidents took place in a League match versus Torquay, who were to finish bottom of the Division. The Cobbler's took a 4-1 lead, only to see it frittered away, and Torquay pull level. Northampton scored two more, but both were disallowed, and the referee had to be escorted from the field, by policemen, at the end of the match.

Loasby was missed, Cockle was brought back, but was past his best, Price was not up to the job, and O'Dell did a good job but was needed in the half-back line. Herbert Chapman was at one particular game, and suggested he had a player who might fit the bill, he was not quite good enough for the Arsenal side, but he felt he could fit in at Northampton. His name was Ted Bowen, and he made his debut away to Norwich, which the Cobblers won 4-3, and Bowen scored a hat-trick, the first man to do so for Northampton in a league match since Fanny Walden.

Millwall were running away with the championship, and it was more a case of waiting for them to slip up rather than overtaking them, but the club made every effort to be up there with them. In a 4-1 defeat at Newport, the Cobblers scored their 100th League goal, but were disappointed to find another team had pipped them at the post, by scoring their 100th goal earlier in their game, the team was Northampton Town reserves; they scored their 100th v Peterborough reserves.

The last game of the season was at home to Coventry, who disputed the Cobbler's winning goal, and each time the referee put the ball on the centre spot, a Coventry player kicked it away. At the end of the game he was hit on the head by a tobacco tin. The club ended up in second place, unfortunately ten points behind Millwall the champions.

They drew crowds of 10,000, and five players - Bowen, Loasby, Hoten, Smith and Wells all had double figures so far as League goals were concerned. The half-back line of Allon, Maloney and O'Dell would be talked of for years to come. One sad note was the premature death of Goldie, the ex amateur international who had played for the club in the Southern League, and had assisted the Nomads. He had taken over his father's waterproofing business in Victoria road, but in a bout of depression took his own life, while still in his mid 30's, leaving behind a young family. It was later stated that he was to have been approached to join the Nomad's management committee.

1928-29

The bulk of last season's team were retained. Joe Daley, the right-winger moved to Luton and full-back Tommy Jeffs called it a day. Jack Harrington, from Wolves, was signed to replace Daley, Andy Lincoln, an inside-forward came from Millwall, and John Weston, a left-winger, was signed as cover for Wells. In all there were six new signings, but none were to make an impact throughout the season, making just 52 appearances between them.

The season kicked off with a 4-1 home win over Charlton, in which both Bowen and new boy, Andy Lincoln claimed to have kicked the ball as it crossed the line for a Cobbler's goal, but it was credited to a Charlton defender, who was making desperate attempts to keep it out.

September saw a clash with the Northamptonshire Football Association. The club's Maunsall Cup Final versus Kettering was held over from the previous year, but Northampton did not want to play the game at Kettering. They stated it was not a replay and the County Ground should be used, but the N.F.A. retorted that the last County Cup Final played at the County ground brought in just £21. Northampton relented and played the game at Kettering, and beat them 4-0.

There was an amazing 8-1 win over Crystal Palace in October, Ralph Hoten scoring five goals, and two weeks later, in the next home game, he hit another four against Torquay. This kind of form was keeping the club up with the leaders, and the talk was of promotion.

The F.A. Cup brought three matches, all against the same club, Millwall. Two draws were followed by a second replay at Highbury, which Millwall won 2-0. The first of the trio, was at Millwall and a group of Cobbler's supporters from Wellingborough walked to the match. They left their home town at 11.00 a.m. on Wednesday to arrive in time for the match.

It was about this time that companies saw a successful football team as a good way of selling their wares. The 'Health Ray Clinic' in Abington street, took a full column advert, complete with team Photograph, stating that prior to their Cup match v Millwall, all the players had 'Health Ray Treatment'. It claimed to cure many ailments, including rheumatics, indigestion, gout, head noises, hair loss and influenza, to name but a few. Unfortunately it did not have the power to win cup games!

The season run-in was tense and exciting, and it was a very small consolation for secretary Arthur Jones, to know that the club he had helped build, from nothing to a League side, was top of the Third Division South, on the day he died. The ex-schoolteacher passed away, after a short illness, and still held the post of club secretary; a sad day at such an exciting time for the club. Lady luck seemed to enjoy teasing the Cobblers, for they were lucky to escape with a point in the home match with Swindon, when the Wiltshire side had two goals disallowed, then they took a 3-0 lead at home to Fulham, only to see the Londoners score a trio in a seven minutes spell - and then had the disappointment of a winning goal being ruled out for offside.

The penultimate away game, at Q.P.R. saw the gates closed before the kick-off. A fence gave way, and several of the 21,916 supporters were hurt, and to cap it all, Rangers won 4-1. On the last day of the season, one of three teams could win the championship. Charlton had 52 points, and were away to mid-table Walsall; Palace also had 52 points, but an inferior goal average, were home to mid-table Brighton, while the Cobblers on 51 points were away to eighth place Watford.

Northampton played a hard game, but could only manage a point, whereas both Palace and Charlton, won their games, and Northampton Town had to be content with third place, but their goal average was better than Charlton's, and just two more points would have seen them in the Second Division. Instead, they could only reflect on some of the incidents that took place over the previous eight months. Like the match at Exeter, when the Devon club signed a winger called Death (pronounced 'Deeath') on the Friday night, whereupon he immediately travelled down from his home in the North-East, arrived in Exeter at 9.00 a.m. on Saturday morning, grabbed two hours sleep, and helped his new side to a win over the Cobblers.

The home match versus Exeter caused some amusement when a dog got onto the pitch, and play was held up as the players ran around, trying to catch it. One enterprising supporter brought a portable wireless to the game against Bristol Rovers, and watched the match, game against Bristol Rovers, and watched the match, while listening to the Cup Final. Once again the club showed its generosity, by inviting Leicester City down, in an effort to raise money for the cricket club.

Most of the players who had joined at the start of the season had left, and Willie Watson retired, the last link with the side that entered the League in 1920.

1929-30

There were no major signings of note, for manager Tresadern relied on the side that came so close to promotion the last season. The season kicked off at the County Ground against Bournemouth, in a rainstorm, which the Cobblers won 2-0, and by mid-september, they topped the League again.

The weather played a major factor on the season, as August was wet, so September was hot, and a game versus Norwich was played on a sun-baked pitch. A 1-1 draw at home to Plymouth saw 21,102 pack the County ground, and ambulance men plus the police, were kept busy.

December the 30th, 1929 is a day to remember in the club's history. An away match at Bournemouth in terrible conditions saw the club race into a 3-0 lead, but before half-time Bournemouth had pulled two goals back from the penalty spot. While the players were taking their break, the referee declared the game abandoned, as the rain was turning the pitch into a mud bath. While the players were returning home, little did they know what was happening at the County Ground.

A Mrs. Abbey, of Birchfield Road, was returning home via Abington Avenue, when she saw smoke coming from under one of the doors at the ground, at 6.30 p.m. She alerted a Mr. Marriott, the landlord of the County Hotel, who promptly phoned the fire brigade. By Seven-o-clock, the fire was at its peak, and it took until 8.30p.m. to get it under control. Stands A, B and C were destroyed, but D was saved, except for some charring. At the time the cause of the fire was unknown, but it was later revealed that it was believed to have come from the ceiling of the away dressing room, which had been used earlier in day for a match between the second eleven and Bournemouth reserves,

Damage was estimated at £5,000, and the Saints offered the use of Franklin Gardens, but the club were going to soldier on, either relocating season ticket-holders, or returning their money. This was the start of unconfirmed rumours that the club were looking for a new ground.

The club's success saw other teams taking interest, not only in the players, but also the manager, and Jack Tresadern, was in line for the Tottenham manager's post, and lost out only by a casting vote, although he did get the job some five years later.

The Third round of the F.A.Cup was reached this season. After beating Aldershot 1-0 away, Northampton then entertained Margate and beat them 6-0 and it could have been more was it not for the heroics of the Margate keeper, a 20-year-old named Keizer. Blackburn ended the clubs Cup interest with a 4-1 win, but £600 was made out of the game.

By February the stand was rebuilt, and things started to get back to normal, but although the club kept up with the leaders, Plymouth were so far in front that everything hinged on them doing badly, rather than any other team doing well. May saw the club end up in fourth place, and provide two very entertaining matches at the County Ground.

The first was against Aberdeen, invited to raise money for the ailing cricket club - it ended 1-1 - with the Cobbler's playing a 'Mr X' at inside-right. It was later announced to be Tommy Boyle the ex-Sheffield United and Manchester United player. The second game was against Arsenal in the Hospital Cup, in which both sets of players toured a shoe factory, and then took tea with the Mayor.

It was all change time again, and after two close calls at promotion, Tresadern decided on a rebuild. Tom Smith moved to Norwich, but only gave them a season before moving back to his home in Whitchurch, where he died at 35. Ralph Hoten moved on to Q.P R., and Frank Brett joined Brighton,

CHAPTER FOUR
1930-1938

1930-31

The club had gone for experience. Tommy Boyle, an inside-forward, aged 34, and Bill Inglis, a defender aged 33, were both signed from Manchester United. Frank Davies a wing-half from Nantwich was a 'youngster' of 27 compared to his new team-mates.

There was a great start to the season, two away matches, both won, by 4-1 at Bristol Rovers, and 4-0 at Brentford, the first Cobblers win against the London club on their own ground since 1928. Ted Bowen had five goals under his belt, and another young goalscorer, emerged, Albert Dawes. The youngster, and his brother Fred, were two youngsters signed from Frimley Green. Albert was the forward, and Fred the full-back, and they were to make history later on in their careers.

By October, Northampton had lost just one of their nine League games, and ironically that was at home to mid-table Torquay, and by 3-0. However, they got back to winning ways when Coventry were beaten 1-0, a shot from Dawes cannoning off the referee to enter the net. The following game, a 3-0 win over Walsall, proved to be Tresedern's last game in charge, for he left to join Crystal Palace, and returning to his roots. He was to give Palace five seasons, and took them to the runners-up spot of Division Three South, but in those days only the champions went up. The next stop was Spurs, a club he had previously applied to join, but his three years there were unhappy, failing to win over the supporters or the board, so he joined Plymouth Argyle, and despite being with them for nine seasons, he only had two as the manager of a League team, those either side of WW2. After a spell as Aston Villa's scout he joined Chelmsford City as manager in 1949, and Hastings in 1951, to whom he gave eight seasons, and finally Tonbridge, where he was still in charge when he died in 1959.

"I Do not believe in too much training"

Cobblers manager Syd Puddefoot, prior to the clubs 6-1 defeat by Walthamstow Avenue November 1936.

This move naturally opened the door to speculation as to who was going to be the next manager at Northampton. Several names were thrown into the ring, including those in the 'veteran' stage, on the playing staff. The club did quite well without a manager, holding Notts County the divisional leaders to a 2-2 draw at Meadow Lane, in front of 21,329, with over 1,500 being Cobblers' supporters.

A young forward named Fred Eyre was signed from Wolverton, and he made his first team bow in the Maunsall Cup Semi-final versus Rushden, He scored two of the goals in a 4-2 win, and ironically the two Rushden goals were scored by Shipley and Seddon, both ex Cobblers.

Jack English became the new manager, who had experience with Nelson and Darlington when his own playing career was cut short at 27 of age. He had played for Sheffield United in the 'Khaki Cup Final' of 1915, and had a brief spell at Watford before retiring as a player; he was the club's first non-playing manager. Under English they started a run of undefeated games, that started with a 6-2 win at Walsall, was followed by a 6-0 home victory against Q.P.R., and ended - eight games later - at Luton. This lifted the club to second place, but ten points behind the leaders, Notts County. Unfortunately, the seven games between Easter and the end of the season, realised just six points, and saw the club drop to sixth place.

The team failed to capitalise on a 'four' pointer home match with Notts County, that attracted 14,284 and was watched by the Mayors of both Northampton and Nottingham; the game ended 0-0.

Several of the fringe players were released. Armitage joined Halifax, and McLachlan moved to Mansfield, he was later to become chairman of the Leicestershire Football Association.

FRED DAWES

1931-32

The only new face in the starting line-up was John Scott, a right-winger from Nottingham Forest, who had also seen service with Sunderland, Darlington, and Kettering. Although the club had also signed centre-half Ollie Park from Newcastle, and winger Bob Mortimer from Bolton, they were to wait a while for their first team debuts. By the end of September, the club had won only three of its nine League games, and fell 4-0 at home to wooden-spoonists elect, Thames. It was to be the East London team's only away win of the season, as well as their last season (of two) in the League. The Northampton supporters were not happy and a missile was thrown at Kemp, their captain, and a linesman.

This resulted in the Football Association, insisting that the club put up posters warning supporters of their conduct. Two new players were signed, for an undisclosed fee, from Notts County - John Dowsey and Harry Lovatt. Dowsey could play winger or wing-half, was 26 years old, and had seen service with Newcastle, West Ham, Carlisle and Sunderland, and he ousted Tom Allon from the right half-spot. Harry Lovatt, an inside-forward, was the same age, and was something of a footballing nomad, having played for Port Vale, Crewe, Bradford City, Wrexham, Scarborough, and Leicester. Lovatt took any forward position, and scored on his debut v Q.P.R.

It was after that particular game against the London side that a sick rumour spread around the town like wildfire, that four of the Cobbler's players had been killed in a car crash. The story gathered so much momentum, that by Monday morning a large band of supporters decided to forsake their work, and watch as the players came into the County Ground for training, and count them in - then breathing a sigh of relief when the last one arrived. It was front page news in the local paper that evening.

When the first round of the F.A.Cup came around, the club had just completed a nine match run without a win, and hoped they could stop this poor form in the home tie with the Metropolitan Police; they did, with vengeance, scoring nine without reply. But despite this morale booster, it was Boxing Day before they recorded their next League win, 1-0 against Gillingham, leaving a run of 13 League games without victory.

Southend were beaten 3-0, in the next round of the F.A.Cup, then came Darlington. Ollie Park had won a place in the first team by this time, and he announced that his family, who lived in Darlington, were going to watch him play, for the first time. He gave a creditable display, in the 1-1 draw, but with Bob Maloney fit again, he was out for the replay, at the County Ground, which

the Cobblers won 2-0. The cup run ended in the next round, with a 4-2 defeat to Bradford.

An away game at Watford caused some amusement, although not at the time, for the team bus broke down at St Albans, and the players had to pile on to a service bus that ran to Watford. The club found a bit of form towards the end of the season, but after beating Torquay 2-0 at home, on a very wet day, it was announced that only 2,882 watched the game, which led the local newspaper to ask; *"Would the crowd have been bigger, if one or more of the terraces, were covered?"*

A 4-3 victory over Clapton Orient in the last home game was almost a victory for the London side, who were so short of players that they fielded one, who had not played since September, another who had not appeared since November, and one who had not played at all!

The end of the season, saw the club finish in 14th place, and several familiar faces left the County Ground. The famous half-back line of Allon, Maloney and O'Dell, all left the club, although Maloney was granted a testimonial, for the match versus Grimsby. He suffered from illness and injury which had restricted his appearances during this season, however he was far from finished as a player, and his career took on an international look, when he turned out for Shelbourne and Dundalk of Ireland, and Racing Club Calais of France. He later returned to the area and set up a small engineering business after the war. Both Allon and O'Dell moved to Wigan Borough, the latter returning to his Hertfordshire home after his playing days, and worked as a bus driver for London Transport.

Ted Bowen left for Bristol City, his place had been taken by Albert Dawes, and the club found him 'surplus to requirements', but he left behind a record of 34 League goals in a season, a record that would stand for some time. The most surprising departure was Harry Lovatt, but he did not enjoy his five months at Northampton and asked to leave. He was put on the transfer list at £1,000, and allowed to join Macclesfield on loan, but when no one was willing to pay the fee, he brought the League management committee in, and they granted him a free transfer; he went on to join Stafford Rangers.

The most disappointing move was that of Colin Russell, he had joined before the transfer deadline from local football, scored eight goals in those last seven games, including a hat-trick in his last versus Swindon. He then threw in his lot with Bournemouth, but by the end of the following season he was back in the area, with Wolverton. Bill Inglis, also retired, but took up a coaching job, with the club.

1932-33

Fred Forbes, a forward, was signed from Leith Athletic, just prior to his 38th birthday. He had seen service with Hearts, Everton, Plymouth and Bristol Rovers, and had returned home to finish his playing days, but the opportunity to play League football again brought him back.

John McFarlane, another Scotsman, arrived from Halifax; he was a forward. Jim McGuire, had the opportunity to emigrate with his parents to America, or join the Cobblers, when Celtic gave him a free transfer, and he decided on the latter, and took over Maloney's mantle at centre-half.

There were also changes on the board, Len Benbow, Len Hawtin, Bill Liddell and R. Hooton, were all elected to the board of directors, and all but the latter were ex-players.

Albert Dawes was finding the net in no uncertain fashion, and during September he scored nine goals including four against Newport, and another quartet against Swindon. The victory over Newport produced a 8-0 score, and history was made, as both Albert, and brother Fred - who had now made the first team - scored. This was the first, and only time, that brothers had scored for the Cobbler's in the same League match.

Running a football team, brought many and varying problems, as the new members of the board were to find. In the home match versus Brighton, storm clouds approached and the game was started five minutes early, there was no half-time break, and it finished in semi-darkness. The second problem saw the traffic commissioners stop buses running into outlying areas on a Saturday, just to pick up Cobbler's supporters. This brought a howl of protest from the supporters and the club, especially when the latter needed all the support it could get.

After a 1-1 draw at Q.P.R, the players returned to Northampton, packed their bags, and left for Holland. They took 12 players, as there was a doubt about Fred Dawes ankle, so Oakley was added to the squad. Also in the party was manager English, trainer Newman, and directors, Gillett, Seal, James, Liddell and Hooton. The team was invited by the Dutch F.A. to play a game against the national side, who it was said were equivalent to our own third division at the time. Northampton were regarded as an average division three side,

Many of the players had never been abroad, and it was a first for Jack English, but Tommy Boyle, who was a seasoned campaigner at foreign travel, used his knowledge of foreign parts, to 'wind up' the management. He informed his manager that the main dish of Holland was mice! This caused the manager to scurry around trying to find a hotel that provided English food, until someone pointed out the joke!

The players arrived in Holland, and were photographed puffing on their duty free cigars; what a difference 60 years makes! The game, in Rotterdam, ended 4-0 in favour of the Cobbler's with Albert Dawes netting all Four goals. So impressed with the club were the Dutch F.A. they sent a representative to the hotel the club were staying in, to congratulate them.

It was back to earth with a bang, when the following Saturday Q.P.R. were the visitors. The game ended 0-0, and Albert Dawes, was carried off injured, forcing the first team change for 11 League games.

MR. CHARLES GYDE DEAD

GREAT WORK FOR THE COBBLERS

FIFTY YEARS LICENSEE

Every football enthusiast in Northamptonshire, as well as a wide circle of personal friends, will learn with deep regret of the death this morning of Mr. Charles Gyde, a founder and director of the Northampton Town Football Club.

MR. GYDE, who was 82 years of age, was for 50 years licensee of the Princess Royal, Wellingborough-road. He had been in failing health for a year and a week ago became seriously ill. He retired from the Princess Royal in February, and since then had lived with his only child, Mrs Payne, at 40 Palmerston-road.

Failing health did not lessen the keenness of his intellect, and up to his last serious illness he was a brilliant and interesting conversationalist.

MR. CHARLES GYDE.

The newspaper of 17th June 1932 announced the sad news.

The F.A. Cup paired Northampton with Lloyds Bank of Sittingbourne, an unknown quantity. They shocked the Cobbler's by taking a 1-0 lead, and the League side struggled to pull one back before half-time, but in the second period, they rattled the goals in, Dawes, netted Five, and Cobblers came away 8-1 winners. It was a different story for the home tie with Doncaster in the second round. Over 10,000 watched the game, Doncaster brought 400, many of them miners who had finished a night shift, then travelled down to watch the game. They were rewarded with a 1-0 win.

It was obvious that the goalscoring feats of Albert Dawes would attract the 'big boys', and national newspapers printed stories of Tottenham and Birmingham who were supposedly interested in the player. But manager English, who himself had been given a new contract, denied this. Again, the club showed its inconsistent form when Bournemouth were beaten 6-0, and a few weeks later Cardiff beat the Cobblers by the same score, although in both cases, the losing side lost key players. By beating Reading 1-0, the club went through the whole season without a home defeat in the League.

It is worth mentioning the goalscoring feats of Albert Dawes, for that season he netted 51 - 32 in the League, 5 in the F.A.Cup 10 in friendlies, and 4 in the County cup competitions. The season ended on a sour note, when the corporation turned down the club's request for money.

During the season, an interesting little story emerged involving 'that man' again, Pat Darnell! Tommy Boyle was taking some other players to the dog racing at South Bridge, when he was stopped by a policeman, accused of erratic and dangerous driving, and was summonsed.

When the case went to court, Boyle was represented by Darnell, who got the policeman so flummoxed, he lost

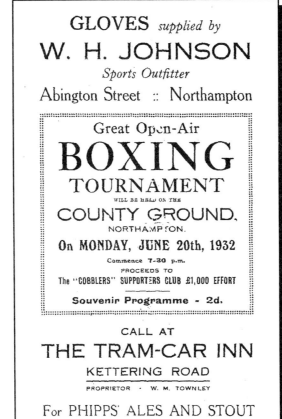

GLOVES *supplied by*

W. H. JOHNSON
Sports Outfitter

Abington Street :: Northampton

Great Open-Air
BOXING
TOURNAMENT
WILL BE HELD ON THE
COUNTY GROUND,
NORTHAMPTON.
On MONDAY, JUNE 20th, 1932
Commence 7-30 p.m.
PROCEEDS TO
The "COBBLERS" SUPPORTERS CLUB £1,000 EFFORT
Souvenir Programme - 2d.

CALL AT
THE TRAM-CAR INN
KETTERING ROAD
PROPRIETOR · W. M. TOWNLEY

For PHIPPS' ALES AND STOUT

The supporters club made use of the County Ground for other fund-raising purposes

his way and the case was dropped - even in his 60's the clubs founder was still involved in helping the club, and its staff.

Forbes, was released, and at 39, he still gave Airdrie a season. Oakley, moved to Kettering, and Mortimer, joined Brentford. It was sad to see 'keeper Len Hammond go, for he had given the club stirling service and joined Notts County for an undisclosed fee. He never really completed a season with County, after a bust-up with the management, making his feelings known after declaring Third Division players were not up to the next level. He returned to the area and played for Rugby.

1933-34
The Balance sheet made dismal reading, with over £600 lost on the season. Biggest expenditures were the entertainment tax of £1,642 and the reserve team travel, at £1,336, surprisingly outweighing the first team by £800. The club had a dilemma with their reserves. If they played them in the Northants League, the opposition was too weak, and if they played them in the London Combination expenses shot through the roof.

Tom Crilly an experienced defender with Hartlepool and Crystal Palace took the full-back spot vacated by Oakley, and Danny Tolland came from Ayr United, a clever, ball playing inside-forward. The first game was at home to Luton. The cricket finished at 5.30p.m. and after a flurry of activity, the football started an hour later, it was the first time that amplifiers were set up for music, and announcements.

It was the Sixth game before the club picked up their first win, 2-1 at home to Q.P.R, but it had a downside, since Fred Dawes was taken off with a broken collar bone. A bad run of defeats resulted in an axe wielding exercise by the manager, and he made four changes. One of the players dropped was new 'keeper, Bill Cave, which was a shame as he had saved penalties in the last two games.

On December the 2nd, Albert Dawes scored a hat-trick against the Palace, yet three weeks later he was a Palace player, joining them for a 'record' fee, which was later revealed at £1,650. The news did not get any better, when Tom Crilly was carried off, but the F.A.Cup run was causing interest. Exeter and Torquay were removed with some ease in the first two rounds, while Southampton proved to be more of a stumbling block, but they fell after a replay. Huddersfield came next, and they were sitting on the top of Division One, at the time. Despite this awesome task, Northampton beat them on their own ground, which must rate as the greatest giant-killing act, in the club's history.

Darnell met the players at the St. Johns station, and wished them all good luck. Two train loads of supporters went, with a combined number of 25 carriages. Over 28,000 watched the game, and the club's share of the gate was £639, the equivalent, of a month of Division Three football. Now the interest was bubbling, and the local Chronicle and Echo ran a 'Limerick' competition, the winner would have two tickets for the game in the next round at Preston. This was the first time the club had ever reached the last 16 of the competition.

An even larger army of supporters left for Preston and 40,180 watched the game at Deepdale - a new ground record for them - the figure including over 2,000 Cobblers supporters. The game ended as a convincing 4-0 win for Preston, Palethorpe hitting a hat-trick, after Jim McGuire opened the scoring by putting the ball past his own 'keeper.

The rest of the season was something of an anti-climax, with small interesting facts emerging here and there, like the match at Charlton, where the home team wore Pink, the Cobblers blue, and the ball was yellow; and at Swindon the players were brought back from the dressing room after the referee discovered he had played four minutes short.

Ernest Clough,
— Menswear —

WEATHERPROOFS BURBERRY and AQUASCUTUM RAINCOATS. From 3 guineas	WOODROW AMYLYTE HATS The Original Lightweight Bowler 18/6	MEN'S SHIRTS of distinction 8/6 to 21/. including two Collars. Shirts to Measure:

Westgate, Huddersfield.

Huddersfield Town.

Goal
1 Turner
Backs
2 Roughton   3 Mountford
Half-Backs
4 Willingham   5 Young   6 Campbell
Forwards
7 Williams   8 McLean   9 Mangnall   10 Luke   11 Bott

News & Chronicle FOR BEST REPORTS

12 Wells   13 Tolland   14 Henson   15 Boyle   16 Mitchell
Forwards
17 Davies   18 McGuire   19 Riches
Half-Backs
20 Dawes   21 Crilly
Backs
22 Allen
Goal

Northampton Town.

Referee—E. V. GOUGH (Staffordshire).   Colours—Claret Shirts, White Knickers.
Linesmen—N. BOOTH (Red Stripe).   J. W. LEGGE (Blue Stripe).

RESTAURANT & GRILL ROOM. 60 BEDROOMS. PRIVATE SITTING ROOMS, &c.
Replete with every comfort for visitors to Huddersfield.

GEORGE HOTEL
(Adjoining Station)
H. A. DUCKSBURY, Resident Proprietor.
Telephones 3574, 3572, 3582.   Telegraphic Address :—" George," Huddersfield.

Programme from the famous F.A.Cup win
Note the player numbering system at this time.

Several of the first and reserve players were 'swapped', for the last game of the season, as the reserves needed to win their last game versus West Ham to stay in the First Division of the London Combination, this they did by winning 1-0. Almost as an act of defiance, the reserve players, won their first team fixture at home to Cardiff 2-0. That game ended the season, as it started, for the football followed the cricket by an hour.

An interesting footnote was the fact that Albert Dawes, was the top goalscorer in Division Three South, but he was not the top scorer for either of his clubs that season. Two old favourites were released, when Fred Davies joined Burton, and Ollie Park returned to his native North-East, and gave Hartlepool four seasons before becoming player-manager of Consett.

1934-35

Billy Baker, a goalkeeper, joined the club from Brentford and James Melville a centre-half from Hull, and Dick Brown a winger arrived from Q.P.R.

Northampton Town had agreed to take over Wellngborough Town as their 'A' team, although the non-Leaguers would still have their own management committee, and select the team and players, but Northampton would be allowed to use these players in their first or reserve teams. Likewise if a first or second team player was recovering from injury, then he would be given a run in the 'A' team. For the first time, the club ran three teams.

Two excursion trains ran from Northampton to Coventry, and nearly 23,000 watched Coventry win 2-0. Two wins in the first Seven games was hardly exciting, but by late September, the club found its form, and started to climb up the League. John Surtees, a ster who had joined from Bournemouth, was unable to break into the League side and asked to be released as he was going to emigrate, but before he did he was offered trials at Sheffield Wednesday, was accepted, and at the end of the season, played in the F.A.Cup final for them; a real rags to riches story.

If that did not upset the supporters too much, then the next move by the club did, for George Henson was sold to Wolves. Henson had joined the club from Wolverton, in October 1932, had taken over as main goalscorer when Albert Dawes left, and in his short time with the club had netted 28 goals. At 22 years he still had a lot of goals left in him. He failed to make an impact at Wolves or his next club Swansea, but became a prolific scorer for Bradford, and netted 32 goals during the 1937-38 season whereupon he was quickly snatched up by Sheffield United, but the war ended the rest of his career. The club tried to counter this departure by signing the Luton forward Tom Bell, who joined the club on his 28th birthday, but did not make an immediate impact.

Barry Town were host to the Cobblers in the F.A. Cup, but they lost their centre-forward Carless after three minutes, and Cobblers won 1-0. Then came two matches against Workington in round two. Hobbs of the Cobblers scored the only goal in the 180 minutes. The next round brought Bolton Wanderers to Northampton. Twenty extra buses were laid on from Brackley, Daventry, Weedon and Bletchley, and 30 extra police were drafted in to cope with the crowd. The gates were opened at 12 noon, and as the first supporters began to arrive, a flurry of snow fell but did not settle. Nearly 18,000 watched Bolton win the match 2-0.

This was the first season of the divisional knock-out cup, where clubs played other clubs from within their division, but it was soon found that clubs were not treating it seriously enough, and in many cases it was a run-out for some reserve players as the attendances reflected. Clapton Orient were beaten after a replay, Newport were overcome 3-0, but the club lost its quarter-final match at home to Bristol Rovers 2-0, in front of 1,000 spectators.

It was Rovers who inflicted a 7-1 defeat on the club, causing nine changes - two positional - for the next match, versus Gillingham. February started badly and Jack English announced he was not going to be given a new contract. He left the club at once, and this phlegmatic character took the manager's job at Exeter,

THE COBBLERS' CHORUS

Despite the successful Cup run, the finances were still in a poor state

later returned to Darlington, but the County Ground had not heard the last of the name English! The day he left, director Russell Seal died at his Cogenhoe home. He had been ill for some time but it was thought that he had started to make a recovery.

On March the 7th, Syd Puddefoot, the ex-England international forward of West Ham, Falkirk and Blackburn, took over as manager. He was the talk of the footballing world when he moved from West Ham to Falkirk for a record fee as it was most unusual for Scottish clubs to pay big fees. However, he found the standard of football somewhat lower and jumped at the chance to join Blackburn. His first game in charge at Northampton was a 3-0 win over Torquay, and the club won nine of their remaining 12 games to finish the season in seventh place. If that form had been maintained earlier in the season they would have been strong contenders for the championship.

Tom Crilly and Tommy Boyle both became player-managers, with Scunthorpe and Scarborough respectively. Billy Baker joined Rochdale and Alex Cochrane went to Swindon.

1935-36
Biggest news was the club broke its record in-coming transfer fee, when they paid £1,000 to Falkirk for James Bartram.

Puddefoot secured him from his old club Falkirk, where the 24-year-old had been a prolific scorer in his three seasons there, netting 65 goals, including six, in one game versus Ayr. Bartram was not a Scotsman, he was born in South Shields, and played for Portsmouth and North Shields, before finding his form at Falkirk.

Another new face was 'keeper Bill Gormlie, once a cinema manager at Blackpool, but he gave it up to take up professional football, after four seasons at Blackburn he had joined Northampton. The most significant signing, was that of Colin Lyman, for he was the first player to play in the first team, who had come through the ranks from the 'A' team. He had actually made his first team debut the previous season, having played as an Amateur when he first joined the club in July 1934, but his potential was soon spotted and he was offered professional terms, making his debut in January 1935 versus Bristol City.

It was a long struggle for Lyman, although born in Northampton he went to West Brom, but failed to make the grade, returning to the area and playing for Rushden. He was tempted away again, this time to Southend, where he actually made one League appearance, but again was released, and once again returned home just in time to sign for the Cobbler's 'A' team.

There were changes again on the board, Chairman Parker stood down, unable to come to terms with the death of his wife, he was replaced by T.C. Gillett. Len Benbow resigned, and E.C. Hawtin, cousin of Len, and H. Lea joined the board.

The start was not good, just one point from their first three games and no goals. The home match against Aldershot produced a 3-0 victory, with Bartram opening his account, but the following game, with Luton, saw the influential Jim McGuire carried off with an injury that could keep him out for three months. If things were not bad enough, a little more salt was rubbed into the wound when a 6-1 beating by Palace saw Albert Dawes net four of the goals.

Richard Deacon, a winger who had played for a host of clubs, joined the Cobblers in October from Glentoran, and was in time to make his debut against Southend, who had

The newspapers of the period were always quick to point out the Cobblers shortcomings!

DR. SCOREM (of the League Academy): Only nine marks out of 28, Cobbler! You'll have to be "sent to Coventry" again.

his brother James in their team.

The supporters club were quick to bring Len Benbow onto their committee as chairman, with their number now up to 419. After five consecutive defeats, the manager decided on wholesale changes for the home F.A.Cup-tie versus Bristol Rovers. Bell, Cave, McGuire, Riches and Robson, were all in the reserve team that beat Chelsea reserves 7-0, they all earned a recall and held Rovers to a 0-0 draw. They lost the replay, but the manager kept faith in them for the next League game at Newport, and they lost that 1-5, the same scoreline as the previous League game with Brighton, after which five players were dropped.

The goals were being conceded at an alarming rate, the gates were going down, and money was becoming tight, something had to happen. James Bartram returned to Scotland, on loan to Queen of the South, and the club hoped this would be a 'shop window' and put him on the transfer list, knowing they would not get a large fee while he was playing in the reserves. A two day period in March saw two players transferred, and a lot of money come in the kitty. Alf Brown went to Mansfield, and Fred Dawes joined his brother, at Crystal Palace, for a record fee of £3,000.

This was followed by a flurry of transfer activity, for in came Bill Thayne and George Turner from Luton. Thayne was a centre-half and came from a family of boxers, he had seen service with Crystal Palace and Hartlepool, before joining Luton; he was 23 years old. Turner, a left-winger, was two years older, and had played for a host of clubs, without making himself a regular first teamer at any. A third new arrival was Freddie Farr, a forward from Bath, his fee was a game against Bath, in which Puddefoot played himself.

It is fair to say the new arrivals made some difference to the club's performance, for they won six of the last ten games, lifting themselves to 15th in the table.

New signing Bill Thayne

James McGuire, was released as a player, but was offered the job as reserve team coach. He was a popular figure at the County Ground and the club appreciated his approach and attitude, but he declined, preferring to return to the United States with his American wife. He joined Brooklyn Wanderers, and then went into Football administration, later emerging as President of the National American Soccer Federation. McGuire also became a member of F.I.F.A. and sat on the 1974 World Cup Committee. One wonders if he ever regretted not taking the job as manager of the Cobbler's 'stiffs'!

McMenemy was also surprisingly released, and he took the well-trodden path to Crystal Palace, whilst Dick Brown threw in his lot with Forest. Two events made news at the end of the season. It was decided to drop the 'A' team, they were a costly exercise, and although the club had signed a few of the players, only Colin Lyman was a regular first teamer, but the 'Wellingborough committee' decided that they would continue, under the name of Wellingborough Town, again. The balance sheet showed that they cost £650 to run, but brought in just £213. The £400 difference, plus a £300 deficit on transfers gave the club a £700 loss on the season. The second event was a Friendly at Buckingham, which the Cobblers won 8-2, and Puddefoot not only played, but scored a hat-trick. He was 41 years and 186 days at the time, an unofficial record age to play first team football.

1936-37
John Mackie joined the club at the tail end of the previous season. The Irish international full-back had seen service with Arsenal and Portsmouth and had over 300 League games under his belt. Colin Cook became yet another ex-'Hatter' on the books, he was an inside-forward who had failed to create an impression at Luton, after being a prolific scorer with Chesterfield.

Charles Rawlings, came to Northampton about 30 years after his father, Archie, and filled the same position on the right-wing, having failed to make an impression at Huddersfield or West Brom. Other new faces were Harold Riley, a much travelled inside-forward who had the ability to turn a game on his own, if it suited him, and Bill Simpson, a wing-half from Villa who cost £200.

The season kicked-off at Swindon, on what was to be the hottest day of the year, and ended 2-0, in favour of the home side. It was 'all change' in the next game, with a 5-3 victory over Aldershot. When Millwall supporters arrived at Castle Station, they walked to the County Ground with a Lion - their mascot - on a chain and decked out in blue; this caused a lot of interest from shoppers in the town centre!

The club were featured on a BBC radio programme, called 'Midland Clubs', when several of the staff, including chairman Gillett were interviewed, it was the first time the national media had ever featured the club at any length.

Jack Little scored what he thought was the equaliser with a 30 yard screamer against Notts County, in the dying minutes of their Meadow Lane clash, only for Hughie Gallagher to net the winner for County with the last kick of the game. Ralph Allen, a prolific scorer, for Fulham, Brentford, and Charlton, joined the club for a £1,000 fee from Reading, whom he had joined just three months earlier, and paid back a large part of the fee with two goals on his debut, in a 2-2 draw at Walsall. Allen was not the first choice, for Aston Villa had agreed the transfer of Jack Palethorpe to Northampton for the same fee, but the player opted for Palace. Palethorpe was the player who scored a hat-trick for Preston when they put the Cobblers out of the F.A.Cup in 1934.

November was to be a month to remember. On the 21st, Palace were beaten 2-0, Ralph Allen scoring one of the goals, and Palethorpe was kept well in check. Also playing that day was John Lauderdale, a ball playing inside-forward who had helped Coventry into Division Two, but was now struggling for a first team spot, so he joined Northampton, and laid on both goals. On the 28th, the club were to travel to Walthamstowe Avenue, an Amateur team, in the F.A.Cup. Asked how he was going to approach the game, manager Syd Puddefoot answered; *"I do not believe in too much training"*.

A case of 'opening one's mouth and putting one's foot in it'; Walthamstowe won 6-1, at the time the biggest win by a non-League team over a Football League club! Since then it has been equalled by Boston (v Derby), Hereford (v Q.P.R.) and Barnet (v Newport). Ironically, Northampton had been knocked out of the Divisional competition, losing to Torquay, also by a five goal margin. It was the kick up the backside the team needed, and five matches in December brought maximum points.

Another new face arrives, Maurice Dunkley, a right winger from Kettering. With two games in the West Country within three days, it was decided to stay in the area, and after beating Exeter 5-2, the team was beaten 5-0 by Torquay, for the second time that season at Plainmoor. Amazingly Torquay were to avoid re-election that season on goal average..... above Exeter!

On March the 11th, Syd Puddefoot resigned, stating that one or two of the directors did not agree with his decisions, although the directors denied a rift. The remainder of the season was an anti-climax, with the club holding a mid-table position.

One particularly interesting event, was in the 3-2 defeat at Luton, when Thayne was dismissed, but he appealed, and his suspension was lifted as he was found not guilty of violent conduct, the 'offence' he was supposed to have committed. This was the first time this had ever happened to a Northampton player, although it had occurred a few seasons back, to Jim McGuire, while playing for the reserves, against Luton Reserves!

Mackie and Turner were released on free transfers, while Simpson moved to Walsall for £100, and the rest of the team were retained

1937-38

Warney Cresswell was the new manager, despite newspaper rumours that Louis Page would return to this post. Cresswell had held a similar position at Port Vale,

Ken Gunn, also from Port Vale, joined the new manager

but in a major cut-back operation, he found himself out of a job. Like Puddefoot, he had also played for England, in a football career that saw him at Hearts, Hibs, Everton and Sunderland. He brought with him Kenn Gunn, a full-back, also released by Vale, and two youngsters, Jack Jones a goalkeeper, and Eddie Blunt a wing-half.

The 'A' team was reformed, but this time the club had full responsibility for it, and games were to be played at the County Ground, but they did not make the most auspicious start, losing 4-0 to Guildford.

By the end of September, the club had played eight games and secured four points; five goals had been scored and top scorer was Ralph Allen with two. Then came another bombshell, when Colin Lyman was sold to 'Spurs for £2,250. He was to give Tottenham three seasons before war broke out, assisted eight clubs during the hostilities, and then played for Nottingham Forest, Port Vale, Notts County, and Nuneaton - as player-manager. There was no immediate replacement for Lyman, although Riley was given a run, but failed to impress, then Dunkley switched wings, allowing Rawlings to take the right-wing. This worked well until the second bombshell was dropped. Danny Tolland and Charles Rawlings were sold over a two day period, Tolland to Bristol Rovers, and Rawlings to Millwall.

Rawlings was to stay with Millwall for two seasons, helping them to the Division Three South Championship, and then after a very brief spell at Everton, played as a 'Pilgrim' at Plymouth for two years. Tolland never really got going at Rovers, he became ill in his second season there, retired from the game, and emigrated to the States, after making less than 50 appearances for Rovers.

The home match versus Crystal Palace the following week was abandoned after 55 minutes due to the weather, but instead of the supporters leaving the ground, they demonstrated outside the directors box. Not because the game was abandoned, but in view of the sale of Tolland and Rawlings. The whole incident overshadowed the fact that John Parris, the first Coloured player to play for Wales, had been signed from Luton and was making his debut on the left-wing. This game produced the first case of a player making his debut in an abandoned game.

Prior to all this, the club faced Cardiff in the F.A.Cup, and having been knocked out of the divisional cup by them, they wanted revenge. Bobby King, a young local lad who had not long won a place in the reserves entered the ground expecting to watch the game, only

John Parris
A 'first' for the Welsh national team

to be told, 'get undressed, you're playing'. Cardiff won 2-1, and again criticism was aimed at the manager for throwing the youngster in at the deep end, but as he stated there was no ready replacement to cover the injured Dunkley. There was a rift growing between the supporters and management, and it was shown up in the 'local Derby' game with Notts County, when only 100 supporters travelled to Meadow Lane.

In March the transfer market became busy, for Maurice Dunkley joined Manchester City in exchange for three players. Colin Rodger was a Scotsman and a winger who in three seasons at City, made just 18 appearances, Keillor McCulloch, an Irishman, was a full-back who had joined City from Belfast Celtic - he too was a reserve player - but Fred Tilson, had given the Maine Road team nearly ten seasons service, having joined them from Barnsley in 1929 for £3,000. In that decade Tilson had won a League championship medal, an F.A.Cup winners medal, had played four times for England and represented the Football League three times. Although he was 33, he still had the skill, most certainly for this Division, he scored three times in his 11 appearances.

Things looked better towards the end of the season, the defence tightened up and only two goals were conceded in the last seven games, a 3-0 defeat at Millwall was made sweeter by the 24,423 crowd, the Cobbler's 20% of the gate was more than some home games.

Ninth place was not bad considering the start and the upheavals of the season, but despite all the transfers out

the club still made a £225 loss, which would have been more had it not been for a £500 donation from the directors, and £300 from the supporters club.

1938-39

The season kicked off with no new players, the nucleus of last season's side was retained and a great start was made with six points from the first three games, the third a 3-0 win over Clapton Orient that required the Cobblers to change into blue shirts at half-time because of a colour clash, that victory saw them top the League. As is the case with most teams that are at the top, lady luck rides with them, and a goal by Bobby King, from an acute angle, was scored at Newport with just 30 seconds left on the clock, giving the Cobblers a share of the points.

In the first round of the divisional knock-out cup, a draw at Southend was followed by a replay at home, in which the Cobblers won 3-2, after extra time. Ralph Allen was brought back for this game, having been dropped at the latter end of the previous season, and scored a hat-trick, but he was still kept out of the next game. The rift between the management and supporters was healing, as these things do, but it generally takes some bad news to do it, and this was no different, for director Len Hawtin died. The supporters hoped to raise £1,000 towards the erecting of a stand at the hotel end, and name it after the director. The supporters club themselves were not too happy, their membership had dropped from 515, to 393, in the past 12 months.

In a 0-0 draw at Brighton, the referee was struck by a missile, and one cynical reporter, claimed it was the only shot on target, all afternoon. In November, after a single goal defeat at Walsall, on what was described as a muck heap, Cresswell made a swap deal signing, when he brought John Haycox from Torquay, and allowed Ralph Allen to go in the opposite direction.

A 2-2 draw at home to Southampton, saw Gormlie injured, he returned later with his leg heavily bandaged but struggled on, it was later discovered he had a small fracture, and would be out for some time. John Jones was promoted to first team 'keeper, and saved a penalty against Exeter on his League debut; he had previously played in the Maunsall cup.

Christmas was accompanied with spirit, and the directors funded a party for the players. In return the players entertained them, Bill Gormlie crooned like Bing Crosby, and Jack Cuff gave them a medley of North Country songs.

A 2-0 defeat at Cardiff was watched by the Welsh selectors, who admit to an interest in Jones, the Cobblers 'keeper, an amazing fact since he had just 14 games under his belt, although his form was tip-top, but bad news was to follow, for he broke his collarbone in a match at Brighton, and for the second time that season, winger Colin Rodger found himself between the sticks. With both 'keepers out injured, the club moved swiftly and signed John Clifford the Palace reserve, he made his debut in a 3-1 defeat by Bournemouth, but in the next game - a 4-1 victory over Walsall - it came to light that seven of the players in the side were under 21 years, including all five forwards.

Disaster struck in the match at Southend when Syd Russell broke his leg. Complications set in, and he had to have it amputated, but the support he got from supporters and other players was overwhelming.

The season ended on a bad run, when the club failed to score in their last seven matches, but they managed four in the draw with Corby in the Maunsall Cup final. The 2,281 crowd was a record for the Corby ground at the time. Northampton Town won the replay 2-1, but in fairness to their opponents, most of the players were from the steelworks, and had all done a full shift before the match. Added to that the club were behind in their Southern League games, and had a punishing eight games to play in a two week period.

Seventeenth position was not good, but only seven points from the last 12 games saw the team tumble down the table, and the position was not helped with only ten goals scored away from home.

Everton sent a strong team to play the Cobblers, in a benefit match for Syd Russell. The 'Toffeemen' included Ted Sager, Joe Mercer, and the man who scored the winning goal, in the 2-1 victory for them, Tommy Lawton.

Only Gunn, and McCulloch were retained, along with all the youngsters. Gormlie joined Lincoln, and after the war moved to Belgium, where he managed several club sides, including Anderlecht, he also coached the National side, and finished his days there. Josh Hewitt moved north to Southport, while Haycox joined neighbours Peterborough, after just nine months as a 'Cobbler'.

John Lauderdale moved to Nuneaton, but made several appearances for Coventry during the war, while Jason McCartney who had joined the club less than a year before, for a substantial fee, moved to South Shields. Postlethwaite moved to Watford, Rodger to Ipswich, Thayne joined Walsall, and Tilson retired, to become York City's trainer. Yet none were to have a lasting relationship with their new clubs, in view of the events, about to happen.

Syd Russell, who's football career ended so tragically

CHAPTER FIVE
1939-1946

1939-1946

Manager Cresswell had moved for experience and signed Harold Miller, an ex-England Amateur international from Chelsea. A wing-half, he had been with Chelsea for 16 seasons, and Charlton for the two before that; he had just passed his 37th birthday, when he signed. Reuben Simons, was a centre-half, and was signed from Swansea, he had spent many years in Welsh non-League football before joining his home town club. He became the first choice centre-half until losing his place at the tail end of the last season, and he was 30 years old. Eugene Melaniphy was an Irishman, who had played centre-forward for Cardiff and Plymouth, but decided to step into non League football with Worcester City, where he scored 30 goals during the season.

Cresswell was quick to bring him back in to League football, at 27 years of age. James Strathie was the fourth new signing, a full-back or wing-half, who came via Luton reserves, and was the 'babe' of the quartet at 26. Cresswell had gone for experience to fit in with his youngsters.

There was activity off the field as well, for Gillett stood down as chairman, and Horace Lea, the meat wholesaler, took his position. Gillett, had suffered ill health over the past few months, and felt he could not carry on, Lea on the other hand, was a newcomer to the board, and fired up with enthusiasm.

The season kicked-off with 3-2 defeat by Q.P.R. in the Jubilee Fund match. As these matches were supposed to be 'Derby' matches in an attempt to attract the crowds, one wonders why Northampton played a team 65 miles away!

The League season kicked off with a home match versus Swindon, which was held up, as the ground had to be searched as a precaution against terrorists. The four new men played, and the Cobbler's won 1-0, Bob Ellwood scoring the only goal of the game.

"If there are any professional footballers in the crowd, would they please come to the home dressing room at once".

Loudspeaker appeal, at half-time, when four of the Cobblers team fail to appear for the match versus Arsenal, November 1940.

The following Monday, Northampton were home again, this time to Exeter City, and the only change was Jim Garvey making his debut for the injured Eddie Blunt, at right-half. Melaniphy opened his account from the penalty spot, but Exeter scored twice, giving them a 2-1, victory, then came the Bournemouth game.

There have been several 'rumours', as to the reason the Cobblers fell to their heaviest defeat of their League career. One was that due to the pending war, the 'no alcohol' rule was lifted on the train journey, another was that the eleven players on the team sheet were not the eleven who played, and a third was that as it was obvious war was going to be declared, so no one bothered.

All these excuses do not hold water, for the team and players were professionals, and the most likely explanation was that they were beaten by a far better team on the day. Prior to their game at Deans Court, the heavens opened, turning the pitch into a mud-bath, one of the linesmen failed to appear and following an appeal, Basil Haywood - the son of the Bournemouth chairman - took the flag.

The Cobblers had made just one change, again at right-half, for McCulloch moved to this position, and A. Smith made his debut at full-back. Bournemouth won, 10-0, they adapted to the conditions better, and it seemed every shot on goal went in. Their sixth goal, not only burst the net, but also laid out a spectator, catching him full in the face.

The following day, war was declared, all contracts were made null and void, some clubs closed down, but the government encouraged all to continue playing, albeit with whoever they could find to play. Many of the players returned home, to join the army, or work on the land, or even like Eddie Blunt, in the mines. Manager Warney Cresswell became a Sergeant instructor and returned up North.

Living in a Northamptonshire village, working his small farm, and bakery, was an ex-Leeds City player Tom Smith. He was approached and he accepted the job as war-time manager. Like most he may well have thought the war was going to be short term, not realizing he was about to face seven seasons of hassle, and trying to find players.

It took the F.A. six weeks to work out a fixture list, and Northampton were put in an eight team, Midland Section league, with Birmingham, Coventry, Leicester, Luton, Walsall, Wolves and West Brom. Over the season, they would play each other four times. In between the Bournemouth game and the start of this new campaign, the club played a couple of friendlies, losing 4-0 at Watford, and beating Notts County 6-0 at home, with whatever players the team could muster.

Bill Barron, who continued to live in the area, and was a frequent player during the War years.

Russell stood in the centre of the County Ground, supported by crutches, his wife by his side, and baby son in his arms. There was not a dry eye in the house as he thanked the people of Northampton, and they in turn gave him a standing ovation. Russell did not wallow in self-pity, for he returned to his Felham home and got a job in local government, and was often seen cycling backwards and forwards, to work. He returned to the town in 1965, when Everton came to the County Ground again, and had a reunion with some of his teammates who still lived in Northampton, such as Bill Barron and Ken Gunn.

History was made on the 21st November, for Bobby King became the first player to be transferred during hostilities, when he joined Wolves for a substantial fee, but nothing like the £3,500, the Cobbler's were asking for him. King could still play for Northampton, but Wolves had first call on him, like many others they thought the war was short term. The 'guest' system, had its drawbacks, for often a player would play for a team one week, and against them the next, such as the case of Pritchard. The last week he played against Northampton, for Leicester, and seven days later he scored the winner for the Cobblers against Luton. one supporter of the time was quoted as saying, *"it was great seeing all these internationals, but I never accepted them as a 'Cobbler's ' team, as they could play for you one match, and against you the next".*

The first war-time league game was home to Coventry, and Northampton were represented by: Joe Calvert in goal, he was from Leicester as was full-back Howe; his left-back partner was Bob Dennison from Fulham. Right-half Grogan and centre-half Heywood were also from Leicester, but Reuben Simons stayed in the town, and took the left-half spot. The forward line was made up of ex-Cobblers, all who had left the club, but as they lived in the town, were able to 'guest' for the team, they were Maurice Dunkley, Jack Billingham, George Henson, Charles Hewitt, and Jack Parris. Hewitt scored in the 1-1 draw.

This was followed by the clubs first ever visit to Molineux, where they met the mighty Wolves, and came off second best in a 7-2 defeat. Wolves had the luxury of a missed penalty, but most of the damage was done by their teenage wingers, namely Jimmy Mullen, and Billy Wright.

After a 1-1 draw at home to West Brom, a presentation was made of £1,500 to Syd Russell, this was money raised just by supporters and players from other teams, as well as the Everton benefit match.

The club were attracting some top quality players, such as Moss and Shell of Villa, and in one game the latter got married in the morning, and brought his new bride to Northampton to watch him play in the 2-0 victory over Wolves in the afternoon. Because of the late start to the season, and five week break, due to the bad weather the season ran on into June. In the final League game, at Leicester, the Cobblers lost 2-0, one of the goals coming from a young colt player, named Logan. He scored with his first touch of the ball, after 30 seconds, but it was to be his only outing ever for City. Sixth out of eight was not a bad position, at all.

1940-41

The F.A. changed the system this year, although games were still played against regional opposition, there would be two tables, a North and South, and positions would be calculated on average points per game. The club A.G.M. took place at the Plough Hotel in August, and it was announced that the club had made a £600 profit, but summer wages and transfer fees, brought it down to an £800 loss.

The first match was away to Luton, and three players failed to appear; Cobblers used their twelfth man, borrowed Smith, an ex-Burnley player then living in Luton, and Tom Smith was about to get changed himself, when Willmott, a Luton reserve walked in and played; Luton won 7-1. The following match, at home to Mansfield, was a little different, for two Scottish internationals - George Cummings and Bill Shankley - played, as did ex-England international Tom Smalley. Coventry 'keeper, Alf Wood, appeared in goal, and Bobby King returned to net a hat-trick, in the 6-1 result. The return match at Field Mill was full of incident, for two Northampton players failed to show, a situation that would often be repeated, and two Mansfield reserves were offered. During the game, Hubbard the Stags' forward broke his wrist, and when Billingham scored for Northampton, the referee awarded a goal, was asked to speak to a linesman, did so, and gave Mansfield a free kick instead.

Bill Barron, one of the young forwards from Cresswell's pre-war side, would well remember the 19th of October. He was just a travelling reserve for the match against Arsenal, who were then playing at White Hart Lane, but when the full contingent of players failed to appear he was drafted in, and scored a hat-trick in the 5-4 defeat.

An away match at Coventry attracted an official crowd of 509, although the Coventry records shows it even lower at 307. Nottingham Forest, came to Northampton with just 10 men, and only two of those were from the original 11 selected, hence Northampton's 7-0 win. Seven days later, the club were to suffer an 8-1 defeat, at home.

Tom Smith wanted his strongest side to play Arsenal, but four failed to appear. They rang to say they were stuck in Rugby but would get a taxi, with this in mind Smith played seven men against one of the country's top teams, but with a five goal deficit at half-time, he had to do something. The manager put over an appeal: *"If there are any professional footballers in the crowd, would they please come to the home dressing room."* This led to a deluge of people claiming to be on the books of some club or another, but in the end Smith chose Pursglove of

Barnsley, and Towl of Hull; his third player was Hart, the colt's player, plus Pryde, the Arsenal 12th man to make up a full team. Arsenal won the game 8-1, but offered the Cobbler's sympathy, as they too had problems trying to get 11 players on the pitch.

By December the club had lost the services of George Cummings, for the Scottish international full-back returned to Scotland, where his home had been bombed. Cummings was one of football's characters, a tall bald headed player, he had an aggressive style that often upset referees, and he had a ritual of smoking a cigarette just before the start of a game. He often entered the field with the ball in one hand, and a cigarette in the other,

Christmas saw a double fixture v Leicester, home in the morning, and away in the afternoon; after winning 5-2, they lost the away match 7-2.

Teams not allowing players to 'guest' for other clubs was also a problem, and Luton - the Cobblers' opponents for a February fixture - were not notified until Saturday morning, that their guests could not play. This caused five youngsters to be drafted in at the last minute, but they gave a creditable display, in a 5-4 defeat, and could have earned a draw had Cobbler's 'keeper Alf Wood not saved a penalty from 'ten goal' Joe Payne.

Another transfer in March, saw Stan Frost an amateur with the Colts, move to Leicester on professional terms. In exchange, Leicester gave the Cobbler's Bedford, a centre-half who had been 'guesting' for the club, until the end of the season. Lincoln City sent a team to play Northampton in a friendly on March the 29th, they also sent a team to play Mansfield on the same day, as they had so many professional footballers to call upon, they won both games.

With little at stake, the end of the season became patchy, and away to Stoke, Northampton had just ten players, the Potteries club lent them Basnett, who scored the side's only goal, in a 2-1 defeat. The following week Chelsea came to Northampton with nine men, borrowed two, and lost 4-1. The end of the season saw the club finish fifteenth out of 34 teams, with a points average of 1.183, and 45 players had been used.

1941-42

The biggest pre-season news was that ex-player George Jobey was suspended by the F.A. for irregular payments while manager of Derby, but the ban was later lifted and he took over at Mansfield. There was also a strong lobby by the London clubs to set up their own league, and break away from the F.A., with Northampton Town being invited to join them.

Club Chairman Horace Lea, knocked the idea on the head, even though he agreed they would be better off, he stated that one game during the last season brought in just 1/9d (8p); there was a £42 loss over the season.

The home and away match versus Norwich that season were beset by transport problems. First the Norwich coach had a puncture in Cambridge on their way to Northampton, and when they arrived they only had ten men, so the Cobblers lent them Curtis, a young winger from the Colts. The following week the Cobbler's coach was involved in an accident at Wymondham, on its way to Norwich, luckily no one was hurt.

On October the 18th, the Czechoslovakian Army arrived in Northampton, well their football team did. The Chairman, Lea and manager Smith, met them at the station, and they were taken to the Grand Hotel for lunch. The match itself was very entertaining, the Eastern European's short passing game, compared to the home sides long ball and use of wingers. Northampton won 5-2, but the man the crowd took to was Michna, the Czech keeper, his acrobatic display left people talking for some time to come.

By April the club had qualified for the final stages of the knock-out cup, the first round of which was two legged, and against Bristol City. But the club were disappointed that Liverpool refused to give their permission for Bill Fagan to play, the Scottish international, and his fellow countryman, Dick Beattie of Preston. However, they managed without them, winning the home leg 3-0, and losing the away tie 1-3, thus giving them a second round tie with Norwich. But the East Anglian club won both legs to end the Cobbler's interest in the competition.

FRANK BROOME

BILL SHANKLY

Two familiar faces that became temporary 'Cobblers' (Broome just two matches and Shankly nine)

During the latter part of the season, Luton were beaten 8-0, after Northampton lent them three players, one of whom was the Colts full-back and captain, Wallington, who was forced to play in goal, and was the star of the game. Stoke City were beaten 10-0, but just seven days later, they made four changes to their team and won 3-2. The season was split into two, the first part, pre-Christmas, saw the club in Third place, but the post-Christmas League had them as high as third, the average crowd was just over 3,000, and seventeen of the 32 players used found the back of the opponents net at least once.

Joining the club towards the end of the season was the Middlesborough centre-half, Harold Shepherdson, who was later to become the England trainer.

1942-43

The club had hoped Eddie Hapgood would turn out for them during the season, but he never made it, despite that the club had many player to choose from.

The season was split into two, and run on the lines of the previous season. In the home match with Walsall, Gilbert Alsop, a Walsall player, scored against his old club, in the return match, he was playing for Walsall, and scored against the Cobblers. Alsop was one of the Walsall players who had been in the famous 'Saddlers' side that had knocked Arsenal out of the F.A.Cup in 1933.

It was the club's poor away form that was stopping their progress up the League, losing 6-3 at West Brom, 5-0 at Coventry and 6-0 at Walsall, and their cause was not helped by the fact that up until Christmas they had used three different goalkeepers.

News broke, in December, that the club had approached Alex James to come out of retirement, and play for the club, but it would have meant returning his pension money, and that could have meant selling his tobacconist and newsagents shop, a heavy price to pay for a few war-time games.

The club unearthed a goalscoring jewel, in Harry Nichols. He was on the books of Sheffield Wednesday and netted five goals in seven games for Northampton, but he found it hard to get to games from his Shrewsbury home, so he was released and joined Walsall. The 1942 part of the season saw the club reach 25th out of 48 clubs, winning eight and drawing one of their 18 games. Harris, a guest from Southend, became the only 'Cobbler' to get his marching orders, when he was sent off - together with Bolieau of Coventry - in a two goal home defeat, but they set the record straight the Cobblers following week, when they beat Coventry 1-0 on their own ground. It was Coventry's first defeat in the '1943' competition, their first defeat at home, all season, and the first time they had conceded a goal at home since 3rd October.

Meanwhile back at the County Ground, Jack English, son of the ex-manager, scored twice for the Colts versus the R.A.O.C, a feat that was to happen quite a bit in the future. Roy Hawtin, son of Len, also scored and made his debut in the match. An away game at Aston Villa, saw the home side score from the kick-off, within five minutes, they had a second, however they failed to score again, and the Cobblers did pull one back. Ironically the scorers for Villa, were Shell and Haycock, two players who had 'guested' for the Cobbler's a couple of years back.

The Cobbler's themselves made some news with quick-scoring goals, for they netted within two minutes against Walsall, when Lowe found the net on his debut. Heavy scoring also made the news when a match against the Eastern Command ended up with the Cobblers losing by the odd goal in 11!

Thirty-seventh out of 54 teams was hardly earth shattering, but there were some good points, for £209-9-0d was made from the 'pool', although the chairman did make comment of the poor sportsmanship of some teams not releasing players who were stationed nearby. Forty six players used during this season, and the average crowd was up to 3,400.

1943-44
The season opened with a home match with Walsall that was delayed 25 minutes due to the 'Saddlers' late arrival. Northampton won 2-1, one goal coming from Dave

Kinnear, a winger from Scotland, and a player destined to be a crowd favourite in his short stay. Kinnear made history by being the 12th man for both Chelsea and Millwall when they played in the war-time cup final of 1945.

The club announced a profit of £1,442 on the 1942-43 season, and were attracting some top names to play for them; Eddie Perry, the Welsh international forward - he scored twice on his debut - Tom Brolly, Millwall's Irish international, Syd Pugh of Arsenal and Harold Sheperdson.

It was the ninth match before the club suffered its first defeat, 3-0, at home to Coventry. The two matches with Forest were of special interest. The Cobblers arrived late in Nottingham, but earned a 2-2 draw, after being two goals down, but the return at the County ground was a different tale. Forest arrived with a 'scratch' side who were no match for the well organised Northampton team, and with ten changes from the side that had drawn one week earlier, they went down 9-1. E. Litchfield, who was a youngster on Newcastle's books, scored four, and was becoming quite a prolific scorer for the club. He netted 11 goals in nine games, before being called away, and stationed in Colombia.

The first championship saw the club pick up 25 points from a possible 36, not a bad record, but the second half of the season was a different story. The club lost Smith and Kinnear, who were in Scotland and assisting Rangers, Perry was injured, and the club struggled to put out 11 men versus Walsall.

Then a young Austrian turned up at the County Ground, and claimed to be on the books of one of the top Austrian sides, the club gave him a trial and he seemed suitable. Although they did wince a bit at his name, Hess! He made his debut in the Walsall match, and was so out of his depth, that had there been substitutes in those days, he would no doubt have been replaced. Hess never played again, either for the first team, or the Colts.

Cliff Britton was invited to join the club, but declined, and meanwhile the Midland clubs decided to have a cup competition, to run along side the League games, making each game a double header. Cooper, a youngster from Aston Villa was the first team goalkeeper now. He was an amateur, having found a job with a firm of solicitors in the town.

In a game with Coventry, he saved a penalty, but the ball squeezed out of his grasp, and trickled along the line, and although Coventry appealed for a goal, the referee waved play on.

A rare, but unfortunately unnamed team group taken at the County Ground during the War years.

The linesman flagged, and after consultation he decided to award a goal, which caused the Cobbler's players to protest. The official changed his mind again, but in any event Coventry eventually won the match 2-0.

Another good find was Wilson of Dundee, who scored four goals on his debut, and netted seven times in his four games, as a Cobbler. Unfortunately, he was only stationed locally for a short spell. Jack Jennings was based at Bedford and was the ex-Wigan Borough, Cardiff and Middlesborough player. He had been Physio/Trainer/Coach at Preston, and Tom Smith asked him if he would like to do a similar job at the County Ground, which he agreed to. However, in a crisis, he was asked to play and made 17 appearances and scored a goal; not bad for a man in his 42nd year.

Another player to help out was Dennis Brooks, the Northants County cricketer, he scored a goal in his two appearances on the 'other' side of the County Ground

The second half of the season was not so successful, The club winning nine of its 19 matches, however they did reach the Semi-final of the Midland Cup, a two legged affair versus Nottingham Forest, but never recovered from the 5-0 defeat at Forest, a match in which the ex-England winger, John Leighton, died while watching from the stands. The home leg was won 3-1, but not enough to get the club to the final.

The tragic news reached the club that Syd Pugh, the loanee from Arsenal was killed while on a training flight with the R.A.F. He was to be the only Second World War victim associated with the club, a plus considering the numbers who died during the First World War. The average attendance was increasing and now 5,300 were watching home games, 800 more than the average at the away games.

1944-45
Seven debutants were played in the opening game against West Bromwich Albion, a 4-1 defeat, in fact the first three games were lost, and it was not until they completed the 'double' with Port Vale, that the team recorded the first win.

A match against Wolves saw both Tom Smalley and Billy Wright score from the penalty spot, ironically one ex-England International and one future, but of course that was not known at the time. Against the Wolves, the Cobbler's borrowed N.Phillips, a right-winger, and in the Coventry game the following week, they had N.Phillips again in the right-wing spot, only this was a different player who came from Plymouth Argyle.

In November, A.J. Darnell tendered his resignation as representative of the Third Division South, he was now reaching 70 and felt the time was right. Club Chairman Horace Lea was elected onto the Division's Management Committee. It was a reflection of the ability of Darnell, whatever League or competition the Cobbler's played in, that he was elected on to that League's committee. First the Northamptonshire Football Association, then the Southern League Management Committee, followed by the Football League - not forgetting local associations like the supporters club, and the Schools Football League, the latter to whom he presented a trophy, 'The Darnell Cup'.

Bad weather saw the postponement of the Christmas programme, and later Tom Smith announced that this had cost the club some £1,200, and he also stated that he failed to see when these games would be played, unless the League relented and allowed mid-week games. The Secretary of State for India watched the match in which Villa beat the Cobblers 5-2, and congratulated both teams on their sporting play.

Jack Billingham, who had a very short first team career at Northampton, was a prolific scorer now in his 'guesting' period for the club. He moved on to Burnley, and was to be their 12th man in the 1945-46 Cup Final. Alex Lee was a giant 'keeper, in both height and weight, being over 6'-3" and close to 14 stone. One of the best finds was Alf Morrall, he came from Redditch and became a prolific scorer.

Several players found themselves at Bedford, at the Rehabilitation Centre recovering from war wounds, and here they came up against Jack Jennings, who would often invite them back to play for the club. One such player was Archie Garrett, who was now with Hearts, but Jennings knew him from his Preston days. Garrett was to net eight goals in an 11 match spell, including four against Coventry. Another find was a young left-winger from Everton, he was shot in France, and while recovering at Bedford was invited to play for the Cobblers. Although he made an inauspicious start, he went on to be a cult figure, his name was Tommy Fowler. Len Hammond, the ex-'keeper of the 1930's recommended a young player from the Rugby area, he was taken on and he too became folklore - Gwyn Hughes was to give the club several seasons,

Northampton did not fare to well in either the pre-Christmas or post-Christmas League, however they did have the chance to stop West Brom. reaching the Semi-final of the Knock-out Cup, as they needed to score five times, without reply to qualify; they in fact scored six!

The following match with Birmingham, saw the club so short of players, they had to play Alex Lee at centre-forward, he did not score, but he helped his side to a 2-2 draw. Tom Smalley missed the game at Coventry in February because of injury, it was his first break in 136 War-time games.

1945-46

A.J. Darnell was awarded an honorary life membership of the club, in this their last War-time season. The League could have gone back to the full programme, but they decided to allow clubs one season to sign new players and sort out their finances.

The Third Division South was itself split into two Divisions, a North and a South section - Northampton were placed in the Division Three South, Northern Section. The first signing of the season was Gordon Roberts, the young draughtsman from Wolves, who realised that he would not find a first team place waiting for him with the First Division club, so he came to Northampton.

The Cobblers had a great start, just one defeat in the first seven games, and a run of five games without conceding a goal. The A.G.M showed a profit of £2,269, and a new director joined the board, R.Seymour, who replaced Gillett, the ex-chairman, whose health was fading. A keen and anonymous supporter offered 1/-(5p) for every goal the club scored.

The club secured Smalley, Fowler and Dennison, the Fulham club were reluctant to let the Cobbler's skipper go but realised that it was best for him. The team's second defeat came at Ipswich, who had six guests in their side, including the complete forward-line, meanwhile, around mid-October, the Colts were also enjoying some success in the United Counties League, beating Peterborough 15-4; Alf Morrall scored nine of the goals.

A Scottish newspaper circulated a story that a Northampton Town director, was in Scotland, with £40,000 to spend on players, of course the club strongly denied this, and actually accounted for all its directors.

An away defeat at Q.P.R. was made worse by a decision that was hard to believe. A free kick was awarded to Northampton, and as the players moved upfield, the referee changed his mind and gave it the other way. With everyone out of position, the Rangers took it quickly and scored. Despite the protests the goal stood. A triple transfer took place in November, when Lowery, Sankey and Heaselgrave were all signed from West

COBBLERS TURN DOWN BIGGEST DEAL IN CLUB'S HISTORY

MILLWALL MAKE FIVE-FIGURE OFFER FOR FIVE PLAYERS

Morrall.

BEHIND the scenes at yesterday's cup-tie at Millwall dramatic moves were being made to bring about what would have been the most sensational transfer deal in the Cobblers' history, writes Flag-Kick.

At the end of the game the offer was put in concrete terms.

The Millwall club made a bid well over the five figure mark for five of the Cobblers' players, a bid which caused hurried consultations between the Northampton directors and manager, Tom Smith.

The offer was a tempting one to put before any Third Division club. It would have dispelled financial worries for several seasons to come.

On the other hand, it would destroy the Cobblers' chances of getting into the Second Division when the promotion system re-starts.

This is undoubtedly the Cobblers' aim, and it was not long before the directors decided to turn down the offer.

Bromwich Albion - the former two were both wing-halves, whilst Heaselgrave was a centre-forward. The trio were in their late twenties, or early thirties, but all had a wealth of experience behind them and cost a combined fee of £4,500. Sam Heaselgrave had joined the Cobblers earlier in the season, as a guest. One of the first games for the three nearly ended in disaster, when they travelled down from their Birmingham homes to Northampton by car, having missed the train.

The coach that was to take the players to Clapton Orient hung on as long as it could, but had to leave with three players short. When the trio arrived they realised the coach had left, and decided to drive to London themselves. They broke down on the way and arrived at the ground at half-time, but the Cobbler's still lost, 1-0.

The F.A.Cup was played over two legs that season, and Chelmsford were the first round opponents. The Cobblers beat them 5-1, but the City's lone goal came straight after the kick-off following the Cobbler's fifth, and never touched a Northampton player. Heaselgrave was helped off, with a leg injury, and it was found he had a twisted knee which kept him out for some weeks. The away leg produced a 5-0 victory, so it was an easy passage to round two, and Notts County.

Notts County were beaten 3-1 at home, but won 1-0 away, giving the Cobbler's a 3-2 aggregate - the only time they lost an F.A.Cup-tie, and still went through to the next round. Round three brought on Millwall, who held the Cobblers to a 2-2 draw at the County Ground, and beat them 3-0 at the Den. But the biggest shock was to come when they made a five figure offer for five of the Cobblers team, with an option on another two. This was rejected by the board, then Millwall came back with a firm offer for Morrall, and that too was turned down.

Sankey and Lowery made their marks in a game with Mansfield, when Sankey scored from 40 yards and Lowery from the halfway line. Mid-table was all the team could reach in the League, but this was a levelling season and it was more important to see what playing staff the club could find.

Jones, who had played for Norwich during the war returned in goal, and Dave Scott, a teacher from Bective School, was number two. Bill Barron, the pre-war winger was now a post-war full-back and also a member of the Northants County Cricket team, Tom Smalley was his partner. As back-up there was Bob Allen, the ex-Wimbledon tennis player, Strathie the pre-war player, and Quinney, from Nuneaton.

Sankey and Lowery were wing-halves, with Eddie Blunt, who had spent his war time down the mine and playing for Bury was also in contention, While Bob Dennison was centre-half, and captain. Gordon Roberts was the right-winger, and Tommy Fowler, the left. Dave Smith, late of Newcastle, and Morrall, were the inside partners of Heaselgrave.

The club was ready for League football. Tom Smith was praised for his efforts in keeping a side together over the past few years, and he in turn revealed that he had twice been approached by First Division teams to be their manager. On a sad note it was reported that Chairman T.C. Gillett passed away in April 1946. During April the Cobblers put Rushden out of the Maunsall Cup and the Senior Cup in a four day period. The Maunsall Cup game, a Semi-final, was won 9-0 with Northampton fielding virtually a reserve side. Pre-war player, Harry Jennings, hit four goals, and Hughes got a hat-trick.

The Senior Cup Final was won 5-0, and the team followed this victory with a 4-2 win against Kettering in the Maunsall Cup Final at Rockingham Road, in what was to be the last game at this venue before the pitch was levelled.

Jack Jennings had a summer job, for he was to become the Cricket Club scorer at away games, since Leo Bullimer no longer wanted to travel, and was also Masseur to the Indian touring side.

CHAPTER SIX
1946 - 1959

1946-47

The League decided to use the same fixture list that was produced for the 1939-40 season, which put the Cobblers at home to Swindon, who were now managed by ex-player Louis Page, for the first match. Nearly 12,000 people watched Heaselgrave and Morrall score a brace a piece, to give the club a 4-1 victory.

The euphoria did not last, for a home defeat by Exeter, and away to Bournemouth, only 2-1 this time, saw them drop down the League again, and Tom Smith was obviously not happy with ten Goals in seven games, so he went out and bought two players from Hearts - Archie Garrett and Jimmy Briscoe. Both players had been on Preston's books and the two had moved to Hearts during the war. Garrett, a centre-forward had a spell at Northampton, as well as Bristol City, and his partner was a winger, who had played for a host of clubs, including Arsenal, during the war. The joint fee was £3,500.

"It was worth a goal start to us"

Ron Patterson, the Cobblers skipper regarding the crowd support when they knocked Arsenal out of the F.A.Cup in January 1958

Roberts and Morrall had to make way for the new boys, who helped defeat Notts County 2-1, with Garrett scoring both goals. Ironically the signings came at a time when the club announced a £3,000 loss on the previous season. Chairman Horace Lea stated, at the A.G.M., that the F.A. would not allow guests in the F.A.Cup, so they had to sign the players on contracts. The club would liked to have signed more, but the housing shortage in the town was a problem.

Only a few weeks after the A.G.M., Lea was voted out of office, but he made his disappointment known, and stated that at some stage during the past seven seasons he had paid the players wages from his own pocket. The directors said there was nothing untowards about the move, there was a change of chairman every so often, and the time was due. Lea did not accept a place on the board, and instead joined Leyton Orient. Hooton refused the Chairmanship, so it fell to E.C. Hawtin.

Back on the field, the club made the national news after two draws with neighbouring non-League Peterborough United, in the F.A.Cup - they eventually beat them 8-1 at Highfield Road, with Archie Garrett netting four.

Those games were the first to mention human - as opposed to animal - mascots, for the three games saw the Cobblers led out by a man in an Apron, while Peterborough had a very 'posh' man fronting their team. By this time ex-York City player, Harry Thompson had signed, after a spell abroad; he was a wing-half or inside-forward.

Following Peterborough, came Preston North End in round three, and nearly 17,000, crammed into the ground to watch this game. Bill Barron had the job of marking Tom Finney, said Bill; *"A few days before the game I felt a bit excited and rather nervous, thinking he might give me the run around. Although we lost the game 2-1, it was one of the best games I ever had for the Cobblers. Once the match started I lost my nervousness, and through the whole game more than held my own, it was an honour to have played against such a great player."*

Just prior to the Cup-tie, the club played the return match at Swindon, and a shot from Dave Smith hit the back of the net and rebounded into play. As the other Northampton players were congratulating him, the Swindon team took the ball down field and scored. The referee awarded Swindon a goal rather than the Cobblers.

The crowds were good, away to Cardiff 29,426 watched them beat Northampton 6-2, while the Wales v England Rugby match was being played at the other end of the city; Cardiff City won the Division Three Championship that season. The only other notable event of 1946-47, was the 8-0 home defeat to Walsall, a record away win or home defeat for a Division Three South match. Amazingly, only the day before the Cobblers had beaten Brighton 6-1, and the only change from the side was Strathie replaced the injured Lowery, at centre-half. It is interesting to note that Strathie never played for Northampton again, although he was to give many of the local clubs, good service.

1947-48

Only fringe players were allowed to leave, for the main body of the side were all retained, and added to the squad was Bill Coley from Torquay who had assisted the club during the war, and had the reputation of a hard tackling wing-half.

The club announced they had spent £2,870 on new players and nearly £1,000 on ground improvements the previous season, hence the loss of £2,942.

The team made an average start to the season, the first item of real excitement coming in November, when the home match versus Notts County coincided with the Nottinghamshire club, signing Tommy Lawton. The crowds started to arrive four hours before the game commenced, and in all 18,272 crammed into the County Ground. County fans were not disappointed when Lawton netted after five minutes, Garrett equalised, but County scored again to come away with both points.

After a 5-1 defeat at Swansea, in which Bill Coley became the first post-war Cobbler to be sent off, there was

Cartoon relating to Newport match (November 1947), but also making reference to the difficulties of obtaining playing kits, etc., in post-War Britain.

transfer activity at Northampton. Archie Garrett joined Birmingham, for a club record fee of £10,000 and reserve 'keeper David Lloyd went with him. Garrett had already netted nine goals during the current season and supporters wondered where the goals would now come from. Bobby King returned from Wolves, he had not made many appearances in the old gold shirt, and found it hard to hold down a first team place, he took Garrett's place.

The F.A.Cup stretched to four games, but the club, never got any further than round two. A draw at Exeter was

followed by a 2-0 home win in the first round, while a 1-1 draw at home to Torquay, saw a Cobblers defeat in the replay. Gordon Lewis, from Washington Street - but who worked as a call boy in London - announced prior to the Torquay replay, that he was going to travel to every away game in the Cup, that Northampton were involved in, the exercise did not last long!

When Jack English was manager of the club, in the thirties, many of the players used to speak of his son, who made a nuisance of himself by trying to get involved in practice games and work-outs. But the interest bore fruit, for that son - also Jack English - became a nuisance to every Third Division defence in the League, and it started when he made his bow versus Bristol City, a team he had assisted during the War.

It was also around this time that the club announced that it was going to buy the 'True form' sports ground, on Kettering Road. They would build it up to League standard, and it would be their new home, and as from next season, they would run a 'Colts' team again. The effort to move to another ground, had been made before, just prior to the outbreak of World War Two, when the club were looking at the barracks, at Barrack Road, and had hostilities not intervened then they may well have taken it up, but this latest idea looked promising, and a pitch was already there.

A match against Watford on 1st January caused a lot of interest, as Watford fielded seven debutants, and still drew 1-1. One of the new boys was Joe Calvert, the goalkeeper, who assisted Northampton during the war. Towards the end, of what became a poor season, a few new faces came into the team; Jack Ansell, a goalkeeper who was spotted playing for Bletchley Brickworks joined the club, he thought as cover for reserve 'keeper Scott, but he ended up in the first team, making his debut in a 3-1 win over Exeter.

Another debutant, was a winger named Dave Bowen. His father ran the Roadmenders Boys Club, and Dave played for them, progressing to the Reserves, and into their first team - he would be around for a long time. There were quite a few players leaving the club at the end of the season. Both 'keepers Jones (Oldham) and Scott(Oxford) moved on, as did Heaselgrave, who returned to his Birmingham home via Boston and Sankey, and joined Hereford. Morrall became a Newport player and Dennison retired to take a job with Hannafy and Co., a timber merchant in the town, but he agreed to run the colts.

1948/49

The two biggest buys of the season consisted of Eddie Freimanis, the Latvian forward who had such a good game for Peterborough against the

New winger - Dave Bowen

Cobbler's in the F.A.Cup, also Norman Aldridge, a full-back from Birmingham joined the club for a 'substantial' fee.

The club made a bad start, with a 5-1 thrashing at Exeter, followed by defeats at Norwich and Bristol City, and there was no doubt that it was Dennison they were missing. The club later admitted they tried many times to try and sign a replacement for Dennison, but the selling club always wanted one of the Cobbler's youngsters in exchange. Harry Lowery was the first choice centre-half, but he was injured and the young Ben Collins was drafted in, both gave creditable displays, but Lowery was a wing-half, and Collins was still a youngster.

October produced two talking points. The match with Leyton Orient saw their full-back Ritson carried from the field with a broken leg, and later the player contracted gangrene, and had to have it amputated. The other point concerned Cheney, a left-winger made his debut for Bournemouth against the Cobblers; the previous season he made his debut for Watford - against Northampton.

Wilf McCoy, who liked to be called Tim, joined the club in December. He was a centre-half aged 27, and cost the club £3,500 from Portsmouth. McCoy had played regularly for Pompey during the War, but had lost his place after the hostilities ceased. At the same time Archie Garrett returned, he had suffered a broken leg at Birmingham and never recovered his place. It was a good choice as far as the Supporters were concerned, for both players made their debut in the goalless home draw with Torquay, but Garrett was back on form with two goals in the next game against Exeter.

Around this time manager Tom Smith resigned, he cited his reason as 'director interference', although the directors strongly denied this. Tom moved and joined Norwich as chief scout, later returning to Northampton when Dave Bowen became manager, in the same capacity. His 'pork pie' hat and cigar would no longer be spotted in the Cobbler's dug out, but no one could take away from him the good job he had done at Northampton, during the war.

As always, there was speculation as to who was going to be next for the hot seat. Jack Jennings, and ex-League referee and Jack Barrick were just two of the names thrown into the hat, but it went to Bob Dennison, the ex-skipper who was now running the colts, and he promised everyone he *"would do the best he could."* He had little time to do much, for the club were struggling to keep out of the re-election zone, and all the new manager could do was 'shuffle the pack'.

It came down to the last game, away to Walsall. Crystal Palace were doomed to seek re-election, but anyone of four teams above them could be their 'bedmates', including the Cobblers. Walsall won 2-0, and the supporters waited with baited breath for the other results. When they were known, the slide rules came out and a sigh of relief could be heard, all over the town. Northampton had avoided re-election by a goal average difference of 0.009, in those pre-goal difference or goals-scored days.

The season ended with a £5,516 loss, and a new director joined the board, Fred York, of Yorks coaches. Now Dennison had a few months to build his new side.

1949/50

Young winger Dave Bowen, joined Arsenal having been recommended to them by the Arsenal manager's son, when the two were in the same R.A.F. unit. Bowen's ability was spotted, and he was more than happy to sign for the top London club. Norman Aldridge, who had joined the club for a substantial fee, moved to Headington, where ex-player Harry Thompson was now the manager.

The new faces included the much travelled defender, Jack Southam, from Birmingham, Maurice Candlin, a hard-tackling defender from Partick, Eddie Murphy, a ball playing inside-forward from Morton, and Adam McCullough, a terrier type centre-forward from third Lanark. In addition there was winger Bert Mitchell, who had preferred to play Southern League football with Kettering rather than play for Blackburn reserves.

All the newcomers, except McCullogh, started off in the first team, with Southam replacing the absent Barron who was still playing cricket for the County. Adam McCullogh made his debut when Archie Garrett went down with flu. The Scotsman seized his chance and netted twice against Newport and kept his place from then on.

Maurice Dunkley also returned to Northampton, the club's pre-war right-winger. He had joined Kettering after the war and gone into the grocery business stating that he had enough of professional football. His return lasted four games, by which time it was obvious his League days were over.

The F.A.Cup saw a 4-1 victory over Walthamstowe Avenue, the victors over Northampton before the war. Arthur Dixon, an Englishman from Hearts, had joined the club and he netted one of the goals.

McCoy had by now handed the captaincy over to Candlin, and the team were creeping up the League with the competition for places hotting up. Barron had won back his left-back spot from Southam, but there was no place for Fowler, Freimanis or Bill Smith, which resulted in the latter moving to Birmingham for £3,000, not a bad fee for a reserve player.

By this time Torquay had been beaten in the F.A.Cup second round, which led to a third round tie at home to Southampton. A crowd of 23,209 crammed into the County ground, creating a new ground record, and they watched a 1-1 draw, with the replay being set for the following Wednesday at Southampton. Gwyn Hughes stated: *"We travelled down by coach, and the sight of thousands of supporters on the way down, was something to behold. Every country pub we passed, had a coachload of supporters outside, waving their Scarves as we went by; they started as early as the Green Man at Syresham."*

Fourteen players made the trip, so three did not play in the game, one of whom was Ben Collins, who recalled... *"The three of us shared the £2.00 between us, 13/4d (67p) each."* The game ended in a 3-2 win for the Cobbler's, with wing-halves Candlin and Hughes netting two of the goals. The fourth round drew Bournemouth in another away match, but this ended in a 1-1 draw, and it was replay time again, but this time at home. Only 600 supporters short of the recent record crowd turned up to watch the match, a very good figure for a Thursday afternoon.

English and McCullogh netted the goals that saw the club into the fifth round, and an away tie at Derby. A new record was set at the Baseball Ground when 38,063 turned up to watch the match, but it was no fairy tale. The 'Rams' raced into a 3-0 lead after 17 minutes, and despite Dixon netting two, Derby scored a fourth and went through to the quarter-finals.

Northampton Town, got back to the business of League football, and an eight match run in February saw the club lose just one game. The turning point came when they played Notts County at Meadow lane. County were top, the Cobblers second, and the game was a 'four pointer'.

Ben Collins, who by now had taken the unhappy McCoy's place at centre-half, remembers the game; *"I was playing against my school boy hero, Tommy Lawton. The match was an evening game, but over 31,000 watched a thrilling match. County won 2-0, and won promotion from the Division as Champions."* There was some revenge two days later, when County came to the County ground and were handed a 5-1 thrashing. By this time both Garrett and Fowler were back in the side, the former scoring one of the goals.

Runners-up spot was very good considering the previous season's flirtation with re-election. Two mid-season incidents are worth mentioning. In the away match at Port Vale over Christmas, Jack Southam rang from his Birmingham home to say he was too ill to travel, this resulted in manager Bob Dennison dragging Bill Barron away from his celebrations and rushing him to Vale Park in his car. The match against the same team, at the County Ground, resulted in a gate being broken, and over a 1,000 people getting in free, which swelled the official crowd of 19,163.

Eddie Freimanis, the Latvian who came to England as an interpreter, left and joined Nuneaton. He first Anglicized his name to Freidman, and then to Freeman.

1950-51

Tim McCoy was in dispute with the club, they wanted him to move to Northampton and he wanted to stay on the South Coast, so he refused to sign a new contract, and went on the list. Ted Duckhouse, a giant centre-half, was signed from Birmingham as a replacement, and he was joined by Jim Davie, a near record buy from Preston, plus Sonny Feehan, an Irish goalkeeper from Manchester United. Jack Smith, a Leicester amateur signed professional terms for Northampton, and amateur winger, Henry Potts, also joined the club; he had been honoured by Oxford University and had played for Pegasus.

Within three games both full-backs had scored, this gave an indication as to how attack-minded the team were. After six weeks McCoy relented and signed a new contract, agreeing to move to Northampton, but it never happened for within a fortnight he became a Brighton player and stayed on the South Coast.

Ben Collins
with happy memories

As with most successful clubs, the national newspapers circulated rumours, and two were that Cardiff had offered £10,000 for McCullough, which the club denied, and another was that Dennison was linked with the vacant Newcastle hot seat, but again this was denied.

The club were exempt from the F.A.Cup until round three, because of their high League position the previous season, and they entertained Barnsley at this stage and beat them 3-1. This brought an exciting fourth round tie, away to Arsenal at Highbury. Murphy and Barron both failed fitness tests, so Gwyn Hughes and Jack Southam came into the side.

A crowd of 72,408 watched the game, the most a Cobblers side have ever played before. Although Arsenal won 3-2, the Cobblers never disgraced themselves; Jack English scored two, and Ted Duckhouse, despite being injured, saw a late shot hit the bar, and bounce to safety.

Barnsley were so impressed with Eddie Murphy they signed him. It was a chain of events, for Barnsley sold Danny Blanchflower to Aston Villa, and bought Murphy with the £8,000 money. He in turn replaced the young Tommy Taylor, who was to put in a transfer request and later joined Manchester United. Murphy's stay at Barnsley was short, for he moved to Exeter in 1952 and gave them four seasons before joining Trowbridge Town.

At one stage the team were eighth in the table, with an outside chance of promotion, but a catalogue of problems saw the team drop down the League. First, Jack Ansell broke his leg playing against Southend, then Jack English was injured, and there was no suitable replacement for Murphy. Garrett, Hughes and young Tommy Mulgrew were all tried, but failed, and this resulted in the team finishing seven points off of a re-election place. Bob Dennison took a firm move and he released all the older players in the side.

Archie Garrett, joined Wisbech then Holbeach, before moving to Bristol to settle and Tom Smalley moved back to Wolverhampton, and played for Gornal, as player-coach, while Bill Barron joined Kettering Town.

1951-52

There was again an element of Scotland in the new signings. Full-back Connell came from Morton, Staroscik, a Polish-born winger joined from Third Lanark, and forward Willie O'Donnell had played for Partick. Jim Wilson signed from Luton, and Freddie Ramscar, a ball playing inside-forward, came via the well-trodden path from Preston. Before a ball was kicked, Bert Mitchell left the club for Luton and he was later to play for the England 'B' team, before returning to his midland home. By the sixties he was working as a salesman, and scouting for the Cobblers.

There was no place in the side for Arthur Dixon, and he moved to Leicester for £10,000. After only 11 games for the City over two seasons, he moved on to Kettering, where he broke a leg and his career was ended. However, he could look back on it with some humour. Dixon was the son of the Hearts trainer, and all his football was played in Scotland prior to his move to Northampton. This prompted Scotland to pick him for their side versus the R.A.F., until it was discovered he was an Englishman!

Connell's first team life was short, for he was soon replaced by Ben Collins, and Jim Davie lost his place to Gwyn Hughes, while Felix Staroscik was replaced by Tommy Fowler, on the left-wing. Joe Payne, an inside-forward, was signed from Scunthorpe, and in his second game for the club he netted a 19-minute hat-trick - against one of his old clubs, Newport County. In December, yet another old face returned, Alf Wood, the 'keeper who had guested for Northampton during the war.

Some supporters questioned the acquisition of a 34-year-old goalkeeper, but he answered his critics on his League debut, a 6-0 win over Shrewsbury, where he knocked out his own skipper, Ted Duckhouse, while trying to punch a ball clear. It led the Droll Duckhouse to remark; *"Our keeper has a good punch."*

The buying and selling did not stop there, for around Christmas Adam McCullough was allowed to join

Two players who both came in to the side for the Arsenal match, Top - Jack Southam and below - Gwyn Hughes.

Shrewsbury, and Cliff Pinchbeck was bought from Port Vale as his replacement. But in his third game for the club he netted his third goal, and was carried off with a broken ankle; he never played for the first team again. McCullough assisted Shrewsbury, Aldershot and Ramsgate, before emigrating to Australia, and his son Andy, played League football in the 1980's for a host of clubs including, Oxford, Q.P.R. and Aldershot.

The club finished eighth, and Norwich had the honour of completing the treble over the club, winning both League games, and the F.A.Cup game - the Cobblers first exit at the first round one stage since 1938! Jack Ansell joined Headington, winning a Southern League championship medal with them, Ted Duckhouse was offered the player-manager's job at Rushden, which he agreed to take if they found him a job, which they did as a coal carrier. Meanwhile full-backs Connell and Wilson drifted out of League football

1952-53

Tommy McLain one of the fastest footballers at the time was signed from Sunderland, he was a wing-half. Ron Patterson, a full-back, was signed from Middlesborough, and the experienced Maurice Edelston was signed from Reading.

The forward line now picked itself; English, Edelston, O'Donnell, Ramscar and Fowler. Realising that it was almost a 'closed shop', Tommy Mugrew - a young player who had joined from Morton - accepted an offer to join Newcastle, and moved for £8,000. His stay was short as a 'Magpie' - just two seasons - but he was to give Southampton eight years and over 300 games and creating one or two records for them on the way. He scored for the Hampshire team within fifteen seconds of his debut, but he was also the first Saint to be sent off in 29 years. He later assisted Aldershot. A ding-dong match with Norwich saw McLain booked, then carried off, return, then was sent off; Gavin of Norwich was also dismissed, and the Cobbler's Patterson carried off. Ramscar saw his goal disallowed, but the Cobbler's won 2-1.

Again the club were keeping up with the leaders, and there were some thrilling games. Palace were beaten 5-1, and it could have been six if Ramscar had not missed a penalty. Freddie always side-footed his penalties, trying to send the 'keeper the wrong way with his run-up. Bristol City were awarded a penalty in the dying minutes of their home game against the Cobblers, but Alf Wood saved it, giving Northampton the two points. Then a home match against Reading looked destined for a 1-1 draw with twenty minutes to go, but the floodgates opened and the Cobblers scored five in the latter part of the game. Once again the press circulated stories of Dennison being linked with the vacant West Bromwich job, that a reserve winger named Hern was wanted by Cardiff, and that out of favour Davie could become a Coventry player, but they were just rumours.

Before the transfer deadline, Frank Upton, a blacksmith's lad, was signed from Nuneaton, in a deal that took wingers Briscoe and Raynes the other way for the remainder of the season. Injury forced Upton to be drafted into the first team, and he helped out in the late rally for promotion, which failed by just two points. Both Bristol Rovers and Millwall won their last game, Northampton could only draw, and they stayed yet another season in Division Three South.

There was little activity on the retained list, although Briscoe became Wolverton's manager, Joe Payne became the Colts coach, and most surprising was Maurice Candlin's move to Shrewsbury, together with Jim Davie. Candlin had two seasons at Shrewsbury, then returned to the area and managed Wellingborough Town. After his football days were over he took first a pub, then a newsagents, before moving to Carlisle where he retired.

1953-54

Bob Dennison broke off his holiday, on the South Coast and took a plane to the North East. There he sought out Sunderland's reserve defenders, Bill Walsh and Maurice Marston, bringing them both back to Northampton. Marston recalled: *"My wife and I were round a relative's house where we were playing cards. Suddenly a knock came on the door, and there was the Northampton manager, offering me terms to come and play for Northampton Town."* The two new men were the only debutants at the start of the season, which had started well.

John Anderson, a quiet spoken Scotsman, arrived from Partick. He was a man of little pace but great skill, and he was followed by a somewhat strange signing, in Jack Cross. Cross was Bournemouth's centre-forward, and Northampton were one of several clubs after his

signature. He agreed to sign in October 1953, for a £6,500 fee. He had a B.A. qualification and had been at Bournemouth for six seasons, netting 64 goals, and he scored on his Cobbler's debut against Colchester United. Although he started the season as captain, Walsh lost both the captaincy and his centre-half spot to Ben Collins, and also out was Maurice Edelston, injury taking its toll. The arrival of Cross prompted Willie O'Donnell to ask for a transfer,

After beating Llanelly in the F.A.Cup, Northampton found themselves at home to Hartlepool, and a 1-1 draw required them to travel to the North-East for the replay. Ron Patterson had the misfortune to see a backpass stick in the mud, and the 'Pool, scored the only goal of the game.

February brought the shock news that Jack Cross had been sold, after ten games and eight goals. He moved to Sheffield United for £13,000, a fee the Cobbler's could not turn down, but it did not go down well with the supporters. Cross scored just 16 goals in two and a half seasons, before moving to Reading.

The club ended the season in fifth position, 12 points behind the leaders Ipswich. Jack Jennings was given a testimonial, that saw both Matthews and Mortenson at the County Ground. Jack remembered; *"The chief constable informed me that all the police, many of whom I had treated, had given their services for free."*

There was a downside, for Dennison was leaving, the frustration of near misses and the chance to return to his native North-East was enough to see him go. He would never enjoy the success he had at Northampton, although he would do well at Middlesborough, as he would with Hereford, and also his short spell in charge at Coventry.

Also leaving the County Ground, was Edelston, who moved to the media, plus Walsh who returned North with Darlington, and O'Donnell who joined Candlin at Shrewsbury.

1954-55

Dave Smith had taken over the job of club secretary when he retired from playing, and now he was team manager replacing Bob Dennison. He made three new signings, George Webber, an experienced goalkeeper from Torquay, Don Hazeldine, an inside-forward, who could not hold a regular place in the Derby side, and Ken Oakley, a Cardiff City reserve forward.

One of Smith's first duties was to transfer Freddie Ramscar to Millwall, after the forward had put in a request. This led to a strange incident.

Ramscar was still living in the town and travelled down with the Cobbler's team to play for Millwall, against his old team mates. He scored the only goal of the game, for the 'Lions', then travelled back home with the Northampton team! Freddie stayed in Northampton, and he later assisted Peterborough, and Wellingborough, and was the Colts' coach for a spell.

After a bright start, things started to fall away, and after the A.G.M., when it was stated that there had been a £4,301 loss, belts had to be tightened.

Debut man - Roly Mills

Smith was not afraid to give his youngsters a run, and in his first season he gave first team debuts to Roly Mills, the young Daventry lad who started with the club's un-official Town League side - he was a winger, but could play anywhere, Ron Newman, a Welsh inside-forward who came through the ranks, and Don Adams. Don was an inside-forward, whose father had played for the Cobbler's as an amateur in the 1920's. Don was also an amateur and was on the books of Chelsea. While undergoing treatment for an injury, under Jack Jennings, it was suggested Adams had a trial with the Cobblers, he did, and was taken on. Unfortunately, although a skilful forward, he was also dogged by injury, and every time he made the first team he then picked up an injury. He well remembered a game versus Orient: *"I left the field after five minutes, to have two stitches over my right eye. Jack English joined me in the dressing room a few minutes later with a dislocated collar bone, and at half-time Ron Patterson was concussed, when a home supporter hit him over the head with a bottle. I returned to the field in the second-half, after treatment, to make up a nine man team, and in another five minutes I clashed with the Orient Centre, Aldous, getting a damaged knee; this time I was out of the game. Strange as it may seem, it was not a dirty game."*

The events of this game overshadowed the debut of Eddie 'Ginger' Smith, the new inside-forward, from Watford. The player appeared for many clubs, but never gave up his newsagents shop in London.

The F.A.Cup-tie, at home to Coventry, made history. Roy Kirk, a Coventry defender, made a clearance from his own area, and sent it goalwards. Alf Wood ran out to catch it, but slipped, and watched the ball sail into the net; it was adjudged to be a 70-yard shot, and Northampton were out of the Cup.

Gwyn Hughes was selected for the Division Three South team, to play the divisional North section; it was the first time the two sides had met. Hughes relayed the tale: *"I was disappointed to be told I was to be substituted at half-time. Unfortunately for me the second-half was to be televised, and all my friends and family in Wales had made arrangements to watch the game. No mean feat as there were few T.V.'s in Wales at the time since reception was poor."*

On the second of April 1955, Northampton Town beat Torquay 1-0, but it was one of the hollowest victories ever for the club, since it was on the same day that Albert Joseph Darnell died, he was 90 years of age. He was the last link with the club's formation, the man who had achieved more than anyone, and although his activity in later years was not great, no one could take away what he had done for the club, it was so sad that in later years he was to be all but forgotten.

When the club faced Bournemouth away, they gave debuts to Ron Newman, and Derek Danks. Newman scored the only goal of the game, and Danks laid it on, yet both players were dropped for the next game - Bournemouth at home. But without them the team won 5-0. Thirteenth place was not the best of positions, but considering the club fell as low as 20th in mid season, it was not too bad. All the new signings left - Webber, Oakley, and Haxeldine, the latter who moved to Boston where he played in the team that beat his old club Derby, 6-1, in the F.A.Cup. Alf Wood accepted a new contract, but asked to be released when he was offered the trainers job at Coventry.

1955-56
Peter Pickering was a record transfer for a goalkeeper when he moved from York City to Chelsea, but he had lost his way, and was by now playing Southern League football for Kettering. Dave Smith gave him the opportunity to return to League football. Jim Wallace, a centre-half from Aberdeen also joined the club, but as cover.

In early September, Derek Draper was signed from Lockheed Leamington, he was to be the first of several part-time players signed in an attempt to keep the wages down. Draper was never out of his depth, and as the season progressed he seemed to improve, and finished the season as top goalscorer, notching one more than the prolific Jack English.

Pickering saved two penalties in a match against Aldershot, but conceded two in open play, while in an away match at Newport, Ron Newman told all his family, from Pontypridd, to come and watch him play. They came, and he obliged with the only goal of the game.

A match against Torquay could have turned into a broadcaster's nightmare had it been on air, for among the 22 players there were four Smiths', three named Collins, and two Mills'. It was also around this time that some of the shoe firms began to sponsor the club with boots and trainers, the start of what was to be big business.

The club made an offer to Hull for Neil Franklin, the ex-England centre-half, and although the clubs agreed a fee, Franklin did not want to move home, and the deal fell through. The transfer deadline in March brought a lot of activity to the County Ground. Ron Newman was allowed to move to Coventry, with centre-forward Charlie Dutton moving to Northampton.

Colin Gale

This was followed by a deal with Cardiff, when they signed Bernard Jones, and in return the Cobblers signed inside-forward Roland Williams and centre-half Colin Gale. Gale was a makeweight in the deal, yet of all the five players involved, he was the only one to settle with his new club and to give a reasonable length of service.

Another mid-table position, without any real challenge for promotion, but the gates were good, with well over 10,000 average, something was going right, for the club.

Gwyn Hughes moved to Bedford, the last playing link with the war sides, and he settled in Northampton. Tommy McLain also left, he was now 34, but still gave Headington a season, and then took over from Candlin, as player-manager of Wellingborough.

It is worth mentioning at this stage the wingers, Jack English and Tommy Fowler, undoubtedly the best wingers to wear a Northampton shirt, since Page and Pease. Fowler was fast, tricky, and had lots of stamina, whilst English was less skilful, but was so cool in the box, knowing where the goal was and had the instinct to be at the right place at the right time.

1956-57

There were three major signings in Hugh Morrow, a right-winger from Lockheed Leamington, Alan Woan a forward from Norwich, and Reg Elvy, an experienced 'keeper from Blackburn.

The team again made an indifferent start. The match at Southampton saw Morrow come off with an ankle injury and by the time he had arrived in Northampton the ankle was so swollen he had to ask Draper to drive his car back to their Leamington homes. A hard fought game at Coventry saw three bookings, three carried off, and two sent off. Yeomans, the player sent off for Northampton, remarked that he only asked the referee about a certain decision.

Dave Smith must have been doing something right, as he was rewarded with a three year contract. Transfer activity came to the fore again. Syd Asher had played against the Cobbler's in the F.A.Cup for Hastings the previous season, and he was signed on. It took him some time to adapt to League football, not scoring until his seventh appearance, but then he netted 11 times in his remaining 16 appearances.

An experiment in March badly backfired. The management broke up the English/Fowler partnership, by dropping Tommy and replacing him with Hugh Morrow for the game versus Walsall. It did not work, but it meant Tommy missed his first team outing for 237 games. It goes without saying, he was back for the next game. At the end of the season, there was a mass clearout, and despite being top goalscorer, Asher was allowed to leave for Bedford, Morrow and Draper joined Kettering, as did Marice Marston - who was later to be the 'Poppies' manager and secretary. Larry Canning, later to work for the BBC, joined Nuneaton after just two first team outings.

Towards the end of the season, four youngsters were given a run-out; winger Miller, an amateur, inside-forward Bobby Tebbutt, full-back Tony Claypole, and forward Gerry Bright. It seemed that the future of the club could lay in the hands of these youngsters.

1957-58

This was to be the last season of the Third Division South, for the following season, the top halves of the South and North sections would merge to become the new Third Division, while the rest would form Division Four. So Northampton knew that nothing lower than 12th would suffice.

Bobby Corbett, the 34-year-old ex-Middlesborough full-back replaced Marston, and two Robinsons' were signed. Terry was a defender, and ex-England amateur international, while Maurice was a winger who came from Kettering.

An indifferent start was made again, including a 1-7 defeat at Brentford, and a 1-5 defeat at Swindon, but also provided victories of 4-0 over Coventry and 4-1 versus Colchester.

Smith tried to sign more players, making an offer for Dave Sexton of Orient, but the player turned down a move saying he wanted to stay in London; a few weeks later he turned up in the Brighton team! Joe O'Neil signed from Leicester, he scored two on his debut - a 5-0 victory over Plymouth - and then fell out of favour. Centre-half Colin Gale was given a run at centre-forward, and scored one in the Cup-tie with Newport, but by the time the second round came about - at home to Bournemouth - Barry Hawkings had established himself in the centre-forward spot. The ex-Lincoln man took some time to settle, as Alan Woan had done the season before. The club need not have worried about scoring against Bournemouth, for in a 4-0 win, the South Coast side scored two of the goals themselves.

Then came the home game with the Arsenal! Dave Bowen still trained with the Northampton team, but he was banned from the Country Ground in the run-up. A few days before the game, top scorer Alan Woan went down with blood poisoning, and was confined to bed; he had to be content with listening to the cheers, from his Abington Avenue flat. Bobby Tebbutt was given his place in the team.

Captain Ron Patterson
One of the heroes in
the Arsenal match

The game took place on Saturday the 4th January. Arsenal wore gold shirts, and the Cobblers an unfamiliar blue. Dave Bowen was made captain, a position he held with the Arsenal until he left, and he won the toss, with the Cobblers kicking towards the hotel end. An all-ticket crowd of 21, 344 watched the game and saw Bobby Tebbut give the home club the lead, putting away Rae Yeomans free kick. Bowen made a desperate lunge to stop the shot, but it went safely into the back of the net. Arsenal equalised soon after, but the Cobblers lead was restored when Hawkings cheekily hooked the ball over his shoulder. The crowd went wild. Arsenal went on an all-out attack, but it was the Cobblers, via Ken Leek, who made the game safe, and the Arsenal had been beaten 3-1.

The B.B.C. had their camera's at the game, and the Cobbler's skipper, Ron Patterson, was interviewed after the match, when he gave a tribute to the enthusiastic and cheering crowd, who got behind the team, by stating: *"It was worth a goal to us."*

One footnote regarding game, was the first goal by Tebbutt. A photographer caught Dave Bowen's desperate attempt to save the goal on film, and the picture appeared in many papers. Bowen admitted to hating it in the end. When he returned to Northampton someone had framed it and put it in his office; at the first opportunity he dumped it, only to find it back in his office, and some proud member of the office staff boasting that he had retrieved it from the rubbish bin!

Round four gave the club an away tie at Liverpool. The club took the players to Southport on the Tuesday for four days training. Tommy Fowler recalled: *"We had four memorable days training there, in about six inches of snow. I was looking forward to the game, I was born about eight miles from Anfield, and saw Liverpool many times in my schooldays."*

The game was somewhat different to the Arsenal match. Goalkeeper Reg Elvy takes up the story; *"Having played at Anfield many times for both Bolton and Blackburn, it was old stamping ground for me. The thing that stood out was the terrible weather conditions, for across the city Everton's game had been cancelled; and the fact that we lost."*

Problems ahead for the Cobblers - unwilling founder-members of the new Fourth Division.

Centre-half Ben Collins concluded the story: *"In front of 57,000, we settled down well at 1-1, then I scored at their famous Kop end, to make it 2-1 - alas the wrong end, it was an own goal, and the match ended 3-1 to the Liverpool team."*

The League form had suffered because of the Cup run, and the team rolled up its sleeves in an effort to remain a Division Three side. Millwall were beaten 7-2, and Exeter 9-0, in fact in the last 11 games eight were undefeated, but it all fell apart in the last two matches, home and away to Southend.

Two points would have made it safe, but Southend also needed them, and the home match was won by Southend 3-1. With everything to play for the Cobblers took an early lead in the away game, but it was shortlived, for the 'Shrimpers' won 6-3, and the Cobblers became founder-members of Division Four.

Most of the players who joined at the beginning of the season left, and only Joe O'Neill remained. Peter Pickering had departed in mid-season, to emigrate to South Africa; he was going to be a sub-editor of a provincial newspaper, but on his way out there the editor died, and he took over the newspaper. The biggest transfer was Ken Leek, who joined Leicester City for £10,000.

1958-59

Several new faces arrived including Tony Brewer, a 'keeper from Millwall, Jack Bannister an experienced full-back from Shrewsbury, and Brian Kirkup from Reading - an inside-forward.

Alan Woan has the record of scoring the first ever goal in the Fourth Division, when he netted in the first minute away to Port Vale, and he was to add another in the Cobbler's 4-1 win. After the game, what gambling man would have put money on Vale to win the championship that season, but they did.

During September Dave Smith brought in two experienced men, Kevin Baron from Southend, and Ollie Norris from Bournemouth; Norris had scored one of the own goals in the Cup match of the previous season.

Although the club were in high mid-table, there seemed no threat of promotion, so it was a case of change again. After a 2-2 draw at Darlington, Rae Yeomans stayed in that area and signed for Middlesborough. He had joined the club four seasons before while serving as a cook in the R.A.F., when he was on the books of St. Johnstone, and joined the Cobbler's on his demob. It was ironic that he should sign for Darlington, as he was later to join the 'Quakers' as both player and manager.

Ralph Phillips, a full-back, moved the other way; winger Bela Olah, an Hungarian refugee came from Bedford, and Alan Loasby, nephew of the famous Harry of pre-war days, joined from Wellingborough, all in an attempt to lift the team to a promotion spot.

After the accolades from the F.A.Cup a year earlier, the club were to see the other side of the coin, with a defeat by Amateurs Tooting and Mitcham. Colin Gale was out with chicken-pox, and during the game, Bannister was injured, and he moved up with the forwards. Mills went to full-back, and Baron to wing-half, but the team was disrupted, and the London side proved to be too strong, winning 2-1. It was small consolation in that the non-Leaguers had beaten Bournemouth in the first round, and then held Nottingham Forest to a draw in the third round, before losing the replay; and Forest went on to win the Cup!

Eighth place, seven points off one of the four promotion spots, and 24 players used. The only good point was Alan Woan's achievement, for he was only two League goals off of Ted Bowen's record.

Dave Smith suggested to the board that they pay £7,000 for Dave Bowen, and bring him back to the County Ground as player coach, but the board had a better idea. They paid the £7,000 and brought him back to the County ground as player-manager; Dave Smith's contract was not renewed!

Mike Everitt

Two long-serving players with Northampton Town, who were to make their mark in the early 1960's.

Barry Lines in action

CHAPTER SEVEN
1959 - 1969

1959-60

Dave Bowen took over the hot seat and got to work at once making three new signings. Frank Griffin, a winger from West Brom. - he had scored the winning goal for the club in the 1954 F.A.Cup final, Richie Ward - a youngster with Scunthorpe schools - and Jim Fotheringham, a centre-half who was a teammate of the manager at Arsenal arrived from Hearts. The latter signing caused regular centre-half Colin Gale to put in a transfer request.

The first game was a 1-1 draw away to Exeter, and it was the first time a manager had played since Jack Tresadern.

Bowen was never afraid to use the transfer market, and became a master at picking up a player at a reasonable price, getting the best out of him and selling him on for a larger fee.

Two games in September were well remembered, for goalkeeper Tony Brewer was injured and Alan Woan went in goal, having scored a goal himself earlier, and in the match versus Millwall, the new 'keeper, Peter Issac, saved a penalty, Tommy Fowler missed one. Some joker in the crowd blew a whistle and the players shook hands and walked off, with the referee desperately trying to get them all back on to finish the last four minutes!

All through the season there was activity on the transfer market; the unsettled Alan Woan moved to Crystal Palace, with Mike Deakin and a cash adjustment coming the other way. Woan came from a footballing family, his brother Don played for Liverpool and Orient, and his son Ian would later play for Nottingham Forest. Another twist of fate would have both Woan and Deakin playing together for Aldershot later in their careers. Peter Kane was signed from Queens Park, a small but gifted inside-forward, with a flair for goals.

The new manager also signed players to replace his ageing stars, Ken Tucker was signed from Shrewsbury, he was to replace Tommy Fowler on the left-wing, but he didn't, and local lad, Tony Haskins took over Ron

Patterson's, left back mantle. Things did not go all his way, for Bobby Tebbutt broke a leg in a match versus Walsall, obscuring the fact that the Champions-elect were beaten on their own ground, and the club made an early exit from the F.A.Cup, losing 7-1 to Torquay United. The three players who scored for the home team, were all Torquay born.

Three new directors joined the board, Dr.Hollingsworth, Eric Northover, and Archie Whatton, at the same time the Claret and White society was formed to raise money for floodlights. Mike Deakin, an old fashioned centre-forward began to find the net regularly towards the end of the season, netting four against Barrow, and scoring within ten seconds of the kick off versus Bradford. Sixth in Dave Bowen's first season was not bad, and only four points off one of the four promotion places.

There was a lot of close season activity. Brian Kirkup, who lost his place early in the season, had joined old manager Dave Smith at Aldershot, Peter Kane moved to Arsenal for £10,000, and that was on the strength of his 16 goals in 28 games.

Griffin returned to the Midlands, and Jack English said goodbye after 135 League goals for the club. Ironically Jack had always been a part-time player, having been released from a full-time contract some years back, and returned part-time, combined with managing a Clothing Manufacturers. He gave Rugby Town a season of service, before quitting the game.

1960-61

The only new face at the start of the season line-up was David Laird from St. Mirren, an inside-forward who had one taste of League football with Aldershot, but then returned to Scotland.

There was a greater incentive to win promotion this season, for rivals Peterborough United had been elected to the Football League in place of Gateshead, and despite being in another County, geographically they came under the umbrella of the Northants F.A.

> *"The miracle of 1966 was not England winning the World Cup, but Northampton Town reaching Division One."*
>
> Joe Mercer, Manager of Manchester City

The team started well, only three defeats before Christmas, and the goals were shared out between, Deakin, Derek Leck - the player who had joined from Millwall, a few seasons earlier - and Micky Wright, who was snatched from local East Anglian football.

Jack Jennings had been in Rome with the British Olympic team, and it was he who suggested that they sign Laurie Brown from Bishop Auckland. The six-footer was equally at home at either centre-half or centre-forward, and was an awesome sight coming forward. 'Topper' was an amateur but had been offered professional terms by several clubs, but he decided to throw his lot in with Northampton Town, maybe because he knew Jack Jennings. Tommy Fowler made his 500th appearance for the club, against Barrow, on the very day his replacement, Barry Lines, signed from Bletchley.

F.A. Amateur Cup star Laurie Brown, later in his career in a Norwich City shirt

On October the eighth, Peterborough and Northampton met for their first ever League meeting. There were 22,959 people there to witness the clash at London Road, and Northampton received some bad news, for Laurie Brown was out. Having stepped on a piece of wood, a nail had penetrated and injured his foot. Then Roly Mills failed a fitness test, so the young Rugby amateur player, Terry Branston, was given a debut, and what a debut.

The Cobblers ran up a 3-0 half-time lead, with goals from Leck, Deakin and Fowler, but a second-half injury to the left-winger saw the 'Posh' pull the three goals back, to end this first encounter all square.

October also saw the floodlights erected, and Arsenal brought a strong team, beating the Cobblers 3-2, and supporters got the first glimpse of the club's two new signings, goalkeeper Norman Coe, and left-winger Barry Lines. Over the next few months, the club 'raided' Norwich. First right-winger Ron Spelman arrived, then came Jimmy Moran, an inside-forward, and finally centre-forward Bob Edwards.

Mike Everitt was signed from Arsenal for £4,000, he was a utility player and Dave Bowen remembered him from his early days. This season was to be the first season of the League Cup, which ended at Wrexham, after a 1-1 draw in the first tie at home. Roly Mills scored the goal, and became the first 'Cobbler', to score in all three major competitions.

In the F.A.Cup, the club fared a little better, after beating Hastings in the first round, managed by ex-manager Tresadern, they won a second round tie at Romford 5-1, with Derek Leck, netting a hat-trick, this brought a round three tie at Luton.

The Bedfordshire constabulary insisted on an all-ticket match, the first at Luton since 1952; they won the tie 4-0. Back in the League the four teams that were to be promoted, Peterborough, Crystal Palace, Northampton and Bradford, were by now running away from the rest of the League, and it was obvious by Easter that these were the quartet who were going up. All that was left to question was in what order?

By now Tony Brewer had lost his place in goal, he went part-time and drifted into non-League football, while Norman Coe now had the number one spot. Ralph Phillips and Tony Claypole, were the full-backs, although the latter broke an ankle just prior to the end of the season; Phillips was the player used in the exchange deal with Yeomans, and had taken some time to settle. Claypole was the youngster from Weldon who had been capped at Schoolboy level. Cooke, Gale and Mills formed the regular half-back line, although Branston had replaced Cooke by the run-in. Tucker, Olah, Spelman and Everitt had all had a run at outside-right, the latter holding down the place by the end of the season, while on the other wing, Barry Lines had taken over the left-wing spot from Tommy Fowler. Deakin, Leck, Brown, Laird and Wright all vied for the three inside-forward positions, although Deakin left in mid-season, to tread the well-walked path to Aldershot. Bob Edwards finished the season at centre-forward, netting eight goals in his 13 games.

There was again a flurry of close season activity, when Laurie Brown moved to Arsenal for £35,000, he later joined Spurs and Norwich, before becoming player-manager of Bradford where news was made when the chairman sacked him, and replaced him with a steward. Brown later moved on to Kings Lynn.

Colin Gale also left, he decided that Third Division football was not for him, and he joined Wisbech as well as taking regular employment. He returned to Cardiff later, and ran an hotel. Tucker joined Hereford, Wright - Kings Lynn, where he was to make over 1,000 appearances for them, and Phillips returned North to Darlington. He would well remember his recall, to the first team in September, when Patterson failed a late fitness test, and a call went out to Phillips' digs, where it was discovered he was out shopping, and a frantic search was launched; he was found on time, and played in the match.

1961/62

There were two new signings for the first Division Three season. Theo Foley, an Irish full-back came from Exeter, for £1,000, and Pat Terry, a well travelled centre-forward joined from Gillingham. Bowen had been trying for some time to capture the London-born front runner.

Things did not start well, for the club had gained just two points from its first five games, and Terry was the only Cobbler to find the net in that time. It was then that Bowen pulled a master stroke, when he signed Cliff Holton. Holton was a team-mate of Dave Bowen's at Arsenal, and had moved to Watford where he was a prolific goalscorer and a great crowd favourite; he had scored 84 League goals in his three seasons at Vicarage Road, but there had been a disagreement between himself and the manager over his commitment, as he had business interests, and the Watford manager claimed he was more involved with this than training, which Holton denied.

The centre-forward takes up the story: *"There was great secrecy involved, as Watford insisted on telling their fans I was not for sale. The local press suspected something, following me to work that day, staying and watching my factory office. Later, Dave Bowen rang to say he had clearance to sign me, and would I play that evening at Crystal Palace? I escaped from the factory and met the team at a Harrow hotel and duly signed on. Later as we were about to go out on the field, Dave Bowen threw me the balls and said 'You're in charge on the field' (Such confidence). History showed we won 4-1, and I got a hat-trick, courtesy of some great players who made up the team. With a start like that, and having some super*

players around me, breaking the club's goalscoring record was made easy for me."

Charles 'Chic' Brodie

Chic Brodie from Wolves was the next major signing, and when he made his debut against Halifax, he made history by playing for three different clubs, in three different divisions in consecutive games. He played his last game for Aldershot in the fourth, next for Wolves in the first - but only played once for them - before joining the Cobbler's in the Third.

This prompted Brian Caine, who had signed on from Coventry in close season, to leave for Barrow, for he could see no future with three keepers on the books. Inside-forward John Reid was signed in November, from Bradford City. He was a talented player with the ability to make and score goals.

As Holton had said, he had some great players around him and that was the reason the club started to climb the division. Holton was finding the net regularly, at one stage he scored in nine consecutive League matches.

With so many new players coming in, some had to go. Pat Terry never settled in Northampton and returned to London, to Millwall, and after 16 years, Tommy Fowler left the club with the words; *"You have to go where the work takes you."* He joined ex-manager Dave Smith at Aldershot, fast becoming the resting home of old Cobblers, and his record of 521 League games has never been threatened,

A deficit of £3,500 was made the previous season, but thanks to a donation from the supporters club it was turned into a £2,131 profit. The transfer deadline brought into the side another ex-player in full-back Arnold Woollard, who had left the club some years earlier, moved to Peterborough, then on to Newcastle, and finally Bournemouth, from where he joined the Cobblers - plus a cash adjustment for winger Ron Spelman. Woollard was to take the left-back spot from the injured Claypole.

Despite all the new players coming in, Dave Bowen was always ready to give his own youth players a break. Terry Branston had taken over the centre-half spot from Gale, and when he left he never looked back. Winger Tommy Robson, and forward Brian Etheridge both made their bows, during the season.

Although the club never threatened to win promotion, they were in the top half of the table and gave all the teams a run for their money. A 7-0 victory over Grimsby was particularly outstanding, for the 'Mariners' were promoted that season. In a 4-1 win over Coventry, Holton scored two goals, the first equalled Ted Bowen's record, the other beat it, and he netted another, away to Q.P.R., and finished the season on 36 League goals, a new club record. Holton also had the distinction of holding the individual goalscoring record with two different clubs, Northampton and Watford. Only two other players have done this - Wally Ardon, (Rotherham and Forest), and Jimmy Greaves (Spurs and Chelsea).

1962-63

The main body of the first team was retained, with the fringe players moving on. Four new players arrived for the start of the season. Vic Cockcroft, a full-back from Wolves, who was unable to break into their first team, Roy Sanders a right-winger from Romford, who had played so well against the Cobblers when they met in the Cup, two seasons earlier. John Kurila was a hard tackling, no frills wing-half, and from Luton came Alec Ashworth. The transfer of the last player was fate, for in both the case of the player, and the club, it was second choice.

Northampton had made a £10,000 offer for Terry Bly to Peterborough, but he turned them down, so they moved for Ashworth.

He in turn was wanted by Southampton, but he felt this was too far away from his Southport home, so he joined the Cobblers. Ashworth was on the books of Everton, and had joined Luton as a makeweight, when Billy Bingham moved the other way.

The start to the season was exceptional, with just one defeat in the first ten games, and these included an 8-0 win over Wrexham, and a 7-1 defeat of Halifax. Holton and Ashworth, were both scoring goals, as was Barry Lines and John Reid, and even Derek Leck, now converted to wing-half, was weighing in with a few.

Around the turn of the year the transfer market became active again. Roy Sanders picked up an injury early in the season, and took some time to shake it off, although it was fair to say that despite his skill he was unhappy at Northampton and he was allowed to return to Romford. Billy Hails was signed from Peterborough to replace Sanders, together with Ray Smith an inside-forward.

No sooner had these players settled in then Q.P.R. made an offer for Cliff Holton. At first it was turned down, but Holton himself then asked for a move. He had business interests in North London, and wanted to return to the capital, he complained that he had worn out two cars, driving up and down the motorway (although he failed to say the cars belonged to the club). The request was granted, and his name was circulated to just the London clubs. Q.P.R. and Fulham made attractive offers, but he decided on Crystal Palace. Despite being 34 years-old, he still had some goals left in him and he went on to assist Watford (again), Charlton, and Orient, before retiring in the late 1960's. He had one of the hardest kicks in football which had been recorded at over 70 m.p.h.

Holton's replacement was Bert Llewellyn, the man who had scored a hat-trick against the Cobblers when Port Vale knocked Northampton out of the Cup a year earlier. Llewellyn was so different from Holton, standing 5'-1" compared to Holton's six feet, he was also a busy

JOHN REID   ALEC ASHWORTH

A goal-scoring pair

tricky forward, compared to the bigger player's, almost elegant canter into the box, where he used to wait for the pass, almost on his toe. Llewellyn will well remember his debut for Northampton, which was away to Q.P.R., for in the first-half he twisted a knee and was carried off, and it was later discovered to be a long-term injury. During the match, at White City, which Northampton won 3-1, others had reason to remember the game.

An angry spectator jumped the fence and attacked both Foley and Branston, but met his match when he tried it on with Chic Brodie, who pinned him against the goalpost, while police officers rushed towards them; it was unsure if they were trying to save the Cobbler's 'keeper, or the spectator!

This gave manager Bowen another problem, with Llewellyn out for some time he needed to find another forward, ironically, he was sitting in the stands at White City watching the game, little knowing by the end of the week he would be replacing the man being carried off. His name was Frank Large.

Frank started as a wing-half with Halifax and scored a lot of goals for them by picking the ball up on a run, and powering through, a big powerful lad, it was hard to knock him off the ball, and he put his head were others were afraid to put their boots!

It did not take long for bigger clubs to hear of his exploits, and Q.P.R. took him to London, but there he was made an out-and-out centre-forward. The game was foreign to him, as he was now playing most of a match with his back towards goal, and hence he found it hard to settle with his new club. But that was not to be the case at Northampton. In his second game he opened his account versus Bradford, and in the following game he netted a hat-trick against Colchester; in a short time the supporters had taken him into their hearts.

Frank, Large in name and in his contribution to the Cobblers' cause.

January, and part of February, were out, as far as football was concerned. Snow drifts and freezing fog blanketed the Country, and Northampton - that often misses so much bad weather - lost six weeks of football. But it did not stop the rhythm of the team, and in their 44th League game, a 2-0 home win over Carlisle, the Third Division Championship was assured. Frank Large hit both goals, and the club were to enter Division Two for the first time in their history.

Promotion was assured when the club did the double over Brighton, in the Easter programme, in both games, the 'Seagulls' defender Roy Jennings, scored an own goal for the club. The Cobblers won the Third with 62 points, four more than runners-up Swindon, and it was the first time they had won a championship since they won the Southern League in 1909, when the r u n n e r s - u p   t h e n   w h e r e ......Swindon!

Only Arnold Woollard was released, having lost his place to Mike Everitt at left-back. Alec Ashworth, who was by now skipper, asked for a move, had it granted, and he joined Preston, for an estimated £20,000.

Another strange but true fact was that on the transfer deadline, the club had signed Vic Rouse, the Welsh international 'keeper from Palace for £1,000. He was signed purely as cover, never made a first team appearance, and moved on to Oxford, during the next season.

1963-64
The season started on a bad note, Dave Bowen, who had got the club this far, quit, he said he had got the club as far as he could, and he wanted a rest. Jack Jennings took over on a temporary basis, and the applications came flooding in, one from ex-manager Bob Dennison.

John Kurila, had gone to play football in Canada, but a problem with his contract stated he could sign for any club on his return, except Northampton, so he joined Bristol City. There was only

*As the successes came, so did the crowds increase,
and it wasn't always easy to get a good vantage point!*

one new signing of note, Joe Kiernan, a midfield/wing-half play-maker from Sunderland, and he was going to have a large say in the history of the club.

The season started well, the double was achieved over Scunthorpe, and Sunderland were beaten 2-0 at Roker Park, with Kiernan made skipper for the day against his old club. There were mixed emotions for the home game against Derby, for it was the club's first defeat, knocking them off the top of the Division, but the game heralded the return of Dave Bowen, who had relented, and returned.

Injury to Billy Hails, saw a young winger, just signed from Pollock, take his place, his name was Billy Best, and he netted goal on his debut against Norwich. Around the same time Peter Kane returned from Arsenal, never making it at Higbury, and scored twice, along with Frank Large, against Swindon; it was the Wiltshire club's first defeat of the season.

Bryan Harvey, a goalkeeper, was signed from Blackpool, as cover for Tony Waiters, and had First Division experience with Newcastle. His signing was forced when Chic Brodie went down with 'flu, and Norman Coe conceded three against Leeds, although it was unfair to judge the cover 'keeper on one game. Again, Harvey's arrival was fate, as the club was about to sign Peter Wakenham from Charlton, but the player could not agree personal terms.

The club lost too many home games to be a threat, but always bobbled around mid-table, and will well remember the 5-0 thrashing of Sunderland, Dave Bowen recalled: *"I spent hours previous to the game experimenting with different forms of footwear, to combat the ice and snow, that lay on the surface of the County Ground. After much deliberation I decided all our players should wear a rib soled canvas basketball boot, which I felt was perfect for the occasion.*

The boots that day made us sure-footed, and we destroyed Sunderland. I could not have been more pleased if I had scored a hat-trick." The 'Sunday People', who marked players out of ten, gave winger Barry Lines maximum points.

Along with Harvey came Bryn Jones, a full-back from Bournemouth, and brother of 'Spurs' Cliff. He was bought to replace the injured Foley, and also on the move was Brodie, not happy with second team football he joined Brentford, where he gave them several seasons, before his League career was ended when a dog ran on the pitch and into him, injuring his leg.

Luton made a raid on the club and took Smith and Reid, making them both 'offers they could not refuse', while Bryn Jones left the club after two months to join Watford, with ex-England amateur International Bobby Brown, moving the other way.

The final piece of transfer activity was to allow Frank Large to join Swindon, and the payment of £15,000, to Colchester for Bobby Hunt, a goal-scoring forward. By this time, John Kurila, had also returned.

Eleventh place was a fair start to their first ever in Division Two, and supporters and players could reflect on some of the incidents that took place over the season.

The arrival at Manchester City eight minutes before kick-off, with the players changing in the coach..... the time that the first and reserve team coaches were leaving the County Ground for away matches, and Joe Kiernan was taken ill - the reserve team coach was flagged down, and Roly Mills swapped coaches....the Brisbane Road incident, where Frank Large was hit in the back by a dart..... the £30,000 that the club turned down when Arsenal came in for Barry Lines, or the £5,000 lost over the last season.

Peter Kane joined Crewe, Bert Llewllyn - Walsall - now managed by ex-Cobbler Alf Wood, and Billy Hails joined the exodus to Luton, Harry Walden coming in the other direction. Sadly, Jack Jennings called it a day at the County Ground, he left to set up his own business as a physio., but still kept his position with the cricket club, and was still active in the late 1980's. He died in 1997.

1964-65

Walden and Charlie Livesey, a centre-forward from Watford, were the only new signings for the start of the season. Both local lads Don Martin and Brian Etheridge were making the first team and vying with Hunt for the two inside-forward positions, and Livesey in the middle.

After picking up just three points from their first four games, the club looked to be struggling, but then they put together a run of 17 League games without defeat, which lifted them into second position.

A lot could be put down to the defence remaining the same throughout the run, only Cockcroft needing to cover Everitt for three of the matches. By this time Tommy Robson had ousted Barry Lines from the outside-left position, it was a shame having two excellent players in the same position, for Lines was a skilful winger who liked to take on his opponent, while Robson preferred to cut inside and go for goal.

The defeat that ended the run, came at Newcastle, the eventual champions, by 5-0, but it was only a stutter, as the club immediately got back to winning ways. Another reason for the good run was the penalty saves of Brian Harvey, seven in all, including two in one game versus Southampton, from Terry Paine who was the England penalty-taker at the time. The final few months saw the return of Ken Leek, he scored one of the goals

in that 2-2 draw with Southampton that also saw Foley score an own goal and Branston move up field to equalise.

The two matches against Bolton made news. In the goalless draw away, the team coach was stoned, causing £1,000 of damage, while at the home match, an evening game, all the reserves and apprentices cleared the snow prior to the clubs 4-0, win, in which Harvey saved a penalty with his legs, from Franny Lee. Bobby Brown had taken over as centre-forward from Livesey, and was finding the net quite regularly.

Promotion to the First Division was achieved when Northampton beat Bury 4-0 at Gigg lane, on the 12th April. As they walked off the pitch Dave Bowen greeted them with the words, *"You're up."* One of the tragedies of the promotion was that chairman Fred York never saw it, after so much work he passed away before he could see the fruits of his labour. Ted Buller stepped up to finish off the good work.

The two games versus Plymouth made news. Firstly the Cobblers flew to a League match, catching a plane from Luton to Exeter, then coaching to Plymouth, where the Argyle won 5-2, including the converting of two penalties, however revenge was sweet, with the Cobblers winning the return 3-1.

The final game was against Portsmouth, who needed a point to stay in the Division. They got it, in what was to be Jimmy Dickenson's last game for the club. The match was played on a Saturday night, and after the match the Cobbler's players went into the stand and threw their shirts in to the crowd. Division one, here we come!

This was the season the club reached the last eight of the League Cup, going out to Plymouth 1-0, and then only due to a terrible mix-up between two defenders that allowed Newman, a 'tap-in' goal. All the players were retained, but Livesey was put on the 'open to offer list'. The players then went on a four match tour of Eastern Europe.

Another goal in the Second Division promotion season. Match action against Carlisle United (another 'unfashionable' club who would reach the lofty height of the First Division)

1965-66

The opening match in Division one, was away to Everton, Bobby Brown scored the club's first goal in the top section, and with 15 minutes to go, the club were only 2-1 down. The floodgates then opened and the 'Toffeemen' rattled in another three. The game finished 5-2, but the club were not too disheartened.

The first home match was a 1-1 draw with Arsenal, in which history was made when Vic Cockcroft replaced Mike Everitt as substitute, the first in a League game for Northampton. Manchester United were held to a 1-1 draw, when Bobby Hunt scrambled a late attempt over the line, with just seven minutes to go.

The club had its first home defeat, since April 1964, when they lost a ding-dong battle with West Brom., in which Barry Lines made national history, being the first player to play and score in all four divisions, for the same club.

The first win came in the League Cup away to Blackburn. Mike Everitt was pushed out to the right-wing and scored the only goal of the game. However, the next round saw a quick exit when the team lost 5-0 at Fulham, it was ironic that they should be drawn against two fellow Division one strugglers, who, like the Cobblers, were fighting for their existence in such company.

The Cobblers thought they had won their first match at Forest, but the Nottingham team scrambled a late equaliser when their winger, Kear, later admitted to pushing the ball over the line with his hand. It was League game number 14, when they picked up their first win 'bonus'. Theo Foley tucked away a penalty, he never missed one for the club. Ken Brown equalised, but Ken Leek made the game safe when he headed on a Barry Lines cross, and the Cobbler's fans went home jubilant.

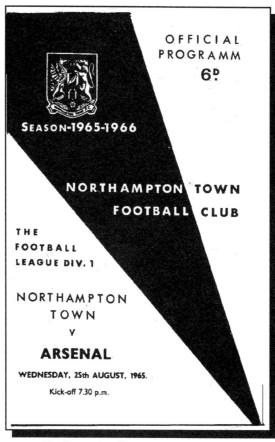

OFFICIAL
PROGRAMM
6ᴰ

SEASON-1965-1966

NORTHAMPTON TOWN
FOOTBALL CLUB

THE
FOOTBALL
LEAGUE DIV. 1

NORTHAMPTON
TOWN
v
ARSENAL

WEDNESDAY, 25th AUGUST, 1965.
Kick-off 7.30 p.m.

Northampton Town versus Arsenal in the Football League Division 1. Who would have thought this fixture could ever have take place!

There had been some activity in the transfer market, for Derek Leck had been asked to play sweeper, which he refused, stating he was an attacking midfield player. He was transfer-listed, and followed Livesey to Brighton. In came outside-right, Joe Broadfoot, he was a £27,000 buy from Ipswich, at the time a club record.

The A.G.M. was held in November, and from it came news of a £19,000 loss, mainly due to the £27,000 spent on new players, this may have prompted the club to accept the £30,000 that Chelsea offered for Tommy Robson. The Geordie was to have a chequered career, he only had a short spell in London before moving home to Newcastle, and then joined Peterborough in 1968, making 562 appearances for them. This established a club record, and at one stage he was contemplating a move back to Northampton.

Northampton had their revenge on Fulham at Craven Cottage, when the Londoners 'keeper, Tony Macedo, was injured and Rodney Marsh went in goal. Bobby Brown netted a hat-trick, the first of his career, and against one of his old clubs. Villa were also beaten 2-1, with Northampton 'keeper Norman Coe making his first Division One appearance, and turning in a star performance. Despite the club letting in an alarming rate of goals, any new faces that arrived at the ground were always forwards; Dave Bowen could never be accused of defensive tactics.

The inside-forward trio was made up of Bobby Brown, Don Martin, who missed the start of the season when he fractured a jaw in pre-season training which ruined his chance of a possible under 23 Cap, and either Jim Hall or Bobby Hunt, but the latter two fell from the picture when Graham Moore arrived from Manchester United. Dave Bowen knew all about Moore, for Bowen was also the Welsh team manager by now, on a part-time basis, and Moore was a regular for his country, although not for his club.

The £15,000, was a bargain. He made his debut and scored in the home defeat by Chelsea, a match that drew a record crowd of 23,325, shortlived though this number was.

It was Bobby Brown who said: *"Every time a new player arrived at the County Ground it was a forward, the turn over of forwards was very high. When I was in the reserves the boss told me Exeter were interested in me, but I said I was not interested, a few months later I was in the first team and scoring, and the boss came up to me again and told me Derby had made an offer for me, but it had been rejected."*

The team suffered two 6-2 defeats, versus Manchester United and Stoke, but beat, Newcastle and Leeds, the latter match being a game to remember. It heralded the arrival of another striker, George Hudson from Coventry. The Stocky centre-forward was on Accrington's books when they lost League status, but he moved on to Peterborough and then Coventry, where he became a popular figure. So popular was he that some of the 21,564 who watched the Leeds match were from Coventry, disappointed that their club had sold their hero. He soon became popular with the Northampton fans, setting up one goal for Barry Lines and scoring another by rounding Jack Charlton.

The run-up to the end of the season saw some good results. Forest thought they had won both points in the home game at, but John Kurila equalised with the last kick of the match. Villa were beaten 2-1 on their own ground, giving the Cobblers their only double of the season, and 'Spurs were held to a 1-1 draw at White Hart Lane, where 'keeper Harvey was carried off, and substitute John Mackin went in goal. Mackin was a 'keeper in his younger days before deciding to play outfield and he proved so that day, for it took a Jimmy Greaves penalty to beat him.

The turning point was the home match against Fulham, played on the 23rd of April 1996. The County Ground attendance record was broken again, this time 24,423 packed in to watch the Cobbler's take a 2-1 lead, in what was classed as a 'four pointer'.

It seemed a third goal had made the game safe, with the Fulham 'keeper McClelland fumbling the ball on the line, and the supporters on the Spion Kop raising their hands in jubilation plus the Cobblers forwards appealing. Joe Kiernan recalled: *"I turned to referee Jack Taylor, but he pointed to the linesman, who had fallen over, and was in no position to see the 'goal'. 'Sorry Joe, I can't give it, sorry'."* The game turned, George Cohen did a destruction job on the club, and laid on three of the four goals, Steve Earl netting a hat-trick, and Bobby Robson scoring another. Although this game did not put the Cobblers down, it was now out of their hands.

Victory over Sunderland, was followed by defeat at Blackpool and relegation.

The club made a determined effort to return to the top flight, for they released just two of their players, Norman Coe - who moved into non-League football with Kings Lynn, and Joe Broadfoot who had been involved in a dressing room dispute and made it clear he did not want to play for the club any more; he joined Millwall.

Match action in the White Hart Lane encounter with 'Spurs.

So the only season in the top flight was over, a season that caused the Manchester City manager, Joe Mercer, to state: *"The miracle of 1966 was not England winning the world cup, but Northampton reaching Division One."*

1966-67

Bobby Hunt moved in the close season to Millwall, and Dave Bowen relied on the same players that had fought so hard to remain in Division One. The manager tried to bring England winger Mike O'Grady to Northampton from Leeds, but the player could not agree personal terms, so Bobby Jones came from Bristol Rovers, for a fee just short of £20,000. The club were not 'pulling up any trees' on the field. In the match at Hull, Barry Lines gave Northampton a two minute lead, and they lost 1-6.

Clive Walker, a full-back was signed from Leicester, and when Bryan Harvey broke two fingers in a 5-1 defeat at Palace, Bill Brown was signed from Spurs. Bill was part of the 'Spurs 1961 double winning side, and was a Scottish international. Bobby Brown joined Cardiff, he was later to coach the Welsh national team, and after a spell at Hull as Community officer he returned to Wales to run a hotel.

One highlight of the season was the 8-0 thrashing of Brighton in the League Cup. Don Martin scored four of the goals, and there was a young debutant on the right wing, Graham Felton, who takes up the story: *"On the day of the match my excitement was coupled with terrible nerves as I arrived for the game. However, we went on to win 8-0 that night, Don Martin scoring four, and I felt I was walking on air, unable to sleep, reliving the game over and over again. The same team was selected to play at Ipswich for the Division Two match. This time I was on the wrong side of the thrashing, as we lost 6-1. In the space of a few days, at such a young age I found out the meaning of the saying 'The ups and downs of football', a hard lesson at the time."*

Four-goal hero Don Martin

Bobby Brown, George Hudson, and Jim Hall had all been given a run at centre-forward, but all the goals were coming via Don Martin, and this prompted Dave Bowen to dip into the purse again to bring Frank Large back, now at Oldham, for £10,000. This allowed George Hudson to leave, he joined Tranmere, and Bobby Jones, who never settled in at Northampton, joined Swindon in an exchange deal that brought the goal-scoring Dennis Brown to Northampton.

Mike Everitt joined Plymouth, and Bill Brown asked to be released from his contract, as he was offered a job in Canada, to which the club obliged.

It is hard to put a finger on the reason the club were relegated to Division Three. It could have been the vast turnover of personnel, or the fact the club had 12 players injured during the season with cartridge operations - Joe Kiernan having two in eight weeks - or to lose Dennis Brown after eight games when he was injured in a car crash which resulted in him losing a knee cap. There were a few good points, for there was a £15,000 profit on the previous season, mainly due to a £29,000 hand out from the supporters club. The club still had players on First Division wages, hence there was a major clear out.

Terry Branston joined Luton, who he helped to win promotion from the Fourth Division, and almost did it again with Lincoln. Vic Cockcroft moved to Rochdale, Theo Foley was offered a coaching job at the club, but preferred to continue playing, and joined Charlton. Graham Moore also joined Charlton and Harry Walden returned to his first club, Kettering.

1967/68

Only full-back Brian Faulkes was signed for the new season, he came from Reading, but was quickly followed by Ron Flowers, the ex-England half-back, who came to Northampton as player-coach. Dave Bowen then announced he was moving upstairs to take the general manager/secretary's job and the team manager's job went to Tony Marchi, the ex-'Spurs wing-half who was a fringe member of the 1961 double team, having recently managed Cambridge City. A shock win over Orient was due to two wind-assisted goals from free kicks by Brian Faulkes, and he almost made a third, but on the down side Barry Lines broke a leg against Scunthorpe, and was expected to be possibly out for some months.

Marchi did not stand on ceremony with anyone, for he sold Don Martin to Blackburn for £36,000, and then Frank Large to Leicester for £20,000. Large did not want to go, but it was his first chance of playing First Division football at 28 years of age. Then Kiernan, Kurila and Hall were put on the list, although John Roberts, a utility player from Swansea, was signed for £13,000, plus John Fairbrother and John Byrne from Peterborough, the former costing £9,000. Byrne was an exchange deal with Jim Hall moving the other way. This was to be a good move for Hall as he would become a prolific scorer for 'Posh', and never regretted the refusal to join Mr.Docherty at Rotherham. Wingers Tommy Knox and Eric Weaver also joined the club from Mansfield and Notts County respectively. They were just the players the manager actually signed, for Tom White and John McCormick of Palace turned the club down on personal terms, Dave Poutney of Villa felt a move would jeopardise his testimonial, and a Cambridge City player, who refused to give up his job to turn professional, never made the journey.

The club finished in 18th position, completing the season with two defeats at the hands of Peterborough in five days, first in the Northants Senior Cup, and then in the last game of the League season, however, the victories were hollow, as Peterborough were relegated that season.

Harvey (to Kettering) plus Kurila and Best (both to Southend) left at the end of the season, together with Marchi, who was told his contract would not be renewed, his parting words were... *"They wanted the slide halting, and I halted it."*

Bill Best, who moved on at the end of the season.

1968-69

Ron Flowers was made player-manager, and he brought in Ray Fairfax, a back from West Brom. plus Frank Rankmore a centre-half from Peterborough. Barry Lines had recovered from his broken leg and had now gone part-time, mixing his football with a salesman's job.

Tommy Knox misses a penalty in the opening game versus Reading, the first Cobbler to do so since 1962. Peter Gordon, who played Town League football before seeking his fortune with Norwich, returned as coach, but left after a few months citing that he could not get a house in the town. He was replaced with 'Mac' McCormick, the local Physio.

Bob Hatton was signed from Bolton, he was a striker and an ex-team mate of Flowers at Wolves; he netted twice on his debut against Tranmere, and fitted in well with Fairbrother who was scoring well that season. Flowers believed in giving youth a chance, and he gave first team opportunities to Phil Neal, Neil Townsend, Peter Hawkings, and Roger Barron, as well as the established youngsters like Graham Felton and John Clarke.

By middle March, the club had an outside chance of promotion, but the final 10 games brought just two points and relegation. One of those matches was a home game with Shrewsbury. Flowers gave a first team place to Stuart Skeete, a goalkeeper from 'Spurs, who was on loan to the club, their first ever loanee. At one stage the Cobblers were 3-1 up, only to lose 4-3 when Skeete conceded own goals from both Flowers and Clarke.

The clubs Third Division life hinged on a match between Gillingham and Shrewsbury, but it produced the wrong result and Northampton returned to the Fourth Division, nine seasons after they left it. Flowers was asked to stay as a player, but was dismissed as manager, an offer he refused, preferring to joined Telford, Byrne went to South Africa, and Roberts became a 'Gunner' for a £30,000 fee.

CHAPTER EIGHT
1969 -1977

1969-70

Dave Bowen once again took over as manager and started to rebuild the side. Eric Brookes a full-back, came from Barnsley, and Dixie McNeil was signed from Corby, having netted 50 goals in the last two seasons. Mcneil had been on the books of Leicester and Exeter City before moving into non-League.

If the 2-0 defeat at Oxford in the League Cup was not enough, then the fact the team coach was turned away from a pub in Weston-on-the-Green on the way back was the final insult.

Frank Large returned for the third time. The 'Happy Wanderer' had left Leicester for Fulham, as a makeweight in the Allan Clarke transfer, and was not making the first team, so was therefore happy to return to Northampton. In a match at Swansea, both he and Peter Hawkins were dismissed, but in Frank's case the ensuing suspension was lifted, when his crime was found to be due to an over-enthusiastic referee. Frank's shot at goal missed its target, and hit a youngster in the crowd, he went over to see if the lad was all right, but was attacked by another spectator. He had to defend himself and hence was cleared of the offence.

It took 18 League games for Northampton to record their first win, which they did in style, with a 4-1 victory over Newport. Dennis Brown got some of his own back for being released by the club, when he netted for Aldershot in 18 seconds, but the Cobblers pulled two back, only to eventually lose 5-2.

The F.A.Cup drew the most interest that season, after two matches against Weymouth, it was Exeter in round two. In the first encounter it took substitute Phil Neal to score an equaliser three minutes from time. In the replay, the Cobblers had three goals disallowed and in the second replay, at Swindon, there was bad news when both Weaver, and his replacement Barry Lines, went down with Flu. Dixie McNeil had started the season in the first team but lost his place, and these circumstances earned him a recall which he took with both hands, scoring the winner against his old club, and cementing his claim for a first team place.

"How can you fine them on the money they earn."

Bill Dodgin speaking regarding the poor pay of some players in the lower divisions.

Brentwood were eliminated next, with a John Fairbrother goal, and it took two games against Tranmere to win the fourth round tie, the winner being headed in by skipper Rankmore who out jumped every other player when a Felton corner came over. Round five saw a home tie versus Manchester United.

The club upset some supporters by increasing their prices for this one-off game, a season ticket seat went from £1.10s (£1.50) to £2.00, the hotel end price jumped from 5/6 (27p) to 12/- (60p), while the Spion Kop doubled from 5/- (25p) to 10/- (50p).

The players were taken for a pre-match steak meal at the Westone Hotel, while the crowds at the County Ground began to build up. George Best had just completed a six week suspension and there was doubt if he would be playing, or not, but he did - as every Northampton supporter would later find out.

Things started to go wrong when Rankmore's penalty was saved and the rebound, that went to Fairbrother, was also taken by the 'keeper. 'Besty' then went on the rampage scoring six of the eight goals that day.

Northampton did pull two back, near the end of the game, which led one cynical (or over-optimistic) radio reporter to state: *"Yes, Northampton Town are making a comeback."* Frank Large and Dixie McNeil scored the Cobbler's goals, and Dixie recalls.....*"Every now and again, they show those goals on T.V. No doubt Frank, like myself, wonders why our goal apiece isn't shown, still, what a memory, to score against Manchester United."*

This started a rumpus when a newspaper article suggested the Chairman, Eric Northover, had called his Northampton team 'disgraceful'. The players demanded an apology, but Northover said his words were 'taken out of context'. Dave Bowen got every player to sign the match ball, and sent it off to George with the words, 'Georgie, you are the greatest'. The League programme was something of an anti-climax after that, but 14th position was attained.

*George Best turns on the style in the F.A.Cup match,
leaving Cobblers' number 2, Ray Fairfax, bemused*

Fairbrother became the first Cobbler to score over 20 League goals since Ashworth in 1963, and their run in the F.A.Cup to round five was the best since the early 50's; ironically they did not win an F.A.Cup match between 1963-68, then a trip to the last 16!

1970-71
Despite the good Cup run, the club lost £47,000, on the season, they had signed Keith East from Bournemouth, for £5,000 and brought in two new directors, Ron Dillegh and Peter Stevenson.

By September the Cobblers were on top of Division Four, and Dave Bowen had won the manager of the month award. Two youngster were signed, Trevor Gould from Coventry and John Buchanan from Ross County, both were midfield players, Gould being the younger brother of Bobby.

Eric Northover stated that the Cobblers would have a new home in five years time, a brave prediction, and 20 years out!

Defeat by non-League Hereford in the F.A.Cup started the club's downfall that season, and it was made worst by the injury to skipper Rankmore, when a broken arm saw complications set in and he had to retire from the game, leaving a big gap in the defence. Several players were tried at centre-half, but the only one who filled the breech was Frank Large, but that in turn made the front line lightweight.

Brian Heslop, younger brother of George, was signed from Sunderland, for £5,000, £1000 of the fee coming from the supporters club. Peter Price was signed on loan from Peterborough, as Leicester had once more made their interest in signing Frank Large be known, but it never materialized, and Price contacted flu and never played for the club at all. The club picked up just 15 points from its last 20 games, and it cost promotion, but Bowen was building a youthful side and released some of the more experienced players; Brookes (to Peterborough), East (to Crewe) and Fairfax (to Olney Town).

1971-72
Alan Starling, a goalkeeper from Luton, joined on a one year loan initially, but was offered a full contract later in the season. It was a similar case with Folds, the Bedford-based Gillingham player, who had a two months trial, and did so well at full-back, that he was signed. John Hold came from Bournemouth. The newcomers were joined by another board member George Taylor, who was once president of Long Buckby F.C.

The season had hardly got under way before Fairbrother moved to Mansfield, and he was followed by goalkeeper Kim Book, who went on loan, and then signed for Doncaster. Lew Chatterley was signed from Villa for £10,000, he came on loan but when offered terms turned them down, later changing his mind he filled the centre-half spot vacated by Rankmore, who was now a Northampton publican.

On the field, things were not going the Cobbler's way. After taking a 40 second lead against Brentford, they fell behind, and lost 6-1, then at home to Aldershot they lost their first ever home game to the 'Shots', when a last minute equaliser was disallowed and the referee had to have a police escort. Hereford, still a non-League side, put the club out of the F.A.Cup again, but this time it took a third game at the Hawthorns.

Dixie McNeil moved on to Lincoln for £12,000, and at the time the club were considering an exchange deal involving the club's old centre-half Terry Branston, but it all came to nothing. Just to prove there was 'life in the old dog yet', Frank Large hit an 18 minute hat-trick against Chester.

Alan Starling, a Luton 'import'.

Lew Chatterley moved to Grimsby for £10,000, five months after joining the club. The previous season he had been on loan to Doncaster, and was about to sign permanently, when their manager - Laurie McMenemy - was sacked, hence he returned to Villa, and then joined the Cobbler's on loan. McMenemy then took over the Grimsby hot seat, and Chatterley went with him, also moving to the manager's next port of call - Southampton - as player and coach, and to Sunderland, as coach, before taking him back to the Saints once again.

A 3-2 home defeat by Lincoln, had a great significance on the future of English football. The Lincoln side included Branston, Kurila and McNeil, but it also contained a full-back, who was injured in this game, and never played again. His name was later put up against Terry Branston's for the managers job, with the 'Imps', which proved so successful, that he was snapped up by Watford and after taking them from four to one, he moved to Aston Villa, and then became England's manager. His name was Graham Taylor, and it all started to happen on a very muddy County Ground pitch.

The last game of the season was at home to Darlington, a win or draw would save the Cobbler's from re-election, but a defeat would place them in the re-election zone for the first time in their League career. They lost 2-1, and were required to apply to remain a League club for the first time in their 52 years Football League career.

Luckily the club still had friends, for the voting went: Northampton 49, Crewe 46, Stockport 46, Barrow 26, Hereford 14 and Wigan 2, Telford and Yeovil 1 and another 8 failing to win a single vote. Joe Kiernan said goodbye, he was the last playing link with the First Division days, and he joined Kettering and skippered them to the Southern League Championship, but he would later return to the County Ground.

1972-73

It was a turnabout as Bowen signed four experienced defenders, Bill Baxter who had won a League Championship medal with Ipswich, Stuart Robertson, a centre-half from Doncaster, Dietmar Bruck a full-back, from Charlton, and formerly Coventry, plus James Burt, ex-Aldershot and Leicester.

The biggest crowd of the season was not to see a match involving Northampton, but a second round, second replay, League Cup match between Birmingham and Luton, the 'Blues' winning 1-0, thanks to a Trevor Francis goal; 11,451 watched the game.

By October, Bill Baxter had taken over as manager, Dave Bowen returned to his job as general manager/secretary, and vowed he would not get involved with team management again. He could look back over his management record with some pride, having turned down the hot seat at Manchester City, Sunderland and even the full-time job as Wales manager, and while at Northampton, it was only the board who stopped him spending money on youngsters like, Mike England, Mike Summerbee, Colin Bell, and Francis Lee; the four all going on to receive England Caps. He also signed on Phil Neal, John Gregory, and later George Reilly, the three cost nothing, but making £250,000 for the club.

Baxter's first move was to release Frank Large to Chesterfield, on the grounds he was no longer needed, and he finished the season, as Chesterfield's joint top scorer. Baxter then brought ex-Cobbler Bobby Hunt and Eamonn Rogers from Charlton on loan, and they made a difference, which led to an offer for Hunt, who in turn joined Reading!

The club was having problems on and off the field, struggling near the basement and a debt that was growing weekly.

The directors set up a £50,000 appeal, with collection boxes being set up in different shops and at matches, with the Mayor, Ken Pearson, being at the forefront of the appeal. It was at this time that Millionaire sportsman John Banks said that he was 'very interested' in buying the club, but after weeks of paper talk and promises he backed out, using the excuse that the newly applied VAT had scuppered his plans, so it was back to normal for the Club.

There was a flurry of new faces, with Gordon Riddick, a forward, coming from Gillingham, Bobby Park, a midfielder from Peterborough, and Tony Buck was signed from Rochdale. Any attempt to score goals had little effect, and a 0-0 draw with Darlington (again) resigned the club to another season of re-election.

Amongst the gloom, one ex-Cobbler - James McGuire - was at least happy!
He had emigrated to the U.S.A. and became the President of their Soccer Federation.
On a National Team visit to Israel in November 1973, McGuire (on the right) met Jerusalem's
Mayor. The ex-player, also a member of F.I.F.A., was appointed to the 1974 World Cup Committee

Once again the club got through the re election voting, which produced the following votes: Colchester 48, Northampton 43, Crewe 36, Darlington 26. The club spelt out the reason for its losses - there was a decline of £9,000 on gate receipts, promotions were down by £17,000, while £71,000 was spent on players. Many of the players were released, and Baxter was asked to stay as a player, after losing his managers job, but declined the offer.

1973-74

Bill Dodgin junior, took the managers job. Bill was the centre-half in the Arsenal team that lost to the Cobblers in 1958, he had a brief spell as manager of Q.P.R. and Fulham, and was then the assistant at Leicester. He knew what had to be done and set about his task. His first task was to get Johnny Petts - who was one of his Arsenal colleagues, and was now manager of Trowbridge.

The Wiltshire club wanted a fee for him, and this was the new man's first wrangle, that took some months to sort out; he saw Petts as the right kind of coach.

The club lost to Grimsby 2-1 in the League Cup, and Grimsby's ex-Cobbler, Lew Chatterley, stated that: *"Northampton were unlucky that Grimsby were not coming to Northampton for a replay."* Billy Best returned to the club, albeit on a part-time basis, whilst Gordon Riddick left for Brentford. Dodgin changed the attitude of many of those involved with the club, including the players, especially Phil Neal who was considering quitting the League game and becoming a P.E.Teacher, who now had a new lease of life. John Gregory was put on full terms and the team was playing better.

Northampton were not the only team with problems, as the attendance at Workington, for their home match with Northampton, numbered only 996. Alan Starling was sent to Leicester and had training with Peter Shilton, meanwhile Dodgin signed David Carlton, a midfield player, from Fulham. So revitalised was John Clarke, that he scored his first goal for the club after eight years, when he netted in the Barnsley match.

Dodgin knew of the financial problems, and used the loan system as much as he could. Robin Wainwright came from Millwall and Malcolm John from Bristol Rovers. Dodgin was also canny, for Rovers wanted a fee for John, but the manager said he would be a free agent at the end of the season. Again it took some wrangling, but again the Cobblers man got his way, and his man. Dodgin was a disciplinarian, but always reasoned.... *"How can you fine them on the money they earn?"*, his words relating to the difference in wages between the divisions.

Promotion that season was missed by sixth points, and fifth position was attained; compared to the re-elections of the last two seasons, that was enough in itself.

Local youngsters, like Paul Stratford, Alan Oman, Barry Tucker and Derrick Christie, were emerging through the ranks and the future looked brighter.

Some highlights of the season were the home match versus Lincoln, where goalkeeper Starling was carried off, and Phil Neal went in goal - now having played in every position, including keeper; the 2-1 home defeat by Bristol Rovers, with their striking partners of Bannister and Warboys, known as 'Smash and Grab' being the main attraction, but it was the consolation goal of John Buchanan's that caused the talking point. He let fly from outside the box and had the 'keeper got a hand to it, the shot would have taken it off! Gone were Bruck, Park and Hawkins.

1974-75

Gary Mabee, a striker, came from 'Spurs, he was a nephew of Cliff Holton, and the experienced John

John Clarke who eventually scored a goal!

One of Northampton's famous 'sons' Phil Neal who joined Liverpool

Moore joined from Luton. The team did not win a game until the fourth match, a 3-0 victory over Darlington, in which their 'keeper, Willie Wigham, had not played football at any level for three years since being released by Middlesborough.

Paul Stratford hit his first hat-trick, and the club's first in three years, when he appeared against Workington, making him the youngest Cobbler ever to achieve that feat. In October, Northampton made the national papers when it was known that Phil Neal was moving to Liverpool for £65,000, a new record for the Cobblers. He was to be Bob Paisley's first signing since taking over from Shankley, and it was hard to believe that 18 months earlier, the player was thinking of packing it all in after a ruck with the then Cobbler's manager Bill Baxter. Baxter was prepared to accept a £6,000 offer from Aldershot for Neal, but the directors turned it down, for they saw the potential in the lad.

Neal well remembered his days as an apprentice at Northampton, how he learned to drive - with the groundsman's tractor - how he once found a 10/-(50p) note on the terracing while sweeping up, and all the apprentices had fish and chips that day. He remembers standing in awe as he watched Colin Milburn smash the West Indies, all over the County Ground. He also wondered if being a utility player was a good idea, as it never guaranteed a first team place and provided the ideal substitute.

It all came good for Phil, who has to go on record as Northampton Town's most famous 'son', winning 50 England caps, every domestic honour, and captaining Liverpool's European cup side. He was disappointed much later when he discovered that it was Kenny Dalglish who was earmarked for the Liverpool manager's job and not him.

However, he was to do well at Bolton, as manager, taking their team to Wembley and winning promotion. He then took the manager's jobs at Coventry and Cardiff, and assistant at Manchester City and Peterborough, and there is little that Phil has not done in football.

The news of this transfer had hardly died down, when the club was involved in another transfer, John Buchanan joining Cardiff and John Farrington, the ex-Leicester and Wolves winger, joining the Cobbler's. Buchanan was a fiery character who became well known to referees, but had an excellent shot and was one of the few players who had the confidence to have a go from outside the area. He was a hard-working midfielder, who's temperament sometimes let him down, but he wanted away, and Dodgin saw this as a good deal.

Another player on the move
- John Buchanan -
but he did return later.

It may well have been for these losses that the club had a poor season, compared to the previous campaign, but the manager still had his eye out for the right player, and he brought Jim Hall back from Peterborough on loan. Hall had scored 137 League and Cup goals for the London Road side, and Dodgin hoped he would do so, back at the County Ground. The manager also signed two players from 'Spurs, Garry Anderson - a full-back on full terms - and Wayne Cegielski, a centre-half on loan until the end of the season.

Robin Wainwright had joined the club on a full contract by now, and slowly the team was taking shape, although the bad news was that an injury to John Clarke put an end to his career, and he was granted a Testimonial match versus Leicester. John had been on the club's books since their First Division days, and the Kingsthorpe lad was snapped up by Dave Bowen when he heard Leeds were interested. He was a solid hard worker, playing in the un-glamorous sweeper position who had only seen the club go down, now they were on the doorstep of promotion he had to quit.

Billy Best won the Club's first ever, 'Player of the Year' award. John Moore moved to Hitchen, and later managed Luton, Alan Oman joined Wellingborough, and Malcolm John, who Dodgin fought hard to get for free, left, not being the same player he was whilst on loan.

1975-76

When Huddersfield scored against the Cobbler's in the opening minutes of the opening game, of this season, the Cobbler's supporters must have wondered what they were in for. However, full-back Barry Tucker sent in a cross-come-shot that found the back of the net, and equalised.

Jeff Parton, a Welsh under-23 goalkeeper had joined the club from Burnley, and he started the season between the posts, but after a 3-1 defeat by Barnsley, Starling returned. September saw the arrival of Neil Davids, a central defender from Norwich on loan, and he made history by becoming the first Northampton loanee to be sent off, when he was sent packing against Tranmere. Next came Steve Phillips, a busy little midfield player who came on loan from Birmingham, and then signed on full terms. The best signing was that of Andy McGowan, another midfielder, he joined from Corby, and was a busy, skilful, player who could be relied on to pop in the odd goal now and again.

When Northampton met Lincoln on the 18th of October, it was the first Saturday game at the County Ground since the 12th of April. All previous games had been played on a Friday or Tuesday, and notably it was the best supported of all the games played thus far.

Northampton Town went top of the Fourth Division after Jim Hall - now signed on permanent terms - scored the only goal of the game at the Abbey Stadium, Cambridge, and now people were sitting up and taking note. Don Martin returned from Blackburn, a more complete player than the one that left. He could play in either defence, midfield or attack, and like Billy Best could give a good account of himself in any of these positions.

Alan Mayes joined the club from Watford, on loan, soon after Davids was despatched back to Norwich. Mayes was a forward, with a flair for goals, netting four in his ten games for the Cobblers, and his last game was against his own club Watford. Dodgin gained permission to play him at Vicarage Road, and he was keen, so much so that he laid on the only goal of the game for Jim Hall to score. This led to a barrage of barracking from Watford fans when he went for a drink in the club, but what hurt the Cobblers fans was the fact that Dodgin did not re-sign him on loan, or offer a full contract. This puzzled the player as to why the Northampton manager played him against his own club, when he had no intention of signing him. Things did turn out right for Mayes in the end, for he was to play in a higher sphere with Chelsea and Carlisle, and he helped Swindon to a Fourth Division championship.

Graham Felton joined Barnsley on loan, having lost his place to Farrington, but rejoined the club, just in time for its promotion push. Promotion was assured in a 2-1 win at Bradford City, where Jim Hall netted twice. An amazing game at home to Hartlepool ended 5-2 in the Cobbler's favour. Three penalties were awarded - two to the Cobbler's, of which one was taken by the club's penalty-taker, Martin, and the other was offered to Alan Starling, the 'keeper, who took it and scored. This goal ensured that every regular member of the first team had scored that season. It was also a nice gesture by Don Martin, as he had already netted two goals from outfield, and had he scored from the second penalty, he would have been the only Cobbler to have scored four goals in a game, twice.

The final match was a Friday night game with Stockport, which the Cobblers won 4-0, when Stratford netted a hat-trick this time. Northampton Town accumulated 68 points, in any other season that would have been the championship, but Lincoln were breaking all records and gained 74; they dropped just 18 points all season, and only two at home, scoring 111 goals compared to Northampton's 87, and had reached the fifth round of the F.A.Cup, compared to Northampton who went out in round one to Brentford. However the club could be proud of its record this season. Jim Hall's 21 League goals was the best since John Fairbrother in 1970, and

Jim Hall returned to the County Ground for a second spell with the Cobblers.

the 6-0 thrashing of Bournemouth, with all the goals coming in the first half, will always be especially remembered.

On the downside, Gary Mabee quit the game with knee problems, at the age of 23, but his sideline of making videos turned into big business, and currently he can still be seen at Northampton's games capturing everything on camera. Graham Felton was released, and had a season at Barnsley, followed by Kettering. He stayed in the area and set up a painting and decorating business, first with Billy Best, and then on his own. He later assisted running one of the club's youth sides and then helped the management team at Wellingborough. Gary Anderson returned to London and played in non-League football.

1976/77

Bill Dodgin resigned. The news broke in the close season, and no reason was given, although it could be fair to assume that it was over money for new players, or in this case the lack of it. With a higher grade of football, it was going to need one or two players of that standard, but the club obviously did not have any spare cash in the kitty, and that was enough to make the amicable manager leave.

Many of the players who played under him held the man in high regard, and he was seen as being a champion of the lower League players, voicing the fact that wages in the Third and Fourth Divisions were closer to what people earned in industrial jobs. On the other hand one ex-player tells how he went in to him for a raise, stating, *"I would be better off, taking a job, and playing non-League football, than playing here"*, to which Dodgin replied; *"Then go and do that, son"*. Which he did! Dodgin was not out of work for long, for he was soon snapped up by Brentford, which pleased him, as his father had also managed the London club.

Meanwhile, back at Northampton, names were being debated by supporters - Theo Foley, who had recently left Charlton, Johnny Petts who was the number two, and two ex-players now managing non-League sides, Graham Carr and Terry Branston. But it was Pat Crerand, the ex-Manchester United number two who got the job. He had recently had a bust up with Tommy Docherty, and quit United.

Joe Mercer recommended him for the Northampton job, which came as a surprise to everyone. There were no new faces in for the start of the season, and the results started off evenly, a draw at Chesterfield, a defeat at Sheffield Wednesday and a victory at Lincoln, but then things started to go wrong, on and off the field.

After the 1-0 win over fellow promotion mates, Lincoln, Northampton had a run of five defeats. They halted this with a 3-1 win over Portsmouth, one of the goals coming via George Reilly, a lanky striker who arrived from Corby, and who was to be one of the season's high points. When York City were beaten 4-1 at York, Crerand stated: *"I knew they would come good."*, but they didn't.

Some of the players were not happy, not liking the list of 'Rules' hung up on the dressing room door, or the fact that Crerand still lived in Manchester and commuted to Northampton, although he was looking to buy a house at the Weston Favell end of town. Dave Carlton was the first to move, he said his wife wanted to return to London, and he was the first to rejoin Dodgin. Jeff Parton, the cover 'keeper, was told he was not wanted, and to find another club, although he still had 18 months of his contract to run. Bobby Owen, a midfielder, was signed on loan from Carlisle, but he made little impression, and was destined to play for four clubs that season - his own, plus Northampton, Workington and Bury; all four clubs were either relegated or had to apply for re-election, a 'Midas in reverse' touch!

Ian Ross, the ex-Liverpool defender joined the club on loan from Villa, and he came with the promise that he would 'stop the goals being shipped in at the back', but he lasted just two games. Non-League Leatherhead ended the club's interest in the F.A.Cup. The third loan of Crerand's, was a first - an exchange loan. Jim Hall went to Canibridge United, the centre forward finding goals hard to come by in the Third Division, and he was swapped with Keith Bowker, who was going through a similar phase at Cambridge. For Hall it was a good move, for he found his goal flair and stayed until the end of the season helping his adopted club to the Fourth Division title, but Bowker became another unimpressive loanee.

The crunch came, after a 2-0 defeat at Brighton, just after the new year. Crerand resigned, he pulled out of his housing move and stayed in Manchester, where he took a pub. He did not leave quietly, for he complained that he lacked co-operation from both the players and directors, and that he had wanted to bring in several newcomers, but no money was available.

Chairman, Neville Ronson, announced there would be no new manager, instead a committee was set-up, consisting the chairman, the coach, and three senior players. They would be responsible for team selection, the coach would be in charge of fitness and tactics, and the chairman would cover the manager's day to day paperwork. Ronson explained, *"It would take a new manager several weeks to sort out a winning team, and by then it could be too late. These lads got themselves into this, they can get themselves out."* The first move was to change the captaincy from Billy Best to Stuart Robertson, this fuelled speculation that the popular utility player was on his way, but Best answered with the comment: *"If they did't want me they would tell me."*

One player who did leave was Steve Phillips, for he showed his disgust at the 'Committee' and joined the exodus to Brentford. The first game under the new 'Management' was a 4-3 defeat at home to Tranmere, the team were praised afterwards for their valiant effort, but it was still a defeat.

Ian Gilligan was signed from Swindon, a midfield player he scored a cracking goal against Chesterfield that gave Northampton their first League win in seven games, but unfortunately in his five games for the club it was his only real highlight. Steve Bryant, Crerand's only signing, from Birmingham, settled into left-back, allowing Barry Tucker to move to the right, which in turn allowed John Gregory to play Sweeper and Billy Best to move in midfield. But no sooner had the changes been made, then there was a lot of movement both in and out of the club. Alan Starling announced he was leaving and joined Huddersfield, and his replacement was Bob Ward, another loan player from West Brom. Keith Williams, an aggressive midfield player came from Aston Villa, and after beating Shrewsbury 5-3, Ray Haywood was signed from the Shropshire club.

Under the committee the club did fairly well, notably losing by the odd goal in nine at Lincoln, Billy Best scoring a hat-trick yet finishing on the losing side. Frank Large did a similar thing for the club against Bristol Rovers in 1968. Victory over Palace was sweet, as their full-back Peter Wall had called the Cobbler's the worst team in the Third Division. The team crept out of the relegation zone, then pinpointed their downfall to a game at Portsmouth. With the score at 1-1, Stratford scored what he believed was his, and the club's second goal. However, a linesman waved play on, and Pompey went on to score the winner; from then on it was all downhill.

The last game was away to Mansfield, who were top of the League, and the Cobbler's needed to win, and even then they would have to rely on Portsmouth picking up no more than one point, and Reading no more than four from their remaining three games. Mansfield won 3-0, and Northampton were relegated.

As expected John Gregory moved on, for he was snapped up by Villa, for £40,000 and had a career that saw him play for Brighton, Q.P.R., manage Portsmouth, assistant at Leicester and Villa, and also manage Wycombe, as well as play for England.

Johnny Petts was made manager, and back the club went to Division Four!

A determined John Gregory in action.

1977-78

Dave Liddle, an ex-youth team player, was given a full contract and promoted to the first team. The only other new face was Stuart Garnham, a goalkeeper, on loan from Peterborough. It was his second spell on loan to the Cobblers, his first was in 1974, when he was a Wolves player. Also returning to the club was Clive Walker, as coach. After a lengthy spell at Mansfield, he gave Gravesend a season, then took up the coaching side of the game.

The side made a good start in the League Cup, beating Southend in both legs, but went down 5-0 to Ipswich in the next round, still currently a joint record defeat by Northampton in this Competition.

Two losses both made news, the first was a 3-2 defeat by the Arsenal, in a benefit match for Dave Bowen, and the other was a 2-0 reverse at the hands of the League's 'new boys', Wimbledon; this was the Dons first victory after eight League games.

Steve Litt was signed from Minnesota Kicks, having had experience with Arsenal and Blackpool, and played alongside Stuart Robertson at the heart of the defence. Petts and skipper Robertson had a falling-out that saw the centre-half transfer listed and stripped of the Captaincy. Litt took over as captain, and David Lyon, a centre-half, was signed from Cambridge.

The experiment backfired, for in the new boy's three games, in place of Robertson, the defence let in nine goals. Garnham had now left, and Parton was re-instated in goal, but just one clean sheet in six appearances saw the arrival of Carl Jayes, a goalkeeper from Leicester. He had been cover for both Peter Shilton and Mark Wallington, and now he came to Northampton for regular first team football, but his debut produced a 4-2 defeat at Doncaster.

"Do you want to buy a football club?"

Mike Conroy, in casual conversation with Derek Banks

The club announced a profit of £12,000 on the previous season, so a small beam of light was showing through in the darkness.

It took nearly 20 years, but revenge was at last taken over Tooting and Mitchum for knocking the Cobblers out of the 1958 F.A.Cup competition; but Enfield put the Cobbler's out in round two, and therefore non-League opposition had beaten the Cobblers for two years running. A 0-2 half-time scoreline at Swansea was converted into a 4-2 win, but a 2-0 lead at Newport ended up 5-3 to the Welsh side. It might well have been the inconsistency that caused Johnny Petts to resign.

Dave Bowen was made caretaker for a month, then Mike Keen arrived from Watford. He had been their player-manager, but after they were relegated to the fourth he failed to lift them and was sacked, now he had to try and accomplish a similar job at Northampton. One of his first moves was to allow Barry Tucker to join Brentford for £10,000, and bring in Tony Geidmintis from his old club, Watford, for £8,000. Geidmintis was a Londoner of Lithuanian parents and he had spent 12 seasons at Workington before joining Watford, and is the only player to have scored a hat-trick in the League, for the 'Reds'.

The club won five and drew two of its last seven games to lift them up to a mid-table position. Keen won the 'Manager of the Month' award, and things looked good for next season.

Many of the older players were released, for Don Martin moved to Hitchen, and then Corby, Billy Best joined Bedford, and Jim Hall finished his footballing career at Cambridge City. Ray Haywood had been released from his contract earlier, he was unable to hold a first team place and when he failed to arrive for a reserve team match, due to a jam on the motorway, it was

Barry Tucker
another export to Brentford

decided it was in both player's and club's interest to release him. Steve Litt returned to the U.S.A., and Geoff Parton moved into non-League football.

The sad news was that both Paul Stratford and Andy McGowan had to quit League football. Stratford at his peak, had West Ham interested in him, but he departed from the game completely, concentrating on his career as a plumber, while Andy McGowan drifted into non-League football and went on to play for a host of clubs, making a Wembley appearance into the bargain.

Meanwhile, Tony Geidmintis, came up from the South, from Watford

1978-79

Allen Woollett signed from Leicester, he was a central defender, with a lot of experience. Also arriving was Northampton-born, Ricky Walker, a full-back, who had joined Coventry but failed to make the grade. Walker would well remember his debut, against Hartlepool, for he was carried off after 16 minutes.

A 4-1 defeat to Wimbledon saw Alan Cork score the 'Dons' first hat-trick in the League, and they were beginning to enjoy their encounters against Northampton. It was around this time that David Liddle was hurt in a traffic accident involving a police car, he suffered a broken wrist and a knee injury, and this in effect was to end his career.

Two new players were signed in September, John Froggatt, and Andy Poole. Froggatt was a six foot centre-forward, and had played for several clubs, before joining from Port Vale for £8,000. Poole was a 'keeper, he was snapped up from Mansfield on a free transfer, and was signed as competition for Carl Jayes.

Manager Mike Keen was always on the lookout for new players, and he raided his old club's youth team, bringing back utility player Paul Saunders. He also made a bid for a young forward in the reserves at Vicarage road. Watford said that if the player had not made the first team by the end of the season, Northampton could have him, but the player did go on to make the grade, and he also moved on to better things, his name was Luther Blissett.

Cambridge United made a £20,000 bid for the club's coloured winger Derrick Christie, the Milton Keynes youngster had gone through the ranks at Northampton and was putting in some stirring performances, hence the club turned it down. When Cambridge came back with a £50,000 offer the club took it.

Portsmouth beat Northampton in consecutive weeks, winning 2-0 in the League encounter, and knocking them out of the F.A.Cup by the same score. Northampton made a bad start to 1979, for it was not until their seventh game that they recorded their first win, and their League position was getting worse. Steve Bryant moved on when he joined Portsmouth for £20,000.

Keen was told his contract was not going to be renewed and he left, leaving Clive Walker to take over. He made a few changes to the team, bringing in Paul Matthews on loan from Rotherham, and then dropped Woollett. Under Walker the club avoided relegation by two points, and it was a case of once again of 'back to the drawing board'.

Stuart Robertson, won the 'Player of the Year' award, and then was handed a free transfer, while Woollett joined Corby but made it very clear what he thought of Northampton Town F.C. in an article in a Leicester newspaper. Froggatt also left, but he had started a painting and decorating business with members of his family, and later joined Boston, whom he went on to manage.

1979-80

There were six new faces at the start of the season, Dennis Byatt a central defender, and Gary Sargent a forward moved from Peterborough in a £10,000 deal. They were joined by Kevin Farmer, a central defender from Leicester, who cost £20,000. Peter Denyer had joined from Portsmouth, as a contra to the money owed for Bryant, he was a midfield player, although he later turned into a very useful utility player. Stephen Ward signed from Brighton, a striker who was unable to break into their first team.

Tony Taylor, a much travelled fullback came too as player coach. These new players, added to the existing staff of George Reilly who was equally at home at centre-forward, or centre-half, Keith Bowen, son of Dave, who was a striker on non-contract terms,

Midfielder Jim Mcaffrey, and local defender Des Waldock, along with the two goalkeepers, were to be the nucleus of the 1979/80 squad. By 5th September, the club had reached the third round of the League Cup, eliminating Millwall, and Oldham - both from the Third Division - yet had picked up only one point in the League. It was to be the eighth League game before Northampton recorded their first win, beating local rivals Peterborough 1-0. The players were disappointed with player-coach Taylor, and felt his place in the side was not warranted, and after seven games he left, moving North to Scotland.

Bill Harvey joined the club as coach, having had experience in management with Grimsby and Luton, while on the field two new faces arrive, Russ Townsend, a £20,000 midfield buy from Barnet, and Phil Sandercock, who was 'rescued' from Huddersfield. Despite all the money splashed out the team were not gelling although they gave Brighton a run for their money in the League cup, going out by the only goal of the game.

Kevin Farmer was struggling in the side and George Reilly was moved back to centre-back. Farmer first became the substitute, then he was dropped all together, but he made a comeback in the forward line in the Hereford match, and scored both goals in a 2-0 win. He did it again in a 4-2 win against Huddersfield and netted his fifth goal in three games in the 2-3 defeat at Rochdale.

Meanwhile there was activity in the transfer market. George Reilly moved on to Cambridge United for £165,000, where the lanky Scotsman stayed for four seasons before joining Watford in the First Division, and winning an F.A.Cup runners-up medal. He later assisted Newcastle, West Brom and Cambridge again, before stepping into non-League football with Barnet, where his career ended after suffering an eye injury. George remembers a game he played for the Cobblers against Bradford City, back in 1977: *"That day I was wearing the number nine shirt. It was a miserable day all round, and we lost 3-1. I lost two teeth when a belligerent City centre-half elbowed me in the face, I could tell the*

'Giant' Wakeley Gage returned

referee had no sympathy for me when he accused me of trying to bite the centre-half's elbow!"

Northampton bought Mike O'Donoghue on loan from Southampton, he was a different player from Reilly, a ball player, and very tricky. He netted once in his four appearances, and the club were interested in signing him, but Southampton wanted £60,000, and this for a player who was not even making the reserve side. Naturally all interest in the player ended.

Russ Townsend never adapted to League football and returned to Barnet and Wakeley Gage joined from Desborough. The six foot five inch centre-half was with the Northampton Town nursery club some years earlier but was allowed to leave, and his transfer fee was £8,000. He was joined by local lad, Adam Sandy.

There was still a familiar, inconsistency about the side, for after beating Huddersfield 4-2 at home, they lost 5-0 away less than two weeks later. February's run of three wins and two draws brought Walker the divisional manager of the month award, and he celebrated by breaking the club record incoming transfer fee, with a £33,000 deal that bought the Arsenal winger Mark Heeley to Northampton, and he was joined by Luton's Godfrey Ingram on loan. The loanee impressed with his four goals in 11 games, but there was no question of a permanent transfer, and he returned to Luton.

The season finished with a home game against the already promoted Portsmouth, and 10,774 watched the game, two-thirds of the crowd being Pompey supporters.

Thirteenth position was poor considering the money spent, with only Keith Bowen finding the net regularly, and he missed part of the season, due to his studies. Farrington, Jayes and youth player Ashenden, moved to Leamington, a club the former was later to manage, whilst Ward joined Halifax. McCaffrey quit the game to take a newsagents in Blackpool, and Clive Walher went back to the drawing board!

1980-81

Steve Phillips returned to the club, for £50,000. He had been converted into an out-and-out striker at Brentford, but after Dodgin had left the London club there was some unrest and Phillips asked for a move; he was automatically made captain. The player was followed by Dodgin himself, who took the coaching job, ousting Bill Harvey; but after a run of just three wins in ten games, Walker and Dodgin swapped positions. Dave Carlton also returned to add bite to midfield, together with Gary Saxby, a free transfer defender/midfielder from Mansfield.

New floodlights were installed, but during the first game, at home to Southend, they failed and the game had to be abandoned, with the fault not being found until the following day. At the home match versus Crewe, the police insisted that no one should stand on the cricket side of the ground as only a rope separated the supporters from the pitch - the crowd numbered 2,179!

Lincoln City put eight past the Cobblers in October, but there was no crying and screaming, Dodgin simply said, *"Blame me."* With Bowen, Farmer and Phillips swapping the forward positions there was no room for Gary Sargent who moved on to Barnet. He would later be involved with a few local teams, including Northampton Spencer.

For the first time in 11 seasons, Northampton got a first round F.A.Cup-tie draw at home, and when Peter Denyer appeared to have given the club the lead, it looked as if the team was going to move on with a victory, but the goal was disallowed, and the 'Posh' went on to win 4-1.

It became obvious that Dodgin was not too impressed with some of the players he had inherited, and slowly they started to leave. Ricky Walker, was followed by Dennis Byatt, who joined Wealdstone. Tenth position at the end was only slightly better than a year earlier, although the wage bill must have been lighter.

The biggest disappointment was the release of Keith Williams, the midfielder who had lost a lot of his career through injury during his stay at the County Ground, but even so he was still a crowd favourite.

1981-82

Three new faces arrived, Paul Brady, a defender from Birmingham, Peter Coffill a midfield player from Torquay, and John Alexander, a forward from Millwall.

The season kicked off with a home match, a rare event at the County Ground, due to the cricket. Scunthorpe were the opponents and the game ended 1-1, and the

results never really improved from then. It took thirteen League games, before the club had its first win, a 3-2 victory over Tranmere, in which the newly returned John Buchanan, scored in the dying seconds.

Buchanan came back as player-coach, and was one of 18 players used in an effort, to find a winning formula. The game also heralded the arrival of Tony Mahoney, a loan striker from Fulham. Mahoney played in six league games for Northampton, without scoring, but netted twice in the League Cup and once in the F.A.Cup. The League Cup saw the scalps of Hartlepool and Bristol Rovers taken, before a plumb third round tie versus Manchester City brightened the fixture list. Many Cobblers supporters were among the 21,000 crowd, and although City won 3-1, the Northampton goal from Mahoney, a volley from outside the box, had everyone in the ground applauding.

The Londoner's career at Northampton, ended when he was stuck in a motorway jam, and failed to arrive at Northampton in time for the coach leaving for Peterborough. The Cobblers lost 1-0, and Mahoney's replacement, John Alexander, missed a sitter, but the Fulham player's loan period was not extended.

By Christmas the club realised that unless action was taken, they were going to be in the re-election zone again. Steve Perrin, a striker, came from Hillingdon Borough. He was a teacher and signed on the agreement he would only play in first team games, scoring on his debut in the match versus Scunthorpe, he maintained a first team place throughout the remainder of the season.

Bill Dodgin left by mutual consent in February, and he was replaced by Walker, who took the hot seat again. It was all hands to the pump as an attempt was made to lift the club from the bottom four.

Steve Phillips joined Southend for £19,000, less than half the fee the club paid for him the previous season, but this released some cash, and Pat Kruse came on a non-contract basis to stiffen up the defence, whilst

Steve Bryant returned until the end of the season. But the problem was goals, or rather the lack of them. Phillips had gone, Keith Bowen had left to join Brentford, and the scoring was down to Perrin, who as a part-timer was not 100% committed.

Earlier in the season, a chance conversation between general manager Dave Bowen, and Bournemouth's Alec Stock, resulted in the latter informing the former of a useful young striker who was stuck in the Peterborough reserve team.

Bowen passed the information on to Bill Dodgin, who did not act on it, however when the club were short of a goalscorer he informed Walker, who signed him. The player did not make an impression straight away, but the next season, was to be his 'red letter season'; his name was Steve Massey.

The last eight games resulted in just three points, and re-election loomed again, although they were voted back in without much trouble. However, the club was back were it had started from a few seasons earlier, but with no money.

Poole, Farmer, Carlton and Alexander were all released, and Heeley went part-time, whilst Buchanan remained player-coach on non-contract terms.

1982-83

Mark Kendall an ex-England youth team 'keeper came from Aston Villa, full-back Ian Phillips, and forward Dave Syrett joined from nearby Peterborough, and Aidy Burrows, a centre-half moved down from Mansfield.

The season kicked off with a new competition, the League Group Cup, in which teams were put into mini-Leagues of four, played each other once, then the winners of each group would continue the competition on a knock-out basis. Northampton were drawn against Peterborough, Norwich, and Mansfield, but as this was a pre-season contest, the County Ground was not available, and all the Cobbler's games had to be played away. The Norwich match ended in a 3-0 defeat, the match at Mansfield produced a 2-1 victory, while at Peterborough, the 'Posh' won 5-2 - hence there was a quick exit from that competition.

The matches also brought up another problem, for 'keeper Kendall was injured and there was no cover, so Walker quickly went out and signed Neil Freeman from Peterborough. The player was born in the County, and actually had a loan spell at the County Ground some years earlier while on Arsenal's books, but he was never used in

A determined Neil Freeman signed for the Cobblers after an earlier loan period

the first team. He had played for several clubs, including Arsenal, Birmingham, and Southend, as well as Peterborough, and he would well remember his debut as a 'Cobbler'. The match was away to Wimbledon, and in the 1-1 draw, he was sent off under the new rule of committing a foul outside the area; he was the first Northampton player to be sent off on his debut, and the first 'keeper to get his marching orders in this way.

Another first was the club's victory over Irthlingborough Diamonds in the Maunsall Cup, clubs were no longer allowed to share the cup for six months after a draw, therefore games had to be played to a result. After 120 minutes of football Northampton lifted the trophy by converting five penalties to the Diamonds four. This was the first time the club had been involved in a penalty shoot-out.

The first League victory, was one to remember. It was on a Sunday afternoon at home to Bristol City, and the Cobblers could not put a foot wrong. Syrett hit four, Massey two, and Denyer another, which was pleasing for the lad who missed three months of the last season due to injury. Nearly 3,000 people watched the game, and they were full of anticipation for the next home game just two days later - which they lost 1-0 to Bury.

Away to Hull, Freeman was sent off again, and having become so disillusioned with the game he decided to quit, after giving the club three month's notice, and instead follow in his father's footsteps with a career in the police force. He covered himself in glory by saving a penalty in his next game against Peterborough, the match ending goalless, and it was agreed by most *supporters* that in his short stay he had become a crowd favourite, and most fans were sorry to see him go.

Barry Tucker returned, first on loan, and Dave Buckanan also came on loan from Peterborough, but then the club hit a snag, for Freeman was suspended for the away match at Scunthorpe, and Kendall was not fit. Therefore an application was made to sign a third loan player, which was granted so long as he was a goalkeeper. Richard Key was signed and played in the 5-1 hammering at the old show ground, although none of the goals could be blamed on the newcomer. He also played in the 2-1 win over Blackpool that was televised, and showed Peter Denyer netting both goals with brave headers.

The F.A.Cup drew some interest that season. Round one was at home to Wimbledon, and the Cobblers were coasting to victory when Heeley and a 'Dons' player were sent off. The game turned at this point, and Wimbledon escaped with a draw. However, a double strike from Peter Coffill in the replay gave Northampton an easy ride into round two - away to Gillingham.

Another draw was followed by a County Ground replay, but when Gillingham swept into a 1-0 lead and Brady was carried off, the situation looked grim. The substitute was young striker, Frankie Belfon, and with two brave diving headers he put the Cobblers in front. Gillingham equalised with a goal that brought howls of protests from players and supporters alike, as they all felt that Freeman was held, and the 'keeper chased the referee to the half-way line in protest, but to no avail, for the goal stood.

With extra time looming, it seemed that everyone was in for another 30 minutes, but Steve Massey got himself into a shooting position and somehow squeezed the ball between the 'keeper and post. The final score was 3-2, and the reward was a home tie in round three with Aston Villa.

Over 14,500 packed the County Ground for the televised match, when the Cobblers never looked like the underdogs, for they gave Villa a run for their money and supporters still speak of the shot of Massey's that hit a post, when a pass to Syrett might have secured a goal. The game was decided by a piece of magic by Mark Walters, the Villa youngster, who 'turned on a sixpence', leaving Burrows for dead, and fired on the volley past the stranded Freeman. If Northampton had to go out, it was worth going out to a goal like that.

Freeman left the club to take up his career as a policeman, and Kendall made his long awaited debut, but it lasted just 10 games, for Peter Gleasure - an ex-F.A.Youth Cup winner - was signed from Millwall, first on loan, then on full terms.

The rest of the season was something of an anti-climax, although a mid-table position was achieved, after the club secured Billy Jeffrey from Blackpool on transfer deadline day.

Coffill and Denyer moved into non-League football, although Denyer also agreed to work on the promotional side with Kettering, as well as play for them. Sanders, Heeley, and Perrin all dropped into non-League football, as did Saxby who took a job in security. Kendall was the only one to move on to another League club when he signed for Birmingham.

1983-84

Tucker's full back partner was Martin Forster, a youngster released by Kettering. Russell Lewis arrived from Swindon, to make up a three man central defence with Burrows and Gage. Brian Mundee, a full-back joined from Bournemouth, while Austin Hayes, an Eire international signed from Millwall, and Terry Austin joined from Doncaster. Bill Dodgin had tried to sign Austin when he was a youngster at Ipswich, and since then he had moved on to Plymouth - in an exchange deal for Paul Mariner - plus Walsall, Mansfield, Huddersfield and Doncaster. He was 29 years-old, and had scored over 80 goals in his career. Tommy O'Neill, was to be Billy Jeffrey's partner in midfield, he was a free transfer from Cambridge United.

Former Swindon player Russell Lewis

The club had lost Steye Massey, the player having joined Hull, and as the clubs could not agree a fee, the Tribunal stepped in and £20,000 was decided. Although Massey had cost the club nothing, his goals would be missed, and £20,000 would hardly buy a striker of his calibre. Massey went on to play for Cambridge and Wrexham, but never had the success he enjoyed at Northampton.

Not the best of season starts was the 2-1 defeat by Corby in the Maunsall Cup, with Barry Tucker missing a penalty. Ritchie Norman joined as Coach, and the club made one of its best starts to a season going 11 matches without a League defeat - even though eight results were draws - with a 3-2 defeat coming at Crewe. By October, Mundee had replaced Tucker, and Syrett had back injuries from which he never recovered, so the attack was made up of Austin, Hayes and Belfon.

The League Cup, and the Associate Members' Cup, saw first round exits, but the F.A.Cup was the season's focal point again. It took three games to shake off non-League Waterlooville, two played at the County Ground and one on the South coast, then it took another two games before going out to Telford. The first encounter at the County Ground finished 1-1 - Burrows putting through his own net - and it seemed that this would win the game until a late goal from Terry Austin forced a replay. Telford took an early lead in the second match second-half, but the Cobblers pulled the goal back, and then went in front, only for the Shropshire side to score two more. Once again Northampton had fallen to non-League opposition.

Aidy Mann in action - on his debut he set a new club record, becoming the youngest-ever first team player.

It is fair to say that the rest of the season was an anti-climax. Terry Austin netted his 100th first team goal and debuts were given to Steve Brown and Aidy Mann, the latter becoming the youngest player ever to appear in a Cobblers shirt.

A run of five games without a win was followed by a 6-0 defeat by Peterborough, and that proved to be the breaking point for Walker who resigned, considering that enough was enough. Neville Ronson went on record as saying that Clive Walker would have a job at Northampton for as long as he was chairman, and Walker was offered the youth team coach which he accepted.

Eighteenth in the table, showed another poor finish to the season, and once again the axe swung and few were retained. Tucker, O'Neill, Jeffrey, Forster, Syrett and Hayes were all released, while Burrows went on record as saying that if he could not find a club outside the Fourth Division he would quit. In the meantime speculation was rife, as to who would replace Walker. Ritchie Norman, the new Coach, was one possibility, and the experienced Ray Train, who had joined on a month's loan from Oxford but was injured training the youth team, was another, but the name on everyone's lips was Graham Carr, who had done such a fine job in non-League football.

A couple of points worth mentioning was that the 4-1 defeat by Aldershot, played at home in thick fog, was the club's 2,500th League game.

*No play today! A snow-covered County Ground
on the day of the F.A.Cup replay with Brentford in 1984*

After the match there was a protest from the fans, demanding something be done about the poor form, this in turn upset the directors, who threatened to sell the club, or move it to Milton Keynes who were keen to have a League club based there. The situation would reach a climax the following season.

1984-85
Tony Barton had been approached at least twice by the directors of Northampton Town Football Club asking him to take the manager's job at Northampton, but he declined. Maybe he felt that the manager who had won the European Cup, as he had with Villa, would have a better offer than that from a struggling Fourth Division club, but when he realised this was as good as he was likely to get, he accepted the offer at £40,000 over two years.

He did not endear himself to the Northampton fans when he announced that all the better free transfer players had gone by now, for it was, after all, his reluctance to accept the job that caused the delay in his appointment.

Phil Cavener came from Gillingham, a winger come-full-back, and Michael Barnes joined from Reading - a centre-back to replace Burrows, who had by now joined Plymouth for £10,000. Trevor Lee was a much travelled striker, who arrived from Cardiff, while Ray Train was to be in midfield, and was made the captain. Paul Shirtliff and Paul Bancroft came from Wednesday and Derby respectively. There was also a young midfielder from Peterborough, who was offered terms by Wimbledon but preferred to join Northampton on trial; his name was Ian Benjamin.

While attending the pre-season friendly match at Shepshed Charterhouse, Barton became ill, and he went home and called the doctor who rushed him to hospital with a suspected heart attack. It meant he was to be out of the game for some time, so Norman and Walker took over the manager's role between them.

The opening game was at Exeter, and Northampton lost 5-0. In their first home game, they scored against Chesterfield with a twice taken Austin Hayes penalty, and the first goal in open play came against Colchester - the ninth (League and cup) game.

Out of the blue Port Vale were beaten 3-0 on their own ground, but if anyone thought this was the turning point they were to be disappointed, as the team lost their next two games. By late October, Barton had returned part-time, and he moved up Benjamin into the forward line, and it worked for he netted two against Wrexham, and three in his next game against Aldershot.

The club was going through 'Valleys' and 'Peaks', for in November they picked up four points and scored eight goals, yet in December just one was recorded. Geoff Scott was signed from Charlton to replace the injured Barnes but failed to improve the club's fortunes.

A disastrous February and March saw just one point from some games, and the supporters had had enough. They proved this for the midweek game versus Chester, when for the first time ever a crowd of less than 1,000 turned up for a League game, a figure of just 942. Things were getting bad and the board insisted on wage pruning.

This measure led to Mark Hutchinson, the non-contract player from Leicester, and Trevor Lee, being released. Lee, had blotted his copybook when he had a puncture on the way to a game and missed the team coach. He had been signed as a striker, but never scored a league goal, yet both he and Ray Train were each successful in both rounds of the F.A.Cup.

Pre-match meals were out, to be replaced by rolls on the coach, and there was talk of players travelling to games in their own cars. There was much happening off the field, with Frank Murphy the chairman of Kettering trying to convince Northampton to merge the two clubs, using the excuse that it would benefit "football in the County". However, the Football League saw this as a back door approach into the League, and the idea was 'knocked on the head' at an early stage.

Meanwhile, two different conversations were to lead to setting the club on stronger foundations. Mike Conroy, a Cobblers supporter was with his life-long friend, Tobacco Importer Derek Banks, when he asked him, *"Do you want to buy a football club?"* The remark was made only in casual conversation, but when the Watford-based family man showed interest, the suggestion snowballed. Around the same time, two local businessmen, Barry Stonhill and Charles Barham were playing pool when it was suggested that there must be many more businessmen in the area who were also fans, and may be prepared to put money into the club - this was the formation of the 'Friends of the Cobblers'.

Chronicle & Echo
Phil Cavener

Two influential players in a period of gloom for the club

Ian Benjamin

In an action-packed month of April, Derek Banks bought the club from Neville Ronson, and the new 'Friends of the Cobblers' made money available, with two of its members joining the board.

The new chairman insisted that Mike Conroy should also be on the board and he was duly elected.

Back on the field, Barton had secured two loan players - Warren Donald, a small midfielder from West Ham, and Keith Thompson a striker from Coventry. The pair played a large part in the end of season revival.

Banks took control, and one of the new board's first moves was to replace Barton with Graham Carr, who took over for the last seven games of the season, of which six were won and one was drawn. Following this run, the Cobblers were able to move above Torquay in bottom place. Although re-election had to be sought, there was a good feeling at the ground, almost a rebirth, as fresh faces and fresh ideas started to put the stability of the club back again.

Brough, Train, Shirtliff, Bancroft, Hayes, Belfon and Scott were all released. Barnes retired through injury and Gage asked for a move, he joined Chester, which left just five of the last season's regular first team on the books.

CHAPTER TEN
1985 -1997

1985-86

Graham Carr, the club's centre-back from the First Division days had spent ten successful years in non-League management, starting at Weymouth, where he was asked to take over the club, and then on to Dartford and Nuneaton. His playing career blossomed after he left Northampton in 1968, when he went on to York and then Bradford P.A., and was with this club when they lost their Football League status in the same week that he received the 'Player of the Year' award; he was then given a free transfer. He played for Altrincham and skippered Telford in the F.A.Trophy Final at Wembley, and from there joined Weymouth. Northampton was to give him his first taste Football League club management.

Carr brought in Trevor Morley and Richard Hill from Nuneaton, for £30,000, plus Graham Reed from Frickley for £6,000. He then picked up Paul Curtis from Charlton, and Ian Dawes from Newcastle on free transfers.

There was a great feeling of optimism, yet when the half-time results were read out for the first games of the season, the Cobblers, were 3-0 down at Burnley. Later goals from Morley and Reed made the score respectable, but this defeat was only to be a 'blip', for the club went on to win three of their next four matches, including a 6-0 hammering of Preston.

Phil Chard, a utility player, was signed from Peterborough, just in time to play against his old club in the League Cup, and Mark Schiavi, a winger

"Our opponents respect us now."

Manager Ian Atkins remarks, a season after his arrival, in 1996.

moved from Bournemouth on a free transfer. Warren Donald returned from West Ham, this time for a fee, and slowly the team started to take shape. Ian Dawes struggled at centre-back, so first Gavin Nebbelling, a South African from Palace, came on loan, followed by Keith McPherson from West Ham. 'Macca', as he became known, made history, for he had been on loan to Cambridge and played against the Cobblers, now he was playing for the Cobblers and he played against Cambridge!

While the team were finding their feet on the field, off it the new directors were coming up against their first snag, and the biggest stumbling block....The County Ground. The Authorities insisted that the old wooden stand was pulled down, after the experiences of the Bradford City disaster, and despite assurances from Dave Bowen that this could not happen at Northampton, the powers that be stood their ground, Unlike Bradford, where the gates were locked up to the end of the game, the County ground gates were secured by shoot bolts, so they could be opened quickly.

This requirement necessitated that the whole of the Abington Avenue end be closed, while the stand was dismantled, and any ambitious plans the board had were shelved. Meanwhile the press had to sit in the cricket pavilion, and watch the game through field glasses!

Derek Banks was perhaps one of the most approachable chairman, the club ever had, and he became a popular figure with supporters for he attended supporters

Harry Warden (left), Cobblers' first gateman in 1920, and still with the club in 1985, is presented with an award by Leslie Underwood of the F.A.

meetings and got involved with the club. He later admitted that in order to buy the club he had borrowed the money from his mother!

Back on the field things were not going all the club's way, and a 3-2 defeat by Swindon saw all three of the Wiltshire club's goals scored from the spot. To add to the problems, one home game was almost cancelled when it was discovered a safety barrier at the Spion Kop was not safe, and it took an eleventh hour repair to keep the game on.

Peterborough were beaten 5-0 at London Road, when their 'keeper John Turner was sent off after six minutes, this helped the goal tally, and by the turn of the year, the club won a cash prize for being the first team to score 50 League goals, which they achieved in the 2-2 draw with Port Vale. Three new directors joined the board, England international fly fisherman, Bob Church, Martin Pell, plus Don Hammond, and they were followed by Graham Wilson, and Dick Underwood.

By January the main stand terracing was opened, turning the ground back into a three-sided ground, and by March the infamous 'Meccano' stand was erected which held just 450 seats. Later dubbed the 'Baden Powell 'stand by Banks, as from it there were so many scouts watching the Northampton Players

Without making a serious challenge for promotion the club finished eighth, but scored 79 goals, and this gave some indication of their attacking qualities. Trevor Morley, was one of the most skilful players ever seen at the County Ground in later years, while Benjamin and Richard Hill were always amongst the goals. Two particular talking points of the season, were the 683 who turned up at Southend to watch the Cobblers in the Associate Members Cup match, and the on-loan transfer of Mick Forsyth from West Brom. Forsyth had hardly had time to find a peg in the dressing room before he was called back to his club and sold to Derby; his stay was for less than 48 hours! Other moves saw Mundee joining Cambridge United, Curtis who went to Corby, and Lewis who went to Kettering.

1986-87

Winger Eddie McGoldrick and 'keeper Alan Harris joined Northampton from Nuneaton in a joint £15,000 deal, they were joined by Dave Gilbert, a midfield player from Boston, and Bob Coy, a centre-back from Chester. Carr arguably made his team the fittest in the League, and any new recruits who were not up to the required standard were soon knocked into shape by 'Sergeant Major' Clive Walker.

The season started well, just one defeat in the first few games, including a 6-3 win at Halifax. This was the most goals the club had scored in an away match since 1931. After losing 1-2 at Swansea, Northampton played another 21 League games undefeated, until they lost 1-0 - at home to Swansea. Russell Wilcox had been signed from Frickley, and he had by now replaced Coy, at centre-half, whilst Graham Reed had converted to right-back, and some hard-working performances had earned him the nickname 'Rambo', meanwhile the goals were coming thick and fast.

Richard Hill was the main scorer, with Benjamin and Morley who were both able to hold up the ball and lay it in the path of the midfield player. Because of his speed and the inability of opponents to knock him off the ball, he went on to score. Morley and Benjamnin themselves were also weighing-in with a few. The ex-Nuneaton man will well remember a goal scored at home to Stockport when the Cobblers kicked-off the second-half, and he started a three man move with Cavener and Benjamin, finishing with a goal, without a Stockport player touching the ball.

The F.A. Cup was memorable that season, for Peterborough were beaten 3-0 in a Sunday afternoon first round tie, and a second round match at Southend ended 4-4. The replay was going in Southend's favour, at 2-1, when the referee had to go off, to be replaced by the senior linesman, who awarded the Cobblers two penalties, and hence victory.

Newcastle were the Third round opponents, but after much planning and arranging of a weekend in Newcastle for the fans, the game was cancelled, due to the weather. It was played the following weekend, and Newcastle took an early lead in the match. Hill equalised, only for a defensive error by loanee full-back Millar, to allow the 'Toons' to score the winner. Worse was the carrying off of Trevor Morley, keeping him out for six weeks. Back to League action, and the promotion bandwagon rolled on, with David Logan, a full-back arriving from Mansfield to provide the final piece of the jigsaw.

Promotion was assured in a 2-1 home win over Crewe, with nearly 9,000 people staying on after the game to celebrate, as the players threw their shirts into the crowd below.

Better was to follow when the town insisted on an open top bus ride, finishing off with a meal at the Town Hall. Thousands lined the streets to wave to their heros with many more at the Hall, and it was hard to believe that two years earlier, the club was close to leaving, merging, or even folding.

Richard Hill joined Watford for a £265,000 fee - a club record. Coy and Schiavi were also released, the former moving into non-League football and following a career as a policeman, whilst the latter joined Cambridge but stayed in the area.

1987-88

Steve Senior, a full-back from York, and David Longhurst, a striker from Halifax, were the only additions to the squad, and they both proved to be good buys as they assisted in the 5-0 defeat of Chester at Sealand road. A 1-0 win versus Port Vale, in the League Cup, resulted in four players being sent off - two from each side. Chard and Senior were the Northampton offenders, and after suspension, they were both made to fight to win their places back, although in Senior's case he failed to shift the popular Reed, hence his dismissal cost him his place in the team and he was sold on to Wigan.

The goals had dried up for Ian Benjamin, finding it hard to score in the Third Division, and over a period of two weeks there was a double transfer, for 'Benjy' moved on to Cambridge United - which was fast becoming a direct route for Northampton players - for £25,000, while Paul Culpin arrived via Coventry for £50,000. Culpin was with Carr at Nuneaton, and the manager had earlier tried to bring him to Northampton, but he preferred to stay with First Division Coventry, but finding it hard to break into their side he came to the County Ground for what was to be a record fee at the time.

The club were saddened to hear of two deaths around this time. Charles Barham, one of the 'Friends of the Cobbler's' passed away, he was a director but had been in ill-health over the previous few months.

Manager Graham Carr (above) had moved around in his time, as both a player and manager. At this time he found it necessary to look far and wide for new blood.

One acquisition was a striker to boost the goals tally, David Longhurst (below)

The other was Harry Warden. Harry was 'Northampton Town', having been a backroom boy since just after the First World War, and he was the club's first gateman in the League. If there was a job description, for Harry, it would take around 50 pages to set-out; from making tea, to polishing the silverware (when the team won any), counting the takings, to locking up - Harry had done it all.

He was every youngster's hero during the 1930's and 40's., for midway through the second-half of a home game, Harry would lower the club flag, and this was a signal for every youngster, who could not afford the entrance fee, to get in free and watch the last 20 minutes of the game. He was awarded a '50 Years Award' by the club just prior to his death, at aged 93.

Martin Singleton arrived from West Brom., he cost £57,500, a new club record. A midfielder, Martin was another piece in an ever-changing jigsaw, as the club tried hard to maintain its position near the top of the Third Division.

Prior to the match at home to Bristol Rovers, Graham Reed was injured and Dave Logan was dropped, this led manager Carr to delve into the loan market again, when he brought two full-backs to the club. Brett Williams came from Forest, and Chris O'Donnell joined from Ipswich. Both players made their debuts in the Rovers match, but at half-time O'Donnell was pulled off, and replaced by McGoldrick. Graham Carr pulled no punches when he described the Ipswich man's performance. The loan was jinxed from the start, since he first failed to turn up for training, claiming he had lost his way, then in the pre-match interview he could not remember whom the opponents were, and his substitution was the last straw.

O'Donnell was despatched back to Ipswich, who sent him back, saying 'you signed him for a month, he's yours'.

Trevor Morley asked for a move and was about to join Hill at Watford, but the day before the move the Watford manager, Bassett, parted company with the club, so Manchester City stepped in. They offered £175,000 with Tony Adcock moving the other way, forming £85,000 of the deal. There was also movement on the board, for Mike Conroy left, as he found the pressure of shift-working and being a director of a football club was too much. Conroy was replaced by Len Banks, father of Derek, and Barry Blundell, manager of the Chairman's firm.

Goals from Paul Culpin included a hat-trick against Aldershot

Cobblers a play-off place, but City won, and it was to be another season in the Third.

Logan was released after being dropped, he joined Halifax, and he was the only departure, at the end of that season.

1988-89

Dean Thomas, a midfield/defender joined the club from Fortuna Dusseldorf, Germany. Dean had played for Nuneaton under Graham Carr and joined Wimbledon, before moving into German football with his brother Wayne, before agreeing to the £50,000 move to Northampton.

Another new arrival was Paul Flexney from Clyde, a centre-half who was signed to cover Wilcox who had an injury that could have keep him out for most of the season.

Phil Chard joined Wolves for £45,000, while Northampton brought Paul Wilson, a full-back from Norwich, firstly on loan and then for a £30,000 fee. Centre-half Trevor Slack also arrived, for a nominal fee, to cover the injured McPherson.

With promotion clearly in sight, the club made a valiant effort. Victories were obtained over Fulham, Grimsby and Mansfield, during the Easter period, but a defeat at Brighton, and a draw at York, meant the club would have to rely on a play-off spot. They still needed the points and it looked like they would lose out in their last home game against Blackpool, when a mistake by Wilcox allowed the seasiders to take a 3-2 lead late in the game, but with almost the last kick of the match, Adcock equalised to give both clubs a point.

Failure to pick up a point in the last game meant the club had to rely on Doncaster beating Bristol City to give the

After beating Aldershot 6-0, which included a Culpin hat-trick, the club hit a bad patch with six consecutive defeats, and were hit with the loss of the influential midfielder, and skipper, Martin Singleton. Like Wilcox's injury, his too was going to be a long job.

Steve Berry was signed from Aldershot for £40,000, and Blair - an experienced player from Aston Villa - came on a free, but only two victories were achieved in nine games, and Blair soon disappeared from the picture. When Eddie McGoldrick moved to Palace for £200,000, it allowed Graham Carr to buy three new players; Mick Bodley, a centre-half from Chelsea, Trevor Quow, a midfielder from Gillingham, and Wayne Williams a full-back from Shrewsbury, and while there were comings and goings on the pitch, there were some also taking place off the pitch.

Derek Banks sold the club, for he was losing sight of his own company and needed to spend more time with it. He had an offer from a chain of hotels, but Vice-Chairman Dick Underwood suggested it would be better staying local, so he bought the club off Banks. Martin Church, David Kerr, and Barry Hancox, were to join the board, with Barry Stonhill as Vice-Chairman, and Stuart Wilson stood down.

Wilcox returned for the final run-in and assisted the side to avoid relegation. In a desperate attempt to avoid the drop and balance the books at the same time, Carr sold Gilbert to Grimsby for £55,000 and bought Darren Collins from Petersfield for £3,000, for it was made clear that any more money for transfers, would have to be first made by selling players. Graham Reed quit through injury, although he was to give Aylesbury, Kettering, Rushden and Dagenham some years more. David Longhurst had moved to Peterborough earlier in the season, and from there he moved to York, where he was to die while playing in a match for them against Lincoln. Flexney had returned to Scotland after being homesick, and he joined Ayr, while Blair finished his days in Malta.

A word about a young striker from Evesham, Andy Preece. He made a couple of substitute appearances at Northampton but never impressed. He joined Worcester, and from there stepped back into League football with Wrexham, before later moving to Palace for a large fee - one that got away!

Dick Underwood, was a local lad who had set up a transport business some years earlier and it proved to be successful. He had played football for several local clubs, in both the Town and the United Counties Leagues. The Kingsthorpe man also went into management, running his firm's team 'Nexday', and walking off with the coveted, F.A. Sunday Cup - the only Northamptonshire club to do so. He confessed to being a Cobblers fan of some years, and his wife Yvonne was crowned the 'Cobblers Queen' a few years earlier.

Despite the wealth of talent available, the club struggled and remained a Third Division club by the skin of its teeth, when 29 players had been used during the season. Russell Wilcox returned for the last month of the season, and Carr was forced to play Darren Collins, the youngster recently purchased from Petersfield, whom he would have preferred to have keep under 'wraps' until he had a few more reserve games under his belt.

1989-90

There were no new faces arriving for the start of the season, just announcements. The first was from the manager, who was disappointed with his strike force, and he put both Adcock and Culpin on the transfer list. The next item of news was from the supporters club, who said they had given the club £6,000 over the previous four years, whilst the club said it was just £1,000. The final newsworthy item was from the bookies, who were offering 33/1 on the Cobbler's winning the championship.

By October, the club were laying in low mid table and the busiest place was on the transfer market. Adcock joined Bradford City for £190,000, despite an alternative offer of £200,000 from Peterborough, but they in turn bought Paul Culpin for £40,000, and a third striker, Glen Donegal, joined Aylesbury, for £10,000. In came Bobby Barnes from Bournemouth for £70,000. Graham Carr had remembered the player when he did a one-man destruction job on the Cobblers whilst playing for Aldershot. Barnes had started his career at West Ham, had a spell at Aldershot, joined Swindon, (in an exchange deal, with Steve Berry), then moved on to Bournemouth. He was tricky, had pace, and had an eye for goals.

Irvin Gernon, arrived from Reading for his second spell with the club, having joined Northampton on loan during their promotion season, but then an Ipswich player. The defender had at the time turned down a permanent move, but was happy to sign this time, and he cost £25,000. Phil Chard returned from Wolves, and it was a case of 'League hopping' for him, for he had left Third Division Northampton, to play for Fourth Division Wolves, who in turn were promoted to the Second, and now he was back in the Third.

The season was not going too badly, the club beating Bolton 3-0, on their own ground - it was the 'Trotters' first defeat in 28 League games at home - then they won 2-1 at Mansfield, their first League win at Field Mill in 21 years. However, the F.A.Cup proved to be the highlight. First the club drew Kettering, where a Dean Thomas goal at Rockingham Road saw the club through to round two and a home tie with Aylesbury United. The 'Ducks' were managed by ex-Cobbler Trevor Gould, with two former players in the side, Reed and Donegal. The game ended all square at the County Ground, but a Bobby Barnes strike secured a third round tie for the Cobblers.

Coventry were the visitors for this match, and over 11,000 forced their way into the ever-decreasing capacity County Ground, where they witnessed a strike from Steve Berry three minutes from time that was enough to put them into the fourth round of the F.A.Cup.

In 1990 there was a re-union of the Cobblers 1965-66 season First Division team

It was around this time that the club announced that they had spent £75,000 getting the County Ground up to scratch, much having come from the surplus realised on transfer deals, and the rest from the directors.

A 3-0 defeat at Rochdale in the fourth round of the F.A. Cup was the turning point of the season, for everything seemed to go downhill from there on. After beating Chester 1-0 on New Year Day, the club were unable to win another League game until the 14th of April - when they beat Chester 1-0 again.

In a last desperate sweep, the manager sold Dean Thomas to Notts County for £175,000, then bought Steve Terry, a centre-half from Hull for £70,000 plus Aidy Thorpe, a forward from Walsall, for £50,000. Also secured was 6'-3" striker Carl Leaburn, on loan from Charlton.

With four games left, Northampton needed maximum points, and they won their two remaining home games, versus Huddesfield and Crewe, but could only draw at Tranmere, and defeat followed at Rotherham; Northampton Town were back in Division Four. Graham Carr resigned, but he left behind him a legacy, for his transfer dealings alone had netted the club over half-a-million pounds. Carr joined Blackpool, and then Maidstone, before a successful spell at Kettering, and his last stop was at Dagenham and Redbridge.

1990-91

Once again names were being mentioned as to who would sit in the manager's chair, and it eventually turned out to be another ex-Cobbler, Theo Foley, who had been number two at Arsenal.

Both centre-backs, McPherson and Wilcox, asked for a move. McPherson joined Reading and Stuart Beavon and Darren Wood joined the Cobblers in exchange plus a cash adjustment. Beavon was an experienced midfield player who scored one of the quickest goals at the County Ground for Reading against the Cobblers, when Wood was a centre-half.

The Wilcox deal went to a tribunal, as deals with Hull generally did, and there it was agreed that Hull would pay £40,000. plus another £40,000, after a set number of appearances. Foley brought Joe Kiernan in as his number two, and offered Clive Walker the youth team coach position, but this was turned down, and he later rejoined Graham Carr at Maidstone and Kettering.

The club made a great start to the season. Foley had brought Kevin Wilkin in from Cambridge City - he was a striker - Terry Angus from V.S.Rugby - he was a centre-half - and Pat Scully, another central defender who was signed on loan from Arsenal. While scoring his first goal for the club, at Maidstone, Darren Wood injured a leg, which eventually required ten operations and ended his career.

Brighton were eliminated from the League Cup, but Sheffield United, complete with Vinney Jones, ended the Cobblers run in that competition. The F.A.Cup saw a first round victory at Littlehampton, then two matches against non-League Barnet. The first, at Barnet, saw three players - Angus, Thorpe, and Williams - missing, for they were all trapped in their Midland homes after a snowstorm.

The game ended 0-0, but Barnet won the replay, 1-0, at the County Ground. Marlon Beresford was signed on loan from Sheffield Wednesday, as first team 'keeper, and when his loan period expired, he was replaced by Kevin Hitchcock from Chelsea, also on loan, who saved a penalty on his debut versus Gillingham.

By the end of February, the club were sitting on top of the Division, but goals were drying up, so Tony Adcock was signed from Bradford City for £75,000, and Trevor Quow, who had been surprisingly loaned out to Kettering, returned to the first team.

The pressure of work, and the effect the chairman's job was having on his family, caused Dick Underwood to put the club up for sale. The A.G.M showed a loss of £53,437, which could have been higher had they not sold the premises in Abington Avenue for £49,000. Enter Michael McRitchie, the Birmingham based ex-market trader, who sold Crockery at the market during the 1960's. In fairness McRitchie did not make any rash promises, and his first game as Chairman was a 3-0 home defeat by Darlington, although unknown at the time, this was a sign of things to come,

A newspaper article appeared, stating that Chard, Terry, Barnes, Adcock and Wilson, were all for Sale, but McRitchie denied this saying it was a back-up; if he had not bought the club, then they would have had to sell these players, to raise the money required to pay-off Underwood.

On the field, automatic promotion, was replaced by a play-off place, but by the end of April the club had fallen to mid-table. Foley released Berry and Williams, while several other players, were all open to offers. Meanwhile the Police were considering court action over a £30,000 unpaid bill, and Barry Stonhill resigned from the board - a sure sign that there was unrest.

1991-92

Peterborough United were keen to sign Adcock and offered Culpin in return, but the club turned the offer down. Marlon Beresford was signed on loan again, as the first team 'keeper, and Jason Burnham was promoted from the youth team. These were the only new faces to arrive until Barry Richardson signed from Scarborough, once Beresford's loan period ended. By November things started to come to a head.

McRitchie sacked the rest of the board, although he claimed they resigned, running the club with himself and his wife as directors. On the field Darren Wood made his long-awaited comeback, but had to go off after 47 minutes, and Crawley knocked the Cobblers out of the F.A.Cup, forcing Foley to threaten his resignation. Just to cap it all, Abbeyfield Press - the programme publishers - threatened court action if their bill was not met. The programme for the home game versus Burnley was a sheet of folded A4 paper.

The players refused to train when their wages were not met, and trained themselves instead. This action brought in the P.F.A., who agreed to pay the players for two months, but the club in turn would have to pay them back.

In 1992, this stark headline appeared in the 'Chronicle and Echo' could this be the end, just five years short of 100 years?

A nine match unbeaten run (ten if the Aldershot game, that was later expunged, is included) saw the club up with the leaders again, but then a trio of players were sold off. Paul Wilson joined Halifax for £30,000, Adcock and Barnes joined Peterborough for £65,000, while Dean Edwards (Torquay), and Christian Mclean (Bristol Rovers), joined the club on non-contract terms.

A home game with Aldershot, who were in a similar plight to Northampton, saw both Chairmen leading the clubs out, to the Monty Python song of 'Look on the brighter side of life'; McRitchie may have done it out of bravado, or misguided humour, but which ever was the case it did not go down well with the supporters.

Mickey Bell, who scored two - rare - goals.

A meeting was arranged by the supporters in January, at the Exeter Rooms, where the future of the club was discussed. McRitchie was invited to attend but declined, although Theo Foley did and he told the supporters there that he did not want to lose Adcock or Wilson, but he had no choice,

From this meeting the 'trust', was formed, and they started to collect money in buckets at games. This in turn angered McRitchie who alienated himself from the trust and stopped the collections inside the ground. He refused meetings, and the money collected, stating it was not their money but money taken from supporters.

Things came to a head when players were being paid with the gate money, and more and more companies were threatening court orders. After a 2-2 draw at home to Rochdale, major changes were made with the Football League telling McRitchie he was to sort the problem out, hence he brought in a firm of administrators, Pannell Foster Kerr. They set to work at once, and Barry Ward, the man in charge, saw the problems, but liked the set up, so set about making plans to save the club.

Ten of the players not in the first team were 'sacked' viz. Quow, Gernon, Wilkin, Campbell, Johnson, Gleasure, Thorpe, Scope Wood, and Mclean and although the last was non-contract. The management team of Foley, Kiernan and Best were also released. Phil Chard was made player-manager, and Stuart Beavon, his assistant.

For the remaining six games, Chard had himself, Terry, Beavon, Brown and Angus, together with goalkeeper Richardson, who were the only ones in the team to have any real experience, with the rest being made up of members of the youth team. The first five games all ended up in defeat, with just one goal scored, but the last game away to Hereford produced a 2-1 win, Micky Bell netting both goals. The new look Cobblers did not win many games, but they were winning friends.

1992-93

The administrators set up a board, with four of the previous directors, and two members of the trust, on it; Barry Ward himself was chairman.

Barry Stonhill, Barry Hancock, Martin Church and Mark Deane, were joined by Trust members Brian Lomax and Phil Frost. There was no money for new players, and all Phil Chard brought in was Morrys Scott from Plymouth, a striker, plus Kevin Wilkin was brought back, who was one of the ten players released the previous season.

A 3-2 opening day victory at Gillingham was followed by two defeats, then came the first home match of the season, against Hereford, that made history. The United had a record number of four players sent off, including player-manager Greg Downes, but still managed a 1-1 draw.

So desperate was the club for experienced players that youth team coach Paul Curtis was pressed back into action, and made several appearances in the full-back spot. Northampton-born Darren Harmon, an aggressive midfield player was signed from Shrewsbury, while Ian McParland, an experienced striker joined from Dunfermline, on non-contract terms. His stay was short but profitable for he netted seven times in his three months with the Cobblers, but was sent off twice. Then, out of the blue, he joined the exodus of ex-players in Hong Kong.

The club could not lift itself out of the bottom four, although the lowest position was the one to avoid, but they were having some success in the F.A.Cup. Fulham were beaten in the first round, and Bath City went out in the second, after a replay, with Rotherham next as the third round opponents, at home.

The original fixture was cancelled, so when the game did take place it was known that the winners were away to Newcastle. This brought Kevin Keegan, Terry McDermott and Sir John Hall to the County Ground to watch the match that Rotherham won in the last minute of the game.

During the McRitchie era, all talk of a new stadium was dropped, but now there were rumblings again, and once again the Council were talking of a community stadium to be used by the Cobblers.

It was no easy ride for Phil Chard, for firstly a director took it on his own back to invite Graham Carr back as manager, which he turned down, then Stuart Beavon resigned as assistant, leaving Chard on his own. John Barnwell had been Chard's manager at Peterborough, and he was happy to join the club as 'Consultant'.

He would be manager on matchdays, and assist with coaching in the week. Stuart Yound was signed from Hull, a striker who scored twice in his seven appearances, then came Pat Gavin. The lanky striker came from Barnet where he could not find a first team spot.

After five years inactivity from the first team, Paul Curtis was called back into action.

By the beginning of April the club were bottom, but victories over Carlisle, Rochdale and Bury, lifted them up the League, but only to be brought down again by winning just two points in a run of four games. The final game, was away to Shrewsbury, who were looking for a play-off place, and the only other club who could go down, was Halifax, and they were at home to Hereford. Coachloads of supporters went to Shrewsbury, swelling the crowd to over 6,000.

Shrewsbury took a 23rd minute lead, and five minutes later, scored a second, and when Martin Aldridge had to go off injured, it looked as though Northampton Town's life was hanging from a thread. Then came 45 minutes that will be etched in the club's history, for many years to come. Phil Chard jumped on a defensive error after 51 minutes and pulled one back, yet hardly had the cheering died down before news came that Hereford were 1-0 up against Halifax.

Twenty minutes after Chard's goal, Pat Gavin brought the scores level at 2-2. Now the atmosphere was electric. Shrewsbury supporters urging their team on to a play-off place, while the Cobblers supporters were encouraging their team on to save their Football League life; meanwhile a third faction, some Bury supporters, were also backing the Cobblers to win, and give their team who would replace Shrewsbury, a shot at the play-offs. The Shrews goalkeeper, Paul Edwards, fly-kicked a ball downfield, but did not see the advancing Gavin, the ball hit the outfield player and bounced into the net; Shrewsbury Town 2, Northampton Town 3. The final seven minutes went on for ever, but at the final whistle the Cobblers supporters flooded on to the pitch, and there was a carnival atmosphere as everyone congratulated each other. Players, supporters and officials, mingled on the pitch, and the same phrase was continually repeated: 'This must never happen again'.

Northampton lifted themselves to 20th position, two places off the bottom with this win and lived to fight another day. Stuart Young, who was signed from Hull in mid-season was given a free transfer, but the surprise was the release of centre-back Terry Angus, and the hero of the Shrewsbury game, Pat Gavin.

1993-94

Two experienced players were signed, Les Phillips, a midfield player from Oxford, and Steve Sherwood, a 39 year-old goalkeeper from Grimsby. The latter was signed when Barry Richardson picked up a virus before the start of the season. Ian Gilzean, son of the Spurs and Scotland forward - Alan - joined after a spell in Scotland, and winger Terry Fleming came from Coventry.

The start to the season was bad, with just two points from the first six games, and the team was out of the Coca-Cola Cup.

A 2-0 home defeat by Wigan, in which Pat Gavin, now a Latic, scored one of the goals, had manager Phil Chard furious, claiming several of the players were just not good enough. By this time a transfer embargo had been put on the club, and no players could sign, and none could leave, until the £60,000 bill to the P.F.A. had been settled.

A meeting between the manager and the directors resulted in Phil Chard leaving the club, and Barnwell was appointed manager, who stressed that all consideration should be given to Phil who had done a good job under very difficult conditions. Barnwell actually convinced the ex-manager to complete his contract as a player.

'Lady (bad) Luck' played a hand again, for Darren Wood made another attempt at a comeback that lasted two games, but this time he had to admit defeat, and Kevin Wilkin was injured in his first game - after being out with injury for nearly two years; he would not play again until the 1st January.

A 5-1 win over Mansfield in October was followed by 19 League and Cup games without a victory, and the team was 14 points adrift at the bottom of the table, having been knocked out of the F.A.Cup, by Bromsgrove Rovers, at home.

It would have been easy for anyone to walk away from Northampton Town at this stage - players, manager or supporters. But it was the much-maligned directors who saved the day, by buying the club out of administration, and clearing the immediate debts.

This allowed the manager to bring in new players, either on contract or on loan, and of these defenders Ray Warburton

At last it was made possible to sign new players, notably Ray Warburton was one.

from York, and Ian Sampson from Sunderland were outstanding, as was a young Cameroon international under-23 player. Diodinne Efon Elad, whom Barnwell likened to a 'bottle of fizzy pop', was kept to a minimum of appearances due to injury, but when he did appear, everyone was excited at the ex-Cologne player, with his unusual ball play, and his big broad smile that made him a favourite in the short time he was at the County Ground.

While all this was happening, across the town, the new Community Stadium, was being built, but things had been put on hold while the future of the club was being decided. However, now it was all systems go, and the builders had promised a close season finish. This left the penultimate game, and the last home game, versus Chester, as the last game at the County ground.

The Cobblers kicked-off, and Efon Elad beat two players and pushed the ball wide to Wilkin, who hammered in an unstoppable shot to give Northampton the only goal of the game. It would have been a fitting end if it was the last game at the County ground, but it was not!

The season finished at Chesterfield, Northampton needed to win but they did not, for they lost 4-0, and for the first time ever they finished bottom of a Football League division. It had taken 74 years, but this was the first time they had finished at the foot of a table since their Southern League days in 1907.

Kidderminster had won the Conference, but because they had not met the necessary ground criteria they were not elected in in Northampton's place. This caused an outcry, with shouts of 'Closed Shop', and 'looking after their own'. However, as the Kettering Chairman stated, Kidderminster spent money on players instead of ground improvements, while clubs like his own brought their grounds up to scratch, and they could hardly complain about the eventual outcome.

There was a massive clearout at Northampton. Gone were Phil Chard (Kettering), Steve Terry (Aylesbury), Les Phillips (Marlow) and Ian Gilzean (Ayr); Sherwood returned to Grimsby as assistant-manager, and Barry Richardson moved to Preston for £20,000.

Steve Brown had moved earlier in the season to Wycombe Wanderers for £40,000. It was a personal triumph for Brown, who was on the Cobbler's books as a youngster, for he was released by Graham Carr in 1986, and played United Counties League football, but he was also a member of Richard Underwood's successful, 'Nexday' Sunday side, and it was the Cobblers chairman who suggested to Graham Carr that he give the midfielder a contract; from then his career bloomed.

1994-95

Peter Morris joined the club as assistant-manager, he had been at Boston and brought several players with him including twin strikers Dean Trott and Neil Grayson. Ray Warburton and Ian Sampson, both centre-backs who had loan spells at Northampton the previous season, returned on full terms, costing £65,000 between them.

Once again, the season started badly, and it was to be the club's tenth, League and cup game before they recorded their first win, and that was against the Division's high flyers Carlisle.

Grayson, who had two previous spells at League football with York and Doncaster, was finding it hard to adapt; Trott was playing well, and he could shield a ball, could not be knocked off it, and was good in the air, but he was a target man and was not going to be a prolific scorer.

A mid-week low key match versus Mansfield was to be the last match the club ever played at the County Ground. The Stags won 1-0, and just under 5,000 turned up. Four days later, a near capacity crowd turned up at Sixfields, the clubs new ground based at Upton.

A crowd of 7,461, watched Martin Aldridge give the Cobblers a 1-0 lead against Barnet, and then watched Doug Freedman equalise.

The Stadium, that the club had been waiting for for decades had arrived. It was smart, it was plush, and it had all the amenities. In fact it had everything, except that which had been left at the County Ground - nearly a hundred years of memories.

The 'bottle of Fizzy pop' - Efon Elad

The Barnet game was Micky Bell's last for Northampton, and the club were involved in two transfer tribunals; Bell moved to Wycombe for £45,000, while David Norton, who had been playing on loan with the Cobblers, joined from Hull for £25,000. This was the third tribunal the club had been involved in that featured Hull. Neil Grayson lost his first team place, but came on as substitute against Cambridge, in the Auto Windshield match, and scored a cracking goal from over 30 yards. He also netted the winner in the following game versus Wigan, and had now become established. But his goals were not putting the club on their winning ways,

A 3-2 home defeat by Chesterfield, in December, saw the team one place off the bottom, and Barnwell parted company with the club. Peter Morris was made caretaker-manager, but a 4-1 thrashing at Darlington did little to promote his cause.

Ian Atkins arrived in January. He had considered signing for the club the previous season, as a player, but opted for the manager's job at Doncaster, which he had since left when the Rovers insisted that he move from his Birmingham home. Atkins swept into Sixfields, bringing in Chris Burns, a midfielder from Portsmouth, Darren Hughes, a full-back from Port Vale, Garry Thompson a centre-forward from Cardiff, Andy Woodman a goalkeeper from Exeter, and Danny O'Shea came from Cambridge as player-coach. Atkins also pleased the fans when he promised: *"We will not finish bottom."*

The new man's first game in charge was at home to Gillingham, which the Cobbler's won 2-1 thanks to a Harmon penalty and a Dean Trott goal. Atkins made history when he loaned a player **from** a non-League side, Nicky Smith, the ex-Colchester midfielder who was signed on loan from Sudbury, and was offered terms but was not keen to give up his job as a postman

Of the last nineteen League games, under Atkins, seven were won, and five drawn, lifting the club to 17th. The new manager was true to his word, but he did not have it his all own way, for a 5-0 thrashing at Home by Bury, was followed by the same score in the away fixture.

THE NEW

(Top) Sixfield nears completion - August 1994

(Above) one of the first matches - versus Doncaster Rovers.

(Left) Sixfields completed

THE OLD

(Above) The demolition of the Main Stand.

(Right) The County Ground as it was (with the 'Meccano' Stand)

(Left) With the demolition now complete, it is difficult to visualise First Division football having once been played here.

The crowds were coming back, an average of 1,500 more a game, on the last season, and the best average since the club was fighting for a Division Three play-off place in 1988. Most of the players John Barnwell signed were released; Goalkeeper Stewart returned to Chester after helping Chesterfield in the play-offs while on loan to them, Peter Morris left for the manager's job at Kings Lynn, taking several players with him, While Trott and winger Ian Brown were released due to the amount of travelling involved, for they had interests near their homes.

1995-96

Hunter and Dean Peer, midfield players from West Brom and Walsall, joined on free transfers, while £35,000 was paid out to Scarborough for Jasson White.

Revenge was sweet when Bury were beaten 4-1 in the opening game. Neil Grayson scored a hat-trick, the first by a Cobblers player since Paul Culpin in 1988. After the two five goal defeats of last season it was a great start.

Unfortunately, injuries and suspensions took their toll, and the club started to reach familiar territory near the bottom the League. Two new players were signed in right-back Lee Maddison, from Bristol Rovers, and Ally Gibb came from Norwich for a combined £65,000 fee.

Slowly the club began to climb up the League, although they were never a challenge for the Championship, they stopped a few celebrations, such as the

'The Last'

PROGRAMMES

'The First'

beating of Preston at Deepdale - for the first time ever - which prevented the Lancashire teams from winning the Division on the day. Also Gillingham were held to a draw which left them a point away from automatic promotion.

Lee Maddison turned on an ankle, which kept him out for the rest of the season, so Mark Taylor joined from Fulham to replace Maddision, only to incur the same injury himself in a reserve game.

Twenty-nine players were used that season, although only 15 were retained. Like the managers that came before him, Atkins used the loan market to its full potential.

Armstrong of Sunderland, and Doherty of Birmingham were two such players, as was Bob Scott, of Sheffield United. The latter player was all set to sign until Fulham stepped in and took him back to London, from where he had started his career.

Derek Mountfield, the experienced central-defender came to the County Ground when released by Carlisle, but before he could sign professional terms he was approached by Walsall and signed for them instead.

As Ian Atkins said, *"Our opponents respect us now."*

Biggest surprise on the 'not retained' list was David Norton, who moved on to Hereford. Aldridge had been allowed to join Oxford after a falling-out with the manager, while Williams joined Scarborough.

1996-97

Sean Parrish, a midfield player, joined after a tribunal set his transfer fee at £45,000. He was joined by Ian Clarkson, a free transfer from Stoke City.

A ground record was set when 7,478 watched the Memorial Match for Dave Bowen, who had died earlier in the year. Arsenal provided the opposition, and the Cobblers won 3-1.

The League season had a bad start, for an away match at Wigan saw the coach stuck in traffic and arrive 30 minutes late. When the game did take place Peer and O'Shea were sent-off, with Sharp of Wigan, and manager Atkins was lectured by referee Laws on the touchline. Things did not help when another new signing, Mark Cooper, was given his marching orders in the second leg of the League Cup match versus Cardiff, which the Cobblers won through young striker Chris Lee who netted both goals.

Back in the League Leyton Orient arrived, to win only their second away game in three years; the previous success was at Sixfields the previous season!

Stoke City were the second round Coca-Cola Cup opponents, and after winning the first leg 1-0, at Stoke, it looked like it was going to be a goalless draw at Northampton, until the Stoke striker John Gayle scored a bizarre own goal. This brought the game into extra time, but Mike Sheron scored twice to make the game safe for the Potters.

By October, the club were in 21st position in the table, and new director Chris Smith recalls: *"My first game as a director was away to Exeter.*

Two of the players who helped to make the dream come true (Top) David Rennie and (Below) Christian Lee.

I drove down with a colleague, we pulled up behind one of the supporters coaches, and there in the back window, was the words 'SACK THE BOARD', causing my companion to add 'welcome to the real world'." The Exeter game, gave the club their first away win, and things started to pick up again.

Darren Roberts of Darlington was a target of Atkins, but a change of management put paid to that deal, and as if to rub salt in the wound he scored twice for the 'Quakers' in the 3-1 victory over Northampton. The club's next defeat was away to Leyton Orient, where Peter Shilton made his 1,001st Football League appearance, but his first against the Cobblers.

January was a great month for the club, for Cardiff were beaten 4-0, and this was followed by a 5-1 victory over Chester. The latter match was marred by an injury to Parrish when he was elbowed, whilst being watched by the Welsh selectors. Hartlepool were beaten 3-0, Neil Grayson netting a four minute hat-trick, and another club record. By February, Northampton had reached the Area Semi-finals of the Auto Windshield Cup, but they fell 2-1 at Colchester, even though the 'U's' had their 'keeper sent off after 24 minutes.

A 1-1 draw at home to Lincoln, saw both Maddison and Parrish carried off, the latter with a broken nose, after just returning from his fractured cheek bone injury. By now John Gayle the striker who had scored the own goal for the club while with Stoke had joined the Cobblers, and also now wearing a Northampton shirt was John Frain.

On the 29th of March, Northampton lost 1-0 to Wigan at Sixfields, but it was to be their last defeat of the season. The following seven games resulted in two draws and five victories, and more importantly, a play-off place. The final League game versus Scunthorpe saw the club one point off the play-offs, but they secured all three in a 1-0 win.

Cardiff were the play-off opponents again, with the first leg in Wales, a game that was played on a very wet Sunday. Sean Parrish scored the only goal of the game, but the talking point was the sending off of Cooper, for he had also been despatched against Cardiff earlier in the season, in the Coca-Cola Cup, and by the same referee, John Kirby. The second leg went 3-2 in Northampton's favour, when both central defenders, Sampson and Warburton scored, as did John Gayle.

Wembley here we come!

Northampton Town had reached Wembley in its Centenary season. The build up had started even before the victories over Cardiff. It has to be said, it was **the** 'Day' and not **the** 'Match' that made the 24th of May 1997, so memorable.

Coaches left from Sixfields with young supporters having their faces painted in claret and white. Train loads of supporters poured into Castle Station, and the Ml was awash with cars with claret and white scarves, waving from the windows.

Wembley way was like Northampton Town centre, as supporters met friends and colleagues, and discussed the pending game.

Cobblers fans mingled with Swansea supporters, and good natured banter took place with the Welshmen who were outnumbered by three to one.

The build-up was good, the pre-match entertainment as expected, but the match itself turned out to be something of a disappointment. Highlights were Woodman's save from Heggs, Chris Lee's header that went just wide, and Rennie's head injury that caused him to be taken off.

With the seconds ticking away, and extra time looming, Northampton were awarded a free kick outside the Swansea penalty area. John Frain took the kick, which was headed away, but the referee adjudged the wall to have moved too early and the kick was taken again. This time it found its mark.

Northampton Town 1
Swansea City 0.

Wembley Stadium erupted, as the final whistle sounded, A sea of claret and white could be seen dancing, singing, and chanting, to the Tina Turner song 'Simply the best'. Celebrations lasted for days. The following day the club took an open-topped bus ride through the town, with thousands greeting the players and officials in the town centre.

Ian Atkins had achieved what he set out for, Division Two football, and had given the fans a Wembley appearance as well as a future.

Goalscorer John Frain

The Goal - One for the scrapbook.

(Right)
The Celebrations -
Jubilant Cobblers fans
leave the stadium.

(Below)
The Flag -'The biggest
in the Football League
(made by supporters
Will Townley and Ally
Campbell)

ONWARDS
TO THE NEXT 100 YEARS!

Things move in circles. Chapman took a team from the bottom of the League to the Championship in two seasons in 1909. Graham Carr did it again in 1987. The club was started by Darnell the Solicitor, Jones the Teacher, and Gyde the Landlord, three different factions. In 1992 the club was saved by Pannell Foster Kerr, The Directors and The Trust - three different factions.

In the twenties the club had two of the best wingers in the division, in Page and Pease, in the 1950's Fowler and English were wingers to be feared by the opposition.

So which course is the club following now? Could it be a repeat of the 1960's, when Dave Bowen took a 'workmanlike' team through the divisions without star players, not unlike today's side.

Whatever the outcome of the next 100 years, supporters should never forget the work put in by, Albert Darnell, Charles Parker, and the current board. Supporters should never forget the goalscorers; Ted Bowen, Albert Dawes, Cliff Holton and Frank Large, or players like Page, Pease and Neal, who went on to play for England. Neither should Herbert Chapman, Dave Bowen, Graham Carr or Ian Atkins, be forgotten in the years to come.

Whatever the view of the supporter, the facts speak for themselves. The effort of Barry Ward, the money and work of the directors, and the enthusiasm of the supporters have saved this club. Had it not been for these three factions Northampton Town would have died.

FACTS, FIGURES AND RECORDS

(Note: All references are taken to close season 1997. Most abbreviations are self-explanatory, the following leagues and competitions are as follows: SL = Southern League. D3S = Division Three South. D4 = Division Four. NL = Northants. League. F = Friendly. AMC = Associate Members Cup, or later sponsored equivalent name)

ABANDONED

Date	Opponents	Comp.	Venue	Time	Reason	Score (At time)
26. 3.98	Kettering Res.	NL	A	60 Mins	Snowstorm	1-0
16.11.01	Burton United	FAC	A	60 Mins	Fog	1-2
22.11.02	Reading	SL	H	82 Mins	Bad Light	0-2
14.3.03	Queens Park R	SL	H	45 Mins	Ground Unfit	2-0
5.12.03	Southampton	Sl	A	45 Mins	Bad Light	1-2
13.2.04	Swindon Town	Sl	A	44 Mins	Waterlogged	3-1
18.1,08	Portsmouth	SL	A	45 Mins	Fog	0-1
1.10.10	Coventry City	SL	H	55 Mins	Bad Light	0-0
26.11.21	Watford	D3S	A	83 Mins	Fog	2-1
28.12.29	Bournemouth	D3S	A.	45 Mins	Waterlogged	3-2
15.2.36	Southend Utd.	D3S	A	38 Mins	Fog	0-2
4.12.37	Crystal Pal	D3S	H.	55 Mins	Waterlogged	1-1
15.12.38	Southend Utd.	D3S	A	38 Mins	Freezing	0-2
26.12.59	Watford	D4	A	50 Mins	Waterlogged	0-1
18.3.69	Oldham Ath.	D3	A	55 Mins	Sleet	1-0
4.12.76	Mansfield Town	D3	H.	45 Mins	Freezing	0-1
29.8.80	Southend Utd.	D4	H.	45 Mins	F/light Fail	0-0
3.12.82	Halifax Town	D4	A.	78 Mins	Fog	0-0
14.8.84	Shepshed Chart.	F	A	45 Mins	Waterlogged	1-0
11.12.84	Brentford	FAC	H.	26 Mins	Fog	0-0

AGE
OLDEST

	Player	Years-days		Opponents	Comp.	Date:
1.	Edwin Lloyd-Davies	42-	V	Brighton	S.L.	1.4.1920
2.	Jack Jennings	41-252	V	Birmingham City	War	6.5.1944
3.	Steve Sherwood	40-24	V	Crewe Alex.	D3	3.1.1994
4.	Alf Wood	39-351	V	Shrewsbury Town	D3S	30.4.1955
5.	Tommy Thorpe	39-307	V	Bristol Rovers	D3S	12.3.1921
6.	Tom Crilly	39-307	V	Torquay Utd.	D3S	9.3.1935
7.	Tom Smalley	39-105	V	Plymouth Arg.	D3S	28.4.1951
8.	Fred Forbes	38-267	V	Reading	D3S	29.4.1933
9.	Reg Elvy	38-31	V	Gillingham	D4	26.2.1958
10.	Tommy Boyle	37-261	V	Newport County	D3S	23.2.1935

To Score:	Tom Crilley	39-195	V	Reading	D3S	30.1.1935
Hat-trick:	Tommy Fowler	34-347	V	Gillingham	D3S	27.12.1958
Debut:	Steve Sherwood	39-264	V	Crewe Alex.	D3	31.8.1993
Manager:	John Barnwell	56-005				29.12.1994

YOUGEST

Player	Years-days		Opponents	Comp.	Date:
1. Aidy Mann	16-297	V	Bury	D4	5.5.1984
2. Mark Bushell	16-308	V	Stockport County	D4	9.4.1985
3. Derrick Christie	16-318	V	Reading	D4	27.1.1974
4. Peter Hawkings	16-351	V	Leyton Orient	D3	14.12.1968
5. James Benton	16-363	V	Crewe Alex.	D2	11.4.1992
6. Mark Parsons	17-005	V	Hereford Utd.	D4	29.2.1992
7. Paul Stratford	17-015	V	Bury	D4	19.9.1972
8. Lee Carter	17-032	V	York City	D3	24.3.1988
9. Maurice Muir	17-037	V	Scunthorpe Utd.	D4	25.4.1980
10. Arthur Poppy	17-054	V	Wimbledon	D4	28.2.1978

To Score:	James Benton	17-09	V	Carlisle Utd.	D4	18.4.1992
Hat-trick;	Paul Stratford	19-03	V	Workington	D4	1.10.1974
Manager;	Herbert Chapman	20-93				1.5.1907

ALEXANDER CUP

Short-lived Competition between Northampton and Hamilton Academicals,
the two towns in which the Company were based.

7.8.89. Hamilton Acc. 0   Northampton Town 0 (Hamilton Won 3-2 on Penalties)
11.8.90. Hamilton Acc 1   Northampton Town 0

APPEARANCES - MOST

Player	Lge.	FAC	Lge.Cup	Others	S.L.	War	Total
1. Tommy Fowler	521	31				31	583
2. Tom Smalley	200	26				201	427
3. Peter Gleasure	344	25	25	18			412
4. Neddy Freeman	25	22			316		363
5. Joe Kiernan	308	19	25				352
6. Willie Watson	326	26					352
7. Phil Chard	277	19	18	16			330
8. Edwin Lloyd-Davies		18			311		329
9. Len Hammond	301	24		2			327
10. Roly Mills	305	16	6				327
11. Jack English	301	20					321
12. Ron Patterson	300	17					317
13. Tommy Wells	277	34		5			316
14. Barry Tucker	277	12	13				302
15. Barry Lines	266	10	18				294
16. Gwyn Hughes	225	20				43	288
17. Graham Felton	254	19	13				286
18. Jock Manning		18			264		282
19. Stuart Robertson	254	11	16				281
20. Bill Lockett	185	20			76		281

Most Consecutive Appearances: Tommy Fowler 237 League and Cup
Shortest First Team Career: Ryan Kirby 3 minutes v Scunthorpe Utd. 15/10/96

GEORGE REILLEY

MARTIN SINGLETON

RICHARD HILL

PETER GLEASURE

*A SELECTION OF
PLAYERS WHO HAVE
MADE IT IN THE
COBBLERS RECORD
BOOK*

TOMMY FOWLER

PETER DENYER

JACK ENGLISH

NEIL GRAYSON

ALBERT DAWES

CLIFF HOLTON

ATTENDANCES

Top Attendances At the County Ground

1.	24,523	V Fulham	D1	23.4.1966	(2-4)
2.	23,275	V Chelsea	D1	?712.1965	(1-2)
3	23,209	V Southampton	FAC	7.1.1950	(1-1)
4.	22,644	V Bournemouth	FAC	2.2.1950	(2-1)
5.	21,965	V Portsmouth	D2	24.4.1965	(1-1)
6.	21,711	V Manchester Utd.	FAC	7.2.1970	(2-8)
7.	21,564	V Leicester City	D1	26.3.1966	(2-2)
8.	21,548	V Leeds United	D1.	5.3.1966	(2-1)
9.	21,344	V Arsenal	FAC	4.1.1958	(3-1)
10.	21,140	V Manchester Utd.	D1	28.8.1965	(1-1)
11.	21,102	V Plymouth Arg.	D3S	19.10.1929	(1-1)
12.	21,000	V Peterborough Utd.	D4	25.2.1961	(0-3)
13.	20,680	V Stoke City	D1	12.,4.1966	(1-0)
14.	19,718	V Plymouth Arg.	D2	20.4.1965	(3-1)
15.	19,488	V Rotherham Utd.	D2	23.3.1965	(1-0)

How the record was broken

15,000	V Sheffield United	FAC	22.1.1902
16,000	V Southampton	FAC	81.1921
16,532	V Stoke City	FAC	28.1.1922
18,123	V Plymouth Arg.	D3S	25.12.1922
21,148	V Sunderland	FAC	19.1.1928
23,209	V Southampton	FAC	7.1.1950
23,275	V Chelsea	D1	27.12.1965
24,523	V Fulham	D1	123.4.1966

Seasons Average Attendances

Best			Position	Worst		
18,584	1965-66	Div.1	1	1,826	1984-85	Div.4
15,393	1964-65	Div.2	2	2,305	1980-81	Div.4
15,366	1963-64	Div.3	3	2,308	1981-82	Div.4
13,420	1961-62	Div.3	4	2,343	1983-84	Div.4
12,680	1962-63	Div.3	5	2,384	1985-86	Div.4
12,677	1949-50	Div.3s	6	2,594	1982-83	Div.4
12,095	1951-52	Div.3s	7	2,789	1991-92	Div.4
12,031	1952-53	Div.3s	8	2,829	1978-79	Div.4
11,977	1966-67	Div.2	9	2,835	1972-73	Div.4
11,319	1955-56	Div.3s	10	3,024	1979-80	Div.4

Attendances - General

The lowest crowd at the County Ground in Recent times is 942 v Chester City in a Division Four Match 19 March 1985.

Only 400 people turned up to watch Northampton's Division 3 South Divisional knock-out cup match v Ipswich, at the County Ground on 23rd January 1939 (a Monday afternoon).

Lowest attendance at an away match in recent times is 683 v Southend in an Associate Members Cup game.

A Southern League match v Southend on Boxing Day 1908 recorded 15,000 at the County Ground, but a gate was broken down at the Wellingborough Road end, and several thousands got in free. If all spectators present had paid admission, it would have been a ground record.

The same thing happened again on 27th December 1949, home to Port Vale. 19,163 paid to watch the game, with several thousand who did not pay for admission

When Northampton Nomads entertained South Bank in the 3rd round of the F.A.Amateur Cup on 11 February 1922, at the County Ground, 7,500 watched the match - a record for two amateur sides at the County Ground.

When Northampton travelled to Deepdale for an F.A.Cup match v Preston 17 February 1934, 40,180 watched the game, at the time a record at Deepdale. A similar situation occurred in February 1950, when Northampton played Derby County in an F.A.Cup match; 38,063 watched the game a record for the Baseball ground at that time.

72,408 watched the Arsenal v Northampton F.A.Cup-tie at Higbury, the largest crowd present at a Northampton Town match.

BASS CHARITY CUP

A short lived Competition, run by the Brewery for Midland clubs. Northampton's record in the Competition is:

1902/03 (Home)	Walsall	0-1	
1903/04 (Away)	Kettering	1-0	
(Home)	Chesterfield	0-1	

BENEFITS/TESTIMONIALS

Date	Opponents	Result	Player
25.10.1906	Northants. County	5-1	Bert Neal
12.10.1908	Leicester City	2-0	Dick Murrell
18.4.1912	Tottenham Hotspur	2-0	'Neddy' Freeman
24.4.1913	Nottingham Forest	3-5	Fred Lessons
20.4.1914	Welsh XI	0-5	Edwin Lloyd-Davies
26.4.1920	Millwall	3-2	Tommy Thorpe, Jock Manning
31.1.1921	Kettering Town	4-1	Eric Tomkins
4.3.1922	Portsmouth*	0-0	Arthur Jones
3.5.1923	Southampton*	2-2	Arthur Lockett
4.1924	Plymouth Argyle	1-1	Harry Smith
8.11.1924	Brighton	1-0	Billy Pease
21.11.1925	Swindon Town*	2-0	Willie Watson
11.4.1927	Cardiff City*	4-1	Billy Williams
24.4.1932	Grimsby Town	5-2	Bob Maloney
26.9.1932	Derby County	4-3	Tommy Wells
1.5.1939	Everton	1-1	Syd Russell
4.5.1950	Combined League XI		Bill Barron
28.4.1952	Combined League XI		Gwyn Rughes, Tommy Fowler
27.4.1953	Alf Ramsey XI		Jack English
13.4.1954	Combined League XI		Jack Jenning
27.4.1954	Sheffield United	1-1	Ben Collins
28.4.1956	Peterborough United	3-3	Jack Smith
18.4.1957	Partick Thistle	2-1	Ron Patterson, Tommy Fowler
29.4.1958	All Star XI	7-5	Roly Mills, Ken Leek
31.10.1962	All Star XI		Ron Patterson
12.4.1976	Leicester City	1-1	John Clarke
22.11.1976	Liverpool	2-2	Dave Bowen
20.9.1977	Arsenal	2-3	Dave Bowen
14.4.1980	Cobblers Past XI	6-3	Paul Stratford
13.10.1986	Luton Town	2-2	Terry Branston
30.11.1987	Watford	3-2	Clive Walker
20.10.1992	Leicester City	0-2	Roly Mills
11.4.1993	Tottenham XIi	3-3	Peter Gleasure
8. 5.1995	Cobblers 86/87	1-1	Graham Reed
13. 8.1996	Arsenal	3-1	Dave Bowen Memorial

CAPTAINS

1897-98	M. Jones	1933-34	F. Dawes	1973-74	G. Riddick
1898-99	T. Minney	1934-35	T. Crilley	1974-77	W. Best
1899-00	Hendry	1935-36	J. McGuire	1977-78	S. Robertson
1900-01	A. Stewart	1936-37	J. Little	1977-78	S. Litt
1901-02	J. Farrell	1937-39	K. Gunn	1978-79	J. Farrington
1902-03	H. Dainty	1946-48	R. Dennison	1979-80	P. Sandercock
1903-05	L. Benbow	1948-49	W. Barron	1980-82	S. Phillips
1905-06	B. Neal	1949-50	W. McCoy	1982-83	L. Phillips
1906-07	W. Perkins	1950-53	M. Candlin	1983-84	W. Jeffrey
1907-10	D. McCartney	1953-55	M. Marston	1984-85	R. Train
1910-20	E. Lloyd-Davies	1955-56	B. Collins	1985-88	T. Morley
1920-21	R. Hewison	1956-61	R. Patterson	1987-88	P. Chard
1921-22	G. Whitworth	1961-62	J. Moran	1988-89	M. Singleton
1922-25	W. Lockett	1962-63	C. Holton	1989-90	T. Adcock
1925-26	W. Pease	1963-64	A. Ashworth		R. Wilcox
1926-27	W. Watson	1964-67	T. Foley	1990-91	P. Chard
1927-28	T. Smith	1967-68	G. Moore	1991-92	S. Beavon
1928-30	W. Watson		T. Branston	1992-93	S. Terry
1930-32	W. Inglis	1968-69	R. Flowers	1993-94	S. Brown
1932-33	J. Dowsey	1969-72	F. Rankmore	1994-	R. Warburton
		1972-73	W. Baxter		

These are appointed Club or Team Captains, and does not cover
Players who may have covered for the occasional game.

CHARITY SHIELD

As Winners of the Southern League in 1909, Northampton were invited to play in the Charity Shield V Newcastle.
28 April 1909 Stamford Bridge Att. 7,000.   Newcastle United (1) 2   Northampton Town (0) 0

NORTHAMPTON TEAM:
Cooch, Bonthron, Lloyd-Davies, Manning, McCartney, Dunkley, McDiarmid, Walker, Lessons, Lewis, Freeman.

COUNTY CUPS

The Maunsell Premier Cup
Winners: 1928, 1930, 1933, 1935, 1937, 1938, 1939, 1946, 1947, 1949,
    1951, 1953, 1956, 1980, 1981, 1985, 1989, 1991, 1995.
Runners-up: 1914, 1921, 1923, 1931, 1932, 1934, 1952, 1954, 1960, 1977,
    1978, 1979, 1983, 1993.
The Hillier Senior Cup
Winners: 1904, 1908, 1910, 1920, 1946, 1964*, 1966, 1970*, 1971, 1972, 1975.
Runners-up: 1899, 1901, 1902, 1912, 1913, 1961, 1962, 1963, 1968, 1968.
The Junior Cup
Winners: 1904
Runners-up: 1901 1902
Youth Football Knock-out Cup
Winners: 1959, 1964
Runners-up: 1968, 1960, 1961
* Joint Winners

COUNTY GROUND

Northampton Town's first home, from 1897 when the club was formed, to 1995 when they moved to Sixfields. Listed below are some of the events and changes that have taken place over the 98 years the club were at Abington Avenue.

1907: Terraces laid at Abington Avenue side, and small stand built costing £2,500.

1909: Banking completed at 'Spion Kop' end, accommodation for 1,000 spectators, also new stand completed to hold 1,750.

1911: Ground holds its first 'non-County' final Crewe v Edge hill in the Railway cup final, (Crewe won 5-3)

1923: £5,000 spent to build a stand with a tunnel underneath. Also west Stand is raised, and flag erected for the first time

1926: 'Spion Kop' end extended again - 6-7,000. Supporters club hand over £650 for building costs.

1929: England Amateurs play 'The Rest' in a trial match. Part of Stand destroyed in a fire causing over £5,000 of damage.

1933: Amplifiers fitted around the ground for announcements to spectators.

1936: Ball boys used for the first time.

1962: England v West Germany International youth match.

1964: Host to the F.A. Xl v New Zealand Touring Party.

1965: 'Spion Kop' end extended again. England v Eire Schoolboy International.

1972: Birmingham v Luton meet in League Cup 2nd replay. First meeting of two Football League clubs (other than Northampton) at ground.

1985: Authorities instruct the demolition of the 65 year-old wooden stand, 450 seater 'Meccano' stand erected in its place.

COACHES AND TRAINERS

LOAKES A. 1897-1906
No record traced as a player. Came from the Nottingham area and took the job as club trainer until 1906, when he took over the town boys. Died in St.Edmunds Hospital in 1944.

MURRELL, Richard 1906-1912
Played for Wellingborough and Northampton, taking over the coaching duties from Loakes in 1906. Coached the club to the Southern League Championship in 1909, followed Herbert Chapman to Leeds City in 1912.

BURROWS, Arthur 1897-1925
Born: Tewkesbury 1879, and was appointed Reserve trainer in 1897, promoted to first team 1912, a position he kept until his death in 1925.

WEBSTER, Joe 1925-1927
Born: Ilkeston 1884, and played for Ilkeston, Watford and West Ham as a goalkeeper. Represented the Southern League three times. Was Watford trainer from 1919-1925, then joined the Cobblers. Died in 1927 when complications set in after an operation.

MELLORS, Ernest 1927-1931
Born: Belper, Derby, no record traced as a player, but coached Mansfield, Notts County and Derby. Left Northampton in May 1931 to take up a similar position with Bristol City.

SCOTT, Harry 1925-1932
Seven seasons with the club with no record of previous or later clubs.

McMULLEN, John 1931-1932
Short stay at Northampton, left when he got the opportunity to return to Ireland and coach Shelbourne.

NEWMAN, Mick 1932-1954
Ex-player, who was on the club's books during the Southern League days. 22 years as trainer to both the first and reserve teams,

INGLIS, William 1932-1934
Born: Kircaldy 1897, played for Kircaldy, Raith, Sheffield Wednesday and Manchester United. Joined Cobblers as a player taking up the trainers job in 1932, which he held for a year before returning to Manchester United in the same capacity, died in Sale 1968.

McKINNELL, James 1934-1935
Born: Dalbeattie 1895. Played for Queen of the South, Dumfries, Blackburn, Darlington and Nelson. One season at Northampton in a 'two trainer system'.

JENNINGS, Jack 1939-1964
Born: Platt Bridge 1902. Played for Wigan Boro., Cardiff, Middlesbrough and Preston, turning to physio and trainer with the latter. Joined the Cobblers and added physio to

the County Cricket team, Indian touring team, and coach to the Great Britain Olympic team of 1960. Had a three match spell as caretaker-manager in 1963 and left the following season to manage Banbury and set up his clinic. Died in Northampton in 1997.

HANFORD, Harry   1948-1954
Born: in Swansea 1907. Played for Swansea, Sheffield Wednesday, Swindon, Exeter and Haverfordwest. Won Welsh caps at full and schoolboy level. Spent six seasons at Northampton, before returning to Wales to set up in business.

PAYNE, Joe   1955-1967
Born: Briton Ferry 1921. Played for Swansea, Newport, Scunthorpe and Northampton. Took up the colts coaching job in 1953, and progressed to first team coach, helping the club into Division 1. Had a brief spell at Banbury in 1967.

FLOWERS, Ron   1967-68
Full record under MANAGERS section

GORDON, Peter   1968-69
Born: Northampton 1932. A wing-half playing for Norwich, Watford, Exeter and Newport, took up coaching with Southend and Hartlepool before returning to his home town, but only briefly.

McCORMICK, 'Mac'   1968-72
Mac was a physio who came via Wellingborough. He never played League football. Left in 1972 to set up his own physio business.

UPTON, Frank   19 69-70
Born: Ainsley Hill 1934, played as a wing-half for Northampton, Derby, Chelsea, Notts County, Worcester and player-manager of Workington. Returned to Northampton as coach-scout in 1969, but the stay was brief, the club claiming his post was a luxury they could not afford.

PETTS, John   1972-77
full record under MANAGERS section

WALKER, Clive   1977-79, 1980-82
Full record under MANAGERS section

HARVEY, Bill   1979-80
Born: Grimsby in 1929. Bill played for his home town club, as well as Boston, Peterborough and Spalding. Was Coach to Bristol City, manager of Luton then had coaching spells at Swindon and Grimsby before joining Northampton, but again it was a short stay for when Bill Dodgin returned, Bill was released and joined Peterborough.

TAYLOR, Tony   1979-80
Born: Glasgow, a defender, he played for Morton, Crystal Palace, Southend, Swindon, Athlone, Bristol Rovers and Portsmouth, but his stay was short at Northampton, who he joined as player-coach.

NORMAN, Richie   1984-85
Born: Newcastle-on-Tyne 1935. A full-back with Leicester, Peterborough and Burton, before taking a coaching job with Derby. Came to Northampton at the time of Tony Barton's illness and was made acting joint manager with Clive Walker, but on Graham Carr's arrival he was released and moved across the County Ground as Physio to the Cricket club.

KIERNAN , Joe   1990-92
Born: Coatbridge 1942. A wing-half with Sunderland, Northampton, Kettering, Atherstone and Wellingborough. Was coach to Irthlingborough Diamonds and to the Cobbler's youth team before accepting Theo Foley's invitation to be the first team coach. Was released in 1992 when the club went into administration.

BEAVON, Stuart   1992-93
Born: Wolverhampton 1958, and played for Wolves, 'Spurs and Reading as an attacking midfielder. Was given the job as Coach to Phil Chard by the Administrators but admitted he did not enjoy it and stepped down after a few months, later to play junior football in Oxfordshire

BARNWELL, John   1992-93
Full record under MANAGERS section

MORRIS, Peter   1995-96
Born: New Houghton, Derby 1943. Midfield player with Mansfield, Ipswich and Norwich. Managed Mansfield, Crewe, Newcastle(Assistant), Peterborough, Nuneaton, Kettering and Boston, and came to Northampton as assistant to John Barnwell, taking over Christmas 1994 when Barnwell was sacked, on a caretaker-basis. Left when Ian Atkins took over, moving on to manage Kings Lynn

O'SHEA, Danny   1996-97
Born: Kennington 1963. A defender playing for Arsenal, Charlton, Exeter, Southend and Cambridge, the latter as player-coach, before coming to Northampton, where he left in 1997 after being offered the coach'es job full-time, but felt he could continue playing and joined Rushden and Diamonds.

COVENTRY NURSING CUP

An invitation Competition that Northampton entered just once, and won it.

1924/25:   Kettering 2-1 (Away)   Coventry 2-0 (Home)

DIRECTORS

DIRECTOR		SPAN	CHAIRMAN	
ADKINS	J.	71-78		Builder
BANKS	Derek	85-89	85-89	Tobacco Importer
BANKS	Len	88-90		Tobacco Importer
BARHAM	Charles	85-87		Building Society Manager
BATES	G.W.	49-57		
BENBOW	Len*	32-35		Accountant
BLUNDELL	Barry	88-90		Manager of tobacco importers
BOWEN	Dave	83-85		General manager of N.T.F.C
BRETT	Bob	59-79	68-69	Farmer
			77-78	
BROWN	C.S.*	23-24		
BULLER	Ted	59-68	65-68	Leather Manufacturer
CAMPLING	F. C.	38-49		
CHURCH	Martin	89-97		Builder
CHURCH	Robert	86-96		Fishing Goods Manufacturer
COLLINS	Barry	94-97		Member of Supporters Trust
CONROY	Martin	85-88		Brewery Worker
CUTLER	F.R	55-58		Leather Manufacturers
COVINGTON	John	23-24		Cinema Proprieter
DEANE	Mark	85-91		Home Improvements
DEAR	K.	36-42		Finance
DILLEGH	Ron	70-79		Local Counciller
FROST	Phil	92-94		Member of Supporters Trust
GILLETT	Thomas C*	23-45	35-39	Farmer
GRIGGS	Max	79-85		Boot Manufacturer
GUNN Dr.	Roger	81-82		Air Conditioning
GYDE	Charles*	23-32		Owner of 'Princess Royal'
HADLAND	Trevor	68-80		Architect
HAMMOND	Don	85-89		Electrical retailer
HANCOCKS	Barry	89-		Packaging retailer
HAWTIN	E.C.	35-58	46-55	
HAWTIN	Len C.	32-39		
HESKETH	Lord	77-79		Racing Motorcycle Manufacturer
HODGSON	T.	27-32		
HOLLINGSWORTH Dr.		60-62		
HOOTON	G.	32-54		
HUTTON	P.	47-59	55-58	Boot and Shoe trade
JAFFA	L.	72-80		
JAMES	Thomas S.*	29-36		Provisions merchant
JOHNSON	J.J.*	23-36		
KERR	David	89-		Accountant
LEA	Horace	39-46	39-46	Meat Wholesaler
LIDDELL	W.S.	26-45		Chairman of Supporters Club
LOMAX	Brian	92-		Chairman of Supporters Trust
MARTIN	John J.*	30-35		Builder

Barry Hancocks

Barry Ward (Chairman)

THE DIRECTORS - 1997

David Kerr

Brian Lomax

Barry Stonhill (Vice-Chairman)

Chris Smith

MILLS	J.H.	36-39			
McRITCHIE	Michael	91-92	91-92		
NORTHOVER	Eric P.	60-90	69-71		Chemist
PARKER	Fred C.*	22-39	22-35		Bookmaker
PELL	Martin	86-89			Leather Goods
PENN	Walter	41-69	58-61		Farmer
PHEE	W.	45-51			
RONSON	Neville J.	67-85	73-77		Builder
			79-85		
SAUNDERS	F*	23-31			
SAUNDERS	Reg.	58-67			Managing Director
SEAL	Russell P.*	23-35			Motor Factor
SEARS	William T.*	23-37			Boot Manufacturer
SEYMOUR	B.T.	45-58			
SMITH	Chris	96-			Builder
STEVENSON	Peter	70-71			Dress Manufacturer
STONHILL	Barry	85-			Estate and Property
TAYLOR	George	71-81			Property
UNDERWOOD	Richard	86-91	89-91		Transport
WARD	Barry	92-	92-		Administrator
WHATTON	Archie	60-72			Timber Merchants
WILSON	Con.	67-79			Bookmaker
WILSON	C.T.	51-68			
WILSON	F. C. T	61-73	71-73		Builder
WILSON	Graham	86-89			Electrical retailer
WILSON	Stuart	79-89			Leather and Tanning business
WOODING	Norman MBE	49-60			
YARDE	Cyril*	24-36			Nursery owner
YORK	Fred	49-65	61-65		Coach operator

* committee member, prior to club going public in 1922

FAMILY LINKS

Brothers who have played for the club:

Leo	(99-05)	and	Lucienrex	(04-05)	Boullemier*
Albert	(29-32)	and	Fred	(29-35)	Dawes
James	(00-07)	and	George	(06-07)	Frost
G	(97-98)	and	T.	(97-98)	Hakes
Richard	(24-25)	and	Bill	(26-27)	Oxley
Louis	(22-24)	and	Bill	(22-23)	Page
Keith	(84-85)	and	Gary	(95-)	Thompson
A. H.	(05-07)	and	B. W	(05-07)	Vann
James	(32-33)	and	Fred	(36-37)	Wallbanks
F	(97-01)	And	Roger	(98-01)	Warner

* Leo Anglicized His Name to Bullimer.

Fathers and Sons Who Have Played for the Club:

Bill	(37-51)	and	Roger	(66-69)	Barron
Dave	(47-50)	and	Keith	(76-82)	Bowen
	(59-85)				
Joe	(63-72)	and	Danny	(91-92)	Kiernan
Archie	(13-14)	and	Charles	(36-38)	Rawlings

Uncles and Nephews Who Have Played for the Club:

Norman	(51-53)	and	Bill	(72-77)	Dodgin
	(81-82)				
Harry	(31-33)	and	Alan (58-59)		Loasby
Cliff Holton (61-63)		and	Gary (74-76)		Mabee

FRIENDLIES

(Northampton First team games only. H= Home, A = Away)

1897/98		
(A)	48th Regiment	7-1
(H)	Earls Barton	4-1
(H)	Earls Barton	3-1
(H)	Finedon Rev.	3-0
(H)	Desborough T.	2-0
(A)	Earls Barton	4-3
(H)	Kettering Res.	5-4
(H)	N'pton Victoria	8-1
(A)	Kettering Res.	3-2
(H)	Leicester 8-1	
(H)	N'thants League	5-4

1898/99		
(A)	Irthlingboro'	3-0
(A)	London Vampires	4-0
(A)	Rothwell Town	5-2
(H)	Burton Wand	0-1
(H)	Market H'boro'	12-1
(H)	3rd Gren. Gds.	10-1
(H)	London Vampires	0-2
(H)	Queens Park R.	3-0
(H)	West Brom. Alb.	6-1
(A)	Rest of League	2-0

1899/00		
(H)	Derby County	1-2
(H)	Kaffirs	7-4
(A)	Luton Town	5-6
(H)	Bullwell	2-2
(H)	Loughborough	4-3
(H)	Wolverton	5-2
(H)	Luton Town	4-4
(H)	Sheffield Utd.	0-3
(H)	Scott. Am. XI	3-0

1900/01		
(H)	Hinckley	3-0
(H)	Bury	1-4
(H)	Leicester	1-6
(H)	Scott. Am. XI	1-2
(A)	Leicester C.	2-4

1901/02		
(A)	Rushden T.	5-0
(H)	Chesterfield	2-4
(A)	Chesterfield	2-4
(H)	Crewe	2-0
(H)	Aston Villa	3-3
(A)	Brighton	0-1

1902/03		
(H)	Notts County	1-4
(H)	Oxford City	6-0
(A)	Oxford City	2-1
(H)	Oxford Univ.	2-0
(A)	Oxford Univ.	2-0
(H)	Sheffield Utd.	0-2
(H)	Arsenal	1-1
(A)	Ilford	1-0

1903/04		
(A)	Rushden Town	8-0
(H)	West Brom. Alb.	2-1
(H)	Corinthians	3-3
(H)	Notts County	2-2
(A)	Luton Town	0-4
(A)	Watford	1-5

1904/05		
(A)	Leicester C.	1-2
(H)	Luton Town	1-3
(H)	Port Vale	1-1
(A)	Watford	0-1
(A)	Norwich City	4-3
(H)	N'pton Thursday	4-1
(H)	Wellingborough	1-1
(A)	Wolverton	8-0

1905/06		
(H)	Southampton	2-2
(A)	Kettering T.	1-0
(H)	D.C. Partisan	9-0
(A)	Ilford	0-0
(A)	Corinthians	2-5
(A)	Irthlingboro	0-3

1906/07		
(A)	Wolverton	2-1
(A)	Luton T. 0-2	
(H)	Nottingham F.	3-4

1907/08		
(A)	Peterboro' C.	1-1
(A)	Towcester T.	6-3

1908/09		
(A)	Wolverton T.	2-2

1909/10		
(A)	Peterborough C.	3-3
(A)	Wellingborough	2-0

1910/11		
(H)	Kettering T.	8-3
(A)	Cardiff C.	0-3

1911/12		
(A)	Rushden W'mill	6-1
(A)	Kettering T.	1-4

1912/13		
(A)	Swansea T.	2-2
(A)	Leeds City	0-4

1913/14		
(H)	Leicester C.	5-1
(H)	Cambridge Univ.	7-3

1914/15		
(A)	Bradford	0-4

1919/20		
(A)	Rotherham	2-2

1920/21		
(A)	Rushden T.	4-3

1922/23		
(A)	Wellingborough	4-1
(H)	Crystal Palace	0-2
(A)	Folkestone	0-0
(H)	Corinthians	2-1

1923/24		
(A)	Oxford Univ.	13-1
(A)	Fletton U.	2-2

1924/25		
(H)	Sth. African XI	1-1
(H)	Oxford Univ.	4-1
(A)	Peterborough C.	2-2

1926-27		
(A)	Clapton Orient	2-3

1928/29		
(H)	Middlesborough	2-2
(H)	Corinthians	3-4

1929/30		
(H)	Bristol City	4-2
(H)	Aberdeen	1-1

1932/33		
(A)	Holland	4-0
(A)	Wolverton	1-1

1933/34		
(A)	Wolverton	2-2

1934/35		
(A)	Towcester T.	9-2

1935/36		
(A)	Bath	6-1
(A)	Buckingham	8-2

1936/37		
(A)	Kettering T.	2-2
(A)	Buckingham	2-1

1947/48		
(A)	Aston Villa	2-4

1949/50		
(A)	Kettering T.	3-0

1950/51		
(A)	St. Neots	3-1
(H)	England Am. XI	4-1
(A)	Headington	1-1
(H)	Progres (Lux)	1-0
(A)	Gillingham	1-3

1951/52		
(H)	Carlisle	1-1

1952/53			**1970/71**			**1982/83**		
(H)	Saints	4-0	(A)	Banbury	1-4	(A)	Brentford	1-7
			(A)	Lincoln C.	1-2	(A)	Luton Town	5-3
1953/54			(A)	Charlton	3-0	(a)	Leicester	4-6
(H)	Saints	5-3	(A)	Leicester C.	2-2	(A)	Luton Town	1-4
			(A)	Swindon	0-0	(H)	Luton Town	2-1
1955/56								
(A)	Saints	2-0	**1971/72**			**1983/84**		
(A)	Bedford T.	2-2	(H)	Hannover 96	1-2	(A)	Leicester U.	2-0
			(A)	Cambridge U.	3-5	(A)	Nuneaton	2-2
1956/57			(H)	Notts County	2-0	(A)	Luton Town	0-1
(A)	Boston Utd.	6-2				(A)	Cambridge U.	0-0
(H)	Rochdale	1-2	**1972/73**			(H)	Wolves XI	2-0
(A)	Bedford	2-2	(A)	Reading	0-0	(A)	Leicester C.	3-0
(A)	Kettering T.	3-4	(A)	Cambridge C.	2-1	(H)	Luton Town	0-5
			(A)	Bedford T.	2-1			
1958/59						**1984/85**		
(H)	N'pton Regent	3-3	**1973/74**			(A)	Wantage	2-0
			(A)	Charlton Ath.	0-1	(A)	Aston Villa	0-3
1959/60						(A)	Nuneaton	1-3
(H)	Norwich	2-0	**1974/75**			(A)	Shepshed Chart.	aban.
(H)	Shrewsbury T.	2-1	(A)	Birmingham	1-0	(A)	Banbury	1-0
(H)	Olympic XI	2-2	(A)	Coventry C.	1-3			
			(A)	Bedford Town	1-0	**1985/86**		
1960/61						(A)	Notts County	4-3
(H)	Arsenal	2-3	**1975/76**			(A)	Leicester C.	2-0
(H)	Norwich	1-3	(A)	Leicester City	0-1	(A)	Luton Town	0-3
(H)	Oxford Utd.	2-2	(A)	Birmingham City	0-1	(A)	Blyth Spartans	4-0
			(A)	Oxford Utd.	1-4	(A)	North Shields	5-1
1963/64			(A)	Bedford Town	1-4	(A)	Blue Star	2-0
(H)	Dundee Utd.	2-1	(H)	Persian Gulf XI	4-0	(A)	Enfield	1-2
			(A)	Corby Town	4-0	(A)	Wimbledon	3-2
1964/65			(H)	Corby Town	2-5			
(A)	Dulka Prague	2-3				**1986/87**		
(A)	Pardubice	1-1	**1976/77**			(A)	Leicester C.	1-5
(A)	P. Bysricas	1-0	(A)	Willingborough	4-0	(A)	Nuneaton	3-1
(A)	L. Vgzkoscise	2-0	(A)	Towcester T.	9-0	(H)	Crystal Palace	5-2
						(A)	Millwall	1-2
1965/66			**1977/78**			(A)	West Brom. Alb.	0-3
(A)	F.C. Rapide	2-2	(A)	West Brom. Alb.	3-0	(A)	Aston Villa	1-3
(A)	Leicester C.	1-6	(A)	Coventry C.	1-2	(A)	Frickley	1-0
(A)	Coventry C.	2-2				(A)	Gretna Green	2-3
(A)	Hannover 96	0-3	**1978/79**			(A)	Blue Star	3-0
(A)	Opel Russlham	3-1	(A)	Hillingdon B.	3-1	(A)	Blythe Spartans	0-1
(A)	SVE Trier E.	2-1	(A)	Cheltenham	2-2	(A)	Ashington	6-2
			(H)	Brentford	3-0	(A)	Whitley Bay	2-1
1966/67			(A)	Luton Town	2-1	(A)	Wimbledon	0-5
(A)	Kings Lynn	6-1				(A)	Tottenham	0-6
(A)	Bedford	5-1	**1979/80**			(A)	Raunds	5-1
(A)	Wellingborough	7-2	(A)	Leicester C.	3-0	(A)	Chelsea	1-0
(H)	Hannover 96	3-1	(A)	Watford	0-2	(A)	Atherstone	1-0
			(A)	Luton Town	1-1	(A)	Wellingborough	1-3
1967/68			(A)	Barnet	1-3	(A)	Timken Duston	2-1
(A)	Colchester	1-3	(A)	Dartford	2-1	(A)	Dartford	6-3
(A)	Southend	0-0	(A)	Tottenham	0-6	(A)	Weymouth	3-1
			(A)	Bedford	2-1	(A)	Llanfarris	2-1
1968/69								
(A)	Bedford	4-1	**1980/81**			**1988/89**		
			(A)	Tottenham	1-3	(H)	Peterborough	1-3
1969/70			(A)	Nuneaton	1-0	(A)	N'pton Spencer	4-1
(A)	Hendon	4-1	(A)	Wellingborough	1-0	(A)	Birmingham	1-3
(A)	Mansfield	0-0	(A)	Watford	0-1	(A)	Enfield	1-1
(H)	Coventry	1-2				(A)	Kettering	1-1
(A)	Wellingborough	2-1	**1981/82**			(A)	Cambridge Utd.	2-2
			(A)	Tottenham	1-3			
			(A)	Nuneaton	2-0			
			(A)	Wellingborough	1-0			
			(A)	Watford	0-1			

1989/90				1992/93				1994/95		
(A)	Rothwell	2-0		(A)	Towcester	11-0		(A)	Cambridge U.	0-1
(H)	Peterborough	2-3		(H)	West Brom. Alb.	2-2		(A)	Notts County	1-1
(A)	Dorchester	6-0		(A)	Aston Villa	2-2		(A)	Luton Town	2-1
(A)	Yeovil	0-1		(A)	Raunds	4-3		(A)	Rushden & Diam.	2-3
(A)	Gloucester City	4-3		(A)	Corby T.	1-1		(A)	Welling	0-2
(A)	Ayr United	4-1		(A)	Aylesbury	1-0		(A)	Gainsborough	0-2
(A)	Ashington	3-3		(A)	Rushden & Diam.	2-2		(A)	Birmingham	2-0
(A)	Petersfield	6-0		(A)	Wellingborough	6-0		(H)	Nottingham F.	2-1
(A)	Ipswich T.	1-1		(A)	N'pton Spencer	7-0		(A)	Moor Green	2-1
								(H)	Oxford U.	0-1
1990/91				1993/94				(A)	Chelmsford	2-0
(A)	Dover	1-2		(A)	Cambridge U.	3-0		(H)	Peterborough	1-1
(A)	Aylesbury	1-2		(H)	Floriana	2-0				
(A)	Welling	1-0		(H)	Ipswich	1-2		1995/96		
(A)	Cambridge C.	0-4		(H)	Grimsby	0-1		(H)	Birmingham C.	1-2
(A)	Cambridge U.	0-3		(A)	Armitage	2-0		(A)	Halesowen	1-0
(A)	Rushden T.	0-0		(A)	Kings Lynn	0-1		(H)	Aston Villa	1-3
				(A)	Frickley	4-5				
1991/92				(A)	Raunds	1-2		1996/97		
(A)	Rushden & Diam.	1-0		(A)	Rushden & Diam.	1-1		(A)	Raunds	1-2
(A)	Margate	1-0		(A)	Aston Villa	3-5		(H)	Norwich	0-0
(A)	Aylesbury	2-0						(A)	Solihull Boro'	2-1
(A)	Telford	3-0						(A)	Raunds	3-2
(A)	Woking	0-0						(A)	Bromsgrove	2-0
								(H)	Chelsea	0-1
								(A)	Evesham	0-0*
								(H)	Ipswich	0-0
								(A)	Telford	0-1

GOALKEEPER REPLACEMENTS

Outfield player substitutes (other than that of a recognised goalkeeper substitute)

Date		Opponent		Player		Replaced
09.10.1899	H.	Kaffirs	(F)	Foster	replaced	Bullimer
03.10.1910	H.	Kettering	(F)	Whittaker	"	Thorpe
23.12.1911	A.	Luton Town	(SL)	Hampson	"	Thorpe
27.12.1920	A.	Gillingham	(3S)	Thomas	"	Thorpe
16.03.1935	A.	Brighton	(3S)	McMenemy	"	Baker
03.12.1938	H.	Southend	(3S)	Rodger	"	Gormlie
04.03.1939	H.	Brighton	(3S)	Rodger	"	Jones
04.11.1950	H.	Gillingham	(3S)	Mitchell	"	Feehan
23.02.1952	H.	Reading	(3S)	Collins	"	Wood
25.09.1958	H.	Reading	(4)	Hawkins	"	Brewer
16.04.1966	A.	Tottenham	(1)	Mackin	"	Harvey
03.03.1969	A.	Barrow	(3)	Roberts	"	Morritt
08.12.1973	H.	Lincoln	(4)	Neal	"	Starling
05.10.1974	A.	Rotherham	(4)	Neal	"	Starling
28.08.1982	A.	Wimbledon	(4)	Phillips	"	Freeman
23.10.1982	A.	Hull City	(4)	Phillips	"	Freeman
13.01.1996	H.	Cardiff	(3)	Burns	"	Woodman

GOALS
Most

Player	League	Fac	Lge Cup	Others	South.Lge.	Total
1. Jack English	135	8				143
2. Ted Bowen	114	6				120
3. Bill Lockett	69	9			32	109
4. Frank Large	88	5	3			96
5. Albert Dawes	82	12				94
6. Albert Lewis		4			85	89
7. Tommy Fowler	84	4				88
8. Ralph Hoten	75	9				84
9. Tommy Wells	72	9		1		82
10. Don Martin	69	1	11			81

Most Goals in A Season: Most Goals in A Game: 5
Cliff Holton 39 (36 League, 3 FAC)   Ralph Hoten V Crystal Palace (Div.3S) 27.10.28
                                    Albert Dawes V Lloyds Bank (FAC)26.11.32

Top Scorers in Each Major Competition

Competition	1st		2nd		3rd	
League	J. English	135	E. Bowen	116	F.large	88
F.A.Cup	A. Dawes	12	3 Players on 9 Goals			
League Cup	D. Martin	11	G. Reilly	9	W. Best	6
Southern Lge	A. Lewis	85	F. Lessons	74	E. Freeman	71
A.M.C.	I. Benjamin	5	R. Hill	3	P.Chard	3
Midland Lge	F. Warner	27	W. Miller	17	A.Stewart	17
Northants. Lge	E. Lawrence	18	A. Dunkley	8	Byles	7
W.W.2	G. Allsop	40	J.Billingham	371	A. Morrall	35

Hat-tricks

First hat-trick for the club was scored by B.Smith v Kettering Reserves, 11.12.1897.
J.Litchfield was the first in a competitive match v Raunds, 15.1.1898. (but never scored another League goal!)
Everard Lawrence was the first in consecutive games v Market Harborough, 28.1.1899 and v Grenadier Guards, 11.2.1899.
In the 10-0 victory over Walsall, 5.11.1928, Alan Loasby, Tom Smith and Tommy Wells all scored hat-tricks.
Tommy Fowler scored two hat-tricks for the Cobblers - ten years apart: v. Millwall, February 1949 and v Gillingham, December 1958

Most hat-tricks:

7:	Albert Dawes, Albert Lewis
5.	Jack English, Cliff Holton, Ralph Hoten
4:	Ted Bowen, Harry King, Frank Large, Alan Woan, Richard Hill
3:	Ralph Allen, Ian Benjamin, Neil Grayson, Bill Lockett, Leslie Robinson, George Reilly, Fred Walden, George Whitworth

Fastest Hat-tricks

4 Mins.	Neil Grayson	V Hartlepool	(D3)	25. 1.1997
11 Mins.	Peter Denyer	V Scunthorpe U.	(D4)	13. 3.1981
15 Mins.	Frank Large	V Chester C.	(D4)	22. 1.1972
19 Mins.	Joe Payne	V Newport C.	(D3S)	20. 8.1951

HONOURS:

Players who have won honours either before, during or after leaving Northampton.
* indicates winning the honour while a Northampton player.

EUROPEAN CUP:
WINNER: P.Neal 77,78.81.84
RUNNER-UP: P.Neal 85
EUROPEAN CUP WINNERS CUP:
WINNER: W.Brown 63, D.Mountfield 85
EUFA CUP:
WINNER: P.Neal 76
DIVISION ONE
WINNER: G.Jobey 11, C.Rodger 37, F.Tilson 37, C.Holton 53, W.Brown 61, R.Flowers 54, 58, 59, J.Roberts 71, P.Neal 76, 77, 79, 80, 82, 83, 84, 86, W.Baxter 62, D.Mountfield 87, H.Johnston 1896, H.Brown 07, W.Perkins 06
DIVISION TWO
WINNER: W.Pease 27,29, J.Cook 23, J.Daley 23, J.Lauderdale 30, T.Duckhouse 48, W.Baxter 61,68, D.Bruck 67,J.Gregory 87, J.Farrington 72, M.Patching 77, R.Train 78, K.McPherson 92, J.Griffiths 05, W.Smith 08, F.Walden 20

DIVISION THREE

WINNER: A.Woollard*63, D.Leck*63, T.Branston*63, M.Everitt*63, B.Lines*63, C,Brodie*63, T.Foley*63, J.Reid*63, J.Kurila*63, W.Hails*63, A.Ashworth*63, R.Smith*63, F.Large*63, D.Martin 75, J.Roberts 78, D.McNeil 76,78, I.Ross,72, P.Matthews 77, D.O'shea 91, P.Chard 89, M.Singleton 85, S.Beavon 86, D.Mountfield 95

DIVISION FOUR

WINNER: T.Branston 68, T.Robson 74, B.Hails 60, R.Smith 60, J.Hall 74, J.Broadfoot 62, C.Walker 75, A.Starling 80, L.Chatterley 73, S.Robertson 69, D.Kryzwicki 76, A.Mayes 78, J.McCaffrey 75, P.Matthews 75, J.Alexander 79, P.Gleasure*87, I.Benjamin *87, W.Donald*87, R.Hill*87, G.Reed*87, T.Morley*87, P.Chard *87,88, K.McPherson 87, E.McGoldrick 87, D.Gilbert*87, R.Wilcox*87, C.Henry 86, S.Senior 84, D.Thomas 83, M.Holmes 88, P.Robinson 88, S.Sherwood 78

DIVISION THREE SOUTH

WINNER: A.Dawes 37, J.Wallbank38, W.Baker 33, J.Payne 49, R.Allen 35, J.Lauderdale 36,C.Rawlings 38, J.McCartney 38

DIVISION THREE NORTH

WINNER: E.Evans 24, J.Harrington 24, W.McNaughton 33, A.Cochrane 29, T.Bell 31, H.Riley 32,R.Burkinshaw 29

DIVISION THREE SOUTH CUP

WINNER: T.Wells 36

F.A.CUP:

WINNER: J.Tresadern 23, T.Boyle 25, F.Tilson 34, R.Corbett 51, F.Griffin 54,W.Brown 61, R.Flowers 60, D.Mountfield 84, W.Brawn 02, L.Benbow 1898, F.Bradshaw 07.

RUNNERS-UP:

G.Jobey ll, J.Mackie 29,34, K.Baron 50, C.Holton 52, A.Ashworth 64, P.Neal 77, J.Gregory 82, G.Reilly 84, A.Woollett 89, S.Terry 84, S.Sherwood 84, A.Stewart 1893, J.Farrell 00, P.Durber 1900, A.Chadwick 1900, J.Turner 02, A. Rawlings 22

LEAGUE   CUP

WINNER: F.Upton 65, K.Leek 63, R.Fairfax 66, P.Neal 81,82,83, I.Ross 75

RUNNERS-UP: C.Walker 65, D.Kryzwicki 70, A.Hayes 79, S.Berry 85

FULL MEMBERS CUP

WINNER: E.McGoldrick 91, S.Beavon 88, G.Thompson 91, D.Martin 83, J.Frain 91

ASSOCIATE MEMBERS CUP

WINNER: P.Neal 86, K.Hitchcock 87, M.Holmes 88, P.Robinson 94, D.Peer 91, J.Gayle 91, I.Clarkson 91

RUNNERS-UP: A.Preece 93, C.McLean 90, D.Edwards 89, P.Robinson 94, A.Flounders 84

F.A. TROPHY

WINNERS: G.Carr 72, R.Flowers 71, B.Fagan 73, R.Wainwright 85, N.Cordice 85, D.Byatt 85, W.Donald 92, D.Gilbert 85, D.Martin 85

RUNNERS-UP: G.Carr 74, R.Knox 71, P.Bancroft 87

F.A. VASE

WINNER: T.Robson 80, A.McGowan 80, A.Flouders 96. D.Logan 97

RUNNERS-UP: S.Garnham 89, D.Lyons 80, T.Lee 75, A.Flounders 97

F.A. AMATEUR CUP

WINNER: W.Tull 09

VAUXHALL CONFERENCE:

WINNER: D.Byatt 85, W.Donald 92, S.Berry 96, N.Smith 92

SOUTHERN LEAGUE

WINNER: A.Lewis*09, R.Bonthron*09, F.Dunkley*09, E.Lloyd-Davies*09, W.Hickleton*09, D.McCartney*09, F.McDiarmid*09, F.Lessons*09, G.Badenoch*09, C.Brittan*09, J.Manning*09, A.Dunkley 05, E.Lawrence 07, J.Farrell 1897,1898, P.Durber 98, A.Chadwick 1898,1899,01,02, J.Turner 1897,1898,03,04, E.Freeman*09, W.Ansell 53,54, M.Robinson 57, J.Kiernan 73

SCOTTISH LEAGUE

WINNER: A.Craig 92

SCOTTISH F.A.CUP

WINNERS: H.Neal 10, H.Dainty 10

SCOTTISHLEAGUE CUP

WINNERS: E.Murphy 49

RUNNERS-UP: D.Laird 57, G.Evans 93

HOSPITAL CUP

From 1910, Northampton entertained a First Division side, in an effort to raise money for the local hospital.

26. 9.1910	V	Nottingham Forest	1-0		3.5.1925	V	Nottingham Forest	(Unknown)
18.9.1911	V	Newcastle United	1-2		7.5.1928	V	Nottingham Forest	2-1
9.10.1912	V	Fulham	1-3		6.8.1929	V	Derby County	3-1
23.9.1913	V	Fulham	1-2		5.5.1930	V	Arsenal	7-0
25.4.1921	V	Fulham	5-1		4.5.1931	V	Arsenal	0-1
13.9.1923	V	Leicester City	2-1		3.5.1933	V	Grimsby Town	2-6
5.2.1924	V	Huddersfield 2-1						

INTERNATIONAL PLAYERS

The following players have represented their Country either before, during or after their period at Northampton.
Those who won honours while a Northampton player are marked:

ENGLAND

FULL: W.Brawn, F.Bradshaw, A.Chadwick, J.Coleman, R.Flowers, J.Gregory, P. Neal L.Page, W.Pease, T.Smalley, F.Tilson, J.Tresadern, F.Walden

U-21:   I.Gernon, G.Thorapson, D.Mountfield

U-23:   R.Flowers

AMATEUR: A.Davies, H.Miller, H.Potts, H.Springthorpe, M.Edelston, T.Robinson, R.Ward, L.Brown, F.Dunkley, A.H.Vann, D.Woods, R.Brown, R.Goldie

YOUTH :   R.Mills*, B Cooke, T.Robson*, D.Clapton, B.Etheridge*, V.Cockcroft, G.Carr*, H.Llewellyn, D.Martin* C.Sharpe*, J.Hall*, J.Clarke*, T.Gould, G.Felton, N.Townsend*, E.Brookes, D.McPartland B.Mundee, L.Chatterley, N.Rioch, A.McGowan, N.Davids, S.Phillips, J.McCaffrey, G.Ingram, A.Mahoney, D.Syrett, M.Kendall, D.Buchanan. M.Patching, I.Benjamin, K.Thompson, M.Schiavi, I.Gernon, M.Singleton, D.Norton, L.Phillips, B.Barnes, T.Quow, D.Marin, A.Smith

SCHOOLBOY:
          E.Tomkins, W.Lockett, H.Riley, R.Allen, P.Vickers, C.Walker E.Brookes, T.Gould, R.Jayes, G.Ingram, M.Muir, M.Hutchinson, W.Donald, I.Dawes, I.Gernon, P.Tisdale

'B'   B.Mitchell, D.Mountfield

VICTORY   M. Edelston

SEMI-PRO: D.Buchanan, P.Shirtliff, P.Bancroft, T.Morley, R.Wilcox, P.Culin, D.Collins, W.Stewart

SCOTLAND

FULL: W.Brown	U-21: A.Blair	'B': J.Fotheringham, W.Brown
YOUTH: W.Jeffries, P.Friar, D.Rennie	SCHOOLBOY: J.McGuire	

WALES

FULL: W.Williams*, J.Parris, D.Bowen, K.Leek*, G.Moore*, J.Roberts, F.Rankmore, R.Kryzwicki, W.Watkins, E.Lloyd Davies*, W.Bailiff

AMATEUR: E.Evans   U-21: J.Roberts, W.Cegielski, J.Parton, K.Bowen   *U-23: K.Leek*, J.Roberts

SCHOOLBOYS: J.Jones, P.Hawkins*, J.Parton, K.Bowen*   SEMI-PRO:R.Lewis

NORTHERN IRELAND - FULL: E.Ross

EIRE:

FULL: T.Foley*, E.Rodger, A.Hayes, E.McGoldrick, P.Scully

U-23:   E.Rodger, P.Scully   U-21: P.Scully, M.Rush   'B': P.Scully

YOUTH: T.Kilkelly   SCHOOLBOY: E.Rodger, P.Scully

IRELAND

FULL: P.Mcilvenny, P.Kavanagh, J.Mackie   AMATEUR: R.Parry

LATVIA: E.Freimanis   HUNGARY (YOUTH): B.Olah   CAMEROON(U-21):   E.Elad

MANAGERS

CHAPMAN, Herbert
APRIL 1907 - MAY 1912
Born: Kiverton Park 19.1.1878. Died London 6.1.1934
Player: Stalybridge, Rochdale, Grimsby, Swindon, Sheppey, Worksop, Northampton, Sheffield United, Notts County, Northampton, Tottenham, Northampton
Manager: Northampton, Leeds City, Huddersfield, Arsenal
Honours: 4 League championship, 2 runners-up, 2 F.A.Cup winners, 2 Runners-up, 1 Southern League.

BULL Walter
MAY 1912 - DECEMBER 1912
Born: Nottingham 19.12.1874 Died Nottingham 25.7.1952
Player: Notts County, Tottenham, South America
Manager: Northampton

LESSONS Fred
AUGU9T 1913 - MAY 1915
Player: Stoke City, Northampton
Manager: Northampton
Honours: Southern League (as player)

Herbert Chapman

HEWISON Robert
MAY 1920 - APRIL 1925
Born: : Backworth 25.3.1889 Died Bristol 1964
Player: Newcastle United, Leeds City, Northampton
Manager: Northampton, Q.P.R., Bristol City, Guildford, Bath
Honours Div.3S runners-up.

TRESADERN Jack
MAY 1925 OCTOBER 1930
Born: Leytonstone 26.9.1890. Died Tonbridge 26.12.1959
Player: West Ham, Burnley, Northampton
Manager: Northampton, Crystal Palace, Tottenham, Plymouth, Chelmesford, Hastings, Tonbridge
Honours: Div.3 S (twice)

Jack Tresadern

ENGLISH Jack
FEBRUARY 1931- MARCH 1935
Born: Hebburn 1887 Died Jan 1953
Player: Preston, Sheffield United, Watford
Manager: Darlington, Nelson, Northampton, Exeter, Darlington
Honours Div.3 N Champions and runners-up

PUDDEFOOT Syd
MARCH 1935 - MARCH 1937
Born: West Ham 17.10.1894. Died Rochdale 2.10.72
Player: West Ham, Falkirk, Blackburn, West Ham
Manager: Galatasary, Northampton

Syd Puddefoot

CRESSWELL Warney
MARCH 1937 - SEPTEMBER 1939
Born: South Shields 5.11.1894   Died:20.10.73
Player: South Shields, Sunderland, Everton
Manager: Port Vale, Northampton

SMITH Tom
SEPTEMBER 1939 - MARCH 1949
Born: : Whitburn
Player: Leeds City
Manager: Northampton

DENNISON Robert
MARCH 1949 - JULY 1954
Born: : Amble 6. 3. 1912.   Died: Kent 19.6.1996
Player: Newcastle, Nottingham Forest, Fulham, Northampton
Manager: Northampton, Middlesborough, Hereford, Coventry
Honours: Div.3 South runners/up. Southern League Championship

Robert Dennison

SMITH Dave
JULY 1954   - JULY 1959
Born: : South Shields12.10.1915
Player: Newcastle, South Shields, Northampton
Manager: Northampton, Aldershot

BOWEN Dave
JULY   1959 - SEPTEMBER 1967
MAY   1969 - MAY 1972
Born: Maestag 7. 6.1928.   Died: Northampton 25.9.1995
Player: Northampton, Arsenal, Northampton,
Manager: Northampton, Wales
Honours: Div2 runners-up, Div3 Championship

Dave Bowen

MARCHI Tony
SEPTEMBER 1967 - MAY 1968
Born: Edmonton 21.1.1933
Player: Tottenham, Lanerossi, Torino
Manager: Cambridge City, Northampton

FLOWERS Ron
MAY 1968 - MAY 1969
Born: Edlington 28.7.1934
Player: Wolves, Northampton
Manager: Northampton, Telford
Honours: F.A.Trophy winner

BAXTER William
OCTOBER 1972 - MAY 1973
Born: Edinburgh 23.4.1939
Player: Ipswich. Hull, Watford
Manager: Northampton

DODGIN Bill
JUNE 1973 - JUNE 1976
OCTOBER 1980 - FEBRUARY 1982
Born: .Durham 4.11.1931
Player: Fulham, Arsenal
Manager: Q.P.R, Fulham, Leicester (asst.), Northampton,
Brentford, Northampton, Woking
Honours: Div.4 runners-up (twice)

Tony Marchi

PETTS John
SEPTEMBER 1977 - JANUARY 1978
Born: Edmonton 2.10.1938
Player: Arsenal, Reading, Bristol Rovers
Manager: Trowbridge, Northampton, Northampton Spencer

CRERAND Pat
SEPTEMBER 1976 - JANUARY 1977
Born: Glasgow 19.2.1939
Player: Celtic, Manchester United,
Manager: Northampton

KEEN Mike
FEBRUARY 1978 - MARCH 1979
Born: High Wycombe 19. 3.1940
Player: Q.P.R., Watford, Luton
Manager: Watford, Northampton, Wycombe, Marlow

Phil Chard

WALKER Clive
MAY 1979 - OCTOBER 1980
MAY 1982 - MAY 1984
Born: Watford 24.10.1945
Player: Leicester, Northampton, Mansfield, Gravesend, Chelmsford
Manager: Northampton, Maidstone

BARTON Tony
JULY 1984   - APRIL 1985
Born: Sutton 8.4.1937
Player: Sutton, Fulham, Nottingham Forest, Portsmouth
Manager: Aston Villa, Northampton, Southampton. Portsmouth
Honours: European Cup Winners

CARR Graham
APRIL 1989 - MAY 1990
Born: Newcastle 25.10.1944
Player: Northampton, York, Bradford, Altrincham, Dartford, Tonbridge, Weymouth
Manager: Weymouth, Dartford, Nuneaton, Northampton, Blackpool, Maidstone, Kettering, Dagenham and Redbridge
Honours Division Four Championship, Southern League Championship

Ian Atkins

FOLEY Theo
MAY 1990 - APRIL 1992
Born: Dublin 2.4.1937
Player: Home Farm, Burnley, Exeter, Northampton, Charlton
Manager: Charlton, Dulwich, Q.P.R., Millwall (asst.), Arsenal (asst.)
Northampton, Fulham (Youth), Southend (asst.)

CHARD Phil
APRIL 1992 - SEPTEMBER 1993
Corby 16.10.60
Player: Nottingham Forest, Peterborough, Northampton, Wolves, Northampton, Kettering
Manager: Northampton

BARNWELL John
SEPTEMBER 1993 - DECEMBER 1994
Born: Newcastle 24.12.1938
Player: Bishop Auckland, Arsenal, Nottingham Forest, Sheffield United.
Manager: Hereford (asst.), Peterborough, Wolves, Notts County, Walsall, A.E.K.Athens, Northampton, Grantham
Honours: League Cup winners

ATKINS Ian
JANUARY 1995 -
Born: Sheldon, 16,1.1957
Player: Shrewsbury, Birmingham, Sunderland, Everton, Birmingham, Redditch
Manager: Colchester (Player/manager), Cambridge United, Doncaster, Northampton

PLAYERS WHO LATER MANAGED LEAGUE CLUBS

Bradshaw Frank	Aberdare (23-24)
Brown Laurie	Bradford (68-69)
Chadwick Arthur	Exeter(08-22), Reading(23-25), Southampton(25-31)
Dawes Fred	Crystal Palace(50-51)
Dodgin, Norman	Exeter (53-57), Barrow(57-58), Oldham (58-59),
Everitt Mike	Brentford (73-75)
Gregory John	Portsmouth(89-90), Plymouth(90-91), Wycombe(96-
Hails Billy	Peterborough (78-79)
Jobey George	Wolves (22-24), Derby C.(25-41), Mansfield (52-53)
Mcintyre James	Southampton (19-24), Coventry(28-31), Fulham(31-34)
Mcneil Dixie	Wrexham (85-89)
Moore John	Luton (86-87)
Neal Phil	Bolton(85-89), Coventry(92-95), Cardiff(95-96)
	Manchester City(96-97 Asst.), Peterborough (97 Asst.)
Page Louis	Newport(35-37), Swindon (45-53), Chester (53-56)
Ross Ian	Huddersfield (92-93)
Upton Frank	Workington (67-68)
Wood Alf	Walsall (63-64)
Yeomans Rae	Darlington(68-70)

MANAGER OF THE MONTH

			P.	W.	D.	L.	F.	A
December 1970	Dave Bowen	Div.4	4	2	1	1	6	4
November 1975	Bill Dodgin	Div.4	5	4	1	0	7	0
April 1978	Mike Keen	Div.4	8	5	2	1	15	7
February 1980	Clive Walker	Div.4	5	3	2	0	6	2
September1986	Graram Carr	Div,4	6	5	0	1	15	7
December 1986	Graham Carr	Div.4	5	4	0	1	17	4
November 1990	Theo Foley	Div.4	3	3	0	0	5	2
January 1991	Theo Foley	Div.4	4	3	1	0	7	1
April 1997	Ian Atkins	Div.3	6	4	2	0	7	1

PAISLEY

7. 8. 1965   ST.MIRREN 0   NORTHAMPTON TOWN 2

PENALTIES

* First player to take a penalty was G.J.Thompson v Finedon in a Friendly 16 Oct. 1897, and he missed. he also converted the first penalty v Wellingborough Reserves in Junior cup 27 Nov. 1897.
* Byles had a penalty saved v Wellingborough Reserves 7 Jan.1899 but headed in the rebound.
* A Southern League game v Northampton and Luton 26 Dec.1904 saw five penalties awarded three to Luton, all converted and two to Northampton, one scored one missed
* Bryan Harvey saved two penalties in a game v Southampton 2 Jan 1965, from Terry Paine, who was at the time, England's penalty taker.
* Peter Pickering also saved two penalties in a match v Aldershot 14 September 1955.
* Freddie Ramscar had two penalties saved by Dave Underwood of Watford 5 September 1953
* Kevin Hitchcock saved a penaly on his Northampton debut v Gillingham 29 Dec.1990.
* Bryan Harvey saved 7 penalties during the 1964/65 season.
* Stuart Beavon converted 10 penalties during the 90/91 season.
* During the 1924/25 season, 8 penalties were missed.

PLAYER OF THE YEAR

Season	'Home Player'		'Home Player'		'Away Player'
1974-75	Billy Best	1988-89	Tony Adcock	1991-92	Jason Burnham
1975-76	Jim Hall	1989-90	Keith Mcpherson	1992-93	Barry Richardson
1976-77	Billy Best	1990-91	Phil Chard	1993-94	Darron Harmon
1977-78	Steve Bryant	1991-92	Steve Terry	1994-95	
1978-79	Stuart Robertson	1992-93	Barry Richardson	1995-96	Ray Warburton
1979-80	Andy Poole	1993-94	Darron Harmon		
1980-81	Keith Williams	1994-95	Neil Grayson		'Press Player'
1981-82	Wakeley Gage	1995-96	Ray Warburton	1990-91	Steve Terry
1982-83	Steve Massey	1996-97	Ian Clarkson	1991-92	Steve Terry
1983-84	Wakeley Gage			1992-93	Barry Richardson
1984-85	Wakeley Gage		'Away Player'	1993-94	
1985-86	Russell Lewis	1988-89	Tony Adcock	1994-95	Neil Grayson
1986-87	Ian Benjamin	1989-90	Keith McPherson	1995-96	Ray Warburton
1987-88	Peter Gleasure	1990-91	Steve Terry	1996-97	Ray Warburton

Lee Colkin (94-95) and Paul Binder (95-96) were under 21 players of the year.

REPRESENTATIVES

The following players have also represented various organisations, those that did so while with Northampton are marked thus*

Southern League:
W. Bailiff(1915), F. Bradshaw(1912*), R. Brittan(1911*,1912*,1913*), E. Freeman(1912*), R. Hughes(1915*), A. Lewis(1910*), E.Lloyd-Davies(1915*), T. Thorpe(1914*,1915*), F. Walden(1913*).
Football League:
F. Bradshaw (1910), J. Coleman(1911), R. Flowers(1964), F. Tilson(1936), F. Walden(1915).
Football Association:
L. Hawtin (1921), M. Edelston (1946), R. Brown (1965).
Division Three South:
J. Bannister(1958), G. Hughes(1955*), R. Mills(1956*), R. Pickering(1957*), R. Yeomans (1958*).
Scottish League:
C. Rodger (1936).
Great Britain Olympics:
M. Edelston (1936), L. Brown (1960).
Football Combination:
T. Mclain (1955).

RESERVES (and COLTS)

11.4.1908:   Reserves fined 10/6 (52p) for playing an ineligible player

13.4.1919:   Play Desborough Town in the Junior Cup Final at Desborough, with the score at 0-0 at half-time the referee deemed the pitch not good enough for a Final and turns it into a Friendly. During the second-half the NFA members present state this can not be done and revert it back again to the Final. When the players and referee come off the field and are told of the change, they all walk off in disgust.

19.3.1927:   Fined £20 for playing A.Gautrey, a professional Rugby player, in the Reserves.

5. 5.1934:   Several first-teamers drafted into the Reserves in an attempt to keep them in the Combination Division One

8.11.1941:   Reverend George Layton, Minister for Gold Street, plays for the Colts v Leicester Colts

20.11.1943:   Nosef-Dujaik, a Czechoslovakian International scored a hat-trick on his Colts debut, he had played against England in 1935

22.12.1945   Northants cricketing legend, Dennis Brooks, scored twice for the Colts v Corby Reserves.

29.12.1945   The Colts found themselves with just 10 men v Corby, and utilised the 'Chronicle and Echo' reporter who was covering the game,

25. 2.1956   Colts beat Wootton Blue Cross 13-1, Brocklebank scoring seven of the goals.

29. 4.1966   Despite winning the Senior cup, the club were fined £250 for fielding a reserve side in the Competition.

SENDING OFF's

#	Player		Opponent	Venue	Comp	Date	#	Player		Opponent	Venue	Comp	Date
1.	C. Baker	V	Raunds	Home	N.L.	15.1.1898	39.	K. Thompson	V	Tranmere R.	Home	D4	20.4.1985
2.	R. Bonthron	V	Millwall	Away	S.L.	2.10.1909	40.	R. Hill	V	Mansfield T.	Away	D4	11.1.1986
3.	R. Walker	V	Brentford	Away	S.L.	25.12.1909	41.	P. Chard	V	Scunthorpe U.	Away	D4	18.3.1986
4.	J. Manning	V	Nottingham F.	Home	FAC	2.1910	42.	D. Gilbert	V	Southend U.	Away	D4	26.12.1986
5.	J. Manning	V	Crystal Pal.	Away	S.L.	24.12.1910	43.	P. Chard	V	Port Vale	Away	L.Cup	17.8.1987
6.	C Myers	V	Newport C.	Home	D3S	17.2.1923	44.	S. Senior	V	Port Vale	Away	L.Cup	17.8.1987
7.	D Tolland	V	Gillingham	Away	D3S	11.4.1934	45.	K. McPherson	V	Notts County	Away	D3	2.1.1988
8.	W. Thayne*	V	Luton T.	Away	D3S	15.3.1937	46.	W. Donald	V	Southend U.	Away	D3	17.1.1989
9.	A. Harris	V	Coventry C.	Home	War	23.1.1943	47.	D. Thomas	V	Chesterfield	Away	D3	28.1.1989
10.	.W. Coley	V	Swansea T.	Away	3S	22.11.1947	48.	D. Thomas	V	Bolton Wand.	Home	D3	17.2.1990
11.	W. Coley	V	Reading	Home	D3S	2.12.1950	49.	W. Donald	V	Bristol Rovers	Home	D3	31.3.1990
12.	T.McLain	V	Norwich C.	Away	D3S	13.12.1952	50.	S. Brown	V	Chesterfield	Away	D4	6.10.1990
13.	R. Patterson	V	Millwall	Home	D3S	17.9.1953	51.	T. Angus	V	Darlington	Away	D4	23.10.1990
14.	R. Yeomans	V	Coventry C.	Away	D3S	12.1.1957	52.	G. Fee	V	Barnet	Away	FAC	8.12.1990
15.	C. Gale	V	Millwall	Away	D4	18.2.1961	53.	P. Wilson	V	Gillingham	Away	D4	29.12.1990
16.	T. Foley	V	Bradford	Away	D3	7.10.1961	54.	A. Thorpe	V	Torquay Utd.	Away	D4	19.2.1991
17.	A. Ashworth	V	Watford	Away	D3	27.10.1962	55.	P. Chard	V	Torquay Utd.	Home	D4	16.4.1991
18.	M. Everitt	V	Chesterfield	Home	L.Cup	4.11.1964	56.	T. Angus	V	Crewe Alex.	Away	D4	17.9.1991
19.	D.Leck	V	Plymouth Arg.	Away	D2	19.4.1965	57.	C. Mclean	V	Burnley	Away	D4	11.2.1992
20.	C. Walker	V	Blackburn R.	Away	D2	22.4.1967	58.	S. Terry	V	Hereford U.	Home	D4	29.2.1992
21.	J. Roberts	V	Rotherham U.	Away	D3	21.1.1969	59.	T. Angus	V	Lincoln C.	Home	D4	31.3.1992
22.	E. Weaver	V	Port Vale	Away	D4	23.8.1969	60.	I. McParland	V	Wrexham	Away	D3	24.10.1992
23.	F. Large*	V	Swansea T.	Away	D4	20.9.1969	61.	D. Harmon	V	Colchester U.	Away	D3	1.12.1992
24.	P. Hawkins	V	Swansea T.	Away	D4	20.9.1969	62.	I. McParland	V	Halifax T.	Away	D3	16.1.1993
25.	.P. Neal	V	Hereford U.	Home	FAC	14.12.1971	63.	T. Angus	V	Lincoln C.	Away	D3	6.3.1993
26.	A. Oman	V	Hartlepool	Away	D4	22.4.1972	64.	S. Brown	V	Colchester U.	Away	D3	20.4.1993
27.	N. Davids	V	Tranmere R.	Away	D4	10.10.1975	65.	K. Gillard	V	Scunthorpe U.	Away	D3	16.10.1993
28.	P. Stratford	V	Cambridge U.	Away	D4	8.11.1975	66.	A. Gilzean	V	Chester C.	Away	D3	20.11.1993
29.	N. Freeman	V	Wimbledon	Away	D4	28.8.1982	67.	C. Burns	V	Hereford Utd.	Away	D3	4.2.1995
30.	M. Heeley	V	Hartlepool U.	Away	D4	11.9.1982	68.	I. Sampson	V	Torquay Utd.	Away	D3	23.9.1995
31.	S. Massey	V	Torquay Utd.	Away	D4	16.10.1982	69.	C. Burns	V	Preston N.E.	Home	D3	31.10.1995
32.	N. Freeman	V	Hull C.	Away	D4	23.10.1982	70.	A. Woodman	V	Cardiff C.	Home	D3	13.1.1996
33.	M. Heeley	V	Wimbledon	Away	FAC	20.11.1982	71.	I. Sampson	V	Mansfield T.	Away	D3	3.2.1996
34.	J. Buchanan	V	Tranmere R.	Away	D4	19.2.1983	72.	D. O'shea	V	Wigan A.	Away	D3	17.8.1996
35.	B. Mundee	V	Aldershot	Away	D4	1.11.1983	73.	D. Peer	V	Wigan A.	Away	D3	17.8.1996
36.	A. Hayes	V	Bristol C.	Away	D4	14.4.1984	74.	M. Cooper	V	Cardiff C.	Home	L.Cup	3.9.1996
37.	W. Gage	V	V. S. Rugby	Away	FAC	21.11.1984	75.	I. Clarkson	V	Carlisle U.	Away	D3	1.2.1997
38.	P. Shirtliff	V	Scunthorpe U.	Away	D4	22.3.1985	76.	M. Cooper	V	Cardiff C.	Away	P/off	14.5.1997

* Later cleared of any offence

SOUTHERN CHARITY CUP

4.10.1909 (A) Brentford 5-3   28 10.1909 (H) Watford 0-1

TRANSFERS - RECORDS

FEE IN-COMING

				Date	Fee (£)
Frank	Howard	to	Derby County	4.1899	50p
Billy	Brawn	to	Sheffield Utd.	1.1900	
	undisclosed				
Albert	Dawes	to	Crystal Palace	12.1933	1,650
Fred	Dawes	to	Crystal Palace	2.1936	2,650
Colin	Lyman	to	Tottenham	10.1938	3,000
Archie	Garrett	to	Birmingham C.	11.1947	10,000
Jack	Cross	to	Sheffield Utd.	1.1954	13,000
Laurie	Brown	to	Arsenal	5.1961	35,000
Don	Martin	to	Blackburn	11.1967	36,000
Phil	Neal	to	Liverpool	10.1974	65,000
George	Reilly	to	Cambridge Utd.	11.1979	165,000
Richard	Hill	to	Watford	4.1987	265,000

FEE OUT-GOING

				Date	Fee (£)
Edwin	Lloyd -Davies	From	Stoke City	11.1907	400
Ted	Bowen	From	Arsenal	2,1928	750
John	Bartram	From	Falkirk	8.1935	1,000
Harry	Lowery				
Jack	Sankey	From	West Brom. A.	4.1946	4,500
Sam	Heaselgrave				
Tim	McCoy	From	Portsmouth	12.1948	3,500
Jack	Cross	From	Bournemouth	10.1954	6,500
Dave	Bowen	From	Arsenal	7.1959	7,000
Alec	Ashworth	From	Luton Town	7.1963	10,000
Bobby	Hunt	From	Colchester Utd.	3.1964	15,000
Joe	Broadfoot	From	Ipswich Town	10.1965	27,000
Mark	Heeley	From	Arsenal	3.1980	33,000
Steve	Phillips	From	Brentford	8.1980	50,000
Paul	Culpin	From	Coventry City	10.1987	55,000
Martin	Singleton	From	West Brom. A.	11.1987	57,500
Tony	Adcock	From	Manchester City	1.1988	85,000

UNITED LEAGUE

The club played in the United League for two seasons, the results were as follows:

	1899-1900		1900-1901	
	H	A	H	A
Desborough T.	9-0	4-1		
Finedon	0-1	4-1	1-1	2-1
Kettering	4-0	1-2	2-2	1-4
Luton Town			0-0	1-2
Rothwell T.	6-0	2-1		
Rushden T.	3-0	4-4	W	3-3
Wellingborough	4-4	2-2	0-2	2-3

WELLINGBOROUGH CHARITY CUP

1897-98	(H)	Wolverton	3-1
	(A)	Kettering	0-2
1898-99	(H)	Rushden T.	0-0
	(A)	Rushden T.	0-2
1899-00	(A)	Wellingborough	2-5

THEY WHO ALSO SERVED

The following have all appeared for the Reserves, and have made their names elsewhere, either in or out the game.

BULLER Ted.
A forward who had his best season during the season of friendlies 1915-16, took up the whistle, moved into local football administration in the 50's then joined the Cobbler's board. Later becoming chairman during their Division One days.

CASEY Dennis
A forward who served time at the County Ground without making the first team, moved on to Wellingborough where he scored many goals. Turned to Physio where he returned to Northampton via Nuneaton.

DOWIE. Ian
Came on trial from Hendon during the 1988/89 season but made no impact. Returned and was later to play for Fulham, West Ham, Southampton, Crystal Palace and Northern Ireland.

GRAHAM Richard
A goalkeeper loaned from Corby in 1938/39 and again during WW2. Was never taken on and sought a career with Crystal Palace and Leicester. Went into management with Crystal Palace, Charlton, Leyton Orient and Walsall, but was best known as manager of the Colchester team that knocked Leeds out of the F.A.Cup in 1971.

HALES Bert
Had a spell at the County ground in 1930 but failed to make the first team. Later appeared for Forest, Peterborough, Stoke, Chesterfield, Stockport and Rochdale.

HARGREAVES Alwyn
Spent four seasons as a reserve wing-half at Northampton just after WW2 without breaking into the first team. Became better known as a councillor and played a large part in getting Northampton Town to Sixfields.

ICKE David;
A goalkeeper loaned to the club from Coventry in 1970/71, and never made the first team. Moved on to Hereford, and then in to T.V Sports journalism before making news with his religious beliefs.

KERNICK Dudley
Joined the club from Torquay, and moved on to Birmingham, without making the first team, but made a name in the midlands as a Commercial Manager.

LAW George
Failed to make an impression during his stay here in 1936, moved on to Norwich giving them five seasons.

MILLER Leslie
Spent the 1929-30 season at Northampton without a first team game, then moved on to Spurs, Chesterfield and Mansfield.

MORGANS Gwyn
Was with Northampton 1954-56, without a first team game. Joined Wrexham and later Southport, where he won honours as a Welsh AmateurInternational.

MURPHY Matt
Ex-youth player of early 1980's who was allowed to go to Corby where he was spotted and signed by Oxford United..

O'CONNER Des.
A right-winger who played for the Colts, but moved into the entertainment business first as a Butlin Redcoat, and then on T.V.

PLATNAUER Nick
A youth player who was allowed to join Bedford in 1979, then onto a host of clubs including Notts County, Leicester, and Cardiff.

RIDDING Bill
His one season at Northampton in 1934/35 bore no fruit and he returned north with Tranmere. But it was when he moved into management that he made his name, taking Bolton Wanderers to two cup finals

SMITH Peter
A goalkeeper on the clubs books for many years, before turning to management with Long Buckby. Became a Physio often to the Reserves and sometimes the first team in those dark days of the 1970's. Ran the youth team with Roly Mills around the same time. Took up refereeing, becoming a class one, and found time to set up his own business and become a class entertainer as well as a J.P. Can be seen as M.C. on match days.

SURTEES John
Joined Northampton from Bournemouth in 1934, but, after failing to make the first team , after a few months he asked to be released, and was about to emigrate to the U.S.A. when Sheffield Wednesday offered him a trial and at the end of the season he played in the Cup Final for them.

WEALANDS Jeff
A loanee goalkeeper from Wolves in 1970. He stayed a month, returned to Wolves, and later played for a host of League clubs including Hull and Manchester United, later joined Altrincham, where he is now a director.

STATISTICAL SECTION
Notes

WHO'S WHO SECTION

This section includes all players who have appeared in the Football League, FA Cup, Football League Cup, Associated Members Cups and other competitive first team matches up to the end of the 1996-97 season. The "first" and "last" seasons are the first year of each season; thus a player with the entry 1966 to 1971 appeared between the seasons 1966-67 and 1971-72. An entry in the first season column only indicates that the player only appeared in a single season. Entries on more than one line indicate a player had more than one spell at the club, with the total number of appearances shown. Substitute appearances have not been shown separately and are included within the totals.

The appearances and goals columns have headings for the Football League, FA Cup, Football League Cup and Other games (or pre-League: SL - Southern League, M.L.- Midland League, or N.L. - Northants League). The 'Other' column includes all first team competitive matches.

The Second World War seasons are covered in a separate section, with alternative headings.

SEASON STATISTICS SECTION

The seasonal statistics pages (that follow the 'Who's Who' section) have been designed for easy reference, and are generally self-explanatory, however the following notes are given to avoid confusion.

Left hand column signifies the match number or the round number in a cup competition, e.g. Qr = qualifying round, R2 = 2nd round, rep = replay, rep2 = second replay, R1/2 = 1st round second leg, PR = preliminary round, etc.

The second column signifies the date (month abbreviated)
The third column shows the opposition team (upper case - capital letters - a Northampton home match, lower case - away match). Neutral, or alternative venues are indicated otherwise.
The fourth column shows the match result (Northampton score first)
The fifth column shows the attendance where known.
The sixth column provides the Northampton goalscorers (where known). Figure in brackets are the number of goals scored by that player, OG ('own goal') indicates a goal credited to the opposition team, (p) indicates a goal scored from a penalty.

Right hand column, the players table: The numbers refer to the shirt number worn by that player in the starting line-up (or the accepted position in pre-War seasons, i.e. 1 = goalkeeper, 2 = right-back, 6 = left-half, 10 = inside-left, etc.). Unused substitutes have not been included. Used substitutes are shown as 12, 14 or 15. Additional players not included are shown at the bottom of the table.

The alternative method of naming each player in an eleven column table is included for the Second World War seasons, in view of the large number of players appearing for the club during this period.

STATISTICS

SECTION

Sheet No.1 - Adams CJ to Braidford

Player			Date of Birth	Place of Birth	Died	First Season	Last Season	Previous Club	Next Club	Appearances				Goals			
										League	FAC	FLC	Other	League	FAC	FLC	Other
Adams	CJ	Craig	9/11/74	Northampton		1991			VS Rugby	1	0	0	0	0	0	0	0
Adams	DF	Don	15/2/31	Northampton	1994	1951	1955		Bedford T	23	0	0	0	7	0	0	0
Adcock	AC	Tony	27/2/63	Bethnal Green		1987	1989	Manchester City	Bradford City	107	2	7	6	40	1	3	2
						1990	1991	Bradford City	Peterborough U								
Adey	TW	Thomas	22/2/01	Hetton-le-Hole	1986	1926		Swindon Town	Durham City	10	1	0	0	0	0	0	0
Aitken	JG	John	19/9/1897	Glasgow	1967	1927		Norwich City	Kilmarnock	10	0	0	0	5	0	0	0
Aldridge	MJ	Martin	6/12/74	Northampton		1991	1994		Oxford United	70	2	3	5	17	1	0	4
Aldridge	NH	Norman	23/2/21	Coventry		1948		West Bromwich A.	Oxford United	2	0	0	0	0	0	0	0
Alexander	JE	John	3/10/55	Liverpool		1981		Reading		21	1	4	0	4	0	1	0
Allan	CE	Charles	1910	Darlington		1932	1933	Darlington	Darlington	15	0	0	0	0	0	0	0
Allen	AR	Robert	11/10/16	Bromley-by-Bow		1946		Brentford	Colchester Utd.	5	0	0	0	0	0	0	0
Allen	PW	Percy	2/7/1895	West Ham	1969	1925	1926	Lincoln C	Peterborough U	44	1	0	0	3	0	0	0
Allen	RSL	Ralph	30/6/06	Newburn	1981	1936	1938	Reading	Torquay United	52	2	0	3	41	0	0	3
Allen	T	Tommy	1/5/1897	Moxley	1968	1933		Accrington Stanley	Kidderminster H.	19	6	0	0	0	0	0	0
Allon	TG	George	27/8/1899	Blyth	1983	1926	1931	Coventry City	Wigan Borough	185	7	0	0	7	0	0	0
Ambridge	FW	Frederick	1900	Wellingborough		1921		(Navy)	Wellingborough	13	4	0	0	0	0	0	0
Anderson	DE	Doug	29/8/63	Hong Kong		1988		Plymouth Arg. (loan)		5	0	0	1	0	0	0	0
Anderson	GL	Gary	20/11/55	Bow		1974	1975	Tottenham H	Barking	14	0	2	0	0	0	0	0
Anderson	JL	John	5/4/28	Glasgow		1953		Partick Thistle	Exeter City	14	1	0	0	5	0	0	0
Angus	TN	Terry	14/1/66	Coventry		1990	1992	VS Rugby	Fulham	116	6	7	9	6	0	0	0
Ansell	W	William 'Jack'	4/8/21	Bletchley		1947	1951	Bletchley Brick Wks	Oxford United	131	11	0	0	0	0	0	0
Anthony	C	Charles	1903	Mansfield		1929	1931	Mansfield Town	Mansfield Town	81	3	0	0	0	0	0	0
Armitage	JH	Jack	21/8/1897	Chapeltown		1930		Southend Utd.	Halifax Town	4	0	0	0	0	0	0	0
Armstrong	GI	Gordon	15/7/67	Newcastle		1995		Sunderland (loan)		4	0	0	1	1	0	0	0
Ashenden	RH	Russell	4/2/61	South Ockendon		1978	1979		Wycombe Wan.	18	0	4	0	0	0	0	0
Asher	SJ	Sid	24/12/30	Portsmouth		1956		Hastings	Bedford	21	1	0	0	11	0	0	0
Ashworth	A	Alec	1/10/39	Southport	1995	1962		Luton Town	Preston NE	30	1	3	0	25	0	1	0
Austin	TW	Terry	1/2/54	Isleworth		1983		Doncaster Rovers	Stamford	43	5	2	1	10	2	0	1
Bailey	RR	Ray	16/5/44	St Neots		1971		Gillingham (loan)		1	0	0	0	0	0	0	0
Baines	SN	Stan	28/7/20	Syston		1946		Leicester City		1	0	0	0	0	0	0	0
Baker	TW	Tommy	17/8/05	Shotton	1975	1934		Brentford	Rochdale	13	0	0	1	0	0	0	0
Bancroft	PA	Paul	10/9/64	Derby		1984		Derby County	Nuneaton	16	0	1	0	0	0	0	0
Bannister	JH	Jack	1/2/29	Chesterfield		1958		Shrewsbury Town	Aldershot	24	1	0	0	0	0	0	0
Barnes	DO	David 'Bobby'	17/12/62	Kingston		1989	1991	Bournemouth	Peterborough Utd.	98	9	5	6	37	3	3	1
Barnes	MF	Michael	17/9/63	Reading		1984		Reading	Basingstoke	19	4	2	0	1	0	0	0
Baron	KP	Kevin	19/7/26	Preston	1971	1958		Southend Utd.	Gravesend	25	2	0	0	4	0	0	0
Barratt	AG	Alf	13/4/20	Corby		1938		Kettering	Stewarts & Lloyds	1	0	0	0	0	0	0	0
Barron	RW	Roger	30/6/47	Northampton		1967	1968		Bedford T	17	0	2	0	0	0	0	0
Barron	W	Bill	26/10/17	Houghton-le-Spring		1938	1950	Charlton Ath.	Kettering	166	23	0	0	4	0	0	0
Bartram	JL	James	1911			1935		Falkirk	Queen of the South	12	0	0	2	3	0	0	3
Baxter	LR	Larry	24/11/31	Leicester		1952	1953		Norwich City	17	0	0	0	2	0	0	0
Baxter	WA	Bill	23/4/39	Edinburgh		1972		Hull City	Nuneaton	41	1	1	0	4	0	0	0
Beavon	DG	David	8/12/61	Nottingham		1982		Lincoln City (loan)		2	0	0	0	0	0	0	0
Beavon	MS	Stuart	30/11/58	Wolverhampton		1990	1992	Reading	Newbury	98	6	6	9	14	1	0	3
Beckford	JN	Jason	14/2/70	Manchester		1995		Millwall	Halifax	1	1	0	2	0	0	0	0
Bedford	SG	Syd	1901	Northampton		1920	1923		Brighton & Hove A.	70	70	0	0	1	1	0	0
Belfon	F	Frank	18/2/65	Wellingborough		1981	1984		Wellingborough	78	9	3	3	15	2	0	1
Bell	M	Mickey	15/11/71	Newcastle		1989	1994		Wycombe Wan.	153	5	9	11	10	1	0	1
Bell	T	Tommy	9/11/06	Seaham Colliery	1983	1934	1937	Luton Town	Wellingborough	73	5	0	1	31	0	0	0
Bellamy	BW	Ben	22/4/1891	Wollaston	1985	1920		Wollaston	Kettering	3	0	0	0	0	0	0	0
Benjamin	IT	Ian	11/12/61	Nottingham		1984	1987	Peterborough Utd.	Cambridge Utd.	150	9	12	9	58	3	2	5
Bennett	J	Jesse		Dronfield		1933	1935	Coventry City		56	2	0	7	0	0	0	0
Benton	J	James	9/4/75	Wexford		1991	1992		Tring	10	0	0	2	1	0	0	0
Beresford	M	Marlon	2/9/69	Lincoln		1990		Sheffield Wed. (loan)		28	0	0	2	0	0	0	0
						1991		Sheffield Wed. (loan)									
Berridge	R	Reginald		Northampton		1929			Wellingborough	1	0	0	0	0	0	0	0
Berry	SA	Steve	4/4/63	Walton		1988	1990	Aldershot	Maidstone Utd.	102	7	5	9	7	2	0	1
Best	WJB	Billy	7/9/43	Glasgow		1963	19673	Pollock	Southend Utd.	243	10	18	0	49	1	6	0
						1973	19773	Southend Utd.	Bedford								
Billingham	J	Jack	3/12/14	Daventry	1981	1935		Stead & Simpson	Bristol City	3	0	0	0	0	0	0	0
Blair	A	Andy	18/12/59	Bedworth		1988		Aston Villa	Naxxar (Malta)	3	0	0	0	0	0	0	0
Blencowe	AG	Arthur	5/11/16	Brackley		1937		Brackley	Banbury	2	0	0	0	0	0	0	0
Blunt	E	Eddie	21/5/18	Tunstall		1937	1948	Port Vale	Accrington Stanley	87	8	0	2	2	3	0	0
Bodley	MJ	Mike	14/9/67	Hayes		1988		Chelsea	Barnet	20	0	0	2	0	0	0	0
Book	K	Kim	12/2/46	Bath		1969	1971	Bournemouth	Doncaster Rovers	78	11	6	0	0	0	0	0
Bosse	PL	Percy	18/10/14	Cardiff		1937	1938	Arsenal		34	1	0	3	3	0	0	0
Bowen	DL	David	7/6/28	Maesteg	1995	1947	1948		Arsenal	34	1	0	0	1	0	0	0
						1959		Arsenal									
Bowen	EC	Eddie 'Ted'	1/7/03	Goldthorpe		1927	1931	Arsenal	Bristol City	162	10	0	0	114	6	0	0
Bowen	KB	Keith	26/2/58	Northampton		1976	1981		Brentford	65	2	9	0	24	0	1	0
Bowker	K	Keith	18/4/51	West Bromwich		1976		Cambridge U (loan)		4	0	0	0	0	0	0	0
Boyd	MS	Malcolm				1926		Harpole	Rushden	2	0	0	0	0	0	0	0
Boyle	TW	Thomas	27/2/1897	Sheffield		1930	1934	Manchester Utd.	Scarborough	142	7	0	2	33	2	0	0
Bradshaw	H	Harold				1925				2	0	0	0	0	0	0	0
Brady	PJ	Paul	26/3/61	Birmingham		1981	1982	Birmingham City	Crewe Alexandra	51	7	8	3	3	0	0	0
Braidford	L	Lowington	1898	Scotland		1923		Hartlepool Utd.		5	0	0	0	1	0	0	0

Sheet No.2 - Branston to Collins

Player			Date of Birth	Place of Birth	Died	First Season	Last Season	Previous Club	Next Club	Appearances				Goals			
										League	FAC	FLC	Other	League	FAC	FLC	Other
Branston	TG	Terry	25/7/38	Rugby		1960	1966		Luton Town	246	8	17	0	2	0	0	0
Brett	FB	Frank	10/3/1899	King's Norton	1988	1923	1929	Aston Villa	Brighton & Hove A.	254	19	0	0	4	0	0	0
Brewer	AP	Anthony	20/5/32	Edmonton		1958	1960	Millwall		87	2	1	0	0	0	0	0
Bright	G	Gerry	2/12/34	Northampton		1956	1957		Wellingborough	4	0	0	0	0	0	0	0
Briscoe	JER	James	23/4/17	St Helens	1981	1946	1948	Preston NE	Wolverton	53	7	0	0	17	1	0	0
Broadfoot	J	Joe	4/3/40	Lewisham		1965		Ipswich Town	Millwall	17	1	0	0	1	0	0	0
Brodie	CTG	Charles 'Chic'	22/2/37	Duntocher		1961	1963	Wolves	Brentford	87	4	6	0	0	0	0	0
Brookes	E	Eric	3/2/44	Mapplewell		1969	1970	Barnsley	Peterborough Utd.	80	11	7	0	1	0	2	0
Brooks	JT	John	23/8/47	Paddington		1967		Ipswich Town	Guildford	1	0	0	0	0	0	0	0
Brough	NK	Neil	22/12/65	Daventry		1983	1984		Long Buckby	12	0	0	1	0	0	0	0
Brown	A	Alf	22/2/07	Chadderton		1933	1935	Oldham Athletic	Mansfield Town	55	3	0	4	1	0	0	0
Brown	AR	Richard	14/2/11	Pegswood		1934	1935	QPR	Nottm. Forest	79	5	0	7	23	0	0	4
Brown	DJ	Dennis	8/2/44	Reading		1966	1968	Swindon Town	Aldershot	46	0	2	0	10	0	1	0
Brown	IO	Ian	11/9/65	Ipswich		1994		Bristol City	Sudbury	23	0	0	0	4	0	0	0
Brown	L	Laurie	22/8/37	Shildon		1960		Darlington	Arsenal	33	3	2	0	22	3	0	0
Brown	RH	Bobby	2/5/40	Streatham		1963	1966	Watford	Cardiff City	50	2	4	0	22	1	1	0
Brown	SF	Steve	6/7/66	Northampton		1983	1993		Wycombe Wan.	173	11	10	11	22	2	1	1
Brown	WDF	Bill	8/10/31	Arbroath		1966		Tottenham H	Toronto Falcons	17	1	3	0	0	0	0	0
Brown	WY	Billy		South Inch		1922		Portsmouth		2	0	0	0	0	0	0	0
Bruck	DJ	Dietmar	19/4/44	Danzig		1972	1973	Charlton Ath.	Nuneaton	41	1	2	0	0	0	0	0
Bryant	SP	Steve	5/9/53	Islington		1976	1981	Birmingham City	Portsmouth	107	2	8	0	5	0	0	0
Buchanan	D	David	23/6/62	Newcastle		1982		Leicester City (loan)		5	0	1	0	0	0	0	0
Buchanan	J	John	19/9/51	Dingwall		1970	1974	Ross County	Cardiff City	183	15	8	3	30	3	1	0
						1981	19823	Cardiff City	Wolverton								
Buck	AR	Tony	18/8/44	Whitwell, Oxon.		1972	1973	Rochdale	Bedford	17	1	0	0	3	0	0	0
Buckby	LC	Leonard	1905	Wellingborough		1926			Wellingborough	4	0	0	0	0	0	0	0
Bukowski	DJ	David	2/11/52	Northampton		1971	1972		Blyth Spartans	13	0	0	0	0	0	0	0
Bulzis	RRB	Riccardo	22/11/74	Bedford		1991			Wellingborough	4	0	0	0	0	0	0	0
Bunce	PE	Paul	7/1/67	Coalville		1986	1987	Leicester City	Weymouth	12	0	2	0	2	0	0	0
Burn	RG	Ralph	9/11/31	Alnwick		1950			Crewe Alexandra	1	0	0	0	0	0	0	0
Burnand	WT	Walter	4/10/1894	Northampton		1920	1921		Rushden	25	1	0	0	5	0	0	0
Burnham	JJ	Jason	8/5/73	Mansfield		1991	1993		Chester City	88	6	6	8	2	0	0	0
Burns	C	Chris	9/11/67	Manchester		1994	1996	Swansea City	Gloucester	66	2	3	3	9	0	1	1
Burrows	AM	Adrian	16/1/59	Sutton-in-Ashfield		1982	1983	Mansfield Town	Plymouth Argyle	88	10	5	3	4	1	0	0
Burt	JHL	Jimmy	5/4/50	Harthill		1972		Aldershot	Rochdale	21	0	1	0	0	0	0	0
Bushell	MJ	Mark	5/6/68	Northampton		1984			Corby	1	0	0	0	0	0	0	0
Byatt	DJ	Dennis	8/8/58	Hillingdon		1979	1980	Peterborough Utd.	Wealdstone	47	2	4	0	3	0	0	0
Byrne	J	John	25/5/39	Cambuslang		1967	1968	Peterborough Utd.	Addington (SA)	40	2	2	0	4	0	0	0
Byrne	R	Ray	4/7/72	Newry		1994		Nottm. Forest	Cork City	11	1	0	3	1	0	0	0
Cahill	OF	Ollie	29/9/75	Clonmel		1994		Clonmel		2	0	1	0	0	0	0	0
Campbell	GR	Greg	13/7/65	Portsmouth		1990	1991	Plymouth Argyle		47	4	2	5	7	1	0	0
Candlin	MH	Maurice	11/11/21	Jarrow	1992	1949	1952	Partick Thistle	Shrewsbury Town	139	13	0	0	1	1	0	0
Canning	L	Larry	1/11/25	Cowdenbeath		1956		Kettering	Nuneaton	2	0	0	0	0	0	0	0
Carlton	DG	David	24/11/52	Stepney		1973	1976	Fulham	Brentford	180	6	8	0	7	1	0	0
						1980	1981	Brentford									
Carr	WG	Graham	25/10/44	Newcastle		1962	1967		York City	85	2	9	0	0	0	0	0
Carson	AM	Alec	12/11/42	Glasgow		1960	1961		Aldershot	8	0	0	0	0	0	0	0
Carter	LR	Lee	22/3/70	Dartford		1987			Boreham Wood	1	0	0	0	0	0	0	0
Cave	W	William	1907	Northampton		1927	1936			93	6	0	5	0	0	0	0
Cavener	P	Phil	2/6/61	Tynemouth		1984	1985	Gillingham	Peterborough Utd.	45	2	6	1	11	0	1	0
Cegielski	W	Wayne	11/1/56	Bedwellty		1974		Tottenham H (loan)		11	0	0	0	0	0	0	0
Chambers	L	Leonard		Northampton		1920	1921	Rushden	Rushden	28	1	0	0	0	0	0	0
Chapman	WJ	Walter		Rothwell		1924		Rothwell	Rothwell	8	1	0	0	0	0	0	0
Chard	PJ	Phil	16/10/60	Corby		1985	1987	Peterborough Utd.	Wolves	278	19	18	16	46	3	1	4
						1989	1993	Wolves	Kettering								
Chatterley	LC	Lew	15/2/45	Birmingham		1971		Aston Villa	Grimsby Town	23	4	0	0	2	0	0	0
Cherry	J	James		Wigan		1933		Wigan Borough	Walsall	10	0	0	0	2	0	0	0
Christie	DHM	Derrick	15/3/57	Bletchley		1973	1978		Cambridge Utd.	138	6	12	0	18	1	2	0
Churchman	EA	Ernest	1891	Northampton	1925	1920		Rushden Town	Wellingborough	2	0	0	0	1	0	0	0
Civil	H	Harry		Northampton		1922				2	0	0	0	0	0	0	0
Clapton	DP	Dennis	12/10/39	Hackney		1961			Arsenal	1	0	0	0	0	0	0	0
Clarke	JL	John	23/10/46	Northampton		1966	1974			233	17	12	0	1	0	0	0
Clarkson	IS	Ian	4/12/70	Solihull		1996		Stoke C		45	1	4	6	0	0	0	0
Claypole	AW	Anthony	13/2/37	Weldon		1956	1961		Cheltenham	116	6	3	0	1	0	0	0
Clifford	JC	John				1938		Crystal Palace	Bournemouth	11	0	0	0	0	0	0	0
Cobb	GE	Gary	6/8/68	Luton		1988		Luton Town (loan)		1	0	0	0	0	0	0	0
Cochrane	AF	Sandy	8/8/03	Glasgow		1933	1934	Chesterfield	Swindon Town	42	4	0	6	7	1	0	0
Cockburn	GW	George	1907	Gateshead		1926		West Ham Utd.		1	0	0	0	0	0	0	0
Cockcroft	VH	Vic	25/2/41	Harbourne		1962	1966	Wolves	Rochdale	47	2	5	0	1	0	0	0
Cockle	ES	Ernest	12/9/1896	East Ham	1966	1924	1927	Luton Town	Wigan Borough	97	7	0	0	46	0	0	0
Coe	NC	Norman	6/12/40	Swansea		1960	1965	Arsenal	King's Lynn	58	3	1	0	0	0	0	0
Coffill	PT	Peter	14/2/57	Romford		1981	1982	Torquay United	Wellingborough	69	6	8	1	3	2	0	0
Coleman	GJ	Geoff	13/5/36	Bedworth		1955	1958	Bedworth	Leamington	18	0	0	0	0	0	0	0
Coley	WE	William	17/9/16	Wolverhampton		1947	1950	Torquay United	Exeter City	104	9	0	0	7	0	0	0
Colkin	L	Lee	15/7/74	Nuneaton		1991	1994			99	4	9	5	3	0	1	0
Collins	BV	Ben	9/3/28	Kislingbury		1948	1958			213	11	0	0	0	0	0	0

Sheet No.3 - Collins D to Fairhurst

Player			Date of Birth	Place of Birth	Died	First Season	Last Season	Previous Club	Next Club	Appearances				Goals			
										League	FAC	FLC	Other	League	FAC	FLC	Other
Collins	D	Darren	24/5/67	Winchester		1988	1990	Petersfield	Aylesbury	51	7	4	6	9	0	0	2
Connell	PM	Peter	26/11/27	East Kilbride		1951		Morton		13	0	0	0	0	0	0	0
Conway	T	Thomas		Belfast		1932		Burnley		3	0	0	0	0	0	0	0
Cook	C	Colin	8/1/09	North Shields		1936	1937	Luton Town		12	0	0	0	3	0	0	0
Cook	J	Jack	27/7/1891	Sunderland		1924		Notts County		20	0	0	0	2	0	0	0
Cooke	BA	Barry	1961	Wolverhampton		1959	1961	West Bromwich A.	Wisbech	58	3	3	0	1	0	1	0
Cooke	PC	Peter		Northampton		1980				5	0	0	0	1	0	0	0
Cooper	MD	Mark	5/4/67	Watford		1996		Barnet	Welling	41	1	3	1	10	0	0	0
Corbett	R	Robert	16/3/22	North Walbottle		1957		Middlesbrough		8	0	0	0	1	0	0	0
Cordice	NA	Neil	7/4/60	Amersham		1978		Tooting & Mitcham	Wealdstone	8	1	2	0	1	0	0	0
Cornwell	JA	John	13/10/64	Bethnal Green		1993		Southend Utd. (loan)		13	0	0	0	1	0	0	0
Cottrell	AT	Alfred				1937		Bristol City	Worcester City	1	0	0	0	0	0	0	0
Cowen	JE	James	1913	Heningham	1950	1927	1928	Nelson	Southport	1	1	0	0	0	1	0	0
Coy	RA	Bobby	30/11/61	Birmingham		1986		Chester City	Aylesbury	17	0	2	1	0	0	1	0
Craig	AH	Albert	3/1/62	Glasgow		1988		Newcastle Utd. (loan)		2	0	0	0	1	0	0	0
Craven	J	Joseph	1935	Glasgow		1934	1935	St. Mirren		2	0	0	2	0	0	0	0
Crawford	GW	George	1906	Sunderland		1930		Bournemouth		2	0	0	0	0	0	0	0
Crilly	T	Tom	20/7/1895	Stockton	1960	1933	1934	Crystal Palace	Scunthorpe U	46	10	0	3	1	0	0	0
Cross	J	Jack	5/2/27	Durham		1953		Bournemouth	Sheffield Utd.	10	2	0	0	8	1	0	0
Croy	J	John	1954	Falkirk	1980	1951	1954	Third Lanark	Corby	25	1	0	0	0	0	0	0
Culpin	P	Paul	8/2/62	Kirby Muxloe		1987	1989	Coventry City	Peterborough Utd.	63	3	5	6	23	0	2	1
Curtis	LH	Leslie		Yorkshire		1938		Barnsley		2	0	0	0	1	0	0	0
Curtis	PAE	Paul	1/7/63	Woolwich		1985	1992	Charlton Ath.	Corby T	49	1	4	4	2	0	0	0
Curtis	R	Robbie	21/5/72	Mansfield		1994		Boston	King's Lynn	13	0	2	2	0	0	0	0
Daly	J	Joseph	28/12/1899	Lancaster		1927		Notts County	Luton Town	33	4	0	0	4	3	0	0
Daniels	SC	Scott	22/11/69	Benfleet		1994		Exeter City	Dover	8	0	0	0	0	0	0	0
Danks	PD	Derek	15/2/31	Cheadle		1954			Corby	1	0	0	0	0	0	0	0
Davids	NG	Neil	22/9/55	Bingley		1975		Norwich City (loan)		9	0	0	0	0	0	0	0
Davie	JG	James	7/9/22	Newton		1950	1952	Preston NE	Shrewsbury Town	75	1	0	0	1	0	0	0
Davies	AT	Arthur		Nelson		1921			Nelson	10	2	0	0	1	0	0	0
Davies	FP	Frank	1/8/03	Swansea	1970	1930	1933	Nantwich	Burton	144	18	0	2	7	6	0	0
Davies	LJ	Llewellyn	1894	Northampton	1965	1921				1	0	0	0	0	0	0	0
Davies	OT	Oliver		St Albans		1933		St. Albans		1	0	0	0	0	0	0	0
Dawes	AG	Bert	23/4/07	Frimley Green	1973	1929	1933	Frimley Green	Crystal Palace	164	18	0	0	82	16	0	0
Dawes	FW	Fred	2/5/11	Frimley Green	1989	1929	1935	Frimley Green	Crystal Palace	162	18	0	5	1	3	0	0
Dawes	IM	Ian	5/1/65	Aldershot		1985		Newcastle United		5	0	1	0	0	0	0	0
Dawson	W	William	5/2/31	Glasgow		1954	1955	Glasgow Ashfold	Corby	14	0	0	0	7	0	0	0
Deacon	R	Dicky	26/6/11	Glasgow	1986	1935		Chelsea	Lincoln City	3	1	0	0	0	1	0	0
Deakin	MRF	Mike	25/10/33	Birmingham		1959	1960	Crystal Palace	Aldershot	44	2	2	0	31	0	0	0
Dennison	RS	Bob	6/3/12	Amble	1996	1946	1947	Fulham		55	12	0	0	0	0	0	0
Denyer	PR	Peter	26/11/57	Haslemere		1979	1982	Portsmouth	Kettering T	148	6	14	2	28	1	4	1
Dickinson	A	Alfred	1915	Lancashire		1937	1938	Everton		19	0	0	3	5	0	0	1
Dixon	A	Arthur	17/11/21	Middleton		1949	1951	Hearts	Leicester City	68	9	0	0	21	5	0	0
Dixon	CH	Cecil	28/3/35	Trowbridge		1961		Newport County	Wisbech T	15	0	1	0	4	0	0	0
Docherty	J	James	21/4/26	Clydebank		1950		Celtic	Stirling Albion	1	0	0	0	0	0	0	0
Dodgin	N	Norman	1/11/21	Gateshead		1951	1952	Reading	Exeter City	19	0	0	0	1	0	0	0
Doherty	N	Neil	21/2/69	Barrow		1995		Birmingham (loan)		9	0	0	0	1	0	0	0
Donald	WR	Warren	7/10/64	Hillingdon		1984	1989	West Ham Utd.	Colchester U	188	10	11	12	13	1	0	0
Donegal	GP	Glen	20/6/69	Northampton		1986	1989		Maidstone Utd.	21	1	2	2	3	0	1	0
Dowsey	J	John	1/5/05	Gateshead	1942	1931	1933	Notts County		86	11	0	0	5	5	1	0
Draper	RW	Richard	26/9/32	Leamington Spa		1955	1956	Leamington	Rugby T	49	3	0	0	20	2	0	0
Duckhouse	E	Ted	9/4/18	Walsall	1980	1950	1951	Birmingham City	Rushden	68	3	0	0	0	0	0	0
Dunkley	MEF	Maurice	19/2/14	Kettering	1989	1936	1937		Manchester City	30	0	0	1	5	0	0	0
						1949		Kettering T	Corby T								
Dutton	CA	Charles	10/4/34	Rugeley		1955	1956	Coventry City	Leamington	10	0	0	0	2	0	0	0
East	KMG	Keith	31/10/44	Southampton		1970		Bournemouth	Crewe Alexandra	29	0	6	0	7	0	2	0
Eccles	J	Joe	1/2/06	Stoke-on-Trent	1970	1928		West Ham Utd.	Coventry City	15	3	0	0	1	0	0	0
Edelston	M	Maurice	27/4/18	Hull	1976	1952	1953	Reading	(retired)	40	5	0	0	17	0	0	0
Edwards	DS	Dean	25/2/62	Wolverhampton		1991		Exeter City	(Hong Kong)	7	0	0	0	0	0	0	0
Edwards	EJ	Evan	14/12/1898	Merthyr Tydfil		1926		Swansea City	Halifax Town	11	1	0	0	2	0	0	0
Edwards	RH	Bob	22/5/31	Guildford		1960	1961	Norwich City	King's Lynn	23	1	0	0	10	0	0	0
Edwards	SC	Sydney	16/8/12	Northampton		1934	1935	Wellingborough	Rushden	4	0	0	2	1	0	0	1
Elad	DE	Efon	5/9/70	Hillingdon		1993		FC Cologne	Cambridge Utd.	10	0	0	0	0	0	0	0
Ellwood	RJ	Reginald	1919	Worcester		1938		Worcester	Guildford	19	0	0	2	2	0	0	0
Elvy	R	Reg	25/11/20	Leeds	1991	1956	1958	Blackburn Rovers	(retired)	67	5	0	0	0	0	0	0
English	J	Jack	19/3/23	South Shields	1985	1947	1959		Rugby Town	301	20	0	0	135	8	0	0
Etheridge	BG	Brian	4/3/44	Northampton		1961	1965		Brentford	17	1	4	0	1	0	0	0
Evans	CJH	Charles	31/1/1897	Cardiff		1924		Cardiff City	Grimsby Town	17	0	0	0	2	0	0	0
Evans	GJ	Gareth	14/1/67	Coventry		1990		Rotherham Utd. (loan)		2	0	0	0	0	0	0	0
Everitt	MD	Mike	16/1/41	Clacton		1960	1966	Arsenal	Plymouth Argyle	207	8	12	0	15	1	1	0
Eyre	FMB	Fred	29/9/03	Northampton		1930		Wolverton	Rushden	1	0	0	0	0	0	0	0
Facer	A	Albert	15/7/01	Northampton		1923			Higham T	2	0	0	0	0	0	0	0
Fagan	B	Bernard	29/11/49	Houghton-le-Spring		1969		Sunderland	Scarborough	6	2	0	0	0	0	0	0
Fairbrother	J	John	12/2/41	Cricklewood		1967	1971	Peterborough Utd.	Mansfield Town	140	14	10	0	56	4	2	0
Fairfax	RJ	Ray	13/1/41	Smethwick		1968	1970	West Bromwich A.	Onley T	116	14	8	0	0	0	0	0
Fairhurst	WS	Bill	1/1/02	New Delaval	1979	1932		Nelson	Hartlepool Utd.	13	2	0	0	0	0	0	0

146

Player			Date of Birth	Place of Birth	Died	First Season	Last Season	Previous Club	Next Club	Appearances				Goals			
										League	FAC	FLC	Other	League	FAC	FLC	Other
Farmer	KJ	Kevin	24/1/60	Ramsgate		1979	1981	Leicester City	Bedworth	77	1	9	0	12	0	0	0
Farr	FE	Fred		Bristol		1935		Bristol City	Southampton	2	0	0	0	0	0	0	0
Farrell	SP	Sean	28/2/69	Watford		1991		Luton Town (loan)		4	0	1	0	1	0	0	0
Farrington	JR	John	19/6/47	Lynemouth		1974	1979	Cardiff City	Leamington	232	8	13	0	29	0	2	0
Faulkes	BK	Brian	10/4/45	Abingdon		1967	1968	Reading	Torquay United	52	3	4	0	2	0	0	0
Fee	GP	Greg	24/6/64	Halifax		1990		Sheffield Wed.(loan)		1	2	0	0	0	0	0	0
Feehan	I	Ignatius 'Sonny'	17/9/26	Dublin	1995	1950	1951	Manchester Utd.	Brentford	39	1	0	0	0	0	0	0
Felton	GM	Graham	1/3/49	Cambridge		1966	1975	Cambridge U	Barnsley	254	19	13	0	25	2	0	0
Ferrari	FW	Fred	22/5/01	Stratford	1970	1925		Leyton Town	Sheffield Wed.	18	0	0	0	0	0	0	0
Fisher	PM	Peter	17/2/20	Edinburgh		1947			Shrewsbury Town	8	0	0	0	0	0	0	0
Fitzpatrick	PJ	Paul	5/10/65	Liverpool		1993		Hamilton	Rushden	2	0	0	0	1	0	0	0
Fleming	TM	Terry	5/1/73	Marston Green		1993		Coventry City	Preston NE	31	1	2	1	1	0	0	0
Flexney	P	Paul	18/1/65	Glasgow		1988		Clyde	Kilmarnock	12	1	4	1	0	0	0	0
Flounders	AJ	Andy	13/12/63	Hull		1994		Halifax T	(Hong Kong)	2	0	0	0	0	0	0	0
Flowers	R	Ron	28/7/34	Edlington		1967	1968	Wolves	Telford U	62	6	3	0	4	0	0	0
Folds	RJ	Bob	18/4/49	Bedford		1971		Gillingham	Telford U	30	1	1	0	0	0	0	0
Foley	TC	Theo	2/3/37	Dublin		1961	1966	Exeter City	Charlton Ath.	204	6	10	0	8	2	1	0
Forbes	FJ	Fred	5/8/1894	Leith		1932		Leith	Airdrie	35	10	2	0	3	10	0	0
Forrest	J	James 'Jack'		Shildon		1922		Leyton Orient	Spennymoor U	2	0	0	0	0	0	0	0
Forster	MG	Martyn	1/2/63	Kettering		1983		Kettering T	Corby T	42	5	1	1	0	0	0	0
Fotheringham	JG	Jim	19/12/33	Hamilton	1977	1959		Arsenal		11	1	0	0	0	0	0	0
Fowler	T	Tommy	16/12/24	Prescot		1946	1961	Everton	Aldershot	521	31	0	0	84	4	0	0
Fox	MC	Matthew	13/7/71	Birmingham		1992		Birmingham City		1	0	0	0	0	0	0	0
Frain	JW	John	8/10/68	Birmingham		1996		Birmingham		13	0	0	6	0	0	0	1
Francis	SR	Sean	1/8/72	Birmingham		1993		Birmingham City		1	0	1	0	0	0	0	0
Fraser	WC	William	3/7/07	Cowpen		1926	1927	East Stirling	Aldershot	20	3	0	0	5	0	0	0
						1933		Fulham	Hartlepools Utd.								
Freeman	E	Edwin	5/6/1886	Northampton	1945	1920				25	3	0	0	2	0	0	0
Freeman	N	Neil	16/2/55	Northampton		1982		Peterborough Utd.	(retired)	22	5	3	0	0	0	0	0
Freeman	NF	Neville	25/1/25	Brixworth		1950			Wellingborough	1	0	0	0	0	0	0	0
French	JR	Jim	27/1/26	Stockton		1951		Middlesbrough	Darlington	1	0	0	0	0	0	0	0
Friar	JP	Paul	6/6/63	Glasgow		1985		Charlton Ath. (loan)		14	0	0	2	0	0	0	0
Friedmanis	E	Eddie	22/2/20	Latvia	1993	1948	1949	Peterborough U	Nuneaton	19	0	0	0	4	0	0	0
Froggatt	JL	John	13/12/45	Sutton-in-Ashfield		1978		Port Vale	Boston U	43	1	0	0	12	0	0	0
Frost	SD	Stan	19/10/22	Northampton		1946		Leicester C	Leicester C	6	0	0	0	1	0	0	0
Gage	WAJ	Wakeley	5/5/58	Desborough T		1979	1984	Desborough T	Chester City	218	17	13	5	17	4	1	0
Gale	CM	Colin	31/8/32	Pontypridd		1955	1960	Cardiff City	Wisbech T	211	9	2	0	0	1	0	0
Gallacher	B	Bernard	22/3/67	Johnstone		1993		Brighton & Hove A.	Bromsgrove Rov.	5	0	0	0	0	0	0	0
Garner	TJ	Tim	30/3/61	Hitchin		1985		Leamington	Aylesbury	2	0	0	0	0	0	0	0
Garnham	SE	Stuart	30/11/55	Selby		1974		Wolves (loan)		12	0	1	0	0	0	0	0
						1977		Peterborough U (loan)									
Garrett	ACE	Archie	17/6/19	Lesmahagow	1994	1946	1947	Hearts	Birmingham City	94	5	0	0	50	6	0	0
						1948	1950	Birmingham C	Wisbech T								
Garwood	J	Jason	23/3/69	Birmingham		1988		Leicester City (loan)		6	0	1	0	0	0	0	0
Gavin	PJ	Pat	5/6/67	Hammersmith		1992		Barnet	Wigan Ath.	14	0	0	0	4	0	0	0
Gayle	J	John	30/7/64	Bromsgrove		1996		Stoke City		13	0	0	5	1	0	0	2
Geidmintis	AJ	Tony	30/7/49	Stepney	1993	1977	1978	Watford	Halifax Town	63	1	5	0	1	0	0	0
George	HS	Herbert	1905	Wellingborough		1924	1927	Wellingborough	Rushden	22	4	0	0	2	2	0	0
Gernon	FAJ	Frederick'Irvin'	30/12/62	Birmingham		1986		Ipswich Town (loan)		57	8	1	6	1	0	0	1
						1989	1991	Reading	Kettering T								
Gibb	AS	Ally	17/2/76	Salisbury		1996		Norwich		32	0	4	3	2	0	0	0
Gilbert	DJ	David	22/6/63	Lincoln		1986	1988	Boston	Grimsby Town	120	6	10	9	21	3	2	1
Gillard	KJ	Ken	30/4/72	Dublin		1992	1993	Luton Town	Chesham	23	1	1	3	0	0	0	0
Gillespie	P	Pat	26/9/22	Bellshill		1947		Watford	Doncaster Rovers	1	0	0	0	0	0	0	0
Gilligan	JJ	John	2/5/57	Abingdon		1976		Swindon Town (loan)		5	0	0	0	1	0	0	0
Gilzean	IR	Ian	10/12/69	London		1993		Dundee	Ayr	33	1	2	3	10	0	0	0
Gleasure	PF	Peter	8/10/60	Luton		1982	1991	Millwall	Hitchin	344	25	25	18	0	0	0	0
Gormlie	WJ	Bill	1/4/11	Blackpool	1976	1935	1938	Blackburn Rovers	Lincoln City	138	3	0	7	0	0	0	0
Gould	TR	Trevor	5/3/50	Coventry		1970	1972	Coventry City	Bedford T	105	4	1	0	6	0	0	0
Graham	W	William		Preston		1921	1923	Lancaster T	Wrexham	45	4	0	0	10	0	0	0
Gray	GR	George		Sunderland		1923		Bury		11	1	0	0	0	0	0	0
Grayson	N	Neil	1/11/64	York		1994		Chesterfield	Hereford	120	3	8	10	31	0	0	3
Gregory	JC	John	11/5/54	Scunthorpe		1972	1976		Aston Villa	187	7	9	0	8	1	1	0
Grendon	FJW	Fred	5/9/1891	Farnham	1984	1920	1921		Rushden T	38	4	0	0	0	0	0	0
Griffin	FA	Frank	28/3/28	Pendlebury		1959		West Bromwich A.	Wellington T	16	1	0	0	0	0	0	0
Groome	JPG	Joseph	1/9/01	Apsley	1956	1926		Apsley T	Watford	13	0	0	0	6	0	0	0
Gunn	K	Kenneth	9/4/09	Dunfermline	1991	1937	1938	Port Vale	(retired)	74	2	0	3	1	0	0	0
Gunnell	RC	Richard	10/4/1889	Harpenden	1977	1926		Hertford	Bedford	11	2	0	0	0	1	0	0
Hails	W	Billy	19/2/35	Nettlesworth		1962	1963	Peterborough Utd.	Luton Town	59	1	3	0	13	0	0	0
Hall	JL	Jim	2/3/45	Northampton		1963	1967	Peterborough Utd.	Peterborough Utd.	124	5	12	0	35	0	4	0
						1974	1977	Peterborough Utd.	Cambridge C								
Hamill	SP	Stewart	22/1/60	Glasgow		1985		Leicester City	Scarborough	3	0	0	1	1	0	0	1
Hammond	L	Leonard	12/9/01	Rugby	1983	1924	1932	Rugby T	Notts County	301	24	0	0	0	1	0	0
Harmon	DJ	Darren	30/1/73	Northampton		1992	1994	Shrewsbury Town	Kettering T	89	5	3	9	12	0	0	1
Harrington	JW	Jack		Hednesford		1928		Wolves	Brierley Hill	8	0	0	0	0	0	0	0
Harrison	GM	Gary	12/3/75	Northampton		1993	1994	Aston Villa	King's Lynn	7	0	0	1	0	0	0	0

Sheet No.5 - Harron to Keirnan J

Player			Date of Birth	Place of Birth	Died	First Season	Last Season	Previous Club	Next Club	Appearances				Goals			
										League	FAC	FLC	Other	League	FAC	FLC	Other
Harron	J	Joe	19/3/1900	Langley Park	1961	1921		Hull City	Sheffield Wed.	18	2	0	0	1	0	0	0
Harvey	BR	Bryan	26/8/38	Stepney		1963	1967	Blackpool	Kettering T	165	3	13	0	0	0	0	0
Haskins	AJ	Anthony	26/7/35	Northampton		1959	1961		Cheltenham T	8	0	0	0	0	0	0	0
Hatton	RJ	Bob	10/4/47	Hull		1968		Bolton Wanderers	Carlisle Utd.	33	3	0	0	7	11	0	0
Hawke	WR	Warren	20/9/70	Durham		1992		Sunderland (loan)		7	0	0	0	1	0	0	0
Hawkings	B	Barry	7/11/31	Birmingham		1957	1958	Lincoln City	Gravesend	64	5	0	0	25	2	0	0
Hawkins	PM	Peter	18/12/51	Swansea		1968	1973		Bedfford	61	3	2	0	10	1	0	0
Hawtin	LC	Leonard	2/7/1892	Northampton		1920	1922			10	2	0	0	0	0	0	0
Haycox	JH	Jack	1910	Cheltenham		1938		Torquay United	Peterborough U	17	1	0	1	6	0	0	0
Hayes	AWP	Austin	15/7/58	Hammersmith	1986	1983	1984	Millwall	Barnet	63	9	4	2	14	0	0	0
Haywood	RJ	Ray	12/1/49	Dudley		1976	1977	Shrewsbury Town	Kidderminster H.	16	0	1	0	2	0	0	0
Hazledine	D	Don	10/7/29	Derby		1954		Derby County	Boston U	22	1	0	0	4	0	0	0
Heaselgrave	SE	Sammy	1/10/16	Smethwick	1975	1946	1947	West Bromwich A.	Boston U	42	5	0	0	4	1	0	0
Heeley	DM	Mark	8/9/59	Peterborough		1979	1982	Arsenal	Aylesbury	92	7	8	3	5	0	1	0
Henry	CA	Charlie	13/2/62	Acton		1986		Swindon Town (loan)		4	0	0	0	1	0	0	0
Henson	GH	George	25/12/11	Stony Stratford		1932	1934	Wolverton	Wolves	43	6	0	3	23	1	0	4
Heslop	B	Brian	4/8/47	Carlisle		1970	1971	Sunderland	Workington	50	4	1	0	8	1	0	0
Hewison	R	Bob	25/3/1889	Backworth	1964	1920	1924	Newcastle United		99	9	0	0	8	1	0	0
Hewitt	JJ	John 'Joss'	15/6/11	Evenwood		1935	1938	Norwich City	Southport	83	2	0	5	14	1	0	0
Hicks	TG	Thomas	1903	Trehafod		1928		Nottm. Forest	Chester	5	0	0	0	0	0	0	0
Higgins	T	Thomas		Glasgow		1934		Hearts	Scunthorpe U	3	0	0	0	0	0	0	0
Hill	DR	David	28/9/53	Kettering		1970			Kettering	1	0	0	0	0	0	0	0
Hill	RW	Richard	20/9/63	Hinckley		1985	1986	Nuneaton	Watford	86	5	6	6	46	3	0	3
Hinson	RH	Ronald	9/10/15	Chelveston		1933	1935	Irchester	Rushden	8	2	0	0	4	0	0	0
Hitchcock	KJ	Kevin	5/10/62	Custom House		1990		Chelsea (loan)		17	0	0	1	0	0	0	0
Hobbs	EC	Ernest	1912	Wellingborough		1934	1935	Wellingborough	Exeter City	9	1	0	3	0	1	0	0
Hobbs	RV	Ralph		Toddington		1923		Toddington		1	0	0	0	0	0	0	0
Hold	JD	John	28/3/48	Southampton		1971	1972	Bournemouth	Weymouth	44	0	1	0	11	0	0	0
Holmes	MA	Mick	9/9/65	Blackpool		1992		Carlisle Utd.	Telford U	6	0	0	0	0	0	0	0
Holt	D	David		Northampton		1936				1	0	0	0	0	0	0	0
Holton	CC	Cliff	29/4/29	Oxford	1996	1961	1962	Watford	Crystal Palace	62	3	3	0	50	3	1	0
Horne	AT	Alf	6/9/26	Brixworth		1948			Corby T	1	0	0	0	0	0	0	0
Hoten	RV	Ralph	27/12/1896	Pinxton	1978	1924	1929	Luton Town	QPR	197	16	0	0	75	9	0	0
Hoult	AA	Alfred	9/7/15	Ashby-de-la-Zouch		1937		Notts County		9	1	0	0	0	0	0	0
Hudson	GA	George	14/3/37	Manchester		1965	1966	Coventry City	Tranmere Rovers	18	0	2	0	6	0	0	0
Huffer	P	Phil	23/1/32	Bedworth		1954		Derby County		1	0	0	0	0	0	0	0
Hughes	DJ	Darren	6/10/65	Prescot		1994		Port Vale	Exeter City	21	0	0	1	0	0	0	0
Hughes	TG	Gwyn	7/5/22	Blaenau Ffestiniog		1946	1955		Bedford T	226	20	0	0	15	4	0	0
Hunt	RR	Bobby	1/10/42	Colchester		1963	1965	Colchester Utd.	Millwall	45	0	2	0	13	0	2	0
						1972		Charlton Ath. (loan)									
Hunter	RI	Roy	29/10/73	Middlesbrough		1995		W.B.A.		70	3	4	8	6	0	0	1
Hurel	E	Eli	10/4/15	Jersey		1938		Everton		12	0	0	2	2	0	0	0
Hurrell	WT	Billy	15/9/55	Newcastle		1972				5	0	0	0	0	0	0	0
Hutchinson	CM	Mark	12/11/63	Stoke-on-Trent		1984		Leicester City	Nuneaton	2	0	0	1	0	0	0	0
Hyslop	CT	Chris	14/6/72	Watford		1993		Southend Utd. (loan)		8	0	0	0	0	0	0	0
Inglis	WW	Bill	2/3/1897	Kirkcaldy	1968	1930	1931	Manchester Utd.	(retired)	62	5	0	0	0	0	0	0
Ingram	GP	Godfrey	26/10/59	Luton		1979		Luton Town (loan)		10	0	0	0	4	0	0	0
Isaac	WH	William	16/5/35	Pontypridd		1959		Stoke City	Hereford U	8	0	0	0	0	0	0	0
Jackson	LW	Len	6/9/22	Birmingham		1948		Birmingham City		2	0	0	0	0	0	0	0
James	R	Ron	16/3/22	Birmingham		1948		Birmingham City	Kidderminster H	4	0	0	0	1	0	0	0
Jayes	CG	Carl	15/3/54	Leicester		1977	1979	Leicester City	Leamington	68	3	6	0	0	0	0	0
Jeffrey	WG	Billy	25/10/56	Clydebank		1982	1983	Blackpool	Kettering	54	5	2	1	6	1	0	0
Jeffs	TE	Thomas	3/8/1900	Peterborough	1971	1921	1927	Rugby		143	17	0	0	0	0	0	0
Jenkins	RJ	Randolph	5/9/23	Sligo		1946	1947	Walsall	Fulham	17	3	0	0	6	1	0	0
Jennings	HW	Bill	7/1/20	Norwich	1969	1938	1946		Ipswich Town	11	0	0	1	2	0	0	0
Jennings	W	Bill	25/2/1891	Bulwell		1926		Luton Town		3	0	0	0	0	0	0	0
Jobey	G	George	1/7/1885	Heddon	1962	1920	1921	Leicester City	Wolves (mgr)	78	5	0	0	2	1	0	0
John	M	Malcolm	9/12/50	Bridgend		1973		Bristol Rovers (loan)		41	2	0	0	8	0	0	0
						1974		Bristol Rovers	Trowbridge								
Johnson	DD	David	10/3/67	Northampton		1989	1991		Rushden	47	2	1	4	0	0	0	0
Johnson	I	Ian	14/2/69	Newcastle		1988		Gateshead	Weymouth	3	0	0	1	0	0	0	0
Johnson	PR	Percy	13/12/1899	Northampton	1983	1921	1922		Wellingborough	11	1	0	0	0	0	0	0
Johnston	WJ	Willie	3/9/48	Sunderland		1967			Durham	1	0	0	0	0	0	0	0
Jones	B	Bernard	10/4/34	Coventry		1953	1955		Cardiff City	43	4	0	0	16	0	0	0
Jones	BR	Bryn	20/5/31	Swansea	1990	1963		Bournemouth	Watford	7	0	0	0	0	0	0	0
Jones	H	Herbert		Wolverton		1926		Wolverton		5	0	0	0	0	0	0	0
Jones	JT	John	25/11/16	Holywell		1938	1947	Port Vale	Oldham Athletic	71	8	0	2	0	0	0	0
Jones	RS	Bobby	28/10/38	Bristol		1966		Bristol Rovers	Swindon Town	17	1	0	0	1	0	0	0
Jordan	G	Gerry	4/4/49	Seaham		1966				1	0	0	0	0	0	0	0
Kane	P	Peter	4/4/39	Petershill		1959		Queen's Park	Arsenal	46	1	2	0	24	1	0	0
						1963		Arsenal	Crewe Alexandra								
Kavanagh	PJ	Peter	1911	Ireland		1932		Celtic		1	0	0	0	0	0	0	0
Kendall	MI	Mark	10/12/61	Nuneaton		1982		Aston Villa	Birmingham City	11	0	1	3	0	0	0	0
Key	RM	Richard	13/4/56	Coventry		1982		Cambridge Utd. (loan)		2	0	0	0	0	0	0	0
Kiernan	DJ	Daniel	16/12/73	Northampton		1991			Ayr	9	0	0	0	0	0	0	0
Kiernan	J	Joe	22/10/42	Coatbridge		1963	1971	Sunderland	Kettering T	308	19	25	0	13	0	1	0

148

Sheet No.6 - Kilkelly to Maddison

Player			Date of Birth	Place of Birth	Died	First Season	Last Season	Previous Club	Next Club	Appearances				Goals			
										League	FAC	FLC	Other	League	FAC	FLC	Other
Kilkelly	TF	Tom	22/8/55	Galway		1974		Leicester City (loan)		4	0	0	0	0	0	0	0
Kilsby	RH	Reginald	23/8/10	Wollaston		1934		Wellingborough	Scunthorpe U	1	0	0	0	0	0	0	0
King	FAR	Fred 'Bobby'	19/9/19	Northampton		1937	1938		Wolves	99	2	0	1	23	0	0	0
						1947	1949	Wolves	Rushden								
Kirby	RN	Ryan	6/9/74	Chingford		1996		Doncaster	Stevenage	1	0	0	0	0	0	0	0
Kirkup	BA	Brian	16/4/32	Slough		1958	1959	Reading	Aldershot	26	2	0	0	7	2	0	0
Knight	BM	Brian	28/3/49	Dundee		1969		Huddersfield T	Cambridge C	12	1	0	0	0	0	0	0
Knox	T	Tommy	5/9/39	Glasgow		1967	1968	Mansfield Town	St. Mirren	30	1	2	0	0	1	0	0
Kruse	PK	Pat	30/11/53	Biggleswade		1981		Brentford (loan)		18	0	0	0	0	0	0	0
Krzywicki	RL	Dick	2/2/47	Penley		1973		Huddersfield T (loan)		8	0	0	0	3	0	0	0
Kurila	J	John	10/4/41	Glasgow		1962		Celtic	Bristol City	148	3	11	0	4	0	0	0
						1963	1967	Bristol City	Southend								
Laird	DS	David	11/2/36	Rutherglen		1960		St. Mirren	Folkestone	12	1	1	0	1	0	0	0
Lamb	PD	Paul	12/9/74	Plumstead		1992			Buckingham	3	0	1	0	0	0	0	0
Large	F	Frank	26/1/40	Leeds		1962	1963	QPR	Swindon Town	220	17	13	0	88	5	3	0
						1966	1967	Oldham Ath.	Leicester City								
						1969	1972	Fulham	Chesterfield								
Lauderdale	JH	Jock	27/11/08	Dumfries	1965	1936	1938	Coventry City	Nuneaton	47	1	0	1	10	0	0	0
Leaburn	CW	Carl	30/3/69	Lewisham		1989		Charlton Ath. (loan)		9	0	0	0	0	0	0	0
Leck	DA	Derek	8/2/37	Northbourne		1958	1965	Millwall	Brighton & Hove A.	246	10	11	0	45	3	1	0
Lee	C	Christian	8/10/76	Aylesbury		1996			Doncaster	34	3	1	7	7	0	2	0
Lee	TC	Trevor	3/7/54	Lewisham		1984		Cardiff City	Fulham	24	4	2	2	0	2	0	0
Leek	K	Ken	26/7/35	Ynysybwl		1955	1957		Leicester City	87	6	1	0	31	2	0	0
						1964	1965	Birmingham C	Bradford C								
Leonard	GE	Gary	23/3/62	Northampton		1979	1980		Kettering T	2	0	0	0	0	0	0	0
Lewis	R	Russell	15/9/56	Blaengwynfi		1983	1985	Swindon Town	Kettering T	132	10	7	6	6	0	0	0
Liddle	DN	David	21/5/57	Bedford		1977	1978		Bedford	31	2	5	0	3	0	0	0
Lincoln	A	Andy	17/5/02	Seaham Harbour	1977	1928		Millwall	Stockport Co.	2	0	0	0	0	0	0	0
Lindsay	DM	Duncan	1907	Cambuslang		1933		Bury	Hartlepool Utd.	1	0	0	0	0	0	0	0
Lines	B	Barry	16/5/42	Bletchley		1960	1969	Bletchley U	Milton Keynes	266	10	18	0	48	1	1	0
Litt	SE	Steve	21/5/54	Carlisle		1977		Minnesota Kicks	Minnesota Kicks	20	2	0	0	0	0	0	0
Little	J	Jack	18/9/04	Dunston-on-Tyne	1988	1935	1937	Chester City	Exeter City	57	1	0	1	1	0	0	0
Livesey	CE	Charlie	6/2/38	West Ham		1964	1965	Watford	Brighton & Hove A.	28	1	4	0	4	0	2	0
Llewellyn	HA	Herbert	5/2/39	Golborne		1962	1963	Port Vale	Walsall	1	0	1	0	0	0	0	0
Loasby	AA	Alan	19/3/37	Wellingborough		1958		Luton Town	Wellingborough	2	0	0	0	0	0	0	0
Loasby	H	Harry		Wellingborough		1927	1929		Gillingham	27	3	0	0	25	3	0	0
Lockett	WC	William	23/4/1893	Tipton	1974	1920	1925	Wolves	Kidderminster H.	185	16	0	0	68	9	0	0
Logan	D	David	5/12/63	Middlesbrough		1986	1987	Mansfield Town	Halifax Town	41	1	3	1	1	0	0	0
Longhurst	DJ	David	15/1/65	Northampton	1990	1987	1988	Halifax Town	Peterborough Utd.	37	2	3	1	7	0	1	1
Lovatt	HA	Harry	18/8/05	Audley		1931		Notts County	Macclesfield	14	4	0	0	7	4	0	0
Lowery	H	Harry	26/2/18	Moor Row		1946	1948	West Bromwich A.	Bromsgrove	76	16	0	0	2	0	0	0
Lyman	CC	Colin	9/3/14	Northampton	1986	1934	1937	Southend Utd.	Tottenham H	86	2	0	5	29	0	0	1
Lyne	NGF	Neil	4/4/70	Leicester		1996		Hereford	Kettering	1	0	0	0	0	0	0	0
Lyon	DG	David	18/1/51	Northwich		1977		Cambridge Utd.	Cambridge C	6	0	0	0	0	0	0	0
Mabee	GL	Gary	1/2/55	Oxford		1974	1975	Tottenham H	(retired)	33	1	4	0	13	0	0	0
McAleer	J	Joseph	8/3/10	Blythswood		1933		Rochdale	Lincoln City	8	0	0	0	6	0	0	0
McCaffrey	J	Jim	12/10/51	Luton		1978	1979	Portsmouth	(retired)	57	1	5	0	6	0	1	0
McCartney	JJ	Jimmy	30/3/09	Washington	1976	1938		Millwall	South Shields	22	0	0	2	7	0	0	0
McClean	CA	Christian	17/10/63	Colchester		1991		Swansea City	Chelmsford	19	1	0	2	3	0	0	1
McCoy	W	Wilf 'Tim'	4/3/21	Birmingham		1948	1949	Portsmouth	Brighton & Hove A.	60	8	0	0	0	0	0	0
McCulloch	ABR	Adam	4/6/20	Crossford		1949	1951	Third Lanark	Shrewsbury Town	89	10	0	0	36	3	0	0
McCulloch	T	Tommy	25/12/21	Dumfries		1949		Queen of the South	Bradford City	2	0	0	0	0	0	0	0
McCullough	K	Keillor		Larne		1937	1938	Manchester City		35	0	0	2	1	0	0	1
McFarlane	J	John		Shettleston		1932		Halifax Town	Kiddermister H.	3	2	0	0	1	1	0	0
McGleish	JJ	John	9/11/51	Airdrie		1970	1972		Wellingborough	8	0	0	0	0	0	0	0
McGoldrick	EJP	Eddie	30/4/65	London		1986	1988	Nuneaton	Crystal Palace	107	7	9	7	9	1	0	1
McGowan	A	Andy	17/5/56	Corby		1975	1977	Corby	Irthlingborough	105	1	5	0	14	0	0	0
McGuire	JP	James	1911	Edinburgh		1932	1935	Celtic	Brooklyn Wan.	70	12	0	3	0	0	0	0
McIlvenny	P	Paddy	1900	Belfast		1928		Shelbourne	Boston	8	0	0	0	2	0	0	0
McKechnie	JP	John		Inverness		1920		Newcastle United	Exeter City	11	0	0	0	0	0	0	0
McKee	RT	Ray	16/2/26	Finchley		1946		Finchley T		5	0	0	0	0	0	0	0
McKenna	MJ	Mike	3/11/16	Darkley	1974	1946		Bromsgrove		4	0	0	0	0	0	0	0
Mackie	JA	Alex	23/2/03	Belfast	1984	1935	1936	Portsmouth	(retired)	19	0	0	0	0	0	0	0
Mackin	J	John	18/11/43	Glasgow		1965	1968		Lincoln City	101	4	7	0	11	0	2	0
McLachlan	ER	Edwin	24/9/03	Glasgow	1970	1930		Mansfield T	Mansfield T	11	0	0	0	1	0	0	0
McLain	T	Tom	19/1/22	Linton	1995	1952	1955	Sunderland	Wellingborough	96	5	0	0	11	0	0	0
McMenemy	F	Frank	1910	Rutherglen		1933	1935	Airdrie	Crystal Palace	57	3	0	5	3	0	0	0
McMenemy	PC	Paul	5/11/66	Farnborough		1986		West Ham Utd. (loan)		4	0	0	0	2	0	0	0
McNamara	B	Brett	8/7/72	Newark		1994		Stamford	King's Lynn	1	0	0	1	0	0	0	0
McNaughton	WF	Bill	8/12/05	Poplar	1980	1928	1929	Peterborough	Gateshead	11	1	0	0	2	0	0	0
McNeil	R	Richard 'Dixie'	16/1/47	Melton Mowbray		1969	1971	Corby T	Lincoln City	85	11	6	0	33	5	0	0
McParland	IJ	Ian	4/10/61	Edinburgh		1992		Lincoln City	(Hong Kong)	11	3	0	3	3	1	0	3
McPartland	D	Des	5/10/47	Middlesbrough		1969		Carlisle Utd.	Hartlepool Utd.	6	0	0	0	0	0	0	0
McPherson	KA	Keith	11/9/63	Greenwich		1985	1989	West Ham Utd.	Reading	182	12	9	13	8	0	1	0
McPhillips	T	Terry	1/10/68	Manchester		1989			Halifax Town (loan)	1	1	0	1	0	0	0	0
Maddison	LR	Lee	8/10/72	Bristol		1995		Bristol Rovers	Dundee	55	3	4	5	0	0	0	0

Player			Date of Birth	Place of Birth	Died	First Season	Last Season	Previous Club	Next Club	Appearances				Goals			
										League	FAC	FLC	Other	League	FAC	FLC	Other
Mahoney	AJ	Tony	29/9/59	Barking		1981		Fulham (loan)		6	0	5	0	0	0	2	0
Malcolm	AA	Alex	13/2/56	Hamilton		1976		Luton Town	Dunstable	2	0	0	0	0	0	0	0
Maloney	RJH	Robert	8/6/03	Thringstone	1981	1926	1931	Peterborough U	Shelbourne	183	11	0	0	4	0	0	0
Mann	AG	Adrian	12/7/67	Northampton		1983	1987		Newport County	81	6	4	6	5	0	0	1
Marston	M	Maurice	24/3/29	Trimdon		1953	1956	Sunderland	Kettering T	149	6	0	0	2	0	0	0
Martin	D	Don	15/2/44	Corby		1962	1967		Blackburn Rovers	228	6	18	0	70	1	11	0
						1975	1977	Blackburn Rovers	Hitchin								
Martin	D	Dave	25/4/63	East Ham		1994		Bristol City (loan)		19	0	0	3	1	0	0	2
Martinez	E	Eugene	6/7/57	Chelmsford		1983		Newport Co. (loan)		12	0	0	0	2	0	0	0
Massey	S	Steve	28/3/58	Denton		1981	1982	Peterborough Utd.	Hull City	60	5	4	3	25	1	3	1
Matthews	PW	Paul	30/9/46	Leicester		1978		Rotherham U (loan)		13	0	0	0	0	0	0	0
Maxwell	K	Ken	11/2/28	Glasgow		1950		Kilmarnock	Bradford	2	0	0	0	0	0	0	0
Mayes	AK	Alan	11/12/53	Edmonton		1975		Watford (loan)		10	0	0	0	4	0	0	0
Mead	PS	Peter	9/9/56	Luton		1977	1978	Luton Town	Hitchin	77	1	6	0	4	0	0	0
Melville	J	Jim	15/3/09	Barrow	1961	1934	1935	Hull City		20	0	0	4	0	0	0	1
Millar	J	John	8/12/66	Coatbridge		1986		Chelsea (loan)		1	1	0	2	0	0	0	0
Miller	RL	Roger	18/8/38	Northampton		1956	1958		Wellingborough	4	0	0	0	1	0	0	0
Mills	RWG	Roly	22/6/33	Daventry		1954	1963			305	13	6	0	30	1	2	0
Mitchell	A	Andrew	20/4/07	Coxhoe	1971	1933		Hull City	Rossendale U	18	4	0	2	3	0	0	0
Mitchell	AJ	Bert	22/1/22	Stoke-on-Trent		1949	1950	Blackburn Rovers	Luton Town	81	9	0	0	21	8	0	0
Molloy	W	William	1900	Gateshead		1924		Spen	Ashington	3	0	0	0	0	0	0	0
Moore	G	Graham	7/3/41	Hengoed		1965	1966	Manchester Utd.	Charlton Ath.	53	1	5	0	10	0	2	0
Moore	J	John	21/12/43	Harthill		1974		Luton Town	Hitchin	14	0	2	0	0	0	0	0
Moran	J	Jimmy	6/3/35	Wishaw		1960	1961	Norwich City	Darlington	24	1	0	0	6	1	0	0
Morley	TW	Trevor	20/3/61	Nottingham		1985	1987	Nuneaton	Manchester City	107	6	10	7	39	2	4	0
Morrall	AD	Alf	1/7/16	Duddeston		1946	1947	Redditch	Newport County	34	10	0	0	11	8	0	0
Morritt	GR	Gordon	8/2/42	Rotherham		1968	1969	Doncaster Rovers	York City	42	3	1	0	0	0	0	0
Morrow	HJE	Hugh	9/7/30	Larne		1956		Leamington	Kettering	30	0	0	0	3	0	0	0
Mortimer	R	Bob	1/4/08	Bolton		1931	1932	Bolton Wanderers	Brentford	62	3	0	0	22	0	0	0
Mountfield	DL	Derek	2/11/62	Liverpool		1995		Carlisle	Walsall	4	0	0	0	0	0	0	0
Muir	M	Malcolm		Campbeltown		1930		Aberdeen		3	0	0	0	0	0	0	0
Muir	M	Maurice	19/3/63	Wimbledon		1979		Crystal Palace	Leamington	28	8	1	0	0	1	0	0
						1981	1983	Banbury	Kettering								
Mulgrew	T	Tommy	13/4/29	Motherwell		1950	1952	Morton	Newcastle United	8	0	0	0	1	0	0	0
Mundee	BG	Brian	12/1/64	Hammersmith		1983	1985	Bournemouth	Cambridge Utd.	100	8	6	4	3	1	0	0
Murphy	E	Eddie	13/5/24	Hamilton		1949	1950	Morton	Barnsley	71	10	0	0	15	1	0	0
Myers	EC	Colin	1894	Chapeltown		1922	1924	Aberdare Ath.	QPR	72	3	0	0	29	3	0	0
Neal	G	George	29/12/19	Wellingborough		1946				3	0	0	0	0	0	0	0
Neal	PG	Phil	20/2/51	Irchester		1968	1974		Liverpool	187	12	9	0	28	1	1	0
Nebbeling	GM	Gavin	15/5/63	Johannesburg, SA		1985		Crystal Palace (loan)		11	0	0	1	0	0	0	0
Needham	GW	George	1894	Staveley		1923	1924	Gillingham	Worksop	35	1	0	0	1	0	0	0
Newman	R	Ron	1/5/33	Pontypridd		1954	1955		Coventry City	18	0	0	0	5	0	0	0
Newton	F	Frank	1902	Romiley		1922	1923	Bradford City	Halifax T	41	4	0	0	0	0	0	0
Norris	OP	Ollie	1/4/29	Derry		1958		Bournemouth	Ashford	14	1	0	0	1	0	0	0
Norton	DW	David	3/3/65	Cannock		1994		Hull City	Hereford United	82	3	4	4	0	0	0	0
Oakley	JE	James	10/11/1901	Tynemouth	1972	1931	1932	Reading	Kettering T	33	1	0	0	0	0	0	0
Oakley	K	Ken	9/5/29	Rhymney		1954		Cardiff City	Ebbw Vale	13	0	0	0	6	0	0	0
Odell	GW	George	1/16/01	Hoddesdon	1971	1927	1931	St. Albans	Wigan Borough	147	11	0	0	10	0	0	0
O'Donnell	C	Chris	26/5/68	Newcastle		1987		Ipswich Town (loan)		1	0	0	0	0	0	0	0
O'Donnell	W	Willie	9/8/24	Clydebank		1951	1953	Partick Thistle	Shrewsbury Town	105	4	0	0	44	0	0	0
O'Donoghue	MG	Mike	13/9/56	Redhill		1979		Southampton (loan)		4	0	0	0	1	0	0	0
Olah	B	Bela	8/6/38	Hungary		1958	1960	Bedford	Wisbech T	42	1	0	0	8	0	0	0
Oman	AJ	Alan	6/10/52	Northampton		1970	1974		Wellingborough	88	7	1	0	3	0	0	0
O'Neil	J	Joe	15/8/31	Glasgow		1957	1958	Leicester City	Bath C	28	0	0	0	4	0	0	0
O'Neill	T	Tommy	2/2/58	Glasgow		1983		Cambridge Utd.	Royston	43	5	2	1	6	1	0	0
O'Rourke	J	John	1912	Bolton		1935	1938	Bury		14	0	0	2	1	0	0	0
O'Rourke	P	Peter	14/3/03	Newmains		1925		Bradford	Norwich C	2	0	0	0	0	0	0	0
O'Shea	DE	Danny	26/3/63	Kennington		1994		Cambridge Utd.	Rushden & D	80	3	6	5	1	0	0	0
Ovendale	MJ	Mark	22/11/73	Leicester		1994		Wisbech T	Barry Town (Barri)	6	0	0	2	0	0	0	0
Owen	R	Bobby	17/10/47	Farnworth		1976		Carlisle U (loan)		5	0	0	0	0	0	0	0
Oxley	RL	Richard	10/4/1893	Wallsend	1953	1924		QPR		1	0	0	0	0	0	0	0
Oxley	W	William		Wallsend		1926		Merthyr T	Durham	3	0	0	0	1	0	0	0
Page	LA	Louis	27/3/1899	Kirkdale	1959	1922	1924	Stoke City	Burnley	122	7	0	0	24	2	0	0
Page	W	William	19/9/1896	Lancashire	1981	1922		Cardiff C	Bideford T	13	0	0	0	1	0	0	0
Park	O	Ollie	7/2/05	Darlington		1931	1933	Newcastle United	Hartlepool Utd.	75	5	2	0	0	0	0	0
Park	RC	Bobby	3/7/46	Edinburgh		1972	1973	Peterborough Utd.	Hartlepool Utd.	24	0	1	0	0	0	0	0
Parker	S	Sean	23/8/73	Newcastle		1991	1992		Rushden	10	0	1	0	0	0	0	0
Parris	JE	Eddie	31/1/11	Chepstow		1937	1938	Luton Town	Cheltenham T	25	0	0	1	7	0	0	0
Parrish	S	Sean	14/3/72	Wrexham		1996		Doncaster		39	1	3	3	8	0	0	1
Parsons	MC	Mark	24/2/75	Luton		1991	1993		Kettering T	51	2	3	4	0	0	0	0
Parton	JJ	Jeff	24/2/53	Swansea		1975	1977	Burnley	Irthlingborough	25	1	4	0	0	0	0	0
Partridge	AE	Albert	2/13/01	Birmingham	1966	1933		Bradford City		2	0	0	0	0	0	0	0
Pascoe	J	Jason	15/2/70	Jarrow		1994		Clipston	King's Lynn	15	1	1	2	0	0	0	0
Patching	M	Martin	1/11/58	Rotherham		1982		Watford (loan)		6	0	0	0	1	0	0	0
Patmore	WJ	Warren	14/8/71	Kingsbury		1993	1994	Millwall	Yeovil T	21	0	0	0	2	0	0	0
Patterson	RL	Ron	30/10/29	Gateshead		1952	1961	Middlesbrough	Rothwell	300	17	0	0	5	0	0	0

Sheet No.8 - Payne to Scott DP

Player			Date of Birth	Place of Birth	Died	First Season	Last Season	Previous Club	Next Club	Appearances				Goals			
										League	FAC	FLC	Other	League	FAC	FLC	Other
Payne	IEH	Irving 'Joe'	29/6/21	Briton Ferry		1951		Scunthorpe Utd.	(coach)	32	1	0	0	6	1	0	0
Peacock	RJ	Robert	18/12/37	Rushden		1957		Rushden T	Kettering T	2	1	0	0	0	0	0	0
Pease	WH	Billy	30/9/1898	Leeds	1955	1920	1925	Leeds City	Middlesbrough	246	19	0	0	45	4	0	0
Peer	D	Dean	8/8/	Stourbridge		1995		Walsall		63	2	5	9	1	0	2	0
Perkins	GS	Glen	12/10/60	Little Billing		1978			Kettering T	1	0	0	0	0	0	0	0
Perrin	SC	Steve	13/2/52	Paddington		1981	1982	Hillingdon	Wycombe	22	3	1	2	6	1	0	0
Perry	MA	Mick	4/4/64	Wimbledon		1984		West Brom. Alb. (loan)		4	0	0	0	0	0	0	0
Perryman	G	Gerry	3/10/47	West Haddon		1966			Colchester Utd.	1	0	0	0	0	0	0	0
Phillips	IA	Ian	23/4/59	Edinburgh		1982	1983	Peterborough Utd.	Colchester Utd.	42	5	5	3	1	0	0	0
Phillips	LM	Les	7/1/63	Lambeth		1993		Oxford United	Marlow	26	1	2	3	0	0	0	0
Phillips	R	Ralph	9/8/33	Houghton-le-Spring		1958	1960	Middlesbrough	Darlington	83	4	2	0	1	0	0	0
Phillips	SE	Steve	4/8/54	Edmonton		1975	1976	Birmingham City	Brentford	126	5	10	0	38	2	3	0
						1980	1981	Brentford	Southend U								
Pickering	PB	Peter	24/3/26	York		1955	1957	Chelsea	(South Africa)	86	5	0	0	0	0	0	0
Pinchbeck	CB	Cliff	20/1/25	Cleethorpes	1996	1951		Port Vale	Bath C	3	0	0	0	3	0	0	0
Platt	R	Richard		Huyton		1937	1938	Tranmere Rovers		3	0	0	2	0	0	0	0
Poole	AJ	Andy	6/7/60	Chesterfield		1978	1981	Mansfield Town	Wolves	141	5	11	0	0	0	0	0
Poole	K	Kevin	21/7/63	Bromsgrove		1984		Aston Villa (loan)		3	0	0	0	0	0	0	0
Poole	KJ	Ken	2/7/33	Blaencwm		1956		Swansea City		4	0	0	0	0	0	0	0
Poppy	APC	Arthur	6/1/61	Yeovil		1977				1	0	0	0	0	0	0	0
Postlethwaite	TW	Tom	4/9/09	Haverthwaite		1937	1938	Bradford	Watford	61	1	0	3	1	0	0	0
Potter	FL	Len		Bedford		1934	1935	Bedford	Wellingborough	20	0	0	0	6	0	0	0
Potts	HJ	Henry	23/1/25	Carlisle		1950		Pegasus	Kettering T	10	0	0	0	0	0	0	0
Poyntz	WI	Bill	18/3/1894	Tylorstown	1966	1924		Doncaster Rovers	Bradford	29	1	0	0	4	0	0	0
Preece	AP	Andy	27/3/67	Evesham		1988		Evesham U	Worcester C	1	0	1	1	0	0	0	0
Preston	RJ	Richard	7/5/76	Basildon		1993			Corby T	1	0	0	1	0	0	0	0
Price	E	Eric	3/9/05	Hemsworth	1976	1927		Norwich City	Torquay United	4	0	0	0	2	0	0	0
Price	RJ	Ray	30/11/48	Northampton		1966	1967		Corby T	7	0	0	0	0	0	0	0
Quinney	HJ	Jesse	15/10/22	Rugby		1946			Banbury U	3	0	0	0	0	0	0	0
Quow	TS	Trevor	28/9/60	Peterborough		1988	1991	Gillingham	(Hong Kong)	88	4	4	4	2	0	0	0
Radford	B	Bernard	1907	West Melton		1931		Sheffield Utd.		8	0	0	0	0	0	0	0
Ramscar	FT	Fred	24/1/19	Salford		1951	1954	Preston NE	Millwall	139	7	0	0	55	4	0	0
Rankmore	FEJ	Frank	21/7/39	Cardiff		1968	1970	Peterborough Utd.	(retired)	103	14	9	0	15	4	0	0
Rawlings	JSD	Syd	5/5/13	Wombwell	1956	1936	1937	West Bromwich A.	Millwall	48	2	0	0	18	0	0	0
Reed	G	Graham	24/6/61	Doncaster		1985	1988	Barnsley	VS Rugby	112	7	12	7	2	0	0	0
Reid	J	John	20/8/32	Newmains		1961	1963	Bradford City	Luton Town	85	1	4	0	14	0	2	0
Reilly	GG	George	14/9/57	Bellshill		1976	1979	Corby T	Cambridge Utd.	127	4	13	0	45	0	9	0
Rennie	D	David	29/8/64	Edingborough		1996		Coventry		43		4	5	4	0	0	0
Richardson	B	Barry	5/8/69	Willington Quay		1991	1993	Stockport Co.	Preston NE	96	5	4	8	0	0	0	0
Riches	LE	Len	1910	Broughton		1929	1937	Kettering T	Kettering T	136	12	0	3	8	1	0	0
Riddick	GG	Gordon	6/11/43	Watford		1972	1973	Leyton Orient	Brentford	28	0	1	0	3	0	0	0
Riley	H	Harry	22/11/09	Hollinwood	1982	1936	1937	Cardiff City	Exeter City	22	0	0	0	4	0	0	0
Rioch	NG	Neil	13/4/51	Paddington		1971		Aston Villa (loan)		14	0	0	0	4	0	0	0
Roberts	DG	Gordon	30/5/25	Foleshill		1946	1948	Wolves	Brighton & Hove A.	57	12	0	0	7	6	0	0
Roberts	JG	John	11/9/46	Abercynon		1967	1968	Swansea City	Arsenal	62	4	0	0	11	2	0	0
Roberts	JT	John	24/3/44	Cessnock, Australia		1972		Southend Utd.		13	0	0	0	0	0	0	0
Robertson	SJ	Stuart	16/12/46	Nottingham		1972	1978	Doncaster Rovers	Bedford T	254	11	16	0	27	1	1	0
Robinson	LStJ	Les	2/5/1898	Romford	1965	1925	1926	West Ham Utd.	Norwich City	73	6	0	0	32	6	0	0
Robinson	M	Maurice	9/11/29	Newark		1957		Kettering T	Bedford T	11	1	0	0	2	1	0	0
Robinson	PJ	Phil	6/1/67	Stafford		1994			Huddersfield(loan)	14	1	1	2	0	0	0	0
Robinson	TE	Tommy	11/2/09	Coalville	1982	1935		Lincoln City	Gillingham	5	0	0	2	2	0	0	0
Robinson	TH	Terry	8/11/29	Woodhams		1957		Brentford	QPR	13	1	0	0	0	0	0	0
Robson	T	Tommy	1909	Morpeth		1934	1937	Yeovil T	Kettering T	38	3	0	5	0	0	0	0
Robson	TH	Tommy	31/7/44	Gateshead		1961	1965		Chelsea	74	1	7	0	20	0	1	0
Rodger	CC	Colin		Ayr		1937	1938	Manchester City		35	0	0	2	4	0	0	0
Rogers	E	Eamonn	16/4/47	Dublin		1972		Charlton Ath. (loan)		4	0	0	0	1	0	0	0
Ross	I	Ian	26/11/47	Glasgow		1976		Aston Villa (loan)		2	0	0	0	0	0	0	0
Ross	WE	Eric	19/9/44	Belfast		1969	1971	Newcastle United	Hartlepool U	57	10	5	0	5	0	0	0
Rush	MJ	Matthew	6/8/71	Hackney		1996		Norwich (loan)		14	0	0	1	3	0	0	1
Russell	CH	Colin		Pottersbury		1931			Wolverton	7	0	0	0	8	0	0	0
Russell	GH	George	1/8/02	Atherstone		1927	1930	Watford	Bristol Rovers	53	4	0	0	0	0	0	0
Russell	R	Roger	20/11/57	Corby		1981				1	0	0	0	0	0	0	0
Russell	SEJ	Sid	1911	Feltham		1935	1938	QPR	(retired)	109	3	0	5	0	0	0	0
Sampson	I	Ian	14/11/68	Wakefield		1993		Sunderland (loan)		126	2	8	11	10	0	0	1
						1994		Sunderland									
Sandeman	BR	Bradley	24/2/70	Northampton		1987	1990		Maidstone Utd.	58	2	5	7	3	0	0	0
Sandercock	PJ	Phil	21/6/53	Plymouth		1979	1980	Huddersfield T	Kettering T	69	2	2	0	3	0	0	0
Sanders	RJ	Roy	22/9/40	Stepney		1962		Romford	Romford	15	1	3	0	2	0	0	0
Sandy	AVC	Adam	22/9/58	Peterborough		1979	1982	Wolverton	Wolverton	104	4	5	0	6	1	1	0
Sankey	J	Jack	19/3/12	Winsford	1985	1946	1947	West Bromwich A.	Hereford U	42	8	0	0	0	0	0	0
Sargent	GS	Gary	11/9/52	Turvey		1979	1980	Peterborough Utd.	Barnet	43	1	7	0	4	0	0	0
Saunders	PB	Paul	17/12/59	Watford		1978	1982	Watford	Aylesbury	125	4	9	3	5	0	0	0
Saxby	GP	Gary	11/12/59	Mansfield		1980	1982	Mansfield Town	Stamford	96	9	6	3	11	1	2	0
Schiavi	MA	Mark	1/5/64	City of London		1985	1986	Bournemouth	Cambridge Utd.	35	0	2	3	5	0	0	1
Scope	DF	David	10/5/67	Newcastle		1989	1991	Blyth Spartans	Gateshead	19	2	0	1	1	0	0	0
Scott	DP	David	6/6/18	Belfast	1977	1946	1947		Oxford U	11	7	0	0	0	0	0	0

Sheet No.9 - Scott GS to Turley

Player			Date of Birth	Place of Birth	Died	First Season	Last Season	Previous Club	Next Club	Appearances				Goals			
										League	FAC	FLC	Other	League	FAC	FLC	Other
Scott	GS	Geoff	31/10/56	Birmingham		1984		Middlesbrough	Cambridge Utd.	17	3	0	2	0	0	0	0
Scott	J	Jack	5/2/08	Sunderland		1931		Nottm. Forest	Exeter City	22	3	0	0	0	0	0	0
Scott	MJ	Morrys	17/12/70	Swansea		1992		Plymouth Argyle	Slough	17	1	2	3	2	0	0	3
Scott	R	Rob	15/8/73	Epsom		1995		Sheffield United (loan)		5	0	0	1	0	0	0	0
Scully	PJ	Pat	23/6/70	Dublin		1990		Arsenal (loan)		15	0	0	1	0	0	0	0
Seabrook	A	Arthur	1897	Luton		1921	1923	Luton Clarence	Halifax T	36	2	0	0	9	0	0	0
Seddon	S	Syd		Kettering		1926		Rushden	Rushden	1	0	0	0	0	0	0	0
Sedgemore	BR	Ben	5/8/75	Wolverhampton		1994		Birmingham C (loan)		1	0	0	0	0	0	0	0
Senior	S	Steve	15/5/63	Sheffield		1987		York City	Wigan Ath.	4	0	2	0	0	0	0	0
Shaw	WH	William	1902	Durham		1925	1930	Barcelona	Kettering T	74	6	0	0	15	0	0	0
Sherwood	S	Steve	10/12/53	Selby		1993		Grimsby Town	Grimsby Town	16	1	1	2	0	0	0	0
Shipley	AG	Arthur		Kettering		1926		Desborough	Wellingborough	1	0	0	0	0	0	0	0
Shirtliff	PR	Paul	3/11/62	Hoyland		1984		Sheffield Wed.	Frickley Ath.	29	0	1	0	0	0	0	0
Simpson	WS	Billy	1/5/07	Cowdenbeath		1936		Aston Villa	Walsall	42	1	0	1	0	0	0	0
Singleton	MD	Martin	2/8/53	Banbury		1987	1989	West Bromwich A.	Walsall	50	4	4	2	4	0	1	0
Sissons	AE	Albert	5/7/03	Kiveton Park	1975	1929		Southport	Worksop	19	2	0	0	4	1	0	0
Skeet	SC	Stuart	6/7/48	Cheshunt		1968		Tottenham H (loan)		1	0	0	0	0	0	0	0
Skelly	RB	Richard	24/3/72	Norwich		1994		Newmarket T	King's Lynn	3	0	0	2	0	0	0	0
Slack	TC	Trevor	26/9/62	Peterborough		1987	1988	Grimsby Town	Chesterfield	13	0	1	0	1	0	0	0
Smalley	T	Tom	13/1/12	Kinsley	1984	1946	1950	Norwich City	Gornell	200	26	0	0	2	0	0	0
Smart	AAC	Allen	8/7/74	Perth		1996		Preston (loan)		1	0	0	0	0	0	0	0
Smith	A	Tony	21/9/71	Sunderland		1995		Sunderland (loan)		2	0	0	0	0	0	0	0
Smith	D	David	12/10/15	Durham		1946	1950	Newcastle United		128	14	0	0	31	2	0	0
Smith	EWA	Eddie	23/3/29	London		1954	1955	Watford	Colchester Utd.	53	3	0	0	12	1	0	0
Smith	HC	Charles	1894	Litchborough		1920	1925		Higham	173	8	0	0	0	1	0	0
Smith	HR	Ray	13/9/34	Hull		1962	1963	Peterborough Utd.	Luton Town	23	0	1	0	7	0	1	0
Smith	JO	John	4/9/28	Leicester		1950	1959			186	9	0	0	9	0	0	0
Smith	NL	Nicky	28/1/69	Berkeley		1994		Sudbury (loan)		6	0	0	0	1	0	0	0
Smith	TG	Tom	18/10/1900	Whitburn	1934	1927	1929	Manchester Utd.	Norwich City	112	9	0	0	22	0	0	0
Smith	WH	Bill	7/9/26	Plymouth		1948		Reading	Birmingham City	26	2	0	0	6	2	0	0
Sorenson	IM			Northampton		1923		Cambridge University		1	0	0	0	0	0	0	0
Southam	JH	James 'Jack'	19/8/17	Willenhall	1982	1949	1954	Birmingham City	Walsall (coach)	145	11	0	0	1	1	0	0
Spelman	RE	Ron	22/5/38	Blofield		1960	1961	Norwich City	Bournemouth	34	4	0	0	3	0	0	0
Sproson	A	Albert	1889	Northampton	1934	1920			Desborough	5	0	0	0	0	0	0	0
Stackman	HS	Scott	16/11/75	Arizona, USA		1993			Bedworth	1	0	0	0	0	0	0	0
Stant	PR	Phil	13/10/62	Bolton		1996		Bury (loan)		5	0	0	0	2	0	0	0
Stanton	SH	Sid	16/6/23	Dudley		1947	1948	Birmingham C		7	0	0	0	0	0	0	0
Starling	AW	Alan	2/4/51	Barking		1971	1976	Luton Town	Huddersfield T	238	11	9	0	1	0	0	0
Starocsik	F	Felix	20/5/20	Poland (Silesia)		1951	1954	Third Lanark	Bedford	49	1	0	0	19	0	0	0
Stewart	WI	Billy	1965	Liverpool		1994		Chester City	Chester City	27	1	2	1	0	0	0	0
Strang	R	Richard		Rutherglen		1932		Halifax T	Darlington	7	0	0	0	0	0	0	0
Stratford	P	Paul	4/9/55	Northampton		1972	1977		(retired)	172	7	9	0	59	1	1	0
Strathie	WJ	James	12/2/13	Beancross	1976	1946		Luton Town	Kettering T	6	0	0	0	0	0	0	0
Sugrue	PA	Paul	6/11/60	Coventry		1985		Portsmouth	Newport County	8	0	1	0	2	0	0	0
Syrett	DK	Dave	20/1/56	Salisbury		1982	1983	Peterborough Utd.	Brackley T	44	1	4	3	13	0	2	2
Taylor	A	Tony	6/9/46	Glasgow		1979		Portsmouth	Canada	4	0	3	0	0	0	0	0
Taylor	A	Andy	4/4/63	Stratford-on-Avon		1981		Aston Villa	Alvechurch	17	2	3	0	0	0	0	0
Taylor	JW					1930				1	0	0	0	0	0	0	0
Taylor	MS	Mark	8/11/74	Saltburn		1995		Fulham		1	0	0	0	0	0	0	0
Taylor	S	Steve	7/1/70	Stone		1995		Crystal Palace (loan)		2	0	0	0	0	0	0	0
Tebbutt	RS	Robert	10/11/34	Irchester		1956	1959		Bedford T	55	3	0	0	21	1	0	0
Terry	PA	Pat	2/10/33	Lambeth		1961		Gillingham	Millwall	24	3	1	0	10	1	0	0
Terry	SG	Steve	14/6/62	Clapton		1989	1993	Hull City	Walton & Hersham	181	9	10	1	17	1	0	0
Thayne	W	Billy	1912	West Hartlepool		1935	1938	Luton Town	Walsall	133	3	0	2	0	0	0	0
Thomas	DR	Dean	19/12/61	Bedworth		1988	1989	Aachen	Notts County	74	6	6	5	12	1	0	0
Thomas	WS	William		Croydon		1920			Millwall	21	3	0	0	2	0	0	0
Thompson	GL	Garry	7/10/59	Birmingham		1994		Cardiff City		50	0	2	1	6	0	0	0
Thompson	H	Harry	29/4/15	Mansfield		1946	1948	York City	Oxford U	38	7	0	0	2	1	0	0
Thompson	KA	Keith	24/4/65	Birmingham		1984		Coventry City (loan)		10	0	0	0	1	0	0	0
Thompson	WJ	Walter	1910	Croydon		1933	1935	Aston Villa	Scarborough	9	0	0	0	0	0	0	0
Thorpe	A	Adrian	20/11/63	Chesterfield		1989	1991	Walsall	Kettering T	52	2	3	4	6	0	0	2
Thorpe	T	Thomas	19/5/1881	Kilnhurst	1953	1920		Barnsley	Barnsley	22	3	0	0	0	0	0	0
Tilson	SF	Fred	19/4/04	Barnsley	1972	1937	1938	Manchester City	York City	41	1	0	0	10	1	0	0
Tisdale	PR	Paul	14/1/73	Malta		1992		Southampton (loan)		5	0	0	0	0	0	0	0
Tolland	D	Donal 'Danny'	19/3/05	Ireland		1933	1937	Ayr U	Bristol Rovers	138	12	0	10	26	1	0	3
Tomkins	EF	Eric	18/12/1892	Rushden	1980	1920	1926	Rushden	Rushden	82	4	0	0	0	1	0	0
Townsend	NR	Neil	1/2/50	Long Buckby		1968	1971		Southend Utd.	67	4	1	0	1	1	0	0
Townsend	RN	Russ	17/1/60	Reading		1979		Barnet	Barnet	13	1	1	0	0	0	0	0
Train	R	Ray	10/2/51	Nuneaton		1984		Oxford United	Tranmere Rovers	46	4	2	2	1	2	0	0
Tresadern	J	Jack	26/9/1890	Leytonstone	1959	1925	1926	Burnley		34	7	0	0	1	0	0	0
Trott	DD	Dean	13/5/67	Barnsley		1994		Boston U	Gateshead	22	1	2	1	4	0	0	0
Tucker	KJ	Ken	15/7/35	Merthyr Tydfil		1959	1960	Shrewsbury Town	Merthyr	10	2	1	0	3	0	0	0
Tucker	WB	Barry	28/8/52	Swansea		1971	1977		Brentford	277	12	13	0	8	0	0	0
						1982	1983	Brentford									
Tumbridge	RA	Ray	6/3/55	Hampstead		1974		Charlton Ath. (loan)		11	0	0	0	0	0	0	0
Turley	WL	Billy	15/7/73	Wolverhampton		1995		Evesham		3	0	0	0	0	0	0	0

152

Sheet No.10 - Turner to Young

Player			Date of Birth	Place of Birth	Died	First Season	Last Season	Previous Club	Next Club	Appearances				Goals			
										League	FAC	FLC	Other	League	FAC	FLC	Other
Turner	G	George	1910	Mansfield		1935	1936	Luton T		22	0	0	1	3	0	0	0
Turner	GM	Mark	4/10/72	Bebington		1994		Wolves	Telford U	4	0	0	1	0	0	0	0
Tysoe	J		13/11/1902	Northampton		1920				1	0	0	0	0	0	0	0
Upton	F	Frank	18/10/34	Ainsley Hill		1952	1953	Nuneaton	Derby County	17	0	0	0	1	0	0	0
Vickers	P	Peter	6/3/34	Kilnhurst		1959		Lincoln C		2	0	0	0	0	0	0	0
Wainwright	RK	Robin	9/3/51	Luton		1973	1974	Millwall	Milton Keynes C	32	2	1	0	5	0	0	0
Walden	Fl	Frederick 'Fanny'	1/3/1888	Wellingborough	1949	SL		Wellingborough	Tottenham H	20	1	0	0	1	1	0	0
						1926		Tottenham H									
Walden	HB	Harry	22/12/40	Walgrave		1964	1966	Luton Town	Kettering T	76	1	7	0	3	0	0	0
Waldock	DH	Des	4/12/61	Northampton		1978	1980			54	2	4	0	4	0	0	0
Walker	DCA	Clive	24/10/45	Watford		1966	1968	Leicester City	Mansfield Town	72	2	6	0	1	0	0	0
Walker	RP	Ricky	4/4/59	Northampton		1978	1980	Coventry City	Corby T	53	1	7	0	0	0	0	0
Wallace	J	James	17/2/33	Kirkintilloch		1955		Aberdeen	Aberdeen	1	0	0	0	0	0	0	0
Wallbanks	J	Jimmy	12/9/09	Platt Bridge	1979	1932		Norwich City	Millwall	2	0	0	0	0	0	0	0
Walsh	W	William	4/12/23	Easington		1953		Sunderland	Darlington	19	0	0	0	0	0	0	0
Walton	RP	Ronnie	12/10/45	Newcastle		1964		Rotherham Utd.	Crewe Alexandra	1	0	0	0	0	0	0	0
Warburton	R	Ray	7/10/67	Rotherham		1993		York City (loan)		135	4	4	12	11	1	0	2
						1994		York City									
Ward	JR	Richard	16/9/40	Scunthorpe		1959		Scunthorpe Utd.	Millwall	6	0	0	0	0	0	0	0
Ward	RA	Bob	4/8/53	West Bromwich		1976		West Brom. A. (loan)		8	0	0	0	0	0	0	0
Ward	SC	Steve	21/7/59	Derby		1979		Brighton & Hove A.	Halifax Town	15	0	4	0	2	0	1	0
Warner	M	Michael	17/1/74	Harrogate		1995		Tamworth		9	1	0	2	0	0	0	0
Warren	E	Ernest	9/14/10	Sunderland		1933		Southampton	Hartlepool Utd.	2	0	0	1	1	0	0	0
Wassell	KD	Kim	9/6/57	Wolverhampton		1977	1978	West Bromwich A.	Aldershot	20	1	2	0	0	0	0	0
Watson	WJ	William		Carlisle		1920	1928			326	26	0	0	4	1	0	0
Watson	WJB	Jimmy	1914	Durham	1979	1934		Bristol Rovers	Gillingham	7	1	0	0	3	0	0	0
Watts	D	Derek	30/6/52	Leicester		1973		Leicester City (loan)		1	0	0	0	0	0	0	0
Weaver	E	Eric	1/7/43	Rhymney		1967	1969	Notts County	Boston U	63	5	3	0	9	0	0	0
Webber	GM	George	28/6/25	Abercynon		1954		Torquay United	Ebbw Vale	13	0	0	0	0	0	0	0
Wells	TC	Tommy		Nunhead		1926	1934	Arsenal	Swindon T	277	34	0	5	73	20	0	0
Weston	CA			Kettering		1920	1921		Kettering T	4	0	0	0	0	0	0	0
Weston	JM	John	19/10/1900	Halesowen		1928	1931	Burnley	Shelbourne	45	5	0	0	15	1	0	0
Wheeler	AJ	Alf		Bilston		1933		Brentford	Southampton	5	0	0	0	1	0	0	0
White	JG	Jason	19/10/71	Meriden		1995		Scarborough		77	3	5	7	18	0	0	0
Whitworth	GH	George	14/7/1896	Northampton		1920	1921	Rushden	Crystal Palace	67	8	0	0	42	4	0	0
Whyte	C	Campbell		Lochgelly		1930		Gillingham	Rochdale	5	0	0	0	1	0	0	0
Wilcox	R	Russell	25/3/64	Hemsworth		1986	1989	Frickley Ath.	Hull City	138	10	6	8	9	0	0	1
Wilkin	K	Kevin	1/10/67	Cambridge		1990	1994	Cambridge C	Rushden	78	4	6	5	11	2	1	0
Williams	B	Brett	19/3/68	Dudley		1987		Nottm. Forestt (loan)		4	0	0	0	0	0	0	0
Williams	DR	Roley	10/7/27	Swansea		1955	1956	Cardiff City	Bath C	15	0	0	0	0	0	0	0
Williams	E	Edgar	20/5/19	Sheffield		1948		Nottm. Forest		3	0	0	0	0	0	0	0
Williams	GJ	Gareth	12/3/67	Cowes		1994		Bournemouth	Scarborough	50	2	2	6	1	0	0	0
Williams	JS			Rugby		1921		Rugby T		2	0	0	0	0	0	0	0
Williams	KD	Keith	12/4/57	Burntwood		1976	1980	Aston Villa	Bournemouth	131	3	8	0	6	0	1	0
Williams	W	Billy	1896	Llantwit Vardre		1921	1926	Cardiff City	Newport County	187	16	0	0	3	0	0	0
Williams	W	Wayne	17/11/63	Telford		1988	1990	Shrewsbury Town (loan)	Walsall	55	1	6	6	1	0	0	0
Wilson	F			Northampton		1926		Rothwell	Higham	1	0	0	0	0	0	0	0
Wilson	JA	James	28/6/22	Musselburgh		1951		Luton Town	Chesterfield	23	1	0	0	0	0	0	0
Wilson	JR	John 'Jock'		Blyth		1927	1929	Reading		24	1	0	0	1	0	0	0
Wilson	PA	Paul	2/8/68	Bradford		1987	1991	Norwich City	Halifax Town	141	8	10	9	6	0	1	0
Woan	AE	Alan	8/2/31	Liverpool		1956	1959	Norwich City	Crystal Palace	119	4	0	0	68	1	0	0
Wonnacott	CB	Clarence	12/31/09	Clowne	1989	1930	1931	Mansfield T	Shelbourne	13	0	0	0	4	0	0	0
Wood	AR	Alf	14/5/15	Aldridge		1951	1954	Coventry City	Coventry City	139	7	0	0	0	0	0	0
Wood	D	Darren	22/10/68	Derby		1990	1993	Reading	(retired)	4	0	2	0	1	0	0	0
Wood	EE	Edmund	10/2/03	King's Norton		1922	1924	Rhyl	Birmingham City	50	0	0	0	3	0	0	0
Wood	JT	John	1902			1921		Daventry		1	0	0	0	0	0	0	0
Wood	W	William	1900	Parkgate		1923		Oldham Athletic	Swansea City	32	5	0	0	6	4	0	0
Woodman	AJ	Andy	11/8/71	Denmark Hill		1994		Exeter City		99	3	6	10	0	0	0	0
Woods	DE	Derek	23/3/41	Northampton		1961			Cambridge U	6	0	0	0	2	0	0	0
Woollard	AJ	Arnold	24/8/30	Bermuda		1950		(Bermuda)	Newcastle United	31	1	2	0	0	0	0	0
						1961	1962	Bournemouth	(retired)								
Woollett	AH	Alan	4/3/47	Wigston		1978		Leicester City	Corby T	23	1	4	0	0	0	0	0
Worboys	GA	Gavin	14/7/74	Doncaster		1995		Darlington	Guisley	13	0	0	0	1	0	0	0
Wright	ME	Mike	16/1/42	Newmarket		1959	1961	Newmarket	King's Lynn	26	0	2	0	7	0	0	0
Wright	RL			Kettering		1923			Kettering T	1	0	0	0	0	0	0	0
Yeoman	RI	Ray	13/5/34	Perth		1953	1958	St. Johnstone	Middlesbrough	169	7	0	0	4	0	0	0
York	R	Roland				1923		Higham	Higham	3	0	0	0	0	0	0	0
Yorke	AE	Andrew	1901	Blyth		1925	1926	Coventry City	Lincoln City	24	2	0	0	0	0	0	0
Young	JW	Joe	1906			1929		Luton T		2	0	0	0	2	0	0	0
Young	SR	Stuart	16/12/72	Hull		1992		Hull City	Scarborough	8	0	0	0	2	0	0	0

Sheet No.11

Played in F.A. Cup only

Player	Date of Birth	Place of Birth	Died	First Season	Last Season	Previous Club	Next Club	League	FAC	FLC	Other	League	FAC	FLC	Other
Gorman K Keith	13/10/66	Bishop Auckland		1986		Ipswich T (loan)		0	1	0	1	0	0	0	0
Roe J		Northampton		1920			Kettering T	0	1	0	0	0	0	0	0
Welsh A Andy	1918	Annfield		1945		Darlington		0	1	0	0	0	0	0	0
Wilson S Sam	16/12/31	Glasgow		1960		Millwall	Lincoln	0	1	0	0	0	1	0	0
Yarker L				1945		(RAF)		0	5	0	0	0	0	0	0

Played in Football League Cup only

Player	Date of Birth	Place of Birth	Died	First Season	Last Season	Previous Club	Next Club	League	FAC	FLC	Other	League	FAC	FLC	Other
Caine B Brian	20/6/36	Nelson		1961		Coventry C	Barrow	0	0	1	0	0	0	0	0
Linnell J John	2/1/44	Holcot		1966			Peterborough U	0	0	1	0	0	0	0	0
Parker K Ken	1954	Newcastle		1972			Milton Keynes	0	0	1	0	0	0	0	0
Scott C Chris	11/9/63	Wallsend		1987		Blyth Spartans	Lincoln C	0	0	1	0	0	0	0	0
Sharpe C Colin	1944	Bugbrooke		1963			King's Lynn	0	0	2	0	0	0	0	0

Played in Miscellaneous Games Only

Player	Date of Birth	Place of Birth	Died	First Season	Last Season	Previous Club	Next Club	League	FAC	FLC	Other	League	FAC	FLC	Other
Cuff J		Lancs.		1938		Everton	Tranmere Rov.	0	0	0	1	0	0	0	0
Hewitt E Edwin				1936		Aston Villa		0	0	0	1	0	0	0	0
Jones H		Wolverton		1935		Wolverton		0	0	0	1	0	0	0	1
Smith A		Northampton		1938				0	0	0	1	0	0	0	0
Wallbanks F Fred	1909	Wigan		1936		Nottm. Forest		0	0	0	1	0	0	0	0

Played in Abandoned Season 1939-1940 Only

Player	Date of Birth	Place of Birth	Died	First Season	Last Season	Previous Club	Next Club
Garvey J Jim	4/6/19	Paisley		1939		Corby Town	Leicester City
Melaniphy E Eugene 'Ted'	2/5/13	Westport		1939		Cardiff City	
Miller HS Harold	20/5/02	St. Albans		1939		Chelsea	
Simons RR Reuben	16/10/08	Swansea		1939		Swansea Town	Swansea Town
Smith A				1939			

Part Two: Pre-League 1897 - 1920

Allen to Chadwick

Player	Date of Birth	Place of Birth	Died	First Season	Last Season	Previous Club	Next Club	S.L.	M.L.	N.L.	FAC	S.L.	M.L.	N.L.	FAC
Allen H				1897			Socialists	0	0	1	0	0	0	0	0
Allen L Len		Northampton		1907	1910			1	0	0	0	0	0	0	0
Anderson A		Scotland		1897			Leith	0	0	2	0	0	0	0	0
Badenoch GH George	9/4/1882	Castlehouse	1915	1907	1909	Tottenham Hotspur	Indianhead	47	0	0	2	1	0	0	3
Bailiff WE William		Ruabon	1972			Druids	Treharris	2	0	0	0	0	0	0	0
Baker C				1897			Rushden Town	0	0	13	0	0	0	5	0
Ball W				1911	1913			3	0	0	0	0	0	0	0
Batson W				1904	1906			2	0	0	1	1	0	0	0
Beadling W William		1885 Sunderland	1944	1909		Grimsby	Grimsby	3	0	0	0	0	0	0	0
Beale RH				1906				4	0	0	0	0	0	0	0
Bellamy BW Ben	22/4/1891	Wollaston	1985	1920		Wollaston	Kettering	56	0	3	0	11	0	0	0
Benbow L Len	1874	Hanley	1946	1902	1907	Nottingham Forest	Retired	68	0	0	5	35	0	0	2
Bennett				1906				4	0	0	0	0	0	0	0
Bennett JW John	29/11/1879	Liverpool		1901	1903	Wellingborough	Luton Town	50	0	0	8	1	0	0	0
Benskin WE William	8/4/1880	Leicester		1906			Wigston	9	0	0	0	0	0	0	0
Benson HL Harry	22/1/1883	Harshill		1907		Stoke	Port Vale	20	0	0	0	0	0	0	0
Best R				1919		Mickley	Mickley	14	0	0	0	0	0	0	0
Birtles TJ Thomas	26/10/1886	Barnsley	1971	1913		Rotherham		14	0	0	1	0	0	0	0
Bishton WH		Northampton		1919				1	0	0	0	0	0	0	0
Blair A		Scotland		1902				1	0	0	0	0	0	0	0
Bonthron RD Robert	1884	Dundee		1908	1910	Sunderland	Birmingham	59	0	0	6	0	0	0	0
Boullemier LE Lucien	1877	Stoke	1949	1904		USA	North Nomads	9	0	0	6	0	0	0	0
Bradshaw F Frank	31/5/85	Sheffield		1910	1912	Sheffield Wednesday	Everton	44	0	0	3	12	0	0	2
Brawn E		1883 Wellingborough		1905		Wellingborough	Gainsborough	13	0	0	0	3	0	0	0
Brawn J		1883 Wellingborough		1904	1907	Wellingborough	Wellingborough	1	0	0	0	0	0	0	0
Brawn WF William	1/8/1878	Wellingborough	1932	1898	1900	Wellingborough	Sheffield United	0	15	12	3	0	8	5	1
Brittan RC Richard	7/8/1887	Isle of Wight	1949	1907	1911	Portsmouth	Tottenham	90	0	0	7	0	0	0	0
Brown DC David		Scotland		1913	1914	Morton		13	0	0	0	4	0	0	0
Brown G George	1885	Wolverton		1903	1905	Wolverton / Watford	Watford / Wolverton	49	0	0	3	9	0	0	1
Brown H Henry	11/1883	Northampton	1934	1900	1903		WBA	34	1	0	2	9	0	0	0
Brown P				1919			Corby Town	0	0	0	0	0	0	0	0
Bryant		Bristol		1898				0	0	3	0	0	0	0	0
Bull W Walter	19/12/1874	Nottingham		1913		South America		2	0	0	0	0	0	0	0
Bullimer L Leo				1899	1905	Brighton	Retired	3	39	0	2	0	0	0	0
Burke PJ				1919	1920			1	0	0	0	0	0	0	0
Burkenshaw R Ralph	26/3/1898	Rotherham	1951	1919	1920	South Shields	Gainsborough	12	0	0	2	1	0	0	0
Byles				1898	1900	Wellingborough	Wellingborough	0	23	16	3	0	0	8	0
Chadwick A Arthur	1875	Church Lane	1936	1904	1906	Plymouth	Exeter	59	0	0	7	1	0	0	0

Sheet No.12 - Chapman to Kerridge

Player			Date of Birth	Place of Birth	Died	First Season	Last Season	Previous Club	Next Club	Appearances				Goals			
										S.L.	M.L.	N.I.	FAC	S.L.	M.L.	N.I.	FAC
Chapman	H	Herbert	19/1/1879	Kiverton Park	1934	1901		Worksop	Sheffield United	58	0	0	10	23	0	0	6
						1904		Notts County	Tottenham								
						1907	1913	Tottenham Hotspur	Leeds City								
Chettle	H					1906		Rushden		9	0	0	0	2	0	0	0
Churchman	EA	Ernest	1891	Northampton	1925	1920		Rushden Town	Wellingborough	22	0	0	0	0	0	0	0
Clark	DC	David				1900			Glossop	0	1	0	1	0	0	0	0
Clarke	WH	William	1880	Kettering		1903	1905	Sheffield United	Southampton	67	0	0	5	4	0	0	0
Clipston	F	Fred	1892	Geddington	1920	1910	1920	Portsmouth	Retired	174	0	0	11	6	0	0	0
Clipstone	M	Matthew				1898		Finedon	Finedon	0	0	14	2	0	0	6	1
Codling	RL	Rowland	10/1879	Durham		1909		Aston Villa	Croydon	3	0	0	0	0	0	0	0
Cole	JS	John	1885	West Bromwich	1943	1905		Wellingborough		9	0	0	2	0	0	0	0
Coleman	JG	John	26/10/1881	Kettering	1940	1901		Kettering	Arsenal	30	0	0	7	14	0	0	3
Cooch	G	George		Wellingborough		1905	1909	Kettering	Norwich	125	0	0	8	0	0	0	0
Cooke	FW	Fred	1880	Rugby		1901	1903		WBA	58	0	0	7	0	0	0	0
Cooper						1903		Irthlingborough		5	0	0	0	0	0	0	0
Cox	M	Mark	10/5/1879	Northampton	1968	1900	1902	48th Regiment		0	9	0	0	0	1	0	0
Crump	F	Fred	1880			1902		Glossop	Stlybridge	27	0	0	1	2	0	0	0
Dainty	HC	Herbert	2/6/1880	Geddington	1957	1902		Leicester	Notts County	29	0	0	1	1	0	0	0
Davies	LJ	Llewellyn				1919		Cambridge University		2	0	0	0	0	0	0	0
Dawson	S	Sidney	1893	Mexborough		1914	1915	Kilnhurst	Grimsby	7	0	0	0	2	0	0	0
Denton	W			Rushden		1905		Rushden	Rushden	4	0	0	0	2	0	0	0
Dickens	RG					1919			Rushden Town	3	0	0	0	4	0	0	0
Dickens	T	Tom		Wovlerton		1903		Wolverton	Wolverton	6	0	0	0	0	0	0	0
						1906		Wolverton	Wolverton								
Didymus	FE	Fred	13/4/1886	Portsmouth		1907		Plymouth	Blackpool	9	0	0	0	2	0	0	0
Dilks	FT	Frank	1880	Daventry		1901	1903		Reading	35	0	0	2	6	0	0	1
						1905		Leicester	Retired								
Drennan	TA	Tom	9/1885	Long Eaton		1905		Aston Villa	Coventry	88	0	0	7	0	0	0	0
Driffield	LT	Lance	10/8/1880	Old, Northants	1917	1900		Cambridge	Cambridge	0	2	0	0	0	0	0	0
Dunkley	AE	Albert	1877	Northampton	1949	1897	1900	Rushden	Leicester	0	24	30	3	0	9	8	0
						1901		Leicester	Gillingham								
Dunkley	F	Fred	1874			1906	1910	Earls Burton	Retired	87	0	0	3	2	0	0	0
Durber	P	Peter	1874	Wood Lane		1902	1906	Glossop	Retired	112	0	0	5	0	0	0	0
Elderton						1905		Wellingborough	Earls Burton	2	0	0	0	0	0	0	0
Ellis						1897				0	0	2	0	0	0	0	0
Emery	J	Jack			1919	1920				6	0	0	0	1	0	0	0
Facer	P	Percy		Northampton	1919	1920				6	0	0	0	0	0	0	0
Faulkner	A					1919			Wellingborough	5	0	0	0	0	0	0	0
Farrell	J	Joe	1875	Tunstall	1933	1901		New Brighton	West Ham United	30	0	0	7	13	0	0	2
Forscutt	AH			Wellingborough		1913	1920	Wellingborough	Wellingborough	2	0	0	0	0	0	0	0
Foster	J	James				1899		Reading	Leicester	0	23	0	1	0	4	0	0
Freeman	E	Edwin	5/7/1886	Northampton	1945	1905	1920			316	0	0	19	17	0	0	2
Frost	G	George		Wolverton		1905		Wolverton	Wolverton	1	0	0	1	0	0	0	0
Frost	J	James	1880	Wolverton	1928	1900	1907	Wolverton	Chelsea	173	16	0	16	16	6	0	0
Garfield	J	James	7/1875	Canterbury	1949	1900	1904	Aston Villa	Kettering	21	0	0	1	2	0	0	0
Gates						1905		Kettering	Raunds	2	0	0	0	0	0	0	0
Gilbert	H					1897				0	0	1	0	0	0	0	0
Gates	RS	Robert	1893	Northampton	1919	1920				1	0	0	0	0	0	0	0
Gilbert						1919				4	0	0	0	0	0	0	0
Goldie	WH	William	1874	Penistone	1969	1905		Arsenal	Retired	22	0	3	0	1	0	0	1
Goldsmith	JE	John	1876	Birmingham	1953	1903		Wellingborough		22	0	0	0	0	0	0	0
Grendon	FJW	Frank	05/09/1891	Farnham	1984	1920	1921		Rushden T	53	0	0	2	0	0	0	0
Hakes	G	George				1897		Hackleton	Hackleton	0	0	1	0	0	0	0	0
Hakes	T	Tom				1897		Hackleton	Hackleton	0	0	1	0	0	0	0	0
Hampson	EJ	John	28/12/1887	Oswestry	1960	1910	1913	Oswestry	Leeds County	77	0	0	7	2	0	0	0
Handley	G	George				1899		Derby	Newark	0	14	0	1	0	9	0	0
Hanger						1903		Kettering	Kettering	5	0	0	0	0	0	0	0
Harris	FM			Desborough		1911	1914		Swansea	4	0	0	0	0	0	0	0
Hartshorne	A	Arthur	1881	Darlaston		1906		Southampton		12	0	0	1	0	0	0	0
Hartwell	W	William				1905	1907	Manchester United	Peterborough United	19	0	0	1	0	0	0	0
Hawtin	R	Rawlings		Northampton		1906				1	0	0	0	0	0	0	0
Haywood	RW	Robert		Kent		1908				1	0	0	0	0	0	0	0
Hendry						1899	1902	Rushden		2	44	0	2	0	0	0	0
Henley	C					1906	1908		Wellingborough	1	0	0	0	0	0	0	0
Henry	W					1906		Notts County		13	0	0	1	0	0	0	0
Hicklton	WH	William		Newcastle		1907	1909	Portsmouth	Coventry	32	0	0	3	2	0	0	0
Howard	F	Frank	12/3/1878	Hardingstone		1897	1899	Rushden	Derby County	2	0	27	2	0	0	1	0
						1904		Wellingborough	Retired								
Howe	R	Ralph	1882	Wellinborough		1901	1906	Wellingborough	Wellingborough	112	43	0	14	0	2	0	0
Howells	S					1900				0	1	0	0	0	0	0	0
Howson	R					1919				1	0	0	0	0	0	0	0
Hughes	R	Robert	5/8/1892	Penlow		1909	1915	Pelaw	Hull City	112	0	0	4	23	0	0	0
Johnston	H			Scotland		1900		Stockport		0	19	0	0	0	0	0	0
Jones	M	Maurice		Wales		1897	1899			0	0	16	0	0	0	5	0
Kent	T					1900	1901			0	2	0	0	0	0	0	0
Kerridge	J			Cosgrove		1905		Cosgrove	Y. Gobian	4	0	0	2	0	0	0	0

Player			Date of Birth	Place of Birth	Died	First Season	Last Season	Previous Club	Next Club	Appearances				Goals			
										S.L.	M.L.	N.I.	FAC	S.L.	M.L.	N.I.	FAC
Kilsby	F	Frank		Fenny Stratford		1907	1909		Reading	6	0	0	0	3	0	0	0
King	HE	Harry	1884	Evesham		1911	1914	Crewe Alexandra	Arsenal	99	0	0	6	68	0	0	2
Langham	F	Francis				1912	1915	Nottingham Forest	Rushden	14	0	0	1	1	0	0	0
Lawrence	ET	Everard				1898	1900	Wellingborough	Kettering	24	11	16	10	7	5	18	2
						1901		Kettering	Arsenal								
Lessons	FG	Fred	1885	Stockport		1907	1915	Nottingham Forest	Retired	234	0	0	15	75	0	0	4
Lester	L					1900				0	2	0	0	0	0	0	0
Lewis	AE	Albert	1884	Wolverhampton		1908	1913	Coventry	WBA	164	0	0	15	85	0	0	5
Letting						1914	1915			2	0	0	0	0	0	0	0
Liddell	WS	William				1897	1901			0	0	8	0	0	0	0	0
Litchfield	J					1897		Rushden Town	Rushden A	0	0	6	0	0	0	3	0
Lloyd-Davies	E	Edwin	1877	Cefn	1957	1907	1920	Swindon Town	Retired	311	0	0	18	3	0	0	0
Lockett	WC	William	23/04/1893	Tipton	1974	1920	1925	Wolves	Kidderminster	77	0	0	4	32	0	0	1
Lovatt						1899				0	0	1	0	0	0	0	0
Lowe	H	Harry				1903	1908			7	0	0	1	2	0	0	1
McCartney	D	David	1881	Ayrshire		1907	1910	Chelsea	Retired	106	0	0	7	8	0	0	1
McDiarmid	F	Fred	1881	Dundee		1907	1911	Tottenham	Distillary	138	0	0	11	18	0	0	1
McIntyre	JA	James	1881	Darleston		1903	1904	Walsall	Reading	21	0	0	0	8	0	0	0
Manning	DJ	'Jock'		Burnt Islant		1908	1920	Blackburn	Retired	264	0	0	18	8	0	0	0
Maris	AJ					1905	1907		Rushden F	19	0	0	0	1	0	0	0
Marriott	W	William	1880			1904		Bristol Rovers	Gillingham	34	0	0	4	1	0	0	1
Martin	A	Albert				1905		Wellingborough	Wellingborough	4	0	0	0	0	0	0	0
Masters	AB					1909	1911			2	0	0	0	0	0	0	0
Miles						1899		Wellingborough	Wellingborough	0	1	0	1	0	0	0	0
Miller	WT	William	15/8/1868	Burton		1899	1902	Kettering	Retired	1	41	0	0	0	16	0	0
Minney	T					1898	1900	Rushden Town	Rushden Town	0	0	19	2	0	0	0	0
Murrell	R	Richard				1900	1905	Wellingborough	Trainer	66	26	0	9	0	6	0	2
Murray	WB	William	1882	Forres		1903	1904	Sunderland	Tottenham	27	0	0	1	0	0	0	0
Napier	D					1910		Sheffield Wednesday		5	0	0	0	0	0	0	0
Neal	H	Herbert	1882	Daventry		1901	1907		Dundee	153	0	0	11	0	8	0	0
Negus						1897	1900			0	0	1	0	0	0	0	0
Newman	WM	'Mick'	1888	Northampton		1910	1915		Trainer	1	0	0	0	0	0	0	0
Nobles	WD	William	1883	Wellingborough	1947	1903		Wellingborough	Wellingborough	5	0	0	0	1	0	0	0
						1906		Barnsley	Wellingborough								
Norton	P	Percy	1884	Wellinborough		1904		Wellingborough	Wellingborough	2	0	0	0	1	0	0	0
Oates	A					1909				1	0	0	0	0	0	0	0
Parkin	G					1897		Earls Burton	Kettering	0	0	1	0	0	0	0	0
Parry						1898				0	0	4	0	0	0	2	0
Parry	JD			Ireland		1902				2	0	0	0	0	0	0	0
Pease	WH	Billy	30/09/1898	Leeds	1955	1920	1925	Leeds City	Middlesbrough	32	0	0	2	1	0	0	2
Pell	W	William				1900	1902	Kettering	Glossop	26	26	0	7	1	5	0	2
Pendred						1900		Rushden Town	Rushden Town	0	17	0	1	0	3	0	0
Perkins						1910		Irthlingborough	Irthlingborough	2	0	0	0	0	0	0	0
Perkins	WH	William		1876	Wellingborough		1903	1906	Liverpool	Retired	100	0	0	8	0	0	0	0
Pettit						1903				1	0	0	0	0	0	0	0
Platt	J	Jack	1880			1905	1908	Portsmouth	Preston	77	0	0	5	22	0	0	6
Randall	C					1897	1901			0	6	4	0	0	0	0	0
Randall	E	Ted				1903	1905		Accrington	9	0	0	0	0	0	0	0
						1906	1907	Accrington	Portsmouth								
Rawlings	A	Archie	2/10/1891	Leicester	1952	1913		Shirebrook	Rochdale	13	0	0	0	1	0	0	0
Rawlings	J	Jack				1907	1913			11	0	0	0	0	0	0	0
Redhead	HA					1910	1913		Kettering	3	0	0	0	0	0	0	0
Robotham						1897	1900	48th Regiment	48th Regiment	1	0	0	0	0	0	0	0
Rushton	RE	Ron				1919	1920			6	0	0	0	2	0	0	0
Sargent	G					1897	1900		Rushden	0	0	29	2	0	0	1	0
Saxon	A	Arthur	1876			1901		Bedminster		6	0	0	0	0	0	0	0
Scott	HJ					1900		48th Regiment		0	1	0	0	0	0	0	0
Scrivens	T	Tom	1876	Walsall		1900		Birmingham City	Retired	0	7	0	1	0	6	0	0
Severn	A					1909	1911	Peterborough		10	0	0	0	4	0	0	0
Sharman	H	Harry				1906	1909	Battersea	Kettering	2	0	0	0	0	0	0	0
Shortland	G					1899		Rothwell	Rothwell	0	5	0	1	0	0	0	0
Smith	B					1897	1901			0	1	13	0	0	0	5	0
Smith	CH	Charles		Small Heath		1912	1915	Nuneaton	Coventry	57	0	0	2	10	0	0	1
Smith	HC	Charles	1894	Litchborough		1920	1925		Higham	17	0	0	0	0	0	0	0
Smith	J	Joe			1920	1919			Died	1	0	0	0	0	0	0	0
Smith	W	Wallace	1883	Allerton	1917	1904		Kettering	Bradford City	29	0	0	4	7	0	0	1
Spencer	F					1897	1899	Wellingborough	Wellingborough	0	0	5	0	0	0	1	0
Spicer						1897		48th Regiment		0	0	1	0	0	0	0	0
Springthorpe	H	Harry	28/4/1886	Stamford	1915	1904	1908	Wolverton	Grimsby	49	0	0	4	9	0	0	3
Sproston	A	Albert	1889	Northampton	1934	1920			Desborough	39	0	0	2	1	0	0	0
Stanbourne	WF					1897	1898			0	0	1	0	0	0	0	0
Stewart	A	Alex	1869	Greenock		1899	1901	Bedminster	Burnley	0	38	0	1	0	17	0	0
Stonley	S		1889			1910		Seaham		1	0	0	0	0	0	0	0
Sutton						1897				0	0	1	0	0	0	0	0
Tebbutt	B	Bryan	2/12/1891	Northampton		1909	1914			12	0	0	0	0	0	0	0
Thomas	WS	William		Croydon		1920			Millwall	8	0	0	0	4	0	0	0

Player			Date of Birth	Place of Birth	Died	First Season	Last Season	Previous Club	Next Club	Appearances				Goals			
										S.L.	M.L.	N.I.	FAC	S.L.	M.L.	N.I.	FAC
Thompson				Daventry		1904		Daventry		1	0	0	0	0	0	0	0
Thompson						1900				0	0	3	0	0	0	1	0
Thompson	GJ					1897				0	0	4	0	0	0	0	0
Thompson	WD			Scotland		1919		Reading		5	0	0	1	0	0	0	0
Thorpe	T	Thomas	19/5/1881	Kilnhurst	1953	1920		Barnsley	Barnsley	254	0	0	16	2	0	0	0
Tirrell	P	Pat				1905	1908	Kettering	West Ham United	96	0	0	6	1	0	0	1
Tomkins	EF	Eric	18/12/1892	Rushden		1920	1926	Rushden	Rushden	144	0	0	9	0	0	0	0
Townley	J	Jack				1906			Higham Town	1	0	0	0	0	0	0	0
Tull	WD	Walter	28/4/1888	Folkestone	1918	1911	1915	Tottenham	KIA	105	0	0	3	9	0	0	0
Turner	EE	Edward	1878	Lancashire		1901		Portsmouth	Portsmouth	27	0	0	7	0	0	0	0
Turner	JH	Joshua	3/1872	Burslem		1905		Southampton		16	0	0	1	2	0	0	0
Vann	AH					1905	1907			17	0	0	0	2	0	0	0
Vann	BW	Bernard	9/7/1887	Rushden	1918	1905	1907		Derby County	7	0	0	1	5	0	0	0
Walden	FI	Fred	1/3/1888	Wellingborough	1949	1909	1913	Wellingborough	Tottenham Hotspur	108	0	0	8	26	0	0	1
Walker	AS					1905	1907	Wolverton		26	0	0	0	2	0	0	0
Walker	R	Robert				1908	1910	Tottenham Hotspur	Millwall	67	0	0	6	24	0	0	1
Warner	F					1897	1901		Rushden Town	0	42	30	3	0	28	4	0
Warner	R	Roger				1898	1901	Rushden Town		0	37	16	4	0	1	0	0
Watkins	WH	Walter	1880	Caersws		1906		Crystal Palace	Stoke City	38	0	0	2	11	0	0	1
Watts						1898				0	0	1	0	0	0	0	0
Westley	WJ					1905		Wolverton	Rushden	1	0	0	0	0	0	0	0
Wheatcroft				Nottingham		1897		Kettering		0	0	1	0	0	0	0	0
Whiting	J					1897	1901			0	7	27	2	0	0	0	0
Whittaker	F	Fred		Nelson		1910	1912	Bradford City	Exeter City	62	0	0	4	18	0	0	0
Whitworth	GH	George	14/07/1896	Northampton		1920	1921	Rushden	Crystal Palace	51	0	0	2	29	0	0	1
Wilson	D		1880			1902			Bristol Rovers	15	0	0	1	2	0	0	0
Wykes	A					1902	1915			2	0	0	0	0	0	0	0
York	A		1883	Walgrave		1903		Walgrave	Peterborough	11	0	0	0	4	0	0	0

Some players who didn't make it on the foregoing pages!
The Northampton Town F.C. Reserve team display their trophies won in 1909

157

WHO'S WHO SECOND WORLD WAR SEASONS:

1939 - 1946

Sheet No.15 - Ainsley to Hart

Player		Date of Birth	Place of Birth	Club	App	Goals	Notes
Ainsley	George	15/4/15	South Shields	Leeds United	1	2	Later managed Workington
Allen	J			Mansfield	1		
Alen	Robert	11/10/16	Bromley Bow	Brentford			Ex tennis pro
Alsop	Gilbert	10/9/08	Frampton Ct	Walsall	61	30	Died April 1920
Amerson	Len			Coventry	18	2	
Ashall	George	29/9/11	Killamarsh	Coventry	3		
Attwell	Reg	23/3/20	Oakengates	West Ham	1		
Baines	Stan	28/7/20	Syston	Leicester	5		Later joined Northampton Town
Baldwin	Harry	17/7/20	Saltey	Brighton	6		
Basnett	AE			Stoke City	1	1	'Borrowed from Stoke
Barratt	Alf	13/4/20	Corby	Northampton Town	1		
Barron	Bill	26/10/17	Houghton LS	Northampton Town	91	23	
Bate					1		
Bates	Edric	3/5/18	Thetford	Southampton	1	1	Later Southampton's manager
Banner	Arthur	28/6/18	Sheffield	West Ham	1		Died in 1980
Beattie	Andy	11/8/13	Kintore	Preston	3		Scottish International
Beattie	Robert	24/1/16	Kilmarnock	Preston	22	21	Scottish International
Bedford	George	1918	Chesterfield	Leicester	33	2	
Billingham	Jack	3/12/14	Daventry	Burnley	57	42	12th man in 1947 Cup Final
Bilton	DH		Midlands	Wolves	14		
Bliss	L			Charlton	1		
Blunt	Eddie	21/5/18	Tunstall	Northampton Town	19	3	
Bollea	Henry	1910	Coventry	Coventry	2		
Bolan	Len	16/3/09	Lowestoft	Southend	30	6	
Bosse	Percy	18/10/14	Cardiff	Northampton Town	2		Offically retired
Brolly	Tom	1/6/12	Belfast	Millwall	2	2	Northern Ireland International
Brookes	Dennis	29/10/15	Leeds		2	1	Northants County Cricketer
Broome	Frank	11/6/15	Berkhampstead	Aston Villa	2	2	England International
Brown	John	8/11/14	Belfast	Birmingham	5	1	Eire/Northern Ireland International
Calvert	Joe	3/2/07	Bullcroft	Leicester	27		Played for Watford at 40
Cansfield	Bill	1914	Liverpool	Blackpool	2	1	
Clark				Northampton Town	1		
Cobley	WA		Leicester	Aston Villa	10		
Coley	Bill	17/9/16	Wolverhampton	Torquay	46	1	Jcined the club post war
Collins	MJ		Kislingbury	Northampton Town	1		
Cooper	Ray			Aston Villa	39		ex England Schoolboy International
Cornish	JA	1919		Corinthians	1		England Amateur International
Coutts	Bill		Edinborough	Leicester	16	4	
Crawford	G			Northampton Town	1		
Cummings	George	5/6/13	Thornbridge	Aston Villa	17		Scottish International
Curtis	FH		Bugbrooke	Northampton Town	8	1	
Dean	WH			Northampton Town	10	4	
Dearson	Don	13/5/14	Ynysybwl	Birmingham	13	10	Welsh International
Dennison	Bob	6/3/10	Amble	Fulham	205	2	Later Northampton Town's manager
Denton	A			Northampton Town	2		
Dixon	Joe	24/9/16	Newcastle Under Lyne	Northampton Town	15	9	
Dunkley	Maurice	19/2/14	Kettering	Manchester City	57	11	
Earl-Chater	R			Northampton Town	2		
Edwards	George	1/4/18	Great Yarmouth	Aston Villa	6	2	
Ellwood	Reg	1919	Worcester	Northampton Town	11		
Fagan	Bill	20/2/17	Musselburg	Liverpool	46	29	Scottish International
Fenton	Ted	7/11/14	Forest Gate	West Ham	2	2	England International
Fowler	Tommy	16/12/24	Prescott	Everton	33	4	
Frame	Bill	7/5/12	Carluke	Leicester	2		
Frost	Stan	19/10/22	Northampton	Northampton Town	2		
Freeman	Harry	4/11/19	Woodstock	Fulham	12		Represented the F.A.
Gardner	Fred	4/6/22	Coventry	Birmingham	32	8	Warwichshire Cricketer
Garrett	Archie	17/6/19	Lemshagow	Hearts	13	8	
Gillespie	J		Scotland	Rangers	13		
Gromlie	Bill	1/4/11	Blackpool	Northampton Town	3		
Greenaway	M				2		
Grogan	John	30/10/15	Paisley	Leicester	13	1	
Grosvenor	P	17/3/11	Evesham	Leicester	4		
Gunn	Ken	9/4/09	Newmains	Northampton Town	1		
Halliwell	LA			Northampton Town	3		
Harris	Arthur	28/7/14	Coventry	Southend	121	7	
Hart	R			Northampton Town	1		

Sheet No.16 - Haycock to Quinney

Player		Date of Birth	Place of Birth	Club	App	Goals	Notes
Haycock	Fred	19/4/12	Liverpool	Aston Villa	49	6	
Heaselgrave	Sam	1/10/16	Smethwick	West Bromwich Albion	12	4	
Henley	Les	26/9/22	Lambeth	Arsenal	2	1	England Schoolboy International
Henson	George	25/12/11	Stone Street	Sheffield United	17	9	
Hess				Austria	1		
Hewitt	Jos	1/7/11	Evenwood	Southport	2	1	
Heywood	Roger	4/5/09	Chorley	Leicester	23		
Hillard	John	3/9/16	Aberdeen	Leicester	3	1	
Hinson	Ron	9/10/15	Chelveston	Rushden	4		
Hobbs					3		
Hornby	Ron	13/3/14	Rochdale	Burnley	1		
Howe	Bert	1/4/16	Rugby	Leicester	13	2	
Hughes	Gwyn	7/5/22	Blaenau F.	Northampton Town	41	8	
Hume	Bill		Bonnyrigg	Aberdeen	4	2	
Hunter	R			R.A.F.	39	2	
Hurrell	W	1919	Dundee	Hibs	4		Respresented both club in 1945 final
Hustwait	Ged		Cardiff	Cardiff	1		Died 1997
Inwood	R		Northampton	Northampton Town	1		
Iverson	Rob	17/10/10	Falkestone	Aston Villa	1		Died 1953
Johnson	Joe	4/11	Bristol	West Bromwich Albion	1		Died 1983
Johnston	Tom		Hearts		22	10	
Jennings	Harry	7/1/20	Norwich	Northampton Town	3		
Jennings	Jack	27/8/03	Platt bridge	Northampton Town	17	1	Northampton Town coach, died 1997
Jones	David	28/10/10	Cardiff	Leicester	4		
Jones	Eric	5/2/15	Birmingham	West Bromwich Albion	4		
Jones	GT		Liverpool	Liverpool	8	3	
Jones				Northampton Town	1		
Kerr	Albert	11/8/17	Lancaster	Aston Villa	1		Died 1979
Kinnear	David	22/2/17	Kircaldy	Rangers	19	9	Scottish International
King	Alf			Coventry	2	1	
King	Sid	1914	Bordesley Green	Birmingham	4		
King	Bobby	19/9/19	Northampton	Wolves	46	20	1st WW2 transfer
Lane	Henry	21/3/09	Hendesford	Plymouth	8		
Lee	Alex	1917		Leeds United	31		
Litchfield	E			Newcastle	9	11	
Liddle	Dan	17/2/12	B'oness	Leicester	29	5	
Littledyke	R		Mansfield	Mansfield	1		Loaned to club for game
Lowe	S			Derby County	2	1	
Lowrie	George	19/12/19	Tonypandy	Coventry	26	25	Welsh International
Lunn	George	28/6/13	Bolton	Aston Villa	1		
Lyman	Colin	9/13/14	Northampton	Notts County	14	6	
Lowery	Harry	26/2/18	Moor Row	West Bromwich Albion	16	2	
MaCauley	Archie	30/17/15	Falkirk	West Ham	24	5	Scottish International
McCullough	K		Larne	Northampton Town	27		
McDonough				Northampton Town	1		
McNab	Alex	27/12/11	Glasgow	West Bromwich Albion	3		Scottish International
McGregor	D		Rossindale	Northampton Town	1		
Maund	John	5/1/16	Hendesford	Aston Villa	12		
Maskall	Les	30/11/18	Cowes	Norwich City	2		Later a Chairman of Diss Town
Melaniphy	Ted	5/2/13	Westport	Northampton Town	1		
Metcalfe	Walter		Scarborough	Coventry	7		
Miller	Harry	20/5/02	St Albans	Northampton Town	2		England Amateur International
Mitchell	Frank	3/6/22	Australia	Coventry	1		
Morgan	Willie	1914	Ryton On Tyne	Coventry	3		Died 1993
Morrall	Alf	1/7/16	Duddeston	Northampton Town	57	28	
Moss	Frank	16/9/17	Birmingham	Aston Villa	17	1	
Mulraney	Ambrose	18/5/16	Wishaw	Ipswich	4	1	
Muncie	William	28/8/11	Carluke	Southend	7		
Newton	B			Northampton Town	2	1	
Nichols	H		Hendesford	Sheffield Wednesday	8	5	
Neal	George	29/12/19	Wellingborough	Northampton Town	17		
O'Neal	W	1923	Liverpool	Northampton Town	1		
Ormond	J		Liverpool	Northampton Town	1		
Parkes	Harry	4/1/20	Erdington	Aston Villa	9	3	Later a Birmingham Director
Parris	Eddie	31/1/11	Chepstow	Northampton Town	8	2	
Peacock	Tom		Clay Cross	Nottingham Forest	1	1	
Perry	Edwin	19/1/09	Rhymney	Doncaster	40	11	Welsh International
Phillips	N			Wolves	1		
Phillips	N			Plymouth	5	1	
Pringle	E			Northampton Town	5		
Pritchard	Harvey	30/1/18	Meridon	Manchester City	114	29	
Pryde	D			Arsenal	1		
Pugh	Sid			Arsenal	42	3	Killed in Action in 1944
Purdie	W			Luton	1		
Pursglove				Hull	1		
Quinney	Jesse	15/10/22	Rugby	Northampton Town	1		

159

Sheet No.17 Roberts to Young

Player		Date of Birth	Place of Birth	Club	App	Goals	Notes
Roberts	Gordon	30/5/25	Foleshill	Wolves	30	12	
Sail	J			Rushden	1		
Sankey	Jack	19/3/12	Winsford	West Bromwich Albion	14	1	Died 1985
Saunders	W	1916	Banbury	West Bromwich Albion	1		
Scott	David	6/6/18	Belfast	Northampton Town	7		Died 1977
Scrinshaw	Stan	7/8/15	Hartlepool	Bradford City	1	2	
Simons	Reuben	16/10/08	Swansea	Northampton Town	24		
Shankley	Bill	2/9/13	Glenbeck	Preston	9		Scottish International
Shaw	Ray	18/5/13	Walsall	Birmingham	33		Later Walsall's manager
Shell	Frank	2/12/12	Hackney	Aston Villa	16	5	
Shepherdson	H	28/10/18	Middlesborough	Middlesborough	70		
Skelton	George	27/11/19	Thurcroft	Hffield	4		
Smalley	Tom	13/1/13	Kinsley	Norwich	207	9	England International
Smith	Bernard	1908	Sileby	Coventry	1		
Smith	C			Northampton Town	1		
Smith	Dave	12/10/15	Durham	Newcastle	38	3	
Smith	Tom			Luton	1		
Sparshott	G			Cardiff	1		
Starling	Ron	11/10/09	Pelaw	Aston Villa	1		
Steele	Fred	6/5/16	Stoke	Stoke City	5	2	England International
Stephens	V	1919		Middlesborough	10		
Strathie	James	12/2/13	Beancross	Northampton Town	1		
Syme	Colin			Torquay	1	1	
Tarrant				Kettering	1		
Thompson	R			Northampton Town	1		
Tidman	DE			Northampton Town	1		
Towl				Northampton Town	1		
Tweed	George			Bristol Rovers	1		
Wallington	I			Northampton Town	1		
Ward				Northampton Town	1		
Ware	Harry	22/10/11	Birmingham	Norwich	27	6	
Welsh	Andy	1918	Annfield	Darlington	32	1	
Wharton	Guy	5/12/16	Broomhill	Portsmouth	13	2	
Willmott	P			Luton	1		
Wilson	Joe	23/3/11	High Spen	Brighton	12	7	
Wood	Alf	14/5/15	Aldridge	Coventry	94		
Wood	Tom	4/08	Wednesbury	Newport	4		
Woodburn	J			Newcastle	12		
Woodgate	John	11/12/19	London	West Ham	2		
Yarker				R.A.F.	5	4	
Young	Richard	17/4/18	Gateshead	Sheffield United	8		

1897/98   4th in Northants League

#	Mon	Day	Opponent	Score	Notes	Allen	Anderson	Baker C	Dunkley A	Ellis	Gilbert	Hakes G	Hakes T	Howard	Jones	Liddell	Litchfield	Minney	Negus	Parkin	Randell	Robotham	Sargent	Smith	Spicer	Stanborough	Sutton	Thompson	Warner	Wheatcroft	Whiting
1	Sep	25	Desborough	0-2				9	11		5			4	10					1	6		3				7	2	8		
2	Oct	9	Rushden Res.	1-4	OG			9	11					5	10	3					6		4	7				2	8		1
3	Nov	6	RUSHDEN RES.	3-1	Jones 2, 1 Unknown		6	9	11					5	10						4		2	7				3	8		1
4		13	WELLINGBORO' RES.	2-2	Baker, Jones		6	9	11					5	10						4		2	7				3	8		1
5	Dec	4	Raunds Unity	2-1	2 Unknown			9	11	4				5	10	3							2	7		8			6		1
6		18	Wellingboro' Res.	1-3	Jones (p)			9	11					5	10	3		4	8				2	7					6		1
7	Jan	1	Finedon Rev.	4-3	Smith 2, Unknown 2	8		9	11	3				5	10			6					2	7					4		1
8		15	RAUNDS UNITY	6-3	Litchfield 3, Baker 2(1p) Smith			8	11					5	10	3	9	6					2	7					4		1
9		22	KETTERING RES.	2-3	Dunkley 2				11					5	10	3	8	6					2	7					4	9	1
10	Feb	5	DESBOROUGH	5-1	Dunkley 2, Baker, Smith, Howard			8	11					5	9	3	10	4					2	7					6		1
11		19	ROTHWELL TOWN	2-1	Jones, Dunkley			10	11					5	9	3	8	4					2	7					6		1
12	Mar	5	Rothwell Town	0-6				9	11			2	4		10	8	5						3	7					6		1
13		12	FINEDON REV.	4-0	Smith, Jones, Dunkley,			9	11					5	10	3	8	4					2	7					6		1
14	Apr	16	Kettering Res.	1-5	Baker			9	11					5	2							4		10	3				6		1
			Apps			1	2	13	14	2	1	1	1	13	14	8	6	8	1	1	4	1	13	13	1	1	1	4	14	1	13
			Goals					5	6					1	6		3							5							

One own goal

Unknown - 2/apps, 6/goals.   7 & 8 (match 14) not recorded

		P	W	D	L	F	A	Pts
1	Kettering Reserves	14	10	2	2	48	22	22
2	Rothwell Town Swifts	14	9	2	3	42	19	20
3	Wellingborough Res.	14	7	4	3	41	28	18
4	NORTHAMPTON TOWN	14	7	1	6	33	35	15
5	Desborough Unity	14	7	0	7	30	39	14
6	Finedone Revellers	14	4	2	8	28	30	10
7	Raunds Unity	14	4	0	10	17	41	8
8	Rushden Reserves	14	2	1	11	21	46	5

1897/98
Back: Smith, Westmorland (Committee), Darnell (President), Whiting, Sargent, Gyde (Treasurer), Jones (Sec)
Middle: Minney, Jones, Howard, Warner, Dunkley
Front: Baker, Remmett, Litchfield

1898/99 1st in Northants League

#			Opponent	Score	Scorers	Att	Brawn W	Bryant	Byles	Clipstone M	Dunkley A	Howard F	Jones M	Lawrence E	Lovatt	Minney T	Parry	Sargent F	Spencer F	Warner F	Warner R	Watts	Whitting J
1	Sep	24	RAUNDS UNITY	2-1	Brawn, Lawrence	650	7		2	10	11	4		9	1	5		3		8	6		
2	Nov	19	Raunds Unity	3-1	Lawrence, Clipstone, OG				2	10	11	5		9		4	7	3		8	6		1
3		26	WELLINGBORO RES.	6-0	F.Warner 3, Lawrence 2, Clipstone				2	10	11	5		9		4	7	3		8	6		1
4	Dec	3	Rothwell Town Swifts	3-3	Byles(p), Parry, Unknown				2	10	11	5		9		4	7	3		8	6		1
5		10	IRTHLINGBORO TOWN	4-0	Brawn, Lawrence, Jones, Byles(p)		7		2		11	5	10	9		4		3		8	6		1
6		24	RUSHDEN RES.	4-1	Lawrence 3, Clipstone		7		2	10	11	5		9		4		3		8	6		1
7	Jan	7	Wellingboro Res.	2-1	Byles, Lawrence		7		2	10	11	5		9		4		3		8	6		1
8		14	Desborough Town	1-2	Lawrence		7		2	10	11	5		9				3	4	8	6		1
9	Feb	4	ROTHWELL TOWN	4-2	Lawrence 2, Byles(p), Clipstone		7		2	10	11	5		9		4		3		8	6		1
10		18	KETTERING RES.	5-0	Byles(2p), Dunkley, F.Warner, *	2000	7		2	10	11	5		9		4		3		8	6		1
11		25	Finedon Rev.	2-2	Lawrence 2				2	10	11	5		9		4	7	3		8	6		1
12	Mar	4	DESBOROUGH TOWN	3-2	Brawn, Lawrence, Dunkley	800	7		2	10	11	5		9		4		3		8	6		1
13		18	Kettering Res.	1-0	Byles(p)		7	4	2	10	11	5		9				3		8	6		1
14	Apr	6	FINEDON REV.	5-1	Brawn 2, Sargent, Lawrence 2	2000	7	6	2		11		10	9				3	4	8	3	1	
15		15	Irthlingboro Town	2-0	Clipstone 2		7		2	10	11	5		9				3	4	8	6		1
16		29	Rushden Res.	2-1	Spencer, Byles(p)		7	4	2	10	11			9				3	5	8	6		1
Apps							12	3	16	14	16	14	2	16	1	11	4	16	4	16	16	1	14
Goals							5		8	6	2		1	18			1	1	1	4			

* Additional scorer: Lawrence

Unknown - 1 goal.

One own goal

F.A. Cup

			Opponent	Score	Scorers		Brawn W	Byles	Clipstone M	Dunkley A	Howard F	Lawrence E	Minney T	Sargent F	Warner F	Warner R	Whitting J
R1	Oct	1	Hinkley T	2-1	Lawrence(p), Clipstone		7	2	10	11	5	9	4	3	8	6	1
R2		24	Wellingborough	1-6	Lawrence		7	2	10	11	5	9	4	3	8	6	1

		P	W	D	L	F	A	Pts
1	NORTHAMPTON TOWN	16	13	2	1	49	17	28
2	Wellingborough Reserves	16	8	3	5	35	25	19
3	Kettering Reserves	16	9	3	4	25	20	*19
4	Rothwell Town	16	7	4	5	36	24	18
5	Desborough Town	16	7	4	5	31	26	18
6	Irthlingborough Town	16	5	2	9	21	37	12
7	Rushden Reserves	16	3	0	11	23	28	10
8	Finedon Revellers	16	4	2	10	18	44	10
9	Raunds Unity	16	2	4	10	21	40	8

* 2 points deducted

1899/1900 3rd in Midland League

#	Month	Opponent	Score	Scorers	Att	Brawn W	Bullimer L	Byles	Dunkley A	Foster J	Handley G	Hendry	Howe R	Lawrence E	Miles	Miller W	Randell C	Shortland	Stewart A	Warner F	Warner R	Whiting J
1	Sep	2 Wellingborough Town	2-2	Howe, Handley	3000	7	1	2	11		8	3	6			10		5		9	4	
2		9 Ilkeston Town	0-3		3000	7	1		11	4	9	3	6			10		5		8	2	
3		16 LINCOLN CITY RES.	3-0	Warner, Miller, Dunkley	3000	7	1	2	11	4	9	3				10		5		8	6	
4		23 Rushden Town	1-0	Handley	3000	7	1	2	11	4	8	3		9		10		5			6	
5	Oct	7 Derby County Res.	1-5	Handley		9	1	2	11	4	7	3				10		5		8	6	
6		21 KETTERING TOWN	1-2	Dunkley				2	11	4	7	3				10	5		9	8	6	1
7	Nov	4 BURTON WANDERERS	5-0	Stewart 2, Foster(p), Brawn,*	1000	7	1	2	11	5		3				10	4		9	8	6	
8		11 RUSHDEN TOWN	1-0	Warner	1500	7	1	2	11	5		3				10	4		9	8	6	
9		25 LEICESTER RES.	4-1	Brawn 3, Foster		7	1	2	11	5		3	4		10				9	8	6	
10	Dec	2 Heanor Town	1-4	Miller		7	1	2	11	5		3				10	4		9	8	6	
11		9 Newark Town	1-3	Stewart		7	1	2	11	5		3	4			10			9	8	6	
12		23 Kettering Town	0-2			7	1	2	11	5		3	4			10			9	8	6	
13		28 WELLINGBOROUGH	6-0	Dunkley 2, Brawn 2, Stewart **	2000	7	1	2	11	5		3	6			10			9	8	4	
14		30 Lincoln City Res.	3-1	Brawn, F.Warner, Lawrence	6000	7	1	2		5		3	6	11		10			9	8	4	
15	Jan	6 DERBY COUNTY RES.	5-3	F.Warner 2 Foster(p), Lawrence +		7	1	2		5		3	6	11		10	4		9	8		
16		20 BARNSLEY RES.	7-1	F.Warner 3, R.Warner, Miller2 #	2000	7	1	2		5		3	6	11		10			9	8	4	
17	Feb	1 Barnsley Res.	2-1	Handley, Miller			1	2		5	7	3	6	11		10			9	8	4	
18		10 DONCASTER ROVERS	4-2	Lawrence 2, F.Warner, Miller			1	2	11	5	7	3	6	9		10				8	4	
19		17 Leicester Res.	6-2	Handley2,Miller2,F.Warner,Dunkley	2000		1	2	11	5	7	3	6	9		10				8	4	
20		24 HEANOR TOWN	3-0	Dunkley 2, Handley	1200		1	2	11	5	7	3	6			10			9	8	4	
21	Mar	10 Burton Wanderers	3-2	F.Warner, Miller, Lawrence			1	2		5	7	3	6	11		10			9	8	4	
22		17 NEWARK TOWN	4-0	Foster(p), Handley, F.Warner ##			1	2		5	7	3	6	11		10			9	8	4	
23	Apr	7 ILKESTON TOWN	2-1	Handley, Howe	1500		1	2		5	7	3	6	11		10			9	8	4	
24		13 Doncaster Rovers	1-1	Unknown			1	2		5	7	3	6	11		10			9	8	4	
				Apps		15	23	23	16	23	14	24	17	11	1	23	5	5	17	23	23	1
				Goals		8			7	4	9		2	5		9			6	14	1	

Additional scorers:
* F.Warner, ** F.Warner, + Brawn, # Stewart, ## Stewart

Unknown - 1 goal.

F.A. Cup

			Opponent	Score	Scorers	Att	Brawn W	Bullimer L	Byles	Dunkley A	Foster J	Handley G	Hendry	Miller W	Randell C	Stewart A	Warner R
Q1	Pre	Sep	30 WELLINGBOROUGH T.	1-2	Unknown	2000	7	1	2	11	4	7	3	9	1	5	6

		P	W	D	L	F	A	Pts
1	Kettering Town	24	16	5	3	57	24	37
2	Wellingborough Town	24	16	4	4	64	38	36
3	NORTHAMPTON TOWN	24	16	2	6	66	36	34
4	Derby County Res.	24	11	5	8	63	46	27
5	Lincoln City Res.	24	11	3	10	45	46	24
6	Heanor Town	24	9	7	8	31	36	25
7	Doncaster Rovers	24	9	6	9	51	42	24
8	Ilkeston Town	24	9	6	9	43	44	24
9	Newark Town	24	10	1	13	51	50	21
10	Burton Wanderers	24	6	6	12	40	62	18
11	Rushden Town	24	7	2	15	38	56	16
12	Barnsley Res.	24	5	6	13	39	58	16
13	Leicester Res.	24	3	3	18	34	74	9

1900/01 3rd in Midland League

#		Date	Opponent	Res	Scorers	Att	Bullimer L	Beale	Brown H	Clarke A	Cox D	Dunkley A	Driffield L	Frost G	Hendry	Howe R	Howell	Johnston	Kent M	Lester	Miller	Murrell R	Pell W	Randell C	Pendered	Scott	Scrivens T	Smith B	Stewart A	Thompson	Warner F	Warner R	Whiting J
1	Sep	1	Wellingborough Town	1-2	Pendered		1							7		6		2				5	4		11		10		9		8	3	
2		8	Ilkeston Town	2-1	Murrell, Scrivens		1							7		6		2				5	4		11		10		9		8	3	
3		22	COALVILLE	7-0	*		1							7		6		2				5	4		11		10		9		8	3	
4		24	Rushden Town	1-1	Murrell	2000	1							7		6		2				5	4		11		10	9			8	3	
5	Oct	6	Sheffield United Res.	2-3	F.Warner 2		1							7	3	6		2				5	4		11		10		9		8		
6		13	WELLINGBOROUGH	2-2	Pell, Frost	2000								7		6		2				5	4		8		10		9			3	1
7		27	LEICESTER RES.	5-1	F.Warner2,Murrell,Scriven, **									7		6		2				5	4		11		10		9		8	3	1
8	Nov	24	Lincoln Res.	5-3	Stewart 2, Frost, F.Warner 2		1							7	3	6		2		8		5	4		11				9		10		
9	Dec	1	RUSHDEN TOWN	5-2	Miller 2, Stewart 2, Murrell									7	3	6		2		8		5	4		11				9		10		1
10		8	Leicester Res.	3-5	Frost 2, F.Warner									7	3	6		2		8		5	4		11				9		10		1
11		15	ILKESTON TOWN	3-1	Frost 2, Stewart						11			7	3	6		2		8		5	4				10		9				1
12		24	DONCASTER ROVERS	0-2		2000					11		1	7	3	6		2		8		5	4						9		10		
13	Jan	12	DERBY COUNTY RES.	2-1	Miller, Stewart						11		1		3	6		2		8		5	4			7			9		10		
14		19	Coalville	4-1	F.Warner 2, Cox, Murrell		1				11				3	6		2		8		5	4						9		10		
15	Feb	9	LINCOLN RES.	3-1	F.Warner 2, Stewart						11				3	6		2		8		5	4	7					9		10		1
16		14	HINKLEY	0-2		400				1	11				3	6		2	7		10	5	4						9		8		
17		16	Burton Wanderers	1-0	Stewart		1				11				3	6		2	7		10	5	4						9		8		
18		23	BURTON WANDERERS	5-1	Miller,Murrell,F.Warner 2,Stewart	1800		7			11				3	6	1	2			10	5	4						9		8		
19	Mar	9	SHEFFIELD UNITED RES.	2-2	Pell 2	2000	1	7			11				3	6			8		10	5	4							9		2	
20		16	WORKSOP	4-2	Miller 3, Pell		1	7			11				3	6					10	5	4						9		8	2	
21		23	Derby County Res.	2-2	Pell, Stewart		1				11				3	6						8	4	5	7				9		10	2	
22		30	NEWARK	2-1	Pendered, Dunkley		1					11		7	3	6					10	5	4		8				9			2	
23	Apr	5	Doncaster Rovers	0-3			1					11		7	3	6					10	5	4		8				9			2	
24		6	Worksop	2-2	Dunkley, Unknown	3000	1					11		7	3	6					10	5	4		8						9	2	
25		9	Hinckley	1-1	Thompson		1					11		7	3	6					10	5	4		8						9	2	
26		18	Newark	1-1	Unknown		1		9		11			7	3	6		2		8		5	4								7		
			Apps				16	3	1	1	9	8	2	16	20	26	1	19	2	2	18	26	26	1	17	1	7	1	21	3	19	13	6
			Goals								1	2		6							7	6	5		3		6		11	1	14		

* Goalscorers: Scrivens (4), Stewart (P), Warner F., Pendered.

** Additional scorer, unknown

Unknown - 3 goals.

F.A. Cup

					Scorers		Bullimer L	Beale	Brown H	Clarke A	Cox D	Dunkley A	Driffield L	Frost G	Hendry	Howe R	Howell	Johnston	Kent M	Lester	Miller	Murrell R	Pell W	Randell C	Pendered	Scott	Scrivens T	Smith B	Stewart A	Thompson	Warner F	Warner R	Whiting J
Q1	Nov	3	Hinckley	0-3						1				7	3	6						5	4		11		10		9		8	2	

			P	W	D	L	F	A	Pts
1	Sheffield United Res		26	21	3	2	78	23	45
2	Doncaster Rovers		26	17	2	7	87	32	36
3	NORTHAMPTON TOWN		26	13	7	6	65	43	33
4	Derby County Res.		26	14	4	8	74	45	32
5	Hinckley		26	12	6	8	55	44	30
6	Newark Town		26	13	2	11	56	50	28
7	Wellingborough Town		26	12	4	10	44	46	25
8	Ilkeston Town		26	10	4	12	70	50	24
9	Leicester Res.		26	11	1	14	60	64	23
10	Lincoln Res.		26	7	7	12	46	49	21
11	Rushden		26	8	5	13	35	61	21
12	Worksop		26	8	4	14	50	75	20
13	Coalville		26	5	2	19	30	102	12
14	Burton Wanderers		26	4	3	19	33	99	11

1901/02 11th in Southern League

#		Date	Opponent	Score	Scorers	Att	Bennett	Brown H	Bullimer L	Cooke F	Coleman J	Chapman H	Dilks J	Farrell	Frost	Grimley	Hendry	Howe	Lawrence	Miller	Murrell	Neal	Pell	Saxon	Turner
1	Sep	7	Reading	1-3	Coleman	5317	2			1	10	8		9	7			6			5		4	11	3
2		14	SOUTHAMPTON	1-2	Coleman	5000	2			1	10	8		9	7			6			5		4	11	3
3		21	Bristol Rovers	2-1	Chapman, Farrell	4000	2			1	10	8		9	7			6			5		4	11	3
4		28	NEW BROMPTON	3-2	Farrell, Lawrence, Pell	2000	2			1	10	8		9	7			6	11		5		4		3
5	Oct	5	WEST HAM UNITED	3-4	Coleman 2, Chapman	2000	2			1	10	8		9	7			6	11		5		4		3
6		12	Watford	1-3	Coleman	3000	2			1	10	8		9	7			6	11		5		4		3
7		19	TOTTENHAM	3-1	Chapman 2, Lawrence	6000	2			1	10	8		9	7			6	11		5		4		3
8		26	Wellingborough	0-1		4000	2			1	10	8		9	7			6	11		5		4		3
9	Nov	9	Swindon Town	3-0	Chapman, Farrell, Coleman		2			1	10	8		9	7			6	11		5		4		3
10		23	Kettering	0-2		2000	2			1	10	8		9	7			6	11		5		4		3
11	Dec	7	Millwall	0-1		2000	2			1	10	8		9	7			6	11			5	4		3
12		21	READING	1-1		3000	2			1	10	8		9	7			6	11		5		4		3
13		26	Luton Town	0-0			2			1	10			9	7			6	11		5		4	8	3
14		28	Southampton	0-11			2			1	10			9	7			6	11		5		4	8	3
15	Jan	4	BRISTOL ROVERS	2-2	Coleman, Lawrence	5000	2			1	10	8		9	7			6	11		5	4			3
16		11	New Brompton	1-0	Farrell		2			1	10	8		9	7			6	11		5	4			3
17		18	West Ham United	1-0	Chapman	4000	2			1	10	8		9	7				11		5	6	4		3
18	Feb	1	Tottenham Hotspur	0-1		3000	2			1	10	8		9	7				11		5	6	4		3
19		8	WELLINGBOROUGH	4-2	Chapman, Farrell 2	1500	2			1	10	8		9	7				11		5	6	4		3
20		15	Portsmouth	1-5	Frost	6000	2			1	10			9	7					8	5	6	4	11	3
21		22	SWINDON TOWN	8-0	Chapman 2,Farrell 2,Dilks 2,Coleman,Frost	2000	2			1	10	8	11	9	7			6			5		4		3
22	Mar	1	Brentford	2-4	Chapman, Coleman	2000	2			1	10	8	11	9	7			6			5		4		3
23		8	KETTERING	2-1	Farrell, Coleman	4000	2			1	10	8		9	7			6	11		5		4		3
24		15	QUEENS PARK RANGERS	4-1	Chapman,Farrell,Coleman,Lawrence	3000				1	10	8		9	7	2		6	11		5		4		3
25		22	MILLWALL	1-0	Frost	2500				1	10	8		9	7	2		6	11		5		4		3
26		29	Queens Park Rangers *	1-5	Coleman	4000				1	10			9	7	3	2		11		5	6	4		
27		31	LUTON TOWN	2-4	Chapman, Coleman					1	10	8		9	7	3	2		11		5	6	4		
28	Apr	1	BRENTFORD	2-2	Brown, Lawrence	1000		8		1	10			9	7	2		6	11		5	4			3
29		5	PORTSMOUTH	3-4	Lawrence, Farrell	3000	2		1		10	8	3	9	7			6	11		5	4			
30		19	Watford	1-1	Coleman	1000	2			1	10	8		9	7			6	11		5		4		3

* Chapman at No.10 in team line-up, but match report stated he did not

	Bennett	Brown H	Bullimer L	Cooke F	Coleman J	Chapman H	Dilks J	Farrell	Frost	Grimley	Hendry	Howe	Lawrence	Miller	Murrell	Neal	Pell	Saxon	Turner
Apps	25	1	1	29	30	25	3	30	30	5	2	24	24	1	29	11	26	6	27
Goals		1			14	12	2	13	3				7				1		

Unknown - 1 app.

F.A. Cup

		Date	Opponent	Score	Scorers	Att	Bennett	Brown H	Bullimer L	Cooke F	Coleman J	Chapman H	Dilks J	Farrell	Frost	Grimley	Hendry	Howe	Lawrence	Miller	Murrell	Neal	Pell	Saxon	Turner
Q3	Nov	2	Gresley Rovers	2-0	Chapman, Coleman		2			1	10	8		9	7			6	11		5		4		3
Q4		20	Burton United	0-0			2			1	10	8		9	7			6	11		5		4		3
Q4		25	BURTON UNITED	2-0	Murrell, Farrell		2			1	10	8		9	7			6	11		5		4		3
Q5		30	Kettering	2-2	Pell, Chapman	3000	2			1	10	8		9	7			6	11		5		4		3
Q5	Dec	2	KETTERING	2-0	Murrell, Farrell		2			1	10	8		9	7			6	11		5		4		3
1R		16	DARWEN	4-1	Coleman 2, Lawrence, Pell	2000	2			1	10	8		9	7				11		5	6	4		3
R1	Jan	22	SHEFFIELD UNITED	0-2		15000	2			1	10	8		9	7			6	11		5		4		3

		P	W	D	L	F	A	Pts
1	Portsmouth	30	20	7	3	67	24	47
2	Tottenham hotspur	30	18	6	6	61	22	42
3	Southampton	30	18	6	6	71	28	42
4	West Ham United	30	17	6	7	45	28	40
5	Reading	30	16	7	7	57	24	39
6	Millwall Athletic	30	13	6	11	48	31	32
7	Luton Town	30	11	10	9	31	35	32
8	Kettering	30	12	5	13	44	39	29
9	Bristol Rovers	30	12	5	13	43	39	29
10	New Brompton	30	10	7	13	39	38	27
11	NORTHAMPTON TOWN	30	11	5	14	53	64	27
12	Queens Park Rangers	30	8	7	15	34	56	23
13	Watford	30	9	4	17	36	60	22
14	Wellingborough	30	9	4	17	34	72	22
15	Brentford	30	7	6	17	34	61	20
16	Swindon Town	30	2	3	25	17	93	7

1902/03 8th in Southern League

#			Result	Scorers	Att	Benbow L	Bennett J	Blair A	Brown H	Bullimer L	Cook F	Crump F	Dainty H	Dilks T	Durber P	Frost J	Garfield	Howe R	Murrell R	Neal H	Parry J	Wilson D
1	Sep	6 BRISTOL ROVERS	1-2	Wilson	3000	9					1		5	11	3	7		6	4		2	10
2		13 Millwall	4-2	Benbow 3(1p), Wilson	5500	9		2	8		1		5	11	3	7		6	4			10
3		20 Watford	0-1		2000	9	2				1	8	5	11	3	7		6	4			10
4		27 BRENTFORD	2-0	Benbow, Brown	3000	9	2		10		1	8	5	11	3	7		6	4			
5	Oct	4 Tottenham Hotspur	0-2		1000	9	2		10		1	8	5		3	7		6	4			11
6		11 WEST HAM UNITED	2-0	Crump, Brown	3000	9	2		10		1	8	5		3	7		6	4			11
7		18 Portsmouth	1-0	Benbow	8000	9	2		10		1	8	5		3	7		6	4			11
8		25 NEW BROMPTON	2-2	Crump, Bennett		9	2		10		1	8	5		3	7		6	4			11
9	Nov	8 KETTERING	1-2	Dilks	3000	9	2		10		1	8	5	11	3	7		6		4		
10		29 Queens Park Rangers	0-0		4000	9	2				1	8	5	11	3	7			4	6		10
11	Dec	6 SOUTHAMPTON	1-4	Garfield	4000		2				1	8	5	11	3	7	10	6	4			9
12		13 Wellingborough	3-1	Benbow 2, Frost		9	2		10		1	8	5	11	3	7		6	4			
13		20 Bristol Rovers	1-1	Benbow	4000	9	2		10		1	8	5	11	3	7		6	4			
14		26 Luton Town	0-4			9			10		1	8	5	3	2	7		6	4			11
15		27 MILLWALL	2-0	Benbow 2	5000	9	2		10		1		5	11	3	7	8	6		4		
16	Jan	3 WATFORD	3-0	Benbow 3	2000	9	2		10		1	8	5	11	3	7		6		4		
17		10 Brentford	2-0	Benbow, Dilks	2000	9	2		10		1	8	5	11	3	7		6	4			
18		17 TOTTENHAM HOTSPUR	3-1	Frost, Brown, Dilks	4000	9	2		10		1	8	5	11	3	7		6		4		
19		24 West Ham United	2-3	Benbow, Dilks	4000	9	2		10		1	8	5	11				6	4	3		7
20		31 PORTSMOUTH	2-5	Benbow 2(1p)	5000	9	2		10		1	8	5	11	3	7		6		4		
21	Feb	7 New Brompton	0-0		3000	9	2				1	8		10	3	7		6	5	4		11
22		14 SWINDON TOWN	1-0	Dainty	2000	9	2		10		1	8	5	11	3	7			4	6		
23		21 Kettering	0-3			9	2				1	8	5	11	3	7			4	6	10	
24	Mar	7 Reading	1-5	Benbow(p)	3500	9	2		10	1			5	11	3	7			4	6		8
25		21 Southampton	0-7		5000	9	2		10		1	8	5	11	3	7		4			6	
26		28 WELLINGBOROUGH	1-0	Benbow		9	2		10		1	8	5	11	3	7		6		4		
27		31 QUEENS PARK RANGERS	1-1	Brown	3000	9	2		10		1	8	5	11	3	7		6	4			
28	Apr	11 Swindon Town	2-0	Benbow(2)	4000	9	2		10		1	8	5		3	7			4	6		11
29		13 LUTON TOWN	0-0			9	2		10		1	8	5		3	7			4	6		11
30		16 READING	1-2	Benbow	1800	9	2		10		1	8	5	11	3	7			4			
		Apps				29	27	1	24	1	29	26	29	24	29	29	4	24	22	15	2	15
		Goals				22	1		4			2	1	4		2	1					2

F.A. Cup

			Result		Att	Benbow L	Bennett J	Blair A	Brown H	Bullimer L	Cook F	Crump F	Dainty H	Dilks T	Durber P	Frost J	Garfield	Howe R	Murrell R	Neal H	Parry J	Wilson D
Q1	Nov	1 Burton United	0-2		2000	9	2		10		1	8	5		3	7		6	4			11

		P	W	D	L	F	A	Pts
1	Southampton	30	20	8	2	83	20	48
2	Reading	30	19	7	4	72	30	45
3	Portsmouth	30	17	7	7	69	32	41
4	Tottenham Hotspur	30	14	7	9	47	31	35
5	Bristol Rovers	30	13	8	9	46	34	34
6	New Brompton	30	11	11	8	37	35	33
7	Millwall Athletic	30	14	3	13	52	37	31
8	NORTHAMPTON TOWN	30	12	6	12	39	48	30
9	Queens Park Rangers	30	11	6	13	34	42	28
10	West Ham United	30	9	10	11	35	49	28
11	Luton Town	30	10	7	14	43	44	27
12	Swindon Town	30	10	7	13	38	46	27
13	Kettering	30	8	11	11	33	40	27
14	Wellingborough	30	11	3	16	36	56	25
15	Watford	30	6	4	20	35	87	16
16	Brentford	30	2	1	27	16	84	5

1903/04 15th in Southern League

#	Mon	Date & Opponent	Score	Scorers	Att	Benbow L	Brown G	Brown H	Clarke D	Cooper	Dickens T	Durber P	Frost S	Garfield J	Griffiths	Hanger	Howe R	McIntyre J	Murray W	Murrell R	Neal H	Nobles W	Pettit	Perkins W	Wykes A	York C
1	Sep	5 Plymouth Argyle	0-2		8000	9		10	3			2		11	5		6	8	7		4			1		
2		12 READING	1-3	McIntyre	3000	9		8	3				7		5	2	6	10	11		4			1		
3		19 Wellingborough	0-4					8	3	11			7		5	2	6	10			4			1		9
4		26 BRISTOL ROVERS	2-1	H.Brown 2				9	3			2	7	8		5	4	10	11		6			1		
5	Oct	3 Brighton	4-0	H.brown 2, McIntyre	5000			9	3		5	2	7	8			6	10	11		4			1		
6		10 PORTSMOUTH	0-3		3000	5		9	3		6	2	7	8				10	11		4			1		
7		17 SWINDON	1-1	Benbow	2500	4		9	3			2	7	8	5			10	11		6			1		
8		24 Brentford	1-4	Neal	6000	9	10		3			2	7	8	5		6		11		4			1		
9	Nov	7 Tottenham Hotspur	1-2	Frost	8000	9	8	10	2	11		3	7				4			5			6	1		
10		14 Queens Park Rangers	1-4	Neal	5000	9	8		2	11		3	7		5		6	10			4			1		
11		21 New Brompton	2-2	Garfield, Benbow	3000	9			2	11		3	7	8			6	10		5	4			1		
12		28 KETTERING	1-0	McIntyre		9			2	11		3	7	8			6	10		5	4			1		
13	Dec	7 Southampton	1-5	McIntyre		9			2			3	7	8			6	10	11	5	4			1		
14		12 SOUTHAMPTON	0-2		2500	9	11		3			2	7	8	4			10		5	4			1		
15		19 Millwall	0-5		1000	9	11		2				7			3	6	10		5	4			1		8
16		26 Luton Town	0-1			9	8		2				7		5		6	10	11	3	4			1		
17		28 QUEENS PARK RANGERS	2-1	Benbow, McIntyre	3000	9	8		2			3	7		5		6	10	11		4			1		
18	Jan	2 PLYMOUTH	1-0	McIntyre	250	6	8		2			3	7		5			10	11		4			1		9
19		9 Reading	1-0	Frost		9			2			3	7		5		6	10	11		4			1		8
20		16 WELLINGBOROUGH	2-0	Benbow 2	4000	9			2			3	7		5		6	10	11		4			1		8
21		23 Bristol Rovers	1-1	York	4000	9			2			3	7		5		6	10	11		4			1		8
22		30 BRIGHTON	2-2	Benbow, York	1000	9			2			3	7		5		6	10	11		4			1		8
23	Feb	20 BRENTFORD	3-0	Frost, Benbow, York	3000	9			2			3	7		5		6	10	11		4			1		8
24		27 West Ham United	0-2		4000	9			2			3	7		5		6	10	11		4			1		8
25	Mar	19 NEW BROMPTON	2-2	Benbow, McIntyre	2000	9						3	7			2	6	10	11	4	5			1		8
26		21 FULHAM	2-1	Benbow, Nobles	2000	9	8		2			3	7				4	10	11		5	6		1		
27		26 Kettering	1-3	G.Brown	2000	9	8		2			3	7				6	10	11		5	4		1		
28	Apr	4 LUTON TOWN	0-0		5000	9	10		2			3	7	8	5		6		11		4			1		
29		7 WEST HAM UNITED	1-3	York	1000	6	10		2			3	7	8	5				11		4			1		9
30		9 Fulham	0-2		9000	4	10		2			3	7	8	5				9	11		6		1		
31		16 MILLWALL	2-0	G.Brown 2	3000	9	10		2			3	7	8	5				11		4			1	6	
32		25 TOTTENHAM HOTSPUR	0-1		3000	9	10		2			3	7	8	5		6		11		4			1		
33		28 Swindon Town	0-2		3000	9	10		2			3	7	8	5		6		11		4			1		
34		30 Portsmouth	1-1	Benbow	4000	9	10		2			3	7	8			6		11	5	4			1		
		Apps				31	16	9	33	5	2	30	33	17	22	5	26	26	27	8	32	5		34	1	11
		Goals				10	3	4					3	1				8			2	1				4

F.A. Cup

	Mon	Date & Opponent	Score		Att	Benbow L	Brown G	Brown H	Clarke D	Cooper	Dickens T	Durber P	Frost S	Garfield J	Griffiths	Hanger	Howe R	McIntyre J	Murray W	Murrell R	Neal H	Nobles W	Pettit	Perkins W	Wykes A	York C
Q3	Oct	31 Wellingborough	0-2		8000	5	10	9	2			3	7	8			6		11		4			1		

	P	W	D	L	F	A	Pts
1 Southampton	34	22	6	6	75	30	50
2 Tottenham Hotspur	34	16	11	7	54	37	43
3 Bristol Rovers	34	17	8	9	66	42	42
4 Portsmouth	34	17	8	9	41	38	42
5 Queens Park Rangers	34	15	11	8	53	37	41
6 Reading	34	14	13	7	48	35	41
7 Millwall *	34	16	8	10	64	42	40
8 Luton Town	34	14	12	8	38	33	40
9 Plymouth Argyle	34	13	10	11	44	34	36
10 Swindon Town	34	10	11	13	30	42	31
11 Fulham	34	9	12	13	33	34	30
12 West Ham United	34	10	7	17	38	43	27
13 Brentford	34	9	9	16	34	48	27
14 Wellingborough	34	11	5	18	44	63	27
15 NORTHAMPTON TOWN	34	10	7	17	36	60	27
16 New Brompton	34	6	13	15	26	43	25
17 Brighton & Hove Albion	34	6	12	16	45	69	24
18 Kettering	34	6	7	21	39	78	19

* Previously known as Millwall Athletic

1904/05 12th in Southern League

							Benbow L	Brown G	Bouillimier L	Bullimer L	Brawn E	Chadwick A	Chapman H	Clark D	Durber P	Frost J	Howard F	Howe R	Lowe	Marriott W	Murrell R	Neal H	Norton	Perkins W	Smith W	Springthorpe H H	Thompson
1	Sep	3	BRISTOL ROVERS	2-0	Neal, Benbow	4000	9	10				5	8	2	3	7		6		11		4		1			
2		10	Brighton	2-1	Smith, OG	6000	9	10				5	8	2		7	3	6		11		4		1			
3		17	Portsmouth	0-3		8000		10				5	9	2		7	3	6		11		4		1	8		
4		24	BRENTFORD	3-2	Brown 2, Frost	4000		10				5	9	2	3	7		6		11		4		1	8		
5	Oct	1	Queens Park Rangers	2-1	Benbow, Marriott	1000	9	10				5		2	3	7		6		11		4		1	8		
6		8	MILLWALL	0-1		5000	9	10				5		2	3	7		6		11		4		1	8		
7		15	Tottenham Hotspur	1-0	Neal	1200	9					5	10	2	3	7		6		11		4		1	8		
8	Nov	5	NEW BROMPTON	2-0	Chapman, Brown	2000		10				5	9	2	3	7		6		11		4		1	8		
9		19	SOUTHAMPTON	0-3		6000		10				5	9	2	3	7		6		11		4		1	8		
10	Dec	3	WATFORD	1-2	Smith	4000	9	10				5		2		7		6		11	3	4		1	8		
11		10	Plymouth Argyle	2-2	Chadwick, Lowe			10				5		2		7		6	9	11	3	4		1	8		
12		17	WEST HAM UNITED	1-0	Lowe	4000		10				5	8	2	3	7		6	9	11		4		1			
13		24	Reading	0-4		4580		10				5	8	2	3	7				11	6	4		1		9	
14		26	Luton	2-4	Clark(p), Chapman	4000		10				5	8	2	3	7				11	6	4		1	9		
15		27	WELLINGBOROUGH	4-0	Clark(p), Chapman 2, Brown	4000		10				5	9	2	3	7		6		11		4		1	8		
16		3	Bristol Rovers	0-3		8000		10				5	9	2	3	7		6		11		4		1	8		
17	Jan	7	BRIGHTON	3-0	Clark(p), Durber, Smith	4000		10				5		2	3	7		6	9	11		4		1	8		
18		21	Brentford	4-3	Smith 2, Chapman, Brown	4000		10				5	9	2	3	7		6		11		4		1	8		
19		28	QUEENS PARK RANGERS	1-1	Chapman	4000		10					9	2	3	7		6		11	4	5		1	8		
20	Feb	11	TOTTENHAM HOTSPUR	0-3		6000		10		1		5	9	2	3	7		6		11		4			8		
21		25	SWINDON TOWN	5-0	Chapman 2, Springthorpe 3	3000			4			5	9	2	3	7		6		11				1	8	10	
22	Mar	4	New Brompton	1-1	Norton	5000		10	4			5		2	3	7				11	6		9	1	8		
23		13	Millwall	0-1		2000		10				5		2	3	7		6		11		4	9	1	8		
24		16	PORTSMOUTH	1-1	Smith				4			5		2	3	7		6		11		9		1	8	10	
25		18	Southampton	1-1	Benbow	5000	5		4					2	3	7				11	6	9		1	8	10	
26		23	FULHAM	0-0		2000	9		4					2	3	7		6		11		5		1	8		
27		25	Fulham	1-4	Clark(p)	8000		10	4					2	3	7		6		9		5		1	8		11
28	Apr	1	Watford	0-1		2500		10	4		9			2	3	7		6		11		5		1	8		
29		8	PLYMOUTH	0-2		4000			4			5		2	3	7		6		11		9		1	8	10	
30		15	West Ham United	1-5	Frost	7000		10	4			5		2	3	7		6		11		9		1	8		
31		22	READING	1-1	Brawn	3000		10			9	5		2	3	7		6		11		4		1	8		
32		24	LUTON TOWN	2-1	Brown, OG			10			9	5		2	3	7		6		11		4		1	8		
33		25	Wellingborough	0-0				10			9	5		2	3	7		6		11		4		1	8		
34		29	Swindon	0-3				10			9	5		2	3	7		6		11		4		1		8	
			Apps				7	29	9	1	5	29	16	34	30	34	2	30	3	24	7	32	2	33	29	7	1
			Goals				3	6			1	1	8	4		2			2	1		2	1		7	3	

Two own goals

F.A. Cup

						Benbow L	Brown G	Chadwick A	Chapman H	Clark D	Durber P	Frost J	Howe R	Marriott W	Neal H	Perkins W	Smith W
Q3	Oct	27	Burton United	3-2	Chapman 2, Brown		10	5	9	2	3	7	6	11	4	1	8
Q4	Nov	12	Kettering	2-2	Benbow 2	9		5	10	2	3	7	6	11	4	1	8
Q5	Nov	26	LEICESTER FOSSE	0-2		3	10	5	9	2		7	6	11	4	1	8
Q5	Dec	1	Leicester Fosse	2-0		9		5	10	2	3	7	6	11	4	1	8

Back: Loakes, Neal, Bouillimer, L.Bullimer, Durber, Chapman, Howe
Front: Clarke, Chadwick, Smith, Perkins, Benbon, Brown, Marriott

	P	W	D	L	F	A	Pts
1 Bristol Rovers	34	20	8	6	74	36	48
2 Reading	34	18	7	9	57	38	43
3 Southampton	34	18	7	9	54	40	43
4 Plymouth Argyle	34	18	5	11	57	39	41
5 Tottenham Hotspur	34	15	8	11	53	34	38
6 Fulham	34	14	10	10	46	34	38
7 Queens Park Rangers	34	14	8	12	51	46	36
8 Portsmouth	34	16	4	14	61	56	36
9 New Brompton.	34	11	11	12	40	40	33
10 Watford	34	15	3	16	44	45	33
11 West Ham United	34	12	8	14	48	42	32
12 Brighton & Hove Albion	34	13	6	15	44	45	32
13 NORTHAMPTON TOWN	34	12	8	14	43	54	32
14 Brentford	34	10	9	15	33	38	29
15 Millwall	34	11	7	16	38	47	29
16 Swindon Town	34	12	5	17	41	59	29
17 Luton Town	34	12	3	19	45	54	27
18 Wellingborough	34	5	3	26	25	107	13

No		Date	Opponent	Score	Scorers	Att	Brawn E	Batson W	Benbow L	Chadwick A	Cole J	Brennan T	Durber P	Dilks T	Denton W	Elperton	Frost G	Frost J	Freeman	Gates	Gooing W	Howe R	Kerridge E	Lowe H	Maris A	Martin R	Neal H	Perkins W	Platt J	Randall E	Springthorpe H	Tirrell P	Turner J
1	Sep	2	Bristol Rovers	0-6		9000				5	10	3	2					7			9						4	1	8			6	11
2		9	PLYMOUTH ARGYLE	1-4	Turner					5	10							7			9	6					2	1	8			4	11
3		16	New Brompton	0-2		4000				5	9		3					7				6					2	1	8		10	4	11
4		23	SOUTHAMPTON	1-2	Frost	4000				5	10	3	2					7			9						6	1	8			4	11
5		30	Portsmouth	0-4		1000					10	3	2					7	5		9	6						1	8			4	11
6	Oct	7	READING	1-0	Platt	4000				5		3	2					7			9						4	1	8		10	6	11
7		10	Swindon Town	2-1	Platt, Brown		9			5		3	2					7									4	1	8		10	6	11
8		21	WATFORD	2-1	Neal(p), Springthorpe	5000	9			5		3	2					7									4	1	8		10	6	11
9		28	Millwall	1-0	Brawn	5000	9			5	10	3	2					7			8						4	1				6	11
10	Nov	4	BRIGHTON	0-0		5000				5		3	2					7			9						4	1	8		10	6	11
11		18	WEST HAM UNITED	2-1	Frost, Springthorpe	5000				5		3	2		11			7			9						4	1	8		10	6	
12		25	Tottenham Hotspur	0-2		8000				5	8		2		11			7			9						4	1			10	6	
13	Dec	2	FULHAM	1-3	Sprinthorpe	3000				5			2		11			7			9	6					4	1	8		10	3	
14		16	Queens Park Rangers	1-6	Platt	8000				5			2					7			9					4		1	8		10	6	11
15		23	NORWICH CITY	0-2		400				5	10		2		11			7			9	4				3		1	8			6	
16		26	Luton Town	0-1			10			5			2		11			7			9	4				3		1	8				
17		30	BRISTOL ROVERS	0-4		5000				5					11	2		7			10			9		3	4	1	8				
18	Jan	6	Plymouth Argyle	0-2		2500	8			5			2					7			9	6	3				4	1			10		
19		20	NEW BROMPTON	0-1		3500				5			2					7	6		9		3				4	1	8		10		
20		27	Southampton	1-9	Batson	5000	9	8		5			2					7			10		3	6			4	1					
21	Feb	3	PORTSMOUTH	0-1			9			5			2		3			7				6					4	1			10		8
22		10	Reading	0-6			9			5	8		2		3			7			10						4	1				6	11
23		17	SWINDON	3-0	Walker, Frost, Denton	8000				5			2		3	9		7			10						4	1			8	6	
24		24	Watford	3-5	Frost, Denton, A.Vann	4000				5			2		3	9		7									4	1			8	6	
25	Mar	8	MILLWALL	0-0		4000				5			2		3	11		7									4	1			8	6	
26		10	Brigton	2-2	P{latt, Gooing	3000				5			2		3	11	9	7			10						4	1			8		
27		12	Brentford	1-2	Frost	2000				5			2		3	11		7			8						4	1	9	10			
28		24	West Ham United	1-4	Springthorpe	4000				5			2		3	11		7			10						4	1	9		8	6	
29		31	TOTTENHAM HOTSPUR	0-0		6000				5			2		3	9		7			10						4	1	8		10	6	
30	Apr	7	Fulham	1-3	A.Vann	1500							2		3			7			10			5			4	1	8			6	
31		14	BRENTFORD	4-0	Platt 2, Turner, Neal(p)	4000			9				2		3			7						5			4	1	8			6	11
32		16	LUTON TOWN	1-2	Maris	9000				5			2		3			7							11		4	1	8			6	9
33		21	QUEENS PARK RANGERS	1-1	Walker	3000				3			2				10	7						9	5		4	1	8			6	
34		28	Norwich City	0-4		5000	9						2		3		11	7						10	5		4	1	8			6	
				Apps			8	2	1	30	9		31	23	9	4	2	1	33	2	2	22	8	4	3	6	4	29	33	25	2	16	30	16
				Goals			2	1							2			5			1				1		3		6		4		2

Additional players: E Brawn 2/3; G Cooch 29/1; A H Vann 18-21,23,24,29,30/11 + 2 goals; B W Vann 25,30/9; A Walker 23-25,31,32/10, 33/11 + 3 goals; W Westley 12/3

F.A. Cup

		Date	Opponent	Score	Scorers	Brawn E	Chadwick A	Cole J	Durber P	Denton W	Frost J	Gooing W	Howe R	Lowe H	Neal H	Perkins W	Platt J	Springthorpe H	Tirrell P	Turner J
Q4	Dec	9	West Stanley	1-1	Dilks		5	10	2		7	9	6		4	1	8		3	11
Q4		14	WEST STANLEY	3-0	Springthorpe 2, Gooing		5		2	11	7	9		3	4	1	8	10	6	
R1	Jan	13	New Brompton	1-2	Sprinthorpe	8	5	6	2		7	9		3	4	1		10		

Additional player: W Hartwell 3/11

Back: Loakes(Trainer), Drennan, Tirrell, Perkins, Durber, Neal, Chadwick
Front: Frost, Platt, Gooing, Cole, Turner

NORTHAMPTON TOWN A.F.C.

		P	W	D	L	F	A	Pts
1	Fulham	34	19	12	3	44	15	50
2	Southampton	34	19	7	8	58	39	45
3	Portsmouth	34	17	9	8	61	35	43
4	Luton Town	34	17	7	10	64	40	41
5	Tottenham Hotspur	34	16	7	11	46	29	39
6	Plymouth Argyle	34	16	7	11	52	33	39
7	Norwich City	34	13	10	11	46	38	36
8	Bristol Rovers	34	15	5	14	56	56	35
9	Brentford	34	14	7	13	43	52	35
10	Reading	34	12	9	13	53	46	33
11	West Ham United	34	14	5	15	42	39	33
12	Millwall	34	11	11	12	38	41	33
13	Queens Park Rangers	34	12	7	15	58	44	31
14	Watford	34	8	10	16	38	57	26
15	Swindon Town	34	8	9	17	31	52	25
16	Brighton & Hove Albion	34	9	7	18	30	55	25
17	New Brompton	34	7	8	19	20	62	22
18	NORTHAMPTON TOWN	34	8	5	21	32	79	21

1906/07 — 4th in Southern League

#		Date	Opponent	Result	Scorers	Att	Beale R	Bennett	Benskin A	Brown G	Chettle	Cooch G	Dickens T	Drennan T	Dunkley F	Freeman E	Frost J	Hartshorne A	Hartwell W	Hawtin R	Henry W	Lowe H	Maris J	Neal H	Platt J	Randall T	Springthorpe H	Tirrell P	Townley J	Vann A	Vann B	Walker A	Watkins W
1	Sep	1	Crystal Palace	0-3		7000						1		2			7	3					5	4			8	6		11		10	9
2		8	BRENTFORD	4-0	Watkins 3, OG	6000			10			1		2			7	3					5	4			8	6				11	9
3		15	Millwall	0-1		5000			10			1		2			7	3					5	4	8			6				11	9
4		22	LEYTON ORIENT	0-0		5000	3					1		2			7						5	4			8	6		11		10	9
5		29	Portsmouth	1-4	Watkins	1000	3			8		1		2			7						6	4				5		11		10	9
6	Oct	6	NEW BROMPTON	1-2	Watkins	4000						1		2	5		7	3						4			8	6		11		10	9
7		13	Plymouth Argyle	1-1	Springthorpe	8000		2				1		2	5		7							4			8	6		11		10	9
8		20	BRIGHTON	1-1	Springthorpe	3000		2				1		2	5		7							4			8	6		11		10	9
9		27	Reading	0-5		4000			3			1		2	5		7							4			8	6		11		10	9
10	Nov	3	WATFORD	1-1	Frost	4000			3			1		2	5		7							4			10	6		11			9
11		10	BRISTOL ROVERS	2-2	Watkins, Tirrell	3000			3			1		2	5		7		11					4			8	6					9
12		17	Queens Park Rangers	0-5								1		2	5		7		11		3			4			8	6				9	9
13		24	FULHAM	0-4		4000						1		2	5		7		11		3			4			8	6				9	9
14	Dec	1	Southampton	0-1		4000			10			1		2	6									4	8			5		11	9		8
15		15	Tottenham Hotspur	0-6		7000						1		2	6	11		3	7					4	8		10	5				9	
16		22	SWINDON	2-1	B.Vann 2	2000						1		2	6	11			7		3			4	8			4			9		10
17		25	Norwich City	1-3	Watkins	1000						1		2	6	11		3	7					4	8			5			9		10
18		27	NORWICH CITY	1-1	B.Vann	3000		5				1		2		11			7	8	3			4				6				11	10
19		29	CRYSTAL PALACE	2-1	B.Vann 2	5000				8		1		2	5	11			7		3			4				6				11	10
20	Jan	5	Brentford	0-2		5000						1		2	5	11			7		3			4	8			6				11	10
21		19	MILLWALL	1-1	Platt	4000						1	5	2		11					3			4	8		7	6				11	10
22		26	Leyton Orient	1-2	Chettle	4000					9	1	5	2							3			4	8		7	6				9	10
23	Feb	9	New Brompton	1-3	Chettle	2000					9	1		2	5						3			4	8		7	6					10
24		16	PLYMOUTH ARGYLE	1-0	Watkins	3000					9	1		2	5						3			4	8		7	6				11	10
25		23	Brighton	0-3		5000					9	1	4		5			2	7		3				8			6					10
26	Mar	2	READING	1-3	Neal(p)	3000						1		2	5	11					3			4	8		7	6					10
27		7	WEST HAM UNITED	0-0		2000					9	1		2	5	11		3					4		8		7						10
28		9	Watford	0-5		4500					9	1		2	5	11		3					4		8								10
29		16	Bristol Rovers	1-6	Watkins	3000					9	1		2	5	11		3						4	8		7	6					10
30		23	QUEENS PARK RANGERS	1-2	Platt						9	1			5			2	7		3			4	8		11	6					10
31		30	Fulham	1-3	Platt	1000	7		3			1		2	5				11				6		8	9	4						10
32	Apr	1	LUTON	0-0		9000			3			1	7	2					11				6	5	8	9	4						10
33		2	Luton	0-1		5000	7		3			1		2	5				11						8	9	4	6					10
34		6	SOUTHAMPTON	2-4	Platt 2				3			1		2	5						7				8	9	11	6					10
35		13	West Ham United	0-4		2500	7	2				1						3			7				8	9	4						10
36		18	PORTSMOUTH	0-2								1		3	5						7		6	2	8	9	11	4					10
37		20	TOTTENHAM HOTSPUR	2-0		3000						1		3	5						7	9	6	2	8		11	4					10
38		27	Swindon Town	0-5		3000	7					1		3	5				11				6	2	8	9	4		1				10
			Apps				4	4	9	4	9	37	4	35	29	10	14	12	19	1	13	1	13	34	24	7	22	38	1	9	5	20	38
			Goals								2						1							1	5		2	1			5		11

One own goal

Additional players: C Henley 28/7; H Sharman 14/9

F.A. Cup

		Date	Opponent	Result	Scorers	Beale R	Bennett	Benskin A	Brown G	Chettle	Cooch G	Dickens T	Drennan T	Dunkley F	Freeman E	Frost J	Hartshorne A	Hartwell W	Hawtin R	Henry W	Lowe H	Maris J	Neal H	Platt J	Randall T	Springthorpe H	Tirrell P	Townley J	Vann A	Vann B	Walker A	Watkins W
Q5	Dec	8	SOUTHPORT CENTRAL	2-1	Platt 2						1		2	6	11		7	3					4	8		10	5					9
R1	Jan	12	Middlesborough	2-4	Platt, Watkins						1		2	5	11					3			4	8		7	6				9	10

Southern League Table

		P	W	D	L	F	A	Pts
1	Fulham	38	20	13	5	58	32	53
2	Portsmouth	38	22	7	9	64	36	51
3	Brighton & Hove Albion	38	18	9	11	53	43	45
4	Luton Town	38	18	9	11	52	*52*	45
5	West Ham United	38	15	14	9	60	41	44
6	Tottenham Hotspur	38	17	9	12	63	45	43
7	Millwall	38	15	6	14	71	50	42
8	Norwich City	38	15	12	11	57	48	42
9	Watford	38	13	16	9	46	43	42
10	Brentford	38	17	8	13	57	56	42
11	Southampton	38	13	9	16	49	56	35
12	Reading	38	14	6	18	57	47	34
13	Leyton	38	it	12	15	38	60	34
14	Bristol Rovers	38	12	9	17	55	54	33
15	Plymouth Argyle	38	10	13	15	43	50	33
16	New Brompton	38	12	9	17	47	59	33
17	Swindon Town	38	11	11	16	43	54	33
18	Queens Park Rangers	38	11	10	17	47	55	32
19	Crystal Palace	38	8	9	21	46	66	25
20	NORTHAMPTON TOWN	38	5	9	24	29	88	19

1907/08 8th in Southern League

#		Date	Opponent	Score	Scorers	Att	Badenoch G	Benson H	Brittan C	Cooch G	Chapman H	Didymus F	Drennan T	Dunkley F	Freeman E	Hickleton W	Kilsby F	Lessons F	Lloyd-Davies E	McCartney D	McDiarmid F	Platt J	Rawlings	Springthorpe H	Tirrell P	Lowe
1	Sep	2	PLYMOUTH ARGYLE	0-1			7	3		1	8		2		11			9		5	6			10	4	
2		4	Crystal Palace	2-0	McCartney(p), Didymus	5000	7		3	1	10	2			11			9		5	6	8			4	
3		7	LUTON TOWN	0-0		5000	7		3	1	10	2			11			9		5	6	8			4	
4		14	Brighton	2-2	McCartney, Chapman	8000	7		3	1	10		2		11			9		5	6	8			4	
5		21	PORTSMOUTH	3-2	Lessons, Platt, McCartney	7500	7		3	1	10	2			11			9		5	6	8			4	
6		28	Bradford Park Avenue	1-1	Lessons	1300	7		3	1	10	2	6		11			9		5		8			4	
7	Oct	5	MILLWALL	2-1	Lessons 2	7000	7		3	1	10	2	6		11			9		5		8			4	
8		7	CRYSTAL PALACE	1-1	Platt	6000	7		3	1	10	2	6		11			9		5		8			4	
9		12	Brentford	1-3	Lessons		7		3	1	10	2			11			9		5	6	8			4	
10		19	BRISTOL ROVERS	2-2	Lessons, Freeman	8000	7	3		1		2			11			9		5	6	8		10	4	
11		26	Leyton	1-1	Chapman	3000	7		3	1	10		2		11			9		5	6	8			4	
12	Nov	2	READING	0-2		7000	7		3	1	8		2		11			9		5	6			10	4	
13		9	Watford	1-2	Platt	5000	7			1	10		2		11	3		9		5	6	8			4	
14		16	NORWICH	0-1		5000	7		3	1	10		2		6			9		5		8		11	4	
15		23	New Brompton	1-0	McDiarmid	6000				1	8	11	2		6			9	3	5	7	10			4	
16		30	Southampton	0-2			7			1	10	2			6			9	3	5	11	8			4	
17	Dec	14	West Ham United	1-1	McDiarmid	4000	7			1	10		2		6			9	3	5	11	8			4	
18		21	QUEENS PARK RANGERS	1-2	Hickleton	6000	7			1	10		2		6			9	3	5	11	8			4	
19		25	Tottenham Hotspur	0-2		2500	7			1	10		2		6			9	3	5	11				4	
20		26	SWINDON TOWN	1-0	McCartney	8760	7			1	10	8	2	5	6				3	9	11				4	
21		28	TOTTENHAM HOTSPUR	2-1	Lloyd-Davies, Freeman	8000	7	3		1	10		2		8	6			5	9	11				4	
22	Jan	25	BRADFORD PARK	1-1	Lessons		7	2		1	10			6	8	4		9	3	5	11					
23	Feb	1	Millwall	0-1		4000	7	2		1	10			6	8	4		9	3	5	11					
24		8	BRENTFORD	0-0		6000	7	2		1				6	10	4		9	3	5	11	8				
25		12	Portsmouth	1-0	Platt	5000	7	2		1	9			6	10	4			3	5	11	8				
26		15	Bristol Rovers	1-1	McDiarmid	5000	7	2		1	9			6	10	4			3	5	11	8				
27		22	LEYTON	5-2	Platt 2, McCartney, Dunkley, Chapman	3000	7	2		1	9			6	10	4			3	5	11	8				
28		29	Reading	1-0	McDiarmid		7	2		1	9				10	4			3	5	11	8			6	
29	Mar	7	WATFORD	0-1		5000	7	3		1	9		2	6	11	4			10	5		8				
30		14	Norwich	1-2	McDiarmid	5000	7	2		1	9			6	10	4			3	5	11	8				
31		21	NEW BROMPTON	2-0	Lessons 2	4000	7	2		1				6	10	4		9	3	5	11	8				
32	Apr	4	Plymouth Argyle	1-1	Platt	4000	7	2		1				6	10	4		9	3	5	11	8				
33		9	SOUTHAMPTON	4-0	McDiarmid 2, Kilsby, Platt		7	2		1				6	10	4	9		3	5	11	8				
34		11	WEST HAM UNITED	4-0	Kilsby 2, Platt, Freeman	6000	7	2		1				6	10	4	9		3	5	11	8				
35		12	Swindon Town	1-3	Platt	6000	7	2		1				6	10	4		9	3	5	11	8				
36		18	Queens Park Rangers	3-2	Freeman 2, Didymus	1500		2	1			7		6	10		9		3	5	11	8	4			
37		20	Luton Town	1-0	Freeman			2	1			7		6	10	4	9		3	5	11	8				
38		21	BRIGHTON	2-0	Platt, Freeman	1000		2	1		9	7		6	10	4			3	5	11	8				
			Apps				34	20	11	38	25	9	22	21	28	17	5	33	23	38	33	28	1	4	28	
			Goals								3	2		1	7	1	3	9	1	5	7	11				

F.A. Cup

		Date	Opponent	Score	Scorers	Att	Badenoch G	Benson H	Brittan C	Cooch G	Chapman H	Didymus F	Drennan T	Dunkley F	Freeman E	Hickleton W	Kilsby F	Lessons F	Lloyd-Davies E	McCartney D	McDiarmid F	Platt J	Rawlings	Springthorpe H	Tirrell P	Lowe
Q5	Dec	7	SUTTON UNITED	10-0	Badenoch 3, Platt 3, Chapman 2,*	7000	7			1	10		2		6				3	5	11	8			4	9
R1	Jan	11	BRISTOL ROVERS	0-1		10000	7			1	9		2	8	6			9	3	5	11				4	

* Additonal scorers: Lowe, Tirrell

Back: Drennan, Cooch, Benson
Middle: Foyle(Fin.Sec.), Tirrell, McCartney, McDiarmid, Brittain, Murrell(Trainer)
Front: Badenoch, Didymus, Platt, Lessons, Springthorpe, Freeman

		P	W	D	L	F	A	Pts
1	Queens Park Rangers	38	21	9	8	82	57	51
2	Plymouth Argyle	38	19	11	8	50	31	49
3	Millwall	38	19	8	11	49	32	46
4	Crystal Palace	38	17	10	11	54	51	44
5	Swindon Town	38	16	10	12	55	40	42
6	Bristol Rovers	38	16	10	12	59	56	42
7	Tottenham Hotspur	38	17	7	14	59	48	41
8	NORTHAMPTON TOWN	38	15	11	12	50	41	41
9	Portsmouth	38	17	6	15	63	52	40
10	West Ham United	38	15	10	13	47	48	40
11	Southampton	38	16	6	16	51	60	38
12	Reading	38	15	6	17	55	50	36
13	Bradfard (P.A.)	38	12	12	14	53	54	36
14	Watford	38	12	10	16	47	59	34
15	Brentford	38	14	5	19	49	52	33
16	Norwich City	38	12	9	17	46	49	33
17	Brighton & Hove Albion	38	12	8	18	46	59	32
18	Luton Town	38	12	6	20	33	56	30
19	Leyton	38	8	11	19	51	73	27
20	New Brompton	38	9	7	22	44	75	25

1908/09   1st in Southern League

#		Date	Opponent	Score	Scorers	Att	Bad	Bai	Bon	Bri	Cha	Coo	Dun	Fre	Hay	Hic	Kil	Les	Lew	LD	Man	McC	McD	Raw	Sha	Wal
1	Sep	2	New Brompton	2-0	Lessons, Freeman	3000			2			1		7		4		9	10	3	6	5	11			8
2		5	COVENTRY	3-1	Walker, Lewis, McDiarmid	1000			2			1		7		4		9	10	3	6	5	11			8
3		10	QUEENS PARK RANGERS	0-0		5000	7		2			1				4		9	10	3	6	5	11			8
4		12	Bristol Rovers	0-1		1200	7		2			1		8				9	10	3	4	5	11	6		
5		19	WATFORD	7-0	Walker 2, Lesson 2, Hickleton,*	8000	7		2			1				6		9	10	3	4	5	11			8
6		26	Norwich City	0-1		6095	7		2			1				6		9	10	3	4	5	11			8
7	Oct	3	READING	3-2	Lewis 2, Lessons	6000	7		2			1	5			6		9	10	3	4		11			8
8		10	Southampton	3-2	Lewis 2, Lessons	6000						1	2	6	7			9	10	3	4	5	11			8
9		17	LEYTON	5-0	Lewis 3, Lessons, Walker	8000						1	2	6	7			9	10	3	4	5	11			8
10		24	West Ham United	1-2	Lewis	9000						1	2	7		6		9	10	3	4	5	11			8
11		31	BRIGHTON	2-1	Walker, Freeman	8000	7		2			1		6		11		9	10	3	4	5				8
12	Nov	7	Crystal Palace	3-2	Lessons 2, McDiarmid	1200	7	1	2	3		1		6				9	10	5	4		11			8
13		14	BRENTFORD	4-2	Lewis 2, Lessons, Walker	7000	7		2	3		1		6				9	10	5	4		11			8
14		21	Luton Town	1-3	McDiarmid	8000	7		2	3		1		6				9	10	5	4		11			8
15		28	SWINDON TOWN	1-1	Walker	8000			2			1		7		6		9	10	3	4	5	11			8
16	Dec	5	Portsmouth	4-3	Lessons 2, Walker, McDiarmid	8000	7		2			1		6				9	10	3	4	5	11			8
17		12	EXETER CITY	1-0	Lewis	8000	7		2			1		6				9	10	3	4	5	11			8
18		19	Plymouth Argyle	2-0	Lewis, Lessons		7		2			1		6				9	10	3	4	5	11			8
19		26	SOUTHEND UNITED	2-1	Dunkley	1500			2			1		6	7			9	10	3	4	5	11			8
20		28	NEW BROMPTON	7-0	Lewis 4, McDiarmid, Lessons	1000			2			1		6	7			9	10	3	4	5	11			8
21	Jan	2	Coventry City	4-1	Lessons 2, Lewis, Walker	6000			2			1			7	6		9	10	3	4	5	11			8
22		9	BRISTOL ROVERS	3-0	Walker, Lessons, Lewis	7000			2			1		7		6		9	10	3	4	5	11			8
23		23	Watford	1-4	Lessons	4000	1		2		7				10		8	9		3	4		11	6		
24		30	NORWICH CITY	1-2	Lewis	7000				3		1		6	7		5	9	10	3	4		11			8
25	Feb	6	Reading	2-1	Walker, Lewis				2			1		6			5	9	10	3	4		11		7	8
26		13	SOUTHAMPTON	1-1	Lewis	8000			2			1		6	7			9	10	3	4	5	11			8
27		20	Leyton	1-0	Lessons	7000	7		2			1				6		9	10	3	4	5	11			8
28		27	WEST HAM UNITED	6-0	McDairmid, Manning, Lessons#	5000			2			1		6		11		9	10	3	4	5	7			8
29	Mar	6	Brighton	4-2	Lewis 3, Lessons	4000			2			1		6		11		9	10	3	4	5	7			8
30		13	CRYSTAL PALACE	1-0	Walker	8000			2			1		6		11		9	10	3	4	5	7			8
31		20	Brentford	1-3	Lewis	7000			2	3		1		6		11		9	10		4	5	7			8
32		27	LUTON TOWN	3-0	McDiarmid 2, Lessons	1400			2			1		6		11		9	10	3	4	5	7			8
33	Apr	3	Swindon Town	0-1		6000			2			1		6		11		9	10	3	4	5	7			8
34		9	Millwall	2-0	Lewis, Freeman	1000			2			1		6		11		9	10	3	4	5	7			8
35		10	PORTSMOUTH	0-1		1200			2			1		6		11	4	9	10	3		5	7			8
36		12	Southend United	2-2	Lewis 2 (1p)	7000			2			1		6		11		9	10	3	4	5	7			8
37		13	MILLWALL	3-1	Freeman, McDiarmid, Lessons	9000			2			1		6		11		9	10	3	4	5	7			8
38		17	Exeter	1-2	Freeman	8000			2			1		6		11		9	10	3	4	5	7			8
39		19	Queens Park Rangers	1-1	Freeman	3000			2			1		6		11	4	9	10	3		5	7			8
40		24	PLYMOUTH	2-1	Walker, McCartney				2			1		6		11	4	9	10	3		5	7			8
			Apps				13	2	31	13	1	37	29	28	1	15	1	40	39	39	37	34	39	2	1	38
			Goals				1						1	7		1		23	30	1	2	2	9			13

* Additonal scorers: Manning, Badenoch
\# Additonal scorers: Freeman, Lewis, Lloyd-Davies

F.A. Cup

		Date	Opponent	Score	Scorers	Att	Bad	Bai	Bon	Bri	Cha	Coo	Dun	Fre	Hay	Hic	Kil	Les	Lew	LD	Man	McC	McD	Raw	Sha	Wal
1R	Jan	16	DERBY COUNTY	1-1	McDiarmid	1479			2			1		7		6		9	10	3	4	5	11			8
1Rr		20	Derby County	2-4	McCartney, Lewis	1125			2			1	4	7				9	10	3	6	5	11			8

CHARITY SHIELD

	Date	Opponent	Score	Att	Bad	Bai	Bon	Bri	Cha	Coo	Dun	Fre	Hay	Hic	Kil	Les	Lew	LD	Man	McC	McD	Raw	Sha	Wal
	Apr	28	Newcastle	0-2	7000			2			1		11		6		9	10	3	4	5	7			8

Back: Brittan, Bailiff, Bonthron, Cooch, Davies
Middle: Foyle(Hon. Financial Sec.), Manning, Hickleton, McCartney, Rawlings, Murrell(Trainer)
Front: Badenoch, Walker, Freeman, Lessons, Lewis, McDiarmid, Kilsby

		P	W	D	L	F	A	Pts
1	NORTHAMPTON TOWN	40	25	5	10	90	45	55
2	Swindon Town	40	22	5	13	96	55	49
3	Southampton	40	19	10	11	67	58	48
4	Portsmouth	40	18	10	12	68	60	46
5	Bristol Rovers	40	17	9	14	60	63	43
6	Exeter City	40	18	6	16	56	65	42
7	New Brompton	40	17	7	16	48	59	41
8	Reading	40	11	18	11	60	57	40
9	Luton Town	40	17	6	17	59	60	40
10	Plymouth Argyle	40	15	10	15	46	47	40
11	Millwall	40	16	6	18	59	61	38
12	Southend United	40	14	10	16	52	54	38
13	Leyton	40	15	8	17	52	55	38
14	Watford	40	14	9	17	51	64	37
15	Queens Park Rangers	40	12	12	16	52	50	36
16	Crystal Palace	40	12	12	16	62	62	36
17	West Ham United	40	16	4	20	56	60	36
18	Brighton & Hove Albion	40	14	7	19	60	61	35
19	Norwich City	40	12	11	17	50	75	35
20	Coventry City	40	15	4	21	64	91	34
21	Brentford	40	13	7	20	59	74	33

1909/10 — 4th in Southern League

#		Date	Opponent	Score	Scorers	Att	Allen L	Beadling W	Bonthron R	Brittan R	Codling R	Dunkley F	Freeman G	Henley C	Hughes R	Lloyd-Davies E	Lewis A	Lessons F	Manning J	McCartney D	McDiarmid F	Oates A	Rawlings J	Redhead H	Severn A	Tebbutt B	Thorpe T	Whittaker F	Walden F	Walker R	Wykes A
1	Sep	2	Coventry	0-1		3000	7	2			6					3	10	9	4	5	11						1	8			
2		4	Leyton	1-2	Lessons	6000	7	2			6					3	10	9	4	5	11						1	8			
3		11	PLYMOUTH	5-1	Lessons 2,Lewis,Walker,Freeman	6000		2					11			3	10	9	4	5	6						1	7		8	
4		18	Southampton	3-2	Freeman 2, Walker	6000		2					11			3	10	9	4	5	6						1	7		8	
5		23	READING	2-0	Lewis, Lessons	5000		2					11			3	10	9	4	5	6						1	7		8	
6		25	CROYDEN COMMON	10-0	Whittaker 3, Lewis 2, *	8000		2					11			3	10	9	4	5	6						1	7		8	
7	Oct	2	Millwall	1-3	Whittaker	3000		2					11			3	10	9	4	5	6						1	7		8	
8		9	NEW BROMPTON	7-1	Lewis 3,Walker 2,Lessons,Freeman	8000		2					11			3	10	9	4	5	6						1	7		8	
9		13	Reading	1-1	Lewis			2					11			3	10	9	4	5	6						1	7		8	
10		16	EXETER CITY	0-0		6000				2			11			3	10	9	4	5	6						1	7		8	
11		23	Queens Park Rangers	0-2		10000				2	5		11			3	10	9	4		6						1	7		8	
12		30	LUTON TOWN	6-1	Walker 3, Lewis 2, Whittaker				3				11			5	10		4		6						1	9	8	7	2
13	Nov	6	Swindon Town	4-1	Lessons, Walker, Whittaker, OG				3	2			11			5	10	9	4		6						1	7		8	
14		13	CRYSTAL PALACE	1-0	Walker	12000			3	2			11			5	10	9	4		6						1	7		8	
15		20	Brighton	0-1		8000	11			2		5				3		9	4		6						1	7	10	8	
16		27	WEST HAM UNITED	3-1	Freeman, Whittaker, Lewis	7000			3	2			11			4				5	6						1	9	8	7	
17	Dec	4	Portsmouth	1-2	Lewis	5000	7			2			11			3	10		4	5	6						1	9		8	
18		11	BRISTOL ROVERS	0-1		7000				2			11			3	10		4	5	6						1	9	8	7	
19		25	Brentford	1-2	Freeman	10000				2			11			3	10	9	4	5	6						1	8		7	
20		27	BRENTFORD	4-1	Lewis 2, Lessons, Walker	11000				2			1			3	10	9	4	5	6						1	7		8	
21		28	WATFORD	3-0	Lewis 2 (1p), Walker	8500															6						1	7		8	
22		30	SOUTHEND UNITED	11-0	Lewis 4, Walden 3, Freeman 2 **	1000				2			11			3	10		4		6						1	7	9	8	
23	Jan	1	Watford	0-2		4000				2			11			3	10		4	5							1	7		8	
24		8	LEYTON	1-0	Walden	4000				2			11						4	5	6					10	1	7	9	8	
25		22	Plymouth	1-0	Walden				2	3			11	7				9			6		5			10	1	4	8		
26		29	SOUTHAMPTON	2-0	Walden, Lessons				2	3			11				10	9	4	5	6						1	7	8		
27	Feb	12	MILLWALL	2-1	Walden, Lewis	4000			2	3			11				10	9	4	5	6						1	7	8		
28		19	New Brompton	1-2	Freeman	4000			2	3			11				10	9	4	5	6						1	7			
29		26	Exeter City	3-2	Lewis, Lessons, Freeman	6000			2	3			11				10	9		5	6						1	4	8	7	
30	Mar	12	Luon Town	3-0	Lewis 2, Freeman				2	3			11				10	9	4	5	6						1	7		8	
31		19	SWINDON TOWN	3-0	Lessons 2, Lewis	7000			2	3			11			3	10	9	4	5	6						1	7		8	
32		23	Croyden Common	2-4	Walker, Lewis				2				11			3	10	9	4	5	6						1	7		8	
33		26	Crystal Palace	0-1		9000			2				11			3	10	9	4	5	6						1	7		8	
34		28	Southend United	2-1	Lessons, OG				2	3			11					9	4	5	6					10	1	7		8	
35		29	COVENTRY	0-1		1400			2	3						6	10	9	4	5	11						1	7		8	
36	Apr	2	BRIGHTON	1-1	Severn	5800				2						3	11	9	4	5	6				10		1	7	8		
37		7	QUEENS PARK RANGERS	0-0		3000				2			11			3	10	9	4	5	6						1	7	8		
38		9	West Ham United	0-1		1000				2			11			3		9	4		6		5		10		1	7	8		
39		14	Norwich City	0-2		3000				2						3	10	9	4	5	6	1	6		8		1	7			
40		16	PORTSMOUTH	2-0	Severn, Whittaker					2					11	3	10		4	5	6	5			8		1	7		8	
41		23	Bristol Rovers	0-1						2						3	9		4	5	6	11		10	8		1	7			
42		30	NORWICH CITY	3-1	McCartney, Severn, Walden	7000				2					11	3	10		4	5	6				9		1	7	8		
			Apps				1	3	28	25	3	3	33	1	2	35	37	32	39	34	41	1	4	1	7	2	42	42	16	29	1
			Goals										13				26	14		1					3			8	11	11	

Three own goals

* Additional scorers: Lessons 2, Freeman 2, Walker
** Additional scorers: Walker, OG

F.A. Cup

		Date	Opponent	Score	Scorers	Att	Brittan R	Bonthron R	Freeman G	Hughes R	Lloyd-Davies E	Lewis A	Lessons F	Manning J	McCartney D	McDiarmid F	Thorpe T	Whittaker F	Walker R
R1	Jan	15	SHEFFIELD WEDNESDAY	0-0		12000	2	3	11		5	10	9	4		6	1	7	8
R1		18	Sheffield Wednesday	1-0	Walker	18533	2	3	11			10	9	4	5	6	1	7	8
R2	Feb	5	NOTTINGHAM FOREST	0-0		15000						10	9	4	5	6	1	7	8
R2		9	Nottingham Forest	0-1		15000						10	9	4	5	6	1	7	8

Back: Whittaker, Bonthron, Thorpe, Davies
Middle: Manning, McCartney, Dunkley, Codling, Brittan
Front: McDiarmid, Walker, Lessons, Lewis, Freeman, Beadling

		P	W	D	L	F	A	Pts
1	Brighton & Hove Albion	42	23	13	6	69	28	59
2	Swindon Town	42	22	10	10	91	46	54
3	Queens Park R.ngers	42	19	13	10	56	47	51
4	NORTHAMPTON TOWN	42	22	4	16	90	44	48
5	Southampton	42	16	16	10	64	55	48
6	Portsmouth	42	20	7	15	70	63	47
7	Crystal Palace	42	20	6	16	69	50	46
8	Coventry City	42	19	8	15	71	60	46
9	West Ham United	42	15	15	12	69	56	45
10	Leyton	42	16	11	15	60	46	43
11	Plymouth Argyle	42	16	11	15	61	54	43
12	New Brompton	42	19	5	18	76	74	43
13	Bristol Rovers	42	16	10	16	37	48	42
14	Brentford	42	16	9	17	50	58	41
15	Luton Town	42	15	11	16	72	92	41
16	Millwall	42	15	7	20	45	59	37
17	Norwich City	42	13	9	20	59	78	35
18	Exeter City	42	14	6	22	60	69	34
19	Watford	42	10	13	19	51	76	33
20	Southend United	42	12	9	21	51	90	33
21	Croydon Common	42	13	5	24	52	96	31
22	Reading	42	7	10	25	38	73	24

1910/11 2nd in Southern League

#	Date		Opponent	Score	Scorers	Att	Bradshaw F	Brittan C	Clipston F	Freeman E	Hampson J	Hughes R	Lessons F	Lewis A	Lloyd-Davies E	Manning J	Masters A	McDiarmid F	Napier D	Perkins	Severn A	Stonley S	Thorpe T	Walden F	Whittaker F
1	Sep	3	WTAFORD	2-0	Freeman, Thorpe(p)	8000	8	2		11			9	10	3	4		6	5				1		7
2		10	Plymouth	0-0		6000	8	2	3	11			9	10	5	4		6					1		7
3		17	SOUTHAMPTON	3-0	Bradshaw, Whittaker, Lewis	1000	8	2	3			11	9	10	5	4		6					1		7
4		24	Southend	0-2		6000	8	2	3			11	9	10	5	4		6					1		7
5	Oct	8	New Brompton	0-0		6000	9	2		11				5	10	3	4	6		7			1	8	
6		15	MILLWALL	0-0		8000	9	2		11				5	10	3	4	6		7			1	8	
7		22	Queens Park Rangers	1-1	Freeman	1100	9	2		8	6			5	10	3	4	11					1		7
8		29	WEST HAM UNITED	2-0	Bradshaw 2	7000	9	2		8	6			5	10	3	4	11					1		7
9	Nov	5	Luton Town	3-1	Whittaker, McDiarmid, Lewis	8000		2	3	8	6			5	10	3	4	11					1	7	9
10		12	PORTSMOUTH	1-0	Whittaker	6000		2	3	8	6			5	10	3	4	11					1	7	9
11		19	Norwich City	0-1		6000	9	2		8	6			5	10	3	4	11					1	7	9
12		26	Brighton	0-5		3000		2		8	6			5	10	3	4	11					1	7	9
13	Dec	1	COVENTRY	4-1	Whittaker 2, Freeman, Lewis			2	3	11	6			5	10		4	11					1	7	9
14		10	Swindon Town	1-2	Lewis	3000	8	2	3	10	6			5	10		4						1	7	9
15		17	BRISTOL ROVERS	3-2	Whittaker, McDiarmid, Thorpe(p)	3000	8	2	3	11	6			5			4	11					1	7	9
16		24	Crystal Palace	0-0		6000	8	2	3	11	6			5	10		4						1	7	9
17		26	BRENTFORD	2-0	Lewis, Whittaker	1200	8	2	3	11	6		9		5		4						1	7	10
18		27	Brentford	0-0		1377	8	2	3	11	6		9		5		4						1	7	10
19		28	EXETER CITY	2-0	Severn, Bradshaw	6000	8	2	3	11	6			5		4					10		1	7	9
20		31	Wtford	2-2	Lessons 2		8	2	3	11	6		9	10	5	4							1	7	
21	Jan	7	PLYMOUTH	0-1			8	2	3	11	6		9	10	5	4							1	7	
22		21	Southampton	0-1			8	2	3		6		9	10	5		4	11					1	7	
23		28	SOUTHEND UNITED	0-0			8	2	3	11	6			5		4						10	1	7	9
24	Feb	11	NEW BROMPTON	2-1	Manning, Bradshaw	4000	8	2	3	11	6		9	10	5	4		11					1	7	
25		18	Millwall	0-0		1000	8	2	3	11	6			10	5	4						9	1	7	
26		25	QUEENS PARK RANGERS	0-0		7000	8	2	3	11	6		9	10	5	4							1	7	
27	Mar	4	West Ham United	2-1	Bradshaw 2	1000	8	2	3	11	6		9	10	5	4							1	7	
28		11	LUTON TOWN	3-1	Lessons 2, OG	6000	8	2	3	11	6		9	10	5	4							1	7	
29		18	Portsmouth	0-0		4000	8	2	3	11	6		9	10	5	4							1	7	
30		25	NORWICH CITY	4-0	Lewis 3, Lessons	3000	8	2	3	11	6		9	10	5	4							1	7	
31		30	Coventry	1-1	Lessons		8	2		11	6		9	10	5	4					3		1	7	
32	Apr	1	BRIGHTON	3-0	Walden 2, Lewis	6000	8	2	3	11	6		9	10	5	4							1	7	
33		8	Exeter City	4-1	Freeman 2, Lewis, Lessons	4500	8	2	3	11	6		9	10	5	4							1	7	
34		14	Leyton	0-2		8000	8	2		11	6		9	10	5	4					3		1	7	
35		15	SWINDON TOWN	0-1		1200	8	2		11	6		9	10	5	4					3		1		7
36		17	LEYTON	3-0	Bradshaw 2, Whittaker		8	2		11	6		9	10	5	4							1		7
37		18	CRYSTAL PALACE	5-0	Lewis 3, Freeman, Lessons	7000	8	2		11	5		9	10	3	4		6					1		7
38		22	Bristol Rovers	1-0	Freeman	6000	9	2		11	4		5	10	3			6			8		1		7
			Apps				34	36	25	34	32	2	33	35	34	35	2	18	5	2	3	1	38	30	19
			Goals				9			7			8	13	1			2			1		2	2	8

One own goal

F.A. Cup

	Date		Opponent	Score	Scorers	Att	Bradshaw F	Brittan C	Clipston F	Freeman E	Hampson J	Hughes R	Lessons F	Lewis A	Lloyd-Davies E	Manning J	Masters A	McDiarmid F	Napier D	Perkins	Severn A	Stonley S	Thorpe T	Walden F	Whittaker F
R1	Jan	14	LUTON TOWN	1-5	Lessons 3, Lewis, Bradshaw	1500	8	2	3		6		9	10	5	4		11					1		7
R2	Feb	4	Newcastle *	1-1	Bradshaw	4202	8	2	3		6		9	10	5	4		11					1		7
		8	Newcastle *	0-1		2988	8	2	3		6		9	10	5	4		11					1		7

* both matches played away

	P	W	D	L	F	A	Pts
1 Swindon Town	38	24	5	9	80	31	53
2 NORTHAMPTON TOWN	38	18	12	8	54	27	48
3 Brighton & Hove Albion	38	20	8	10	58	36	48
4 Crystal Palace	38	17	13	8	55	48	47
5 West Ham United	38	17	11	10	63	46	45
6 Queens Park Rangers	38	13	14	11	52	41	40
7 Leyton	38	16	8	14	57	52	40
8 Plymouth Argyle	38	15	9	14	54	55	39
9 Luton Town	38	15	8	15	67	63	38
10 Norwich City	38	15	8	15	46	48	38
11 Coventry City	38	16	6	16	65	68	38
12 Brentford	38	14	9	15	41	42	37
13 Exeter City	38	14	9	15	51	53	37
14 Watford	38	13	9	16	49	65	35
15 Millwall	38	11	9	18	42	54	31
16 Bristol Rovers	38	10	10	18	42	55	30
17 Southampton	38	11	8	19	42	67	30
18 New Brompton	38	11	8	19	34	65	30
19 Southend United	38	10	9	19	47	64	29
20 Portsmouth	38	8	11	19	34	53	27

Back: Hampson, Clipston, Newman, Thorpe, Brittan, Davies, Napier
Middle: Tebbutt, Bradshaw, Manning, Ewing, Lewis, Rawlings, Hughes
Front: Redhead, Walden, Whittaker, Lessons, Severn, MacDiarmid, Freeman

1911/12 3rd in Southern League

#		Date	Opponent	Res	Scorers	Att	Ball W	Bradshaw F	Brittan C	Clipstone F	Freeman E	Hampson J	Harris F	Hughes R	King H	Lessons F	Lewis A	Lloyd-Davies E	Manning J	Redhead H	Tebbott B	Thorpe T	Tompkins E	Tull W	Walden F	Whittaker
1	Sep	2	Coventry	2-1	Bradshaw, Lessons	1000		8	2	3	11	6			9	10		5	4			1			7	
2		9	LEYTON	3-0	King, Walden, Bradshaw	8000		8	2	3	11	6			9	10		5	4			1			7	
3		16	Norwich	0-1		5000		8	2	3	11	6			9	10		5	4			1			7	
4		23	CRYSTAL PALACE	1-1	King	9000		8	2	3	11	6			9	10		5	4			1			7	
5		30	Southampton	1-2	Lessons			8			11	6			5	10		2	4			1	3		7	
6	Oct	7	PLYMOUTH ARGYLE	4-1	Whittaker 2, Bradshaw, Freeman	6000		8	2		11	6			5	10		3	4			1			7	9
7		14	Reading	0-3		4000		9	2		11	6			5	10		3	4			1			7	8
8		21	WATFORD	2-2	Walden(p), Freeman	6000		10	2		11	6			5			3	4			1		9	7	
9		28	New Brompton	1-3	Tull	5000		10	2		11	4		8	5			3			6	1		9	7	
10	Nov	4	EXETER CITY	2-1	King 2	5000		10	2		11	4		8	5			3			6	1		9	7	
11		11	Brentford	2-2	Lessons, Hampson	4000				2	11	5			8	9	10	3	4			1	6		7	
12		18	QUEENS PARK RANGERS	5-1	King 3, Lewis 2	8000				2	11	5			8	9	10	3	4			1	6		7	
13		25	Millwall	4-0	Lessons 2, Lewis 2	6000				2	11	5			8	9	10	3	4			1	6		7	
14	Dec	2	WEST HAM UNITED	3-2	Lessons, Manning, Freeman	6000				2	11	5	7		8	9	10	3	4			1	6			
15		9	Bristol Rovers	0-0		1200				2	11	5	7		8	9	10	3	4			1	6			
16		16	SWINDON TOWN	4-0	Lessons 3, King	1200				2	11	5			8	9	10	3	4			1	6		7	
17		23	Luton Town	3-3	Freeman 2, Manning	6000				2	11	5			8	9	10	3	4			1	6			7
18		25	Brighton	1-2	Lessons	1150				2	11	5			8	9	10	3	4			1	6			7
19		26	BRIGHTON	1-0	Lessons	1400	3			2	11	5			8	9	10		4			1	6			7
20		30	COVENTRY	2-1	Freeman, Tull	1000	2			3	11	5			8	9			4			1	6	10		7
21	Jan	6	Leyton	1-1	King					3	11	5			8	9	10		4		2	1	6			7
22		20	NORWICH CITY	1-0	Lewis	5000				2	11	5			8	9	10	3	4			1	6			7
23		27	Crystal Palace	2-1	King, Lewis	1000				2	11	5			8	9	10	3	4			1	6			7
24	Feb	10	Plymouth Argyle	0-2		1400				2		5			8	9	11	3	4			1	6	10	7	
25		17	READING	7-0	Freeman 2, Lessons 2, King 2, Tull	8000				2	11	5			8	9		3	4			1	6	10	7	
26	Mar	2	NEW BROMPTON	1-2		5000				3		5	11		8	9	10		4		2	1	6		7	
27		9	Exeter City	2-0	Lessons, Walden	5000				2	11	5			8	9	10	3	4			1	6		7	
28		16	BRENTFORD	6-3	King 3, Lessons 2, Walden	5000				2	11	5			8	9	10	3	4			1	6		7	
29		23	Queens Park Rangers	1-2	Lewis	5000				2	11	5			8	9	10	3	4			1	6		7	
30		30	MILLWALL	2-0	King 2	5000				2		5			8	9	11	3	4			1	6	10	7	
31	Apr	6	West Ham United	2-0	Lewis, Lessons	1000				2	11	5				9	10	3	4			1	6	8	7	
32		8	Stoke City	0-1		7000				2	11	5				9	10	3	4			1	6	8	7	
33		9	STOKE CITY	3-1	Lessons, Freeman, Manning	3000				2	11	5				9	10	3	4			1	6		7	8
34		10	Watford	0-3						2	8	5	11				10	3	4			1	6		7	9
35		13	BRISTOL ROVERS	5-0	Tull 4, Lewis	6000				2	11	5					10	3	4		8	1	6	9	7	
36		20	Swindon	1-1	Tull					2	11	5				9	10	3	4			1	6	8	7	
37		25	SOUTHAMPTON	4-0	Lessons, Tull, Walden, Hampson					2	11	5				9	10	3	4			1	6	8	7	
38		27	LUTON TOWN	1-0	OG					2	11	5			8	9	10	3	4			1	6		7	
			Apps				2	10	6	35	35	38	2	2	26	36	29	34	35	2	5	38	29	12	31	11
			Goals					3			10	2			19	19	9		3					9	5	2

One own goal

F.A. Cup

		Date	Opponent	Res	Scorers	Att	Ball W	Bradshaw F	Brittan C	Clipstone F	Freeman E	Hampson J	Harris F	Hughes R	King H	Lessons F	Lewis A	Lloyd-Davies E	Manning J	Redhead H	Tebbott B	Thorpe T	Tompkins E	Tull W	Walden F	Whittaker
R1	Jan	13	BRISTOL CITY	1-0	Lewis	1400				2	11	5			8	9	10	3	4			1	6		7	
R2	Feb	3	Darlington	1-1	King	8000				2	11	5			8	9	10	3	4			1	6		7	
R2r		8	DARLINGTON	2-0	Lessons, King	7000				2	11	5			8	9	10	3	4			1	6		7	
R3		24	Fulham	1-2	Lewis	3203				2	11	5			8	9	10	3	4			1	6		7	

Back: Murrel (Trainer), Smith, Manning, Lewis, Thorpe, Lessons, Brittan, Clipston, Burrows (Trainer)
Front: Walden, Bradshaw, Whittaker, Davies, King, Hampson, Freeman

		P	W	D	L	F	A	Pts
1	Queens Park Rangers	38	21	11	6	59	35	53
2	Plymouth Argyle	38	23	6	9	63	31	52
3	NORTHAMPTON TOWN	38	22	7	9	82	41	51
4	Swindon Town	38	21	6	11	82	50	48
5	Brighton & Hove Albion	38	19	9	10	73	35	47
6	Coventry City	38	17	8	13	66	54	42
7	Crystal Palace	38	15	10	13	70	46	40
8	Millwall	38	15	10	13	60	37	40
9	Watford	38	13	10	15	56	68	36
10	Stoke	38	13	10	15	51	63	36
11	Reading	38	11	14	13	43	59	36
12	Norwich City	38	10	14	14	40	60	34
13	West Ham United	38	13	7	18	64	69	33
14	Brentford	38	12	9	17	60	65	33
15	Exeter City	38	11	11	16	48	62	33
16	Southampton	38	10	11	17	46	63	31
17	Bristol Rovers	38	9	13	16	41	62	31
18	New Brompton	38	11	9	18	35	72	31
19	Luton Town	38	9	10	19	49	61	28
20	Leyton	38	7	11	20	27	62	25

1912/13   10th in Southern League

#		Date	Opponent	Score	Scorers	Att	Ball W	Bull W	Churchman E	Clipston F	Freeman E	Harris F	Hampson J	Hughes R	King H	Langham F	Lessons F	Lewis A	Lloyd-Davies E	Manning J	Rawlings J	Smith C	Tebbutt B	Tomkins E	Thorpe T	Tull W	Walden F
1	Sep	4	Southampton	2-2	Lewis 2					2	11		5		8			9	10	3				6	1	4	7
2		7	GILLINGHAM	2-1	Lloyd-Davies, Lewis	8000				2	11		5		8			9	10	3				6	1	5	7
3		12	SOUTHAMPTON	1-2	Lewis	1500		5		2	11				8			9	10	3				6	1		7
4		14	Stoke City	0-1		8000				2	11		5		8			9	10	3				6	1	9	7
5		18	Watford	0-2						2	11	7	5		8			9	10	3				6	1		
6		21	Queens Park Rangers	2-3	Lessons 2	1200		2			11		5		8		9		10	3				6	1	4	7
7		28	BRENTFORD	2-0	Walden, King	7000				2	11		5		8		9		10	3				6	1		7
8	Oct	5	Millwall	1-0	King	9000				2			5	11	8		9		10	3				6	1	4	7
9		12	BRISTOL ROVERS	2-1	King, Smith	6000				2			5	11	9				10	3		8		6	1	4	7
10		19	Swindon Town	1-2	King	7000	2						5	11	9				10	3		8		6	1	4	7
11		26	PORTSMOUTH	1-2	King	5000				2			5	11	9				10	3		8		6	1	4	7
12	Nov	2	Exeter City	1-1	Freeman	5000				2	8			11	9	5			10	3				6	1	4	7
13		9	WEST HAM UNITED	4-3	King 2, Lewis, Walden	6000				2	8			11	9	5			10	3	5			6	1	4	7
14		16	Brighton	1-2	OG	8000				2	8			11	9	5			10	3	5			6	1	4	7
15		23	COVENTRY CITY	0-1		8000				2	8			11	9	5			10	3				6	1	4	7
16	Dec	7	MERTHYR	3-0	King, Freeman, Langham	3500				2	8			11	9	5			10	3				6	1	4	7
17		14	Crystal Palace	2-2	King 2(1p)	5500				2	8			11	9	5			10	3				6	1	4	7
18		21	PLYMOUTH ARGYLE	1-1	Lewis	4500				2	8			11	9	5			10	3	4			6	1		7
19		25	Reading	0-1		5000				2	8			11	9	5			10	3	4			6	1		7
20		26	READING	4-1	Freeman 2, Walden, King					2	8			11	9	5			10	3	4			6	1		7
21		28	Gillingham	1-2	King(p)					2	8			11	9	5			1	3	4			6	1		7
22	Jan	4	STOKE CITY	9-0	Walden 4, King 3, Lewis, Freeman	2500				2	8			11	9	5			10	3				6	1		7
23		25	Brentford	0-0		7000				2	8			11	9	5	10			3				6	1	4	7
24	Feb	8	MILLWALL	1-2	Freeman	6000				2	8			11	9	5	10			3				6	1	4	7
25		15	Bristol Rovers	0-2		5000				2	10			11	8			9	3		5			6	1	4	7
26		22	QUEENS PARK RANGERS	0-0		5000				2	10			11	8			9	3		5			6	1	4	7
27	Mar	1	Portsmouth	1-1	King	1000				2	8			11	9			10	3		5			6	1	4	7
28		8	EXETER CITY	4-0	Smith, Freeman, Hughes, King	6000				2	8			11	9				3			5	10	6	1	4	
29		15	West Ham United	0-0		7000			7	2	8				9				3		11	5	10	6	1	4	
30		22	BRIGHTON	1-0	King	7000				2	8			11	9				3			5	10	6	1	4	
31		24	Norwich	2-2	King 2	5000				2	8			11	9				3			5	10	6	1	4	
32		25	NORWICH	3-0	Walden, King, Freeman 1(p)	9000				2	8			11	9				3			5	10	6	1	4	7
33		29	Coventry	4-4	King 3, Hughes					2	8			11	9			10	3			5		6	1		7
34	Apr	5	WATFORD	1-1	King	4000				2	8			11	9			10	3			5	10	6	1	4	7
35		12	Merthyr	1-2	King	8000				2	8			11	9			10	3			5	10	6	1		7
36		17	SWINDON TOWN	1-1	King					2	8			11	9			10	3			5	10	6	1		7
37		19	CRYSTAL PALACE	2-1	Freeman 2	6000				2	8			11	9			10	3			5	10	4	6	1	7
38		26	Plymouth	0-2		5000				3	8			11	9			10	2			5		10	4	6	1	7
			Apps				1	2	1	36	32	1	7	32	38	11	12	24	38	25	4	14	5	38	38	28	31
			Goals								10			2	27	1	2	7	1			2					8

One own goal

F.A. Cup

		Date	Opponent	Score	Scorers	Att	Clipston F	Freeman E	Hughes R	King H	Langham F	Lloyd-Davies E	Manning J	Tomkins E	Thorpe T	Walden F
R1	Jan	18	Blackburn Rovers	2-7	Walden, Lewis	23623	2	8	11	9	5	10	3	6	1	7

Back: Tull, Clipston, Lloyd-Davies, Hughes
Middle: Manning, Tebbutt, Hampson, Rawlings, Tomkins, Burrows(Trainer)
Front: Bull(Manager), Redhead, Walden, King, Lessons, Lewis, Smith, Freeman, Jones(Secretary)

		P	W	D	L	F	A	Pts
1	Plymouth Argyle	38	22	6	10	77	36	50
2	Swindon Town	38	20	8	10	66	41	48
3	West Ham United	38	18	12	8	66	46	48
4	Queens Park Rangers	38	18	10	10	46	35	46
5	Crystal Palace	38	17	11	10	55	36	45
6	Millwall	38	19	7	12	62	43	45
7	Exeter City	38	18	8	12	48	44	44
8	Reading	38	17	8	13	59	55	42
9	Brighton & Hove Albion	38	13	12	13	48	47	38
10	NORTHAMPTON TOWN	38	12	14	12	48	48	38
11	Portsmouth	38	14	8	16	41	49	36
12	Merthyr Town	38	12	12	14	42	60	36
13	Coventry City	38	13	8	17	53	59	34
14	Watford	38	12	10	16	43	50	34
15	Gillingham *	38	12	10	16	36	53	34
16	Bristol Rovers	38	12	9	17	55	64	33
17	Southhampton	38	10	11	17	40	72	31
18	Norwich City	38	10	9	19	39	50	29
19	Brentford	38	11	5	22	42	55	27
20	Stoke	38	10	4	24	39	75	24

* Previously known as New Brompton

1913/14 3rd in Southern League

#	Date	Opponent	Res	Scorers	Att	Bellamy B	Birtles T	Brown D	Clipson F	Freeman E	Harris J	Hughes R	King G	Langham H	Lessons F	Lloyd-Davies E	Manning J	Rawlings A	Smith C	Smith H	Thorpe T	Tomkins E	Tull W
1	Sep 4	CRYSTAL PALACE	1-1	Freeman	7000		7	10	2	8		11	9			3	5				1	6	4
2	6	Norwich City	1-1	King	7000		7	10	2	8		11	9			3	5				1	6	4
3	13	GILLINGHAM	3-1	Freeman 2(1p), Brown	6000			10	2	8	7	11	9			3	5				1	6	4
4	17	Crystal Palace	0-3		5000			10	2	8	7	11	9			3	5				1	6	4
5	20	QUEENS PARK RANGERS	2-2	King, Freeman(p)	5000			10	2	8	7	11	9			3	5				1	6	4
6	27	Southend United	3-1	Hughes, King, Freeman					2	8		11	9		5	3	4				1	6	7
7	Oct 4	BRIGHTON	2-0	Manning, King(p)	6000				2	8		11	9		5	3	4		10		1	6	7
8	11	Portsmouth	0-3		6400				2	8		11	9		5	3	4		10		1	6	7
9	18	MILLWALL	5-1	King 2, Brown 2, Hughes	7000		7	10	2	8		11	9		5	3	4				1	6	
10	25	Exeter City	0-2		4000			10	2	8		11	9		5	3	4				1	6	7
11	Nov 1	CARDIFF CITY	2-1	King 2	6000			10	2	8		11	9		5	3	4				1	6	
12	8	Swindon Town	1-1	King	1000	11		10	2	8			9		5	3	4	7			1	6	
13	15	BRISTOL ROVERS	2-0	King, Brown	4000	11		10	2	8			9		5	3	4	7			1	6	
14	22	Merthyr Town	2-2	King 2	5000			10	2	8		11	9		5	3	4	7			1	6	
15	29	WEST HAM UNITED	0-0		4000			10	2	8		11	9		5	3	4	7			1		6
16	Dec 6	Plymouth	0-2		8000			10	2	8		11	9		5	3	4	7			1		6
17	13	SOUTHAMPTON	0-0			10			2	8		11	9		5	3	4	7			1		6
18	20	Reading	1-1	King		10	7		2	8		11	9		5	3	4				1		6
19	25	Coventry	1-0	King	9000	10	7		2	8		11	9		5	3	4				1		6
20	26	COVENTRY	0-0		9000	10	7		2	8		11	9		5	3	4				1		6
21	27	NORWICH CITY	1-1	King	9000	10	7		2	8		11	9		5	3	4				1		6
22	Jan 3	Gillingham	1-1	Bellamy	5000	10	7		2	8		11	9		5	3	4				1		6
23	17	Queens Park Rangers	0-0		7000	10	7		2	8		11	9		5	3	4				1		6
24	24	SOUTHEND	2-0	Bellamy, King		10	7		2	8		11	9		5	3	4				1		6
25	Feb 7	Brighton	1-1	Hughes	3000	10	7		2	8		11			5	3	4	9			1		6
26	14	PORTSMOUTH	0-0			10	7		2	8		11	9		5	3	4				1		6
27	28	EXETER CITY	2-1	King, OG	5000	10	7		3	8		11	9		5		4	7			1	2	6
28	Mar 7	Cardiff City	0-0		1400	10	7		2	8		11	9		5	3	4				1		6
29	14	SWINDON	1-0	Freeman		10	7		2	8		11	9		5	3	4				1		6
30	16	Millwall	1-2	King	8000	10	7		3	8		11	9	2	5	3	4				1		6
31	21	Bristol Rovers	1-1	Hughes	7000	10	7		2	8		11	9		5	3	4				1		6
32	28	MERTHYR TOWN	1-0	King		10			2	7		11	9		5	3	4		8		1		6
33	Apr 4	West Ham United	1-1	Hughes	1000	10			2	8		11	9		5	3	4	7	1	1			6
34	10	Watford	3-3	Bellamy 2, Hughes	7000	10			2	8		11	9		5	3	4	7		1			6
35	11	PLYMOUTH	2-2	King, Freeman	6000	10			2	8		11	9		5	3	4	7		1			6
36	14	WATFORD	2-0	Bellamy, Hughes		10			2	8		11	9		5	3	4	7		1			6
37	18	Southampton	2-1	Clipston, Rawlings	6000	10			2	8		11	9		5	3	4	7		1			6
38	25	READING	3-1	King 2, Hughes	4000	10			2			11	9		5	3	4	7	8		1		6
				Apps		24	17	13	38	37	3	36	35	1	35	36	38	13	6	5	33	14	34
				Goals		5		4	1	7		8	22				1	1					

One own goal

F.A. Cup

#	Date	Opponent	Res	Scorers	Att	Bellamy B	Birtles T	Brown D	Clipson F	Freeman E	Harris J	Hughes R	King G	Langham H	Lessons F	Lloyd-Davies E	Manning J	Rawlings A	Smith C	Smith H	Thorpe T	Tomkins E	Tull W
R1	Jan 10	Derby County	0-1		15000	10	7		2	8		11	9		5	3	4				4		6

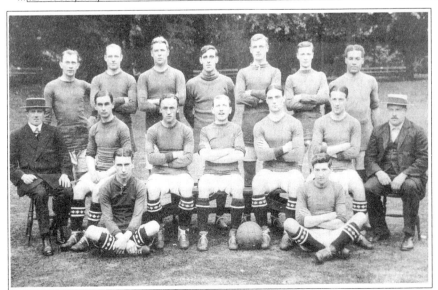

	P	W	D	L	F	A	Pts
1 Swindon Town	38	21	8	9	81	41	50
2 Crystal Palace	38	17	16	5	60	32	50
3 NORTHAMPTON TOWN	38	14	19	5	50	37	47
4 Reading	38	17	10	11	43	36	44
5 Plymouth Argyle	38	15	13	10	46	42	43
6 West Ham United	38	15	12	11	61	60	42
7 Brighton & Hove Albion	38	15	12	11	43	45	42
8 Queens Park Rangers	38	16	9	13	45	43	41
9 Portsmouth	38	14	12	12	57	48	40
10 Cardiff City	38	13	12	13	46	42	38
11 Southampton	38	15	7	16	55	54	37
12 Exeter City	38	10	16	12	39	38	36
13 Gillingham	38	13	9	16	48	49	35
14 Norwich City	38	9	17	12	49	51	35
15 Millwall	38	11	12	15	51	56	34
16 Southend United	38	10	12	16	41	66	32
17 Bristol Rovers	38	10	11	17	46	67	31
18 Watford	38	10	9	19	50	56	29
19 Merthyr Town	38	9	10	19	39	61	28
20 Coventry City	38	6	14	18	43	68	26

Back: Manning, Lessons, Clipston, Thorpe, Langham, Tebbett, Tull
Front: Jones(Secretary), Tomkins, Freeman, Lloyd-Davies, King, Brown, Burrows(Trainer)
Sitting: C.Smith, Hughes

1914/15 5th in Southern League

No		Date	Opponent	Score	Scorers	Att	Bellamy B	Clipston F	Dawson S	Freeman E	Grendon R	Hughes R	Langham D	Lessons F	Letting	Lloyd-Davies E	Lockett W	Manning J	Newman R	Smith D	Thorpe T	Tomkins E	Tull W	Whitworth G
1	Sep	5	Swindon Town	2-2	Lockett, Hughes		10	2	8			11		5		3	9	4		7	1	6		
2		12	SOUTHEND UNITED	1-0	Dawson			2	8			11		5		3	10	4		7	1	6		9
3		19	Queens Park Rangers	0-0		5000		2	8	7		11		5		3	9	4		10	1	6		
4		23	Exeter City	1-2	Clipston(p)	2000	8	2		10		7		5		3		4		11	1	6		9
5		26	Millwall	1-2	OG	1000	10	2		8		11		5		3		4		7	1	6		9
6	Oct	3	Bristol Rovers	3-2	Dawson, Smith, Hughes	7000		2	10	11		7				3	9	5		8	1	6	4	
7		10	CROYDON COMMON	3-2	Clipston(p), Lockett, Smith			2	10	11		7		5		3	9	4		8	1	6		
8		17	Reading	1-2	Smith	6000		2	10	11		7				3	9	5		8	1	6		
9		24	SOUTHAMPTON	2-1	Lockett, Clipston(p)			2	10	11		7				3	9	5		8	1	6		
10		31	CRYSTAL PALACE	2-1	Hughes 2		10	3		11		7		2			9	5		8	1	6	4	
11	Nov	7	Watford	0-0		5000	10	2		11		7				3	9	5		8	1	6		
12		11	PLYMOUTH	1-1	Lockett		10	2		11		7				3	9	5		8	1	6		
13		21	West Ham United	0-1		7000		2		11		7	10			3	9	5		8	1	6	4	
14		28	NORWICH CITY	4-1	Lockett 2, Hughes, Smith	3000		2		11		7		9		3	10	5		8	1	6		
15	Dec	5	Gillingham	2-2	Lockett, Freeman	2000		2		11		7		9		3	10	5		8	1	6		
16		12	BRIGHTON	2-1	Clipston 2(1p)	5000		2		11		7		9		3	10	5		8	1	6		
17		19	Cardiff City	0-5		5000		2		11		7		9		3	10	5		8	1	6		
18		25	Luton City	1-1	Hughes			2		11		7		9		3	10	5		8	1	6		
19		26	LUTON TOWN	0-3			10	2		11		7		5		3	9			8	1	6		
20		28	EXETER CITY	1-1	Bellamy	3000	10	2		11		7		5		3	8	4			1	6		9
21	Jan	2	SWINDON TOWN	2-3	Bellamy, Smith	5000	10	2		11		7				3	9	5		8	1	6	4	
22		23	QUEENS PARK RANGERS	1-1	Bellamy	3000	10	2		11	4	7				3	9	5		8	1	6		
23	Feb	6	BRISTOL ROVERS	2-0	Freeman, Lockett	1000	10	2		11		7				3	9	5		8	1	6		
24		13	Croydon Common	1-0	Lockett	2000	10	2		11		7				3	9	5		8	1	6		
25		17	Southend United	2-1	Bellamy, Freeman		10	2		11		7				3		5		8	1	6	4	9
26		20	READING	2-1	Freeman, Smith	8500	10	2		11	4	7				3	9	5		8	1	6		
27	Mar	6	Crystal Palace	1-1	Lockett	4000	10	2		11	4	7				3	9	5		8	1	6		
28		13	WATFORD	1-1	Smith		10	2		11	4	7				3	9	5		8	1	6		
29		20	Plymouth	1-0	Smith	4000	10	2		11		7				3	9	5	1	8		6	4	
30		27	WEST HAM UNITED	1-1	Lockett	1500	10	2		11	4	7				3	9	5		8	1	6		
31	Apr	2	Portsmouth	0-2				2		11	5	7				3	10	5		8	1		4	9
32		3	Norwich City	1-0	Whitworth	4000		2		11	5	7			3		10			8	1	6	4	9
33		5	PORTSMOUTH	1-0	Whitworth	1000		2		11	4	7				3	10	5		8	1	6		9
34		10	GILLINGHAM	4-0	Hughes 3, Whitworth			2		11	4	7				3	10	5		8	1	6		9
35		17	Brighton	0-1		2000		2		11		7				3	10	5		8	1	6	4	9
36		21	Southampton	2-5	Hughes, Whitworth			2		11	4	7				3	10	5		8	1			9
37		24	CARDIFF CITY	2-5	Hughes, Freeman	5000				11	4	7	2		3		10	5		8	1	6		9
38	May	1	MILLWALL	5-0	Hughes 2, Whitworth 2, Lockett	8000		2		11		7				3	10	5		8	1	6	4	9
			Apps				18	37	7	36	11	38	2	13	2	36	35	36	1	37	37	30	31	11
			Goals				4	5	2	5		13					12			8				6

One own goal

F.A. Cup

No		Date	Opponent	Score	Scorers	Att	Bellamy B	Clipston F	Freeman E	Hughes R	Lloyd-Davies E	Lockett W	Manning J	Newman R	Smith D	Tomkins E	Tull W
R1	Jan	9	Grimsby Town	3-0	Smith, Lockett, Freeman(p)	5000	10	2	11	7	3	9	5	1	8	6	4
R2		30	Hull City	1-2	Freeman	8000	10	2	11	7	3	9	5	1	8	6	4

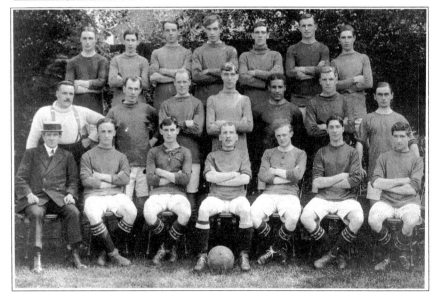

	P	W	D	L	F	A	Pts
1 Watford	38	22	8	8	68	46	52
2 Reading	38	21	7	10	68	43	49
3 Cardiff City	38	22	4	12	72	38	48
4 West Ham United	38	18	9	11	58	47	45
5 NORTHAMPTON TOWN	38	16	11	11	56	51	43
6 Southampton	38	19	5	14	78	74	43
7 Portsmouth	38	16	10	12	54	42	42
8 Millwall	38	16	10	12	50	51	42
9 Swindon Town	38	15	11	12	77	59	41
10 Brighton & Hove Albion	38	16	7	15	46	47	39
11 Exeter City	38	15	8	15	50	41	38
12 Queens Park Rangers	38	13	12	13	55	56	38
13 Norwich City	38	11	14	13	53	36	36
14 Luton Town	38	13	8	17	61	73	34
15 Crystal Palace	38	13	8	17	47	61	34
16 Bristol Rovers	38	14	3	21	53	75	31
17 Plymouth Argyle	38	8	14	16	51	61	30
18 Suthend United	38	10	8	20	44	64	28
19 Croydon Common	38	9	9	20	47	63	27
20 Gillingham	38	6	8	24	43	83	20

Back: C.Smith, Barrett, Tomblin, H.Smith, Thorpe, Langham, Whitworth
Middle: Burrows (Trainer), Manning, Lessons, York, Tull, Clipston, Tomkins
Front: Jones(Sec), Freeman, Dawson, Davies, Lockett, Bellamy, Hughes

1919/20   19th in Southern League

Match results

#	Date		Opposition	Score	Scorers	Att
1	Aug	30	Crystal Palace	2-2	Rushton, Whitworth	1000
2	Sep	1	WATFORD	1-2	Lockett	5000
3		6	SOUTHEND UNITED	2-1	Whitworth, Freeman	6000
4		8	Watford	2-3	Rushton, Lockett	
5		13	Norwich City	1-3	Freeman	8000
6		15	Millwall	2-4	Manning, Whitworth	6000
7		20	BRENTFORD	1-1	Lockett	6000
8		27	Merthyr	2-2	Lockett, Bellamy	
9	Oct	4	PLYMOUTH ARGYLE	0-4		6000
10		11	Bristol Rovers	0-3		9000
11		18	READING	1-3	Whitworth	4000
12		25	Southampton	6-2	Whitworth 3, Dickens 3	7000
13	Nov	1	LUTON TOWN	1-4	Dickens	
14		8	Gillingham	0-0		
15		15	SWANSEA	2-2	Freeman(p), Lockett	
16		22	Exeter City	4-2	Lockett 2, Whitworth 2	6000
17		29	CARDIFF CITY	2-2	Whitworth, Pease	4000
18	Dec	6	Queens Park Rangers	1-5	Buckinshaw	7000
19		13	SWINDON	2-3	Emery, Whitworth	
20		25	Newport County	0-3		1000
21		26	NEWPORT COUNTY	5-1	Whitworth 3, Lockett 2	8000
22		27	BRIGHTON	1-5	Whitworth(p)	7000
23	Jan	3	CRYSTAL PALACE	0-1		
24		17	Southend United	0-0		4000
25		24	NORWICH CITY	0-0		5000
26		31	brentford	0-5		4000
27	Feb	7	MERTHYR	2-4	Lockett 2	
28		14	Plymouth	0-4		
29		21	BRISTOL ROVERS	3-2	Lockett 2, Bellamy	
30		28	Reading	0-5		9000
31	Mar	6	SOUTHAMPTON	3-1	Whitworth 2, Freeman	
32		13	Luton Town	2-0	Whitworth, Lockett	6000
33		20	GILLINGHAM	1-0	Freeman	
34		27	Swansea	1-1	Lockett	
35	Apr	2	Portsmouth	0-6		1600
36		3	EXETER CITY	3-1	Lockett, Whitworth, Thomas	6000
37		6	PORTSMOUTH	0-1		1000
38		10	Cardiff City	1-6	Whitworth(p)	8000
39		17	QUEENS PARK RANGERS	2-0	Whitworth 2(1p)	7000
40		24	Swindon	2-5	Lockett 2	
41		26	MILLWALL	3-2	Lockett, Whitworth, Thomas	6000
42	May	1	Brighton	3-2	Thomas 2, Lockett	9000

Appearances grid (match # : player = shirt no.)

#	Bellamy B	Best R	Brown P	Burkinshaw R	Churchman E	Clipston F	Davies L	Dickens R	Emery J	Facer P	Faulkner A	Forscutt A	Freeman E	Coldsmith	Grendon E	Lloyd-Davies	Lockett W	Manning J	Pease W	Rushton R	Smith H	Sproston A	Thomas W	Thompson W	Thorpe T	Tompkins E	Whitworth G
1										7	2		11		4	3	10	5		8					1	6	9
2										7	2		11		4	3	10	5		8					1	6	9
3										7			11		4	3	10	5		8		2			1	6	9
4										7			11		4	3	10	5		8	1	2				6	9
5	8												11		4	3	10	5			1	2				6	9
6	8												11		4	3	10	5			1	2				6	9
7	11								8				7		4	3	10	5			1	2				6	9
8	8				7								11		4	3	10	5			1	2				6	9
9					7				8				11		4	3	10	5			1	2				6	9
10	8						7	5					11		4	3	10				1	2				6	9
11	8					2							11		5		10	4	7		1	3				6	9
12						2		8					11		5		10	4	7			3			1	6	9
13						2		8					11		5		10	4	7			3			1	6	9
14									6				11		5	3	10	4	7		8	2			1		9
15													11		5	3	10	4	7		8	2			1	6	9
16				8									11		5	3	10	4	7			2			1	6	9
17				8									11		5	3	10	4	7		1	2				6	9
18				8									11		5	3	10	4	7			2			1	6	9
19				8					5				11		4	3	10		7		1	2				6	9
20				8									11		4	5	10		7			2	3		1	6	9
21				8									11		4	5	10		7		1	2	3			6	9
22				8									11		4	5	10		7		1	2				6	9
23				8			5						11		4	5	10		7			2			1	6	9
24				8									11	3	4	5	10		7			2			1	6	9
25				8				5					11	3	4		10		7			2			1	6	9
26				8				6					11	2	4	3	10		7						1		9
27	10							5		1			11	3	4	6	9		7			2					8
28	10	5								1			11		4		9	8	7			2	3		6		
29	10	5	2							1			11		4	6	9		7			3					8
30	10		2							1			11		4	5	9		7			3			6		8
31	10	5								1			11		4	3	9		7			2			6		8
32	10	5											11		4	3	9		7			2			1	6	8
33	10	5											11		4	3	9		7			2			1	6	8
34	10	5											11		4	3	9		7			2			1	6	8
35		5											11		4	3	9		7			2	10		1	6	8
36	6						5						11		4	3	9		7			2	10		1		8
37	6												11		4	5	9		7			2	10	3	1		8
38	6				8								11		4	5			7			2	10	3	1		9
39	5												11		4	3	9		7			2	10		1	6	8
40	5												11		4	3	9		7			2	10		1		8
41	6												11		4	3	9	5	7			2	10		1		8
42	5												11		4	3	9		7			2	10		1	6	8
Apps	14	14	3	12	2	3	2	3	6	6	5	2	41	4	42	36	41	19	32	6	12	39	8	5	25	34	41
Goals	2			1				4	1				5				20	1	1	2			4				23

Additional players: W Bishton 22/3; P Burke 5/7; R Goldie 6/7; R Howson 25/5; J Smith 23/11

F.A. Cup

#	Date		Opposition	Score	Scorers	Att	Bellamy B	Freeman E	Grendon E	Lloyd-Davies	Lockett W	Manning J	Pease W	Sproston A	Thomas W	Thorpe T	Tompkins E	Whitworth G
P6	Dec	20	BRISTOL ROVERS	2-2	Sproston, Pease	8000	8	11	5	2	10	4	7	3		1	6	9
P6r		24	Bristol Rovers	2-3	Whitworth, Pease	14000	8	11	4	5	10		7	2	3	1	6	9

TEAM GROUP FOR 1920/21 SEASON
Back: Burrows(Train.), Watson, Jobey, Smith, Hewison(Capt.), McKechnie, Jones(Sec)
Front: Pease, Grendon, Whitworth, Lockett, Thomas, Tompkins, Freeman

League table

		P	W	D	L	F	A	Pts
1	Portsmouth	42	23	12	7	73	27	58
2	Watford	42	26	6	10	69	42	58
3	Crystal Palace	42	22	12	8	69	43	56
4	Cardiff City	42	18	17	7	70	43	53
5	Plymouth Argyle	42	26	10	12	57	29	50
6	Queens Park Rangers	42	18	10	14	62	50	46
7	Reading	42	16	13	13	51	43	45
8	Southampton	42	18	8	16	72	63	44
9	Swansea Town	42	16	11	15	53	45	43
10	Exeter City	42	17	9	16	57	51	43
11	Southend United	42	13	17	12	46	48	43
12	Norwich City	42	15	11	16	64	57	41
13	Swindon Town	42	17	7	18	65	68	41
14	Millwall	42	14	12	16	52	55	40
15	Brentford	42	15	10	17	52	59	40
16	Brighton & Hove Albion	42	14	a	20	60	72	36
17	Bristol Rovers	42	11	13	18	61	78	35
18	Newport County	42	13	7	22	45	70	33
19	NORTHAMPTON TOWN	42	12	9	21	64	103	33
20	Luton Town	42	10	10	22	51	76	30
21	Merthyr Town	42	9	11	22	47	78	29
22	Gillingham	42	10	7	25	34	74	27

1920/21
14th in Division 3 (S)

#		Date	Opponent	Score	Scorers	Att	Thorpe T	Sproson A	McKechnie JP	Hewison R	Jobey G	Tomkins EF	Pease WH	Whitworth GH	Lockett WC	Thomas WS	Freeman E	Watson WJ	Bellamy BW	Grendon FJW	Smith HC	Churchman E	Tysoe J	Weston CA	Burnard WT	Chambers L	Bedford SG	Hawtin LC
1	Aug	28	Grimsby Town	0-2		12000	1	2	3	4	5	6	7	8	9	10	11	2										
2	Sep	2	Queen's Park Rangers	2-1	Lockett 2	10000	1		3	4	5	6	7	8	9	10	11	2										
3		4	GRIMSBY TOWN	4-1	Whitworth 2, Lockett, Freeman	10000	1		3	4	5	6	7	8	9	10	11	2										
4		6	QUEEN'S PARK RANGERS	0-3		6000	1		3	4	5	6	7	8	9	10	11	2										
5		11	WATFORD	0-1		9000	1		3	4	5	6	7	8	9	10		2	11									
6		13	MILLWALL	0-2		6000	1	2	3	4	5	6	7	8	9		11		10									
7		18	Watford	1-7	Pease	7000	1	2	3	4	5	6	7	8	9	10	11											
8		25	SWANSEA TOWN	2-0	Whitworth, Lockett	6000	1		3		5	6	7	8	9	10	11	2		4								
9	Oct	2	Swansea Town	2-2	Whitworth 2	12000			3		5	6	7	8	9	10	11	2		4	1							
10		9	PORTSMOUTH	1-0	Jobey	7000	1		3		5	6	7	8	9	10	11	2		4								
11		16	Portsmouth	0-2		15000	1		3		5	6	7	8	9	10	11	2		4								
12		23	Southend United	2-1	Pease, Lockett	9000			3	6	5		7	8	9	10	11	2		4		1						
13		30	SOUTHEND UNITED	1-0	Lockett	9000			3		5	6	7	8	9	10	11	2		4		1						
14	Nov	6	Merthyr Town	0-1		13000	1		3		5	6	7	8	9	10	11	2		4		1						
15		13	MERTHYR TOWN	2-2	Whitworth, Lockett	8000	1		3		5	6	7	8	9	10	11	2		4								
16		20	Plymouth Argyle	2-0	Hewson, Pease	12000	1		3	10	5	6	7	8	9		11	2		4								
17		27	PLYMOUTH ARGYLE	1-1	Jobey	8000	1		3	10	5	6	7	8	9		11	2		4								
18	Dec	4	Exeter City	0-4		6000	1		3	10	5	6	7	8	9		11	2		4								
19		11	EXETER CITY	3-3	Pease, Whitworth, Thomas	6000	1		3		5	6	7	8	9	10	11	2		4								
20		25	Gillingham	5-2	Whitworth 2, Lockett 2, Freeman	8000	1		3		5	6	7	8	9	10	11	2		4								
21		27	GILLINGHAM	2-0	Whitworth, Lockett	13290	1		3		5	6	7	8	9	10	11	2		4								
22	Jan	1	Millwall	0-1		3000			3		5	6	7	8	9	10	11	2		4		1						
23		15	LUTON TOWN	1-0	Whitworth	7000	1		3		5	6	7	8	9	10		2		4						11		
24		22	Luton Town	1-3	Churchman	12000	1		3		5	6	7	8	9	10		2	11	4								
25		29	Newport County	1-1	Whitworth	8000	1	3			5	6	7	8		10	11	2		4				9				
26	Feb	5	NEWPORT COUNTY	0-2		8000	1	3			5	6	7	8		10	11	2		4				9				
27		12	SOUTHAMPTON	2-0	Whitworth, Burnard	7000			3		5	6	7	9		10		2		4		1			8	11		
28		26	READING	1-0	Whitworth	6000			3		5	6	7	9		10		2		4		1			8	11		
29	Mar	5	Reading	0-4		4000			3		5	6	7			10		2		4		1		9	8	11		
30		9	Southampton	1-3	Whitworth	7000			3		5	6	7	9		10		2		4		1			8	11		
31		12	BRISTOL ROVERS	1-2	Thomas	5000	1		3		5	6	7	9			8	2		4					10	11		
32		19	Bristol Rovers	2-4	Whitworth, 1 og	5000			3		5	6	7	9		10	11	2		4		1			8			
33		26	Brentford	1-1	Whitworth	8000			3		5	6	7	9		10	11	2		4		1			8			
34		28	Swindon Town	1-2	Burnard	5000			3		5		7	9		10	11	2		4		1			8		6	
35		29	SWINDON TOWN	1-2	Whitworth	10000			3		5		7	9		10		2		4		1			8	11	6	
36	Apr	2	BRENTFORD	6-2	Whitworth 4, Lockett, Burnard	6000			3		5	6	7	9		10		2		4		1			8	11		
37		9	Norwich City	3-3	Whitworth 2, Lockett	6000			3		5	6	7	9		10		2		4		1			8	11		
38		16	NORWICH CITY	1-0	Whitworth	5000			3		5		7	9		10		2		4		1			8	11	6	
39		23	Crystal Palace	1-5	Whitworth	20000		2			5		7	9		10				4		1			8	11	4	3
40		30	CRYSTAL PALACE	2-2	Pease, Whitworth	8000			3		5	6	7	9		10		2				1			8	11	4	
41	May	2	BRIGHTON & HOVE ALB	1-0	Lockett	6000			3		5	6	7	9		10		2				1			8	11	4	
42		7	Brighton & Hove Albion	2-3	Whitworth, Burnard	7000			3		5	6	7	9		10		2				1			8	11	4	

| Apps | | | | | | | 22 | 5 | 11 | 40 | 42 | 37 | 42 | 40 | 41 | 21 | 25 | 38 | 3 | 32 | 20 | 2 | 1 | 3 | 16 | 13 | 7 | 1 |
| Goals | | | | | | | | | | 1 | 2 | | 5 | 28 | 13 | 2 | 2 | | | | | 1 | | | 4 | | | |

One own goal

F.A. Cup

		Date	Opponent	Score	Scorers	Att	Thorpe T	McKechnie JP	Jobey G	Tomkins EF	Pease WH	Whitworth GH	Lockett WC	Thomas WS	Freeman E	Watson WJ	Grendon FJW
Q6	Dec	18	GILLINGHAM	3-1	Tomkins, Whitworth 2	8000	1	3		6	7	9	10	8	11	2	4
R1	Jan	8	SOUTHAMPTON	0-0		16000	1	3	5	6	7	9	10	8	11	2	4
rep		12	Southampton	1-4	Whitworth	16000	1	3	5	6	7	9	10	8	11	2	4

Played in Q6: Roe (number 5)

		P	W	D	L	F	A	W	D	L	F	A	Pts
1	Crystal Palace	42	15	4	2	45	17	9	7	5	25	17	59
2	Southampton	42	14	5	2	46	10	5	11	5	18	18	54
3	Queen's Park Rgs.	42	14	4	3	38	11	8	5	8	23	21	53
4	Swindon Town	42	14	5	2	51	17	7	5	9	22	32	52
5	Swansea Town	42	9	10	2	32	19	9	5	7	24	26	51
6	Watford	42	14	4	3	40	15	6	4	11	19	29	48
7	Millwall	42	11	5	5	25	8	7	6	8	17	22	47
8	Merthyr Town	42	13	5	3	46	20	2	10	9	14	29	45
9	Luton Town	42	14	6	1	51	15	2	6	13	10	41	44
10	Bristol Rovers	42	15	3	3	51	22	3	4	14	17	35	43
11	Plymouth Argyle	42	10	7	4	25	13	1	14	6	10	21	43
12	Portsmouth	42	10	8	3	28	14	2	7	12	18	34	39
13	Grimsby Town	42	12	5	4	32	16	3	4	14	17	43	39
14	NORTHAMPTON TOWN	42	11	4	6	32	23	4	4	13	27	52	38
15	Newport County	42	8	5	8	20	23	6	4	11	23	41	37
16	Norwich City	42	9	10	2	31	14	1	6	14	13	39	36
17	Southend United	42	13	2	6	32	20	1	6	14	12	41	36
18	Brighton & Hove A.	42	11	6	4	28	20	3	2	16	14	41	36
19	Exeter City	42	9	7	5	27	15	1	8	12	12	39	35
20	Reading	42	8	4	9	26	22	4	3	14	16	37	31
21	Brentford	42	7	9	5	27	23	2	3	16	15	44	30
22	Gillingham	42	6	9	6	19	24	2	3	16	15	50	28

1921/22   17th in Division 3(S)

League matches

#	Date	Opponent	Score	Scorers	Att
1	Aug 27	Millwall	0-0		22000
2	29	Swindon Town	2-4	Pease, Lockett	5000
3	Sep 3	MILLWALL	0-3		8000
4	5	SWINDON TOWN	2-1	Whitworth, Harron	7000
5	10	Reading	0-0		12000
6	17	READING	2-1	Lockett 2	10000
7	24	Bristol Rovers	0-2		10000
8	Oct 1	BRISTOL ROVERS	2-2	Pease, Burnard	8000
9	8	Brentford	0-1		16000
10	15	BRENTFORD	2-0	Whitworth 2	8000
11	22	ABERDARE ATHLETIC	2-0	Pease, Whitworth	10000
12	29	Aberdare Athletic	2-4	Whitworth, Lockett	6000
13	Nov 5	Brighton & Hove Albion	0-7		7000
14	12	BRIGHTON & HOVE ALB	2-0	Whitworth 2	8000
15	19	WATFORD	1-0	AT Davies	6000
16	Dec 10	Charlton Athletic	2-2	Watson, Lockett	10000
17	24	Southampton	0-8		10000
18	26	Gillingham	2-3	Hewison 2	10000
19	27	GILLINGHAM	3-1	Watson, Whitworth 2	12000
20	31	Queen's Park Rangers	0-4		9000
21	Jan 14	QUEEN'S PARK RANGERS	1-0	Whitworth	7000
22	19	CHARLTON ATHLETIC	1-0	Whitworth	4000
23	21	EXETER CITY	2-3	Lockett 2	4000
24	Feb 4	SWANSEA TOWN	0-1		3000
25	11	Swansea Town	2-2	Whitworth 2	8000
26	18	SOUTHEND UNITED	0-2		6000
27	25	Southend United	1-1	Whitworth	6000
28	Mar 4	PORTSMOUTH	0-0		8000
29	11	Portsmouth	1-1	Pease	6000
30	18	Merthyr Town	1-2	Lockett	6000
31	25	MERTHYR TOWN	2-0	Lockett 2	7000
32	Apr 1	Plymouth Argyle	0-2		10000
33	3	Exeter City	0-2		4000
34	8	PLYMOUTH ARGYLE	1-3	Lockett	5000
35	14	Watford	2-2	Lockett, Graham	8000
36	15	Newport County	2-2	Lockett, Graham	6000
37	17	Norwich City	0-2		14000
38	18	NORWICH CITY	3-0	Hewson 3	7000
39	22	NEWPORT COUNTY	2-0	Lockett, Graham	3000
40	24	SOUTHAMPTON	0-0		7000
41	29	LUTON TOWN	2-0	Lockett 2	7000
42	May 6	Luton Town	0-3		0

Appearances / Goals grid

#	Smith HC	Watson WI	Williams W	Bedford SG	Jobey G	Tomkins EF	Pease WH	Seabrook A	Whitworth GH	Lockett WC	Harron J	Hewison R	Ambridge FW	Hawtin LC	Davies LJ	Grendon FW	Burnard WT	Davies AT	Chambers L	Jeffs TE	Williams JS	Johnson PR	Wood JT	Graham W	Weston CA
1	1	2	3	4	5	6	7	8	9	10	11														
2	1	2	3	4	5	6	7	8	9	10	11														
3	1	2	3	4	5	6	7	8	9	10	11														
4		2			5	6	7	8	9	10	11	4	1	3											
5		2			5		7	8	9	10	11	4	1	3	6										
6	1	2			5	6	7	8	9	10	11		1	3			4								
7	1	2			5	6	7	8	9	10	11	3					4								
8	1	2		4	5	6	7		9	10	11			3			8								
9	1	2			5	6	7	8	9	10	11			3			4								
10	1	2	3		5	6	7		9	10		4						8	11						
11	1	2	3		5	4	7		9	10		6						8	11						
12	1	2	6		5		7		9	10	3					4	8		11						
13	1	2			5	6	7		9	10		4		3			8		11						
14		2	6		5		7		9	10		4		3			8		11						
15		2	6		5		7		9	10		4	1					8	11	3					
16		2	6	4			7		9	10	11	5	1					8		3					
17		2	6	4			7		9	10	11	5	1							3	8				
18		2	6		5		7		9	10	11	4	1							3	8				
19		2	6		5		7		9	10	11	4	1					8		3					
20		2	6	4	5		7	8	9	10	11		1							3					
21			3	4	5	6	7		9	10	11		1					8				2			
22		2	3	4	5	6	7		9	10	11		1					8							
23		2	3	4	5	6	7	9		10			1				8		11						
24	1		6		5				9	10	11		2			4	8			3			7		
25	1	2	6	4	5		7		9	10							8		11	3					
26	1	2	6	4	5		7		9			8				10	11					3			
27	1	2	6		5	4	7		9	10							8		11	3					
28	1	2	6		5		7		9	10		4							11	3				8	
29	1	2	6		5	4	7		9	10									11	3				8	
30	1	2	6		5	4	7		9	10									11	3				8	
31	1	2	6		5	4	7		9	10								11		3				8	
32	1	2	6		5	4	7		9	10									11	3				8	
33	1	2	6		5	4	7		9	10									11	3				8	
34	1	2	6	4	5		7		9	10									11	3				8	
35	1	2	6		5		7		9	10									11	3				8	4
36	1	2	6	4	5		7		9	10									11	3				8	
37	1	2	6	4	5		7		9	10									11	3				8	
38	1	2	6	4	5		7		9	10									11	3				8	
39	1	2	6	4	5		7		9	10								11		3				8	
40	1	2	6	4	5		7		9	10									11	3				8	
41	1	2	6	4	5		7		9	10									11	3				8	
42	1	2	6	5			7		9	10						4			11	3				8	
Apps	29	40	35	21	36	25	40	10	27	40	18	34	13	8	1	6	9	10	15	24	2	2	1	15	1
Goals		2					4		14	16	1	5					1	1						3	

F.A. Cup

Round	Date	Opponent	Score	Scorers	Att	Smith HC	Watson WI	Williams W	Bedford SG	Jobey G	Tomkins EF	Pease WH	Seabrook A	Whitworth GH	Lockett WC	Harron J	Hewison R	Ambridge FW	Hawtin LC	Davies LJ	Grendon FW	Burnard WT	Davies AT	Chambers L	Jeffs TE
Q5	Dec 3	Lincoln City	2-1	Whitworth, Lockett	6800		2	6				4	7	8	9	10		5	1					11	3
Q6	17	LANCASTER T	1-0	Jobey	12000		2	6		5		7	9		10		4	1				8	11		3
R1	Jan 7	READING	3-0	Lockett 3	8895		2	6	4	5		7		9	10	11	8	1							3
R2	28	STOKE	2-2	Hewison, Lockett	16532			6	4	5		7		9	10		8	1	2					11	3
rep	Feb 2	Stoke	0-2		20000	1		6	5			7		9	10	11	8	2			4				3

League table

		P	W	D	L	F	A	W	D	L	F	A	Pts
1	Southampton	42	14	7	0	50	8	9	8	4	18	13	61
2	Plymouth Argyle	42	17	4	0	43	4	8	7	6	20	20	61
3	Portsmouth	42	13	5	3	38	18	5	12	4	24	21	53
4	Luton Town	42	16	2	3	47	9	6	6	9	17	26	52
5	Queen's Park Rgs.	42	13	7	1	36	12	5	6	10	17	32	49
6	Swindon Town	42	10	7	4	40	21	6	6	9	32	39	45
7	Watford	42	9	9	3	34	21	4	9	8	20	27	44
8	Aberdare Ath.	42	11	6	4	38	18	6	4	11	19	33	44
9	Brentford	42	15	2	4	41	17	1	9	11	11	26	43
10	Swansea Town	42	11	8	2	40	19	2	7	12	10	28	41
11	Merthyr Town	42	14	2	5	33	15	3	4	14	12	41	40
12	Millwall	42	6	13	2	22	10	4	5	12	16	32	38
13	Reading	42	10	5	6	28	15	4	5	12	12	32	38
14	Bristol Rovers	42	8	8	5	32	24	6	2	13	20	43	38
15	Norwich City	42	8	10	3	29	17	4	3	14	21	45	37
16	Charlton Athletic	42	10	6	5	28	19	3	5	13	15	37	37
17	NORTHAMPTON TOWN	42	13	3	5	30	17	0	8	13	17	54	37
18	Gillingham	42	11	4	6	36	20	3	4	14	11	40	36
19	Brighton & Hove A.	42	9	6	6	33	19	4	3	14	12	32	35
20	Newport County	42	8	7	6	22	18	3	5	13	22	43	34
21	Exeter City	42	7	5	9	22	29	4	7	10	16	30	34
22	Southend United	42	7	5	9	23	23	1	6	14	11	51	27

1921/22
Back: Williams, Bedford, Grendon
Middle: Burrows (Trainer), Watson, Hewison (Player/Man.), Ambridge, Jobey, Burnard
Front: Pease, Hawtin, Seabrook, Whitworth, Lockett, Harron, Tomkins

1923/24
Back: Burrows (Trainer), Newton, Watson, Smith, Brett, Wood (), Hewison (Player/Man.), Unknown
Middle: Gype (Director), Pease, Wood (W), Lockett, Myers, Page, Seal (Director)
Front: Williams

1922/23   8th in Division 3 (S)

#	Date		Opponent	Score / Scorers	Att	Smith HC	Watson WJ	Jeffs TE	Bedford SG	Newton F	Williams W	Pease WH	Seabrook A	Brown WY	Myers EC	Page LA	Graham W	Tomkins EF	Lockett WC	Civil H	Hewison R	Johnson PR	Forrest J	Page W	Wood EE	Hawtin LC
1	Aug	26	Swindon Town	0-2	10000	1	2	3	4	5	6	7	8	9	10	11										
2		28	GILLINGHAM	1-0 Graham	10000	1	2	3		5	6	7	8	9		11	10	4								
3	Sep	2	SWINDON TOWN	1-2 L Page	11000	1	2	3		5	6	7			10	11	8	4	9							
4		6	Gillingham	3-0 Seabrooke, Lockett 2	6000	1	2	3	5			7	8		10	11		4	9	6						
5		9	WATFORD	1-1 Lockett	8000	1	2	3	5		6	7	8		10	11		4	9							
6		16	Watford	0-0	10000	1	2	3	5		6	7	8		10	11		4	9							
7		23	BRENTFORD	1-1 Myers	6000	1	2	3	5		6	7			10	11	8	4	9							
8		30	Brentford	1-2 L Page	7000	1	2	3	5			7	8		10	11		4	9	6						
9	Oct	7	Norwich City	0-1	9000	1	2	3	5		6	7			10	11	8	4	9							
10		14	NORWICH CITY	1-1 Graham	8000	1	2		5		6	7			10	11	8	4	9			3				
11		21	Aberdare Athletic	2-0 Seabrooke, Lockett	7000	1	2		5	6		7	8		10	11			9		4	3				
12		28	ABERDARE ATHLETIC	3-1 Watson, Williams, Myers	7000	1	2		5		6	7	8		10	11			9		4	3				
13	Nov	4	Southend United	2-1 Myers 2	7000	1	2		5		6	7	8		10	11			9		4	3				
14		11	SOUTHEND UNITED	5-2 Bedford, Williams, L Page, Graham 2	8000	1	2		5		6	7			10	11	8		9			3	4			
15		25	EXETER CITY	3-0 Watson, Myers, Lockett	7000	1	2	3	5		6	7			10	11	8		9				4			
16	Dec	9	MERTHYR TOWN	1-1 Lockett	7000	1	2		5		6	7			10	11		4	9			3		8		
17		16	Reading	0-0	6000	1	2	3	5		6	7			10	11		4	9					8		
18		23	READING	5-0 Pease, Myers, L Page, Lockett, W Page	10000	1	2	3	5		6	7			10	11		4	9					8		
19		25	Plymouth Argyle	0-1	6000	1	2	3	5		6	7			10	11		4	9					8		
20		26	PLYMOUTH ARGYLE	1-0 Pease	18123	1	2	3	5		6	7			10	11			9		4			8		
21		30	BRIGHTON & HOVE ALB	0-0	5000	1	2	3	5		6	7	9		10	11					4			8		
22	Jan	6	Brighton & Hove Albion	0-1	10000	1	2	3	5		6	7			10	11			9		4			8		
23		13	Exeter City	2-1 Pease, Lockett	6000	1	2	3	5		6	7			10	11			9		4			8		
24		20	Bristol Rovers	0-0	8000	1	2	3	5		6	7			10	11			9		4			8		
25		27	BRISTOL ROVERS	1-0 Myers	7000	1	2		5		6	7			10	11			9		4	3		8		
26	Feb	3	Swansea Town	0-4	15000	1	2	3	5		6	7			9	11	10				4			8		
27		10	SWANSEA TOWN	1-3 Myers	5000	1	2		5		6	7			10	11	8		9		4	3				
28		17	NEWPORT COUNTY	2-1 Lockett 2	6000	1	2	3	4	5	6	7	9		8	11			10							
29		24	Newport County	1-1 Pease	4000	1	2	3	4	5	6	7	9			11	8		10							
30	Mar	3	Bristol City	0-1	14000	1	2	3		5	6	7	9			11			10		4			8		
31		5	Merthyr Town	0-3		1	2	3		5	6	7	9			11			10		4			8		
32		10	BRISTOL CITY	2-1 Pease, Lockett	10000	1	2	3	5	4	6	7			10	11			9							
33		17	PORTSMOUTH	3-0 Seabrooke, L Page, Lockett	7000	1		3	4		6	7	8			11	10		9		2				5	
34		24	Portsmouth	0-0	7790	1		3	4		6	7	8			11	10		9						5	2
35		31	MILLWALL	2-1 Seabrooke, one og	7000	1	2	3	4		6	7	8			11	10		9						5	
36	Apr	2	Charlton Athletic	0-2	8000	1	2	3	4		6	7	8			11	10		9						5	
37		3	CHARLTON ATHLETIC	0-0	10000	1	2	3	4		6	7	8			11	10		9						5	
38		7	Millwall	0-2	12000	1	2	3	4		6	7	8			11	10		9						5	
39		14	LUTON TOWN	2-0 Pease, Lockett	10000	1	2	3	4		6	7			10	11	8		9						5	
40		21	Luton Town	1-2 Myers	8000	1	2	3	4		6	7			10	11	8		9						5	
41		28	QUEEN'S PARK RANGERS	4-2 Pease, Seabrooke 2, Lockett	8000	1	2	3	4		6	7	8		10	11			9						5	
42	May	5	Queen's Park Rangers	2-3 Myers, Wood	9000	1	2		4		6	7	8		10	11			9			3			5	
			Apps			42	40	33	29	18	39	42	23	2	32	39	21	13	38	2	14	9	2	13	10	1
			Goals				2		1		2	7	6		10	5	4		14					1	1	

One own goal

F.A. Cup

	Date		Opponent	Score	Att	Smith HC	Watson WJ	Jeffs TE	Bedford SG	Newton F	Williams W	Pease WH	Seabrook A	Brown WY	Myers EC	Page LA	Graham W	Tomkins EF	Lockett WC	Civil H	Hewison R	Johnson PR	Forrest J	Page W	Wood EE	Hawtin LC
Q5	Dec	2	Charlton Athletic	0-2	5000	1	2	3	5		6	7			10	11	8		9		4					

		P	W	D	L	F	A	W	D	L	F	A	Pts
1	Bristol City	42	16	4	1	43	13	8	7	6	23	27	59
2	Plymouth Argyle	42	18	3	0	47	6	5	4	12	14	23	53
3	Swansea Town	42	13	6	2	46	14	9	3	9	32	31	53
4	Brighton & Hove A.	42	15	3	3	39	13	5	8	8	13	21	51
5	Luton Town	42	14	4	3	47	18	7	3	11	21	31	49
6	Millwall	42	9	10	2	27	13	5	8	8	18	27	46
7	Portsmouth	42	10	5	6	34	20	9	3	9	24	32	46
8	NORTHAMPTON TOWN	42	13	6	2	40	17	4	5	12	14	27	45
9	Swindon Town	42	14	4	3	41	17	3	7	11	21	39	45
10	Watford	42	10	6	5	35	23	7	4	10	22	31	44
11	Queen's Park Rgs.	42	10	4	7	34	24	6	6	9	20	25	42
12	Charlton Athletic	42	11	6	4	33	14	3	8	10	22	37	42
13	Bristol Rovers	42	7	9	5	25	19	6	7	8	10	17	42
14	Brentford	42	9	4	8	27	23	4	8	9	14	28	38
15	Southend United	42	10	6	5	35	18	2	7	12	14	36	37
16	Gillingham	42	13	4	4	38	18	2	3	16	13	41	37
17	Merthyr Town	42	10	4	7	27	17	1	10	10	12	31	36
18	Norwich City	42	8	7	6	29	26	5	3	13	22	45	36
19	Reading	42	9	8	4	24	15	1	6	14	12	40	34
20	Exeter City	42	10	4	7	27	18	3	3	15	20	66	33
21	Aberdare Ath.	42	6	8	7	25	23	3	3	15	17	47	29
22	Newport County	42	8	6	7	28	21	0	5	16	12	49	27

1923/24   8th in Division 3 (S)

#	Date	Opponent	Score	Scorers	Att	Smith HC	Watson WJ	Brett FB	Newton F	Wood EE	Williams W	Pease WH	Wood W	Lockett WC	Myers EC	Page LA	York R	Hewison R	Jeffs TE	Bedford SG	Hobbs RV	Gray GR	Seabrook A	Graham W	Facer A	Sorenson IM	Needham GW	Wright RL	Braidford L
1	Aug 25	BRIGHTON & HOVE ALB	3-0	Myers 2, Pease	14256	1	2	3	4	5	6	7	8	9	10	11													
2	27	Luton Town	1-1	Lockett		1	2	3	4	5	6	7	8	9	10	11													
3	Sep 1	Brighton & Hove Albion	0-2		8712	1	2	3	4	5	6	7	8	9	10	11													
4	3	LUTON TOWN	2-0	Myers, W Wood	9968	1	2	3	4	5	6	7	8		10	11	9												
5	8	Swansea Town	1-2	W Wood	18000	1	2	3	4	5	6	7	8			11	9	10											
6	10	BRISTOL ROVERS	0-0		10000	1	2		4	5	6	7	8	9	10	11			3										
7	15	SWANSEA TOWN	2-0	Myers 2	11951	1	2	3	4	5	6	7	8	9	10	11													
8	22	Newport County	1-1	Lockett	9500	1	2	3	4	5	6	7	8	9	10	11													
9	29	NEWPORT COUNTY	0-0		10000	1	2	3	4	5	6	7	8	9	10	11													
10	Oct 6	Gillingham	1-1	Myers	7000	1		3	4	5	6	7	8	9	10	11		2											
11	13	GILLINGHAM	2-0	Lockett, W Wood	10000	1	2	3	4	5	6	7	8	9	10	11													
12	20	QUEEN'S PARK RANGERS	3-0	Myers 2, Pease	8000	1	2	3			6	7	8	9	10	11				5									
13	27	Queen's Park Rangers	2-3	Page, W Wood	5000	1	2	3	4		6	7	8	9	10	11				5									
14	Nov 3	Plymouth Argyle	0-0		11000	1	2	3	4		6	7	8	9	10	11				5									
15	10	PLYMOUTH ARGYLE	1-0	Myers	11000	1	2	3	4		6	7	8	9	10	11				5									
16	17	MERTHYR TOWN	3-0	Lockett, Myers, Newton	7000	1	2	3	4		6	7	8	9	10	11				5									
17	24	Merthyr Town	0-0			1	2		4		6	7	8	9	10	11			3	5									
18	Dec 8	Bristol Rovers	1-1	W Wood	8000	1	2	3	4		6	7	8	9		11				5	10								
19	22	Charlton Athletic	0-0		10000	1	2	3	4		6	7	8	9	10	11				5									
20	26	Swindon Town	0-2		10000	1	2	3	4		6	7	8	9	10	11				5									
21	27	SWINDON TOWN	1-1	Myers	9000	1	2	3			6	7		9	10	11				5		4	8						
22	29	NORWICH CITY	1-0	Lockett	10796	1	2	3			6	7		9		11	9			5		4		8					
23	Jan 5	Norwich City	4-1	Graham, Lockett, Page 2	6000	1	2	3	4		6	7		10	9	11				5				8					
24	19	READING	3-1	Graham, Lockett, Pease	7000	1	2		5		6	7		10	9	11			3			4		8					
25	26	Reading	0-1		7000	1	2	3			6	7		10	9	11						4	8	5					
26	Feb 2	BOURNEMOUTH	3-1	Myers, Page, Pease	7663	1	2	3			6	7	8		10	11						4		5	9				
27	9	Bournemouth	1-2	Lockett	5000	1	2	3			6	7	8	9		11						4		5			10		
28	16	Millwall	3-4	Myers, Page, Pease	15000	1	2	3			6	7		9	10	11						4		8			5		
29	23	MILLWALL	2-1	Myers 2	8000	1	2	3			6	7		9	10	11						4		8			5		
30	Mar 8	Aberdare Athletic	2-2	Pease 2	8000	1	2	3			6	7	8	9		11						4		10			5		
31	13	CHARLTON ATHLETIC	1-0	Braidford	5000	1	2	3			6	7		9		11			5			4		10					8
32	15	Southend United	1-5	Lockett	9000	1	2	3			6	7		9		11						4					5		8
33	22	SOUTHEND UNITED	8-0	*see below	7000	1	2	3	5		6	7		9	10	11							8				4		
34	29	Exeter City	1-2	Pease	4000	1	2	3	5		6	7			10	11							8		9		4		
35	Apr 5	EXETER CITY	1-0	Lockett	7000	1	2	3			6	7		9		11											4		8
36	7	ABERDARE ATHLETIC	1-2	Brett		1	2	3			6	7		9	10	11											4		8
37	12	Portsmouth	3-1	Lockett, Myers, W Wood	11704	1	2	3	5		6	7	8	9	10	11											4		
38	19	PORTSMOUTH	0-4		13500	1	2	3	5		6	7	8	9	10	11											4		
39	21	Watford	2-0	Lockett 2		1		3	5		6	7	8	9	10	11	2										4		
40	22	WATFORD	1-2	Lockett	8000	1		3	5		6	7	8	9	10	11	2										4		
41	26	Brentford	0-1		3000	1		3	4	5	6	7	8	9	10	11	2										4		
42	May 3	BRENTFORD	2-3	Graham, Lockett	6000	1		3	5		6	7	8	9		11								10			4		
		Apps				42	37	39	23	21	42	42	32	38	32	42	3	1	8	13	1	11	3	9	2	1	14	1	5
		Goals					1					9	6	18	17	5							3	3					1

Scorers in game 33: Lockett 3, Seabrook 3, Myers, Pease.

F.A. Cup

#	Date	Opponent	Score	Scorers	Att	Smith HC	Watson WJ	Brett FB	Newton F	Wood EE	Williams W	Pease WH	Wood W	Lockett WC	Myers EC	Page LA	York R	Hewison R	Jeffs TE	Bedford SG	Graham W
Q5	Dec 1	LINCOLN CITY	5-1	Bedford, Myers 2, Page, Pease	11000	1	2	3	4		6	7	8	9	10	11				5	
Q6	15	Wigan Borough	6-0	Myers, Page, Pease 2, W Wood 2	18000	1	2	3	4		6	7	8	9	10	11				5	
R1	Jan 12	HALIFAX TOWN	1-1	Lockett	11000	1	2	3	4		6	7	8	9		11				5	10
rep	15	Halifax Town	1-1	W Wood	10000	1	2	5	4		6	7	8	9		11		3			10
rep2	21	Halifax Town	2-4	Lockett, W Wood	7500	1	2				6	7	8	9		11	4	3		5	10

Replay 2 at Bramall Lane, Sheffield

League Table

		P	W	D	L	F	A	W	D	L	F	A	Pts
1	Portsmouth	42	15	3	3	57	11	9	8	4	30	19	59
2	Plymouth Argyle	42	13	6	2	46	15	10	3	8	24	19	55
3	Millwall	42	17	3	1	45	11	5	7	9	19	27	54
4	Swansea Town	42	18	2	1	39	10	4	6	11	21	38	52
5	Brighton & Hove A.	42	16	4	1	56	12	5	5	11	12	25	51
6	Swindon Town	42	14	5	2	38	11	3	8	10	20	33	47
7	Luton Town	42	11	7	3	35	19	5	7	9	15	25	46
8	NORTHAMPTON TOWN	42	14	3	4	40	15	3	8	10	24	32	45
9	Bristol Rovers	42	11	7	3	34	15	4	6	11	18	31	43
10	Newport County	42	15	4	2	39	15	2	5	14	17	49	43
11	Norwich City	42	13	5	3	45	18	3	3	15	15	41	40
12	Aberdare Ath.	42	9	9	3	35	18	3	5	13	10	40	38
13	Merthyr Town	42	11	8	2	33	19	0	8	13	12	46	38
14	Charlton Athletic	42	10	7	4	26	20	3	8	10	12	25	37
15	Gillingham	42	11	6	4	27	15	1	7	13	16	43	37
16	Exeter City	42	14	3	4	33	17	1	4	16	4	35	37
17	Brentford	42	9	8	4	33	21	5	0	16	21	50	36
18	Reading	42	12	2	7	35	20	1	7	13	16	37	35
19	Southend United	42	11	7	3	35	19	1	3	17	18	65	34
20	Watford	42	8	8	5	35	18	1	7	13	10	36	33
21	Bournemouth	42	6	8	7	19	19	5	3	13	21	46	33
22	Queen's Park Rgs.	42	9	6	6	28	26	2	3	16	9	51	31

1924/25   9th in Division 3 (S)

#	Date	Opponent	Score	Scorers	Att	Smith HC	Watson WJ	Brett FB	Needham GW	Wood EE	Williams W	Pease WH	Cook J	Lockett WC	Myers EC	Page LA	Poyntz WJ	Jeffs TE	Hewison R	Molloy W	Oxley RL	George HS	Cockle ES	Hoten RV	Hammond L	Chapman WJ	Evans CJH
1	Aug 30	Watford	0-1			1	2	3	4	5	6	7	8	9	10	11											
2	Sep 1	Charlton Athletic	0-0		5000	1	2	3	4	5	6	7	8		10	11	9										
3	4	ABERDARE ATHLETIC	5-0	Cook, Lockett 4		1	2	3	4	5	6	7	8		10	11	9										
4	6	SOUTHEND UNITED	0-1		8000	1	2	3	4	5	6	7	8		10	11	9										
5	8	CHARLTON ATHLETIC	2-1	Pease, Cook	5189	1	2	3	4	5	6	7	8		10	11	9										
6	13	Newport County	0-1		6000	1	2	3	4	5	6	7	8		10	11	9										
7	15	LUTON TOWN	1-0	Pease	5340	1	2		4	5	6	7	8	9	10	11		3									
8	20	BRISTOL ROVERS	5-0	Wood, Myers, Page	7000	1	2	3	4	5	6	7	8	9	10	11											
9	22	Luton Town	0-2		5000	1	2	3	4	5	6	7		9	10	11		8									
10	27	Exeter City	0-0		7000	1	2	3	4	5	6	7		9	10	11		8									
11	Oct 4	SWANSEA TOWN	1-3	Pease	10000	1	2			5	6	7	8	9	10	11		3	4								
12	11	Reading	1-0	Lockett	10000	1	2			5	6	7	8	9	10	11		3	4								
13	18	MERTHYR TOWN	2-0	Wood, Page	7781	1	2			5	6	7	8	9	10	11		3	4								
14	25	GILLINGHAM	1-0	Lockett	5000	1	2	3	10	5	6	7		9		11		8	4								
15	Nov 1	Bournemouth	2-1	Needham, Pease	2000	1	2	3	4	5	6	7	8		10	11	9										
16	8	BRIGHTON & HOVE ALB	1-0	Hewison	9000	1	2	5	4		6	7	8	9		11			10	3							
17	15	Plymouth Argyle	1-2	Hewison	9000	1	2	5	4		6	7	8	9		11			10	3							
18	22	BRISTOL CITY	1-2	Page	8000	1	2	6	4	5		7	8	9		11			10	3							
19	29	Swindon Town	0-5		7000	1	2	3	4	5	6		8			11	9				10	7					
20	Dec 20	BRENTFORD	0-2		6000	1	2	3		5	6	7	8	9		11			4						10		
21	25	Millwall	1-3	Page	15000	1	2	3	4	5	6	7	8			11							9	10			
22	26	MILLWALL	0-2		11534		2		4		6	7		9		11	8	3					10		1		5
23	27	WATFORD	1-1	Page	2000		2		4		6	7		9		11	8	3					10		1		5
24	Jan 3	Southend United	1-0	Pease	6000	1	2				6	7				11	8	3					9	10		5	4
25	17	NEWPORT COUNTY	0-2		6000	1	2				6	7				11	8	3					9	10		5	4
26	24	Bristol Rovers	2-0	Pease, Poyntz	6000	1	2	5				7				11	8	3					9	10		6	4
27	31	EXETER CITY	2-1	Page, Hoten	5000	1	2	5				7				11	8	3					9	10		6	4
28	Feb 7	Swansea Town	1-2	Cockle	18000	1	2	5				7				11	8	3					9	10		6	4
29	14	READING	2-0	Page, Cockle	6000	1	2	5				7				11	8	3					9	10		6	4
30	21	Merthyr Town	2-0	Pease, Cockle	3500	1	2	5			6	7				11	8	3					9	10			4
31	28	Gillingham	1-0	Pease	6000	1	2	5			6	7				11	8	3					9	10			4
32	Mar 7	BOURNEMOUTH	3-0	Page 2, Evans	5000	1	2	5			6	7				11	8	3					9	10			4
33	14	Brighton & Hove Albion	1-0	Page	7000	1	2	5			6	7				11	8	3					9	10			4
34	21	PLYMOUTH ARGYLE	5-2	Pease, Page 2, Cockle, Hoten	9221	1	2	5			6	7				11	8	3					9	10			4
35	28	Bristol City	0-1		11000	1	2	5			6	7				11	8	3					9	10			4
36	Apr 4	SWINDON TOWN	0-0		8000	1	2	5			6	7				11	8	3					9	10			4
37	11	Aberdare Athletic	1-1	Evans	7000	1	2	5			6	7				11	8	3					9	10			4
38	13	Queen's Park Rangers	0-2		8000	1	2	5			6	7				11	8	3					9	10			4
39	14	QUEEN'S PARK RANGERS	1-0	Poyntz	8000	1	2	5			6	7				11	8	3					9	10			4
40	18	NORWICH CITY	1-1	Page	6000	1	2	5	4		6	7				11	8	3					9	10			
41	23	Norwich City	0-4		5500		2	5			6	7				11	8	3					9	10		1	4
42	25	Brentford	3-1	Poyntz 2, OG	5000	1	2	5			6	7				11	8	3					9	10			4
		Apps				39	42	34	21	19	37	39	20	23	8	41	29	28	10	3	1	1	18	21	3	8	17
		Goals							1	2		9	2	6	2	14	4		2				4	2			2

One own goal

F.A. Cup

Rnd	Date	Opponent	Score	Att	Smith HC	Watson WJ	Needham GW	Williams W	Pease WH	Lockett WC	Page LA	Poyntz WJ	Jeffs TE	Cockle ES	Evans CJH
R1	Jan 10	Tottenham Hotspur	0-3	32718	1	2	4	6	7	9	11	8	3	10	5

		P	W	D	L	F	A	W	D	L	F	A	Pts
1	Swansea Town	42	17	4	0	51	12	6	7	8	17	23	57
2	Plymouth Argyle	42	17	3	1	55	12	6	7	8	22	26	56
3	Bristol City	42	14	5	2	40	10	8	4	9	20	31	53
4	Swindon Town	42	17	2	2	51	13	3	9	9	15	25	51
5	Millwall	42	12	5	4	35	14	6	8	7	23	24	49
6	Newport County	42	13	6	2	35	12	7	3	11	27	30	49
7	Exeter City	42	13	4	4	37	19	6	5	10	22	29	47
8	Brighton & Hove A.	42	14	3	4	43	17	5	5	11	16	28	46
9	NORTHAMPTON TOWN	42	12	3	6	34	18	8	3	10	17	26	46
10	Southend United	42	14	1	6	34	18	5	4	12	17	43	43
11	Watford	42	12	3	6	22	20	5	6	10	16	27	43
12	Norwich City	42	10	8	3	39	18	4	5	12	14	33	41
13	Gillingham	42	11	8	2	25	11	2	6	13	10	33	40
14	Reading	42	9	6	6	28	15	5	4	12	9	23	38
15	Charlton Athletic	42	12	6	3	31	13	1	6	14	15	35	38
16	Luton Town	42	9	10	2	34	15	1	7	13	15	42	37
17	Bristol Rovers	42	10	5	6	26	13	2	8	11	18	36	37
18	Aberdare Ath.	42	13	4	4	40	21	1	5	15	14	46	37
19	Queen's Park Rgs.	42	10	6	5	28	19	4	2	15	14	44	36
20	Bournemouth	42	8	6	7	20	17	5	2	14	20	41	34
21	Brentford	42	8	7	6	28	26	1	0	20	10	65	25
22	Merthyr Town	42	8	3	10	24	27	0	2	19	11	50	21

1925/26 — 12th in Division 3(S)

No	Date	Opponent	Score	Scorers	Att	Allen PW	Bradshaw H	Brett FB	Cockle ES	Ferrari FW	George HS	Hoten RV	Hammond L	Jeffs TE	Lockett WC	O'Rourke P	Pease WH	Robinson LStJ	Shaw WH	Smith H	Tomkins EF	Tresadern J	Watson WJ	Williams W	Yorke AE
1	Aug 29	Brentford	4-3	Cockle 4	12317	4		5	9			10		3	11		7	8		1			6	2	
2	Sep 5	CRYSTAL PALACE	4-0	Cockle, Hoten, Robinson 2	9005	4		5	9			10	1	3	11		7	8					6	2	
3	Sep 12	Bristol City	1-1	Robinson	14954	5		3	9			10	1		11		7	8					6	2	4
4	Sep 14	ABERDARE ATHLETIC	3-2	Cockle 2, Shaw	7339	4		5	9			10	1	3			7	8	11				6	2	
5	Sep 19	PLYMOUTH ARGYLE	2-1	Pease, Robinson	6344	4		5	9			10	1				7	8	11				6	2	3
6	Sep 21	Aberdare Athletic	0-1		4432	4		5	9			10	1				7	8	11				6	2	3
7	Sep 26	Southend United	1-6	Cockle	7332	4	11	5	9			10	1				7	8					6	2	3
8	Sep 30	Gillingham	1-1	Cockle	4347	4	11	5	9			10	1				7	8					6	2	3
9	Oct 3	NORWICH CITY	3-2	Robinson 3	10805	4		5	9		11	10	1				7	8					6	2	3
10	Oct 10	Millwall	1-4	Pease	18675	4		5	9		11	10	1				7	8					6	2	3
11	Oct 17	Merthyr Town	3-5	Cockle, Robinson, Shaw	5288	5		3	9			11	1				7	8	10				4	2	6
12	Oct 24	NEWPORT COUNTY	2-0	Cockle 2	7987	4		5	9			11	1				7	8	10				6	2	3
13	Oct 31	BOURNEMOUTH	1-1	Hoten	6495	4		5	9			11	1				7	8	10				6	2	3
14	Nov 7	CHARLTON ATHLETIC	2-1	Pease, Robinson	6201			5	9	4	11		1	3			7	8	10				6	2	
15	Nov 14	Bristol Rovers	2-1	Cockle, Hoten	6695			5	9	4	11	10	1	3			7	8					6	2	
16	Nov 21	SWINDON TOWN	2-0	Pease, Robinson	8782			5	9		11	10	1	3			7	8					4	2	6
17	Dec 5	READING	0-1		7494			5	9		11	10	1	3			7	8					4	2	6
18	Dec 19	QUEEN'S PARK RANGERS	3-2	George, Pease, Robinson	5495	4		5	9		11		1				7	8	10				6	2	3
19	Dec 25	Watford	2-3	Pease, Robinson	7771	4		5	9	3	11		1				7	8	10				6	2	
20	Dec 26	WATFORD	2-2	Allen, Cockle	12335	4		5	9	3	11		1				7	8	10				6	2	
21	Dec 28	GILLINGHAM	1-2	Robinson	7075	4		5	9	3	11		1				7	8	10				6	2	
22	Jan 2	BRENTFORD	6-1	Cockle 2, Pease 2, Robinson 2	4649			5	9	6		10	1	3	11		7	8					4	2	
23	Jan 16	Crystal Palace	0-1		7113	4		5	9	3	11		1	2		10	7	8						6	
24	Jan 23	BRISTOL CITY	1-2	Cockle	5027	4		5	9	2	11		1	3			7	8	10			6			
25	Jan 30	Plymouth Argyle	4-2	Allen, George, Robinson, Shaw	10670	4		5	9		11		1	3			7	8	10				6	2	
26	Feb 6	SOUTHEND UNITED	3-3	Cockle 2, Hoten	7414	4		5	9		11	10	1	3			7	8					6	2	
27	Feb 13	Norwich City	1-2	Pease	6032	6			9	5	11		1	3			7	8	10		4			2	
28	Feb 22	Luton Town	2-3	Pease, one og	5549	6			9	5	11	10	1	3			7	8			4			2	
29	Feb 27	MERTHYR TOWN	4-1	Cockle, Robinson 3	5778	6			9	5	11		1	3			7	8	10		4			2	
30	Mar 6	Newport County	0-3		5293	4			9	5	11		1	2			7	8	10		6			3	
31	Mar 13	Bournemouth	2-4	Robinson, Williams	5376	4		3	9	5		10	1				7	8	11				6	2	
32	Mar 20	Charlton Athletic	3-3	Hoten, Pease, one og	5869	4		5	9	3		10	1				7	8	11				6	2	
33	Mar 27	BRISTOL ROVERS	2-0	Cockle, Hoten	5241	4		5	9	3		10	1				7	8	11				6	2	
34	Apr 2	Brighton & Hove Albion	2-2	Cockle, Shaw	10450	4			9	5		10	1				7	8	11				6	2	3
35	Apr 3	Swindon Town	2-1	Cockle, Robinson	6192	4			9	5		10	1				7	8	11				6	2	3
36	Apr 6	BRIGHTON & HOVE ALB	1-2	Cockle	8434	4		5	9	2		10	1				7	8	11					6	3
37	Apr 10	EXETER CITY	2-1	Cockle, Robinson	4717			5	9		11		1				7	8	10			4	6	2	3
38	Apr 14	Exeter City	0-1		2977			5	9			10	1				7	8	11			4	6	2	3
39	Apr 17	Reading	2-4	Cockle, Shaw	13722	4		5	9			10	1			8	7		11				6	2	3
40	Apr 24	LUTON TOWN	0-1		6697	4		5	9		11	10	1				7	8					6	2	3
41	Apr 26	MILLWALL	3-1	Hoten 2, Robinson	3155	4		5	9			11	1					8	10			7	6	2	3
42	May 1	Queen's Park Rangers	2-3	Cockle, Lockett	4586	4		5	9			10	1		11		7	8					6	2	3
		Apps				35	2	36	42	18	19	31	41	16	5	2	41	41	26	1	4	20	38	31	13
		Goals				2			27		2	8			1		11	23	5					1	

Two own goals

F.A. Cup

Rd	Date	Opponent	Score	Scorers	Att	Allen PW	Bradshaw H	Brett FB	Cockle ES	Ferrari FW	George HS	Hoten RV	Hammond L	Jeffs TE	Lockett WC	O'Rourke P	Pease WH	Robinson LStJ	Shaw WH	Smith H	Tomkins EF	Tresadern J	Watson WJ	Williams W	Yorke AE
R1	Nov 28	BARNSLEY	3-1	George 2, Robinson	14000			5	9		11	10	1	3			7	8					4	2	6
R2	Dec 12	NEWPORT COUNTY	3-1	Robinson 3	11000			5	9		11	10	1	3			7	8					4	2	6
R3	Jan 9	CRYSTAL PALACE	3-3	Lockett, Robinson 2	14467			5	9		11		1	3	10		7	8					4	2	6
rep	Jan 13	Crystal Palace	1-2	Pease		4		5	9		11		1	2			7	8	10				6		3

League table

		P	W	D	L	F	A	W	D	L	F	A	Pts
1	Reading	42	16	5	0	49	16	7	6	8	28	36	57
2	Plymouth Argyle	42	16	2	3	71	33	8	6	7	36	34	56
3	Millwall	42	14	6	1	52	12	7	5	9	21	27	53
4	Bristol City	42	14	3	4	42	15	7	6	8	30	36	51
5	Brighton & Hove A.	42	12	4	5	47	33	7	5	9	37	40	47
6	Swindon Town	42	16	2	3	48	22	4	4	13	21	42	46
7	Luton Town	42	16	4	1	60	25	2	3	16	20	50	43
8	Bournemouth	42	10	5	6	44	30	7	4	10	31	61	43
9	Aberdare Ath.	42	11	6	4	50	24	6	2	13	24	42	42
10	Gillingham	42	11	4	6	36	19	6	4	11	17	30	42
11	Southend United	42	13	2	6	50	20	6	2	13	28	53	42
12	NORTHAMPTON TOWN	42	13	3	5	47	26	4	4	13	35	54	41
13	Crystal Palace	42	16	1	4	50	21	3	2	16	25	58	41
14	Merthyr Town	42	13	3	5	51	25	1	8	12	18	50	39
15	Watford	42	12	5	4	47	26	3	4	14	26	63	39
16	Norwich City	42	11	5	5	35	26	4	4	13	23	47	39
17	Newport County	42	11	5	5	39	27	3	5	13	25	47	38
18	Brentford	42	12	4	5	44	32	4	2	15	25	62	38
19	Bristol Rovers	42	9	4	8	44	28	6	2	13	22	41	36
20	Exeter City	42	13	2	6	54	25	2	3	16	18	45	35
21	Charlton Athletic	42	9	7	5	32	23	2	6	13	16	45	35
22	Queen's Park Rgs.	42	5	7	9	23	32	1	2	18	14	52	21

1925/26
Back: Res., Res., Res., Res., Res., Watson, Res., Jeffs, Res.
Middle: Seal (Director), Newman (Trainer), Res., Res., Hammond, Smith, Shaw,
Brett, Unknown, Unknown, Jones (Sec.)
Front: Pease, Williams, Res., Res., Cockle, Res. Lockett, Hoten, Res.

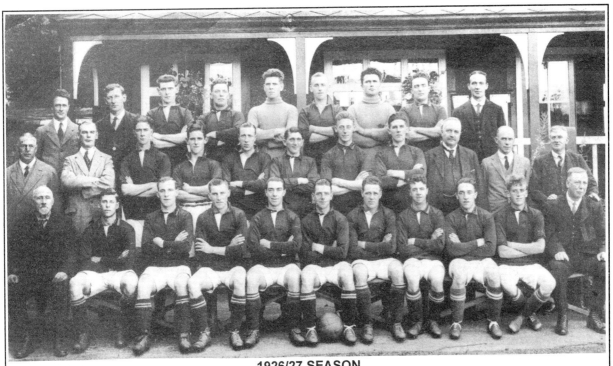

1926/27 SEASON
Back: Tresadern(Man.), Webster(Train.), Yorke, Watson, Hammond, Jeffs, Jelley, Allen, Marlow(Asst. Sec)
Middle: Seal(Dir), Newman(Asst. Train), Wilson, Andrews, Shipley, Williams,
Robinson, Brett, Johnson(Dir), Benbow, A.Jones(Sec)
Front: Gyde(Dir), Boyd, Adey, Austin, Robinson, Cockle, Hoten, Cockburn, Edwards, H.Jones, Gillitt(Dir)

1926/27 — 18th in Division 3(S)

#		Date	Opponent	Score	Scorers	Att	Adey TW	Allen PW	Allon TG	Boyd MS	Brett FB	Buckby LC	Cockle ES	Edwards EJ	Fraser WC	Groome JPG	Gunnell RC	Hammond L	Hoten RV	Jeffs TE	Jennings W	Jones H	Maloney RJH	Oxley W	Robinson LSJ	Shaw WH	Tomkins EF	Tresadern J	Walden FI	Watson WJ	Wells TC	Williams W	Yorke AE
1	Aug	28	Coventry City	3-0	Robinson, Shaw, one og	16330	5				3		9	11				1							8	10		4		7	2	6	
2	Sep	1	Plymouth Argyle	0-3		9380	5				3		9	11				1							8	10		4		7	2	6	
3		4	BRENTFORD	2-3	Cockle, Edwards	10082	5				3		9	11				1							8	10		4			2	6	
4		6	NORWICH CITY	3-0	Cockle, Hoten 2	4491	6	4		7	3	5	9	11				1	10						8						2		
5		11	Millwall	2-4	Allen, Cockle	14271		4		7	3	5	9	11				1	10						8				6		2		
6		13	Luton Town	0-2		8856		4			5		9	11				1	10						8	7			6		2		3
7		18	BRISTOL ROVERS	3-0	Edwards, Robinson, Shaw	6318		4			5		9	11				1			3				8	10			6	7	2		3
8		20	Norwich City	1-6	Tresadern	5123		4			5	6	9					1	11						8	10		7			2		3
9		25	Swindon Town	1-3	Cockle	8298	6	4			5		9	11				1	10	3		7			8					2		
10	Oct	2	EXETER CITY	2-2	Shaw 2	5616		4			5		9	11				1	6						8	10			6	7	2		3
11		9	Merthyr Town	0-2		2840		4			5		9	11				1	6						8	10				7	2		3
12		16	Watford	0-4		8022					3	5	9				11	1		2					8	10	6	4	7				
13		23	CRYSTAL PALACE	0-1	Shaw	5676		4			3		8				11	1	6			5				10			7				2
14		30	Queen's Park Rangers	2-4	Cockle, Oxley	10058					3		8				11	1	6			5		9		10			7				
15	Nov	6	CHARLTON ATHLETIC	0-1		2147					3		8				11	1	6			5		9		10	6	4	7	2			
16		13	Bristol City	3-4	Cockle, Hoten, Robinson	8280			4		3		9		7		11	1	6				5		8	10					2		
17		20	BOURNEMOUTH	2-2	Hoten, Robinson	4165			4		3		9		7		11	1	6				5		8	10					2		
18	Dec	4	NEWPORT COUNTY	1-2	Hoten	5508			4		3		9		7		11	1	6				5			10					2		
19		18	GILLINGHAM	2-1	Brett 2	4979			4		9				11	7		1	6	3			5						8	2			10
20		25	Brighton & Hove Albion	0-2		12991			4		9		10					1	6	3		7	5					11	8	2			
21		27	BRIGHTON & HOVE ALB	0-0		12782			4		9		10					1	6	3		7	5					11	8	2			
22		28	LUTON TOWN	2-1	Hoten, Shaw	8700			4		9		10					1	6	3		7	5		8	11				2			
23	Jan	1	Newport County	0-1		5006	10		4		2		9					1	6	3		7	5		8	11							
24		8	Aberdare Athletic	1-6	Robinson	1724	6		4		2		10		7			1		3			5		8								
25		15	COVENTRY CITY	2-1	Cockle 2	8386			4		2		9		7		11	1	6	3			5		8	10							
26		22	Brentford	1-1	Hoten	4775			4		2		9		7		11	1	6	3			5		8	10							
27	Feb	5	Bristol Rovers	2-5	Groome 2	3972	5		4		2		8		7	9		1	6	3							11	10					
28		12	SWINDON TOWN	1-0	Cockle	5267			4		2		10			9	11	1	6	3			5		8				7			
29		19	Exeter City	2-3	Groome, Wells	5483			4		2		10			9	7	1	6	3			5		8					11		
30		26	MERTHYR TOWN	2-0	Groome, Robinson	5062			4		3				7	9		1	6				5		8	10				2	11		
31	Mar	5	WATFORD	3-2	Cockle, Groome, Robinson	5829			4		3		9		7	9		1	6				5		8					2	11		
32		12	Crystal Palace	0-3		11460			4		3		10			9		1	6				5		8				7	2	11		
33		19	QUEEN'S PARK RANGERS	1-0	Allon	5369			4		3		9					1	6				5		8	10			7	2	11		
34		26	Charlton Athletic	2-5	Hoten, Shaw	4442			4		3				9			1	6				5		8	10			7	2	11		
35	Apr	2	BRISTOL CITY	2-0	Groome, Robinson	7191			4		3				9			1	6				5		8	10			7	2	11		
36		7	MILLWALL	1-4	Brett	3543			4		3				9			1	6				5		8	10			7	2	11		
37		9	Bournemouth	1-3	Robinson	3579			4		3				9			1	6				5		8	10			7	2	11		
38		16	PLYMOUTH ARGYLE	2-1	Cockle 2	4680	6		4		2		8		9			1	10				5						7		11		3
39		18	Southend United	0-2		7809	6		4		2		8		9			1	6				5						7		11		3
40		19	SOUTHEND UNITED	2-1	Cockle 2	6710			4		2		9					1	6				5		8	10			7		11		3
41		30	ABERDARE ATHLETIC	2-1	Shaw, Walden	4608			4		5		9					1	6						8	10			7	2	11		3
42	May	7	Gillingham	2-1	Cockle, Wells	4128			4		2		9		7			1	6				5		8	10					11		3
			Apps				10	9	27	2	42	4	36	11	10	13	11	42	34	14	3	5	25	3	32	31	3	14	20	29	14	3	11
			Goals				1	1			3		15	2		6			8						1	9		8	1	1		2	

Played in one game: GW Cockburn (game 24, at 11), S Seddon (2,7)
AG Shipley (24,9), F Wilson (18,8).

One own goal

F.A. Cup

	Date	Opponent	Score	Scorers	Att	Adey TW	Brett FB	Cockle ES	Buckby LC	Fraser WC	Gunnell RC	Hammond L	Hoten RV	Jeffs TE	Robinson LSJ	Shaw WH	Tresadern J	Walden FI	Watson WJ	Wells TC	Yorke AE
R1	Nov 27	Boston	1-1	Gunnell	6000		5	9		7	11	1	6		10	8		4		2	3
rep	30	BOSTON	2-1	Hoten, Watson	4533		5	9	11	7		1	6		10		4	8		2	3
R2	Dec 11	Exeter City	0-1		11314	4	5	9			11	1	6	3	10			8	7	2	

		P	W	D	L	F	A	W	D	L	F	A	Pts
1	Bristol City	42	19	1	1	71	24	8	7	6	33	30	62
2	Plymouth Argyle	42	17	4	0	52	14	8	6	7	43	47	60
3	Millwall	42	16	2	3	55	19	7	8	6	34	32	56
4	Brighton & Hove A.	42	15	4	2	61	24	6	7	8	18	26	53
5	Swindon Town	42	16	3	2	64	31	5	6	10	36	54	51
6	Crystal Palace	42	12	6	3	57	33	6	3	12	27	48	45
7	Bournemouth	42	13	2	6	49	24	5	6	10	29	42	44
8	Luton Town	42	12	9	0	48	19	3	5	13	20	47	44
9	Newport County	42	15	4	2	40	20	4	2	15	17	51	44
10	Bristol Rovers	42	12	4	5	46	28	4	5	12	32	52	41
11	Brentford	42	10	9	2	46	20	3	5	13	24	41	40
12	Exeter City	42	14	4	3	46	18	1	6	14	30	55	40
13	Charlton Athletic	42	13	5	3	44	22	3	3	15	16	39	40
14	Queen's Park Rgs.	42	9	8	4	41	27	6	1	14	24	44	39
15	Coventry City	42	11	4	6	44	33	4	3	14	27	53	37
16	Norwich City	42	10	5	6	41	25	2	6	13	18	46	35
17	Merthyr Town	42	11	5	5	42	25	2	4	15	21	55	35
18	NORTHAMPTON TOWN	42	13	4	4	36	23	2	1	18	23	64	35
19	Southend United	42	12	3	6	44	25	2	3	16	20	52	34
20	Gillingham	42	10	5	6	36	26	1	5	15	18	46	32
21	Watford	42	9	6	6	36	27	3	2	16	21	60	32
22	Aberdare Ath.	42	8	2	11	38	48	1	5	15	24	53	25

1927/28   2nd in Division 3(S)

#	Date	Opponent	Score	Scorers	Att	Aitkin IG	Allon TG	Bowen EC	Brett FB	Cave W	Cockle ES	Daley J	Fraser WC	George HS	Hammond L	Hoten RV	Jeffs TE	Loasby H	Maloney RJH	Odell GW	Price E	Russell GH	Shaw WH	Smith TG	Watson WJ	Wells TC	Wilson JR
1	Aug 27	MILLWALL	5-2	Aitken, Hoten, Loasby 2, Smith	12188	11	4					7			1	10	3	9	5	6				8	2		
2	29	Brentford	0-3		7220	11	4					7			1		3	9	5	6	10			8	2		
3	Sep 3	Crystal Palace	0-1		13771	11	4					7			1	10	3	9	5	6				8	2		
4	5	BRENTFORD	3-2	Aitken, Loasby, Smith	7220	11	4					7			1	10	3	9	5	6				8	2		
5	10	EXETER CITY	5-0	Daley, Hoten, Loasby, Smith, Wilson	10249		4		2			7			1	10	3	9	5					8		11	6
6	17	Torquay United	5-1	Loasby 2, Wells 2, one og	4625		4		2			7			1	10	3	9	5					8		11	6
7	24	NORWICH CITY	4-2	Loasby 2, Wells 2	13921		4		2			7			1	10	3	9	5					8		11	6
8	Oct 1	Gillingham	3-1	Loasby 2, Smith	4226		4		2			7			1	10	3	9	5					8		11	6
9	8	Southend United	0-2		8768		4		2			7			1	10	3	9	5					8		11	6
10	15	BRIGHTON & HOVE ALB	1-0	one og	13214	11	4		2			7			1	10	3	9	5	6				8			
11	22	PLYMOUTH ARGYLE	2-1	Hoten, Maloney	9434		4		2			7			1	10	3	9	5	6				8		11	
12	29	Merthyr Town	3-1	Allon, Loasby 2	5000		4		2			7			1	10	3	9	5	6				8		11	
13	Nov 5	WALSALL	10-	*see below	11340		4		5			7			1	10	3	9		6				8	2	11	
14	12	Bristol Rovers	2-2	Loasby, Smith	7846		4		5			7			1	10	3	9		6				8	2	11	
15	19	CHARLTON ATHLETIC	2-1	Loasby, O'Dell	10210		4		5			7			1	10	3	9		6				8	2	11	
16	Dec 3	QUEEN'S PARK RANGERS	1-0	Loasby	9737		4		5			7			1	10	3	9		6				8	2	11	
17	17	NEWPORT COUNTY	1-2	Maloney	8945		4		3		9	7			1	10			5	6				8	2	11	
18	24	Coventry City	4-2	O'Dell 2, Daley, Smith	9250		4		3			7			1	10			5	9				8	2	11	6
19	26	LUTON TOWN	6-5	Allon, Daley, Hoten, Maloney, Smith 2	10153		4		3			7			1	10			5	9				8	2	11	6
20	31	Millwall	0-3		26334		4		3			7			1	10			5	9				8	2	11	6
21	Jan 7	CRYSTAL PALACE	1-1	O'Dell	9860	11	4					7			1	10			5	9		3		8	2		6
22	21	Exeter City	1-1	Wells	10231							7			1		3		5	6	9		10	8	2	11	4
23	28	TORQUAY UNITED	4-4	Allon, Price 2, Wells	4832		4						7		1		3		5	6	9		10	8	2	11	
24	Feb 4	Norwich City	4-3	Bowen 3, Wells	6760		4	9					7		1		3		5				10	8	2	11	6
25	11	GILLINGHAM	1-0	Shaw	9538		4	9				7			1		3		5				10	8	2	11	6
26	18	SOUTHEND UNITED	2-1	Allon, Wells	13133		4	9		1			7			10			5	6		3		8	2	11	
27	25	Brighton & Hove Albion	1-2	Wells	12631	7		9	3						1	10			5	6				8	2	11	4
28	Mar 3	Plymouth Argyle	3-3	Bowen 2, Fraser	13942		4	9	3				7		1				5	6				8	2	11	
29	10	MERTHYR TOWN	6-0	Aitken 2, Bowen, Fraser, O'Dell	8549	11	4	9	3				7		1				5	6			10	8	2		
30	17	Walsall	1-1	Fraser	7800		4	9	3				7		1				5	6			10	8	2	11	
31	19	Luton Town	0-2		8194	11	4	9	3				7		1				5	6			10	8	2		
32	24	BRISTOL ROVERS	2-0	Bowen, Fraser	9770		4	9	3				7	11	1	10			5	6				8	2		
33	31	Charlton Athletic	2-2	Bowen, Wells	7121		4	9				7			1	10			5	6		3		8	2	11	
34	Apr 7	SWINDON TOWN	3-0	Bowen 2, Hoten	14174		4	9				7			1	10			5	6		3		8	2	11	
35	9	Bournemouth	1-1	Bowen	9099	11	4	9				7			1	10			5	6		3		8	2		
36	10	BOURNEMOUTH	1-1	Aitken	11693	11	4	9				7			1	10			5	6		3		8	2		
37	14	Queen's Park Rangers	4-0	Bowen, Hoten 2, O'Dell	8399		4	9				7			1	11			5	10		3		8	2		6
38	18	Watford	0-2		4221		4	9				7			1	11			5	10		3		8	2		6
39	21	WATFORD	5-0	Allon, Bowen, Hoten 2, Smith	6255		4	9				7			1	10			5	6		3		8	2	11	
40	25	Swindon Town	0-4		5289		4	9				7			1	10			5	6		3		8	2	11	
41	28	Newport County	1-4	Bowen	2753		4	9				7			1	10			5	6		3		8	2	11	
42	May 5	COVENTRY CITY	2-1	Bowen, Daley	7583		4	9				7			1	10			5	6		3		8	2	11	
			Apps			10	41	19	22	1	1	33	7	2	41	34	20	16	38	35	4	13	6	42	33	29	15
			Goals			5	5	15				4	4			10		18	3	6	2		2	12		13	1

Scorers in game 13: Loasby 3, Smith 3, Wells 3, Hoten

Two own goals

F.A. Cup

R	Date	Opponent	Score	Scorers	Att	Aitkin IG	Allon TG	Bowen EC	Brett FB	Cave W	Cockle ES	Daley J	Fraser WC	George HS	Hammond L	Hoten RV	Jeffs TE	Loasby H	Maloney RJH	Odell GW	Price E	Russell GH	Shaw WH	Smith TG	Watson WJ	Wells TC	Wilson JR
R1	Nov 26	LEYTON	8-0	*See below	12043		4		5			7			1	10	3	9		6				8	2	11	
R2	Dec 10	BRIGHTON & HOVE ALB.	1-0	Daley	16092		4		3			7			1	10		9	5	6				8	2	11	
R3	Jan 14	Sunderland	3-3	Cowen, Daley, Wells	20000		4					7			1	10	3		5	6				8	2	11	
rep	19	SUNDERLAND	0-3		21148		4					7		9	1	10	3		5	6				8	2	11	

Scorers in R1: Daley, Hoten 2, Loasby 3, Wells, one og

Played in R3: JE Cowen (at 9)

	P	W	D	L	F	A	W	D	L	F	A	Pts
1 Millwall	42	19	2	0	87	15	11	3	7	40	35	65
2 NORTHAMPTON TOWN	42	17	3	1	67	23	6	6	9	35	41	55
3 Plymouth Argyle	42	17	2	2	60	19	6	5	10	25	35	53
4 Brighton & Hove A.	42	14	4	3	51	24	5	6	10	30	45	48
5 Crystal Palace	42	15	3	3	46	23	3	9	9	33	49	48
6 Swindon Town	42	12	6	3	60	26	7	3	11	30	43	47
7 Southend United	42	14	2	5	48	19	6	4	11	32	45	46
8 Exeter City	42	11	6	4	49	27	6	6	9	21	33	46
9 Newport County	42	12	5	4	52	38	6	4	11	29	46	45
10 Queen's Park Rgs.	42	8	5	8	37	35	9	4	8	35	36	43
11 Charlton Athletic	42	12	5	4	34	27	3	8	10	26	43	43
12 Brentford	42	12	4	5	49	30	4	4	13	27	44	40
13 Luton Town	42	13	5	3	56	27	3	2	16	38	60	39
14 Bournemouth	42	12	6	3	44	24	1	6	14	28	55	38
15 Watford	42	10	5	6	42	34	4	5	12	26	44	38
16 Gillingham	42	10	3	8	33	26	3	8	10	29	55	37
17 Norwich City	42	9	8	4	41	26	1	8	12	25	44	36
18 Walsall	42	9	6	6	52	35	3	3	15	23	66	33
19 Bristol Rovers	42	11	3	7	41	36	3	1	17	26	57	32
20 Coventry City	42	5	8	8	40	36	6	1	14	27	60	31
21 Merthyr Town	42	7	6	8	38	40	2	7	12	15	51	31
22 Torquay United	42	4	10	7	27	36	4	4	13	26	67	30

1927/28 SEASON
Back: Daly, Tresadern(Manager), Watson, Hammond, Brett, Mellors(Trainer), O'Dell
Front: George, Smith, Bowen, Shaw, Wells, Maloney

1929/30 SEASON
Back: Gillitt(Dir.),Andrews,Hoten Wells,Hammond,Cave,Maloney,A.Dawes,F.Dawes,Newman(Train.)
Middle: Tresadern(Man.), Bowen, Brett, Smith, Anthoney, Russell, Odell, Wilson, Eyre, Mellors(Train.)
Front: Sissons, Berridge, Allon, McNaughton, Loasby, Watson, Shaw, Waite, Weston, Riches, Seal(Dir.)

1928/29   3rd in Division 3(S)

#	Date	Opponent		Scorers	Att	Allon TG	Bowen EC	Brett FB	Cave W	Cowen IE	Eccles J	Hammond L	Harrington JW	Hicks TG	Hoten RV	Lincoln A	Loasby H	Maloney RJH	McIlvenny P	McNaughton WF	Odell GW	Russell GH	Shaw WH	Smith TG	Watson WJ	Wells TC	Weston JM	Wilson JR
1	Aug 25	CHARLTON ATHLETIC	4-1	Bowen, O'Dell, Smith, one og	15135	4	9	5				1	7	3		10					6			8	2		11	
2	30	LUTON TOWN	2-2	Bowen 2	12220	4	9	5				1	7	3		10					6			8	2		11	
3	Sep 1	Norwich City	1-1	Hoten	11120		9	5				1	7	3	10						6			8		11		6
4	3	Luton Town	0-4		10931		9	5			7	1		3						10	6	2		8			11	4
5	8	BRIGHTON & HOVE ALB	1-1	Bowen	11214		7	3		9		1			10			5			6			8	2	11		4
6	15	Exeter City	0-2		6282		9	3				1	7		10			5			6			8	2	11		4
7	17	PLYMOUTH ARGYLE	3-0	Bowen 2, O'Dell	7110	4	9	3			7	1			11			5			10	2		8				6
8	22	SOUTHEND UNITED	2-3	Hoten 2	10711	4	9	2				1			11			5			10	3		8		7		6
9	29	Merthyr Town	2-2	Bowen 2	3983	4	9	3				1	7		10			5						8	2		11	6
10	Oct 6	BOURNEMOUTH	2-0	Bowen 2	8519	4	9	3				1	7		10			5			6			8	2	11		
11	13	Brentford	2-2	Allon, Bowen	9260	4	9	3				1	7		10			5			6			8	2	11		
12	20	Newport County	3-0	Bowen, McIlvenny 2	4405	4	9	3				1			10			5	7		6			8	2	11		
13	27	CRYSTAL PALACE	8-1	Bowen, Hoten 5, Smith, Wells	7299	4	9	3				1			10			5	7		6			8	2	11		
14	Nov 3	Swindon Town	1-0	Bowen	7099	4	9	3				1			10			5	7		6			8	2	11		
15	10	TORQUAY UNITED	6-1	Bowen Hoten 4, Smith	8384	4	9	3				1			10			5	7		6			8	2	11		
16	17	Gillingham	1-2	Smith	5312	4	9	3				1			10			5	7		6			8	2	11		
17	Dec 1	Fulham	1-2	Bowen	16952	4	9	3				1			10			5	7		6			8	2	11		
18	8	QUEEN'S PARK RANGERS	4-2	Bowen 2, Hoten, Wells	10124	4	9	3			7	1			10			5			6			8	2	11		
19	15	Bristol Rovers	2-1	Hoten, one og	4970	4	9	3			7	1			10			5			6	2		8			11	
20	22	WATFORD	3-0	Bowen 2, Weston	9438	4	9	3			7	1			10			5			6	2		8			11	
21	25	Walsall	3-4	Bowen, Hoten 2	8419	4	9	3			7	1			10			5			6	2		8			11	
22	26	WALSALL	4-2	Bowen 2, Hoten, Smith	15987	4	9	3			7	1			10			5			6			8	2	11		
23	29	Charlton Athletic	1-3	Bowen	12073		9	3			7	1			10			5			6		10	8	2		11	4
24	Jan 5	NORWICH CITY	2-0	Bowen, Hoten	7057		9	3				1			10			5	7		4		6	8	2		11	
25	19	Brighton & Hove Albion	3-0	Hoten, Loasby, Weston	7197	4		3			7	1			10		9	5		8		2	6				11	
26	26	EXETER CITY	4-0	Hoten, Loasby 2, Weston	9477	4		3				1			10		9	5	7			2	6	8			11	
27	Feb 2	Southend United	2-2	Eccles, Loasby	5944			3			7	1			10		9	5					6	8	2		11	4
28	9	MERTHYR TOWN	4-1	Bowen, Hoten 2, Weston	6372	4	9	3			7	1			10			5			6			8	2		11	
29	23	BRENTFORD	1-1	Maloney	8555	4	9	3			7	1			10			5			6			8	2		11	
30	Mar 2	NEWPORT COUNTY	7-0	Bowen 2, Hoten 3, Wells 2	8864	4	9				7	1			10			5			6	3		8	2	11		
31	9	Crystal Palace	0-1		25072	4	9				7	1		3	10			5			6	2		8			11	
32	16	SWINDON TOWN	1-1	Bowen	10070	4	9	3			7	1			10			5			6	2		8			11	
33	20	Bournemouth	0-2		3196	4	9	3				1			10			5			6		7	8	2	11		
34	23	Torquay United	1-0	Loasby	3655	4	9	3	1						10		9	5			6	2		8		11		
35	30	GILLINGHAM	1-0	Hoten	10058	4	9	3	1				7		10			5			6			8	2	11		
36	Apr 1	Coventry City	2-0	Bowen, Loasby	20227	4	7	3	1						10		9	5			6			8	2	11		
37	2	COVENTRY CITY	3-3	Bowen 2, Hoten	17152	4	9	3	1						10		7	5			6			8	2	11		
38	6	Plymouth Argyle	1-1	Bowen	11376	4	9	3	1						10		7	5			6			8	2	11		
39	13	FULHAM	3-3	Hoten, Wells 2	9436	4	9	3	1						10		7	5			6			8	2	11		
40	20	Queen's Park Rangers	1-4	Wells	21916	4	9	3				1			10			5			6			8	2	11	7	
41	27	BRISTOL ROVERS	3-1	Bowen, Wells 2	9566	4	9	3				1			10		7	5			6			8	2	11		
42	May 4	Watford	1-1	Hoten	10926	4	9					1			10			5			6	3		8	2	11		
		Apps				35	39	39	6	1	15	36	8	5	38	2	10	38	8	2	39	15	6	40	29	28	14	9
		Goals				1	34				1				29		6	1	2		2			5		9	4	

Two own goals

F.A. Cup

	Date	Opponent		Scorers	Att	Bowen EC	Brett FB	Eccles J	Hammond L	Hoten RV	Maloney RJH	McNaughton WF	Odell GW	Shaw WH	Smith TG	Watson WJ	Weston JM	Wilson JR
R3	Jan 12	Millwall	1-1	Weston	28784	9	3	7	1	10	5		4	6	8	2	11	
rep	17	MILLWALL	2-2	Hoten 2	18261		3	7	1	10	5	9		6	8	2	11	4
rep2	21	Millwall	0-2		32391	9	3	7	1	10	5		4	6	8	2	11	

Replay a.e.t.   Second replay at Highbury

		P	W	D	L	F	A	W	D	L	F	A	Pts
1	Charlton Athletic	42	14	5	2	51	22	9	3	9	35	38	54
2	Crystal Palace	42	14	2	5	40	25	9	6	6	41	42	54
3	NORTHAMPTON TOWN	42	14	6	1	68	23	6	6	9	28	34	52
4	Plymouth Argyle	42	14	6	1	51	13	6	6	9	32	38	52
5	Fulham	42	14	3	4	60	31	7	7	7	41	40	52
6	Queen's Park Rgs.	42	13	7	1	50	22	6	7	8	32	39	52
7	Luton Town	42	16	3	2	64	28	3	8	10	25	45	49
8	Watford	42	15	3	3	55	31	4	7	10	24	43	48
9	Bournemouth	42	14	4	3	54	31	5	5	11	30	46	47
10	Swindon Town	42	12	5	4	48	27	3	8	10	27	45	43
11	Coventry City	42	9	6	6	35	23	5	8	8	27	34	42
12	Southend United	42	10	7	4	44	27	5	4	12	36	48	41
13	Brentford	42	11	4	6	34	21	3	6	12	22	39	38
14	Walsall	42	11	7	3	47	25	2	5	14	26	54	38
15	Brighton & Hove A.	42	14	2	5	39	28	2	4	15	19	48	38
16	Newport County	42	8	6	7	37	28	5	3	13	32	58	35
17	Norwich City	42	12	3	6	49	29	2	3	16	20	52	34
18	Torquay United	42	10	3	8	46	36	4	3	14	20	48	34
19	Bristol Rovers	42	9	6	6	39	28	4	1	16	21	51	33
20	Merthyr Town	42	11	6	4	42	28	0	2	19	13	75	30
21	Exeter City	42	7	6	8	49	40	2	5	14	18	48	29
22	Gillingham	42	7	8	6	22	24	3	1	17	21	59	29

1929/30   4th in Division 3(S)

#	Date	Opponent	Score	Scorers	Att	Hammond L	Anthony C	Brett FB	Allon TG	Maloney RJH	Odell GW	Sissons AE	Dawes AG	Bowen EC	Hoten RV	Weston JM	Smith TG	Berridge R	Dawes FW	Loasby H	McNaughton WF	Riches LE	Russell GH	Shaw WH	Wells TC	Young JW
1	Aug 31	BOURNEMOUTH	2-0	Bowen, Smith	14397	1	2	3	4	5	6			9	10		8					7			11	
2	Sep 2	Merthyr Town	0-1		6817	1	2	3	4	5	6			9	10		8					7			11	
3	7	Walsall	2-1	Bowen 2	10025	1	2	3	4	5	6	7		9	10		8								11	
4	9	MERTHYR TOWN	2-0	Sissons, Bowen	8215	1	2	3	4	5	6	7		9	10		8								11	
5	14	QUEEN'S PARK RANGERS	2-1	Hoten, Smith	12876	1	2	3	4		5		10	9	6		8				7				11	
6	16	Southend United	2-1	Bowen, McNaughton	8145	1	2	3	4		5		10	9	6		8				7				11	
7	21	Fulham	0-1		20406	1	2	3	4		5		10	9	6		8				7				11	
8	28	NORWICH CITY	4-0	O'Dell, Hoten 2, Wells	12302	1	2	3	4	5	6			9	10		8				7				11	
9	Oct 5	Crystal Palace	3-1	Bowen 2, Smith	17562	1	2	3	4	5	6			9	10		8				7				11	
10	12	GILLINGHAM	3-1	Bowen, Hoten 2	10663	1	2	3	4	5	6			9	10		8				7				11	
11	19	PLYMOUTH ARGYLE	1-1	Bowen	21102	1	2	3	4	5			10	9	6		8				7				11	
12	26	Swindon Town	0-2		7695	1		3	4	5		7		9	10		8						2	6	11	
13	Nov 2	BRIGHTON & HOVE ALB	1-3	Wells	4704	1	2	3	4	5		7		9	10		8							6	11	
14	9	Bristol Rovers	3-2	Wells 3	7483	1	2	3	4	5	6	7	10	9			8								11	
15	16	BRENTFORD	1-1	Sissons	6165	1	2	3	4	5	6	7	10	9			8								11	
16	23	Clapton Orient	0-0		8497	1		3		5	4	7	10	9	6						8		2		11	
17	Dec 7	Watford	2-1	Bowen, Hoten	6989	1		3	4	5	6	7		9	10		8						2		11	
18	21	Torquay United	1-0	Wells	3730	1		3	4	5	6	7		9	10		8						2		11	
19	25	Luton Town	0-1		9473	1		3	4	5	6	7	10	9			8						2		11	
20	26	LUTON TOWN	4-1	Hoten 3, Smith	19251	1		3	4	5	6			9	10		8					7	2		11	
21	31	NEWPORT COUNTY	2-0	Bowen 2	5797	1		3	4	5	6			9	10		8					7	2		11	
22	Jan 4	WALSALL	1-0	Hoten	9433	1		3	4	5	6			9	10	7						8	2		11	
23	18	Queen's Park Rangers	2-0	A Dawes, Wells	11696	1		3	4	5	6		8	9	10	7							2		11	
24	Feb 1	Norwich City	3-4	A Dawes, Hoten, Wells	11681	1		3	4	5	6	7	8	9	10								2		11	
25	8	CRYSTAL PALACE	2-0	A Dawes, Bowen	8480	1		3	4	5	6		8	9	10	7							2		11	
26	15	Gillingham	2-5	Bowen, Hoten	4665	1		3	4	5	6	7	8	9	10								2		11	
27	22	Plymouth Argyle	0-1		15376	1		3	4	5		7	10	9	6		8						2		11	
28	26	Bournemouth	1-3	Loadsby	3889	1		3	4	5		7	10		6	11	8			9			2			
29	Mar 1	SWINDON TOWN	3-3	Sissons, Young 2	9254	1	2	3	4	5		7	10		6		8								11	9
30	8	Brighton & Hove Albion	1-2	McNaughton	10622	1		3		5	6			9	10			4			7		2		11	8
31	13	FULHAM	3-1	Bowen, Weston, Smith	4727	1		3		5	6		4	9	10	7	8						2		11	
32	15	BRISTOL ROVERS	6-1	Bowen 3, Hoten, Weston 2	5402	1		3		5	6		4	9	10	7	8						2		11	
33	22	Brentford	0-2		16460	1		3		5	6		4	9	10	7	8						2		11	
34	29	CLAPTON ORIENT	3-0	Bowen 2, Wells	6763	1		3		5	6		4	9	10	7	8						2		11	
35	Apr 5	Coventry City	2-2	Hoten 2	13085	1		3		5	6		4	9	10	7	8						2		11	
36	7	COVENTRY CITY	2-2	Bowen 2	4649	1		3		5	6		4	9	10	7	8						2		11	
37	12	WATFORD	2-0	A Dawes, Bowen	6134	1		3	4	5	6		8	9	10	7							2		11	
38	19	Newport County	1-2	Weston	3282	1		3	4	5	6		8	9	10	7							2		11	
39	21	Exeter City	4-6	Sissons, Weston 3	8258	1	2	3	4	5	6	7	8	9	10	11										
40	22	EXETER CITY	2-0	Bowen, Hoten	7621	1	2	3	4	5	6	7		9	10	11	8									
41	26	TORQUAY UNITED	2-2	Hoten, Weston	4100	1	2		4	5	6	7	8	9	10	11			3						11	
42	May 3	SOUTHEND UNITED	5-1	A Dawes, Bowen 2, Hoten, Weston	3454	1		3		5	4	7	8	9	10	11			2					6		

| | Apps | | | | | 42 | 17 | 42 | 33 | 39 | 36 | 19 | 26 | 40 | 39 | 16 | 30 | 1 | 2 | 1 | 9 | 5 | 23 | 3 | 37 | 2 |
| | Goals | | | | | | | | | | 1 | 4 | 5 | 26 | 18 | 9 | 5 | | | 1 | 2 | | | | 9 | 2 |

F.A. Cup

#	Date	Opponent	Score	Scorers	Att	Hammond L	Anthony C	Brett FB	Allon TG	Maloney RJH	Odell GW	Sissons AE	Dawes AG	Bowen EC	Hoten RV	Weston JM	Smith TG	Berridge R	Dawes FW	Loasby H	McNaughton WF	Riches LE	Russell GH	Shaw WH	Wells TC	Young JW
R1	Nov 30	Aldershot	1-0	Hoten	8000	1		3	4	5	6	7			10		8			9			2		11	
R2	Dec 14	MARGATE	6-0	Sissons, Bowen 2, Hoten 3	11012	1		3	4	5	6	7		9	10		8						2		11	
R3	Jan 11	Blackburn Rovers	1-4	Wells	27000	1		3		5	6		8	9	10	7							2		11	

Played in R3: JR Wilson (at 4)

		P	W	D	L	F	A	W	D	L	F	A	Pts
1	Plymouth Argyle	42	18	3	0	63	12	12	5	4	35	26	68
2	Brentford	42	21	0	0	66	12	7	5	9	28	32	61
3	Queen's Park Rgs.	42	13	5	3	46	26	8	4	9	34	42	51
4	NORTHAMPTON TOWN	42	14	6	1	53	20	7	2	12	29	38	50
5	Brighton & Hove A.	42	16	2	3	54	20	5	6	10	33	43	50
6	Coventry City	42	14	3	4	54	25	5	6	10	34	48	47
7	Fulham	42	12	6	3	54	33	6	3	10	33	50	47
8	Norwich City	42	14	4	3	55	28	4	6	11	33	49	46
9	Crystal Palace	42	14	5	2	56	26	3	7	11	25	48	46
10	Bournemouth	42	11	6	4	47	24	4	7	10	25	37	43
11	Southend United	42	11	6	4	41	19	4	7	10	28	40	43
12	Clapton Orient	42	10	8	3	38	21	4	5	12	17	41	41
13	Luton Town	42	13	4	4	42	25	1	8	12	22	53	40
14	Swindon Town	42	10	7	4	42	25	3	5	13	31	58	38
15	Watford	42	10	4	7	37	30	5	4	12	23	43	38
16	Exeter City	42	10	6	5	45	29	2	5	14	22	44	35
17	Walsall	42	10	4	7	45	24	3	4	14	26	54	34
18	Newport County	42	9	9	3	48	29	3	1	17	26	56	34
19	Torquay United	42	9	6	6	50	38	1	5	15	14	56	31
20	Bristol Rovers	42	11	3	7	45	31	0	5	16	22	62	30
21	Gillingham	42	9	5	7	38	28	2	3	16	13	52	30
22	Merthyr Town	42	5	6	10	39	49	1	3	17	21	86	21

1930/31   6th in Division 3(S)

#	Date	Opponent	Res	Scorers	Att	Allon TG	Anthony C	Armitage JH	Bowen EC	Boyle TW	Cave W	Crawford GW	Davies FP	Dawes AG	Eyre FMB	Hammond L	Inglis WW	McLachlan ER	Maloney RJH	Muir, Malcolm	Odell GW	Riches LE	Russell GH	Shaw WH	Taylor JW	Wells TC	Weston JM	Whyte C	Wonnacott CB
1	Aug 30	Bristol Rovers	4-1	Bowen 2, Wells, Boyle	7649	4	3		9	8				10		1		7	5	2	6					11			
2	Sep 3	Brentford	4-0	Bowen 3, Dawes	11356	4	3		9	8		5	6	10		1	2	7								11			
3	6	NEWPORT COUNTY	1-0	Dawes	13239	4	3		9	8			6	10		1	2	7	5							11			
4	8	CRYSTAL PALACE	0-0		10040	4	3		9	8			6	10		1	2	7	5							11			
5	13	Gillingham	2-0	Bowen 2	4821		3		9	8			6	10		1	2	7	5			4				11			
6	17	Crystal Palace	0-0		11253		3		9				6	10		1	2	8	5			4				11		7	
7	20	EXETER CITY	1-0	Bowen	7346		3		9				6	10		1	2	7	5			4	8			11			
8	27	Brighton & Hove Albion	1-1	Wells	10105		3		9	8			6	10		1	2	7	5			4				11			
9	Oct 4	TORQUAY UNITED	0-3		11852		3		9				8	10		1	2	7	5			4		6		11			
10	11	Coventry City	1-0	Dawes	19569		3		9				6	8		1	2		5			4				11		7	10
11	18	WALSALL	3-0	Dawes, Bowen 2	9341		3		9				6	8		1	2		5			4				11		7	10
12	25	Queen's Park Rangers	2-0	Dawes, Whyte	8362		3		9	8			6	10		1	2		5			4				11		7	
13	Nov 1	NORWICH CITY	3-1	Dawes 2, Bowen	9393		3		9	8			6	10		1	2		5			4				11		7	
14	8	Thames	1-2	McLaughlin	2168		3		9	8			6	10		1	2	7	5			4				11			
15	15	CLAPTON ORIENT	0-0		6820	4	3		9				10	8		1	2	7	5		6					11			
16	22	Notts County	2-2	Dawes 2	21329	4	3		9	8			6	10		1			5						2	11	7		
17	Dec 6	Bournemouth	3-1	Wells 2, Bowen	4850	4	3		9	8			6	10		1	2		5							11	7		
18	13	SWINDON TOWN	3-0	Bowen 3	7625	4	3		9	8			6	10		1	2		5		7					11			
19	20	Fulham	2-4	Bowen 2	9646	4	3		9	8				10		1	2		5		7			6		11			
20	25	Southend United	1-2	Boyle	10068	4		5	9	8			6	10		1	3				7		2			11			
21	26	SOUTHEND UNITED	4-0	Dawes 3, Riches	9976	4		5	9	8			6	10		1	2				7					11			
22	27	BRISTOL ROVERS	1-1	Bowen	10863	4	3	5	9	8			6	10		1				2	7					11			
23	Jan 3	Newport County	2-5	Dawes, Bowen	2977	4	3	5	9	8			6	10		1	2				7					11			
24	15	Watford	2-3	Riches, Wells	3952	4	3		9	8			6	10		1			5	2	7					11			
25	17	GILLINGHAM	0-1		6452	4	3		9	8			6	10		1	2		5		7					11			
26	28	Exeter City	3-3	Wonnacott, Weston, Bowen	3595		3		9	8	1		6	4			2		5		7						11		10
27	31	BRIGHTON & HOVE ALB	2-1	Bowen, Weston	5868		3		9	8	1		6	4	10		2		5		7						11		
28	Feb 7	Torquay United	0-3		4270		3		9	8			6	10		1	2		5		7						11		
29	14	COVENTRY CITY	0-3		7033	4	3		9				10	8		1	2		5		6	7				11			
30	21	Walsall	6-2	Wells 2, Bowen 2, Dawes 2	6345	4	3		9	8				10		1	2		5		6	7				11			
31	28	QUEEN'S PARK RANGERS	6-0	Boyle 2, Riches 2, Wells, Bowen	5198	4	3		9	8				10		1	2		5		6	7				11			
32	Mar 7	Norwich City	1-1	Dawes	6033	4	3		9	8				10		1	2		5		6	7				11			
33	14	THAMES	4-1	Dawes 2, O'Dell, Boyle	5587	4	3		9	8				10		1	2		5		6	7				11			
34	21	Clapton Orient	2-2	Boyle, Bowen	5542	4	3		9	8	5		6	10		1	2					7				11			
35	28	NOTTS COUNTY	0-0		14284	4	3		9	8			6	10		1	2		5			7				11			
36	Apr 4	Watford	2-1	Bowen, Wells	8157	4	3		9	8			6	10		1	2		5			7				11			
37	6	Luton Town	0-4		12292	4	3		9	8			6	10		1	2		5			7				11			
38	7	LUTON TOWN	0-0		8614	4	3		9	8			6			1	2		5			7				11			10
39	11	BOURNEMOUTH	2-2	Bowen, Wells	4830	4	3		9	8			6			1	2		5			7				11			10
40	18	Swindon Town	1-5	Wonnacott	3330	4	3		9	8			6			1	2		5			7				11			10
41	25	FULHAM	4-2	Dawes 2, Boyle, Wonnacott	2753	4	3			8			6	10		1	2		5							11	7		9
42	May 2	BRENTFORD	1-2	Dawes	3698	4	3					1	10	9			2		5		6				8	11	7		
		Apps				30	41	4	40	34	3	2	33	42	1	39	38	11	36	3	18	24	2	2	1	39	7	5	7
		Goals							27	7				21			1				1	4				10	2	1	3

F.A. Cup

#	Date	Opponent	Res	Scorers	Att	Allon TG	Anthony C	Armitage JH	Bowen EC	Boyle TW	Cave W	Crawford GW	Davies FP	Dawes AG	Eyre FMB	Hammond L	Inglis WW	McLachlan ER	Maloney RJH	Muir, Malcolm	Odell GW	Riches LE	Russell GH	Shaw WH	Taylor JW	Wells TC	Weston JM	Whyte C	Wonnacott CB
R1	Nov 29	COVENTRY CITY	1-2	Bowen	8807	4	3		9	8			6	10		1			5				2			11	7		

		P	W	D	L	F	A	W	D	L	F	A	Pts
1	Notts County	42	16	4	1	58	13	8	7	6	39	33	59
2	Crystal Palace	42	17	2	2	71	20	5	5	11	36	51	51
3	Brentford	42	14	3	4	62	30	8	3	10	28	34	50
4	Brighton & Hove A.	42	13	5	3	45	20	4	10	7	23	33	49
5	Southend United	42	16	0	5	53	26	6	5	10	23	34	49
6	NORTHAMPTON TOWN	42	10	6	5	37	20	8	6	7	40	39	48
7	Luton Town	42	15	3	3	61	17	4	5	12	15	34	46
8	Queen's Park Rgs.	42	15	0	6	57	23	5	3	13	25	52	43
9	Fulham	42	15	3	3	49	21	3	4	14	28	54	43
10	Bournemouth	42	11	7	3	39	22	4	6	11	33	51	43
11	Torquay United	42	13	5	3	56	26	4	4	13	24	58	43
12	Swindon Town	42	15	5	1	68	29	3	1	17	21	65	42
13	Exeter City	42	12	6	3	55	35	5	2	14	29	55	42
14	Coventry City	42	11	4	6	55	28	5	5	11	20	37	41
15	Bristol Rovers	42	12	3	6	49	36	4	5	12	26	56	40
16	Gillingham	42	10	6	5	40	29	4	4	13	21	47	38
17	Walsall	42	9	5	7	44	38	5	4	12	34	57	37
18	Watford	42	9	4	8	41	29	5	3	13	31	46	35
19	Clapton Orient	42	12	3	6	47	33	2	4	15	16	58	35
20	Thames	42	12	5	4	34	20	1	3	17	20	73	34
21	Newport County	42	10	5	6	45	31	1	1	19	24	80	28
22	Norwich City	42	10	7	4	37	20	0	1	20	10	56	28

1930/31 SEASON
Back: Allon, English(Manager), Inglis, Hammond, Mellors(Trainer), Anthony, Davies, O'Dell
Front: Riches, Boyle, Bowen Dawes, Wells, Maloney

1931/32 SEASON
Back: Scott, Bowen, Boyle, Hammond, Cave, Davies, F.Dawes
Middle: English(Man), McMullen(Trainer), Todd, Wonnacott, Anthony, Inglish,
Berridge, Oakley, Park, Newman(Train), Marlow(Sec)
Front: Gillett(Dir), Riches, Allon, Mortimer, Radford, O'Dell, Taylor, A.Dawes, Weston, Wells, Seal(Dir)

1931/32   14th in Division 3(S)

Results

#	Date	Opponent	Score	Scorers	Att
1	Aug 29	CARDIFF CITY	1-0	Wells	13448
2	31	Luton Town	0-1		11235
3	Sep 5	Norwich City	0-0		12455
4	7	EXETER CITY	2-1	Bowen, Dawes	7037
5	12	Reading	2-3	Dawes 2	6486
6	16	Exeter City	0-0		5024
7	19	SOUTHEND UNITED	1-2	Wonnacott	8779
8	26	Fulham	3-1	Bowen, Wells, Dawes	19742
9	28	LUTON TOWN	1-2	Bowen	6503
10	Oct 3	THAMES	0-4		7160
11	10	Brentford	0-2		12694
12	17	BRIGHTON & HOVE ALB	0-1		5714
13	24	Mansfield Town	0-2		7015
14	31	WATFORD	1-1	Bowen	5927
15	Nov 7	Crystal Palace	0-4		16119
16	14	BOURNEMOUTH	1-1	Bowen	6161
17	21	Queen's Park Rangers	2-3	Dawes, Lovatt	12117
18	Dec 5	Torquay United	1-4	Dawes	2547
19	19	Swindon Town	0-3		3919
20	25	Gillingham	2-3	Bowen, Mortimer	6823
21	26	GILLINGHAM	1-0	Lovatt	12491
22	28	BRISTOL ROVERS	6-0	Bowen 2, Lovatt 2, Wells 2	6087
23	Jan 2	Cardiff City	0-5		3917
24	16	NORWICH CITY	2-2	Bowen 2	4905
25	28	READING	2-4	Lovatt, Bowen	2672
26	30	Southend United	1-0	Bowen	6465
27	Feb 6	FULHAM	0-1		6239
28	13	Thames	2-0	Boyle, Dawes	1203
29	20	BRENTFORD	3-0	Boyle, Lovatt, Davies	6533
30	27	Brighton & Hove Albion	0-0		7966
31	Mar 5	MANSFIELD TOWN	3-0	Boyle 2, England (og)	5777
32	12	Watford	2-1	Wells, Mortimer	7600
33	19	CRYSTAL PALACE	5-0	Mortimer 2, Boyle, Wells, Lovatt	6685
34	26	Bournemouth	1-1	Dawes	3272
35	28	Coventry City	1-4	Dawes	17062
36	29	COVENTRY CITY	3-2	Wells, Dawes, Mortimer	7854
37	Apr 2	QUEEN'S PARK RANGERS	6-1	Boyle, Russell 2, Wells, Mortimer 2	6444
38	9	Bristol Rovers	2-3	Dowsey 2	3614
39	16	TORQUAY UNITED	2-0	Dawes, Russell	2882
40	21	CLAPTON ORIENT	4-3	Russell, Dawes, Wells, Mortimer	2883
41	23	Clapton Orient	2-3	Mortimer, Russell	4453
42	30	SWINDON TOWN	4-1	Dawes, Russell 3	5058

Player appearances (shirt numbers)

#	Allon TG	Anthony C	Bowen EC	Boyle TW	Cave W	Davies FP	Dawes AG	Dowsey J	Hammond L	Inglis WW	Lovatt HA	Maloney RJH	Mortimer R	Oakley JE	Odell GW	Park O	Radford B	Riches LE	Russell C	Scott J	Wells TC	Weston JM	Wonnacott CB	Dawes FW
1	4	3	9	8		6	10		1	2					5						7	11		
2	4	3	9	8		6	10		1	2					5						7	11		
3	4	3	9			6	8		1	2					5		10				7	11		
4	4		9			6	8		1	2					5		10				7			3
5	4	3	9			5	8		1	2					6		10				7	11		
6	4	3				6	8		1	2			9		5						7	11	10	
7	4					6	8		1	2			9		5						7	11	10	3
8	4	3	9	8		6	10		1	2					5						7	11		
9	4	3	9	8		6	10		1	2					5						7	11		
10	4	3	9	8		6	10		1					2	5						7	11		
11	4			8			10		1	2			9		6	5					7	11		3
12	4			8			9		1	2					6	5	10				7	11		3
13	4	2		8			10		1				9		6	5					7	11		3
14		2	9			6	8		1					4	5		10				7	11		3
15		2				6			1				9		5	10	4				7	11	8	3
16		2	9			6	8	4	1						5		10				7	11		3
17	4		9			6	11	10	1		8			2	5						7			3
18	4	2	9			6	10	5	1									8		11	7			3
19			9			6	10	4	1	2	8	5								11	7			3
20			9			6	4		1	2	8	5	7							11			10	3
21			10			6	4		1	2	9	5	7					8		11				3
22			9			6	4		1		8			2	5					11	7		10	3
23			9			6	4		1	2	8	5								11	7		10	3
24		3	9	8		6	10	4	1		5			2	6			7		11				
25			9	8		6	11		1	2	10	5	7		4									3
26	4		9	8		6	10		1	2			7		5					11				3
27	4		9	8		6	10		1	2			7		5					11				3
28	4		9	8		6	10		1	2					5					11	7			3
29				8		6	10	4	1	2	9		7		5					11				3
30		2		8		6	10	4	1		9		7		5					11				3
31		2		8		6	10	4	1		9		7		5					11				3
32		2		8		6	10	4	1		9		7		5					11				3
33		2		8		6	10	4	1		9		7		5					11				3
34		2	9	8		6	10	4	1				7		5					11				3
35		2	9	8		6	10	4	1				7		5					11				3
36	4			8	1	6	10						7		5				9	11				3
37				8	1	6	10	4		2			9		5				9	11	7			3
38		2		8		6	10	4	1				7		5				9	11				3
39		2		8		6	10	4	1				7		5				9	11				3
40				8		6	10	4	1	2	7	5							9		7			3
41				8		6	10	4	1	2			7			5		11	9					3
42		2		8		6	10	4	1				7			5			9	11				3
Apps	19	23	24	27	2	32	38	27	40	24	14	7	22	4	19	21	8	4	7	22	31	8	6	33
Goals			12	6		1	13	2			7		9						8		9		1	

One own goal

F.A. Cup

Rnd	Date	Opponent	Score	Scorers	Att
R1	Nov 28	METROPOLITAN POLICE	9-0	*See below	6000
R2	Dec 12	SOUTHEND UNITED	3-0	Bowen, Dawes, Lovatt	12627
R3	Jan 9	Darlington	1-1	Lovatt	8792
rep	14	DARLINGTON	2-0	Dawes, Lovatt	
R4	23	Bradford Park Ave.	2-4	Lovatt, Wells	20487

Rnd	Anthony C	Bowen EC	Davies FP	Dawes AG	Dowsey J	Hammond L	Inglis WW	Lovatt HA	Mortimer R	Oakley JE	Odell GW	Riches LE	Wells TC	Scott J	Dawes FW
R1		9	6	10	4	1	2				5	8	7	11	3
R2	3	9	6	10	4	1	2	8		5			7	11	
R3		9	6	10	4	1	2	8			5		7	11	3
rep		9	6	10	5	1	2	8	7		4			11	3
R4	3	9	6	10	4	1	2	8			5	7		11	3

Scorers in R1: Bowen 2, Dawes 3, Riches, Wells 2, 1 og

Division 3(S) final table

		P	W	D	L	F	A	W	D	L	F	A	Pts
1	Fulham	42	15	3	3	72	27	9	6	6	39	35	57
2	Reading	42	19	1	1	65	21	4	8	9	32	46	55
3	Southend United	42	12	5	4	41	18	9	6	6	36	35	53
4	Crystal Palace	42	14	7	0	48	12	6	4	11	26	51	51
5	Brentford	42	11	6	4	40	22	8	4	9	28	30	48
6	Luton Town	42	16	1	4	62	25	4	6	11	33	45	47
7	Exeter City	42	16	3	2	53	16	4	4	13	24	46	47
8	Brighton & Hove A.	42	12	4	5	42	21	5	8	8	31	37	46
9	Cardiff City	42	14	2	5	62	29	5	6	10	25	44	46
10	Norwich City	42	12	7	2	51	22	5	5	11	25	45	46
11	Watford	42	14	4	3	49	27	5	4	12	32	52	46
12	Coventry City	42	17	2	2	74	28	1	6	14	34	69	44
13	Queen's Park Rgs.	42	11	6	4	50	30	4	6	11	29	43	42
14	NORTHAMPTON TOWN	42	12	3	6	48	26	4	4	13	21	43	39
15	Bournemouth	42	8	8	5	42	32	5	4	12	28	46	38
16	Clapton Orient	42	7	8	6	41	35	5	3	13	36	55	35
17	Swindon Town	42	12	2	7	47	31	2	4	15	23	53	34
18	Bristol Rovers	42	11	6	4	46	30	2	2	17	19	62	34
19	Torquay United	42	9	6	6	49	39	3	3	15	23	67	33
20	Mansfield Town	42	11	5	5	54	45	0	5	16	21	63	32
21	Gillingham	42	8	6	7	26	26	2	2	17	14	56	28
22	Thames	42	6	7	8	35	35	1	2	18	18	74	23

1932/33 8th in Division 3(S)

#	Date	Opponent	Score	Scorers	Att	Allan CE	Boyle TW	Cave W	Conway T	Davies FP	Dawes AG	Dawes FW	Dowsey J	Fairhurst WS	Forbes FJ	Hammond L	Henson GH	Kavanagh PJ	McFarlane J	McGuire JP	Mortimer R	Oakley JE	Park O	Riches LE	Strang R	Wallbank J	Wells TC
1	Aug 27	Luton Town	1-2	A Dawes	11414		8		4	6	9	3			10	1					7	2	5				11
2	29	EXETER CITY	5-3	Boyle, A Dawes 2, Mortimer 2	7330		8			6	9	3	4		10	1					7	2	5				11
3	Sep 3	NEWPORT COUNTY	8-0	Boyle 2, A Dawes 4, F Dawes, Mortimer	8920		8			6	9	3	4		10	1					7	2	5				11
4	7	Exeter City	1-3	Mortimer	6180		8			6	9	3	4		10	1					7	2	5				11
5	10	Bournemouth	1-1	Mortimer	6623		8			6	9	3	4	2	10	1					7		5				11
6	17	SWINDON TOWN	6-0	Boyle, A Dawes 4, Forbes	7955		8			6	9	3	4	2	10	1					7		5				11
7	22	BRIGHTON & HOVE ALB	0-0		3784		8			6	9	3	4	2	10	1					7		5				11
8	24	Clapton Orient	2-2	A Dawes, Mortimer	8981		8			6	9	3	4	2	10	1					7		5				11
9	Oct 8	BRISTOL CITY	2-1	A Dawes, Forbes	9033		8			6	9	3	4	2	10	1					7		5				11
10	15	Coventry City	1-3	Boyle	14552		8			6	9	3	4	2	10	1					7		5				11
11	22	Bristol Rovers	3-4	A Dawes 2, Mortimer	8461		8			6	9	3	4	2	10	1					7		5				11
12	29	ALDERSHOT	5-2	Boyle, A Dawes 2, Dowsey, Mortimer	6673		8			6	9	3	4	2	10	1					7		5				11
13	Nov 5	Queen's Park Rangers	1-1	Wells	8895		8			6	9	3	4	2	10	1					7		5				11
14	12	SOUTHEND UNITED	0-0		6474		8			6	9	3	4	2	10	1					7		5				11
15	19	Crystal Palace	0-2		6483					6		3	4	2	10	1	9				7		5	8			11
16	Dec 3	Watford	0-4		7571		8			6	9	3	4		10	1					7	2	5				11
17	17	Reading	0-4		7544		8	1		6	9	3	4	2	10					5							11
18	24	NORWICH CITY	2-2	A Dawes 2	6237	2		1		6	9	3	4		10						7		5	8			11
19	26	BRENTFORD	1-0	A Dawes	14210			1		6	9	3	4		10						7	2	5	8			11
20	27	Brentford	0-1		18747			1		6	9	3	4					11			7	2	5	8			
21	31	LUTON TOWN	1-0	Wells	8321		10	1		6	9	3	4		7							2	5	8			11
22	Jan 7	Newport County	3-0	Boyle 2, Wells	4217		10	1		6	9	3	4		8						7	2	5				11
23	14	GILLINGHAM	1-0	Mortimer	3289		10	1		6	9	3	4		8						7	2	5				11
24	21	BOURNEMOUTH	6-0	Boyle, Davies, A Dawes 3, Wells	5018		10	1		6	9	3	4		8						7	2	5				11
25	28	Swindon Town	1-2	Wells	2937		10	1		6	9	3	4		8						7	2	5				11
26	Feb 4	CLAPTON ORIENT	3-0	Mortimer, Riches, Wells	5039		10	1			9	3	4								7	2	5	8	6		11
27	11	Brighton & Hove Albion	1-2	Riches	6755		10	1			9	3	4								7	2	5	8	6		11
28	18	Bristol City	4-5	A Dawes, Dowsey, Forbes, Mortimer	6334			1		4	9	3	8		10						7	2	5	6			11
29	25	COVENTRY CITY	5-1	Boyle, Davies, A Dawes, Mortimer, Wells	2791		8	1		6	9	3	4		10						7	2	5				11
30	Mar 4	BRISTOL ROVERS	1-1	A Dawes	5919		8	1		6	9	3	4		10						7	2	5				11
31	11	Aldershot	1-0	A Dawes	5045		8	1		6	9	3	4						10		7	2	5				11
32	18	QUEEN'S PARK RANGERS	2-1	A Dawes, McFarlane	5293		8	1		6	9	3	4						10		7	2	5				11
33	25	Southend United	0-1		5670		8	1		6	9	3	4						10		7	2	5				11
34	Apr 1	CRYSTAL PALACE	1-0	A Dawes	4799	3	8	1		6	9		4		10						7	2	5				11
35	8	Gillingham	1-5	Boyle	7352	3	8	1		6	9		4		10							2	5		7		11
36	10	CARDIFF CITY	2-0	A Dawes 2	2304	3	8	1		6	9		4		10						7	2	5				11
37	15	WATFORD	0-0		6197		8	1		6	9		4		10						7	2	5			3	11
38	17	Torquay United	1-5	Mortimer	3553		8	1		6	9		4		10						7	2			5	3	11
39	18	TORQUAY UNITED	2-0	Boyle, A Dawes	4049		8	1	2	6	9		4		10						7	3			5		11
40	22	Cardiff City	0-6		6631		8	1	2	6	9		4		10					5	7	3					11
41	29	READING	1-0	Boyle	3543	3	8	1		6	9		4		10						7	2	5				11
42	May 6	Norwich City	0-2		7913					6	9		4		10	1					7	2	5				11
		Apps				6	38	25	3	40	41	32	41	13	35	17	2	1	3	2	40	29	36	8	7	2	41
		Goals					13			2	32	1	2		3				1		13			2			7

F.A. Cup

#	Date	Opponent	Score	Scorers	Att	Allan CE	Boyle TW	Cave W	Conway T	Davies FP	Dawes AG	Dawes FW	Dowsey J	Fairhurst WS	Forbes FJ	Hammond L	Henson GH	Kavanagh PJ	McFarlane J	McGuire JP	Mortimer R	Oakley JE	Park O	Riches LE	Strang R	Wallbank J	Wells TC
R1	Nov 26	LLOYDS	8-1	A Dawes 5, Dowsey, McFarlane, Wells	6000					6	9	3	4	2	10	1			8		7		5				11
R2	Dec 10	DONCASTER ROVERS	0-1		10008					6	9	3	4	2	10	1			8		7		5				11

		P	W	D	L	F	A	W	D	L	F	A	Pts
1	Brentford	42	15	4	2	45	19	11	6	4	45	30	62
2	Exeter City	42	17	2	2	57	13	7	8	6	31	35	58
3	Norwich City	42	16	3	2	49	17	6	10	5	39	38	57
4	Reading	42	14	5	2	68	30	5	8	8	35	41	51
5	Crystal Palace	42	14	4	3	51	21	5	4	12	27	43	46
6	Coventry City	42	16	1	4	75	24	3	5	13	31	53	44
7	Gillingham	42	14	4	3	54	24	4	4	13	18	37	44
8	NORTHAMPTON TOWN	42	16	5	0	54	11	2	3	16	22	55	44
9	Bristol Rovers	42	13	5	3	38	22	2	9	10	23	34	44
10	Torquay United	42	12	7	2	51	26	4	5	12	21	41	44
11	Watford	42	11	8	2	37	22	5	4	12	29	41	44
12	Brighton & Hove A.	42	13	3	5	42	20	4	5	12	24	45	42
13	Southend United	42	11	5	5	39	27	4	6	11	26	55	41
14	Luton Town	42	12	8	1	60	32	1	5	15	18	46	39
15	Bristol City	42	11	5	5	59	37	1	8	12	24	53	37
16	Queen's Park Rgs.	42	9	8	4	48	32	4	3	14	24	55	37
17	Aldershot	42	11	6	4	37	21	2	4	15	24	51	36
18	Bournemouth	42	10	7	4	44	27	2	5	14	16	54	36
19	Cardiff City	42	12	4	5	48	30	0	3	18	21	69	31
20	Clapton Orient	42	7	8	6	39	35	1	5	15	20	58	29
21	Newport County	42	9	4	8	42	42	2	3	16	19	63	29
22	Swindon Town	42	7	9	5	36	29	2	2	17	24	76	29

1933/34

13th in Division 3(S)

#		Date	Opponent	Score	Scorers	Att	Allan CE	Allen T	Boyle TW	Bennett J	Brown A	Cave W	Cherry J	Cochrane AF	Crilly T	Davies FP	Dawes AG	Dawes FW	Dowsey J	Fraser WC	Henson GH	McGuire JP	McAleer J	McMenemy F	Mitchell A	Park O	Partridge AE	Riches LE	Thompson WJ	Tolland D	Warren E	Wells TC	Wheeler AJ
1	Aug	26	LUTON TOWN	2-3	Tolland 2	16823			8				1	7		2	6	9	3	4						5				10		11	
2		30	Aldershot	1-1	Cherry	5444			8				1	7		2	6	9	3	4			11			5				10			
3	Sep	2	Bournemouth	0-4		7925			8			4	1			2	6	9	3							5		7		10		11	
4		4	ALDERSHOT	0-0		5499						4	1			2	6	9	3							5		7		8		11	10
5		9	Torquay United	2-3	A Dawes, Wheeler	4104						4	1			2	6	9	3							5		7		8		11	10
6		16	QUEEN'S PARK RANGERS	2-1	A Dawes, Wells	7025			10				1	7		2	6	9	3	4			5							8		11	
7		23	Newport County	0-2		4842	3		10				1	7		2	6	9		4			5							8		11	
8		30	NORWICH CITY	2-2	Cherry, Henson	7606	3		8				1	7		2	6	10		4	9	5										11	
9	Oct	7	Bristol City	3-2	A Dawes 2, Henson	8598	3		8				1	7		2	6	10		4	9					5						11	
10		14	CLAPTON ORIENT	3-0	Boyle, A Dawes 2	5336	3		8				1	7		2	6	10		4	9					5						11	
11		21	CHARLTON ATHLETIC	1-2	Henson	6956	3		8				1			2	6	10		4	9					5	7					11	
12		28	Watford	0-2		7027	3		8				1			2	6	10		4	9					5	7					11	
13	Nov	4	READING	2-4	Boyle, Fraser	6244	3		8				1	7		2	6	9		4	10					5						11	
14		11	Coventry City	1-3	Henson	17975	3	1	8					7		2		10		6	9	5						4				11	
15		18	SOUTHEND UNITED	2-0	A Dawes, Henson	3520	3	1	8					7		2		10		6	9	5						4				11	
16	Dec	2	CRYSTAL PALACE	4-2	A Dawes 3, Henson	5034		1	8							2	6	10	3	7	9	5						4				11	
17		16	EXETER CITY	5-3	A Dawes, Riches, Wells 3	4989		1	8								6	10	3	7	9	5				2		4				11	
18		23	Cardiff City	3-1	Boyle, Dowsey, Henson	6168		1	8								6		3	7	9	5				2		4		10		11	
19		25	BRIGHTON & HOVE ALB	1-1	Boyle	5755		1	8								6		3	7	9	5				2		4		10		11	
20		26	Brighton & Hove Albion	3-3	F Davies, McAleer, Wells	7907		1									6		3	8	9	5	7			2		4		10		11	
21		30	Luton Town	1-3	Henson	7696		1									6		3	8	9	5		7		2		4		10		11	
22	Jan	6	BOURNEMOUTH	4-1	F Davies, Henson, Tolland, Wells	11978		1	8							2	6		3		9	5		7				4		10		11	
23		20	TORQUAY UNITED	1-1	Tolland	6480		1	8							2	6		3		9	5		7				4		10		11	
24		31	Queen's Park Rangers	1-2	Wells	5368		1	8							2	6				9	5		7				4	3	10		11	
25	Feb	3	NEWPORT COUNTY	5-3	Boyle, Henson 2, McAleer, Wells	5048		1	8							2	6		3		9	5	7					4		10		11	
26		10	Norwich City	0-2		13174		1	8							2	6		3		9	5	7					4		10		11	
27		22	BRISTOL CITY	2-3	Boyle, Henson	3072		1	8						10	2	6		3		9	5			7			4				11	
28		24	Clapton Orient	1-5	Cochrane	8746		1	9					10		2	6		3			5	7					4				11	
29		28	Bristol Rovers	1-1	Wells	5463			8	2		1			10		6		3		9				5	7		4				11	
30	Mar	3	Charlton Athletic	1-1	Henson	11012			8	2		1			10		6		3		9				5	7		4				11	
31		10	WATFORD	1-0	F Davies	4756			8	2		1					6		3		9				5	7		4		10		11	
32		17	Reading	2-2	Henson, Mitchell	7297						1		8		2	6		3		9				5	7		4		10		11	
33		24	COVENTRY CITY	2-2	Henson, Mitchell	6930						1		8		2	6		3		9				5	7		4		10		11	
34		30	Swindon Town	1-1	Mitchell	10858					2	1					6		3		9				5	7		4		10		11	
35		31	Southend United	0-2		6513					2	1					6		3		9				5	7		4		10		11	8
36	Apr	2	SWINDON TOWN	2-2	Henson, Tolland	7059					2	1		8			6		3		9				5	7		4		10		11	
37		7	BRISTOL ROVERS	1-2	Wells	4894			8		2	1					6		3		9				5	7		4		10		11	
38		11	Gillingham	1-5	Tolland	3398			8		2	4	1		10			3					5		6	7				9		11	
39		14	Crystal Palace	2-1	F Davies, Henson	7984		1	8		2	4					6		3		9				7	5				10		11	
40		21	GILLINGHAM	1-0	McAleer	3702		1			2	4					6		3		9		11		7	5				10			8
41		28	Exeter City	2-0	McAleer 2	3018		1			2						6		3	8		5	11		7					10	4		9
42	May	5	CARDIFF CITY	2-0	McAleer, Warren	2992		1			2						6			8		9	11			5			3		4		

Played in one game: OT Davies (42, at 10), DM Lindsay (28,8), RH Hinson (42, 7).

	Allan CE	Allen T	Boyle TW	Bennett J	Brown A	Cave W	Cherry J	Cochrane AF	Crilly T	Davies FP	Dawes AG	Dawes FW	Dowsey J	Fraser WC	Henson GH	McGuire JP	McAleer J	McMenemy F	Mitchell A	Park O	Partridge AE	Riches LE	Thompson WJ	Tolland D	Warren E	Wells TC	Wheeler AJ
Apps	9	19	30	12	6	23	10	9	25	39	17	31	18	3	30	21	8	10	18	18	2	27	2	27	2	38	5
Goals			6				2	1			4	11	1	1	17		6		3			1		6	1	10	1

F.A. Cup

		Date	Opponent	Score	Scorers	Att	Allan CE	Allen T	Boyle TW	Davies FP	Dawes AG	Dawes FW	Dowsey J	Fraser WC	Henson GH	McGuire JP	McMenemy F	Riches LE	Tolland D	Wells TC
R1	Nov	25	EXETER CITY	2-0	Dowsey, Wells	8801		1	8	2	6	10	3	7	9	5		4		11
R2	Dec	9	TORQUAY UNITED	3-0	Boyle, A Dawes 2	9782		1	8	2	6	10	3	7	9	5		4		11
R3	Jan	13	Southampton	1-1	Wells	21847		1	8	2	6		3		9	5	7	4	10	11
rep		17	SOUTHAMPTON	1-0	Henson	16161		1	8	2	6		3		9	5	7	4	10	11
R4		27	Huddersfield Town	2-0	Boyle, Wells	28143		1	8	2	6		3		9	5	7	4	10	11
R5	Feb	17	Preston North End	0-4		40180		1	8	2	6		3		9	5	7	4	10	11

Third Division (South) Cup

		Date	Opponent	Score	Scorers	Bennett J	Cave W	Crilly T	Dawes AG	Dowsey J	Henson GH	McGuire JP	Mitchell A	Park O	Riches LE	Tolland D	Warren E	Wells TC
R2	Mar	8	Bournemouth	2-1	Henson 2	2	1	8	6	3	9		5	7	4	10		11
R3		21	Norwich City	2-3	Wells, og	2	1	8	6	3	9	5		7	4	10	4	11

		P	W	D	L	F	A	W	D	L	F	A	Pts
1	Norwich City	42	16	4	1	55	19	9	7	5	33	30	61
2	Coventry City	42	16	3	2	70	22	5	9	7	30	32	54
3	Reading	42	17	4	0	60	13	4	8	9	22	37	54
4	Queen's Park Rgs.	42	17	2	2	42	12	7	4	10	28	39	54
5	Charlton Athletic	42	14	5	2	53	27	8	3	10	30	29	52
6	Luton Town	42	14	3	4	55	28	7	7	7	28	33	52
7	Bristol Rovers	42	14	4	3	49	21	6	7	8	28	26	51
8	Swindon Town	42	13	5	3	42	25	4	6	11	22	43	45
9	Exeter City	42	12	5	4	43	19	4	6	11	25	38	43
10	Brighton & Hove A.	42	12	7	2	47	18	3	6	12	21	42	43
11	Clapton Orient	42	14	4	3	60	25	2	6	13	15	44	42
12	Crystal Palace	42	11	6	4	40	25	5	3	13	31	42	41
13	NORTHAMPTON TOWN	42	10	6	5	45	32	4	6	11	26	46	40
14	Aldershot	42	8	6	7	28	27	5	6	10	24	44	38
15	Watford	42	12	4	5	43	16	3	3	15	28	47	37
16	Southend United	42	9	6	6	32	27	3	4	14	19	47	34
17	Gillingham	42	8	8	5	49	41	3	3	15	26	55	33
18	Newport County	42	6	9	6	25	23	2	8	11	24	47	33
19	Bristol City	42	7	8	6	33	22	3	5	13	25	63	33
20	Torquay United	42	10	4	7	32	28	3	3	15	21	65	33
21	Bournemouth	42	7	7	7	41	37	2	2	17	19	65	27
22	Cardiff City	42	6	4	11	32	43	3	2	16	25	62	24

1934/35   7th in Division 3(S)

#	Date		Opponent	Score	Scorers	Att	Baker TW	Bell T	Bennett J	Boyle TW	Brown A	Brown AR	Cave W	Cochrane AF	Crilly T	Dawes FW	Edwards SC	Henson GH	Higgins T	Hobbs EC	Kilsby RH	Lyman CC	McGuire JP	McMenemy F	Melville J	Potter FL	Riches LE	Robson T	Tolland D	Watson WJB	Wells TC	Craven J
1	Aug 25		Coventry City	0-2		22789	1		2	8		7				3		9						6	5		4		10		11	
2	27		EXETER CITY	2-1	McMenemy, Tolland	7685	1		2	8		7				3		9						6	5		4		10		11	
3	Sep 1		CLAPTON ORIENT	3-1	R Brown, Henson 2	9301	1		2	8		7				3		9						6	5		4		10		11	
4	5		Exeter City	0-3		6093	1		2	8		7		10		3		9						6	5		4				11	
5	8		Gillingham	1-3	Henson	3783			2	8		7	1	10		3		9						6	5		4				11	
6	15		READING	1-3	Watson	7832			2	8		7	1			3		9						6	5		4			10	11	
7	22		Aldershot	0-2		3350			3	10	4	7	1	8	2			9					6	5							11	
8	29		Bournemouth	1-0	Boyle	3641			3	10	4	7	1	8	2			9					6	5							11	
9	Oct 6		WATFORD	1-0	Cochrane	5534			3	10	4	7	1	8	2			9					6	5							11	
10	13		Newport County	3-1	R Brown, Henson, Wells	6365			3		4	7	1	8	2			9					6	5					10		11	
11	20		SWINDON TOWN	4-2	R Brown, Cochrane, Tolland, Wells	7033			3		4	7	1	8	2			9					6	5					10		11	
12	27		Torquay United	0-2		3561			3		4	7	1	8	2			9					6	5					10		11	
13	Nov 3		BRIGHTON & HOVE ALB	4-1	Cochrane, Henson 2, McMenemy	7366			3		4	7	1	8	2			9					6	5					10		11	
14	10		Cardiff City	2-2	Edwards, Tolland	9378		9			4	7	1	8	2		3						6	5					10		11	
15	17		CHARLTON ATHLETIC	1-1	Wells	8895		9			4	7	1	8	2	3							6	5					10		11	
16	Dec 1		SOUTHEND UNITED	1-1	Tolland	5933		9			4		1	8	2	3					7		6	5					10		11	
17	15		QUEEN'S PARK RANGERS	1-0	Riches	5008		9				7	1	8	2	3							6	5			4		10		11	
18	22		Crystal Palace	0-2		9318					4	7	1	8	2	3				9			6	5					10		11	
19	25		Bristol City	1-1	Bell	11914		9			4	7	1	8	2	3							6	5					10		11	
20	26		BRISTOL CITY	2-2	Bell, R Brown	13604		9			4	7	1	8	2	3							6	5					10		11	
21	29		COVENTRY CITY	3-4	Bell, A Brown, Wells	10683		9			4	7	1	8	2	3							6	5					10		11	
22	Jan 5		Clapton Orient	2-3	R Brown 2	8436		9			4	7	1	8	2	3							6	5					10		11	
23	16		Bristol Rovers	1-7	Bell	3109		9				11	1	8	2								7	5	6		4		10			3
24	19		GILLINGHAM	2-1	Watson 2	3783	1	9		10	4	7		8	2	3							6	5						11		
25	30		Reading	1-3	Crilly	5196	1	9		10	4	7		8	2	3							6	5						11		
26	Feb 2		ALDERSHOT	0-0		3526	1	9	2	8	4	7				3								5			6		10		11	
27	9		BOURNEMOUTH	0-1		3641	1		2		4	9		10		3							7	5	6		8				11	
28	16		Watford	1-1	Lyman	9442	1	9	2		4	7		8		3						11	5		6				10			
29	23		NEWPORT COUNTY	2-0	R Brown, Lyman	2925	1	9	2		4	7		8		3						11	5		6				10			
30	Mar 2		Swindon Town	3-5	Bell, R Brown, one og	5661	1	9	2		4	7		8		3						11	5		6				10			
31	9		TORQUAY UNITED	3-0	Bell, Lyman, Tolland	2853	1	9	2		4	7		8		3						11	5		6				10			
32	16		Brighton & Hove Albion	3-2	Bell 2, Lyman	5550	1	9	2		4	7		8		3						11	5		6				10			
33	23		CARDIFF CITY	3-0	R Brown, Cochrane, Lyman	3476		9	2		4	7	1	8		3						11	5		6				10			
34	30		Charlton Athletic	1-0	Bell	14926		9	2		4	7	1	8		3						11	5		6				10			
35	Apr 6		BRISTOL ROVERS	1-0	Lyman	4946		9	2		4	7	1	8		3						11	5		6				10			
36	13		Southend United	1-2	R Brown	5992		9	2		4	7	1			3						11	5		6				10	8		
37	19		Millwall	1-0	Bell	16140		9	2		4	7	1	8		3			6			11	5						10			
38	20		LUTON TOWN	2-1	Cochrane 2	7240		9	2		4	7	1	8		3			6			11	5						10			
39	22		MILLWALL	1-0	R Brown	8922		9	2		4	7	1	8		3			6			11	5						10			
40	23		Luton Town	2-2	Bell, Lyman	8168		9	2			7	1	8		3						11	5				4	6	10			
41	27		Queen's Park Rangers	1-3	Lyman	3603		9	2			7	1	8		3						11	5				6		10			
42	May 4		CRYSTAL PALACE	3-2	Bell 2, Potter	4629		9			4	7	1			3							5			10	6		8			

Played in one game: WJ Thompson (42, at 2).

	Baker TW	Bell T	Bennett J	Boyle TW	Brown A	Brown AR	Cave W	Cochrane AF	Crilly T	Dawes FW	Edwards SC	Henson GH	Higgins T	Hobbs EC	Kilsby RH	Lyman CC	McGuire JP	McMenemy F	Melville J	Potter FL	Riches LE	Robson T	Tolland D	Watson WJB	Wells TC	Craven J
Apps	13	26	27	13	32	40	29	33	21	34	3	11	3	2	1	17	36	28	7	1	11	10	35	7	20	1
Goals		13		1	1	11		6	1		1	6				8		2		1	1		5	3	4	

One own goal

F.A. Cup

	Date		Opponent	Score	Scorers	Att	Baker	Bell	Bennett	Boyle	Brown A	Brown AR	Cave	Cochrane	Crilly	Dawes	Edwards	Henson	Higgins	Hobbs	Kilsby	Lyman	McGuire	McMenemy	Melville	Potter	Riches	Robson	Tolland	Watson	Wells	Craven
R1	Nov 24		Barry	1-0	Cochrane	9877		9			4	7	1	8	2	3							5		6				10		11	
R2	Dec 8		WORKINGTON	0-0		8000		9					1	8	2	3							5		6		4		10	7	11	
rep	13		Workington	1-0	Hobbs						4	7	1	8	2	3				9			5				6		10		11	
R3	Jan 12		BOLTON WANDERERS	0-2		17962		9			4	7	1	8	2	3							5		6				10		11	

Third Division (South) Cup

	Date		Opponent	Score	Scorers	Att	Baker	Bell	Bennett	Boyle	Brown A	Brown AR	Cave	Cochrane	Crilly	Dawes	Edwards	Henson	Higgins	Hobbs	Kilsby	Lyman	McGuire	McMenemy	Melville	Potter	Riches	Robson	Tolland	Watson	Wells	Craven
R1	Sep 24		Clapton Orient	1-1	R Brown				3	10		11	1	8	2		7	9						5	6		4					
rep	Oct 1		CLAPTON ORIENT	4-0	R Brown 2, Edwards, Tolland	3000			3	10	4	11	1	8	2		7							5	6				9			
R2	22		NEWPORT COUNTY	3-0	Henson 2, Tolland	2500			3		4		1	8	2		7	9						5	6				10		11	
R3	Feb 21		BRISTOL ROVERS	0-2		1000	1		2		4	7		8		3			9			11	5		6				10			

		P	W	D	L	F	A	W	D	L	F	A	Pts
1	Charlton Athletic	42	17	2	2	62	20	10	5	6	41	32	61
2	Reading	42	16	5	0	59	23	5	6	10	30	42	53
3	Coventry City	42	14	5	2	56	14	7	4	10	30	36	51
4	Luton Town	42	12	7	2	60	23	7	5	9	32	37	50
5	Crystal Palace	42	15	3	3	51	14	4	7	10	35	50	48
6	Watford	42	14	2	5	53	19	5	7	9	23	30	47
7	NORTHAMPTON TOWN	42	14	4	3	40	21	5	4	12	25	46	46
8	Bristol Rovers	42	14	6	1	54	27	3	4	14	19	50	44
9	Brighton & Hove A.	42	15	4	2	51	16	2	5	14	18	46	43
10	Torquay United	42	15	2	4	60	22	3	4	14	21	53	42
11	Exeter City	42	11	5	5	48	29	5	4	12	22	46	41
12	Millwall	42	11	4	6	33	26	6	3	12	24	36	41
13	Queen's Park Rgs.	42	14	6	1	49	22	2	3	16	14	50	41
14	Clapton Orient	42	13	3	5	47	21	2	7	12	18	44	40
15	Bristol City	42	14	3	4	37	18	1	6	14	15	50	39
16	Swindon Town	42	11	7	3	45	22	2	5	14	22	56	38
17	Bournemouth	42	10	5	6	36	26	5	2	14	18	45	37
18	Aldershot	42	12	6	3	35	20	1	4	16	15	55	36
19	Cardiff City	42	11	6	4			2	3	16	20	55	35
20	Gillingham	42	10	7	4	36	25	1	6	14	19	50	35
21	Southend United	42	10	4	7	40	29	1	5	15	25	49	31
22	Newport County	42	7	4	10	36	40	3	1	17	18	72	25

1934/35 SEASON
Back: Kilsby, Craven, Cave, Baker, A.Brown, Dawes, Crilly, Riches
Middle: Watson, McMenamy, Melville, McGuire, Surtees, Bennett, Higgins
Front: Cockrane, R.Brown, Boyle, Henson, Tolland, Potter, Wells

1935/36 SEASON
Back: A.Brown, J.Bartram, Bennett, Gormlie, Davies, McMenemy
Front: R.Brown, Tolland, McGuire, Robinson, Lyman

1935/36 15th in Division 3(S)

	Date		Opponent	Score	Scorers	Att	Bartram IL	Bell T	Bennett J	Brown A	Brown AR	Cave W	Dawes FW	Deacon R	Farr FE	Gormlie WJ	Hewitt JJ	Hinson RH	Hobbs EC	Little J	Lyman CC	Mackie JA	McGuire JP	McMenemy F	Melville J	O'Rourke J	Potter FL	Riches LE	Robinson TE	Robson T	Russell SEJ	Thayne W	Thompson WJ	Tolland D	Turner G
1	Aug	31	GILLINGHAM	0-0		15826	9		2	4	7		3		8	1					11		5	6										10	
2	Sep	2	Aldershot	0-2		3838	9	8	2	4	7		3			1					11		5	6										10	
3		7	Bournemouth	0-4		9547	9	8	2	4	7		3			1					11		5	6										10	
4		9	ALDERSHOT	3-0	Bartram, Robinson, one og	7210	9	8	2	4	7		3			1					11		5					10	6						
5		14	LUTON TOWN	0-0		13595	9	8	2	4	7		3			1					11		5					10	6						
6		16	CRYSTAL PALACE	3-1	Bartram, Lyman, Robinson	6319	9	8			7		3			1					11			4	5				10	6			2			
7		21	Notts County	0-3		8929	9	8			7		3			1					11			4	5				10	6			2			
8		23	Crystal Palace	1-6	Lyman	5134	8	9			7		3			1					11			4	5		10			6			2			
9		28	BRISTOL ROVERS	3-3	Bell, Hinson, Potter	7102		9		5	7		3			1		8			11			6			10	4					2			
10	Oct	5	Clapton Orient	0-4		8102	9	8		2	11		3			1								5			4		6						10	
11		12	SOUTHEND UNITED	2-0	Bartram, R Brown	6991	8	9	2	4	11		3	7		1								5					6						10	
12		19	TORQUAY UNITED	2-1	R Brown, Tolland	6075		9	2	4	7		3			1	8				11			5					6						10	
13		26	Millwall	1-2	Bell	10123		9	2	4	7		3			1	8				11			5					6						10	
14	Nov	2	BRISTOL CITY	0-2		6160		9	2		7		3			1	8				11			5			4		6						10	
15		9	Swindon Town	1-3	Lyman	7670		9	2	4	7		3			1	10	8	5		11			6												
16		16	QUEEN'S PARK RANGERS	1-4	Lyman	6472	9		2	4	7		3			1	10		5		11			6									8			
17		23	Brighton & Hove Albion	1-5	Hewitt	5886	9		2	4	7		3			1	10		5		11			6									8			
18	Dec	7	Newport County	1-5	Bell	3780		9	2		7	1	3	11			8						5				4		6				10			
19		14	COVENTRY CITY	2-4	Bell, R Brown	6803		9	2		7	1	3	11			10	8					5				4		6							
20		21	Watford	1-4	Tolland	4759		9	2	4		1	3					8			11			5					6				10			
21		25	READING	4-2	Bell 2, R Brown, Lyman	7003		9	2		7		3			1					11		5				10	4	6				8			
22		26	Reading	2-5	R Brown 2	18364		9	2		7		3			1			5		11						10	4	6				8			
23		28	Gillingham	3-2	Bell 3	6763		9		2			3			1					11			5			10	4	6							
24	Jan	4	BOURNEMOUTH	2-1	Bell, one og	6167		9			7	-	3			1					11			5			10	4	6				2	8		
25		11	EXETER CITY	1-1	R Brown	6054		9			7		3			1		5			11						10	4	6				2	8		
26		18	Luton Town	3-3	R Brown, Lyman, Potter	12781		9		2	7		3			1					11			5			10	4	6					8		
27		25	NOTTS COUNTY	3-1	Potter 2, Tolland	6285		9		2	11		3			1					7			5			10	4	6					8		
28	Feb	1	Bristol Rovers	2-5	Lyman, Potter	5958		9		2	7		3		5	1					11						10	4	6					8		
29		8	CLAPTON ORIENT	2-0	Bell, Tolland	6131		9			7		3			1			5	2	11						10	4	6					8		
30		22	Torquay United	3-3	Bell 2, Lyman	1977		9					3			1			5	2	11						10	4	6					8		
31		29	SWINDON TOWN	0-0		4226		9			7					1			3	11		5				8		4		6	2			10		
32	Mar	7	Coventry City	0-4		14647		9			7					1			2	11		5			8	10	4		6	3						
33		14	MILLWALL	2-4	R Brown, Turner	6111		9			8					1			2	7								4		5			10	11		
34		21	Queen's Park Rangers	1-0	McMenemy	13687		9			7					1	4		3			2		6			10					5		8	11	
35		28	BRIGHTON & HOVE ALB	1-0	Bell	6306		9			7					1	4		3			2		6			10					5		8	11	
36	Apr	4	Exeter City	1-3	R Brown	2421		9			7					1	4		3			2		6			10					5		8	11	
37		10	Cardiff City	0-0		11302		9			7					1	4		3			2		6			10					5		8	11	
38		11	NEWPORT COUNTY	3-0	Hinson 3	5219		9			7				8	1	4	8	3			2		6			10					5			11	
39		13	CARDIFF CITY	2-0	Bell, Turner	7890		9			7				8	1	4	8	3			2		6		10						5			11	
40		18	Bristol City	2-3	R Brown 2	6463		9			7				8	1	4	8	3					6			10				2	5			11	
41		22	Southend United	1-0	O'Rourke	4134		9			7					1	4		3			2		6		8						5		10	11	
42		25	WATFORD	2-0	Bell, Tolland	4109		9			7					1	4		3			2	5	6		8								10	11	

Played in one game: SC Edwards (game 10, at 7), J Craven (33,3).
Played in games 20, 23 and 30: J Billingham (at 7).

					Apps	12	38	17	17	39	3	30	2	2	39	17	7	7	14	29	8	11	19	13	5	19	19	5	26	3	9	6	30	10
					Goals	3	16			12						1	4			8			1			1	5		2				5	2

Two own goals

F.A. Cup

	Date		Opponent	Score	Scorers	Att	Bartram IL	Bell T	Bennett J	Brown A	Brown AR	Cave W	Dawes FW	Deacon R	Farr FE	Gormlie WJ	Hewitt JJ	Hinson RH	Hobbs EC	Little J	Lyman CC	Mackie JA	McGuire JP	McMenemy F	Melville J	O'Rourke J	Potter FL	Riches LE	Robinson TE	Robson T	Russell SEJ	Thayne W	Thompson WJ	Tolland D	Turner G
R1	Nov	30	BRISTOL ROVERS	0-0		9093		9	2		7	1	3				8				11		5				4		6					10	
rep	Dec	4	Bristol Rovers	1-3	Deacon	8000		9	2		7	1	3	11			8						5				4		6					10	

Third Division (South) Cup

	Date		Opponent	Score	Scorers	Att	Bartram IL	Bell T	Bennett J	Brown A	Brown AR	Cave W	Dawes FW	Deacon R	Farr FE	Gormlie WJ	Hewitt JJ	Hinson RH	Hobbs EC	Little J	Lyman CC	Mackie JA	McGuire JP	McMenemy F	Melville J	O'Rourke J	Potter FL	Riches LE	Robinson TE	Robson T	Russell SEJ	Thayne W	Thompson WJ	Tolland D	Turner G
R1	Oct	2	TORQUAY UNITED	4-1	Bartram, R Brown, Jones, Melville		9				11		3			1								5			4	8	6					10	
R3		14	READING	4-0	Bartram 2, Lyman, Tolland	1000	9		2	4	7		3			1	10		5		11			6										8	
SF	Feb	26	Swindon Town	0-1				9			7					1	4			2	11			6	5			10						8	

Bye in R2

Played in R1: Jones (at 7). Played in R1 (at 2) and SF (at 3): J Craven.

		P	W	D	L	F	A	W	D	L	F	A	Pts
1	Coventry City	42	19	1	1	75	12	5	8	8	27	33	57
2	Luton Town	42	13	6	2	56	20	9	6	6	25	25	56
3	Reading	42	18	0	3	52	20	8	2	11	35	42	54
4	Queen's Park Rgs.	42	14	4	3	55	19	8	5	8	29	34	53
5	Watford	42	12	3	6	47	29	8	6	7	33	25	49
6	Crystal Palace	42	15	4	2	64	20	7	1	13	32	54	49
7	Brighton & Hove A.	42	13	4	4	48	25	5	4	12	22	38	44
8	Bournemouth	42	9	6	6	36	28	7	5	9	24	30	43
9	Notts County	42	10	5	6	40	25	5	7	9	20	32	42
10	Torquay United	42	14	4	3	41	27	2	5	14	21	35	41
11	Aldershot	42	9	6	6	29	21	5	6	10	24	40	40
12	Millwall	42	9	8	4	33	21	5	4	12	25	50	40
13	Bristol City	42	11	5	5	32	21	4	5	12	16	38	40
14	Clapton Orient	42	13	2	6	34	15	3	4	14	21	46	38
15	NORTHAMPTON T.	42	12	5	4	38	24	3	3	15	24	66	38
16	Gillingham	42	9	5	7	34	25	5	4	12	32	52	37
17	Bristol Rovers	42	11	6	4	48	31	3	3	15	21	64	37
18	Southend United	42	8	7	6	38	21	5	3	13	23	41	36
19	Swindon Town	42	10	5	6	43	33	4	3	14	21	40	36
20	Cardiff City	42	11	5	5	37	23	2	5	14	23	50	36
21	Newport County	42	8	4	9	36	44	3	5	13	24	67	31
22	Exeter City	42	7	5	9	38	41	1	6	14	21	52	27

1936/37 7th in Division 3(S)

	Date		Opponent	Result	Scorers	Att	Allen RSL	Bell T	Cave W	Cook C	Dunkley MEF	Gormlie WJ	Hewitt JJ	Holt D	Lauderdale JH	Little J	Lyman CC	Mackie JA	Riches LE	Rawlings JSD	Robson T	Russell SEJ	Simpson WS	Thayne W	Tolland D	Turner G	Riley H
1	Aug	29	Swindon Town	0-2		11150				9		1	4	8		3		2		7			6	5		11	10
2		31	ALDERSHOT	5-3	Cook,Rawlings 2,Tolland,one og	8107				9		1	4			3		2		7			6	5	10	11	8
3	Sep	5	MILLWALL	2-2	Rawlings, Riley	10486				9		1	4			3		2		7			6	5	10	11	8
4		9	Aldershot	2-0	Cook, Tolland	3594				9		1				3		2	4	7			6	5	10	11	8
5		12	Bristol Rovers	0-2		11420				9		1				3		2	4	7			6	5	10	11	8
6		16	Southend United	0-2		6627				9		1				3		2	4	7			6	5	10	11	8
7		19	TORQUAY UNITED	3-0	Rawlings, Tolland, Turner	8260		9				1				3		2	4	7			6	5	10	11	8
8		26	BOURNEMOUTH	0-0		9764		9				1				3			4	7		2	6	5	10	11	8
9	Oct	3	Brighton & Hove Albion	2-1	J Hewitt, Rawlings	10499		9				1	8			3			4	7		2	6	5		11	10
10		10	WATFORD	0-1		8958		9				1	8			3			4	7		2	6	5		11	10
11		17	Notts County	2-3	Little, Riley	14557						1	9			3		2	4	7			6	5	8	11	10
12		24	CLAPTON ORIENT	1-1	Bell	8004		9				1				3		2	4	7			6	5	8	11	10
13		31	Walsall	2-2	Allen 2	5765	9					1				3	11		4	7		2	6	5	8		10
14	Nov	7	LUTON TOWN	3-1	Lyman, Rawlings	18885	9					1	8			3	11		4	7		2	6	5	10		
15		14	Cardiff City	1-2	Allen	18200	9					1	8			3	11		4	7		2	6	5	10		
16		21	CRYSTAL PALACE	2-0	Allem, Tolland	14163	9					1			8	3	11		4	7		2	6	5	10		
17	Dec	5	READING	2-1	Allen, Lyman	8543	9					1			8	3	11		4	7		2	6	5	10		
18		19	BRISTOL CITY	5-1	Allen 3, Rawlings, one og	7148	9					1			8	3	11		4	7		2	6	5	10		
19		25	NEWPORT COUNTY	3-2	Allen, Lauderdale, Rawlings	12371	9		1						8	3	11		4	7		2	6	5	10		
20		26	SWINDON TOWN	4-0	Allen,Lauderdale,Lyman,Tolland	16177	9					1			8	3	11		4	7		2	6	5	10		
21		28	Newport County	3-1	Allen, Dunkley, Lyman	8756	9				7	1	8			3	11		4			2	6	5	10		
22	Jan	2	Millwall	0-1		16485	9				7	1			10	3	11		4			2	6	5	8		
23		9	BRISTOL ROVERS	4-1	Allen 2, Lyman, Tolland	8926	9					1			10		11	2	4	7		3	6	5	8		
24		20	Exeter City	5-2	Allen,Lauderdale 2,Rawlings 2	2348	9					1			8	3	11		4	7		2	6	5	10		
25		23	Torquay United	0-5		2265	9					1			10	3	11		4	7		2	6	5	8		
26	Feb	6	BRIGHTON & HOVE ALB	2-0	Rawlings 2	13034	9					1			10	3	11		4	7		2	6	5	8		
27		13	Watford	1-4	J Hewitt	10430	9					1	8			3	11		4	7		2	6	5	10		
28		18	Queen's Park Rangers	2-3	Allen, Lyman	3751	9				7	1	4		10	3	11	2					6	5	8		
29		20	NOTTS COUNTY	1-1	Allen	18435	9					1	8		10	3	11		4	7		2	6	5			
30		27	Clapton Orient	1-3	Lyman	5095	9					1			10	3	11		4	7		2	6	5	8		
31	Mar	6	WALSALL	6-3	Allen 3, Lyman 2, Rawlings	6247	9					1			10	3	11		4	7		2	6	5	8		
32		13	Luton Town	2-3	Tolland, one og	19579	9					1			10	3	11		4	7		2	6	5	8		
33		20	CARDIFF CITY	2-0	Allen, Lyman	7334	9					1			10	3	11		4	7		2	6	5	8		
34		26	Gillingham	0-2		9426	9					1	8		10	3	11		4	7		2	6	5			
35		27	Crystal Palace	2-2	Allen 2	9523	9					1	8		10	3	11		4	7		2	6	5			
36		29	GILLINGHAM	5-0	Allen,J Hewitt 2,Lyman,Rawlings	10164	9					1	8		10	3	11			7	4	2	6	5			
37	Apr	3	EXETER CITY	2-1	Allen, Tolland	6349	9					1	4		10	3	11			7		2	6	5	8		
38		10	Reading	1-3	Rawlings	6291	9					1	4		10	3	11			7		2	6	5	8		
39		17	QUEEN'S PARK RANGERS	0-1		4056	9					1	4		10	3	11			7		2	6	5	8		
40		21	Bournemouth	2-3	Allen, Lauderdale	3684	9					1			10	3	11		4	7		2	6	5	8		
41		24	Bristol City	1-0	Rawlings	6729	9					1			10	3	11		4	7		2	6	5	8		
42	May	1	SOUTHEND UNITED	4-3	Allen 2, Lauderdale, Tolland	3751	9					1			8	3	11		4	7		2	6	5	10		
					Apps		30	5	1	6	3	41	18	1	25	41	30	11	34	39	1	32	42	42	35	12	13
					Goals		27	1		2	1		4		6	1	11			17					9	1	2

Three own goals

F.A. Cup

	Date		Opponent	Result	Scorers	Att	Allen RSL	Hewitt JJ	Holt D	Little J	Lyman CC	Riches LE	Rawlings JSD	Simpson WS	Thayne W	Tolland D
R1	Nov	28	Walthamstow Avenue	1-6	J Hewitt	7568	9	1	8	3	11	4	7	2	6	5	10

Third Division (South) Cup

	Date		Opponent	Result			Gormlie WJ	Lyman CC	Riches LE	Russell SEJ	Simpson WS	Thayne W	Tolland D	Turner G
R1	Sep	30	Torquay United	0-5			1	7	4	6	2	9	8	11

Played at 5: E Hewitt. At 3: F Wallbanks. At 10: J O'Rourke

		P	W	D	L	F	A	W	D	L	F	A	Pts
1	Luton Town	42	19	1	1	69	16	8	3	10	34	37	58
2	Notts County	42	15	3	3	44	23	8	7	6	30	29	56
3	Brighton & Hove A.	42	15	5	1	49	16	9	0	12	25	27	53
4	Watford	42	14	4	3	53	21	5	7	9	32	39	49
5	Reading	42	14	5	2	53	23	5	6	10	23	37	49
6	Bournemouth	42	17	3	1	45	20	3	6	12	20	39	49
7	NORTHAMPTON TOWN	42	15	4	2	56	22	5	2	14	29	46	46
8	Millwall	42	12	4	5	43	24	6	6	9	21	30	46
9	Queen's Park Rgs.	42	12	2	7	51	24	6	7	8	22	28	45
10	Southend United	42	10	8	3	49	23	7	3	11	29	44	45
11	Gillingham	42	14	5	2	36	18	4	3	14	16	48	44
12	Clapton Orient	42	10	8	3	29	17	4	7	10	23	35	43
13	Swindon Town	42	12	4	5	52	24	2	7	12	23	49	39
14	Crystal Palace	42	11	7	3	45	20	2	5	14	17	41	38
15	Bristol Rovers	42	14	3	4	49	20	2	1	18	22	60	36
16	Bristol City	42	13	3	5	42	20	2	3	16	16	50	36
17	Walsall	42	11	3	7	38	34	2	7	12	25	51	36
18	Cardiff City	42	10	5	6	35	24	4	2	15	19	63	35
19	Newport County	42	7	7	7	37	28	5	3	13	30	70	34
20	Torquay United	42	9	5	7	42	32	2	5	14	15	48	32
21	Exeter City	42	9	5	7	36	37	1	7	13	23	51	32
22	Aldershot	42	5	6	10	29	29	2	3	16	21	60	23

1936/37 SEASON
Back: Rawlings, Hinson, E.Hewitt, Thompson, Puddefoot(Man), Gormlie, Cave, McGuire, Cook, Thayne, Potter, Lea(Dir)
Middle: Newman(Train), Hoult, Billingham, Turner, Little, Wallbanks, Blencowe, J.Hewitt, Russell, Bell, Hawtin(Dir)
Front: Hooton(Dir), Simpson, Lyman, Robson, Tolland, Gillitt(Chair), Mackie, Riley, Riches, O'Rourke, Marlow(Sec)

1938/39 SEASON
Back: Gunn, Barron, Platt, Tilson, Allen, Jones, Gormlie, Cuff, Rodger, Hewitt, Russell
Middle: McKinnell(Asst.Train), Ford, Dickenson, McCullough, Parris,
Postlethwaite, Hawtin(Dir), Newman(Train)
Front: Marlow(Sec), Hurel, O'Rourke, Bosse, King, Gillitt(Chair), Lauderdale, Blunt, Thayne, Hooton(Dir)

1937/38   9th in Division 3(S)

#	Date		Opponent	Score	Scorers	Att.	Allen RSL	Bell T	Blencowe AG	Blunt E	Bosse PL	Cook C	Dickinson A	Dunkley MEF	Gormlie WJ	Gunn K	Hewitt JJ	Hoult AA	King FAR	Lauderdale JH	Little J	Lyman CC	McCulloch K	O'Rourke J	Parris JE	Postlethwaite TW	Rawlings JSD	Riches LE	Riley H	Rodger C	Russell SEJ	Thayne W	Tolland D	Tilson SF
1	Aug	28	Mansfield Town	1-4	Lyman	9619	9								1	2			4			11				6	7			10	3	5	8	
2		31	Bristol Rovers	0-0		7690	9								1	2			4			11				6	7			10	3	5	8	
3	Sep	4	TORQUAY UNITED	0-3		10650	9							7	1	2			4			11				6				10	3	5	8	
4		6	BRISTOL ROVERS	2-0	Allen, J Hewitt	5596	9	4						7	1		8					11				6				10	3	5		
5		11	Clapton Orient	0-1		8939	9								1	2	8					11				6	7	4			3	5		
6		13	Cardiff City	1-4	Lauderdale	20693						9			1	2	8					11				6		7	4		3	5		
7		18	SOUTHEND UNITED	0-2		7680			9	4				7	1	2	8					11				6					3	5	8	
8		25	Queen's Park Rangers	1-1	Allen	13982	9	10		4				7	1	2						11				6					3	5	8	
9	Oct	2	BRIGHTON & HOVE ALB	3-1	Allen 2, Lyman	7998	9			4				7	1	2		8				11				6					3	5	10	
10		9	Bournemouth	0-0		7417	9			4				7	1	2		8				11				6					3	5	10	
11		16	Watford	3-1	Allen, Rawlings, Riley	11100	9			4					1	2		8								6	7		11		3	5	10	
12		23	GILLINGHAM	4-1	Allen 2, Riley, Tolland	7618	9			4					1	2		8								6	7		11		3	5	10	
13		30	Exeter City	1-4	Allen	5946	9						10	7	1	2		4	8							6			11		3	5		
14	Nov	6	SWINDON TOWN	1-0	Allen	7806	9			4					1	2	11	8								6	7				3	5	10	
15		13	Aldershot	2-0	Allen, Dunkley	5571	9			4					1	2	11	8								6	7				3	5	10	
16		20	MILLWALL	0-1		12726	9			4					1	2	11	8								6	7				3	5	10	
17	Dec	11	Notts County	0-5		9988	9			4			10		1	2		8	7						11	6					3	5		
18		18	NEWPORT COUNTY	2-0	Dunkley 2	4989	9			4			10	7	1	2	8									6				11	3	5		
19		27	Bristol City	0-1		20135	9			4			10	7	1	2	8					11				6					3	5		
20	Jan	1	MANSFIELD TOWN	3-0	Dickinson 2, Parris	6401				4	9		10	7	1	2	8					11				6					3	5		
21		8	Reading	3-4	Dickinson, Dunkley, Parris	8298				4	9		10	7	1	2	8					11				6					3	5		
22		15	Torquay United	2-1	Allen, J Hewitt	2321	9			4			10	7	1	2	8					11				6					3	5		
23		22	CLAPTON ORIENT	2-0	Dickinson, Parris	6769	9			4			10	7	1	2	8					11				6					3	5		
24		29	Southend United	2-4	Allen 2	5933	9			4			10	7	1	2	8					11				6					3	5		
25	Feb	3	CRYSTAL PALACE	1-1	Allen	3672	9			4			10	7	1	2	8					11				6					3	5		
26		5	QUEEN'S PARK RANGERS	0-2		9270	9			4			10	7	1	2	8					11									3	5		
27		12	Brighton & Hove Albion	2-1	Cook, J Hewitt	8447				4	9		10	7	1	2	8									6					3	5		
28		19	BOURNEMOUTH	1-3	Postlethwaite	5337				4	9		10	7	1	2	8									6					3	5		
29		26	WATFORD	3-2	Bosse 2, Parris	7085	8				10				9	7	1	2								6				4	3	5		
30	Mar	5	Gillingham	1-2	Bell	4582	8				10				9	7	1	2								6				4	3	5		
31		12	EXETER CITY	1-0	Dickinson	8603					8		9		1	2							4			6				7	11	3	5	10
32		19	Swindon Town	0-1		7678		5			8		9	8	1	2							4			6				7	11	3		10
33		26	ALDERSHOT	1-0	Tilson	5446			8		10				1	2							4	3	7	6					11		5	10
34	Apr	2	Millwall	0-3		24425				6					1	2	9			10			4	3	7					11	3	5		8
35		9	READING	2-2	J Hewitt, Tilson	5014									1	2	9			10			4		7	6					11	3	5	8
36		15	Walsall	1-1	Parris	3799									1	2	9			10			4		7	6					11	3	5	8
37		16	Crystal Palace	1-0	Tilson	14057					4				1	2	9			10					7	6					11	3	5	8
38		18	WALSALL	1-1	Bosse	6574			8	4					1	2	9			10					7						11	3	5	8
39		19	BRISTOL CITY	1-0	J Hewitt	8907					4				1	2	9		7	10						6				11	3	5	8
40		23	NOTTS COUNTY	2-0	Parris 2	11175					4				1	2	9			10					7	6				11	3	5	8
41		30	Newport County	0-0		4436									1		9			10			4	3	7	6				11	2	5	8
42	May	7	CARDIFF CITY	0-0		6410					4				1	2	9			10					7	6				11	3	5	8
			Apps				22	4	2	2	30	6	18	23	42	40	28	9	2	13	2	10	7	3	23	38	9	4	9	11	39	41	11	11
			Goals				14	1			3	1	5	4		5				1		2			7	1	1		2				1	3

Played in one game: AT Cotterill (26, at 6), R Platt (6,6), T Robson (38, 6).

F.A. Cup

	Date		Opponent	Score	Scorer	Att.	Allen	Bosse	Gormlie	Gunn	Hewitt	Hoult	Lauderdale	Postlethwaite	Rawlings	Russell	Thayne	Tolland
R1	Nov	27	CARDIFF CITY	1-2	Tolland	14000	9	4	1	2		8	11	6	7	3	5	10

Division Three (South) Cup

	Date		Opponent	Score		Att.	Allen	Blencowe	Bosse	Dunkley	Gormlie	Gunn	Lyman	Postlethwaite	Russell	Thayne	Tolland
R1	Sep	27	Cardiff City	0-1		3869	9	10	4	7	1	2	11	6	3	5	8

		P	W	D	L	F	A	W	D	L	F	A	Pts
1	Millwall	42	15	3	3	53	15	8	7	6	30	22	56
2	Bristol City	42	14	6	1	37	13	7	7	7	31	27	55
3	Queen's Park Rgs.	42	15	3	3	44	17	7	6	8	36	30	53
4	Watford	42	14	4	3	50	15	7	7	7	23	28	53
5	Brighton & Hove A.	42	15	3	3	40	16	6	6	9	24	28	51
6	Reading	42	17	2	2	44	21	3	9	9	27	42	51
7	Crystal Palace	42	14	4	3	45	17	4	8	9	22	30	48
8	Swindon Town	42	12	4	5	33	19	5	6	10	16	30	44
9	NORTHAMPTON T.	42	12	4	5	30	19	5	5	11	21	38	43
10	Cardiff City	42	13	7	1	57	22	2	5	14	10	32	42
11	Notts County	42	10	6	5	29	17	6	3	12	21	33	41
12	Southend United	42	12	5	4	43	23	3	5	13	27	45	40
13	Bournemouth	42	8	10	3	36	20	6	2	13	20	37	40
14	Mansfield Town	42	12	5	4	46	26	3	4	14	16	41	39
15	Bristol Rovers	42	10	7	4	28	20	3	6	12	18	41	39
16	Newport County	42	9	10	2	31	15	2	6	13	12	37	38
17	Exeter City	42	10	4	7	37	32	3	8	10	20	38	38
18	Aldershot	42	11	4	6	23	14	4	1	16	16	45	35
19	Clapton Orient	42	10	7	4	27	19	3	0	18	15	42	33
20	Torquay United	42	7	5	9	22	28	2	7	12	16	45	30
21	Walsall	42	10	4	7	34	37	1	3	17	18	51	29
22	Gillingham	42	9	5	7	25	25	1	1	19	11	52	26

1938/39 17th in Division 3(S)

League Matches

No	Date	Opponent	Score	Scorers	Att
1	Aug 27	Torquay United	2-1	King, Lauderdale	4569
2	29	WATFORD	2-0	King, Rodgers	10784
3	Sep 3	CLAPTON ORIENT	3-0	Hewitt 2, Lauderdale	13298
4	7	Crystal Palace	0-2		14570
5	10	Newport County	1-1	King	11534
6	17	IPSWICH TOWN	2-0	King, Tilson	13428
7	24	NOTTS COUNTY	2-1	Hewott, Tilson	13949
8	Oct 1	Aldershot	0-3		7580
9	8	BRISTOL CITY	2-2	Gunn, McCulloch	10309
10	15	Reading	1-5	McCartney	11228
11	22	CARDIFF CITY	2-1	Curtis, McCartney	10262
12	29	Brighton & Hove Albion	0-1		9204
13	Nov 5	BOURNEMOUTH	2-0	Lauderdale, Tilson	8645
14	12	Walsall	0-1		8996
15	19	Mansfield Town	3-4	King 2, Tilson	8774
16	Dec 3	SOUTHEND UNITED	2-2	Hewitt, McCartney	5568
17	10	Exeter City	2-3	McCartney, one og	3560
18	17	BRISTOL ROVERS	2-1	Barron, McCartney	5305
19	24	TORQUAY UNITED	4-1	Haycox 3, McCartney	3593
20	26	PORT VALE	2-0	Barron, Haycox	4734
21	27	Port Vale	2-0	McCartney, Rodgers	10717
22	31	Clapton Orient	0-3		6922
23	Jan 9	Queen's Park Rangers	0-3		3492
24	14	NEWPORT COUNTY	1-0	Tilson	9025
25	21	Ipswich Town	0-2		11168
26	28	Notts County	0-1		10924
27	Feb 4	ALDERSHOT	5-0	Elwood 2, Haycox, Rodgers 2	6476
28	11	Bristol City	0-0		10549
29	18	READING	1-1	Tilson	8427
30	25	Cardiff City	0-2		10282
31	Mar 4	BRIGHTON & HOVE ALB	1-4	Tilson	5044
32	11	Bournemouth	1-3	Haycox	4983
33	18	WALSALL	4-1	Barron, Blunt, Hurel, Jennings	5550
34	25	Mansfield Town	1-1	Jennings	4039
35	Apr 1	QUEEN'S PARK RANGERS	1-0	Hurel	7381
36	7	Swindon Town	0-1		14910
37	8	Southend United	0-2		7031
38	10	SWINDON TOWN	0-2		9203
39	15	EXETER CITY	0-0		4207
40	22	Bristol Rovers	0-1		4620
41	29	Watford	0-2		3465
42	May 6	CRYSTAL PALACE	0-0		4056

Player Appearances (shirt numbers)

No	Barratt AG	Barron W	Bosse PL	Blunt E	Clifford JC	Curtis LH	Dickinson A	Ellwood RJ	Gormlie WJ	Gunn K	Haycox JH	Hewitt JJ	Hurel E	Jennings HW	Jones JT	King FAR	Lauderdale JH	McCartney JJ	McCulloch K	O'Rourke J	Parris JE	Platt R	Postlethwaite TW	Rodger C	Thayne W	Tilson SF	Russell SEJ
1			4						1	2		9				7	10						6	11	5	8	3
2			4						1	2		9				7	10						6	11	5	8	3
3			4						1	2		9				7	10						6	11	5	8	3
4			4						1	2		9				7	10						6	11	5	8	3
5									1	2		9				7	10		4				6	11	5	8	3
6									1	2		9				7	10		4				6	11	5	8	3
7									1	2		9				7	10		4				6	11	5	8	3
8							5		1	2		9				7	10		4				6	11		8	3
9									1	2						7	10	9	4				6	11	5	8	3
10									1	2						7	10	9	4		3		6	11	5	8	
11						9			1	2						7		10	4		3		6	11	5	8	
12				6		9			1	2						7		10	4	11					5	8	3
13									1	2		9				7	10	11	4				6		5	8	3
14									1	2	9					7	10	11	4				6		5	8	3
15									1	2	9					7	10	11	4				6		5	8	3
16				6					1	2		9				7	10	11	4						5	8	3
17				6						2	9				1	7	10	11		4					5	8	3
18		8		6						2	9				1	7		10		4				11	5		3
19				6						2	9				1	7		10		4				11	5	8	3
20		11		6						2	9				1	7		10		4					5	8	3
21				6						2	9				1	7		10		4				11	5	8	3
22				6						2	9				1	7		10		4				11	5	8	3
23		8		6						2	9		11		1	7		10		4					5		3
24				6						2	9		11		1	7		10	4						5	8	3
25				6						2	9		11		1	7		10	4						5	8	3
26				6						2	9		11	7	1			10	4						5	8	3
27				6				10		2	9				1	7				4				11	5	8	3
28								10		2	9				1	7			4				6	11	5	8	3
29				6				10		2	9				1	7			4					11	5	8	3
30				6				10		2	9				1	7			4					11	5	8	3
31				6				10		2	9				1	7			4					11	5	8	3
32				6	1			10		2	9					7			4					11	5	8	3
33		11		6	1			10		2			8	9		7		4						3	5		
34		11		6	1			10		2			8	9		7		4							5		3
35		11		4	1			10		2	9		8			7							6		5		3
36		11		4	1			10		2	9		8			7							6		5		3
37	1	11		4				10		2	9		8			7							6		5		3
38					1			4		2	9		8			7		10				3	6	11	5		
39		11		4	1			10		2	9		8			7							6	3	5		
40		11		4	1			10		2	9		8			7							6	3	5		
41		11		4	1			10		2	9		8			7							6	3	5		
42		11		4	1			10		2	9		8			7		10				3	6	3	5		

	Barratt AG	Barron W	Bosse PL	Blunt E	Clifford JC	Curtis LH	Dickinson A	Ellwood RJ	Gormlie WJ	Gunn K	Haycox JH	Hewitt JJ	Hurel E	Jennings HW	Jones JT	King FAR	Lauderdale JH	McCartney JJ	McCulloch K	O'Rourke J	Parris JE	Platt R	Postlethwaite TW	Rodger C	Thayne W	Tilson SF	Russell SEJ
Apps	1	12	4	26	11	2	1	19	16	34	17	20	12	10	15	40	9	22	28	6	2	2	23	24	41	30	35
Goals		3		1		1		2		1	6	4	2	2		6	3	7	1					4		7	

One own goal

F.A. Cup

Round	Date	Opponent	Score	Scorers	Att
R1	Nov 26	Watford	1-4	Tilson	9000

F.A. Cup R1 line-up (shirt numbers): Barron 11, Blunt 6, Gormlie 1, Gunn 2, Hewitt 9, O'Rourke 4, King 7, McCartney 10, Thayne 5, Tilson 8, Russell 3

Third Division (South) Cup

Round	Date	Opponent	Score	Scorers	Att
R1	Sep 26	SOUTHEND	1-1	McCulloch	
rep	Oct 5	Southend	3-2	Allen 3	1000
R2	Jan 23	IPSWICH TOWN	1-1	Dickinson	400
rep	Feb 1	Ipswich Town	0-1		2858

R1 replay a.e.t.

Played in R1: Cuff (at 7), RSL Allen (at 8). In R1 replay: RSL Allen (at 9). In R2 replay: Smith (at 5).

Final Table — Third Division (South)

	P	W	D	L	F	A	W	D	L	F	A	Pts
1 Newport County	42	15	4	2	37	16	7	7	7	21	29	55
2 Crystal Palace	42	15	4	2	49	18	5	8	8	22	34	52
3 Brighton & Hove A.	42	14	5	2	43	14	5	6	10	25	35	49
4 Watford	42	14	6	1	44	15	3	6	12	18	36	46
5 Reading	42	12	6	3	46	23	4	8	9	23	36	46
6 Queen's Park Rgs.	42	10	8	3	44	15	5	6	10	24	34	44
7 Ipswich Town	42	14	3	4	46	21	2	9	10	16	31	44
8 Bristol City	42	14	5	2	42	19	2	7	12	19	44	44
9 Swindon Town	42	15	4	2	53	25	3	4	14	19	52	44
10 Aldershot	42	13	6	2	31	15	3	6	12	22	51	44
11 Notts County	42	12	6	3	36	16	5	3	13	23	38	43
12 Southend United	42	14	5	2	38	13	2	4	15	23	51	41
13 Cardiff City	42	12	1	8	40	28	3	10	8	21	37	41
14 Exeter City	42	9	9	3	40	32	4	5	12	25	50	40
15 Bournemouth	42	10	8	3	38	22	3	5	13	14	36	39
16 Mansfield Town	42	10	8	3	33	19	2	7	12	11	43	39
17 NORTHAMPTON T.	42	13	5	3	41	20	2	3	16	10	38	38
18 Port Vale	42	10	5	6	36	23	4	4	13	16	35	37
19 Torquay United	42	7	5	9	27	28	7	4	10	27	42	37
20 Clapton Orient	42	10	9	2	40	16	1	4	16	13	39	35
21 Walsall	42	9	6	6	47	23	2	5	14	21	46	33
22 Bristol Rovers	42	8	8	5	30	17	2	5	14	25	44	33

SEASON 1939-40

Comp	Date	Opposition	F.T.	Att.	Goalscorers	J.Jones	K.Gunn	J.Strathie	K.McCullough	R.Simons	H.Miller	R.King	H.Jennings	E.Melaniphy	R.Ellwood	W.Barron
J	19 Aug	Queens Park	2-3	8000	2 not known	J.Jones	K.Gunn	J.Strathie	K.McCullough	R.Simons	H.Miller	R.King	H.Jennings	E.Melaniphy	R.Ellwood	W.Barron
D3S	26	SWINDON TOWN	1-0	8315	Ellwood	J.Clifford	K.McCullough	"	E.Blunt	"	"	"	"	"	"	"
D3S	28	EXETER CITY	1-2	5000	Melaniphy(p)	"	"	"	B.Garvie	"	"	"	"	"	"	"
D3S	3 Sep	Bournemouth	0-10	3000		"	A.Smith	"	K.McCullough	"	"	"	"	"	"	"
F	30	Watford	0-4	2000		Tarrant	Hobbs	H.Howe	McDonough	"	"	"	Ward	G.Henson	W.Barron	J.Parris
F	7 Oct	NOTTS COUNTY	6-0	2000	Billingham(2),Henson(2),Dunkley,Barron	J.Calvert	Frame	Hobbs	J.Grogan	G.Bedford	R.Simons	M.Dunkley	J.Billingham	"	"	"
F	14	Norwich City	1-6	1000	Henson	"	C.Hewitt	"	"	"	"	"	"	"	"	"
M	21	COVENTRY CITY	1-1	3000	Hewitt	"	H.Howe	R.Dennison	"	R.Heywood	"	"	"	"	C.Hewitt	"
M	28	Wolves	2-7	3500	Billingham, Parris	"	K.McCullough	"	"	"	"	"	"	"	H.Howe	"
M	4 Nov	WEST BROMWICH A.	1-1	4000	Parris	"	"	"	"	"	P.Grosvenor	"	"	"	C.Lyman	"
M	11	Walsall	1-1	2730	Lyman	"	"	"	"	"	"	"	"	C.Lyman	D.Liddle	"
M	18	LEICESTER CITY	2-2	3000	Henson, Lyman	"	"	"	"	"	H.Howe	"	J.Billingham	"	C.Lyman	"
M	25	LUTON TOWN	2-1	4000	Billingham, Pritchard	"	"	"	"	"	P.Grosvenor	"	"	"	R.Simons	H.Pritchard
M	2 Dec	BIRMINGHAM	1-1	4000	Liddle	"	"	"	"	"	"	"	"	"	R.Liddle	W.Barron
M	9	Coventry City	4-1	1000	Billingham(2), Henson, Liddle	"	"	"	R.Simons	"	H.Howe	"	"	"	"	C.Lyman
M	16	WOLVES	1-2	6657	Billingham	"	"	"	J.Grogan	"	"	"	"	"	"	"
M	23	West Bromwich Albion	1-4	4120	Henson	"	"	H.Howe	R.Simons	"	W.Coutts	"	"	"	"	"
F	25	Port Vale	1-1		Not known											
F	27	PORT VALE	5-1	1000	Lyman(2,1p), Barron, Henson, Howe	J.Calvert	K.McCullough	Frame	R.Simons	R.Heywood	H.Howe	M.Dunkley	J.Billingham	G.Henson	W.Barron	C.Lyman
M	30	WALSALL	6-1	1000	Dunkley(2),Howe,Lyman,Billingham,Henson	"	"	B.Smith	"	"	"	"	"	"	R.Liddle	"
M	6 Jan	Leicester City	1-1	1500	Billingham	W.Gromlie	"	R.Dennison	"	"	"	"	"	"	"	W.Barron
M	13	Luton Town	2-6	3000	Billingham, Henson	"	"	"	W.Coutts	"	R.Simons	"	"	"	"	C.Lyman
M	20	BIRMINGHAM CITY	3-0	1500	Lyman(p), Barron, Dunkly	"	"	R.Shaw	"	F.Moss	"	W.Coutts	"	D.Liddle	F.Shell	W.Barron
M	24	LEICESTER CITY	4-2	3500	Billingham(2), Shell, Liddle	J.Calvert	"	R.Dennison	"	"	"	"	J.Billingham	"	R.Liddle	W.Barron
M	2 Mar	LUTON TOWN	1-1	3000	Billingham	"	"	"	"	"	"	"	"	"	"	"
M	9	Birmingham City	1-3	3117	Moss	"	"	"	"	"	"	"	"	"	"	"
M	16	Coventry City	3-6	1000	Billingham, Barron, Shell	"	"	"	"	"	"	"	"	"	"	"
F	22	Swindon Town	1-3		Not known	"	"	"	"	"	R.Simons	A.Barratt	"	D.Jones	"	"
M	23	WOLVES	2-0	5870	Billingham, Coutts	"	D.Jones	"	"	"	"	J.Billingham	D.Liddle	F.Shell	W.Coutts	"
F	25	SWINDON TOWN	5-2		Shell(2), Coutts(2), King	"	K.McCullough	D.Jones	"	R.Dennison	"	R.King	"	"	R.Liddle	"
M	26	COVENTRY CITY	2-0	4000	Shell, Liddle	"	"	"	"	R.Simons	F.Moss	W.Coutts	G.Edwards	J.Billingham	R.Liddle	"
M	30	West Bromwich Albion	1-2	3000	Shell	"	"	R.Dennison	"	F.Moss	R.Heywood	R.Simons	"	"	W.Coutts	R.Liddle
M	6 Apr	WALSALL	2-2	3000	Edwards, Billingham	"	"	"	"	"	"	W.Coutts	M.Dunkley	G.Edwards	"	J.Billingham
C	13	WATFORD	1-1	4799	Liddle	"	"	"	"	R.Simons	F.Moss	L.Armeson	D.Liddle	"	W.Coutts	Bate
C	15	Watford	1-2		Coutts	"	W.Cobley	"	K.McCullough	"	"	"	"	"	"	S.Baines
F	27	Queens Park Rangers	0-2	1500		"	"	"	"	R.Simons	"	"	"	"	"	"
M	1 May	Birmingham	1-3	4067	Edwards	"	W.Barron	W.Cobley	W.Coutts	R.Simons			G.Edwards		R.Liddle	C.Lyman
M	11	Walsall	0-1	2000		"	K.McCullough			F.Moss	R.Dennison				H.Howe	R.Liddle
M	13	Luton Town	2-3	1500	Broome, Dunkley	"	W.Cobley	R.Dennison	"					F.Broome		
F	25	SHEFFIELD WED.	2-7		Grogan, Billingham	"			J.Grogan	C.Smith	R.Simons	S.Frost	M.Dunkley	J.Billingham	R.Liddle	S.Baines
M	1 Jun	Wolves	0-1	2016		"		G.Cummings	F.Moss	R.Dennison	R.Iverson	M.Dunkley	J.Grogan	F.Shell	R.Starling	R.Liddle
M	5	West Bromwich Albion	1-2	1374	Broome	"				R.Simons	H.Howe	L.Armeson	C.Lyman	F.Broome	R.Liddle	S.Baines
M	8	Leicester City	0-2			"				J.Grogan	R.Dennison		R.Inwood	J.Billingham		

J = Jubilee match. F = Friendly. M = Midland League. C = War Cup.

SEASON 1940-41

Comp	Date	Opposition	F.T.	Att.	Goalscorers	Morgan	T.Smith	G.Cummings	P.Wilmott	A.Barratt	R.Dennison	M.Dunkley	J.Billingham	Earl-Chater	S.Haycock	Newton
S	31	Luton Town	1-7	1200	Newton											
S	7 Sep	MANSFIELD TOWN	6-1	1500	King(3), Billingham(2), Dennison	A.Wood	T.Smalley	"	W.Shankley	G.Bedford	"	"	"	G.Hinson	"	R.King
S	14	West Bromwich Albion	1-4	2607	Billingham	"	W.Cobley	"	"	T.Smalley	"	"	"	"	L.Armerson	Newton
S	21	WEST BROMWICH A.	1-1	3200	Dunkley	"	T.Smalley	"	"	R.Dennison	L.Armerson	"	A.Kerr	"	S.Haycock	W.Barron
S	28	Mansfield	1-3	2000	Billingham	Morgan	"	"	L.Armerson	"	W.Barron	"	R.Allen	J.Billingham	Littledyke	R.King
S	5 Oct	LUTON TOWN	7-1	2700	Billingham(2),Armerson(2),Barron(2),Wharton	"	"	"	W.Shankley	"	G.Wharton	"	J.Billingham	L.Armerson	S.Haycock	W.Barron
S	12	Nottingham Forest	0-1	1500		A.Wood	"	"	"	"	"	"	"	"	"	"
S	19	Arsenal	4-5	2191	Barron(3), Dunkley	"	"	R.Dennison	"	G.Wharton	L.Armerson	"	R.King	J.Billingham	"	"
S	26	WATFORD	2-1	2500	Beattie(2)	"	"	G.Cummings	"	R.Dennison	G.Wharton	"	R.Beattie	"	"	"
S	2 Nov	Coventry	2-1	509	Haycock(2)	"	"	"	L.Armerson	"	"	"	"	G.Alsop	"	R.King
F	9	R.A.F.	3-5		Billingham(2), Dunkley	"	Clark	"	"	"	F.Mitchell	"	J.Billingham	G.Hinson	"	S.Frost
S	16	NOTTINGHAM FOREST	7-0	2500	Alsop(2), Cummings(p), Dunkley, *	"	T.Smalley	"	W.Shankley	"	G.Wharton	"	"	G.Alsop	R.Beattie	W.Barron
S	23	ARSENAL	1-8	7000	Alsop(p)	"	Pursglove	Towl	L.Armerson	Hunter	J.Pryde	"	"	"	Hart	"
S	7 Dec	BIRMINGHAM	2-1	2000	Wharton, Billingham	"	T.Smalley	G.Cummings	W.Shankley	R.Dennison	G.Wharton	"	"	"	S.Haycock	"
S	21	NOTTS COUNTY	2-1	1500	Billingham(2)	"	"	R.Young	Hunter	L.Armerson	"	"	J.Fagan	J.Billingham	"	"
S	25	LEICESTER CITY	5-2	1500	Billingham(2), Alsop(2), Dunkley	"	"	"	"	R.Dennison	"	"	J.Billingham	G.Alsop	"	"
S	25	Leicester City	2-7	2500	Billingham(2)	"	"	"	"	"	G.Bedford	"	"	"	"	"
S	4 Jan	Mansfield	1-3	1000	Alsop	"	"	"	"	G.Bedford	"	"	"	"	"	"
S	11	MANSFIELD	3-3	1500	Billingham, King, Beattie	"	"	R.Dennison	"	"	"	R.King	S.Haycock	J.Billingham	R.Beattie	G.Alsop
S	25	Luton Town	2-2	1200	Billingham, Alsop	"	"	"	S.Haycock	"	"	M.Dunkley	J.Billingham	G.Alsop	"	W.Barron
S	1 Feb	LUTON TOWN	5-2	2000	Billingham(3), Dunkley, Barron	"	"	"	Hunter	"	S.Haycock	"	"	"	"	"
W	15	Luton Town	5-4	1000	Ware(2), Billingham, King, og	"	"	"	S.Haycock	"	Hunter	"	"	H.Ware	R.King	"
W	22	LUTON TOWN		2000	Ware(3), Billingham(2)	"	"	"	"	"	"	"	"	"	"	"
W	1 Mar	Tottenham Hotspur	0-4	4379		"	"	R.Dennison	"	"	"	"	J.Cornish	"	W.Barron	S.Frost
W	8	TOTTENHAM H.	1-3	4000	Smalley(p)	"	"	"	Hunter	"	S.Haycock	"	J.Billingham	"	R.King	W.Barron
S	15	WALSALL	1-3	2500	King	"	"	"	S.Haycock	"	Hunter	"	"	"	"	"
S	22	Walsall	0-2	2500		"	"	A.Beattie	Hunter	R.Dennison	R.Shaw	"	D.Dearson	J.Billingham	S.Haycock	G.Ashall
F	29	LINCOLN CITY	2-4	700	Alsop(2)	"	"	R.Dennison	D.Dearson	G.Bedford	"	Earl-Chater	J.Billingham	G.Alsop	"	W.Barron
S	12 Apr	WEST BROMWICH A.	3-1	2000	Dearson, Ware, Alsop	"	"	A.Beattie	R.Shaw	"	R.Dennison	J.Billingham	D.Dearson	H.Ware	G.Alsop	S.Haycock
S	14	STOKE CITY	7-1	2000	Beattie(3),King,Alsop,Curtis,Smalley(p)	"	"	"	Hunter	"	"	S.Curtis	R.King	G.Alsop	R.Beattie	G.Ashall
S	19	West Bromwich Albion	2-3	2000	King, Alsop	"	"	R.Dennison	"	"	R.Shaw	"	"	"	S.Haycock	W.Barron
S	26	Millwall	4-1	5000	Alsop(3), Haycock	"	"	"	"	"	"	"	"	"	"	W.Barron
S	3 May	MILLWALL	5-1	3000	Ware(2), Billingham, Beattie, King	"	"	W.Barron	"	R.Dennison	D.Dearson	"	J.Billingham	H.Ware	R.Beattie	R.King
S	7	Stoke City	1-2	4000	Basnett	"	"	R.Dennison	"	G.Bedford	J.Fagan	Basnett	"	G.Alsop	S.Curtis	"
S	17	CHELSEA	4-1	3000	Ware(2), Alsop, og	"	"	Ormond	"	R.Dennison	D.Dearson	J.Billingham	H.Ware	"	J.Fagan	"
S	31	Leicester	2-3		King(2)	"	"	R.Dennison	"	G.Bedford	R.Shaw	"	"	"	S.Haycock	"

* Additional goalscorers: Billingham, Beattie, Barron.   S - Southern Section.   W - Southern Section Cup.   F - Friendly.

Back:Shankley,Smith(Manager), Cummings, Wood, Newman(Trainer), Dennison, Mitchell, Armerson. Front: Dunkley, Hinson, Billingham,Cobley, Newton,Smalley

SEASON 1941-42

Comp	Date	Opposition	F.T.	Att.	Goalscorers	A.Wood	T.Smalley	G.Cummings	R.Hunter	R.Dennison	G.Bedford	F.Curtis	W.Fagan	G.Lowerie	S.Haycock	W.Barron
FLS	30 Aug	WALSALL	3-2	3203	Fagan, Lowrie, Haycock	A.Wood	T.Smalley	G.Cummings	R.Hunter	R.Dennison	G.Bedford	F.Curtis	W.Fagan	G.Lowerie	S.Haycock	W.Barron
FLS	6 Sep	Walsall	2-2	2500	Alsop, og	"	"	R.Dennison	"	G.Bedford	F.Shaw	A.King	S.Haycock	G.Alsop	G.Lowerie	"
FLS	13	Nottingham Forest	3-2	2116	Lowrie, Alsop, Fagan	"	"	"	"	"	"	"	G.Lowerie		W.Fagan	S.Haycock
FLS	20	NOTTINGHAM FOREST	4-3	2000	Lowrie(3), Fagan	"	"	"	S.Haycock	"	"	"	"	H.Ware	"	R.Beattie
FLS	27	NORWICH	3-1	3908	Lowrie(2), Haycock	"	"	"	A.Harris	"	"	"	"	G.Alsop	S.Haycock	W.Barron
FLS	4 Oct	Norwich	1-3	4099	og	"	"	"	"	"	"	"	"	H.Ware	W.Fagan	S.Haycock
F	11	Birmingham City	1-4		Beattie	"	"	"	S.Haycock	"	"	"	W.Fagan	R.Beattie	G.Alsop	
F	18	CZECH ARMY	5-2	2000	Lowrie, Alsop, Fagan, King(2)	"	"	F.Shaw	R.Hunter	H.Boileau	S.Haycock	F.Curtis	"	G.Alsop	W.Fagan	King
FLS	25	Leicester City	0-1	4000		"	"	G.Cummings	"	G.Bedford	F.Shaw	S.Haycock	"	F.Steele	"	G.Alsop
FLS	1 Nov	LEICESTER CITY	0-1	2000		"	"	F.Shaw	"	R.Dennison	S.Haycock	A.King	"	"	R.Beattie	"
FLS	8	BRISTOL CITY	5-2	2000	Fagan(2), Bedford(2), Alsop	"	"	R.Young	"	"	F.Shaw	F.Curtis	W.Fagan	G.Bedford	"	"
FLS	15	Bristol City	1-5	2744	Fagan	"	"	I.Wallington	A.Harris	"	F.Shaw	F.Curtis			W.Fagan	King
FLS	22	WOLVES	1-2	3000	Steele	"	"	R.Dennison	"	G.Bedford	"	J.Pritchard	S.Haycock	F.Steele	"	G.Alsop
FLS	29	Wolves	1-2	5000	Fagan	"	"	R.Young	"	R.Dennison	"	"	"	G.Alsop	"	King
FLS	6 Dec	West Bromwich Albion	0-7	1766		"	"	G.Lunn	F.Shaw	"	H.Boileau	"	A.Harris	G.Bedford	F.Steele	S.Haycock
FLS	13	WEST BROMWICH A.	4-1	3000	Fagan, Alsop, Pritchard(2)	"	"	R.Young	R.Hunter	"	F.Shaw	A.Harris	W.Fagan	G.Alsop	R.Beattie	J.Pritchard
FLS	20	Luton Town	3-3	1700	Fagan, Steele, Pritchard	"	"	R.Dennison	"	F.Shaw	S.Haycock	"	"	F.Steele	"	"
FLS	25	LUTON TOWN	8-1	3000	Fagan(3),Pritchard(2),Alsop(2),Lowrie	"	"	F.Shaw	A.Harris	H.Ware	R.Hunter	J.Pritchard	"	G.Lowerie	"	G.Alsop
W	27	NORIWCH CITY	3-2	4000	Lowrie(2), Beattie	"	"	S.Haycock	"	"	F.Shaw	"	"	"	"	King
W	3 Jan	Norwich	1-4	3549	King	"	"	R.Dennison	"	"	"	"	G.Lowerie	G.Alsop	S.Haycock	King
W	10	WALSALL	6-1	3000	Dearson(3), Smalley(p), Fagan, King	"	"	"	R.Hunter	"	"	"	W.Fagan	D.Dearson	R.Beattie	"
W	17	Walsall	2-1	1500	Lowrie(2)	"	"	"	A.Harris	"	J.Pritchard		"	"	G.Lowerie	"
F	14 Feb	A.A. COMMAND	7-1	2000	King(2),Lowrie(2),Fagan,Beattie,Smalley	"	"	"	H.Ware	"	F.Shaw	W.Fagan	D.Dearson	G.Lowerie	R.Beattie	"
W	21	LUTON TOWN	3-0	1500	Fagan, Lowrie, Smalley	"	"	"	D.Dearson	"	"	A.Harris	W.Fagan	"	"	"
W	28	Luton Town	5-1	3000	Lowrie(3), Pritchard, og	"	"	"	A.Harris	"	"	J.Pritchard	"	"	"	"
W	7 Mar	WEST BROMWICH A.	4-3	1500	Pritchard(p), Fagan, Dearson, Lowrie	"	"	"	"	"	"	"	"	D.Dearson	G.Lowerie	"
W	14	West Bromwich Albion	2-2	5000	Harris, King	"	"	"	R.Hunter	"	"	"	"	A.Harris	R.Beattie	"
W	21	Nottingham Forest	1-0	1500	Fagan	"	"	"	A.Harris	J.Woodburn	"	"	"	A.Macauley	R.King	A.King
L	28	LEICESTER CITY	1-1	2500	Fagan	"	"	"	R.Hunter	R.Attwell	A.Harris	"	H.Ware	R.Beattie	J.Pritchard	
L	4 Apr	BRISTOL CITY	3-0	4000	Hunter(2), Alsop	"	"	"	A.Harris	J.Woodburn	J.Pritchard	R.Hunter	G.Alsop	G.Lowerie	W.Muncie	"
L	6	Bristol City	1-3	7488	Dennison	"	"	"	D.Dearson	"	"	"	A.Macauley	G.Lowerie	F.Shaw	"
L	11	NORWICH CITY	3-4	6000	Dearson(2), Pritchard	"	"	"	"	"	"	"	"	"	"	"
L	18	Norwich City	1-3	9871	Lowrie	"	"	"	A.Harris	"	"	"	W.Fagan	"	A.Macauley	King
L	23	Cardiff City	1-0	3000	Lowrie	"	"	"	J.Woodburn		A.Harris	W.Muncie	G.Lowerie	G.Alsop	W.Fagan	J.Pritchard
L	2 May	CARDIFF CITY	6-1	4000	Lowrie(3), Smalley(p), Pritchard, King	"	"	"	A.Harris		J.Woodburn	J.Pritchard	H.Ware	G.Lowerie	A.Macauley	King
L	9	LUTON TOWN	8-0	3000	Ware(4), Fagan(2), King, Smalley(p)	"	"	"	"	"	"	"	W.Fagan	H.Ware	T.Johnson	A.King
L	16	LEICESTER CITY	3-1	3000	Pritchard, Johnson, Alsop	"	"	"	"	"	"	"	"	G.Lowerie	"	G.Alsop
L	23	STOKE CITY	10-0	3000	Dearson(3),Ware(2),Fagan,Pritchard, *	"	"	"	"	"	"	"	D.Dearson	H.Ware	W.Fagan	"
L	25	Leicester City	4-1	2500	Fagan, Also, Johnson, Harris	"	"	R.Young	"	R.Dennison	"	"	W.Fagan	G.Alsop	T.Johnson	C.Lyman
L	30	Stoke City	2-3	1500	Alsop(2)	"	"	R.Dennison	"	"	H.Ware	"	"	"	"	"

* Additional goalscorers: Harris, Alsop, og

FLS = Football League South Cup Qualifier. W = War Cup Proper. L = (War) Football League. F = Friendly.

SEASON 1942-43

Comp	Date	Opposition	F.T.	Att.	Goalscorers											
FLN	29 Aug	WEST BROMWICH A.	2-0	2000	Alsop, Barron	A.Wood	T.Smalley	W.Dennison	A.Harris	S.Pugh	A.Macauley	H.Pritchard	R.Hunter	G.Alsop	T.Johnson	W.Barron
FLN	5 Sep	West Bromwich Albion	3-6		Johnson(2), Muncie	"	"	W.Barron	"	G.Bedford	S.Pugh	"	"	"	"	W.Muncie
FLN	12	WALSALL	4-2		Ainsley(2), Scrimshaw(2)	"	"	"	"	S.Pugh	R.Hunter	A.Mulraney	R.Ainsley	S.Scrimshaw	"	H.Pritchard
FLN	19	Walsall	2-0	3000	Alsop, Peacock	"	"	G.Tweed	"	W.Dennison	S.Pugh	H.Pritchard	T.Johnson	G.Alsop	T.Peacock	W.Barron
FLN	26	BIRMINGHAM	4-1	3000	Macauley(2), Alsop(2)	"	"	W.Dennison	"	H.Shepherdson	"	"	R.Ellwood	A.Macauley	T.Johnson	G.Alsop
FLN	3 Oct	Birmingham	2-0	5000	Fagan(2)	H.Baldwin	"	"	"	"	"	"	"	W.Fagan	"	"
FLN	10	Coventry	0-5	10800		"	"	"	"	"	"	"	W.Fagan	A.Macauley	R.Ellwood	"
FLN	17	COVENTRY	2-1	3000	Alsop(p)	"	"	"	"	"	"	"	R.Ellwood	G.Alsop	T.Johnson	W.Barron
FLN	24	Walsall	0-6	2000		"	"	"	"	"	A.Macauley	"	F.Gardner	"	"	W.Muncie
FLN	31	WALSALL	2-2	4000	McCauley, Nicholls	"	"	"	"	"	"	"	"	H.Nicholls	W.Barron	"
FLN	7 Nov	ASTON VILLA	3-5	4000	Pritchard, Nicholls, Johnson	"	"	W.Barron	"	"	S.Pugh	"	King	"	T.Johnson	G.Alsop
FLN	14	Aston Villa	1-4	5000	Johnson	A.Hallwall	"	"	S.Pugh	"	"	"	A.Harris	"	"	"
FLN	21	COVENTRY	1-2	4000	Harris	"	"	"	W.Dennison	S.Pugh	"	"	"	"	"	"
FLN	28	Coventry	1-2	6936	Nicholls	"	"	W.Dennison	A.Harris	"	"	"	H.Nicholls	W.Dean	R.Ellwood	W.Barron
FLN	5 Dec	NOTTS COUNTY	5-2	2000	Nicholls(2), Pritchard, Barron, og	L.Bliss	"	"	"	"	"	"	G.Alsop	H.Nicholls		"
FLN	12	Notts County	0-2	2500		R.Cooper	"	"	"	"	"	"	L.Bolan	"	T.Johnson	"
FLN	19	NOTTINGHAM FOREST	5-2	2000	Alsop(2), Pritchard(2), Bolan	"	"	"	"	"	"	"	"	G.Alsop	A.Macauley	"
FLN	25	Nottingham Forest	1-2		Hillard, Alsop	"	"	"	"	"	Hillard	"	T.Johnson	"	"	"
C	26	BIRMINGHAM	5-1	7000	Barron(3), McCauley, Johnson	"	"	"	Hillard	"	P.Bosse	"	"	"	"	"
C	2 Jan	Birmingham	4-2		Pugh(2), Johnson, Alsop	"	"	"	A.Harris	"	"	"	"	"	"	"
C	9	WALSALL	2-2	4000	Alsop, Johnson	"	"	"	"	S.Pugh	Hillard	L.Bolan	R.Hunter	"	"	H.Pritchard
C	16	Walsall	0-2	2500		"	"	"	"	"	A.Macauley	"	W.Fagan	"	T.Johnson	"
C	23	COVENTRY	0-2	4000		"	"	"	"	H.Shepherdson	S.Pugh	H.Pritchard	"	W.Dean	"	W.Barron
C	30	Coventry	1-0	8505	Johnson	"	"	"	"	"	"	"	L.Bolan	W.Fagan	A.Macauley	W.Barron
C	6 Feb	ASTON VILLA	2-1	6000	Bolan, Barron,	"	"	A.Banner	"	W.Dennison	"	J.Woodgat	"	G.Alsop	T.Johnson	W.Barron
C	13	Aston Villa	1-2		Alsop	"	"	W.Metcalf	"	"	"	"	"	"	H.Pritchard	H.Pritchard
C	20	LEICESTER CITY	2-3	3000	McCauley, og,	"	"	W.Dennison	"	H.Shepherdson	A.Macauley	H.Pritchard	"	"	A.Macauley	W.Barron
C	27	Leicester City	2-4		Harris, Alsop	"	"	"	"	"	"	"	"	"	H.Lane	"
F	13 Mar	EAST COMMAND	5-6		Dean(3), Barron(2)	"	"	J.Quinney	"	W.Dennison	S.Pugh	"	"	W.Dean	"	"
C	20	WALSALL	2-4	1500	Alsop, Lowe	"	"	W.Dennison	"	H.Shepherdson	"	W.Dean	"	G.Alsop	A.Macauley	H.Pritchard
C	27	Walsall	5-2	1000	Pritchard(2), Mulraney, Bolan, Alsop	"	"	W.Metcalf	"	W.Dennison	"	A.Mulraney	"	"	S.Lowe	"
C	3 Apr	Leicester City	0-3	3000		"	"	"	"	"	"	"	H.Shepherdson	"	"	"
C	10	LEICESTER CITY	2-2	3000	Harris, og	King	"	"	"	H.Shepherdson	"	"	"	W.Dennison	"	"
C	17	Birmingham	0-1	2000		"	W.Coley	"	"	T.Smalley	W.Dennison	H.Pritchard	"	G.Bedford	H.Lane	G.Alsop
C	24	BIRMINGHAM	1-0	2000	Pugh	"	T.Smalley	"	"	W.Dennison	W.Coley	H.Lane	"	S.Pugh	A.Macauley	H.Pritchard
C	26	West Bromwich Albion	1-6	2468	og	"	"	"	"	"	"	"	"	"	"	"

FLN = Football League North. C = Cup Qualifier. F = Friendly.

SEASON 1943-44

Comp	Date	Opposition	F.T.	Att.	Goalscorers											
LN1	28 Aug	WALSALL	2-0	3000	Kinnear, og	R.Cooper	T.Smalley	J.Jennings	A.Harris	H.Shepherdson	S.Pugh	H.Pritchard	D.Smith	W.Dean	L.Bolan	D.Kinnear
LN1	4 Sep	Walsall	0-0	3000		"	"	"	"	"	"	"	"	L.Bolan	H.Lane	"
LN1	11	West Bromwich Albion	4-4	6222	Perry(2), Dean, Kinnear	D.Bilton	"	W.Barron	"	"	"	W.Dean	"	E.Perry	H.Pritchard	"
LN1	18	WEST BROMWICH A.	2-1	3721	Bolan, Smith	"	"	J.Jennings	"	"	L.Bolan	H.Pritchard	"	"	W.Fagan	"
LN1	25	Birmingham	3-1	4000	Barron(2), Parkes	"	"	R.Dennison	"	"	S.Pugh	"	"	"	H.Parkes	W.Barron
LN1	2 Oct	BIRMINGHAM	2-1	4000	Perry, Pritchard	"	"	"	"	"	"	L.Bolan	"	"	"	H.Pritchard
LN1	9	WALSALL	2-0	4000	Perry, Pritchard	R.Cooper	"	J.Jennings	L.Bolan	R.Dennison	"	W.Dean	"	"	"	"
LN1	16	Walsall	0-0	3000		"	"	"	A.Harris	"	"	H.Pritchard	"	"	L.Bolan	D.Tidman
LN1	23	COVENTRY	0-3	6000		"	"	E.Jones	"	"	"	W.Dean	"	"	"	H.Pritchard
LN1	30	Coventry	1-4	8220	Pritchard	"	"	R.Dennison	"	S.Pugh	H.Nicholls	J.Maund	"	"	"	"
LN1	6 Nov	Aston Villa	0-4	14000		D.Bilton	"	J.Jennings	T.Brolly	R.Dennison	T.Wood	"	"	"	"	D.Kinnear
LN1	13	ASTON VILLA	5-0	6000	Brolley(2), Perry(2), Smith	"	"	R.Dennison	A.Harris	H.Shepherdson	T.Brolly	"	"	"	J.Litchfield	"
LN1	20	Coventry	1-0	5320	Perry	"	"	"	"	"	T.Wood	"	"	"	"	"
LN1	27	COVENTRY	4-1	4224	Kinnear(3), Litchfield	"	"	"	"	"	W.Coley	"	"	H.Pritchard	"	"
LN1	4 Dec	Notts County	5-2	5000	Litchfield(2), Kinnear, Pritchard, Smith	"	"	J.Jennings	"	R.Dennison	"	"	"	"	"	"
LN1	11	NOTTS COUNTY	1-1	3000	Litchfield	"	"	R.Dennison	"	H.Shepherdson	"	"	"	"	"	"
LN1	18	Nottingham Forest	2-2	1637	Perry, Bolan	"	"	"	W.Coley	"	S.Pugh	"	"	E.Perry	L.Bolan	"
LN1	25	NOTTINGHAM FOREST	9-1	4000	Litchfield(4), Perry(3), Pritchard(2)	"	H.Freeman	J.Jennings	D.Smith	T.Smalley	"	"	A.Denton	"	J.Litchfield	H.Pritchard
LN2	26	Aston Villa	1-2	14000	Litchfield	"	"	"	A.Harris	"	T.Wood	H.Pritchard	D.Smith	"	"	D.Kinear
LN2	4 Jan	ASTON VILLA	1-2	8000	Litchfield	"	"	"	A.Harris	"	T.Wood	H.Pritchard	D.Smith	"	"	D.Kinear
LN2	8	Birmingham	1-5	1500	Perry	R.Cooper	T.Smalley	H.Freeman	"	R.Dennison	W.Coley	J.Maund	"	"	S.Pugh	"
LN2	22	Walsall	0-3			"	"	R.Dennison	"	J.Jennings	"	J.Hess	L.Bolan	H.Pritchard	T.Wood	J.Maund
LN2	29	WALSALL	2-0	3000	Litchfield, Fagan	"	"	H.Freeman	"	R.Dennison	"	W.Dean	H.Parkes	J.Litchfield	W.Fagan	H.Pritchard
LN2	5 Feb	WEST BROMWICH A.	2-0	4381	Fagan, og	"	"	R.Dennison	D.Smith	H.Shepherdson	A.Harris	H.Pritchard	"	E.Perry	"	D.Kinnear
LN2	12	West Bromwich Albion	1-3	4503	Kinnear	"	"	"	A.Harris	"	W.Coley	"	D.Smith	"	H.Parkes	"
LN2	19	Coventry	0-2	2500		"	"	"	"	"	H.Pritchard	W.Coley	F.Gardner	H.Parkes	D.Smith	W.Barron
LN2	26	COVENTRY	1-2	5701	Perry	"	"	H.Freeman	"	R.Dennison	W.Coley	H.Pritchard	D.Smith	E.Perry	H.Parkes	D.Kinnear
LN2	4 Mar	Wolves	4-1	3492	Perry(2), Parkes, Gardner	"	"	J.Jennings	D.Smith	"	A.Harris	"	A.Harris	F.Gardner	E.Perry	D.Brookes
LN2	11	WOLVES	7-2	3666	Wilson(4), Coley, Pritchard, Gardner	"	"	H.Freeman	A.Harris	"	W.Coley	H.Pritchard	L.Henley	J.Wilson	J.Hume	F.Gardner
LN2	18	Notts County	4-1	2000	Wilson(2), Henley, Jennings	"	"	"	D.Smith	"	"	E.Perry	"	"	"	J.Jennings
LN2	25	NOTTS COUNTY	4-1	3000	Hume(2), Wilson, Kinnear	"	"	"	"	"	"	R.King	F.Gardner	"	"	D.Kinnear
LN2	1 Apr	Leicester City	2-0	3000	Perry, Brookes	"	"	R.Dennison	A.Harris	J.Jennings	"	H.Pritchard	D.Smith	E.Perry	D.Brookes	"
LN2	8	LEICESTER CITY	3-1	7000	Fenton(2), Barron	"	"	H.Freeman	"	R.Dennison	"	"	B.Fenton	"	F.Gardner	W.Barron
LN2	16	Nottingham Forest	0-5	10000		"	"	R.Dennison	"	J.Jennings	"	"	R.Thompso	"	D.Brookes	F.Gardner
LN2	22	NOTTINGHAM FOREST	3-1	10000	Pritchard, Bolan, Perry	"	"	H.Freeman	"	R.Dennison	"	"	L.Bolan	"	F.Gardner	J.Jennings
LN2	29	Birmingham City	1-3	6000	Gardner	"	"	R.Dennison	"	J.Jennings	"	"	B.Fenton	"	F.Haycock	F.Gardner
LN2	6 May	BIRMINGHAM CITY	0-5	1850		"	"	H.Freeman	L.Bolan	R.Dennison	"	"	F.Gardner	J.Wilson	R.Hornby	D.Kinnear

LN1 – League North 1943. LN2 – League North 1944.

SEASON 1944-45

Comp	Date	Opposition	F.T.	Att.	Goalscorers	A.Lee	T.Smalley	A.Welsh	A.Harris	V.Stephens	W.Coley	G.Roberts	G.Jones	E.Perry	W.Cansfield	W.Hurrell
LN1	26 Aug	WEST BROMWICH A.	1-4	4000	Cansfield	A.Lee	T.Smalley	A.Welsh	A.Harris	V.Stephens	W.Coley	G.Roberts	G.Jones	E.Perry	W.Cansfield	W.Hurrell
LN1	2 Sep	West Bromwich Albion	1-3	3000	og	"	"	"	V.Stephens	H.Shepherdson	A.Harris	"	W.Hurrell	W.Cansfield	Greenaway	H.Pritchard
LN1	9	Stoke City	0-5	9000		"	"	"	A.Harris	"	W.Coley	"	W.O'Neil	E.Perry	"	"
LN1	16	STOKE CITY	1-1	2500	Perry	"	"	R.Dennison	"	"	"	H.Pritchard	J.Billingham	"	A.Welsh	W.Hurrell
LN1	23	PORT VALE	3-1	3000	Smalley, Pritchard, Perry	"	"	"	"	"	V.Stephens	"	W.Hurrell	"	A.Morrall	F.Gardener
LN1	30	Port Vale	2-1	6000	Perry, Gardner	"	"	"	"	"	A.Welsh	"	G.Hughes	"	"	"
LN1	7 Oct	Wolves	2-2	3500	Smalley(p), Perry	"	"	"	"	V.Stephens	"	"	A.Morrall	"	"	"
LN1	14	WOLVES	1-1	3000	Welsh	"	"	"	"	H.Shepherdson	W.Coley	N.Phillips	G.Hughes	A.Welsh	"	H.Pritchard
LN1	21	COVENTRY	4-1	3000	Smalley, Harris, Morrall, Gardner	"	"	"	"	"	"	H.Pritchard	"	N.Phillips	"	F.Gardener
LN1	28	Coventry	1-3	4816	Gardner	"	"	"	"	"	"	"	"	"	"	"
LN1	4 Nov	WALSALL	1-1	3000	Pritchard	"	"	"	"	"	"	"	"	"	"	"
LN1	11	Walsall	2-3	2000	Phillips, Gardner	"	"	"	"	A.Welsh	"	"	"	"	"	"
LN1	18	LEICESTER	3-1	3000	Morrall(2), Hughes	A.Wood	"	"	"	V.Stephens	"	"	"	E.Perry	"	"
LN1	25	Leicester	2-2	5000	Hughes, Morrall	"	"	Pringle	"	R.Dennison	"	"	"	"	"	"
LN1	2 Dec	Birmingham	0-0	2000		"	"	R.Dennison	"	H.Shepherdson	"	"	"	A.Garrett	"	"
LN1	9	BIRMINGHAM	2-1	5000	Smalley(p), Morrall	"	"	W.Barron	"	W.O'Neil	"	"	"	G.Hustwait	"	"
LN1	16	Aston Villa	2-5	8000	Hughes, Gardner	"	"	Pringle	"	V.Stephens	"	"	"	A.Garrett	"	"
LN1	23	ASTON VILLA	2-3	6000	Garrett, Morrall	"	"	A.Welsh	"	H.Shepherdson	W.Coley	"	A.Garrett	E.Perry	"	"
LN2	30	ASTON VILLA	2-0	6000	Perry, Morrall	A.Lee	"	R.Dennison	"	"	"	"	"	"	"	"
LN2	6 Jan	WALSALL	2-1	5000	Perry, Morrall	"	"	"	"	"	"	G.Roberts	"	"	"	"
LN2	13	Walsall	1-0	2000	Garrett	"	"	A.Welsh	"	R.Dennison	"	"	"	"	"	"
LN2	3 Feb	Birmingham	0-4	2000		"	"	"	"	"	"	"	"	"	"	H.Pritchard
LN2	10	BIRMINGHAM	2-1	5000	Garrett, Pritchard	A.Wood	"	R.Dennison	"	H.Shepherdson	"	H.Pritchard	G.Hughes	A.Garrett	"	F.Gardener
LN2	17	COVENTRY	8-1	7000	Garrett(4), Morrall(2), Fagan, Harris	"	"	"	"	"	"	G.Hughes	W.Fagan	"	"	"
LN2	24	Coventry City	0-3	4959		A.Lee	Pringle	"	"	V.Stephens	A.Welsh	G.Roberts	G.Hughes	"	"	"
LN2	3 Mar	Aston Villa	2-2	20000	Fagan, Morrall	A.Wood	A.Welsh	"	"	"	W.Coley	G.Hughes	W.Fagan	"	"	J.Johnson
LN2	10	WEST BROMWICH A.	2-2	7000	Garrett, Morrall	"	"	"	V.Stephens	H.Shepherdson	"	"	"	"	"	F.Gardener
LN2	17	West Bromwich Albion	0-6	6000		"	T.Smalley	A.Welsh	G.Hughes	R.Dennison	"	J.Brown	"	"	"	T.Fowler
LN2	24	BIRMINGHAM	0-2	8000		"	"	Pringle	A.Harris	H.Shepherdson	"	E.Jones	A.Macauley	E.Perry	"	J.Brown
LN2	31	Birmingham	2-2	18000	Syme, Morrall,	"	"	E.Jones	"	"	"	C.Syme	G.Hughes	A.Lee	"	T.Fowler
F	2 Apr	WATFORD	3-3		Brown, Dixon, og	"	"	"	F.Gardener	V.Stephens	"	J.Brown	J.Dixon	"	"	"
LN2	21	DERBY COUNTY	2-1	5000	Dixon, Fowler	"	"	R.Dennison	A.Harris	H.Shepherdson	"	"	"	G.Sparshot	"	"
LN2	28	Derby County	0-5	5000		"	"	A.Welsh	"	"	"	H.Pritchard	G.Crawford	J.Dixon	"	J.Brown

LN1 = League North 1944. LN2 = League North 1945. F = Friendly.

SEASON 1945-46

Comp	Date	Opposition	F.T.	Att.	Goalscorers											
3SN	25 Aug	Walsall	1-1	4000	Dixon	Lee	Pringle	Smalley	Welsh	Dennison	Neal	Fowler	Morrall	Dixon	Ellwood	Maskell
3SN	29	Watford	2-4	2768	Dixon(2)	"	Smalley	Jones	Harris	Shepherdson	Barron	Maskell	Dixon	Phillips	Morrall	Fowler
3SN	1 Sep	WALSALL	1-0	6000	Roberts	"	"	Barron	Neal	Dennison	Welsh	Roberts	Ellwood	Dixon	"	"
3SN	5	Southend United	1-0	5000	Morrall	"	"	Dennison	"	Shepherdson	Barron	"	"	"	"	"
3SN	8	PORT VALE	1-0	7000	Roberts	"	"	Welsh	"	Dennison	"	"	"	"	"	"
3SN	15	Port Vale	0-0	7000		"	"	"	"	"	"	"	Wilson	"	"	"
3SN	18	WATFORD	3-0	7000	Roberts, Dixon, Barron	"	"	Dennison	"	Shepherdson	Welsh	"	"	"	"	Barron
3SN	22	Ipswich Town	1-2	12000	Roberts	"	"	Welsh	"	Dennison	Barron	"	"	"	"	Fowler
3SN	29	IPSWICH TOWN	3-3	7000	Heaselgrave, Haycock, Barron	"	"	"	"	"	McNab	"	Hughes	Heaselgrave	Haycock	Barron
3SN	6 Oct	NOTTS COUNTY	1-2	7151	Roberts	"	"	Allen	McNab	Neal	Coley	"	"	"	"	Fowler
3SN	13	Notts County	1-7	10000	Dixon	Wood	"	"	Neal	Dennison	McNab	"	Heaselgrave	Dixon	"	Barron
3SN	20	QUEENS PARK R.	0-2	9000		"	"	Welsh	"	"	Barron	"	Blunt	"	Morrall	Fowler
3SN	27	Queens Park Rangers	1-4	10000	Roberts	"	"	Dennison	Lowrey	Sankey	Allen	"	"	Heaselgrave	"	Barron
3SN	3 Nov	Orient	0-1	5000		Scott	"	Welsh	Neal	Dennison	"	"	"	Dixon	Barron	Fowler
3SN	10	ORIENT	6-1	6000	Roberts(3), Heaselgrave(2), Morrall	"	"	Barron	Lowrey	Sankey	Yarker	"	Heaselgrave	Morrall	Wilson	"
FAC	17	CHELMSFORD	5-1	6700	Morrall(2), Hughes(2), Roberts	"	"	"	"	"	"	"	"	"	Hughes	"
FAC	24	Chelmsford	5-0	2000	Morrall(2), Roberts, Smith, Fowler	"	"	"	"	Dennison	"	"	Smith	"	"	"
F	1 Dec	Aldershot	7-2		Morrall(2),Roberts,Smith,Hughes,Fowler,og	"	"	Welsh	Sankey	"	"	"	"	"	"	"
FAC	8	NOTTS COUNTY	3-1	10000	Morrall(2), Blunt	"	"	Barron	Lowrey	"	Sankey	"	Blunt	"	"	"
FAC	15	Notts County	0-1	17000		"	"	Welsh	"	"	"	"	"	"	"	Allen
3SN	22	Norwich	1-2	10000	Blunt	"	"	barron	"	"	"	"	"	"	"	Allen
3SN	25	Mansfield	0-2			Lee	Neal	Welsh	Harris	Skelton	Yarker	"	"	Ellwood	Wilson	Fowler
3SN	27	MANSFIELD	4-0	7000	Sankey, Lowrey, Roberts, Blunt	Scott	Smalley	Barron	Sankey	Dennison	Lowrey	"	"	Morrall	Hughes	"
3SN	29	SOUTHEND	6-2	7000	Morrall(3), Blunt, Roberts, Hughes	"	"	"	"	Skelton	Welsh	"	"	"	"	"
3SN	1 Jan	NORWICH	4-1	2000	Dixon(2), Roberts, Hughes	Lee	Collins	Allen	Neal	"	Yarker	"	Wilson	Dixon	"	"
FAC	5	MILLWALL	2-2	13000	Blunt, Hughes	Scott	Smalley	Barron	Lowrey	Sankey	"	"	Blunt	Morrall	"	"
FAC	7	Millwall	0-3	15384		"	"	"	"	"	"	"	"	"	"	"
3SC	12	Southend	3-4		Morrall(2), Smalley	"	"	"	Blunt	Skelton	Lowrey	"	Hughes	"	Wilson	"
3SC	19	SOUTHEND	0-1	4000		"	"	"	Bosse	Dennison	"	"	"	"	"	"
3SC	26	Norwich City	1-2	7748	og	Gillespie	"	"	Neal	"	Yarker	"	Blunt	"	Hughes	"
3SC	2 Feb	NORWICH CITY	1-1	4000	Smalley(p)	"	"	"	"	"	Lowrey	"	"	"	"	"
3SC	9	Watford	0-1	4500		"	"	"	Lowrey	"	Yarker	Hughes	"	McGregor	Morrall	"
3SC	16	WATFORD	4-1	5500	Morrall(2), Bates, Fowler	"	"	"	Sankey	"	Lowrey	"	Heaselgrave	Morrall	Bates	"
3SC	23	Swindon	4-1	8865	Morrall(3), Jones	"	"	"	Hughes	"	Blunt	Roberts	"	Jones	Morrall	"
3SC	2 Mar	SWINDON	5-1	4000	Lowrey, Hughes, Jones, Morrall, og	"	"	"	Lowrey	"	"	Hughes	Smith	Heaselgrave	"	"
3SC	9	NOTTS COUNTY	2-1		Morrall, Fowler	Saunders	"	"	Sankey	"	"	"	"	Jones	"	"
3SC	16	Notts County	2-1	8000	Hughes, Jones	Gillespie	"	"	"	"	Lowrey	"	"	"	"	"
3SC	23	MANSFIELD	1-1	10000	Hughes	"	"	"	Lowrey	Sankey	Blunt	"	"	"	Heaselgrave	"
3SC	30	Mansfield	1-2	4000	Morrall	"	"	"	Sankey	Dennison	Lowrey	"	"	"	Morrall	"
3SC	6 Apr	ORIENT	0-2	5000		"	"	"	Lowrey	Sankey	Blunt	"	"	"	"	"
3SC	13	Orient	1-2	10000	Jennings	"	Smith	"	"	"	"	"	Heaselgrave	"	"	Dean
3SC	20	WALSALL	1-4	8000	Fowler	"	"	"	Hughes	"	"	Pritchard	"	"	"	Fowler

3SN = Division 3 South (North Section). 3SC = Division 3 South Cup. FAC = F.A.Cup. F= Friendly

1946/47 13th in Division 3(S)

Player columns (left→right): Allen AR, Baines SN, Barron W, Blunt E, Briscoe JER, Dennison RS, Fowler T, Frost SD, Garrett ACE, Heaselgrave SE, Hughes TG, Lowery H, McKee RT, McKenna MJ, Morrall AD, Neal G, Quinney HJ, Roberts DG, Sankey J, Scott DP, Smalley T, Smith D, Strathie WJ, Thompson H, Jenkins RJ, Jennings HW, Jones JT

#	Date	Opponent	Res	Scorers	Att	Alln	Bns	Barn	Blnt	Bris	Denn	Fowl	Frst	Garr	Heas	Hugh	Lowe	McKe	McKn	Morr	Neal	Quin	Robe	Sank	Scot	Smal	Smth	Stra	Thom	Jnks	Jngs	Jnes
1	Aug 31	SWINDON TOWN	4-1	Heaselgrave 2, Morrall 2	12013			3	6		5	11			10					9			7	4		2	8					1
2	Sep 2	EXETER CITY	1-2	Morrall	9730			3	6		5	11			10					9			7	4		2	8					1
3	7	Bournemouth	1-2	Morrall	13461				6		5	11			9					10			7	4		2	8	3				1
4	9	Port Vale	1-1	Blunt	8709				6		5	11			10					9	4		7		1	2	8	3				
5	14	CARDIFF CITY	0-2		8853			3	6			11			10					9			7	5	1	4	8	2				
6	18	Exeter City	0-1		7933	3			6	10		11								9	4		7	5		2	8					1
7	21	Norwich City	3-2	Fowler 2, Smith	16215			3	6			11			10						4		7	5		2	8				9	1
8	28	NOTTS COUNTY	2-1	Garrett 2	11906			3	6	7	5	11		9	10									4		2	8					1
9	Oct 5	Walsall	0-2		12521			3	10	7	5	11		9			6							4		2	8					1
10	12	Aldershot	1-1	Fowler	5498			3	6	7	5	11		9						10						2	8					1
11	19	WATFORD	4-1	Garrett 2, Morrall, Smith	9776			3	6		5	11		9			4			10			7			2	8					1
12	26	Ipswich Town	2-1	Garrett 2	13280			3	6		5	11		9			4			10			7			2	8					1
13	Nov 2	LEYTON ORIENT	4-1	Garrett 2, Smith 2	10173			3	6		5	11		9			4			10			7			2	8					1
14	9	Queen's Park Rangers	0-1		17796			3	6		5	11		9	10		4						7			2	8					1
15	16	SOUTHEND UNITED	2-3	Garrett 2	11338			3	6		5	11		9			4			10			7			2	8					1
16	23	Bristol Rovers	3-0	Garrett, Morrall, Smith	7886			3	6		5	11		9			4			7						2	8		10			1
17	Dec 7	Torquay United	1-2	Garrett	5265			3	6		5	11		9						7						2	8		10			1
18	21	Reading	0-3		5374			3	6					9				4		7		2	11	5					10	8		
19	25	BRISTOL CITY	2-2	Garrett, Smith	13501			3	6		5			9			4			7			11			2	8		10			1
20	26	Bristol City	3-2	Garrett, Morrall, Smith	23109			3			5	11		9					6	10			7			2	8		4			1
21	28	Swindon Town	1-3	Garrett	15456						5	11		9					6	10		3	7			2	8		4			1
22	Jan 4	BOURNEMOUTH	2-1	Garrett, Roberts	7176					7	5			9				1		10			3	11	4	2	8			6		
23	18	Cardiff City	2-6	Lowery, Smith	29426			3			5			9			4			10				11	1	2	8		6			
24	23	MANSFIELD TOWN	3-0	Fowler, Garrett, Jenkins	2713			3			5	11		9					6	7					1	2	4		10	8		
25	25	NORWICH CITY	1-0	Smith	6023				6		5	11		9						10			7	3		2	8					1
26	Feb 1	Notts County	0-1		13096				6		5	11		9									7	3	1	2	8		10			
27	Mar 8	Leyton Orient	1-2	Garrett	8567			3		7	5	11		9			4						6			2	8		10			1
28	15	QUEEN'S PARK RANGERS	4-4	Garrett 2, Smith 2	9907			3		7	5	11		9					6				4			2	8		10			1
29	22	Southend United	0-4		8465			3		7	5	11		9					6				4			2	8		10			1
30	29	BRISTOL ROVERS	2-1	Smalley	6846			3		7		11		9			4	1		10						2	8	5	6			
31	Apr 4	Brighton & Hove Albion	2-2	Roberts, Thompson	9152	3				7				9	10			1					11			2	4	5	6	8		
32	5	Mansfield Town	2-3	Briscoe, Garrett	5625	3			6	7				9	10		5	1					11			2	4					
33	7	BRIGHTON & HOVE ALB	6-1	*See below	8754	3			6					9	10		5	1		7			11			2	8		4			
34	8	WALSALL	0-8		5757	3			6					9	10				1	7			11			2	8	5	4			
35	12	TORQUAY UNITED	0-0		5808			3	6		5		7	9	10								11			2	8		4			
36	19	Crystal Palace	2-2	Roberts, Smith	10920			3			5		7	9	10								11	4		2	8		6			
37	26	READING	4-0	Heaselgrave, Roberts, Smith 2	5290			3					7	9	10		5						11			2	8		6			1
38	May 3	PORT VALE	1-0	Frost	6258			3	6				7	9	10		5						11			2	8					1
39	10	Watford	1-1	Garrett	5655				6				7	9	10		5						11	3		2	8		4			
40	17	CRYSTAL PALACE	1-0	Smith	5690				6				7	9	10		5						11	3		2	8		4			
41	29	ALDERSHOT	2-2	Garrett, Roberts	4240				6	7				9	10								11	3		2	8		4			
42	31	Ipswich Town	2-2	Garrett 2	3216				6	7				9	10		5		4				11	3		2	8					
		Apps				5	1	28	30	13	27	25	6	35	20	1	24	5	4	24	3	3	31	23	6	41	41	6	24	4	1	31
		Goals						1	1			4	1	26	3		1			9			6			1	17		1	1		

Scorers in game 33: Garrett, Morrall 2, Roberts, Smith 2

F.A. Cup

Rd	Date	Opponent	Res	Scorers	Att	Barn	Blnt	Bris	Denn	Fowl	Garr	Heas	Lowe	McKe	Morr	Robe	Sank	Scot	Smal	Smth	Thom	Jnks	Jnes
R1	Nov 30	MANSFIELD TOWN	2-0	Blunt, Garrett	15600	3	10		5	11	9		6		7		4		2	8			1
R2	Dec 14	Peterborough Utd.	1-1	Garrett	10000	3	11		5		9		4		7	6			2	8	10		1
rep	19	PETERBOROUGH UTD.	1-1	Thompson	6800	3	11		5		9		6		7	4			2	8	10		1
rep 2	23	Peterborough Utd.	8-1	Garrett 4, Morrall 2, Roberts 2	13150	3			5		9		4		7	11	6		2	8	10		1
R3	Jan 11	PRESTON NORTH END	1-2	Roberts	16858	3		7	5		9	10	4			11		1	2	8	6		

League Table — Division 3 (South)

		P	W	D	L	F	A	W	D	L	F	A	Pts
1	Cardiff City	42	18	3	0	60	11	12	3	6	33	19	66
2	Queen's Park Rgs.	42	15	2	4	42	15	8	9	4	32	25	57
3	Bristol City	42	13	4	4	56	20	7	7	7	38	36	51
4	Swindon Town	42	15	4	2	56	25	4	7	10	28	48	49
5	Walsall	42	11	6	4	42	25	6	6	9	32	34	46
6	Ipswich Town	42	11	5	5	33	21	5	9	7	28	32	46
7	Bournemouth	42	12	4	5	43	20	6	4	11	29	34	44
8	Southend United	42	9	7	5	38	22	8	3	10	33	38	44
9	Reading	42	11	6	4	53	30	5	5	11	30	44	43
10	Port Vale	42	14	4	3	51	28	3	5	13	17	35	43
11	Torquay United	42	11	5	5	33	23	4	7	10	19	38	42
12	Notts County	42	11	4	6	35	19	4	6	11	28	44	40
13	NORTHAMPTON T.	42	11	5	5	46	33	4	5	12	26	42	40
14	Bristol Rovers	42	9	6	6	31	26	7	2	12	25	43	40
15	Exeter City	42	11	6	4	37	27	4	3	14	23	42	39
16	Watford	42	11	4	6	39	27	6	1	14	22	49	39
17	Brighton & Hove A.	42	8	7	6	31	35	5	5	11	23	37	38
18	Crystal Palace	42	9	7	5	29	19	4	4	13	20	43	37
19	Leyton Orient	42	10	5	6	40	28	2	3	16	14	47	32
20	Aldershot	42	6	7	8	25	26	4	5	12	23	52	32
21	Norwich City	42	6	3	12	38	48	4	5	12	26	52	28
22	Mansfield Town	42	8	5	8	31	38	1	5	15	17	58	28

1946/47 SEASON Back: Ashley, Neal, Quinney, Scott, Strathie, McGregor, McKenna, Newman, White
Middle: Williams, Heaselgrave, Allen, Jennings (Trainer)
Front: Jenkins, Baines

1947/48 SEASON Back: Candlin, McCoy, Barron, Coley, Maxwell, Smith
Middle: Ansell, Hughes, Freimanis, Fisher, Horn, Jennings(Coach)
Front: Mitchell, Fowler, Garrett

1947/48 14th in Division 3(S)

#	Date		Opponent	Score	Scorers	Att.	Ans	Bar	Blu	Bow	Bri	Col	Den	Eng	Fis	Fow	Gar	Gil	Hea	Hug	Jen	Jon	Kin	Low	Mor	Rob	San	Sco	Sma	Smi	Sta	Tho
1	Aug	23	Swindon Town	0-0		18138					7	6	5				9					1		4	11	3			2	8		10
2		28	TORQUAY UNITED	1-0	Garrett	10255			6		7		5				9				10	1		4	11	3			2	8		
3		30	PORT VALE	4-1	Briscoe, Jenkins 2, Thompson	9404	11		6		7		5				9				10	1		4		3			2			8
4	Sep	3	Torquay United	2-4	Jenkins 2	7019	11		4			6	5				9				10	1				7	3		2	8		
5		6	Queen's Park Rangers	0-2		21419					7	6	5				9				10			4	11	3		1	2	8		
6		11	ALDERSHOT	2-1	Garrett 2	7333		3	4			6	5				9							10	11			1	2	7		8
7		13	WATFORD	0-1		7861		3	6				5				9				10			4	11			1	2	7		8
8		17	Aldershot	1-1	Roberts	4333		3					5				9				10	1	6	7	11	4			2	8		
9		20	Brighton & Hove Albion	3-2	Garrett, Jenkins, Smith	8575		3					5				9				10	1	4	7	11	6			2	8		
10		27	NORWICH CITY	1-0	Garrett	9757		3					5				9				10	1	6	7	11	4			2	8		
11	Oct	4	Bristol Rovers	2-1	Briscoe, Morrall	15098		3			9		5								10	1	6	7	11	4			2			8
12		11	Walsall	0-2		15202		3			9	6	5									1		10	7	11	4			2			8
13		18	LEYTON ORIENT	1-1	Garrett	9419		3			9	6	5				7				10	1		4	11				2	8		
14		25	Exeter City	1-1	Garrett	10391		3				6	5			11	9		10			1		4		7			2	8		
15	Nov	1	NEWPORT COUNTY	1-1	Smith	9289		3					4			11	9		10			1	7		7	5			2	8		6
16		8	Southend United	1-3	Smith	10481		3					5			11	9		10			1	7		7	4			2	8		6
17		15	NOTTS COUNTY	1-2	Garrett	18272		3					5			11	9					1		4	7				2	8		10
18		22	Swansea Town	1-5	Garrett	13826	11					6	5				9		10							7	3		2	8		
19	Dec	25	Crystal Palace	0-1		15095		3			9	6				11						1	8	5		7	4		2			
20		27	CRYSTAL PALACE	3-1	Briscoe, King, Morrall	9631		3	6		7											1	8	5	9	11	4		2			
21	Jan	3	Port Vale	0-1		12905			6		7	4										1	8	5	9	11	3		2			
22		24	BRISTOL CITY	0-4		7522		3				4	5	7					10			1	9	6	8	11			2			
23		31	Watford	1-1	Hughes	13834					7	4	5			6	11			9	10	1	8	3					2			
24	Feb	7	BRIGHTON & HOVE ALB	4-0	Briscoe 2, Hughes, Lowery	6661					7	4	5			6	11			9	10	1	8	3					2			
25		14	Norwich City	3-2	Briscoe, Hughes, Fowler	23470		3			9	4		7		11			6			1	8	5					2		10	
26		21	BRISTOL ROVERS	1-3	Briscoe	5149		3			9	4		7		11			6			1	8	5					2		10	
27		28	WALSALL	2-1	Hughes, King	8253		3	6		7	4				11				10	9	1	8	5					2			
28	Mar	6	Leyton Orient	0-5		14714		3	4		9	6				11						10		1	7	5			2	8		
29		13	EXETER CITY	3-1	Briscoe 2, Hughes	6136	1	3			9	4	5			11			10	8				7	6				2			
30		18	SWINDON TOWN	0-0		6241	1	3			9	6	5			11			10	8				7	4				2			
31		20	Newport County	2-1	Briscoe, Coley	8567	1	3			9	6	5			11			10					7	4				2	8		
32		26	Reading	1-1	King	16774	1	3			9	6	5			11			10					7			4		2	8		
33		27	SOUTHEND UNITED	2-0	Coley 2	9104	1	3			9	6	5			11			10					7			4		2	8		
34		29	READING	1-1	Briscoe	8855	1	3			9	6	5			11			10					7	4				2	8		
35	Apr	3	Notts County	2-3	Fowler, Smith	30903	1			6	9	4			3	11			10					7	5				2	8		
36		8	QUEEN'S PARK RANGERS	1-1	Coley	11260	1	3		6		4	5			9							8	10					2	7		
37		10	SWANSEA TOWN	0-1		8506	1	3		6			5			11			10		9			7	4				2	8		
38		17	Bournemouth	0-2		14818	1		4	6				8	5	11			10					9	3		7		2			
39		21	Ipswich Town	2-5	King 2	9285	1		6						5	11		3	10	9			8			7			2			4
40		24	IPSWICH TOWN	4-2	Heaselgrave, King 3	4410			4	6					3	11			10	9			8	5		7		1	2			
41		29	BOURNEMOUTH	3-6	Hughes 3	6674			4						3	11			10	6			9	5		7		1	2	8		
42	May	1	Bristol City	1-1	King	8392	1		4	6			7		3	11			9	10			8	5					2			
			Apps				12	29	14	6	23	28	28	5	8	25	16	1	22	12	13	25	24	35	10	25	19	5	42	24	2	9
			Goals								11	4				2	9		1	8	5		9	1	2	1				4		1

F.A. Cup

	Date		Opponent	Score	Scorers	Att.		Bar			Bri	Col	Den			Fow			Hea			Jon	Kin	Low		Rob			Sma	Smi	Sta	Tho
R1	Nov	29	Exeter City	1-1	Roberts	13143		3			9	6	5			11						1		4		7			2	8		10
rep	Dec	6	EXETER CITY	2-0	Briscoe, Jenkins	9500		3			9	6	5			11			8		10	1		4		7			2			
R2		13	TORQUAY UNITED	1-1	Heaselgrave	12000		3			9	6	5			11			8		10	1		4		7			2			
rep		20	Torquay United	0-2		7000		3			9	6	5			11			8		10	1		4		7			2			

First games of both rounds a.e.t.

		P	W	D	L	F	A	W	D	L	F	A	Pts
1	Queen's Park Rgs.	42	16	3	2	44	17	10	6	5	30	20	61
2	Bournemouth	42	13	5	3	42	13	11	4	6	34	22	57
3	Walsall	42	13	5	3	37	12	8	4	9	33	28	51
4	Ipswich Town	42	16	1	4	42	18	7	2	12	25	43	49
5	Swansea Town	42	14	6	1	48	14	4	6	11	22	38	48
6	Notts County	42	12	4	5	44	27	7	4	10	24	32	46
7	Bristol City	42	11	4	6	47	26	7	3	11	30	39	43
8	Port Vale	42	14	4	3	48	18	2	7	12	15	36	43
9	Southend United	42	11	8	2	32	16	4	5	12	19	42	43
10	Reading	42	10	5	6	37	28	5	6	10	19	30	41
11	Exeter City	42	11	6	4	34	22	4	5	12	21	41	41
12	Newport County	42	9	8	4	38	28	5	5	11	23	45	41
13	Crystal Palace	42	12	5	4	32	14	1	8	12	17	35	39
14	NORTHAMPTON TOWN	42	10	5	6	35	28	4	6	11	23	44	39
15	Watford	42	6	6	9	31	37	8	4	9	26	42	38
16	Swindon Town	42	6	10	5	21	20	4	6	11	20	26	36
17	Leyton Orient	42	8	5	8	31	32	5	5	11	20	41	36
18	Torquay United	42	7	6	8	40	29	4	7	10	23	33	35
19	Aldershot	42	5	10	6	22	26	5	5	11	23	41	35
20	Bristol Rovers	42	7	3	11	39	34	6	5	10	32	41	34
21	Norwich City	42	8	3	10	33	34	5	5	11	28	42	34
22	Brighton & Hove A.	42	8	4	9	26	31	3	8	10	17	42	34

1948/49   20th in Division 3(S)

#		Date	Opponent	Res	Scorers	Att	Aldridge NH	Ansell W	Barron W	Blunt E	Bowen DL	Briscoe JER	Coley WE	Collins BV	English J	Fowler T	Freimanis E	Garrett ACE	Horne AT	Hughes TG	Jackson LW	James R	King FAR	Lowery H	McCoy W	Roberts DG	Smalley T	Smith D	Smith WH	Stanton SH	Thompson H	Williams E
1	Aug	21	Exeter City	1-5	Fowler	9586	3						6			11	9			10		4		5		7	2	8				1
2		25	Norwich City	1-2	Freimanis	22517	3			4			6			11	9			10		5	7						8		2	1
3		28	Bristol City	0-3		22663			3	4			6			11	9			10			7	5			2	8				1
4	Sep	2	NORWICH CITY	1-0	WH Smith	7127		1	3	4			6	5	7	11	9										2		8		10	
5		4	SWINDON TOWN	0-1		9410		1	3	4			6	5	7	11	9										2		8		10	
6		7	Southend United	1-0	Freimanis	8454		1	3		4		6	5		11	9			10				7			2		8			
7		11	Leyton Orient	3-0	Fowler, Freimanis, Hughes	12747		1	3				6			11	9			10				7	5		2		8			
8		16	SOUTHEND UNITED	2-2	Coley, James	8861		1	3		4		6			11	9			10		8		7	5		2					
9		18	PORT VALE	2-2	Briscoe, one og	9964		1	3		4	7	6			11	9			10					5		2	8				
10		25	Millwall	2-3	Hughes, D Smith	25690		1	3		4	7	6			11	9			10							2	8				
11	Oct	2	ALDERSHOT	2-0	Briscoe, D Smith	7924		1	3			7	6	5		11	9				2			4					8	10		
12		9	IPSWICH TOWN	1-1	D Smith	9589		1	3				6	5		11	9				2			4					8	10		
13		16	Bournemouth	2-5	D Smith 2	16803		1	3			7	6	5		11				10				4			2	8	9			
14		23	NEWPORT COUNTY	2-1	WH Smith 2	8178		1	3			7	6	5		11				10				4			2	8	9			
15		30	Bristol Rovers	0-1		15363		1	3			7	6			11				10				5			2	8	9		4	
16	Nov	6	READING	1-2	WH Smith	8365		1	3				6	5		11	9			10							2	8	7		4	
17		13	Swansea Town	0-1		23095		1	3				6			11	9			10				5			2	8	7	4		
18		20	WATFORD	1-1	D Smith	8437		1	3				6			11	9			10		4		5			2	8	7			
19	Dec	4	TORQUAY UNITED	0-0		11943		1	3						7	11		9						6	5		2	8	10	4		
20		18	EXETER CITY	4-0	English, Fowler, Garrett 2	7876		1	3						7	11	10	9							5		2	6	8	4		
21		25	NOTTS COUNTY	1-2	Garrett	17724		1	3						7	11		9						6	5		2	8	10	4		
22		27	Notts County	0-2		31171		1	3						7			9		10				8	5		2	4		6		
23	Jan	1	BRISTOL CITY	3-1	Fowler, Garrett, King	6901		1	3	6					7	11		9		10			8		5		2	4				
24		15	Swindon Town	2-2	King, one og	14306		1	3	6					7	11		9		10			8		5		2	4				
25		22	LEYTON ORIENT	4-1	English, Garrett, D Smith, King	8661		1	3	4			6		7	11		9					10		5		2	8				
26		29	Crystal Palace	2-2	Garrett 2	13972		1	3	4			6		7	11		9					10		5		2	8				
27	Feb	5	Port Vale	0-1		9369		1	3	4			6		7	11		9					10		5		2	8				
28		12	WALSALL	0-1		8694		1	3	4			6			11		9					10		5		2	8	7			
29		19	MILLWALL	4-0	Fowler 3, WH Smith	10775		1	3	4	9		6			11							10		5		2	8	7			
30		26	Aldershot	1-3	Briscoe	5635		1	3	4	9		6			11							10		5		2	8	7			
31	Mar	5	Ipswich Town	2-4	Fowler, Garrett	10439		1	3	4	7		6			11		9					10		5		2	8				
32		12	BOURNEMOUTH	1-0	WH Smith	8473		1	3				6			11		9					10	4	5		2	8	7			
33		19	Newport County	0-2		14869		1	3				6			11		9					10	4	5		2	8	7			
34		26	BRISTOL ROVERS	0-1		7425		1	3	6						11		9					10	4	5		2	8	7			
35	Apr	2	Reading	0-1		14148		1	3				6		7	11		9					10		5		2	4	8			
36		9	SWANSEA TOWN	0-1		10194		1	3		9		6		7	11	10								5		2	4	8			
37		15	Brighton & Hove Albion	0-0		18271		1	3		9		6		7	11	10						8		5		2	4				
38		16	Watford	1-0	Coley	9609		1	3		9		6		7		10		11				8		5		2	4				
39		18	BRIGHTON & HOVE ALB	1-1	King	9184		1	3		9		6		7		10				11		8		5		2	4				
40		23	CRYSTAL PALACE	3-2	Briscoe 2, English	7717		1	3		9		6		7		10						8		5		2	4	11			
41		30	Torquay United	0-3		6526		1	3		4	9	6		7		10						8		5		2		11			
42	May	7	Walsall	0-2		5995		1	3		4	9	6		7		10						8		5		2		11			
			Apps				2	39	40	15	6	17	35	9	19	37	16	21	1	19	2	4	25	17	24	1	39	35	26	5	5	3
			Goals										5	2	3	8	3	8		2			1	4				7	6			

Two own goals

F.A. Cup

	Date	Opponent	Res	Scorers	Att	An	Ba	Bo	Co	En	Fo	Lo	Mc	Sm	SD	SW	St
R1	Nov 27	DULWICH HAMLET	2-1	D Smith, WH Smith	10300	1	3	9	6	7	11	5		2	8	10	4
R2	Dec 11	Mansfield Town	1-2	WH Smith	13501	1	3	9	6	7	11		5	2	8	10	4

		P	W	D	L	F	A	W	D	L	F	A	Pts
1	Swansea Town	42	20	1	0	60	11	7	7	7	27	23	62
2	Reading	42	17	1	3	48	18	8	4	9	29	32	55
3	Bournemouth	42	15	2	4	42	17	7	6	8	27	31	52
4	Swindon Town	42	11	9	1	38	20	7	6	8	26	36	51
5	Bristol Rovers	42	13	5	3	42	23	6	5	10	19	28	48
6	Brighton & Hove A.	42	11	5	5	32	26	4	13	4	23	29	48
7	Ipswich Town	42	14	3	4	53	30	4	6	11	25	47	45
8	Millwall	42	12	7	2	42	23	5	4	12	21	41	45
9	Torquay United	42	12	5	4	45	26	5	6	10	20	44	45
10	Norwich City	42	11	6	4	32	10	5	6	10	35	39	44
11	Notts County	42	15	3	3	68	19	4	2	15	34	49	43
12	Exeter City	42	12	5	4	45	26	3	5	13	18	50	40
13	Port Vale	42	11	3	7	32	21	3	8	10	19	33	39
14	Walsall	42	9	5	7	34	28	6	3	12	22	36	38
15	Newport County	42	8	6	7	41	35	6	3	12	27	57	37
16	Bristol City	42	8	9	4	28	24	3	5	13	16	38	36
17	Watford	42	6	9	6	24	21	4	6	11	17	33	35
18	Southend United	42	5	10	6	18	18	4	6	11	23	28	34
19	Leyton Orient	42	9	6	6	36	29	2	6	13	22	51	34
20	NORTHAMPTON TOWN	42	9	6	6	33	20	3	3	15	18	42	33
21	Aldershot	42	6	5	10	26	29	5	6	10	22	30	33
22	Crystal Palace	42	7	8	6	27	27	1	3	17	11	49	27

1948/49 SEASON
Back: Res, Res, Res, Res, Res, Res, Williams, Ansell, Coley, Collins, Res, Res, Res
Middle: Newman(Trainer), Smith(Manager), Roberts, Res, English, Res, Smalley,
Res, Hughes, Res, Res, Smith, Jennings
Front: Bowen, Res, Briscoe, (5 Directors), Blunt, Barron, Fowler

1949/50 SEASON
Back: Smalley, McCoy, Ansell, Coley, Dixon
Front: Barron, English, McCulloch, Candlin, Murphy, Mitchell

1949/50   2nd in Division 3(S)

No	Date	Opponent	Score	Scorers	Att	Ansell W	Barron W	Candlin MH	Coley WE	Collins BV	Dunkley MEF	Dixon A	English J	Fowler T	Freimanis E	Garrett ACE	Hughes TG	King FAR	McCoy W	McCulloch ABR	McCulloch T	Mitchell AJ	Murphy E	Smalley T	Smith D	Southam JH
1	Aug 20	Bristol City	1-3	King	27463	1		4	6							9		7	5			11	10	2	8	3
2	25	NEWPORT COUNTY	4-3	Garrett 2, King, Smith	12718	1		4	6							9		7	5			11	10	2	8	3
3	27	Brighton & Hove Albion	1-1	Garrett	18661	1		4	6							9		7	5			11	10	2	8	3
4	Sep 1	Newport County	4-1	A McCulloch 2, Mitchell, Murphy	12536	1		4	6									7	5	9		11	10	2	8	3
5	3	Walsall	3-1	King, Mitchell, Murphy	14066	1		4	6									7	5	9		11	10	2	8	3
6	8	NOTTM. FOREST	0-0		19228	1		4	6		7								5	9		11	10	2	8	3
7	10	MILLWALL	1-0	Smith	13957	1		4	6		7								5	9		11	10	2	8	3
8	14	Nottingham Forest	1-0	Murphy	23394	1		4	6		7								5	9		11	10	2	8	3
9	17	Swindon Town	1-6	one og	15219	1		4	6		7								5	9		11	10	2	8	3
10	24	TORQUAY UNITED	3-0	A McCulloch 2, Mitchell	11781	1		4	6									7	5	9		11	10	2	8	3
11	Oct 1	Aldershot	0-0		6990	1			6								4	7	5	9		11	10	2	8	3
12	8	IPSWICH TOWN	1-2	King	13773	1		4	6					11				7	5	9			10	2	8	3
13	15	Exeter City	3-1	A McCulloch 2, Murphy	8353	1		4	6					11		8			5	9			10	2	7	3
14	22	LEYTON ORIENT	3-0	Garrett, A McCulloch, Murphy	11950	1		4	6					11		8			5	9			10	2	7	3
15	29	Reading	1-3	A McCulloch	18636	1		4						11		8	6		5	9			10	2	7	3
16	Nov 5	WATFORD	0-0		9722	1		4						11		8	6		5	9			10	2	7	3
17	12	Crystal Palace	4-0	Freimanis, A McCulloch, Mitchell 2	12486	1		4	6						8				5	9		11	10	2	7	3
18	19	BOURNEMOUTH	2-3	Murphy 2	15103	1			6						8		4		5	9		11	10	2	7	3
19	Dec 3	SOUTHEND UNITED	2-0	Mitchell, Murphy	12075	1			6			8	7						5	9		11	10	2	4	3
20	17	BRISTOL CITY	4-2	Mitchell 2, Murphy, Smith	11141	1		4	6										5	9	7	11	10	2	8	3
21	24	BRIGHTON & HOVE ALB	2-1	A McCulloch, Murphy	14958	1		4	6			8							5	9		11	10	2	7	3
22	26	Port Vale	1-3	A McCulloch	17212	1	3	4	6			10							5	9	7	11		2	8	
23	27	PORT VALE	1-1	English	19263	1	3	4				8	7						5	9		11	10	2	6	
24	31	WALSALL	2-0	Dixon 2	12349	1	3	4	6			8							5	9		11	10	2	7	
25	Jan 14	Millwall	2-0	A McCulloch, Mitchell	22109	1	3	4				8					6		5	9		11	10	2	7	
26	21	SWINDON TOWN	0-1		14633	1	3	4				8					6		5	9		11	10	2	7	
27	Feb 4	Torquay United	0-1		8732	1		4				8	7				6		5	9		11	10	2		3
28	18	ALDERSHOT	1-1	English	14451	1	3	4				8	7				6		5	9		11	10	2		
29	25	Ipswich Town	2-2	Dixon, A McCulloch	11174	1	3	4				8	7				6		5	9		11	10	2		
30	Mar 4	EXETER CITY	3-3	English, A McCulloch 2	11537	1	3	4				8	7				6		5	9		11	10	2		
31	11	Leyton Orient	0-1		9914	1	3	4	6			8	7		9				5			11	10	2		
32	18	READING	2-0	English, Mitchell	8938	1	3	4	6			8	7						5	9		11	10	2		
33	25	Watford	0-0		13630	1	3	4				8	7				6		5	9		11	10	2		
34	Apr 1	CRYSTAL PALACE	2-2	Dixon 2	10277	1	3	4	6			8	7						5	9		11	10	2		
35	8	Bournemouth	2-1	Dixon, Mitchell	12540	1	3	4	6			8	7						5	9		11	10	2		
36	10	Norwich City	1-2	Dixon	21015	1	3	4	6			8	7						5	9		11	10	2		
37	11	NORWICH CITY	3-1	Coley, Murphy 2	11167	1	3	4	6	5		8		11						9		7	10	2		
38	15	BRISTOL ROVERS	2-0	Fowler, Mitchell	9622	1	3	4	6	5		8		11						9		7	10	2		
39	22	Southend United	2-1	Garrett, Murphy	13195	1	3	4	6	5		8		11		9						7	10	2		
40	27	Notts County	0-2		31928	1	3	4	6	5		8		11		9						7	10	2		
41	29	NOTTS COUNTY	5-1	Dixon 2, Garrett, Mitchell 2	9971	1	3	4	6	5		8		11		9						7	10	2		
42	May 1	Bristol Rovers	0-0		11679	1	3	4	6	5		8		11		9						7	10	2		
Apps						42	20	39	32	6	4	23	12	11	3	11	11	8	36	34	2	37	41	42	26	22
Goals									1			9	4	1	1	6		4		15		14	13		3	

One own goal

F.A. Cup

Rd	Date	Opponent	Score	Scorers	Att	Ansell W	Barron W	Candlin MH	Coley WE	Collins BV	Dunkley MEF	Dixon A	English J	Fowler T	Freimanis E	Garrett ACE	Hughes TG	King FAR	McCoy W	McCulloch ABR	McCulloch T	Mitchell AJ	Murphy E	Smalley T	Smith D	Southam JH
R1	Nov 26	WALTHAMSTOW AVE.	4-1	Dixon, A McCulloch, Mitchell 2	15000	1		4	6			8							5	9		11	10	2	7	3
R2	Dec 10	TORQUAY UNITED	4-2	Dixon, Mitchell 3	16000	1		4	6			8							5	9		11	10	2	7	3
R3	Jan 7	SOUTHAMPTON	1-1	A McCulloch	23209	1	3	4				8					6		5	9		11	10	2	7	
rep	11	Southampton	3-2	Candlin, Dixon, Hughes	23406	1	3	4				8					6		5	9		11	10	2	7	
R4	28	Bournemouth	1-1	Mitchell	22260	1	3	4				8					6		5	9		11	10	2	7	
rep	Feb 2	BOURNEMOUTH	2-1	English, A McCulloch	22644	1	3	4				8	7				6		5	9		11	10	2		
R5	11	Derby County	2-4	Dixon 2	38063	1	3	4				8	7				6		5	9		11	10	2		

		P	W	D	L	F	A	W	D	L	F	A	Pts
1	Notts County	42	17	3	1	60	12	8	5	8	35	38	58
2	NORTHAMPTON TOWN	42	12	6	3	43	21	8	5	8	29	29	51
3	Southend United	42	15	4	2	43	15	4	9	8	23	33	51
4	Nottingham Forest	42	13	0	8	37	15	7	9	5	30	24	49
5	Torquay United	42	13	6	2	40	23	6	4	11	26	40	48
6	Watford	42	10	6	5	26	13	6	7	8	19	22	45
7	Crystal Palace	42	12	5	4	35	21	3	9	9	20	33	44
8	Brighton & Hove A.	42	9	8	4	32	24	7	4	10	25	45	44
9	Bristol Rovers	42	12	5	4	34	18	7	0	14	17	33	43
10	Reading	42	15	2	4	48	21	2	6	13	22	43	42
11	Norwich City	42	11	5	5	44	21	5	5	11	21	42	42
12	Bournemouth	42	11	6	4	38	19	5	4	12	19	37	42
13	Port Vale	42	12	6	3	33	13	3	5	13	14	29	41
14	Swindon Town	42	9	7	5	41	30	6	4	11	18	32	41
15	Bristol City	42	12	4	5	38	19	3	6	12	22	42	40
16	Exeter City	42	9	8	4	37	27	5	3	13	26	48	39
17	Ipswich Town	42	9	6	6	36	36	3	5	13	21	50	35
18	Leyton Orient	42	10	6	5	33	30	2	5	14	20	55	35
19	Walsall	42	8	8	5	37	25	1	8	12	24	37	34
20	Aldershot	42	10	5	6	30	16	3	3	15	18	44	34
21	Newport County	42	11	5	5	50	34	2	3	16	17	64	34
22	Millwall	42	11	1	9	39	29	3	3	15	16	34	32

1950/51   21st in Division 3(S)

#	Date	Opponent	Res	Scorers	Att	Ansell W	Barron W	Burn RG	Candlin MH	Coley WE	Collins BV	Davie JG	Dixon A	Docherty J	Duckhouse E	English J	Feehan I	Fowler T	Freeman NF	Garrett ACE	Hughes TG	Maxwell K	McCulloch ABR	Mitchell AJ	Mulgrew T	Murphy E	Potts HJ	Smalley T	Smith D	Smith JO	Southam JH	Woollard AJ
1	Aug 19	Ipswich Town	1-1	Smalley	15325	1	3		4			6	8		5								9	11		10		2		7		
2	23	Norwich City	0-0		27300	1	3		4			6	8		5								9	11		10		2		7		
3	26	Port Vale	3-0	Barron, A McCulloch, J Smith	21424	1	3		4			6	8		5								9	11		10		2		7		
4	31	NORWICH CITY	1-2	A McCulloch	17696	1	3		4			6	8		5								9	11		10		2		7		
5	Sep 2	NOTTM. FOREST	2-2	A McCulloch, Mitchell	17887	1	3		4			6	8		5								9	11		10	7	2				
6	7	Leyton Orient	0-1		17867	1	3		4			6	8		5								9	11		10	7	2				
7	9	Torquay United	1-1	Mitchell	9219	1	3		4			6	8		5								9	11		10		2		7		
8	14	LEYTON ORIENT	3-3	Dixon, A McCulloch, Murphy	11344	1	3		4			6	8		5								9	11		10	7	2				
9	16	ALDERSHOT	1-0	Dixon	12072	1	3		4			6	8		5								9	11		10	7	2				
10	21	Newport County	2-2	A McCulloch 2	13845	1	3		4			6	8		5								9	11		10	7	2				
11	23	Swindon Town	0-1		13708	1	3		4			6	8		5								9	11		10	7	2				
12	30	COLCHESTER UNITED	2-1	Candlin, Dixon	10160	1	3		4			6	8		5								9	11		10	7	2				
13	Oct 7	WALSALL	1-1	Dixon	12190	1	3		4			6	8		5								9	11		10	7	2				
14	14	Watford	1-0	Dixon	14409	1	3		4			6	8		5								9	11		10	7	2				
15	21	MILLWALL	1-2	Dixon	16346	1	3		4		5	6	8										9	11		10	7	2				
16	28	Bristol City	0-1		20798		3		4		5	6	8			7	1						9	11		10		2				
17	Nov 4	GILLINGHAM	4-1	Dixon, English 2, Mitchell	10785		3		4			6	8		5	7	1						9	11		10		2				
18	11	Bournemouth	0-1		13004	1	3		4			6	8		5	7							9	11		10		2				
19	18	EXETER CITY	4-1	Dixon, English 2, A McCulloch	11503	1	3		4		6		8		5	7						10	9	11				2				
20	Dec 2	READING	1-1	Mitchell	11106	1	3		4	6			8		5	7						10	9	11				2				
21	16	IPSWICH TOWN	2-1	Dixon 2	7123	1	3		4	6			8		5	7							9	11		10		2				
22	23	PORT VALE	1-1	Mitchell	8785	1	3		4	6			8		5	7							9	11		10		2				
23	25	Crystal Palace	0-0		11001	1	3		4	6			8		5	7							9	11		10		2				
24	26	CRYSTAL PALACE	2-0	A McCulloch 2	12607	1	3		4	6			8		5	7							9	11		10		2				
25	Jan 13	TORQUAY UNITED	1-0	Dixon	10976	1			4	6			8		5	7							9	11		10		2			3	
26	20	Aldershot	0-3		7875	1	3		4			6		8	5	7							9	11		10		2				
27	Feb 3	SWINDON TOWN	1-2	English	7195	1			4			6	8			7				5			9	11		10		2			3	
28	10	Southend United	0-3		9185	1			4			6	8			7				5	9			11		10		2			3	
29	17	Colchester United	1-2	Mitchell	7048				4			6	8			7	1			5	9			11		10		2				3
30	24	Walsall	0-1		11941		3					6	8		5	7	1			4	9			11		10		2				
31	Mar 3	WATFORD	6-0	*See below	9136		3		4			6	8		5	7	1			9				11		10		2				
32	10	Millwall	1-2	English	13187		3		4				8		5	7	1			6	9			11		10		2				
33	17	BRISTOL CITY	2-2	English 2	8042				4				8		5	7	1	10			6		9	11				2				3
34	23	Brighton & Hove Albion	1-5	one og	15511				4				8		5		1	10			6		9	11				2	7			3
35	24	Gillingham	1-3	Fowler	10657				4				8		5		1	10			6		9	11				2	7		3	
36	27	BRIGHTON & HOVE ALB	0-0		8966		3		4				8		5		1	10			6		9	11	7			2				
37	31	BOURNEMOUTH	0-1		6260		3			6			8		5		1	10			4		9	11	7			2				
38	Apr 5	NEWPORT COUNTY	1-4	Fowler	6425		3			6			8		5		1	10			4		9	11	7			2				
39	7	Exeter City	0-1		6141		3		4				8		5		1	10			6		9	11	7			2				
40	9	Plymouth Argyle	1-4	A McCulloch	7846		3		4				8		5		1	10			6		9	11	7			2				
41	14	SOUTHEND UNITED	1-1	A McCulloch	7342		3			6			8		5		1	10			4		9	11	7			2				
42	19	BRISTOL ROVERS	1-1	Hughes	6796		3			6			8		5		1	10			4		9	11	7			2				
43	21	Reading	0-2		13401		3		4				8		5		1	10			6		9	11	7			2				
44	25	Nottingham Forest	2-2	Fowler, Mulgrew	27244					6			8		5		1	10			4		9	11	7			2			3	
45	28	PLYMOUTH ARGYLE	1-3	A McCulloch	6342		3			6			8		5		1	10			4		9	11	7			2				
46	May 5	Bristol Rovers	1-1	A McCulloch	10739			8	4	2		6			5		1		3		10		9	11	7							
Apps						26	37	1	30	9	3	39	43	1	41	18	19	13	1	11	22	2	41	44	5	30	10	36	2	5	14	3
Goals							1		1			1	12			9		3		1	1		13	7	1	2		1		1		

Scorers in game 31: Davie, Dixon, English, Garrett, Mitchell, Murphy

One own goal

F.A. Cup

	Date	Opponent	Res	Scorers	Att	Ansell W	Barron W	Candlin MH	Coley WE	Davie JG	Dixon A	Duckhouse E	English J	Feehan I	Maxwell K	McCulloch ABR	Mitchell AJ	Murphy E	Smalley T	Southam JH
R3	Jan 6	BARNSLEY	3-1	Mitchell 2(1p), Murphy	16818	1	3	4	6		8	5	7			9	11	10	2	
R4	27	Arsenal	2-3	English 2	72408	1		4	6		8	5	7		10	9	11		2	3

		P	W	D	L	F	A	W	D	L	F	A	Pts
1	Nottingham Forest	46	16	6	1	57	17	14	4	5	53	23	70
2	Norwich City	46	16	6	1	42	14	9	8	6	40	31	64
3	Reading	46	15	6	2	57	17	6	9	8	31	36	57
4	Plymouth Argyle	46	16	5	2	54	19	8	4	11	31	36	57
5	Millwall	46	15	6	2	52	23	8	4	11	28	34	56
6	Bristol Rovers	46	15	7	1	46	18	5	8	10	18	24	55
7	Southend United	46	15	4	4	64	27	6	6	11	28	42	52
8	Ipswich Town	46	15	4	4	48	24	8	2	13	21	34	52
9	Bournemouth	46	17	5	1	49	16	5	2	16	16	41	51
10	Bristol City	46	15	4	4	41	25	5	7	11	23	34	51
11	Newport County	46	13	4	6	48	25	6	5	12	29	45	47
12	Port Vale	46	13	6	4	35	24	3	7	13	25	41	45
13	Brighton & Hove A.	46	11	8	4	51	31	2	9	12	20	48	43
14	Exeter City	46	11	4	8	33	30	7	2	14	29	55	42
15	Walsall	46	12	4	7	32	20	3	6	14	20	42	40
16	Colchester United	46	12	5	6	43	25	2	7	14	20	51	40
17	Swindon Town	46	15	4	4	38	17	3	0	20	17	50	40
18	Aldershot	46	11	8	4	37	20	4	2	17	19	68	40
19	Leyton Orient	46	13	2	8	36	28	2	6	15	17	47	38
20	Torquay United	46	13	2	8	47	39	1	7	15	17	42	37
21	NORTHAMPTON TOWN	46	8	8	6	39	30	2	7	14	16	37	36
22	Gillingham	46	10	7	6	41	30	3	2	18	28	71	35
23	Watford	46	8	5	10	29	28	1	6	16	25	60	29
24	Crystal Palace	46	6	5	12	18	39	2	6	15	15	45	27

1950/51 SEASON
Back: Newman(Asst.Train), Woollard, Duckhouse, Garrett, Collins, Candlin, Ansell, Freeman, Hughes, Soloman, Croy, Docherty, McCulloch, Jennings(Train)
Middle: Coley, Smalley, Southam, Adams, Jeffrey, J.Smith, Davie, Briscoe, Maxwell, Fowler
Front: Mitchell, Dixon, Murphy, D.Smith, English, Hargrave, T.Smith, Burn

1951/52 SEASON
Back: Duckhouse, Ansell, Collins, Hughes, Davies, Ramscar
Middle: Raines, Briscoe, Bowen, Mitchell, Maxwell, Candlin, Croy, McCullouch, Woollard
Front: Dixon, Fowler, Feehan, Smith, Connell, O'Donnell

1951/52   8th in Division 3(S)

#	Date		Opponent	Score	Scorers	Att	Ansell W	Candlin MH	Collins BV	Connell PM	Croy J	Davie JG	Dixon A	Dodgin N	Duckhouse E	English J	Feehan I	Fowler T	French IR	Hughes TG	McCulloch ABR	O'Donnell W	Payne IEH	Pinchbeck CB	Ramscar FT	Smith JO	Southam IH	Starocsik F	Wilson JA	Wood AR	Adams DF
1	Aug	18	Aldershot	1-0	Ramscar	10047		4		2		6	8		5	7	1					9			10			11	3		
2		20	Newport County	0-2		10870		4		2		6	8		5	7	1					9			10			11	3		
3	Sep	1	BRISTOL CITY	1-2	Ramscar	14152	1	4		2		6			5	7						9	8		10			11	3		
4		6	NEWPORT COUNTY	5-0	English 2, Payne 3	10374	1	4		2		6			5	7						9	8		10			11	3		
5		8	IPSWICH TOWN	1-0	Starocsik	13917	1	4		2		6			5	7						9	8		10			11	3		
6		11	Southend United	0-2		6690	1	4		2		6			5	7		11				9	8		10				3		
7		15	Torquay United	2-1	O'Donnell 2	7627	1	4	2						5	7		11		6		9	8		10				3		
8		20	SOUTHEND UNITED	4-3	English 2, Hughes, Ramscar	10466	1	4	2						5	7		11		6		9	8		10				3		
9		22	GILLINGHAM	2-1	Fowler	12853	1	4	2						5	7		11		6		9	8		10				3		
10		27	PORT VALE	3-1	English, Fowler 2	8082	1	4	2						5	7		11		6		9	8		10				3		
11		29	Brighton & Hove Albion	0-2		15861	1	4	2						5	7		11		6		9	8		10				3		
12	Oct	6	Bristol Rovers	2-2	Fowler, A McCulloch	20905	1	4	2						5	7		11		6	9		8		10				3		
13		13	PLYMOUTH ARGYLE	3-1	English 2, Ramscar	14661	1	4	2						5	8		11		6	9				10			7	3		
14		20	Norwich City	1-2	Ramscar	28078	1	4	2						5	8		11		6	9				10			7	3		
15		27	EXETER CITY	3-1	English, Fowler, Ramscar	12943		4	2						5	7	1	11		6	9		8		10				3		
16	Nov	3	Colchester United	5-2	English 2, A McCulloch, Ramscar 2	10326		4	2						5	7	1	11		6	9		8		10				3		
17		10	CRYSTAL PALACE	5-2	English, A McCulloch 2, Ramscar 2	14845		4	2						5	7	1	11		6	9		8		10				3		
18		17	Swindon Town	1-1	Ramscar	11226		4	2						5	7	1	11		6	9		8		10				3		
19	Dec	1	Walsall	0-3		7676		4	2						5		1	11		6	9		8		10			7	3		
20		8	SHREWSBURY TOWN	6-0	*See below	13715		4	2						5	7		11		6	9		8		10				3	1	
21		22	Port Vale	0-0		8973		4	2						5	7		11		6	9		8		10				3	1	
22		25	Watford	4-2	English, A McCulloch 2, one og	7847		4	2						5	7		11		6	9		8		10				3	1	
23		26	WATFORD	1-4	Payne	18295		4	2						5	7		11		6	9		8		10				3	1	
24		29	Bristol City	0-2		7893		4	2	3				6	5	7		11			9		8		10					1	
25	Jan	5	Ipswich Town	2-3	Fowler, Pinchbeck	10071		4	3	2				6	5	7		11					8	9	10					1	
26		12	MILLWALL	1-1	English	13329		4	3	2				6	5	7		11					8	9	10					1	
27		19	TORQUAY UNITED	2-4	English, Fowler	10535			3	2		4			5	7		11		6	9				10		8			1	
28		24	ALDERSHOT	6-2	English, Fowler, Pinchbeck 2, Ramscar 2	4490			3	2	5	4				7		11		6				9	10		8			1	
29		26	Gillingham	1-2	O'Donnell	9625			3	2	5	4				7		11		6		9			10		8			1	
30	Feb	2	Reading	0-2		15932		5	3	2		4				7		11		6		9			10		8			1	
31		9	BRIGHTON & HOVE ALB	3-0	O'Donnell, Ramscar, Starocsik	13639		5	2			4				7				6		9	8		10			11	3	1	
32		16	BRISTOL ROVERS	2-0	English, Hughes	11704		5	2			4				7				6		9	8		10			11	3	1	
33		23	READING	0-3		15696		5	2			4				7				6		9	8		10			11	3	1	
34	Mar	1	Plymouth Argyle	0-2		22133		5	2			4		6		7	1						8		10			11	3		9
35		8	NORWICH CITY	1-2	Payne	14625		5	2			4				7	1			6			8		10			11	3		9
36		15	Exeter City	3-0	Starocsik, Adams 2	7908		5	2			4				7	1			6			8		10			11	3		9
37		22	COLCHESTER UNITED	2-0	Ramscar, Starocsik	10160		5	2			4				7	1			6			8		10			11	3		9
38	Apr	5	SWINDON TOWN	1-0	Starocsik	7419		5	2			4				7	1			6			8		10			11	3		9
39		12	Leyton Orient	1-2	Adams	8776		5	2			4				7	1			6			8		10			11	3		9
40		14	Bournemouth	0-3		9933		5	2			4				7	1			6			8		10			11	3		9
41		15	BOURNEMOUTH	5-3	English, O'Donnell, Ramscar 3	9524		5	2			4				8	1	11		6		9			10			7	3		
42		19	WALSALL	4-1	English, Fowler, O'Donnell 2	8311			2		5	4				8	1	11		6		9			10			7	3		
43		24	LEYTON ORIENT	4-0	English, O'Donnell, Ramscar 2	6907		5	2			4				8	1	11		6		9			10			7	3		
44		26	Shrewsbury Town	1-3	O'Donnell	9514		5	2			4				8	1	11		6		9			10			7	3		
45		30	Millwall	1-2	Ramscar	10389		5	2					6			1	11	4			9	8		10			7	3		
46	May	3	Crystal Palace	3-3	O'Donnell, Ramscar, Starocsik	7214		5	2			4				8	1	11		6		9			10			7	3		
			Apps				12	42	40	13	3	25	2	5	27	43	20	32	1	36	14	22	32	3	46	4	16	24	23	14	7
			Goals													21		10		2	8	10	6	3	23			6			3

Scorers in game 20: English, Fowler, A McCulloch, Payne, Ramscar

One own goal

F.A. Cup

| R1 | Nov | 24 | Norwich City | 2-3 | Payne, Ramscar | 27120 | | 4 | 2 | | | | | | 5 | | 1 | 11 | | 6 | 9 | | 8 | | 10 | 7 | | | 3 | | |

	P	W	D	L	F	A	W	D	L	F	A	Pts
1 Plymouth Argyle	46	19	3	1	70	19	10	5	8	37	34	66
2 Reading	46	19	2	2	73	23	10	1	12	39	37	61
3 Norwich City	46	18	1	4	55	15	8	8	7	34	35	61
4 Millwall	46	16	5	2	46	21	7	7	9	28	32	58
5 Brighton & Hove A.	46	15	4	4	57	24	9	6	8	30	39	58
6 Newport County	46	13	7	3	45	28	8	5	10	32	50	54
7 Bristol Rovers	46	14	5	4	60	20	6	7	10	29	33	52
8 NORTHAMPTON T.	46	17	1	5	65	31	5	4	14	28	43	49
9 Southend United	46	16	6	1	56	17	3	4	16	19	49	48
10 Colchester United	46	12	7	4	32	22	5	5	13	24	55	46
11 Torquay United	46	10	3	10	53	42	7	7	9	33	56	44
12 Aldershot	46	11	4	8	40	27	7	4	12	38	62	44
13 Port Vale	46	11	11	1	33	16	3	4	16	17	50	43
14 Bournemouth	46	11	4	8	42	30	5	6	12	27	45	42
15 Bristol City	46	13	6	4	44	26	2	6	15	14	43	42
16 Swindon Town	46	9	9	5	29	22	5	5	13	22	46	42
17 Ipswich Town	46	12	4	7	45	31	4	5	14	18	43	41
18 Leyton Orient	46	12	5	6	39	26	4	4	15	16	42	41
19 Crystal Palace	46	9	7	7	32	28	6	2	15	29	52	39
20 Shrewsbury Town	46	11	3	9	35	29	2	7	14	27	57	36
21 Watford	46	7	7	9	34	37	6	3	14	23	44	36
22 Gillingham	46	10	7	6	47	31	1	6	16	24	50	35
23 Exeter City	46	10	4	9	40	36	3	5	15	25	50	35
24 Walsall	46	11	3	9	38	31	2	2	19	17	63	31

1952/53   3rd in Division 3(S)

#	Date	Opponent	Score	Scorers	Att	Adams DF	Baxter LR	Candlin MH	Collins BV	Croy J	Davie JG	Dodgin N	Edelston M	English J	Fowler T	Hughes TG	McLain T	O'Donnell W	Patterson RL	Ramscar FT	Southam JH	Starocsik F	Upton F	Wood AR	Mulgrew T
1	Aug 23	Bournemouth	1-0	English	14771			4			6			7	11		5	9	3	8	2			1	10
2	27	Exeter City	0-2		12729			5			4			7	11		6	9	3	10	2			1	8
3	30	SOUTHEND UNITED	4-3	Fowler 2, Ramscar 2	13611			5			4			7	11		6	9	3	10	2			1	8
4	Sep 4	EXETER CITY	3-1	Edelston, O'Donnell, Ramscar	11988			5			4		8	7	11		6	9	3	10	2			1	
5	6	Watford	1-2	English	21959			5			4		8	7	11		6	9	3	10	2			1	
6	11	COVENTRY CITY	3-1	Edelston, English, O'Donnell	13280			5			4		8	7	11		6	9	3	10	2			1	
7	13	BRIGHTON & HOVE ALB	5-3	Edelston 2, O'Donnell 3	14342			5			4		8	7	11		6	9	3	10	2			1	
8	15	Coventry City	1-1	Ramscar	18217			5			4		8	7	11		6	9	3	10	2			1	
9	20	Newport County	1-4	O'Donnell	10479				5		4		8	7	11		6	9	3	10	2			1	
10	25	SWINDON TOWN	3-1	Edelston 2, Fowler	8746				5		4		8	7	11		6	9	3	10	2			1	
11	27	CRYSTAL PALACE	5-1	English 2, Fowler, Edelston, Southam	12805				5		4		8	7	11		6	9	3	10	2			1	
12	Oct 1	Torquay United	0-3		4784				5				8	7	11	4	6	9	3	10	2			1	
13	4	Bristol City	3-2	English, O'Donnell, one og	21795				5				8	7	11	4	6	9	3	10	2			1	
14	11	BRISTOL ROVERS	2-2	English, McLain	19064				5				8	7	11	4	6	9	3	10	2			1	
15	18	Millwall	2-1	English, Ramscar	22948				5				8	7	11	4	6	9	3	10	2			1	
16	25	GILLINGHAM	3-1	Edelston, English, Ramscar	13689				5				8	7	11	4	6	9	3	10	2			1	
17	Nov 1	Walsall	5-1	Edelston, English, O'Donnell 2	8420			5					8	7	11	4	6	9	3	10	2			1	
18	8	SHREWSBURY TOWN	3-1	Edelston 2, English	13988			5					8	7	11	4	6	9	3	10	2			1	
19	15	Queen's Park Rangers	2-2	Edelston, O'Donnell	14661			5					8	7	11	4	6	9	3	10	2			1	
20	29	Aldershot	1-2	Fowler	3263		8	5						7	11	4	6	9	3	10	2			1	
21	Dec 13	Norwich City	2-1	English 2	21093			5						7	11	4	6	9	3	10	2			1	
22	20	BOURNEMOUTH	5-1	O'Donnell 2, Ramscar 3	8649			5				6	8		11	4		9	3	10	2	7		1	
23	26	READING	6-1	Edelston, English 2, O'Donnell 2, Ramscar	19242			5				6	8	7	11	4		9	3	10	2			1	
24	Jan 3	Southend United	1-3	O'Donnell	7425	10		5					8	7	11	4	6	9	3		2			1	
25	10	Leyton Orient	1-0	English	7826			5					8	7	11	4	6	9	3	10	2			1	
26	17	WATFORD	4-1	Edelston, English, O'Donnell 2	13250			5					8	7	11	4	6	9	3	10	2			1	
27	24	Brighton & Hove Albion	1-1	Starocsik	18750			5				6	8	7	11	4		9	3	10	2			1	
28	31	LEYTON ORIENT	3-1	Fowler, Ramscar 2	9868			5				6		7	11	4	8	9	3	10	2			1	
29	Feb 7	NEWPORT COUNTY	5-0	Edelston, English 2, Ramscar 2	11977			5				6	8	7	11	4		9	3	10	2			1	
30	14	Crystal Palace	3-4	Adams, O'Donnell 2	6409	8		5				6		7	11	4		9	3	10	2			1	
31	21	BRISTOL CITY	0-2		15291		8	5				6		7	11	4		9	3	10	2			1	
32	29	Bristol Rovers	1-1	Ramscar	31115		8	5				6		7	11	4		9	3	10	2			1	
33	Mar 7	MILLWALL	1-1	O'Donnell	13687				5			6	8	7	11	4		9	3	10	2			1	
34	14	Gillingham	1-1	Ramscar	10250				5			6	8	7	11	4		9	3	10	2			1	
35	21	WALSALL	2-1	O'Donnell, Ramscar	9717				5			6	8	7	11	4		9	3	10	2			1	
36	28	Shrewsbury Town	4-2	English, O'Donnell 2, Ramscar	7329		8		5			6		7	11	4		9	3	10	2			1	
37	Apr 4	QUEEN'S PARK RANGERS	4-2	Baxter, Dodgin, English, Fowler	12546		8		5			6		7	11	4		9	3	10	2			1	
38	6	Ipswich Town	1-1	Ramscar	12048				5			6	8	7	11	4		9	3	10	2			1	
39	7	IPSWICH TOWN	2-0	Fowler, McLain	12307		4		5				8	7	11		6	9	3	10	2			1	
40	11	Swindon Town	0-3		9564		4		5				8	7	11		6	9	3	10	2			1	
41	13	Reading	0-2		9020		4		5				8	7	11		6	9	3	10	2			1	
42	16	COLCHESTER UNITED	2-0	O'Donnell 2	7982		8	5						7	11	4	6	9	3	10	2			1	
43	18	ALDERSHOT	4-0	Hughes, O'Donnell, Ramscar 2	10040		8		5					7	11	4		9	3	10	2		6	1	
44	23	TORQUAY UNITED	3-3	English, Fowler, O'Donnell	11510		8			5				7	11	4		9	3	10	2		6	1	
45	25	Colchester United	2-1	English, Fowler	8122		8		5					7	11	4		9	3	10	2		6	1	
46	30	NORWICH CITY	3-3	Baxter, English, Fowler	9555		8			5				7	11	4		9	3	10	2		6	1	
				Apps		2	11	28	19	2	11	14	30	45	46	29	32	46	46	45	46	1	4	46	3
				Goals		1	2					1	15	24	11	1	2	27		22	1	1	1		

One own goal

F.A. Cup

	Date	Opponent	Score	Scorers	Att	Candlin MH	Edelston M	English J	Fowler T	Hughes TG	McLain T	O'Donnell W	Patterson RL	Ramscar FT	Southam JH	Wood AR
R1	Nov 22	Hendon	0-0		9000	5	8	7	11	4	6	9	3	10	2	1
rep	27	HENDON	2-0	Fowler, Ramscar	6100	5	8	7	11	4	6	9	3	10	2	1
R2	Dec 6	Swindon Town	0-2		12936	5	8	7	11	4	6	9	3	10	2	1

		P	W	D	L	F	A	W	D	L	F	A	Pts
1	Bristol Rovers	46	17	4	2	55	19	9	8	6	37	27	64
2	Millwall	46	14	7	2	46	16	10	7	6	36	28	62
3	NORTHAMPTON TOWN	46	18	4	1	75	30	8	6	9	34	40	62
4	Norwich City	46	16	6	1	56	17	9	4	10	43	38	60
5	Bristol City	46	13	8	2	62	28	9	7	7	33	33	59
6	Coventry City	46	15	5	3	52	22	4	7	12	25	40	50
7	Brighton & Hove A.	46	12	6	5	48	30	7	6	10	33	45	50
8	Southend United	46	15	5	3	41	21	3	8	12	28	53	49
9	Bournemouth	46	15	3	5	49	23	4	6	13	25	46	47
10	Watford	46	12	8	3	39	21	3	9	11	23	42	47
11	Reading	46	17	3	3	53	18	2	5	16	16	46	46
12	Torquay United	46	15	4	4	61	28	3	5	15	26	60	45
13	Crystal Palace	46	12	7	4	40	26	3	6	14	26	56	43
14	Leyton Orient	46	12	7	4	52	28	4	3	16	16	45	42
15	Newport County	46	12	4	7	43	34	4	6	13	27	48	42
16	Ipswich Town	46	10	7	6	34	28	3	8	12	26	41	41
17	Exeter City	46	11	8	4	40	24	2	6	15	21	47	40
18	Swindon Town	46	9	5	9	38	33	5	7	11	26	46	40
19	Aldershot	46	8	8	7	36	29	4	7	12	25	48	39
20	Queen's Park Rgs.	46	9	9	5	37	34	3	6	14	24	48	39
21	Gillingham	46	10	7	6	30	26	2	8	13	25	48	39
22	Colchester United	46	9	9	5	40	29	3	5	15	19	47	38
23	Shrewsbury Town	46	11	5	7	38	35	1	7	15	30	56	36
24	Walsall	46	5	9	9	35	46	2	1	20	21	72	24

1953/54   5th in Division 3(S)

No	Date	Match	Score	Scorers	Att	Anderson JL	Baxter LR	Collins BV	Cross J	English I	Edelston M	Fowler T	Hughes TG	Jones B	Marston M	McLain T	O'Donnell W	Patterson RL	Ramscar FT	Southam JH	Smith IO	Starocsik F	Upton F	Walsh W	Wood AR	Yeoman RI
1	Aug 20	Crystal Palace	2-2	English 2	13935					7	8	11	4		2	6	9	3	10					5	1	
2	22	Southend United	0-2		10295					7	8	11	4		2	6	9	3	10					5	1	
3	26	Bournemouth	1-2	English	14409		8			7		11	4		2	6	9	3	10					5	1	
4	29	Brighton & Hove Albion	2-3	O'Donnell, Ramscar	16709		8			7		11	6		2		9	3	10	4				5	1	
5	Sep 3	BOURNEMOUTH	2-1	English 2	12618		8			7		11	6		2		9	3	10	4				5	1	
6	5	WATFORD	4-1	English 3, O'Donnell	13831					7	8	11	6		2		9	3	10	4				5	1	
7	7	Millwall	0-1		11909					7	8	11	6		2		9	3	10	4				5	1	
8	12	Torquay United	1-1	English	8148					7	8	11	6		2		9	3	10	4				5	1	
9	17	MILLWALL	4-2	English 3, Edelston	10131					7	8	11	6		2		9	3	10	4				5	1	
10	19	NEWPORT COUNTY	1-0	English	13138					7	8	11	6		2		9	3	10	4				5	1	
11	21	READING	1-1	Fowler	8778					7	8	11	6		2		9	3	10	4				5	1	
12	26	GILLINGHAM	1-1	English	12096					7	8	11	6		2		9	3	10	4				5	1	
13	30	Reading	0-2		8755		8			7		11	6		2		9	3	10		4			5	1	
14	Oct 3	Coventry City	0-0		17540		8			7		11	6		2		9	3	10	4				5	1	
15	10	Queen's Park Rangers	1-1	Fowler	13300		8			7		11	6		2		9	3	10	4				5	1	
16	17	SOUTHAMPTON	3-0	Fowler, O'Donnell, one og	14403	8				7		11	6		2		9	3	10	4				5	1	
17	24	Colchester United	1-1	Cross	7599	8			9	7		11	6		2			3	10	4				5	1	
18	31	CRYSTAL PALACE	6-0	Anderson, Cross, English 3, Ramscar	12450	8		5	9	7		11	6		2			3	10	4					1	
19	Nov 7	Bristol City	1-2	Smith	17380	8		5	9	7		11	6		2			3	10		4				1	
20	14	ALDERSHOT	6-2	*See below	11695	8		5		7		11	6		2		9	3	10	4					1	
21	28	WALSALL	5-1	Cross 3, Ramscar 2	12561	8		5	9	7		11	6		2			3	10	4					1	
22	Dec 5	Shrewsbury Town	4-2	Cross, Edelston, Ramscar, one og	7825	8		5	9	7	8	11	6		3				10	2	4				1	
23	19	SOUTHEND UNITED	5-0	English 4, McLain	9181	8		5		7		11	4			6	9	3	10	2					1	
24	25	LEYTON ORIENT	2-2	English, Hughes	13809			5	9	7		11	4			6	8	3	10	2					1	
25	26	Leyton Orient	0-2		14768			5	9	7		11	4			6		3	10	2	8				1	
26	Jan 2	BRIGHTON & HOVE ALB	4-2	Cross, Starocsik, two og	10989			5	9			11	4			6		3	10	2	8	7			1	
27	16	Watford	1-1	Cross	13134	8		5	9	7		11	4		2	6			10	3					1	
28	23	TORQUAY UNITED	3-1	Anderson, English, Marston	11162	8		5	9	7		11	4		2	6			10	3					1	
29	Feb 6	Newport County	0-2		10221	8		5		7		11	4		2	6	9		10	3					1	
30	13	Gillingham	1-2	English	9558	8		5		7		11	4		2	6	9		10	3					1	
31	20	COVENTRY CITY	0-1		10539	8		5		7		11	4		2	6	9		10	3					1	
32	27	QUEEN'S PARK RANGERS	2-1	English 2	8259			5		7		11	4		2	6	8		10	3				9	1	
33	Mar 6	Southampton	0-1		14196			5		7		11	4		2	6	8		10	3				9	1	
34	13	SWINDON TOWN	2-0	McLain, Ramscar	6821			5		7		11	4		2	9	8		10		3		6		1	
35	20	Walsall	1-0	Ramscar	10032			5		7		11	4		2	9	8		10		3		6		1	
36	25	IPSWICH TOWN	1-0	McLain	5968			5		7		11	4		2	9	8		10		3		6		1	
37	27	BRISTOL CITY	3-0	English, McLain, O'Donnell	8283			5		7		11	4		2	9	8		10		3		6		1	
38	Apr 3	Aldershot	1-3	Englsih	5728			5		7		11	4		2	9	8		10		3		6		1	
39	8	EXETER CITY	2-2	English, Ramscar	5597			5		7		11	4		2	9	8		10		3		6		1	
40	10	SHREWSBURY TOWN	1-0	O'Donnell	8088			5		7		11			2	9	8		10		3	4	6		1	
41	17	Exeter City	0-1		8844			5		7		11	4		2	9			10		3	8	6		1	
42	19	Norwich City	1-4	O'Donnell	22961			5		7		11	4		2	9	8		10		3		6		1	
43	20	NORWICH CITY	2-0	Ramscar, Upton	8906			5		7		11	4		2	9	10		8		3		6		1	
44	24	COLCHESTER UNITED	3-0	Anderson, English, Fowler	7344	10		5		7		11	4		2		9		8		3		6		1	
45	28	Swindon Town	0-0		5195	10		5		7		11	4		2		9		8		3		6		1	
46	May 1	Ipswich Town	1-2	one og	22133			5		7		11		10	2		9		8		3		6		1	4
		Apps				14	6	29	10	45	10	46	44	1	42	24	37	24	44	26	23	2	13	19	46	1
		Goals				5			8	31	2	5	1		1	4	7		10		1	1	1			

Scorers in game 20: Anderson 2, English, Fowler, O'Donnell, Ramscar.

Five own goals

F.A. Cup

	Date	Match	Score	Scorers	Att	Anderson JL	Baxter LR	Collins BV	Cross J	English I	Edelston M	Fowler T	Hughes TG	Jones B	Marston M	McLain T	O'Donnell W	Patterson RL	Ramscar FT	Southam JH	Smith IO	Starocsik F	Upton F	Walsh W	Wood AR	Yeoman RI
R1	Nov 21	LLANELLY	3-0	Cross, Fowler, Ramscar	16302	8		5	9	7		11	6		2			3	10	4					1	
R2	Dec 12	HARTLEPOOLS UNITED	1-1	Ramscar	18772			5	9	7	8	11	6		2				10	3	4				1	
rep	16	Hartlepools United	0-1		12169			5		7	8	11	4			6	9	3	10	2					1	

		P	W	D	L	F	A	W	D	L	F	A	Pts
1	Ipswich Town	46	15	5	3	47	19	12	5	6	35	32	64
2	Brighton & Hove A.	46	17	3	3	57	31	9	6	8	29	30	61
3	Bristol City	46	18	3	2	59	18	7	3	13	29	48	56
4	Watford	46	16	3	4	52	23	5	7	11	33	46	52
5	NORTHAMPTON TOWN	46	18	4	1	63	18	2	7	14	19	37	51
6	Southampton	46	17	5	1	51	22	5	2	16	25	41	51
7	Norwich City	46	13	5	5	43	28	7	6	10	30	38	51
8	Reading	46	14	3	6	57	33	6	6	11	29	40	49
9	Exeter City	46	12	2	9	39	22	8	6	9	29	36	48
10	Gillingham	46	14	3	6	37	22	5	7	11	24	44	48
11	Leyton Orient	46	14	5	4	48	26	4	6	13	31	47	47
12	Millwall	46	15	3	5	44	24	4	6	13	30	53	47
13	Torquay United	46	10	10	3	48	33	7	2	14	33	55	46
14	Coventry City	46	14	5	4	36	15	4	4	15	25	41	45
15	Newport County	46	14	4	5	42	28	5	2	16	19	53	44
16	Southend United	46	15	2	6	46	22	3	5	15	23	49	43
17	Aldershot	46	11	5	7	45	31	6	4	13	29	55	43
18	Queen's Park Rgs.	46	10	5	8	32	25	6	5	12	28	43	42
19	Bournemouth	46	12	5	6	47	27	4	3	16	20	43	40
19	Swindon Town	46	13	5	5	48	21	2	5	16	19	49	40
21	Shrewsbury Town	46	12	8	3	48	34	2	4	17	17	42	40
22	Crystal Palace	46	11	7	5	41	30	3	5	15	19	56	40
23	Colchester United	46	7	7	9	35	29	3	3	17	15	49	30
24	Walsall	46	8	5	10	22	27	1	3	19	18	60	26

1954/55   13th in Division 3(S)

Results

#	Date	Opponent	Score	Scorers	Att
1	Aug 21	Newport County	1-0	English	12709
2	26	CRYSTAL PALACE	1-1	English	11735
3	28	EXETER CITY	2-0	Fowler, Oakley	9764
4	Sep 1	Crystal Palace	1-3	English	11626
5	4	Colchester United	1-4	Haseldine	7468
6	9	MILLWALL	0-1		8108
7	11	NORWICH CITY	1-1	Oakley	9560
8	13	Millwall	0-1		9558
9	18	Southend United	1-4	McLain	10519
10	21	Watford	1-1	McLain	10692
11	25	ALDERSHOT	2-1	Haseldine, Jones	8235
12	30	WATFORD	0-1		4128
13	Oct 2	Swindon Town	1-0	Jones	8899
14	9	GILLINGHAM	4-1	Fowler, Haseldine 2, McLain	7827
15	16	Reading	1-0	Starocsik	9864
16	23	SHREWSBURY TOWN	3-1	Jones, Starocsik 2	8468
17	30	Southampton	0-4		16039
18	Nov 6	BRISTOL CITY	2-0	Starocsik 2	11608
19	13	Torquay United	2-5	McLain, J Smith	7264
20	27	Brentford	3-1	English 2, McLain	10029
21	Dec 4	COVENTRY CITY	1-0	Starocsik	11008
22	11	SWINDON TOWN	1-0	Starocsik	6609
23	18	NEWPORT COUNTY	2-2	English, Starocsik	6947
24	25	Queen's Park Rangers	0-1		8718
25	27	QUEEN'S PARK RANGERS	1-3	Brown (og)	12623
26	Jan 1	Exeter City	1-3	Douglas (og)	7040
27	8	LEYTON ORIENT	2-2	Adams, Yeoman	8864
28	22	Norwich City	2-3	English 2	11159
29	29	Leyton Orient	1-2	Jones	17969
30	Feb 5	SOUTHEND UNITED	6-2	Jones 2, E Smith 2, Oakley 2	7709
31	12	Aldershot	4-3	Jones 3, E Smith	5237
32	26	Gillingham	2-2	Jones 2	8523
33	Mar 5	READING	2-6	Oakley 2	7191
34	12	Shrewsbury Town	0-4		7778
35	19	SOUTHAMPTON	2-1	Fowler, Ellerington (og)	6855
36	26	Bristol City	1-5	Patterson	20955
37	Apr 2	TORQUAY UNITED	1-0	Adams	5361
38	4	Walsall	1-6	English	5159
39	9	Brighton & Hove Albion	1-2	Starocsik	13120
40	11	Bournemouth	1-0	Newman	8759
41	12	BOURNEMOUTH	5-0	Jones 4, Starocsik	6618
42	16	BRENTFORD	1-2	Dawson	6980
43	18	COLCHESTER UNITED	6-1	Dawson 3, E Smith, Starocsik, Harris (og)	3198
44	23	Coventry City	0-0		11631
45	27	BRIGHTON & HOVE ALB	1-0	Wilson (og)	4349
46	30	WALSALL	1-1	Dawson	6842

Player appearances / shirt numbers

(Columns: Adams DF, Collins BV, Croy J, Danks PD, Dawson W, English J, Fowler T, Hazledine D, Huffer P, Hughes TG, Jones B, McLain T, Marston M, Mills RWG, Newman R, Ramscar FT, Smith EWA, Smith JO, Southam JH, Starocsik F, Webber GM, Wood AR, Yeoman RI, Patterson RL, Oakley K)

#	Ad	Co	Cr	Da	Dw	En	Fo	Ha	Hu	Hg	Jo	Mc	Ma	Mi	Ne	Ra	SE	SJ	So	St	We	Wo	Ye	Pa	Ok
1		5				7	11	8		4		6	2			10			3			1			9
2		5				7	11	8		4		6	2			10			3			1			9
3		5				7	11	8		4		6	2			10			3			1			9
4		5				7	11	8		4		6	2			10			3			1			9
5		5				9	11	8		6	10		2	7					3			1	4		
6		5				9	11	8		6	10		2	7								1	4	3	
7		5				7	11	8		6	10		2									1	4	3	9
8		5				7	11	8		6	10		2									1	4	3	9
9		5				7	11	8		6	10	9	2									1	4		
10		5				7	11	8		6	10	9	2						3			1	4		
11		5				7	11	8		6	10	9	2						3			1	4		
12			5				11	8		6	10	9							2	7		1	4	3	
13			5				11	8		6	10	9							2	7		1	4	3	
14			5				11	8		6	10	9							2	7		1	4	3	
15			5				11	8		6	10	9							2	7		1	4	3	
16			5				11	8		6	10	9						4	2	7		1		3	
17			5				11	8		6	10	9						4	2	7		1		3	
18			5				11	8		6	10	9						4	2	7		1		3	
19			5				11	8		6	10	9						4	2	7		1		3	
20			5			8	11			6	10	9							2	7	1		4	3	
21		2	5			8	11			6	10	9								7	1		4	3	
22		2	5			8	11			6	10	9								7	1		4	3	
23		2	5			8	11	10		6										7	1		4	3	9
24		2	5			8	11			6		10								7	1		4	3	9
25		2	5			8	11			6		10								7	1		4	3	
26	9	2	5			7	11	8		6											1		4	3	
27	9	2	5			7	11			4	10	6									1		8	3	
28	9	5				7	11			4	10	6	2								1		8	3	
29	9	5				7	11				10	6	2				8	4			1			3	
30			5				11			4	10	6	2	7			8				1				9
31			5				11			4	10	6	2	7			8				1				9
32			5				11			4	10	6	2	7					2		1			3	9
33			5				11			4	10	6	2	7					2		1		8	3	
34	9	2	5				11			4	10	6		7							1		8	3	
35	9	5					11			4	10	6	2	7			8				1			3	
36	9	5					11			4	10	6	2	7			8				1			3	
37	9					7	11	10				5					8	4			1			3	
38	9					7	11		5				6	2			10	4			1		8	3	
39	9		5				11				10	6					8	4	2	7	1			3	
40	9		5	10		7	11					3		8			6	2			1		4		
41			5	10	9		11				10	6	2				8	4		7	1			3	
42					9		11			5	10	6	2				8	4	3	7	1				
43					9		11			5		6	2		8		10	4		7				3	
44					9		11			5	10	6	2				8	4		7				3	
45					9	8	11			5		6	2				10	4		7				3	
46					9	8	11			5		6	2				10	4		7				3	
Apps	11	27	20	1	6	26	46	22	1	41	34	38	26	9	2	4	15	15	21	22	13	33	23	37	13
Goals	2				5	9	3	4			15	5			1		4	1		11			1	1	6

Five own goals

F.A. Cup

	Date	Opponent	Score		Att	Co	En	Ha	Hg	Jo	Mc	SJ	So	St	Pa
R1	Nov 20	COVENTRY CITY	0-1		14667	5		11	8	6	10	9	4	2	7	3

League table

		P	W	D	L	F	A	W	D	L	F	A	Pts
1	Bristol City	46	17	4	2	62	22	13	6	4	39	25	70
2	Leyton Orient	46	16	2	5	48	20	10	7	6	41	27	61
3	Southampton	46	16	6	1	49	19	8	5	10	26	32	59
4	Gillingham	46	12	8	3	41	28	8	7	8	36	38	55
5	Millwall	46	14	6	3	44	25	6	5	12	28	43	51
6	Brighton & Hove A.	46	14	4	5	47	27	6	6	11	29	36	50
7	Watford	46	11	9	3	45	26	7	5	11	26	36	50
8	Torquay United	46	12	6	5	51	39	6	6	11	31	43	48
9	Coventry City	46	15	5	3	50	26	3	6	14	17	33	47
10	Southend United	46	13	5	5	48	28	4	7	12	35	52	46
11	Brentford	46	11	6	6	44	36	5	8	10	38	46	46
12	Norwich City	46	13	5	5	40	23	5	5	13	20	37	46
13	NORTHAMPTON TOWN	46	13	5	5	47	27	6	3	14	26	54	46
14	Aldershot	46	12	6	5	44	23	4	7	12	31	48	45
15	Queen's Park Rgs.	46	13	7	3	46	25	2	7	14	23	50	44
16	Shrewsbury Town	46	14	5	4	49	24	2	5	16	21	54	42
17	Bournemouth	46	7	8	8	32	29	6	5	10	8	25	36	42
18	Reading	46	7	10	6	32	26	6	5	12	33	47	41
19	Newport County	46	8	8	7	32	29	3	8	12	28	44	38
20	Crystal Palace	46	9	11	3	32	24	2	5	16	20	56	38
21	Swindon Town	46	10	8	5	30	19	1	7	15	16	45	37
22	Exeter City	46	9	7	7	30	31	2	8	13	17	42	37
23	Walsall	46	9	6	8	49	36	1	8	14	26	50	34
24	Colchester United	46	7	6	10	33	40	2	7	14	20	51	31

1955/56   11th in Division 3(S)

#	Date	Opponent	Score	Scorers	Att	Adams DF	Coleman GI	Collins BV	Dawson W	Draper RW	Dutton CA	English J	Fowler T	Gale CM	Hughes TG	Jones B	Leek K	McLain T	Mills RWG	Marston M	Newman R	Patterson RL	Pickering PB	Smith EWA	Smith JO	Wallace J	Williams DR	Yeoman RI
1	Aug 20	Crystal Palace	3-2	Dawson, English 2	13841			5	9			7	11			8				2		3	1	10	6			4
2	24	Swindon Town	1-0	English	8642			5	9			7	11							2	8	3	1	10	6			4
3	27	BRIGHTON & HOVE ALB	3-0	English, Fowler, Yeoman	10694			5	9			7	11							2	8	3	1	10	6			4
4	Sep 1	SWINDON TOWN	2-1	Fowler, E Smith	11102			5	9			7	11							2	8	3	1	10	6			4
5	3	Southampton	3-2	English, Newman, E Smith	12373			5	9			7	11							2	8	3	1	10	6			4
6	8	ALDERSHOT	3-2	Dawson, English, E Smith	12534			5	9			7	11							2	8	3	1	10	6			4
7	10	SHREWSBURY TOWN	1-0	Fowler	13144				9			7	11							2	8	3	1	10	6	5		4
8	14	Aldershot	0-2		5811			5	9			7	11							2	8	3	1	10	6			4
9	17	Ipswich Town	0-1		17629					10			11			5	9			2	7	3	1	8	6			4
10	19	QUEEN'S PARK RANGERS	5-2	Draper, Fowler, Newman 2, J Smith	9735					9			11			5			7	2	8	3	1	10	6			4
11	24	WALSALL	3-1	Mills, E Smith 2	14247					9			11			5			7	2	8	3	1	10	6			4
12	29	Newport County	1-0	Newman	8076			5		9			11						7	2	8	3	1	10	6			4
13	Oct 1	Torquay United	1-3	Draper	9686			5		9			11						7	2	8	3	1	10	6			4
14	8	COVENTRY CITY	2-1	Draper 2	20370			5		9			11						7	2	8	3	1	10	6			4
15	15	Southend United	0-2		17009			5		9			11						7	2	8	3	1	10	6			4
16	22	EXETER CITY	3-0	Draper, E Smith, Yeoman	10804			5		9			11			8			7	2		3	1	10	6			4
17	29	Leyton Orient	1-1	Draper	24030			5		9			11			10			7	2		3	1	8	6			4
18	Nov 5	COLCHESTER UNITED	0-2		14091			5		9			11			8			7	2		3	1	10	6			4
19	12	Norwich City	1-4	Fowler	21845			5		9		8	11						7	2		3	1	10	6			4
20	26	Gillingham	2-0	Draper, Fowler	8429			5		9		7	11			8				2		3	1	10	6			4
21	Dec 3	MILLWALL	4-0	Draper, English 2, Jones	10759			5		9		7	11			10				2		3	1	8	6			4
22	17	CRYSTAL PALACE	1-1	English	9302					9		7	11	5						2	8	3	1	10	6			4
23	24	Brighton & Hove Albion	0-4		11004			5		9		7	11							2	8	3	1	10	6			4
24	26	Watford	2-2	Adams, English	7041	10		5		9		7	11							2		3	1	8	6			4
25	27	WATFORD	1-3	English	13778	10		5		9		7	11							2		3	1	8	6			4
26	31	SOUTHAMPTON	3-1	Draper, English, E Smith	11035					9		7	11	5	10					2		3	1	8	6			4
27	Jan 14	Shrewsbury Town	1-1	Fowler	7974			5	8	9		7	11					6		2		3	1	10				4
28	21	IPSWICH TOWN	0-5		13103			5		9		7	11						8	2		3	1	10	6			4
29	28	Reading	1-4	Mills	6807			5		9		7	11	6					8	2		3	1				10	4
30	Feb 11	TORQUAY UNITED	2-0	Draper, E Smith	5656			3		9		7	11	5					8	2			1	10	6			4
31	18	Coventry City	1-0	English	19366			3		9		7	11	5					8	2			1	10	6			4
32	25	SOUTHEND UNITED	1-1	English	9535			3		9		7	11	5					8	2			1	10	6			4
33	Mar 3	Exeter City	1-3	Doyle (og)	6996	9		3				7	11	5					8	2			1	10	6			4
34	10	LEYTON ORIENT	0-1		13544			5		9		7	11						8	2		3	1	10	6			4
35	17	Colchester United	0-2		8333					9		7	11	5						2		3	1	10	6		8	4
36	24	NORWICH CITY	1-1	Marston	9387					9		7	11	5			10			2		3	1	8	6			4
37	31	Bournemouth	0-0		9010					9		7	11	5			10		8	2		3	1		6			4
38	Apr 2	Brentford	1-2	Dutton	9527					9	8		11	5					7	2		3	1	10	6			4
39	3	BRENTFORD	1-0	J Smith	8248					9		7	11	5			10			2		3	1	8	6			4
40	7	GILLINGHAM	0-2		6553					9		7	11	5			10			2		3	1	8	6			4
41	12	BOURNEMOUTH	2-1	Draper 2	4179					10	9		11	5					7	2		3	1		6		8	4
42	14	Millwall	1-4	Dutton	3682						9		11	5			10		7	2		3	1		6		8	4
43	16	Walsall	0-2		11934			3		10	9		11	5					7	2			1		6		8	4
44	21	READING	1-2	Leek	5612					9		7	11	5			10			2		3	1		6		8	4
45	26	NEWPORT COUNTY	5-0	Draper 3, Leek 2	3536					9			11	5			10		7	2		3	1		6		8	4
46	28	Queen's Park Rangers	2-3	Leek, Mills	7157			2		9			11	5			10		7			3	6		1		8	4
	Apps					3	1	38	8	32	9	30	46	12	10	8	7	2	24	42	16	36	46	38	44	1	7	46
	Goals					1			2	15	2	14	7			1	4		3	1	4			8	2			2

One own goal

F.A. Cup

Rd	Date	Opponent	Score	Scorers	Att	Collins BV	Draper RW	English J	Fowler T	Gale CM	Jones B	Marston M	Patterson RL	Pickering PB	Smith EWA	Smith JO	Yeoman RI
R1	Nov 19	MILLWALL	4-1	English 3, Hurley (og)	12878	5	9	7	11		8	2	3	1	10	6	4
R2	Dec 10	HASTINGS	4-1	Draper 2, English, E Smith	15534	5	9	7	11		8	2	3	1	10	6	4
R3	Jan 7	BLACKBURN ROVERS	1-2	English	14087		9	7	11	5	8	2	3	1	10	6	4

		P	W	D	L	F	A	W	D	L	F	A	Pts
1	Leyton Orient	46	18	3	2	76	20	11	5	7	30	29	66
2	Brighton & Hove A.	46	20	2	1	73	16	9	5	9	39	34	65
3	Ipswich Town	46	16	6	1	59	28	9	8	6	47	32	64
4	Southend United	46	16	4	3	58	25	5	7	11	30	55	53
5	Torquay United	46	11	10	2	48	21	9	2	12	38	42	52
6	Brentford	46	11	8	4	40	30	8	6	9	29	36	52
7	Norwich City	46	15	4	4	56	31	4	9	10	30	51	51
8	Coventry City	46	16	4	3	54	20	4	5	14	19	40	49
9	Bournemouth	46	13	6	4	39	14	6	4	13	24	37	48
10	Gillingham	46	12	3	8	38	28	7	7	9	31	43	48
11	NORTHAMPTON TOWN	46	14	3	6	44	27	6	4	13	23	44	47
12	Colchester United	46	14	4	5	56	37	4	7	12	20	44	47
13	Shrewsbury Town	46	12	9	2	47	21	5	3	15	22	45	46
14	Southampton	46	13	6	4	60	30	5	2	16	31	51	44
15	Aldershot	46	9	9	5	38	33	3	7	13	34	57	40
16	Exeter City	46	10	6	7	39	30	5	4	14	19	47	40
17	Reading	46	10	2	11	40	37	5	7	11	30	42	39
18	Queen's Park Rgs.	46	10	7	6	44	32	4	4	15	20	54	39
19	Newport County	46	12	2	9	32	26	3	7	13	26	53	39
20	Walsall	46	13	5	5	43	28	2	3	18	25	56	38
21	Watford	46	8	5	10	31	39	5	6	12	21	46	37
22	Millwall	46	13	4	6	56	31	2	2	19	27	69	36
23	Crystal Palace	46	7	3	13	27	32	5	7	11	27	51	34
24	Swindon Town	46	4	10	9	18	22	4	4	15	16	56	30

1955/56 SEASON
Back: Patterson, Smith, Res, Marston, Pickering, Res, Issac, Res, Res, Res, Collins, McLain
Middle: English, Res, Res, Res, Fowler, Res, Smith(Man.), Leek, Draper, Tebbutt, Res, Mills, Yeoman
Front: Res, Adams, Claypole, Res, Res.

1956/57 SEASON
Back: Draper, Res, Marston, Elvy, Pickering, Gale, Leek, Payne(Trainer), Res, Collins, Claypole, Res
Front: Patterson, English, Mills, Woan, unknown, unknown, Smith(Man),
Yeomans, unknown, Smith, Fowler, unknown, unknown

1956/57   14th in Division 3(S)

#	Date	Opponent	Score	Scorers	Att	Asher SJ	Bright G	Canning L	Claypole AW	Coleman GJ	Collins BV	Draper RW	Dutton CA	Elvy R	English J	Fowler T	Gale CM	Leek K	Marston M	Miller RL	Mills RWG	Morrow HJE	Patterson RL	Pickering PB	Poole KJ	Smith JO	Tebbutt RS	Williams DR	Woan AE	Yeoman RI
1	Aug 18	Newport County	0-3		11371						3	9				11	5	10	2			7		1		6		8		4
2	23	READING	3-0	Leek, J Smith, Davies(og)	8914					3		9				11	5	10	2			7		1		4		8		6
3	25	COLCHESTER UNITED	1-0	Draper	9269					2		9				11	5	10	3			7		1		6		8		
4	29	Reading	1-1	Woan	11698					2		9				11	5	10	3			7		1		6			8	4
5	Sep 1	Norwich City	1-2	Draper	15246					2		9				11	5	10	3			7		1		6			8	4
6	6	QUEEN'S PARK RANGERS	3-0	Leek, J Smith, Woan	7591					2		9				11	5	10	3			7		1		6			8	4
7	8	COVENTRY CITY	4-0	Draper 2, Morrrow 2	15291					2		9				11	5		3			7	8	1		6			10	4
8	10	Queen's Park Rangers	0-1		10785					2		9				11	5		3			7	8	1		6			10	4
9	15	Southampton	0-2		16018					2		9				11	5	8	3			7		1		6			10	4
10	17	PLYMOUTH ARGYLE	2-0	English, Mills	7736					2		9			7	11	5		3	8				1		6			10	4
11	22	EXETER CITY	1-1	Draper	9421					2		9			7	11	5		3	8				1		6			10	4
12	24	Plymouth Argyle	3-4	English, Mills, Woan	13727							8			7	11	5		2		9		3	1		6			10	4
13	29	Crystal Palace	1-1	Woan	13904					2	5				7	11			3		9			1		6		8	10	
14	Oct 6	Brentford	1-2	English	10733					2	5	9			7	11			3					1		6		8	10	
15	13	ALDERSHOT	4-2	English, Fowler, Mills, J Smith	8825					2					7	11	5		3		9			1		6		8	10	4
16	20	Watford	1-2	English	9906			4		2					7	11	5		3		9			1		6		8	10	
17	27	SHREWSBURY TOWN	1-1	Woan	8951			4		2		9			7	11	5		3					1		6		8	10	
18	Nov 3	Walsall	2-2	English, Leek	9842	9									7	11	5	8	2				3	1		6			10	4
19	10	IPSWICH TOWN	2-1	Fowler	9655	9									8	11	5	10	2			7	3	1		6				4
20	24	TORQUAY UNITED	3-0	Fowler, Leek 2	8524	9										11	5	10	2			7	3	1		6				4
21	Dec 1	Millwall	0-1		10940	9										11	5	10	2		8	7	3	1		6				4
22	15	NEWPORT COUNTY	0-3		6289	9										11	5	10	2			7	3	1		6			8	4
23	22	Colchester United	1-5	Leek	5899										8	11	5	9	2			7	3	1		6			10	4
24	25	SOUTHEND UNITED	2-2	Mills 2	5165					2						11	5	9			10	7	3	1		6			8	4
25	26	Southend United	1-0	J Smith	8696	8									7	11	5	10	2		9		3	1		6				4
26	29	NORWICH CITY	1-1	Asher	7603	8										11	5	10	2		9	7	3	1		6				4
27	Jan 5	GILLINGHAM	4-1	Asher 2, Fowler, Morrow	6601	9										11	5	10	2		8	7	3	1		6				4
28	12	Coventry City	1-3	Leek	15371	9										11	5	10	2		8	7	3	1		6				4
29	19	SOUTHAMPTON	2-1	Asher, Fowler	8923	9										11	5	10	2		8	7	3	1	6					4
30	26	Gillingham	2-1	Asher 2	5724	9										11	5	10	2		8	7	3	1	6					4
31	Feb 2	Exeter City	0-0		5931	9										11	5	10	2		8	7	3	1	6					4
32	9	CRYSTAL PALACE	1-0	Woan	8651	9										11	5	6	2		8	7	3	1					10	4
33	16	BRENTFORD	5-1	Asher 2, Woan 2, Bragg(og)	9306	9										11	5	6	2		8	7	3	1					10	4
34	Mar 2	WATFORD	1-2	Asher	9309	9										11	5	6	2		8	7	3	1					10	4
35	9	Brighton & Hove Albion	0-5		11922	9										11		6	2		8	7	3	1	5				10	4
36	16	WALSALL	2-3	Asher, Leek	9177	9									7		5	10	2		11		3	1		6			8	4
37	23	Ipswich Town	1-0	Asher	17144	9									7	11	5		2		8		3	1		6			10	4
38	30	BOURNEMOUTH	2-2	Mills, Woan	7549	9									7	11	5		2		8		3	1		6			10	4
39	Apr 6	Torquay United	0-2		7612	9				2					1	7	11	5			8		3			6			10	4
40	10	Aldershot	0-4		2677					2					1	7	11	5	10		8	7	3			6				4
41	13	MILLWALL	2-1	Mills, Woan	5465					2	9				1	11	5	6			8	7	3						10	4
42	20	Shrewsbury Town	0-2		7214					2	9				1	11	5	6			8	7	3						10	4
43	22	Swindon Town	0-4		7523					2	9				1	11	5	6			8	7	3			4			10	
44	23	SWINDON TOWN	2-0	English, Miller	4950										1	7	11	5	6	2	8	9	3			4		10		
45	27	Bournemouth	1-4	English	8392										1	7	11	5	6	2	8	9	3			4		10		
46	30	BRIGHTON & HOVE ALB	1-0	Fowler	4463	9		2							7	11	5	6			8		3	1		4		10		
		Apps				21	1	2	1	16	8	17	1	14	20	45	43	32	39	2	31	30	30	32	4	38	2	8	29	40
		Goals				11						5			8	6		9		1	7	3				4			10	

Two own goals

F.A. Cup

R	Date	Opponent	Score	Att	Asher SJ	English J	Fowler T	Gale CM	Leek K	Marston M	Patterson RL	Pickering PB	Smith JO	Woan AE	Yeoman RI
R1	Nov 17	Southampton	0-2	16757	9	7	11	5	10	2	3	1	6	8	4

		P	W	D	L	F	A	W	D	L	F	A	Pts
1	Ipswich Town	46	18	3	2	72	20	7	6	10	29	34	59
2	Torquay United	46	19	4	0	71	18	5	7	11	18	46	59
3	Colchester United	46	15	8	0	49	19	7	6	10	35	37	58
4	Southampton	46	15	4	4	48	20	7	6	10	28	32	54
5	Bournemouth	46	15	7	1	57	20	4	7	12	31	42	52
6	Brighton & Hove A.	46	15	6	2	59	26	4	8	11	27	39	52
7	Southend United	46	14	3	6	42	20	4	9	10	31	45	48
8	Brentford	46	12	9	2	55	29	4	7	12	23	47	48
9	Shrewsbury Town	46	11	9	3	45	24	4	9	10	27	55	48
10	Queen's Park Rgs.	46	12	7	4	42	21	6	4	13	19	39	47
11	Watford	46	11	6	6	44	32	7	4	12	28	43	46
12	Newport County	46	15	6	2	51	18	1	7	15	14	44	45
13	Reading	46	13	4	6	44	30	5	5	13	36	51	45
14	NORTHAMPTON TOWN	46	15	5	3	49	22	3	4	16	17	51	45
15	Walsall	46	11	7	5	49	25	5	5	13	31	49	44
16	Coventry City	46	12	5	6	52	36	4	7	12	22	48	44
17	Millwall	46	13	7	3	46	29	3	5	15	18	55	44
18	Plymouth Argyle	46	10	8	5	38	31	6	3	14	30	42	43
19	Aldershot	46	11	5	7	43	35	4	7	12	36	57	42
20	Crystal Palace	46	7	10	6	31	28	4	8	11	31	47	40
21	Exeter City	46	8	8	7	37	29	4	5	14	24	50	37
22	Gillingham	46	7	8	8	29	29	5	5	13	25	56	37
23	Swindon Town	46	12	3	8	43	33	3	3	17	23	63	36
24	Norwich City	46	7	5	11	33	37	1	10	12	28	57	31

1957/58   13th in Division 3(S)

#	Date	Opponent	Score	Scorers	Att	Bright G	Claypole AW	Collins BV	Corbett R	Elvy R	English J	Fowler T	Gale CM	Hawkings B	Leek K	Mills RWG	O'Neil J	Patterson RL	Peacock RJ	Pickering PB	Robinson M	Robinson TH	Smith JO	Tebbutt RS	Woan AE	Yeoman RI
1	Aug 24	Walsall	1-2	Woan	13059	9							5	8	6	7		3		1		11	2		10	4
2	29	ALDERSHOT	0-0		7907						7		5	9	6	8		3		1		11	2		10	4
3	31	COVENTRY CITY	4-0	M Robinson 2, Woan, Kirk(og)	12037							11	5	9	10			3		1	7	2	6		8	4
4	Sep 4	Aldershot	0-0		4188				3			11	5	9	10					1	7	2	6		8	4
5	7	Shrewsbury Town	1-3	Woan	9542				3			11	5	9	10					1	7	2	6		8	4
6	10	Brentford	1-7	Woan	10697				3			11	5	9	10					1	7	2	6		8	4
7	14	READING	1-2	Leek	6986						2	1	11	5	9	10	7	3					6		8	4
8	16	BRENTFORD	3-1	English 2, Leek	4528	9					1	7	11	5	10			3					2	6	8	4
9	21	Swindon Town	1-5	Leek	9967	9					1	7	11	5	10		6	3					2		8	4
10	26	COLCHESTER UNITED	4-1	Corbett, Hawkings, Leek, Mills	3454			2	1				11	5	7	8	9	3					6		10	4
11	28	Watford	2-0	Hawkings, Woan	11579			2	1				11	5	7	8	9	3					6		10	4
12	30	Colchester United	0-1		4391			2	1				11	5	7	10	9	3					6		8	4
13	Oct 5	CRYSTAL PALACE	1-2	Patterson	7594			1					11	5	7	10	9	3				2	6		8	4
14	9	Norwich City	2-2	Leek 2	22850		2		1				11	5	7	10	9	3					6		8	4
15	12	PLYMOUTH ARGYLE	5-0	Hawkings, Leek, O'Neil 2, Woan	9692		2		1				5	7	8		9	3			11				10	4
16	19	Port Vale	0-3		12443		2		1				5	7		8	9	3			11	6			10	4
17	26	NEWPORT COUNTY	0-3		7953		2		1				5	7	6		9				11	3		10	8	4
18	Nov 2	Southampton	1-2	English	13469		2	3	1		7		9	8					6			11	5	10		4
19	9	BRIGHTON & HOVE ALB	2-4	Hawkings, Leek	7088		2		1		7	11	5	9	10			3						6	8	4
20	23	QUEEN'S PARK RANGERS	1-5	Woan	7525		2						9	7	10	6		3	4	1	11	5			8	
21	30	Exeter City	1-0	Leek	7933		2					7	11	5	9	10	6	3		1					8	4
22	Dec 14	Millwall	0-0		6761		2		1			7	11	5	9	10	6	3							8	4
23	21	WALSALL	3-0	Hawkings, Tebbutt 2	7058		2		1			7	11	5	9	10	6	3						8		4
24	26	NORWICH CITY	0-1		11125		2		1			7	11	5	9	10	6	3						8		4
25	28	Coventry City	1-1	Leek	20375		2		1			7	11	5	9	10	6	3						8		4
26	Jan 11	SHREWSBURY TOWN	2-0	Hawkings, Leek	8391		2		1			7	11	5	9	10	6	3						8		4
27	18	Reading	2-5	Hawkings, Tebbutt	10846		2		1			7	11	5	9	10	6	3						8		4
28	Feb 1	SWINDON TOWN	3-0	Fowler, Hawkings, Leek	9845		2		1			7	11	5	9	10	6	3						8		4
29	8	WATFORD	2-3	Leek 2	8400		2		1			7	11	5		10	6	3					9	8		4
30	15	Crystal Palace	3-1	Hawkings 2, Tebbutt	16245		2		1				11	5	9	10	6	3						7	8	4
31	22	Plymouth Argyle	0-3		16667		2		1				11	5	9	10	6	3						7	8	4
32	Mar 1	PORT VALE	3-2	Hawkings 2, O'Neil	8711		2		1			7	11	5	9		6	10						4	8	
33	8	Newport County	1-0	Hawkings	7011		2		1			7	11	5	9	10	6	8	3					4		
34	15	SOUTHAMPTON	1-3	Patterson	9374		2		1				11	5	9	10	6	8	3					7		4
35	22	Queen's Park Rangers	0-1		7531		2		1				11	5	9	10	6	3						7	8	4
36	27	GILLINGHAM	3-1	English, Fowler, Woan	2412		2		1		7	11	5	9			6	3						8	10	4
37	29	MILLWALL	7-2	English, Hawkings 2, Tebbutt, Woan 3	6393		2		1		7	11	5	9			6	3						8	10	4
38	Apr 4	Bournemouth	1-1	Yeoman	15196		2		1		7	11	5	9			6	3						8	10	4
39	5	Brighton & Hove Albion	4-1	Mills, Patterson, Woan 2	20066		2		1				11	5	9		7	3						6	8	10	4
40	8	BOURNEMOUTH	4-0	Hawkings, Patterson, Tebbutt, Woan	9888		2		1				11	5	9		7	3						6	8	10	4
41	12	EXETER CITY	9-0	Hawkings, Mills 2, Tebbutt 3, Woan 3	9465		2		1				11	5	9		7	3						6	8	10	4
42	16	Torquay United	0-1		6598		2		1				11	5	9		7	3						6	8	10	4
43	19	Gillingham	2-1	Hawkings, Woan	5721		2		1				11	5	9		7	3						6	8	10	4
44	24	TORQUAY UNITED	1-0	Woan	10123		2		1				11	5	9		7	3						6	8	10	4
45	26	SOUTHEND UNITED	1-3	Hawkings	10975		2		1				11	5	9		7	3						6	8	10	
46	May 2	Southend United	3-6	Hawkings, Tebbutt, Woan	9391	3	2		1		7	11	5	9			6							4	8	10
				Apps		3	10	24	8	38	20	39	46	43	32	37	6	40	2	8	11	13	24	26	34	42
				Goals				1			5	2		20	14	4	3	4						10	20	1

One own goal

F.A. Cup

R	Date	Opponent	Score	Scorers	Att	Claypole AW	English J	Fowler T	Gale CM	Hawkings B	Leek K	Mills RWG	O'Neil J	Patterson RL	Peacock RJ	Pickering PB	Robinson M	Robinson TH	Tebbutt RS	Yeoman RI
R1	Nov 10	NEWPORT COUNTY	3-0	Gale, Mills, M.Robinson	9345	2			9	7	10	6		3	4	1	11	5	8	
R2	Dec 7	BOURNEMOUTH	4-1	Leek, Woan, Hughes(og), Norris(og)	12691	2		7	11	5	9	10	6	3		1			8	4
R3	Jan 4	ARSENAL	3-1	Hawkings, Leek, Tebbutt	21344	2	1	7	11	5	9	10	6	3					8	4
R4	25	Liverpool	1-3	Hawkings	56939	2	1	7	11	5	9	10	6	3					8	4

		P	W	D	L	F	A	W	D	L	F	A	Pts
1	Brighton & Hove A.	46	13	6	4	52	30	11	6	6	36	34	60
2	Brentford	46	15	5	3	52	24	9	5	9	30	32	58
3	Plymouth Argyle	46	17	4	2	43	17	8	4	11	24	31	58
4	Swindon Town	46	14	7	2	47	16	7	8	8	32	34	57
5	Reading	46	14	5	4	52	23	7	8	8	27	28	55
6	Southampton	46	16	3	4	78	31	6	7	10	34	41	54
7	Southend United	46	14	5	4	56	26	7	7	9	34	32	54
8	Norwich City	46	11	9	3	41	28	8	6	9	34	42	53
9	Bournemouth	46	16	5	2	54	24	5	4	14	27	50	51
10	Queen's Park Rgs.	46	15	6	2	40	14	3	8	12	24	51	50
11	Newport County	46	12	6	5	40	24	5	8	10	33	43	48
12	Colchester United	46	13	5	5	45	27	4	8	11	32	52	47
13	**NORTHAMPTON TOWN**	46	13	1	9	60	33	6	5	12	27	46	44
14	Crystal Palace	46	12	5	6	46	30	3	8	12	24	42	43
15	Port Vale	46	12	6	5	49	24	4	4	15	18	34	42
16	Watford	46	9	8	6	34	27	4	8	11	25	50	42
17	Shrewsbury Town	46	10	6	7	29	25	5	4	14	20	46	40
18	Aldershot	46	7	9	7	31	34	5	7	11	28	55	40
19	Coventry City	46	10	6	7	41	24	3	4	16	20	57	39
20	Walsall	46	10	7	6	37	24	4	2	17	24	51	37
21	Torquay United	46	9	7	7	33	34	2	6	15	16	40	35
22	Gillingham	46	12	5	6	33	24	1	4	18	19	57	35
23	Millwall	46	6	6	11	37	36	5	3	15	26	55	31
24	Exeter City	46	10	4	9	37	35	1	5	17	20	64	31

1957/58 SEASON
Back: Ramscar(Colts Coach), Gale, Claypole, Issac, Elvy, unknown, Collins, Patterson
Middle: Yeomans, Mills, English, Hawkings, Smith(Man), Leek, Woan, Smith
Front: unknown, unknown, unknown, Tebbutt, Fowler, unknown, unknown

1960/61 SEASON
Back: Gale, Patterson, Coe, Phillips, Branston
Front: Mills, Spelman, Moran, Brown, Wright, Fowler

1958/59 8th in Division 4

#		Date	Match	Score	Scorers	Att	Baron KP	Bannister JH	Brewer AP	Claypole AW	Coleman GI	Collins BV	English J	Fowler T	Gale CM	Elvy R	Hawkings B	Kirkup BA	Leck DA	Loasby AA	Miller RL	Mills RWG	Norris OP	O'Neil J	Olha B	Patterson RL	Phillips R	Smith JO	Yeoman RI	Tebbutt RS	Woan AE
1	Aug	23	Port Vale	4-1	Hawkings, Kirkup, Woan 2	15018		2						11	5	1	9	8				7		6		3			4		10
2		28	CREWE ALEXANDRA	3-0	Hawkings, Kirkup, Woan	11916		2	1					11	5		9	8				7		6		3			4		10
3		30	CRYSTAL PALACE	3-0	Fowler, Kirkup, Woan	11288		2	1					11	5		9	8				7		6		3			4		10
4	Sep	1	Crewe Alexandra	2-1	Woan 2	7016		2	1					11	5		9	8				7		6		3			4		10
5		6	Chester	3-2	Fowler, Mills, Woan	9723		2	1					11	5		9	8				7		6		3			4		10
6		9	Carlisle United	1-2	Woan	11238		2	1					11	5		9	8				7		6		3			4		10
7		13	WATFORD	2-1	Hawkings, Mills	11106		2	1					11	5		9	8				7		6		3			4		10
8		20	Hartlepools United	0-3		7463		2	1					11	5		9	8				7		6		3			4	10	
9		25	WORKINGTON	1-1	Baron	6487	8	2	1					11	5		7						9	6		3			4		10
10		27	SOUTHPORT	3-1	Fowler, Woan 2	10999	8	2						11	5	1	9					7		6		3			4		10
11	Oct	1	Workington	3-3	Fowler, Mills, Woan	6613	8	2						11	5	1		9				7		6		3			4		10
12		4	Torquay United	2-4	Baron, Norris	5399	8	2						11	5	1						7	9	6		3			4		10
13		9	YORK CITY	1-2	Baron	5826	8	2						11	5	1						7	9	6		3			4		10
14		11	EXETER CITY	1-1	Woan	10077	8	2				5		11		1	7					6	9			3			4		10
15		18	Coventry City	0-2		22305	8	2				5		11		1						6		7		3			4		10
16		25	SHREWSBURY TOWN	3-3	Tebbutt 2, Woan	9897		2				5	7	11		1	9					6				3			4	8	10
17	Nov	1	Darlington	2-2	Fowler, Hawkings	5579		2				5	7	11		1	9					6				3			4	8	10
18		8	WALSALL	3-2	Tebbutt, Woan, Gutteridge(og)	11858	10			2		5		11		1	9					6				3			4	8	7
19		22	ALDERSHOT	1-0	Kirkup	7598	10			2		5		11		1	9					6				3			4	8	7
20		29	Gateshead	1-4	Kirkup	2870	10	2				5		11		1		9				6	8		4	3					7
21	Dec	13	Barrow	2-2	Mills, Tebbutt	4209	10			2		5		11		1	7	9				6	4			3				8	
22		20	PORT VALE	2-4	Fowler 2	6907	10			2		5		11		1	7	9				6	4			3				8	
23		26	Gillingham	1-4	Mills	6947	10			2		5		11		1		9				4	6	7		3					8
24		27	GILLINGHAM	4-2	Fowler 3, Woan	9538	7		1	2				11	5			9				4	10	6		3					8
25	Jan	3	Crystal Palace	1-1	Hawkings	17162	7		1	2				11	5		9					4	10			3		6			8
26		10	Millwall	0-3		11388	7		1	2				11	5		9					4	10			3		6			8
27		24	OLDHAM ATHLETIC	2-1	Claypole, Woan	7168	7		1	2				11	5			9				4	10			3		6			8
28		31	Watford	1-3	Woan	6200	10		1	2				11	5			9				7			4	3		6			8
29	Feb	7	HARTLEPOOLS UNITED	2-1	Baron, Woan	6055	8	2	1					11	5							4	9	7		3		6			10
30		14	Southport	2-1	Woan 2	3630	7	2	1					11	5							4	9			3		6		8	10
31		21	TORQUAY UNITED	1-1	Woan	6329	7	2	1					11	5							4	9			3		6		8	10
32		28	Exeter City	4-3	English, Fowler, Leek, Woan	9870	8	2	1	3			7	11	5				9			4						6			10
33	Mar	7	COVENTRY CITY	4-0	Fowler, Leek 2, Woan	14365	8	2	1	3			7	11	5				9			4						6			10
34		14	Shrewsbury Town	0-4		7227	8	2	1	3			7	11	5				9			4						6			10
35		21	DARLINGTON	1-3	Woan	6399	8	2	1	3			7	11	5				9			4		4				6			10
36		27	Bradford Park Avenue	2-1	O'Neil, Woan	5988			1	2			7	11	5				9			4		8		3		6			10
37		28	Walsall	1-2	English	5991			1	2			7	11	5							4		8		3		6		9	10
38		31	BRADFORD PARK AVE.	4-1	English, Fowler, Leek, Woan	7544			1	2			7	11	5				9			4		8		3		6			10
39	Apr	4	MILLWALL	0-1		7284			1	2			7	11	5				9			4		8		3		6			10
40		6	CARLISLE UNITED	0-0		3450			1				7		5					11		4	9			3	2	6		8	10
41		11	Aldershot	3-1	Leek, Phillips, Woan	2567			1	2				11	5				7			8	9			3	4	6			10
42		13	CHESTER	4-0	Fowler, Woan 3	3865			1	2				11	5				7			8	9			3	4	6			10
43		18	GATESHEAD	1-0	Mills	5799			1	2				11	5				7			8	9			3	4	6			10
44		20	York City	1-2	Woan	9123			1	2				11	5				7			8	9			3	4	6			10
45		25	Oldham Athletic	1-2	Fowler	2671			1	2			7	11	5							4	9			3	4	6		8	10
46		30	BARROW	2-0	English, Woan	4324			1	2			7	11	5							4	9			3	4	6		8	10
					Apps		25	24	31	26	1	10	13	45	36	15	21	17	14	2	2	42	14	22	2	38	10	23	17	14	42
					Goals		4			1			4	15			5	5	5			6	1	1			1				4	32

One own goal

F.A. Cup

		Date	Match	Score	Scorers	Att	Baron KP	Bannister JH	Brewer AP	Claypole AW	Coleman GI	Collins BV	English J	Fowler T	Gale CM	Elvy R	Hawkings B	Kirkup BA	Leck DA	Loasby AA	Miller RL	Mills RWG	Norris OP	O'Neil J	Olha B	Patterson RL	Phillips R	Smith JO	Yeoman RI	Tebbutt RS	Woan AE
R1	Nov	15	WYCOMBE WANDERERS	2-0	Fowler, Kirkup	12934	10			2				11	5	1	9	8				6				3			4		7
R2	Dec	6	Tooting & Mitcham	1-2	Kirkup	10203	10	2				5	7	11		1		9				6	4			3					8

	P	W	D	L	F	A	W	D	L	F	A	Pts
1 Port Vale	46	14	6	3	62	30	12	6	5	48	28	64
2 Coventry City	46	18	4	1	50	11	6	8	9	34	36	60
3 York City	46	12	10	1	37	17	9	8	6	36	35	60
4 Shrewsbury Town	46	15	5	3	59	24	9	5	9	42	39	58
5 Exeter City	46	16	4	3	55	24	7	7	9	32	37	57
6 Walsall	46	13	5	5	56	25	8	5	10	39	39	52
7 Crystal Palace	46	12	8	3	54	27	8	4	11	36	44	52
8 NORTHAMPTON TOWN	46	14	5	4	48	25	7	4	12	37	53	51
9 Millwall	46	13	6	4	46	23	7	4	12	30	46	50
10 Carlisle United	46	11	6	6	37	30	8	6	9	25	35	50
11 Gillingham	46	14	6	3	53	27	6	3	14	29	50	49
12 Torquay United	46	11	5	7	45	32	5	7	11	33	45	44
13 Chester	46	10	5	8	39	33	6	7	10	33	51	44
14 Bradford Park Ave.	46	15	1	7	51	29	3	6	14	24	48	43
15 Watford	46	10	6	7	46	36	6	4	13	35	43	42
16 Darlington	46	7	8	8	37	36	6	8	9	29	32	42
17 Workington	46	9	10	4	40	32	3	7	13	23	46	41
18 Crewe Alexandra	46	11	5	7	52	32	4	5	14	18	50	40
19 Hartlepools United	46	11	4	8	50	41	4	6	13	24	47	40
20 Gateshead	46	11	3	9	33	30	5	5	13	23	55	40
21 Oldham Athletic	46	15	0	8	39	29	1	4	18	20	55	36
22 Aldershot	46	8	4	11	37	45	6	3	14	26	52	35
23 Barrow	46	6	6	11	34	45	3	4	16	17	59	28
24 Southport	46	7	8	8	26	25	0	4	19	15	61	26

1959/60   6th in Division 4

#	Date	Opponent	Score	Scorers	Att	Bowen DL	Brewer AP	Claypole AW	Cooke BA	Deakin MRF	English J	Fotheringham JG	Fowler T	Gale CM	Griffin FA	Haskins AJ	Isaac WH	Kane P	Kirkup BA	Leck DA	Mills RWG	Olha B	Patterson RL	Phillips R	Smith JO	Tebbutt RS	Tucker KJ	Vickers P	Ward JR	Woan AE	Wright ME
1	Aug 22	Exeter City	1-1	Leck	9678	6	1	2				5	11		7					9	4		3						8	10	
2	27	TORQUAY UNITED	3-0	Leck 2, Tebbutt	12974	6	1	2				5	11		7				10	9	4		3			8					
3	29	Doncaster Rovers	2-3	Leck, Woan	7033		1	2					11	5	7				8	9	4		3		6					10	
4	Sep 2	Torquay United	3-5	Kirkup 2, Leck	7447		1	2					11	5	7		3		8	9	4				6					10	
5	5	WORKINGTON	0-0		11298	6	1	2				5	11		7				8	9	4		3							10	
6	10	GILLINGHAM	2-1	Mills, Woan	9622	6	1					5	11		7				8	9	4		3	2						10	
7	12	Rochdale	2-2	Leck 2	5686	6	1					5	11		7				10	9	4		3	2		8					
8	16	Gillingham	1-2	Woan	5970	6	1					5	11		7				8	9	4		3	2						10	
9	19	GATESHEAD	2-0	Leck 2	9426	6						5	11		7		1		8	9	4		3	2						10	
10	21	MILLWALL	0-3		8675							5	11		7		1		8	9	4		3	2	6					10	
11	26	Darlington	2-3	English 2	7199						7	5	11				1			9	4		3	2	6	8				10	
12	28	Millwall	1-2	English	18950	6					7		11	5		3	1			9	4			2		8				10	
13	Oct 3	ALDERSHOT	2-0	Leck, Woan	8316						7		11	5		3	1			9	4			2	6	8				10	
14	10	Oldham Athletic	1-0	Ferguson (og)	5419						7		11	5		3	1			9	4			2	6	8				10	
15	17	CARLISLE UNITED	2-2	Fowler, Woan	8789						7		11	5		3	1			9	4			2	6	8				10	
16	24	Notts County	1-2	Woan	14867	6	1						11	5		3		8		9	4	7		2						10	
17	31	WALSALL	0-1		13041	6	1			10	7		11	5		3		8		9	4			2							
18	Nov 7	Hartlepools United	4-1	Deakin 2, Kane, Leck	1953	6	1			9		5	11		7			8		10	4		3	2							
19	21	Chester	1-1	Deakin	7283	6	1			9			11	5			1	8		10	4		3	2							
20	28	CRYSTAL PALACE	0-2		8121	6	1			10			11	5				8		9	4	7	3	2							
21	Dec 12	STOCKPORT COUNTY	1-1	Olha	6383	6	1		4					5	7			9			8	11	3	2			10				
22	19	EXETER CITY	1-1	Kane	4709	6	1	2	4					5	7			8			9	11	3				10				
23	28	WATFORD	1-2	Tebbutt	8369		1		4	9			11	5				8			6		3	2		7	10				
24	Jan 2	DONCASTER ROVERS	3-1	Fowler, Mills, Tebbutt	6253		1		4				11	5	7			10			6	9	3	2		8					
25	16	Workington	1-5	Bowen	3788	6	1		4				11	5	7							9	3	2		8					10
26	23	ROCHDALE	3-1	Deakin, Olha, Kane	5355	6	1		4	10			11	5				8			9	7	3	2							
27	Feb 6	Gateshead	3-1	Kane 2, Mills	3164	6	1		4	10			11	5				8			9	7	3	2							
28	13	DARLINGTON	3-1	Kane, Olha 2	3477	6	1		4	9			11	5				8				7	3	2				10			
29	20	Aldershot	0-3		4197	6	1		4	9		5	11					8				7	3	2				10			
30	27	OLDHAM ATHLETIC	8-1	*See below	6746		1		4	9			11	5				8			6	7	3	2		10					
31	Mar 1	Watford	1-3	Kane	13024		1		4	9			11	5				8			6	7	3	2		10					
32	5	Carlisle United	2-0	Deakin, Mills	3503		1		4	9			11	5				8			6	7	3	2		10					
33	12	NOTTS COUNTY	4-2	Deakin 2, Kane, Tebbutt	8902		1		4	9			11	5				8			6	7	3	2		10					
34	19	Walsall	2-1	Deakin 2	9852		1		4	9			11	5				8			6	7	3	2		10					
35	26	HARTLEPOOLS UNITED	3-0	Deakin, Kane, Wright	5954		1		4	9			11	5				8			6	7	3	2							10
36	Apr 2	Crewe Alexandra	1-0	Deakin	5901		1		4	9			11	5				8		10	6	7	3	2							
37	7	Bradford Park Avenue	0-3		4916		1		4	9			11	5				8			6	7	3	2					10		
38	9	CHESTER	1-0	Deakin	7037		1	2	4	9			11	5				8			6	7	3						10		
39	11	BARROW	6-0	Deakin 4, Kane 2	5710		1	2	4	9			11	5				8		10	6	7	3								
40	15	Southport	4-0	Kane 3, Olha	3612		1	2	4	9			11	5				8		10	6	7	3								
41	16	Crystal Palace	1-0	Deakin	15943		1	2	4	9				5				8		10	6	7	3						11		
42	19	SOUTHPORT	2-2	Leck 2	12373		1	2	4	9				5				8		10	6	7	3						11		
43	23	BRADFORD PARK AVE.	3-1	Deakin, Fowler 2	8667		1	2	4	9			11	5				8		10	6	7	3								
44	25	Barrow	1-0	Leck	5400		1	2	4	9			11	5				8		10	6	7	3								
45	28	CREWE ALEXANDRA	0-0		10847	6	1	2		9			11	5				8		10	4	7	3								
46	30	Stockport County	0-3		3853		1	2	4	9				5				8		10	6	7	3					11			
				Apps		22	38	15	25	25	6	11	41	35	16	7	8	28	9	30	41	26	39	31	11	15	3	2	6	14	2
				Goals		1				20	3		4					16	2	14	4	5				7				6	1

Scorers in game 30: Deakin 2, Kane 2, Tebbutt 3, Ferguson (og).

Two own goals

F.A. Cup

#	Date	Opponent	Score	Scorers	Att	Bowen DL	Brewer AP	Deakin MRF	Fotheringham JG	Fowler T	Griffin FA	Kane P	Leck DA	Mills RWG	Patterson RL	Phillips R
R1	Nov 14	Torquay United	1-7	Kane	5661	6	1	10	5	11	7	8	9	4	3	2

	P	W	D	L	F	A	W	D	L	F	A	Pts
1 Walsall	46	14	5	4	57	33	14	4	5	45	27	65
2 Notts County	46	19	1	3	66	27	7	7	9	41	42	60
3 Torquay United	46	17	3	3	56	27	9	5	9	28	31	60
4 Watford	46	17	2	4	62	28	7	7	9	30	39	57
5 Millwall	46	12	8	3	54	28	6	9	8	30	33	53
6 NORTHAMPTON TOWN	46	13	6	4	50	22	9	3	11	35	41	53
7 Gillingham	46	17	4	2	47	21	4	6	13	27	48	52
8 Crystal Palace	46	12	6	5	61	27	7	6	10	23	37	50
9 Exeter City	46	13	7	3	50	30	6	4	13	30	40	49
10 Stockport County	46	15	6	2	35	10	4	5	14	23	44	49
11 Bradford Park Ave.	46	12	10	1	48	25	5	5	13	22	43	49
12 Rochdale	46	15	4	4	46	19	3	6	14	19	41	46
13 Aldershot	46	14	5	4	50	22	4	4	15	27	52	45
14 Crewe Alexandra	46	14	3	6	51	31	4	6	13	28	57	45
15 Darlington	46	11	6	6	40	30	6	3	14	23	43	43
16 Workington	46	10	8	5	41	20	4	6	13	27	40	42
17 Doncaster Rovers	46	13	3	7	40	23	3	7	13	29	53	42
18 Barrow	46	11	8	4	52	29	4	3	16	25	58	41
19 Carlisle United	46	9	6	8	28	28	6	5	12	23	38	41
20 Chester	46	10	8	5	37	24	4	5	14	22	51	40
21 Southport	46	9	7	7	30	32	1	7	15	18	60	34
22 Gateshead	46	12	3	8	37	27	0	6	17	21	59	33
23 Oldham Athletic	46	5	7	11	20	30	3	5	15	21	53	28
24 Hartlepools United	46	9	2	12	40	41	1	5	17	19	68	27

1960/61   3rd in Division 4

#	Date	Opponent	Score	Scorers	Att	Branston TG	Brewer AP	Brown L	Carson AM	Claypole AW	Coe NC	Cooke BA	Deakin MRF	Edwards RH	Everitt MD	Fowler T	Gale CM	Laird DS	Leck DA	Lines B	Moran J	Mills RWG	Olha B	Patterson RL	Phillips R	Spelman RE	Tucker KJ	Wright ME
1	Aug 20	Oldham Athletic	2-1	Deakin 2	8929		1			2		4	8			11	5	9				6		3			7	10
2	24	Workington	0-3		3439		1			2		4	8			11	5	7	9			6		3				10
3	27	ALDERSHOT	2-1	Deakin, Leck	8092		1			2		4	8			11	5		9			6		3	7			10
4	29	WORKINGTON	3-2	Leck 2, Wright	6835		1			2		4	8			11	5		9			6		3	7			10
5	Sep 3	STOCKPORT COUNTY	4-2	Deakin 2, Wright 2	8661		1			2		4	9			11	5		8			6		3	7			10
6	7	Crewe Alexandra	2-0	Deakin, Leck	8499		1			2		4	9			11	5		8			6		3	7			10
7	10	Bradford Park Avenue	3-1	Deakin, Mills, Wright	7616		1			2		4	9			11	5		8			6		3	7			10
8	13	CREWE ALEXANDRA	4-1	Deakin, Fowler, Leck, one og	9034		1			2		4	9			11	5		8			6		3	7			10
9	17	GILLINGHAM	3-1	Olha, Wright 2	9575		1			2		4	9			11	5		8			6		3	7			10
10	19	CHESTER	3-2	Fowler, Olha, Leck	9320		1			2		4	9			11	5		8			6		3	7			10
11	24	Barrow	0-1		5583		1			2		4				11	5	9	8			6		3	7			10
12	Oct 1	MILLWALL	2-2	Brown, Leck	11558		1	9		2		4				11	5		8			6		3	7			10
13	3	Accrington Stanley	2-3	Brown, Leck	4603		1	9		2		4				11	5		8			6		3	7			10
14	8	Peterborough United	3-3	Deakin, Fowler, Leck	22959	6	1			2		4	9			11	5		8					3	7			10
15	15	SOUTHPORT	3-1	Olha, Tucker 2	11014		1			2		4	9				5		8			6		3	7		11	10
16	22	Darlington	1-1	Brown	8858		1	6		2		4	9				5						8	3	7		11	10
17	29	CRYSTAL PALACE	1-2	Tucker	13943		1	6		2		4	9				5		8					3	7		11	10
18	Nov 12	HARTLEPOOLS UNITED	3-3	Brown 3	9484		1	9		2		4					5	10	8	11		6		3	7			
19	19	Wrexham	2-2	Brown 2	6328			9		2	1	4					5	10	8	11		6		3	7			
20	Dec 3	Rochdale	1-1	Lines	2173			9		3	1	4					5	10	8	11		6		2	7			
21	10	MANSFIELD TOWN	1-0	Laird	8129			9		3	1	4					5	10	8	11		6		2	7			
22	17	OLDHAM ATHLETIC	1-0	Spelman	9710			9		3	1	4					5	10	8	11		6		2	7			
23	26	York City	1-0	one og	7291			9		3	1	4					5	10	8	11		6		2	7			
24	27	YORK CITY	3-0	Brown 2, Lines	18384			9		3	1	4					5	10	8	11		6		2	7			
25	31	Aldershot	2-2	Brown, Deakin	7117			9		3	1	4			10		5		8	11		6		2	7			
26	Jan 21	BRADFORD PARK AVE.	0-1		9749					3	1	4	9		10		5		8	11		6		2	7			
27	28	Doncaster Rovers	2-0	Brown, Deakin	3028			9		3	1	4			10	11	5		8			6		2	7		.	
28	Feb 11	BARROW	3-0	Brown, Moran	9255	4		9		3	1					11	5		8		10	6		2	7			
29	18	Millwall	1-3	Cooke	11707					3	1	4	9		10	11	5		8			6		2	7			
30	25	PETERBOROUGH UTD.	0-3		21000					3	1	4		9	10	11	5		8			6		2	7			
31	Mar 4	Southport	0-2		4693			9		3	1	4		8	10	11	5					6		2	7			
32	8	Chester	2-0	Everitt, Leck	5455	4		9		3	1			7			5		8	11		6		2				10
33	11	DARLINGTON	1-1	Brown	10124	4		9		3	1			7			5		8	11		6		2				10
34	18	Crystal Palace	3-2	Edwards 2, Leck	20668	4				3	1			9		7	5		8	11		6		2				10
35	21	CARLISLE UNITED	0-0		11593	4				3	1			9		7	5		8	11		6		2				10
36	25	DONCASTER ROVERS	3-0	Edwards, Leck 2	8604	4				3	1			9		7	5		8	11	10	6		2				
37	Apr 1	Hartlepools United	2-4	Edwards 2	3460	4				3	1			9		7	5	10	8	11		6		2				
38	3	Exeter City	3-1	Edwards, Everitt, Moran	5903	4		10		3	1			9	7		5		8	11		6		2				
39	4	EXETER CITY	3-1	Brown 3	12402	4		10		3	1			9	7		5		8	11		6		2				
40	8	WREXHAM	3-0	Brown, Everitt, Lines	11507	4				3	1			9	7		5			11	10	6		2				
41	12	Gillingham	1-0	Lines	4831	4				3	1			9	8		5			11	10	6		2			7	
42	15	Carlisle United	1-2	Mills	3985	4				3	1			9	8		5			11	10	6		2			7	
43	17	Stockport County	1-1	Edwards	4307	5	8		6	1		4		9						11	10	7		3	2			
44	22	ROCHDALE	5-1	Brown 2, Moran 3	9535	4		9		1				7	8		5			11	10	6		3	2			
45	25	ACCRINGTON STANLEY	2-1	Brown, Lines	8167	4		8		1				9	7		5			11	10	6		3	2			
46	29	Mansfield Town	2-4	Edwards, Everitt	4872	4		8		1				9	7		5			11	10	6		3	2			
		Apps				17	18	33	1	42	28	31	19	13	16	19	39	12	29	24	15	45	14	8	42	14	8	23
		Goals						22				1	11	8	4	3		1	13	5	5	2	3			1	3	6

Two own goals

F.A. Cup

#	Date	Opponent	Score	Scorers	Att	Branston	Brewer	Brown	Carson	Claypole	Coe	Cooke	Deakin	Edwards	Everitt	Fowler	Gale	Laird	Leck	Lines	Moran	Mills	Olha	Patterson	Phillips	Spelman	Tucker	Wright
R1	Nov 5	HASTINGS	2-1	Brown, Wilson	11141		1	9		2		4					5		8			6		3	7		11	
R2	26	Romford	5-1	Brown 2, Leck 3	11073			9		3	1	4					5	10	8	11		6		2	7			
R3	Jan 7	Luton Town	0-4		26220			9		3	1	4			10		5		8	11		6		2	7			

Played in R1: Wilson (10)

F.L. Cup

#	Date	Opponent	Score	Scorers	Att	Branston	Brewer	Brown	Carson	Claypole	Coe	Cooke	Deakin	Edwards	Everitt	Fowler	Gale	Laird	Leck	Lines	Moran	Mills	Olha	Patterson	Phillips	Spelman	Tucker	Wright
R2	Oct 18	WREXHAM	1-1	Mills	12029		1	6		2		4	9				5		8					7			3	11	10
rep	25	Wrexham	0-2		7518			6		2	1	4	9				5		8	11				7			3		10

	P	W	D	L	F	A	W	D	L	F	A	Pts
1 Peterborough Utd.	46	18	3	2	85	30	10	7	6	49	35	66
2 Crystal Palace	46	16	4	3	64	28	13	2	8	46	41	64
3 NORTHAMPTON TOWN	46	16	4	3	53	25	9	6	8	37	37	60
4 Bradford Park Ave.	46	16	5	2	49	22	10	3	10	35	52	60
5 York City	46	17	3	3	50	14	4	6	13	30	46	51
6 Millwall	46	13	3	7	56	33	8	5	10	41	53	50
7 Darlington	46	11	7	5	41	24	7	6	10	37	46	49
8 Workington	46	14	3	6	38	28	7	4	12	36	48	49
9 Crewe Alexandra	46	11	4	8	40	29	9	5	9	21	38	49
10 Aldershot	46	16	4	3	55	19	2	5	16	24	50	45
11 Doncaster Rovers	46	15	0	8	52	33	4	7	12	24	45	45
12 Oldham Athletic	46	13	4	6	57	38	6	3	14	22	50	45
13 Stockport County	46	14	4	5	31	21	4	5	14	26	45	45
14 Southport	46	12	6	5	47	27	7	0	16	22	40	44
15 Gillingham	46	9	7	7	45	34	6	6	11	19	32	43
16 Wrexham	46	12	4	7	38	22	5	4	14	24	34	42
17 Rochdale	46	13	7	3	43	19	4	1	18	17	47	42
18 Accrington Stanley	46	12	4	7	44	32	4	4	15	30	56	40
19 Carlisle United	46	10	7	6	43	37	3	6	14	18	42	39
20 Mansfield Town	46	10	3	10	39	34	6	3	14	32	44	38
21 Exeter City	46	12	3	8	39	32	2	7	14	27	62	38
22 Barrow	46	10	6	7	33	28	3	5	15	19	51	37
23 Hartlepools United	46	10	4	9	46	40	2	4	17	25	63	32
24 Chester	46	9	7	7	38	35	2	2	19	23	69	31

1961/62 8th in Division 3

No	Date		Opponent	Score	Scorers	Att
1	Aug	19	Watford	0-0		16849
2		22	Bristol City	0-1		14415
3		26	Hull City	0-1		8027
4		29	BRISTOL CITY	0-1		12832
5	Sep	2	PORT VALE	1-1	Terry	9573
6		6	Crystal Palace	4-1	Holton 3, Terry	25535
7		9	LINCOLN CITY	2-2	Dixon 2	11850
8		16	Torquay United	2-1	Holton, Terry	5707
9		18	BOURNEMOUTH	0-3		14350
10		23	SWINDON TOWN	1-2	Holton	9263
11		27	Bournemouth	2-3	Holton 2	14112
12		30	Halifax Town	3-1	Leck, Lines 2	5737
13	Oct	3	BARNSLEY	3-1	Holton, Terry 2	11448
14		7	Bradford Park Avenue	2-1	Holton, Lines	10738
15		11	Barnsley	2-3	Holton 2	2371
16		14	GRIMSBY TOWN	7-0	Holton 3, Leck, Spelman, Edwards, Mills	11201
17		17	CRYSTAL PALACE	1-1	Holton	13827
18		21	Shrewsbury Town	3-1	Holton, Edwards, Mills	6872
19		28	PETERBOROUGH UTD.	2-2	Everitt, Holton	17324
20	Nov	11	NEWPORT COUNTY	5-0	Holton 2, Lines, Reid 2	7845
21		18	Southend United	3-1	Holton, Spelman, Terry	5974
22	Dec	2	Coventry City	0-1		13693
23		9	Brentford	5-0	Holton 2, Lines 2, Terry	10059
24		16	WATFORD	2-0	Terry 2	12509
25		23	HULL CITY	2-0	Lines, Terry	10203
26		26	Portsmouth	1-4	Lines	17428
27	Jan	13	Port Vale	1-1	Holton	8229
28		20	Lincoln City	0-0		5720
29		27	NOTTS COUNTY	1-2	Lines	11813
30	Feb	3	TORQUAY UNITED	1-2	Lines	8910
31		10	Swindon Town	2-2	Everitt, Holton	8985
32		17	HALIFAX TOWN	3-1	Holton, Lines, Moran	7900
33		24	BRADFORD PARK AVE.	2-0	Holton, Reid	7563
34	Mar	3	Grimsby Town	2-3	Holton 2	9318
35		10	SHREWSBURY TOWN	3-1	Dixon, Lines, one og	8173
36		17	Peterborough United	2-0	Everitt, Robson	17009
37		20	PORTSMOUTH	2-2	Dixon, Everitt	13622
38		24	READING	1-0	Holton	9746
39		31	Newport County	0-0		2568
40	Apr	7	SOUTHEND UNITED	3-1	Everitt, Holton, Lines	7657
41		11	Reading	0-2		5586
42		14	Notts County	4-1	Holton 3, Woods	5974
43		21	COVENTRY CITY	4-1	Holton 2, Lines, Woods	10388
44		23	Queen's Park Rangers	0-2		10953
45		24	QUEEN'S PARK RANGERS	1-1	Holton	12533
46		27	Brentford	0-3		6715

Player appearances (shirt numbers)

No	Branston TG	Brodie CTG	Carson AM	Claypole AW	Clapton DP	Coe NC	Cooke BA	Dixon CH	Etheridge BG	Everitt MD	Fowler T	Foley TC	Haskins AJ	Holton CC	Leck DA	Lines B	Moran J	Patterson RL	Reid J	Robson TH	Spelman RE	Terry PA	Woods DE	Woollard AJ	Wright ME	Edwards RH	Mills RWG
1	5			3		1				6		2			4	11	10					7	9			8	
2	5			3		1				6		2			4	11	10					7	9	8			
3	5			3		1		7		6	11	2			4		10									9	8
4	5			3	8	1		7		4	11	2			6		10					9					
5	5			3		1		7		8	11	2			6		10					9					4
6	5			3		1		7		4	11	2		8	6		10					9					
7	5			3		1		7		4	11	2		8	6							9		10			
8	5			3		1	4	7		10		2		8	6	11						9					
9	5			3		1	4	7		10		2		8	6	11						9					
10	5			3		1		7		4		2		8	6	11						9					10
11	5		4	3		1						2		8	6	11					7					9	10
12	5	1	4	3								2		8	6	11					7					9	10
13	5	1	4	3								2		8	6	11					7	9					10
14	5	1	4	3								2		8	6	11					7	9					10
15	5	1	4	3								2		8	6	11					7	9					10
16	5	1		3						4		2		8	6	11					7					9	10
17	5	1		3						4		2		8	6	11					7					9	10
18	5	1		3						4		2		8	6	11					7					9	10
19	5	1	4	3						10		2		8	6	11					7	9					
20	5			3		1				4		2		8	6	11			10		7	9					
21	5	1		3						4		2		8	6	11			10		7	9					
22	5	1		3						4		2		8	6	11			10		7	9					
23	5	1								4		2		8	6	11			10		7	9					3
24	5	1								4		2		8	6	11			10		7	9					3
25	5	1								4		2		8	6	11			10		7	9					3
26	5	1								4		2		8	6	11			10		7	9					3
27	5	1								4		2		8	6	11			10		7	9					3
28	5	1								4		2		8	6	11			10		7	9					3
29	5	1								4		2		8	6	11			10		7	9					3
30	5	1								4		2		8	6	11			10		7					9	3
31	5	1								7		2	3	8	6	11	9		10								4
32	5	1								7		2		8	4	11	9	3	10								6
33	5	1										2		8	4	11	9	3	10		7						6
34	5	1						7				2		8	4	11			10					3		9	6
35	5	1						7		9		2		8	4	11			10					3			6
36	5	1						7		9		2		8	4				10	11				3			6
37	5	1						7		9		2		8	4				10	11				3			6
38	5	1						7		9		2		8	4				10	11				3			6
39	5	1						7		9		2		8	4	11			10					3			6
40	5	1						7		9		2		8	4	11			10					3			6
41	5					1						2		8	4	10				11			7	3		9	6
42	5					1			10			2		8	4	11			9				7	3			6
43	5	1								9		2		8	4	11			10				7	3			6
44	5	1								9		2		8	4	11			10				7	3			6
45		1	5							9		2		8	4	11			10				7	3			6
46	5	1								9		2		8	4	11			10				7	3			6
Apps	45	32	7	22	1	14	2	15	1	37	5	46	1	41	46	38	9	2	26	4	23	24	6	13	1	10	35
Goals								4		5				36	2	14	1		3	1	2	10	2			2	2

One own goal

F.A. Cup

No	Date		Opponent	Score	Scorers	Att
R1	Nov	4	MILLWALL	2-0	Lines, Terry	11844
R2		25	KETTERING TOWN	3-0	Holton 3	18825
R3	Jan	6	Port Vale	1-3	Moran	19442

No	Branston TG	Brodie CTG	Claypole AW	Everitt MD	Foley TC	Holton CC	Leck DA	Lines B	Moran J	Spelman RE	Terry PA	Edwards RH	Mills RWG
R1	5	1	3	4	2	8	6	11		7	9	10	2
R2	5	1	3	4	2	8	6	11		7	9		10
R3	5	1		4	2	8	6	11	10	7	9		3

F.L. Cup

No	Date		Opponent	Score	Scorers	Att
R1	Sep	13	Luton Town	1-2	Cooke	7512

R1: Branston 5, Claypole 3, Cooke 6, Dixon 7, Etheridge 8, Foley 2, Holton 4, Lines 11, Terry 9, Mills 10

Played at no. 1: B Caine

Final Table – Division 3

		P	W	D	L	F	A	W	D	L	F	A	Pts
1	Portsmouth	46	15	6	2	48	23	12	5	6	39	24	65
2	Grimsby Town	46	18	3	2	49	18	10	3	10	31	38	62
3	Bournemouth	46	14	8	1	42	18	7	9	7	27	27	59
4	Queen's Park Rgs.	46	15	3	5	65	31	9	8	6	46	42	59
5	Peterborough Utd.	46	16	0	7	60	38	10	6	7	47	44	58
6	Bristol City	46	15	3	5	56	27	8	5	10	38	45	54
7	Reading	46	14	5	4	46	24	8	4	11	31	42	53
8	NORTHAMPTON T.	46	12	6	5	52	24	8	5	10	33	33	51
9	Swindon Town	46	11	8	4	48	26	6	7	10	30	45	49
10	Hull City	46	15	2	6	43	20	5	6	12	24	34	48
11	Bradford Park Ave.	46	13	5	5	47	27	7	2	14	33	51	47
12	Port Vale	46	12	4	7	41	23	5	7	11	24	35	45
13	Notts County	46	14	5	4	44	23	3	4	16	23	51	43
14	Coventry City	46	11	6	6	38	26	5	5	13	26	45	43
15	Crystal Palace	46	8	8	7	50	41	6	6	11	33	39	42
16	Southend United	46	10	7	6	31	26	3	9	11	26	43	42
17	Watford	46	10	9	4	37	26	4	4	15	26	48	41
18	Halifax Town	46	9	5	9	34	35	6	5	10	33	33	40
19	Shrewsbury Town	46	8	7	8	46	37	5	5	13	27	47	38
20	Barnsley	46	9	6	8	45	41	4	6	13	26	54	38
21	Torquay United	46	9	4	10	48	44	6	2	15	28	56	36
22	Lincoln City	46	4	10	9	31	43	5	7	11	26	44	35
23	Brentford	46	11	3	9	34	29	2	5	16	19	64	34
24	Newport County	46	6	5	12	29	38	1	3	19	17	64	22

1961/62 SEASON
Back: Jennings(Trainer), Osborne(Secretary), Edwards, Leck, Branston, Coe, Foley, Brodie,
Woollard, Robson, Mills, Bowen(Manager), Payne(Asst. Trainer)
Front: Everitt, Woods, Holton(Captain), Reid, Lines

1962/63 SEASON
Back: Bowen(Manager), Jennings(Coach), Ashworth, Leck, Large, Brodie, Branston,
Kurila, Cockroft, Osborne(Secretary), Payne(Trainer)
Front: Everitt, Hails, Smith, Foley(Captain), Lines, Reid, Mills

1962/63 Champions of Division 3

#	Date	Opponent	Score	Scorers	Att	Ashworth A	Branston TG	Brodie CTG	Carr WG	Cockcroft VH	Everitt MD	Foley TC	Hails W	Holton CC	Kurila J	Large F	Leck DA	Llewellyn HA	Martin D	Mills RWG	Reid J	Sanders RJ	Smith HR	Robson TH	Etheridge BG	Woollard AJ	Lines B
1	Aug 21	Bristol Rovers	2-2	Holton, Lines	11649	9	5	1				2		8	6		4				10	7				3	11
2	25	Swindon Town	3-2	Ashworth, Holton, Sanders	13174	9	5	1				2		8	6		4				10	7				3	11
3	28	BRISTOL ROVERS	2-0	Ashworth 2	15661	8	5	1				2		9	6		4				10	7				3	11
4	Sep 1	PETERBOROUGH UTD.	2-3	Holton, Reid	16064	9	5	1			7	2		8	6		4				10					3	11
5	8	Barnsley	1-1	Ashworth	7674	9	5	1				2		8	6		4				10	7				3	11
6	11	WREXHAM	8-0	Ashworth 2, Holton 2, Reid, Lines 3	9555	9	5	1				2		8	6		4				10	7				3	11
7	15	Colchester United	2-2	Ashworth 2	5413	9	5	1				2		8	6		4				10	7				3	11
8	17	HALIFAX TOWN	7-1	Ashworth 2, Holton 3, Lines, Leck	13975	9	5	1				2		8	6		4				10	7				3	11
9	22	QUEEN'S PARK RANGERS	1-0	Ashworth	15469	9	5	1				2		8	6		4				10	7				3	11
10	24	Halifax Town	3-1	Holton 2, Lines	4202	9	5	1				2		8	6		4					7			10	3	11
11	29	Hull City	0-2		9536	9	5	1				2		8	6		4					7			10	3	11
12	Oct 2	CRYSTAL PALACE	3-1	Holton, Leck, Evans (og)	14204		5	1				2		8	6		4			9	10	7				3	11
13	6	BOURNEMOUTH	2-2	Holton, Lines	12199		5	1				2		8	6		4			9	10	7				3	11
14	10	Crystal Palace	2-1	Ashworth, Lines	13319	9	5	1				2		8			4			6	10	7				3	11
15	13	Coventry City	1-1	Ashworth	22163	9	5	1				2		8	6		4				10	7				3	11
16	20	BRADFORD PARK AVE.	3-1	Ashworth, Reid, Williamson (og)	12634	9	5	1		3		2		8	6		4				10	7					11
17	24	Wrexham	4-1	Ashworth 2, Holton 2	18841	9	5	1		3		2		8			4			6	10	7					11
18	27	Watford	2-4	Lines, Sanders	19015	9	5	1		3		2		8	6		4				10	7					11
19	Nov 10	Reading	1-2	Ashworth	7402	8	5	1		3	9	2					4			6	10	7					11
20	17	PORT VALE	0-0		8718	9	5	1		3		2		8			4			6	10	7					11
21	Dec 1	MILLWALL	1-1	Hails	10198	9	5	1			3	2	7	8	6		4				10						11
22	8	Southend United	1-5	Ashworth	8203	9	5	1			3	2	7	8	6		4				10						11
23	15	Carlisle United	2-1	Ashworth, Reid	3933	9	5	1			3	2	7		6		4		8		10						11
24	26	Notts County	1-2	Lines	6614	10	5	1			3	2	7		6		4		9	8							11
25	Feb 9	Queen's Park Rangers	3-1	Ashworth, Lines 2	14238	8	5	1			3	2	7		6		4	9			10						11
26	23	Bournemouth	0-3		10230	8		1	5		3	2	7		6		4			9	10						11
27	Mar 2	COVENTRY CITY	0-0		18717		5	1			3	2	7		6	9	4			8	10						11
28	9	Bradford Park Avenue	3-2	Large, Lines 2	6551		5	1			3	2	7		6	9	4				10		8				11
29	12	COLCHESTER UNITED	3-1	Large 3	9981		5	1			3	2	7		6	9	4				10		8				11
30	16	WATFORD	1-0	Everitt	12230		5	1			3	2	7		6	9	4				10		8				11
31	23	Bristol City	1-3	Reid	9642		5	1			3	2	7		6	9	4				10		8				11
32	26	SWINDON TOWN	1-1	Hails	16812		5	1			3	2	7		6	9	4				10		8				11
33	30	READING	5-0	Ashworth 3, Large 2	7845	8	5	1			3	2	7		6	9	4				10						11
34	Apr 2	NOTTS COUNTY	2-2	Ashworth, Lines	14606	8	5	1			3	2	7		6	9	4				10						11
35	6	Port Vale	1-3	Lines	8781		5	1			3	2	7		6	9	4				10			8			11
36	8	BRISTOL CITY	5-1	Large 2, Mills, Smith 2	12366		5	1			3	2	7			9	4			6	10		8				11
37	12	Brighton & Hove Albion	5-0	Hails, Large, Leck 2, Jennings (og)	16354		5	1			3	2	7		6	9	4			8	10						11
38	13	SHREWSBURY TOWN	1-0	Large	13350		5	1			3	2	7		6	9	4			8	10						11
39	16	BRIGHTON & HOVE ALB	3-0	Kurila, Large, Jennings (og)	17520	8	5	1			3	2	7		6	9	4				10						11
40	20	Millwall	3-1	Hails, Reid 2	9992		5	1			3	2	7		6	9	4				10		8				11
41	23	BARNSLEY	4-2	Large 2, Reid 2	15939		5	1			3	2	7		6	9	4				10		8				11
42	27	SOUTHEND UNITED	5-3	Large 3, Reid, Smith	13498		5	1			3	2	7		6	9	4				10		8				11
43	May 1	Shrewsbury Town	0-1		6052		5	1		2	3		7		6	9	4				10		8				11
44	9	CARLISLE UNITED	2-0	Large 2	15094		5	1		2	3		7		6	9	4				10		8				11
45	11	Peterborough United	4-0	Hails, Leck, Smith, Rayner (og)	17518		5	1		2	3		7		6	9	4				10		8				11
46	24	HULL CITY	3-0	Ashworth, Foley, Reid	12110	8	5	1			3	2	7			9	4			6	10						11
		Apps				30	45	46	1	8	28	43	26	21	40	20	42	1	2	19	41	15	14	1	2	15	46
		Goals				25					1	1	5	14	1	18	5			1	11	2	4				16

Five own goals

F.A. Cup

	Date	Opponent	Score	Scorers	Att	Ashworth A	Branston TG	Brodie CTG	Carr WG	Cockcroft VH	Everitt MD	Foley TC	Hails W	Holton CC	Kurila J	Large F	Leck DA	Llewellyn HA	Martin D	Mills RWG	Reid J	Sanders RJ	Smith HR	Robson TH	Etheridge BG	Woollard AJ	Lines B
R1	Nov 3	TORQUAY UNITED	1-2	Everitt	11844	9	5	1			2			8	6		4				10	7				3	11

F.L. Cup

	Date	Opponent	Score	Scorers	Att	Ashworth A	Branston TG	Brodie CTG	Carr WG	Cockcroft VH	Everitt MD	Foley TC	Hails W	Holton CC	Kurila J	Large F	Leck DA	Llewellyn HA	Martin D	Mills RWG	Reid J	Sanders RJ	Smith HR	Robson TH	Etheridge BG	Woollard AJ	Lines B
R2	Sep 26	COLCHESTER UTD.	2-0	Ashworth, Holton	7771	9	5	1				2		8	6		4					7			10	3	11
R3	Oct 16	PRESTON NORTH END	1-1	Lines	12418	9	5	1				2		8	6		4				10	7				3	11
rep	29	Preston North End	1-2	Reid	7040	9	5	1			3	6	2	8			4				10	7					11

		P	W	D	L	F	A	W	D	L	F	A	Pts
1	NORTHAMPTON TOWN	46	16	6	1	64	19	10	4	9	45	41	62
2	Swindon Town	46	18	2	3	60	22	4	12	7	27	34	58
3	Port Vale	46	16	4	3	47	25	7	4	12	25	33	54
4	Coventry City	46	14	6	3	54	28	4	11	8	29	41	53
5	Bournemouth	46	11	12	0	39	16	7	4	12	24	30	52
6	Peterborough Utd.	46	11	5	7	48	33	9	6	8	45	42	51
7	Notts County	46	15	3	5	46	29	4	10	9	27	45	51
8	Southend United	46	11	7	5	38	24	8	5	10	37	53	50
9	Wrexham	46	14	6	3	54	27	6	3	14	30	56	49
10	Hull City	46	12	6	5	40	22	7	4	12	34	47	48
11	Crystal Palace	46	10	7	6	38	22	7	6	10	30	36	47
12	Colchester United	46	11	6	6	41	35	7	5	11	32	58	47
13	Queen's Park Rgs.	46	9	6	8	44	36	8	5	10	41	40	45
14	Bristol City	46	10	9	4	54	38	6	4	13	46	54	45
15	Shrewsbury Town	46	13	4	6	57	41	3	8	12	26	40	44
16	Millwall	46	11	6	6	50	32	4	7	12	32	55	43
17	Watford	46	12	3	8	55	40	5	3	15	27	45	42
18	Barnsley	46	12	6	5	39	28	3	5	15	24	46	41
19	Bristol Rovers	46	11	8	4	45	29	4	3	16	25	59	41
20	Reading	46	13	4	6	51	30	3	4	16	23	48	40
21	Bradford Park Ave.	46	10	9	4	43	36	4	3	16	36	61	40
22	Brighton & Hove A.	46	7	6	10	28	38	5	6	12	30	48	36
23	Carlisle United	46	12	4	7	41	37	1	5	17	20	52	35
24	Halifax Town	46	8	3	12	41	51	1	9	13	23	55	30

1963/64 11th in Division 2

#	Date	Opponent	Score	Scorers	Att	Best WJB	Branston TG	Brodie CTG	Brown RH	Carr WG	Cockcroft VH	Coe NC	Etheridge BG	Everitt MD	Hails W	Harvey BR	Hunt RR	Jones BR	Kane P	Kiernan J	Kurila J	Large F	Leck DA	Lines B	Martin D	Mills RWG	Reid J	Robson TH	Smith HR	Foley TC	Hall JL
1	Aug 27	Scunthorpe United	2-1	Large, Lines	8738		5	1						3	7					4		9	6	11			10		8	2	
2	31	Sunderland	2-0	Hails, Smith	39201		5	1						3	7				6			9	4	11			10		8	2	
3	Sep 3	SCUNTHORPE UNITED	2-0	Hails, Large	16032		5	1		2				3	7				6			9	4	11			10		8		
4	7	DERBY COUNTY	0-1		14672		5	1		2				3	7				6			9	4	11			10		8		
5	11	Norwich City	3-3	Large, Leck, Smith	19669		5	1		2				3	7				6			9	4	11			10		8		
6	13	BURY	1-2	Smith	14886		5	1		2				3	7				6			9	4	11			10		8		
7	16	NORWICH CITY	3-2	Best, Large 2	14928	7	5	1		2				3								9	4	11		6	10		8		
8	21	Manchester City	0-3		21340	7	5	1		2				3								9	4	11		6	10		8		
9	28	SWINDON TOWN	4-0	Kane 2, Large 2	18177		5	1		2				3	7				8			9	4	11		6	10				
10	Oct 1	LEEDS UNITED	0-3		15079		5			2		1		3	7				8			9	4	11		6	10				
11	5	Cardiff City	0-1		10178		5			2				3	7	1			8			9	4	11		6	10				
12	8	HUDDERSFIELD T	1-0	Large	13257		5							3	7	1			8			9	4			6	10	11		2	
13	12	Plymouth Argyle	3-0	Hails 2, Kane	13224		5							2	7	1		3	9			4				6	10	11	8		
14	19	CHARLTON ATHLETIC	1-2	Large	15221		5							2	7	1		3	8			9	4	11		6	10				
15	26	Newcastle United	3-2	Hails, Kane, Martin	25743		5							2	7	1		3	9	6			4		8		10	11			
16	Nov 2	PRESTON NORTH END	0-3		13693		5							2	7	1		3	9	6			4		8		10	11			
17	9	Leyton Orient	0-0		11532		5							2	7	1		3	9			10	4		8	6		11			
18	16	SWANSEA TOWN	2-3	Kane, Lines	10985		5							2	7	1		3	8			9	4	11		6	10				
19	23	Southampton	1-3	Martin	18025		5							2	7	1		3		6		9	4	11	8		10				
20	30	MIDDLESBROUGH	3-2	Leck, Martin 2	10346						5		8	3	7	1				6		10	4		9			11		2	
21	Dec 7	Grimsby Town	1-4	Hails	6305		5						8	3	7	1				6		10	4		9			11		2	
22	14	Leeds United	0-0		21208		5							3	7	1			10	6		9	4	11	8				2	
23	21	SUNDERLAND	5-1	Everitt, Hails, Large, Martin 2	12130		5							3	7	1			10	6		9	4	11	8				2	
24	26	ROTHERHAM UNITED	1-3	Large	15089		5							3	7	1			10	6		9	4	11	8				2	
25	28	Rotherham United	0-1		10618		5		10					3	7	1				6		9	4	11	8				2	
26	Jan 11	Derby County	0-0		10195		5		10				8	3	7	1						9	4	11	6				2	
27	18	Bury	1-1	Foley	6077		5		9					3	7	1						8	4	11	10	6			2	
28	Feb 1	MANCHESTER CITY	2-1	Kane, Martin	12330	7	5		9					3					10	6			4	11	8				2	
29	8	Swindon Town	3-2	Kane, Large, Lines	17455		5							3	7	1			10	6		9	4	11	8				2	
30	15	CARDIFF CITY	2-1	Hails, Kane	11871		5							3	7	1			10	6		9	4	11	8				2	
31	18	PLYMOUTH ARGYLE	0-0		9261		5							3	7	1			10	6		9	4	11	8				2	
32	Mar 7	NEWCASTLE UNITED	2-2	Hunt, Leck	11440		5							3	7	1	10		9	6			4	11	8				2	
33	21	Leyton Orient	1-2	Robson	9014		5		9					3	7	1	8			6			4		10			11		2	
34	28	Charlton Athletic	1-1	Everitt	15142	7	5						10	3		1	8			6			4					11		2	9
35	30	Portsmouth	0-3		13633	7	5						10	3		1	8			6			4					11		2	9
36	31	PORTSMOUTH	2-1	Mills, Foley	10245	7	5							3		1	8				6		4	9		10		11		2	
37	Apr 4	SOUTHAMPTON	2-0	Hunt, Kurila	8047	7	5							3		1	8				6		4	9		10		11		2	
38	7	Swansea Town	1-1	Hunt	11398		5							3	7	1	10				6		4	9	8			11		2	
39	10	Middlesbrough	0-1		9220		5							3	7	1	10				6		4	9	8			11		2	
40	13	Huddersfield Town	1-0	Best	6762	7	5							3		1	8				6		4	9				11		2	10
41	18	GRIMSBY TOWN	1-2	Robson	10092		5							3	7	1	8				6		4	9				11		2	
42	25	Preston North End	1-2	Robson	12933	7	5		10					3		1	8				6		4	9				11		2	
		Apps				9	41	9	6	1	9	1	5	42	33	32	11	7	18	19	18	27	33	25	20	22	18	17	9	26	4
		Goals				2								2	8		3		8			1	12	3	3	7	1		3	3	2

F.A. Cup

	Date	Opponent	Score		Att	Best WJB	Branston TG	Brodie CTG	Brown RH	Carr WG	Cockcroft VH	Coe NC	Etheridge BG	Everitt MD	Hails W	Harvey BR	Hunt RR	Jones BR	Kane P	Kiernan J	Kurila J	Large F	Leck DA	Lines B	Martin D	Mills RWG	Reid J	Robson TH	Smith HR	Foley TC	Hall JL
R3	Jan 4	Sunderland	0-2		40683		5		10				8	3	7	1				6		9	4	11						2	

F.L. Cup

	Date	Opponent	Score	Scorers	Att	Best WJB	Branston TG	Brodie CTG	Brown RH	Carr WG	Cockcroft VH	Coe NC	Etheridge BG	Everitt MD	Hails W	Harvey BR	Hunt RR	Jones BR	Kane P	Kiernan J	Kurila J	Large F	Leck DA	Lines B	Martin D	Mills RWG	Reid J	Robson TH	Smith HR	Foley TC	Hall JL
R2	Sep 25	Brighton & Hove Albion	1-1	Mills	5496		5	1		2				3	7							9	4	11		6	10				
rep	Oct 14	BRIGHTON & HOVE ALB.	3-2	Leck, Reid, Smith	5569		5	1						2	7				9				4			6	10	11	8		
R3	Nov 4	Colchester United	1-4	Robson	6237		5	1	10						7				9	6			4					11	8	2	

Played in R2: HA Llewellyn (at 8). Played in R2 replay and R3: Sharpe (at 3).

		P	W	D	L	F	A	W	D	L	F	A	Pts
1	Leeds United	42	12	9	0	35	16	12	6	3	36	18	63
2	Sunderland	42	16	3	2	47	13	9	8	4	34	24	61
3	Preston North End	42	13	7	1	37	14	10	3	8	42	40	56
4	Charlton Athletic	42	11	4	6	44	30	8	6	7	32	40	48
5	Southampton	42	13	3	5	69	32	6	6	9	31	41	47
6	Manchester City	42	12	4	5	50	27	6	6	9	34	39	46
7	Rotherham United	42	14	3	4	52	26	5	4	12	38	52	45
8	Newcastle United	42	14	2	5	49	26	6	3	12	25	43	45
9	Portsmouth	42	9	7	5	46	34	7	4	10	33	36	43
10	Middlesbrough	42	14	4	3	47	16	1	7	13	20	36	41
11	NORTHAMPTON TOWN	42	10	2	9	35	31	6	7	8	23	29	41
12	Huddersfield Town	42	11	4	6	31	25	4	6	11	26	39	40
13	Derby County	42	10	6	5	34	27	4	5	12	22	40	39
14	Swindon Town	42	11	5	5	39	24	3	5	13	18	45	38
15	Cardiff City	42	10	7	4	31	27	4	3	14	25	54	38
16	Leyton Orient	42	8	6	7	32	32	5	4	12	22	40	36
17	Norwich City	42	9	7	5	43	30	2	6	13	21	50	35
18	Bury	42	8	5	8	35	36	5	4	12	22	37	35
19	Swansea Town	42	11	4	6	44	26	1	5	15	19	48	33
20	Plymouth Argyle	42	6	8	7	26	32	2	8	11	19	35	32
21	Grimsby Town	42	6	7	8	28	34	3	7	11	19	41	32
22	Scunthorpe United	42	8	8	5	30	25	2	2	17	22	57	30

1963/64 SEASON
Back: Osborne(Sec), Martin, Branston, Harvey, Leck, Large, Kurila, Bowen(Man), Jennings
Front: Everitt, Kane, Foley, Hails, Lines

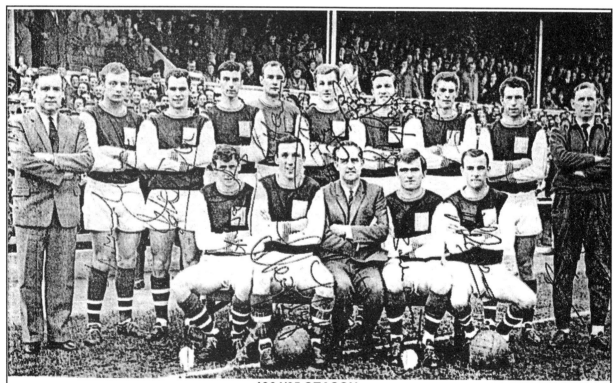

1964/65 SEASON
Back: Osborne(Sec), Carr, Kiernan, Leck, Harvey, Branston, Brown, Martin, Everitt, Payne(Train)
Front: Walden, Foley(Captain), Bowen(Manager), Hunt, Robson

1964/65   2nd in Division 2: Promoted

#		Date	Opponent	Score	Scorers	Att	Best WJB	Branston TG	Brown RH	Carr WG	Cockcroft VH	Etheridge BG	Everitt MD	Foley TC	Hall JL	Harvey BR	Hunt RR	Kiernan J	Kurila J	Leck DA	Leek K	Lines B	Livesey CE	Martin D	Robson TH	Walden HB	Walton RP
1	Aug	24	Middlesbrough	0-1		27122		5					3	2		1	8	6		4			11	9	10		7
2		29	Manchester City	2-0	Foley, Hunt	20935		5					3	2		1	8	6		4			11	9	10		7
3	Sep	1	MIDDLESBROUGH	1-1	Martin	17028		5					3	2		1	8	6		4			11	9	10		7
4		5	Southampton	0-2		13989		5					3	2		1	8	6		4			11	9	10		7
5		8	NEWCASTLE UNITED	1-0	Etheridge	15977	8	5				10	3	2		1		6		4			11	9			7
6		11	HUDDERSFIELD T	3-2	Livesey, Robson 2	12984	8	5				10	3	2		1		6		4			9		11		7
7		15	Ipswich Town	0-0		13520	8	5				10	3	2		1		6		4				9	11		7
8		19	Coventry City	1-0	Robson	30113		5				10	3	2		1	8	6		4				9	11		7
9		26	CARDIFF CITY	1-0	Everitt	12328		5				10	3	2		1	8	6		4				9	11		7
10		29	IPSWICH TOWN	3-2	Hunt 3	14886		5				10	3	2		1	8	6		4				9	11		7
11	Oct	3	Preston North End	2-2	Robson, Walden	15953		5				10	3	2		1	8	6		4				9	11		7
12		7	Portsmouth	3-3	Branston, Livesey, Robson	12262		5				10	3	2		1	8	6		4				9	11		7
13		10	CHARLTON ATHLETIC	1-0	Robson	13552		5			3	10		2		1	8	6		4				9	11		7
14		17	Leyton Orient	2-2	Hall, Martin	8390		5					3	2	10	1		6		4			9	8	11		7
15		24	Bury	2-0	Foley, Martin	11324		5					3	2	10	1		6		4			9	8	11		7
16		31	Crystal Palace	2-1	Livesey, Robson	21331		5					3	2		1	8	6		4			9	10	11		7
17	Nov	7	NORWICH CITY	0-0		16774		5					3	2		1	8	6		4			9	10	11		7
18		14	Rotherham United	1-1	Leck	11273	7	5					3	2		1		6		4		11	10	9	8		
19		21	SWANSEA TOWN	2-1	Martin, Robson	13427		5					3	2		1		6		4		11	10	9	8	7	
20		28	Derby County	2-2	Brown 2	17367		5	10		3			2		1		6		4		11	9		8	7	
21	Dec	5	SWINDON TOWN	2-1	Brown, Walden	9586		5	8		3			2		1		6		4		11	9	10		7	
22		12	Newcastle United	0-5		40376		5	8				3	2		1		6		4		11	9	10		7	
23		19	MANCHESTER CITY	2-0	Everitt, Leck	12665		5			3		8	2		1		6		4	10	11	9			7	
24		26	Bolton Wanderers	0-0		24487		5			3		8	2		1		6		4	10		9		11	7	
25	Jan	2	SOUTHAMPTON	2-2	Branston, Leek	15245		5			3		8	2		1		6		4	10		9		11	7	
26		16	Huddersfield Town	0-2		7359		5	9				3	2		1		6		4	10	11			8		7
27		23	COVENTRY CITY	1-1	Leck	18741		5	9				3	2		1		6		4	10	11			8	7	
28	Feb	6	Cardiff City	2-0	Brown 2	7427		5	9				3	2		1		6		4	10	11			8	7	
29		13	PRESTON NORTH END	2-1	Brown, Robson	14010		5	9				3	2		1			6	4	10		11		8	7	
30		20	Charlton Athletic	1-1	Robson	8958		5	9				3	2		1		6		4	10		11		8	7	
31		27	LEYTON ORIENT	2-0	Leck, Robson	13517		5	9				3	2		1		6		4	10		11		8	7	
32	Mar	2	BOLTON WANDERERS	4-0	Foley, Leck, Martin 2	15515		5	9				3	2		1		6		4			11	10	8	7	
33		13	CRYSTAL PALACE	1-1	Brown	17350		5	9				3	2		1		6		4	10		11		8	7	
34		20	Norwich City	1-1	Robson	25199		5	9				3	2		1		6		4	10		11		8	7	
35		23	Swindon Town	2-4	Brown 2	17886			9	5			3	2	10	1		6		4				8	11	7	
36		27	ROTHERHAM UNITED	1-0	Brown	19488			9	5			3	2	10	1		6		4				8	11	7	
37	Apr	3	Swansea Town	2-1	Brown, Martin	10516			9	5			3	2	10	1		6		4				8	11	7	
38		10	DERBY COUNTY	2-2	Brown, Martin	17917			9	5			3	2	10	1		6		4				8	11	7	
39		17	Bury	4-1	Brown, Kiernan, Martin 2	6800			9	5			3	2		1	10	6		4				8	11	7	
40		19	Plymouth Argyle	2-5	Kiernan, Martin	10547			9	5			3	2		1	10	6		4				8	11	7	
41		20	PLYMOUTH ARGYLE	3-1	Brown, Martin, one og	19718			9	5			3	2		1	10	6		4				8	11	7	
42		24	PORTSMOUTH	1-1	one og	20660			9	5			3	2		1	10	6		4				8	11	7	

	Best WJB	Branston TG	Brown RH	Carr WG	Cockcroft VH	Etheridge BG	Everitt MD	Foley TC	Hall JL	Harvey BR	Hunt RR	Kiernan J	Kurila J	Leck DA	Leek K	Lines B	Livesey CE	Martin D	Robson TH	Walden HB	Walton RP
Apps	4	34	20	8	6	9	39	42	6	42	16	41	1	42	12	9	25	30	36	39	1
Goals		2	13			1	2	3	1		4	2		3	3		3	13	13	1	

Two own goals

F.A. Cup

		Date	Opponent	Score	Scorers	Att	Best WJB	Branston TG	Cockcroft VH	Everitt MD	Foley TC	Harvey BR	Kiernan J	Leck DA	Leek K	Livesey CE	Robson TH	Walden HB
R3	Jan	9	Chelsea	1-4	Foley	44335		5	3	8	2	1	6	4	10	9	11	7

F.L. Cup

		Date	Opponent	Score	Scorers	Att	Best WJB	Branston TG	Brown RH	Cockcroft VH	Etheridge BG	Everitt MD	Foley TC	Hall JL	Harvey BR	Hunt RR	Kiernan J	Leck DA	Lines B	Livesey CE	Martin D	Robson TH	Walden HB
R2	Sep	23	Bournemouth	2-0	Hunt, Livesey	8807		5			10	3	2		1	8	6	4		9		11	7
R3	Oct	20	PORTSMOUTH	2-1	Livesey, Martin	7380		5				3	2	10	1		6	4		9	8	11	7
R4	Nov	4	CHESTERFIELD	4-1	Foley, Hunt, Martin 2	6695		5				3	2		1	8	6	4		9	10	11	7
R5		25	Plymouth Argyle	0-1		21698		5	8	3			2	10	1		6	4	11	9			7

		P	W	D	L	F	A	W	D	L	F	A	Pts
1	Newcastle United	42	16	4	1	50	16	8	5	8	31	29	57
2	NORTHAMPTON T.	42	14	7	0	37	16	6	9	6	29	34	56
3	Bolton Wanderers	42	13	6	2	46	17	7	4	10	34	41	50
4	Southampton	42	12	6	3	49	25	5	8	8	34	38	48
5	Ipswich Town	42	11	7	3	48	30	4	10	7	26	37	47
6	Norwich City	42	15	4	2	47	21	5	3	13	14	36	47
7	Crystal Palace	42	11	6	4	37	24	5	7	9	18	27	45
8	Huddersfield Town	42	12	4	5	28	15	5	6	10	25	38	44
9	Derby County	42	11	5	5	48	35	5	6	10	36	44	43
10	Coventry City	42	10	5	6	41	29	7	4	10	31	41	43
11	Manchester City	42	12	3	6	40	24	4	6	11	23	38	41
12	Preston North End	42	11	8	2	46	29	3	5	13	30	52	41
13	Cardiff City	42	10	7	4	43	25	3	7	11	21	32	40
14	Rotherham United	42	10	7	4	39	25	4	5	12	31	44	40
15	Plymouth Argyle	42	10	7	4	36	28	6	1	14	27	51	40
16	Bury	42	9	4	8	36	30	5	6	10	24	38	38
17	Middlesbrough	42	8	8	5	40	31	5	4	12	30	45	35
18	Charlton Athletic	42	8	5	8	35	34	5	4	12	29	41	35
19	Leyton Orient	42	10	4	7	36	34	2	7	12	14	38	35
20	Portsmouth	42	11	4	6	36	22	1	6	14	20	55	34
21	Swindon Town	42	12	3	6	43	30	2	2	17	20	51	33
22	Swansea Town	42	9	7	5	40	29	2	3	16	22	55	32

1965/66   21st in Division 1: Relegated

No	Date	Opponent	Res	Scorers	Att	Best WJB	Branston TG	Broadfoot J	Brown RH	Carr WG	Cockcroft VH	Coe NC	Everitt MD	Foley TC	Hall JL	Harvey BR	Hudson GA	Hunt RR	Kiernan J	Kurila J	Leck DA	Leek K	Lines B	Livesey CE	Mackin J	Martin D	Moore G	Walden HB	Robson TH
1	Aug 21	Everton	2-5	Brown, Hunt	48489		5		9				3	2		1		8	6	4			10					7	11
2	25	ARSENAL	1-1	Brown	17352			9		5	12		3	2		1		8	6		4		10					7	11
3	28	MANCHESTER UNITED	1-1	Hunt	21245			9		5			3	2		1		8	6		4		10					7	11
4	Sep 4	Newcastle United	0-2		28051			9		5			3	2		1		8	6		4		10					7	11
5	7	Burnley	1-4	Livesey	14792			9		5	12		3	2		1		8	6		4		11	10				7	
6	10	WEST BROMWICH ALB.	3-4	Lines, Robson 2	18528	7	5		9				3	2		1			6		4		10		8				11
7	15	BURNLEY	1-2	Robson	19336	7			9	5			3	2		1			6		4		10		8				11
8	18	Nottingham Forest	1-1	Cockcroft	19669				9	5	7		3	2	8	1			6		4		10						11
9	25	SHEFFIELD WEDNESDAY	0-0		16299				9	5	7		3	2	8	1			6		4		10						11
10	28	Arsenal	1-1	Hall	33240					5			3	2	9	1			6		4		10		8			7	11
11	Oct 2	Leicester City	1-1	Foley	27484		12			5			3	2	9	1			6		4		10		8			7	11
12	9	SHEFFIELD UNITED	0-1		17300		5			4			3	2	9	1			6				10		8			7	11
13	16	Leeds United	1-6	Best	33748	7				5			3	2		1		9	6		4	10			8				11
14	23	WEST HAM UNITED	2-1	Foley, Leek	15367	7				5			3	2		1		9	6		4	8	10						11
15	30	Sunderland	0-3		32216					5			3	2		1		9	6		4	8	10					7	11
16	Nov 6	ASTON VILLA	2-1	Hall 2	18836					5	3	1		2	9			8	6		4		11			10		7	12
17	13	Liverpool	0-5		41904		4			5	3	1		2	9			8	6				10			11		7	
18	20	TOTTENHAM HOTSPUR	0-2		17611	4		7	9	5	3	1		2	10				6				11			8			
19	27	Fulham	4-1	Brown 3, Hunt	11389		5	7	9	4	3	1		2	10			8	6				11						11
20	Dec 4	BLACKPOOL	2-1	Broadfoot, Lines	14504		5	7	9	4	3	1		2	10			8	6				11						
21	11	Blackburn Rovers	1-6	Lines	10685		5	7	9	4	3	1		2	10			8	6				11						
22	27	CHELSEA	2-3	Brown, Moore	23325		5	7	9	4	3	1		2	10				6				11				8		
23	28	Chelsea	0-1		17635		5	7	9	4		1	3	2					6				11			10	8		
24	Jan 1	Sheffield United	2-2	Lines, Martin	16143		5	7	9	4	3	1		2					6				11			10	8		
25	8	BLACKBURN ROVERS	2-1	Brown, Kiernan	15820		5	7	9	4		1	3	2					6				11			10	8		
26	15	West Ham United	1-1	Brown	20745		5	7	9	4		1	3	2	10				6				11				8		
27	29	EVERTON	0-2		16309		5	7		4		1	3	2	10				6				11			8	9		
28	Feb 5	Manchester United	2-6	Martin, Moore	35273			7		5	3	1		2	9				6		4		11			10	8		
29	12	Stoke City	2-6	Brown, Moore	16522			7	9	5	3	1		2					6		4		11			10	8		
30	19	NEWCASTLE UNITED	3-1	Martin 2, Moore	14541		5	7	9		3			2		1			6		4		11			10	8		
31	26	West Bromwich Albion	1-1	Martin	18923		5	7	9		3			2		1			6		4		11			10	8		
32	Mar 5	LEEDS UNITED	2-1	Hudson, Lines	21548		5	7			3			2		1	9		6		4		11			10	8		
33	12	NOTTM. FOREST	3-3	Kurila, Martin, Moore	18670		5	7			3			2		1	9		6	4			11			10	8		
34	19	Sheffield Wednesday	1-3	Hudson	16283		5	7			3			2		1	9		6		4		11		12	10	8		
35	26	LEICESTER CITY	2-2	Hudson, Moore	21564		5				3			2		1	9		6		4		11		12	10	8	7	
36	Apr 2	Aston Villa	2-1	Mackin, Moore	10438		5				3					1	9		6		4		11		2	10	8	7	
37	9	LIVERPOOL	0-0		20029		5				3					1	9		6		4		11		2	10	8	7	
38	12	STOKE CITY	1-0	Martin	20680		5				3					1	9		6		4		11		2	10	8	7	
39	16	Tottenham Hotspur	1-1	Hudson	29749		5				3				12	1	9		6		4		11		2	8	10	7	
40	23	FULHAM	2-4	Hudson, Kiernan	24523		5				3					1	9		6		4		11		2	8	10	7	
41	25	SUNDERLAND	2-1	Everitt, Hudson	17921		5						3			1	9		6		4		11		2	8	10	7	
42	30	Blackpool	0-3		15295		5						3			1	9		6		4		11		2	8	10	7	
		Apps				4	28	17	21	27	18	15	32	31	15	27	11	13	42	20	10	4	40	3	9	26	21	19	16
		Goals				1			9		1		1	2	3		6	3	2	1	1	1	5	1	1	7	7		3

F.A. Cup

Rd	Date	Opponent	Res	Scorers	Att	Branston	Broadfoot	Brown	Carr	Cockcroft	Coe	Foley	Hall	Kiernan	Lines	Moore
R3	Jan 22	NOTTM. FOREST	1-2	Brown	17873	5	7	9	4	3	1	2	10	6	11	8

F.L. Cup

Rd	Date	Opponent	Res	Scorers	Att	Branston	Broadfoot	Brown	Carr	Cockcroft	Everitt	Foley	Harvey	Kiernan	Leck	Lines	Mackin	Walden	Robson
R2	Sep 21	Blackburn Rovers	1-0	Everitt	8814		9		5	7	3	2	1	6	4	10	8		11
R3	Oct 13	Fulham	0-5		7835	5		9	4		3	2	1	6		10		7	11

Played in R3: BG Etheridge (at 8).

	Team	P	W	D	L	F	A	W	D	L	F	A	Pts
1	Liverpool	42	17	2	2	52	15	9	7	5	27	19	61
2	Leeds United	42	14	4	3	49	15	9	5	7	30	23	55
3	Burnley	42	15	3	3	45	20	9	4	8	34	27	55
4	Manchester United	42	12	8	1	50	20	6	7	8	34	39	51
5	Chelsea	42	11	4	6	30	21	11	3	7	35	32	51
6	West Bromwich Alb.	42	11	6	4	58	34	8	6	7	33	35	50
7	Leicester City	42	12	4	5	40	28	9	3	9	40	37	49
8	Tottenham Hotspur	42	11	6	4	55	37	5	6	10	20	29	44
9	Sheffield United	42	11	6	4	37	25	5	5	11	19	34	43
10	Stoke City	42	12	6	3	42	22	3	6	12	23	42	42
11	Everton	42	12	6	3	39	19	3	5	13	17	43	41
12	West Ham United	42	12	5	4	46	33	3	4	14	24	50	39
13	Blackpool	42	9	5	7	36	29	5	4	12	19	36	37
14	Arsenal	42	8	8	5	36	31	4	5	12	26	44	37
15	Newcastle United	42	10	5	6	26	20	4	4	13	24	43	37
16	Aston Villa	42	10	3	8	39	34	5	3	13	30	46	36
17	Sheffield Wed.	42	11	6	4	35	18	3	2	16	21	48	36
18	Nottingham Forest	42	11	3	7	31	26	3	5	13	25	46	36
19	Sunderland	42	13	2	6	36	28	1	6	14	15	44	36
20	Fulham	42	9	4	8	34	37	5	3	13	33	48	35
21	NORTHAMPTON TOWN	42	8	6	7	31	32	2	7	12	24	60	33
22	Blackburn Rovers	42	6	1	14	30	36	2	3	16	27	52	20

1965/66 SEASON
Back: Everitt, Leck, Harvey, Branston, Kiernan, Livesey
Front: Walden, Hunt, Foley, Etheridge, Robson
Insets: Brown, Lines, Carr

1966/67 SEASON
Back: Perryman, Brown, Inwood, Jordan, Fagan, Mackin, Carr, Price, Cockroft
Middle: Everitt, Hunt, Linnell, Moore, Hall, Harvey, Clarke, Kurila, Branston, Martin
Front: Payne(Trainer), Walden, Hudson, Best, Bowen (Man.), Kiernan, Lines, Felton, Mills(Asst.Trainer)

1966/67 — 21st in Division 2: Relegated

#	Date	Opponent	Score	Scorers	Att	Best WJB	Branston TG	Brown DJ	Brown RH	Brown WDF	Carr WG	Clarke JL	Cockcroft VH	Everitt MD	Foley TC	Felton GM	Hall JL	Harvey BR	Hudson GA	Jones RS	Jordon G	Kiernan J	Kurila J	Large F	Lines B	Mackin J	Martin D	Moore G	Perryman G	Price RJ	Walden HB	Walker DCA
1	Aug 20	Preston North End	1-2	Best	12192	7	5							3					1	9		6	4		11	2	8	10				
2	27	ROTHERHAM UNITED	3-1	Best 2, Martin	13954	7	5							3					1	9		6	4		11	2	8	10				
3	30	BURY	0-0		10025	7	5							3					1	9		6	4		11	2	8	10				
4	Sep 3	Millwall	0-1		11121	7	5						3		9		1					6	4		11	2	8	10				
5	6	NORWICH CITY	1-2	Martin	14767	10	5						3		9		1					6	4		11	2	8				7	
6	10	DERBY COUNTY	0-2		10975	7	5						3		8		1		9			6	4		11	2		10			7	
7	17	PLYMOUTH ARGYLE	2-1	Lines, Walden	9802	10	5		9		3			2			1					6			11		4	8			7	
8	20	Bury	2-1	Best, Mackin	8580	10	5		9		3						1					6			11	2	4	8			7	
9	23	Hull City	1-6	Lines	29122	10	5		9		3						1					12			11	2	4	8			7	
10	Oct 1	PORTSMOUTH	2-4	Kiernan, Martin	10364		5				3	4		2			1	10	7			6			11	12	8	9				3
11	8	Crystal Palace	1-5	Martin	18507	10	5				4								9		1	7			11	2	8					3
12	15	HUDDERSFIELD T	0-1		13355		5			1				2			9	8	7			6	4		11		10					3
13	29	WOLVERHAMPTON W.	0-4		16761		5			1				2				8	9			6	5		11		4	10			7	3
14	Nov 5	Ipswich Town	1-6	Best	12820	10	5			1				2	7							6	4		11		8	9				3
15	12	BRISTOL CITY	2-1	Jones, Kurila	10004	10	5			1								7				6	4		11	2	8	9				3
16	19	Carlisle United	0-2		11946	10	5			1								7				6	4		11	2	8	9				3
17	26	BLACKBURN ROVERS	2-1	Martin, Moore	9470		5			1						10						6	4		11	2	8	9			7	3
18	Dec 3	Bolton Wanderers	2-1	Mackin, Martin	10352		5			1						10		7				6	4		11	2	8	9				3
19	14	Cardiff City	2-4	Mackin, Martin	7954		5			1						10		7				6	4		11	2	8	9				3
20	17	PRESTON NORTH END	1-5	Martin	10050		5			1						10		7				6	4		11	2	8	9				3
21	26	Birmingham City	0-3		24302		5			1						7	11	10				6	4	9		2	8					3
22	27	BIRMINGHAM CITY	2-1	Large, Martin	15433				1	5						7		10				6	4	9	11	2	8					3
23	31	Rotherham United	2-1	Large, Martin	9497	12			1	5						7		10				6	4	9	11	2	8					3
24	Jan 7	MILLWALL	1-2	Kiernan	11343				1	5						7		8				6	4	9	11	2	10					3
25	14	Derby County	3-4	Kiernan, Large, Martin	14533				1	5						7		10				6	4	9	11	2	8					3
26	17	CHARLTON ATHLETIC	1-1	Martin	11578				1	5			3			2	7	10				6	4	9	11		8					
27	21	Plymouth Argyle	0-1		12830		5			1						2						6	4	9	11	3	8	10			7	
28	Feb 4	HULL CITY	2-2	Best, Moore	12396	8	5			1				4	2	7						10			6	9		11				
29	11	Portsmouth	2-3	D Brown, Moore	18979		5	10						4	2				1				6	9	11	3		8			7	
30	25	CRYSTAL PALACE	1-0	D Brown	13081		5	8						3	2	7			1				4	9		6		10			11	
31	Mar 4	Wolverhampton Wan.	0-1		25672		5	8						3	2				1				4	9	11	6		10			7	
32	11	COVENTRY CITY	0-0		20100		5	8						3	2				1				6	9	11	4		10			7	
33	18	CARDIFF CITY	2-0	D Brown, Large	11787	8	5	10							2				1				6	9	11	12	4				7	3
34	25	Huddersfield Town	2-0	Large 2	18214		5	8							2				1				6	9	11	4		10			7	3
35	28	Coventry City	0-2		38566		5	8							2				1				6	9	11	4		10			7	3
36	Apr 1	IPSWICH TOWN	1-1	Hall	13129		5	8							2		9		1				6		11	4		10			7	3
37	7	Bristol City	0-1		23750		5								2	7	10	1				6	9			4		8			11	3
38	15	CARLISLE UNITED	3-3	Large, Walden, Mackin	10752		5								2			1				6	9	11	4	10	8			7	3
39	22	Blackburn Rovers	0-3		9883		5								2			1				6	9	11	4	8	10			7	3
40	29	BOLTON WANDERERS	2-1	Large, Martin	9387		5						3		2	7		1				6	9	11	4	8	10				
41	May 6	Charlton Athletic	0-3		15098		5						3		2	7		1				6	9	11	4	8	10				
42	13	Norwich City	0-1		13544						4	5			7		1				3	6	9	11		8		2	10		

	Best WJB	Branston TG	Brown DJ	Brown RH	Brown WDF	Carr WG	Clarke JL	Cockcroft VH	Everitt MD	Foley TC	Felton GM	Hall JL	Harvey BR	Hudson GA	Jones RS	Jordon G	Kiernan J	Kurila J	Large F	Lines B	Mackin J	Martin D	Moore G	Perryman G	Price RJ	Walden HB	Walker DCA
Apps	15	36	8	3	17	11	2	6	13	16	13	13	25	7	17	1	26	37	21	38	36	31	32	1	1	18	22
Goals	6		3							1		1					3	1	8	2	4	13	3			2	

F.A. Cup

R	Date	Opponent	Score	Scorers	Att	Best WJB	Branston TG	Carr WG	Everitt MD	Foley TC	Felton GM	Jones RS	Kiernan J	Kurila J	Mackin J	Martin D
R3	Jan 25	WEST BROMWICH ALB.	1-3	Foley	16899	9	5	1	10	2	7	11	6	4	3	8

F.L. Cup

R	Date	Opponent	Score	Scorers	Att	Best WJB	Branston TG	Brown DJ	Brown RH	Brown WDF	Carr WG	Clarke JL	Everitt MD	Felton GM	Hall JL	Hudson GA	Kiernan J	Kurila J	Lines B	Mackin J	Martin D	Moore G	Walden HB	Walker DCA
R2	Sep 14	PETERBOROUGH UTD.	2-2	Best, R Brown	5778	8	5		9		4	3			1		6		11	2	10	12	7	
rep	26	Peterborough Utd.	2-0	Best, Martin	9484	7	5				4	2	3		1	9	6		11		8	10		
R3	Oct 5	ROTHERHAM UNITED	2-1	Hall, Mackin	5631	8	5				4			9	1		6		11	3	10		7	
R4	26	Brighton & Hove Alb.	1-1	Hall	17235	8	5			1			2			9	6	5	11		4	10	7	3
rep	Nov 1	BRIGHTON & HOVE ALB.	8-0	Best, Martin 4, Moore 2, 1 o	6889	8	5			1			2	7			6	4	11		10	9		3
R5	Dec 7	WEST BROMWICH ALB.	1-3	Hall	14706	7	5			1				10			6	4	11	2	9	8		3

Played in R3; Linnell (at 2).

		P	W	D	L	F	A	W	D	L	F	A	Pts
1	Coventry City	42	17	3	1	46	16	6	10	5	28	27	59
2	Wolverhampton Wan.	42	15	4	2	53	20	10	4	7	35	28	58
3	Carlisle United	42	15	3	3	42	16	8	3	10	29	38	52
4	Blackburn Rovers	42	13	6	2	33	11	6	7	8	23	35	51
5	Ipswich Town	42	11	8	2	45	25	6	8	7	25	29	50
6	Huddersfield Town	42	14	3	4	36	17	6	6	9	22	29	49
7	Crystal Palace	42	14	4	3	42	23	5	6	10	19	32	48
8	Millwall	42	14	5	2	33	17	4	4	13	16	41	45
9	Bolton Wanderers	42	10	7	4	36	19	4	7	10	28	39	42
10	Birmingham City	42	11	5	5	42	23	5	3	13	28	43	40
11	Norwich City	42	10	7	4	31	21	3	7	11	18	34	40
12	Hull City	42	11	5	5	46	25	5	2	14	31	47	39
13	Preston North End	42	14	3	4	44	23	2	4	15	21	44	39
14	Portsmouth	42	7	5	9	34	37	6	8	7	25	33	39
15	Bristol City	42	10	8	3	38	22	2	6	13	18	40	38
16	Plymouth Argyle	42	12	4	5	42	21	2	5	14	17	37	37
17	Derby County	42	8	6	7	40	32	4	6	11	28	40	36
18	Rotherham United	42	10	5	6	39	28	3	5	13	22	42	36
19	Charlton Athletic	42	11	4	6	34	16	2	5	14	15	37	35
20	Cardiff City	42	9	7	5	43	28	2	2	16	18	59	33
21	NORTHAMPTON TOWN	42	8	6	7	28	33	4	0	17	19	51	30
22	Bury	42	9	3	9	31	30	2	3	16	18	53	28

1967/68   18th in Division 3

#	Date		Opponent	Score	Scorers	Att	Harvey BR	Mackin J	Walker DCA	Kurila J	Flowers R	Kiernan J	Best WJB	Martin D	Large F	Carr WG	Hall JL	Faulkes BK	Felton GM	Lines B	Roberts IG	Barron RW	Weaver E	Byrne J	Fairbrother J	Brown DJ	Knox T	Price RJ	Johnson WJ	Clarke JL	Brookes IT
1	Aug	19	Gillingham	0-2		7890	1	2	3	4		6		8	9	5	10		7	11											
2		26	GRIMSBY TOWN	3-0	Martin 2, Large	10206	1	2		4		6		8	9	5	10	3	7	11											
3	Sep	2	Torquay United	0-0		9449	1	2		4	5	6		8	9		10	3	7	11											
4		5	MANSFIELD TOWN	1-1	Mackin	12205	1	2		6	5	10		8	9	4		3	7	11											
5		9	READING	1-2	Large	12625	1	2		6	5			8	9	4	10	3	7	11											
6		16	Swindon Town	0-4		13457	1	2		4	5	6		8	9	7	10	3	12	11											
7		23	SHREWSBURY TOWN	2-2	Martin 2	8922	1	2		6	5			8	9	4	10	3	7	11											
8		25	Mansfield	2-3	Large, Hall	5506	1	2		4	5	6		8	9	10	11	3	7												
9		30	Brighton & Hove Albion	2-0	Mackin, Martin	13546	1	2		4	5	6		8	9	10	11	3	7												
10	Oct	3	ORIENT	2-1	Faulkes 2	8079	1	2		4	5	6		8	9	10	11	3	7												
11		7	Southport	3-1	Martin 2, Hall	6052	1	2		4	5	6		8	9	10	11	3	7												
12		14	SCUNTHORPE UNITED	1-0	Flowers	10097	1	2		4	5	6		8	9	10	11	3	7										12		
13		21	Oldham Athletic	0-2		5019	1	2		4	5	6	7	8	9	10	11	3													
14		24	Orient	3-1	Best 2, Large	4708	1	2	3	4	5	6	7	8	9	10	11														
15		28	BRISTOL ROVERS	4-5	Mackin, Large 3	9126	1	2	3	4	5	6	7	8	9	10	11	12													
16	Nov	4	Barrow	0-4		5851	1	2	3	4	5	6	7	8	9	10	11														
17		11	OXFORD UNITED	1-1	Martin	11318	1	11	3	4	5	6		8			10		2			7						9			
18		14	TORQUAY UNITED	1-0	Martin	8475	1	11	3	4	5	6		8			10		2			7						9			
19		18	Bury	1-3	Kiernan	6642	1	11	3	4	5	6	9	8			10		2			7									
20		25	BOURNEMOUTH	1-0	Roberts	9042	1		3	4	5	6	11	8			10		2		9	7									
21	Dec	2	Colchester United	1-2		3505	1	11	3	4	5	6	8	7			10		2		9										
22		16	GILLINGHAM	1-1	Martin	7411	1	4	3			6		8		5	11		2		9	7					10				
23		23	Grimsby Town	0-0		3595	1		3			6			10	4	9		2		5	7					11	8			
24		26	TRANMERE ROVERS	0-1		12367	1	12	3			6			10	4	9		2		5						11	8			
25		30	Tranmere Rovers	2-2	Weaver, one og	7011	1	2	3			6	7		10	4					5		8	9			11				
26	Jan	20	SWINDON TOWN	2-0	Kiernan, Martin	10339	1		3		5	6		10		4					2		7	8	9		11				
27	Feb	3	Shrewsbury Town	0-2		5382	1	2				6		10		4		3			5		7	8	9		11				
28		10	BRIGHTON & HOVE ALB	2-2	Weaver, Byrne	7882	1		3		5	6		10		4					2		7	8	9		11				
29		14	Reading	0-0		8093	1		3		5	6		10		4					2		7	8	9		11				
30		17	Stockport County	0-4		7121	1		3		5	6		10		4					2		7	8	9		11				
31		24	SOUTHPORT	1-1	Byrne	6387	1		3		5	6		10		4					2		7	8	9		11				
32	Mar	2	Scunthorpe United	1-1	Brown	2745	1		3	4		6				5					2		7	8	9	10	11				
33		9	WALSALL	3-0	Roberts, Fairbrother, Brown	8536	1	12	3	4		6				5			11		2		7	8	9	10					
34		16	OLDHAM ATHLETIC	1-2	Weaver	7558	1		3	4		6				5			11		2		7	8	9	10					
35		19	STOCKPORT COUNTY	4-1	Felton, Roberts, Fairbrother, Brown	6536			3	4		6				5			11		2	1	7	8	9	10					
36		23	Bristol Rovers	0-2		5413		12	3			6				5			11		2	1	7	8		10			9	4	
37		30	BARROW	3-0	Mackin, Roberts, Fairbrother	8283		12	3	4		6				5					2	1	7	8	9	10	11				
38	Apr	2	Walsall	0-4		5552	1		3	4		6				5					2		7	8	9	10	11				
39		6	Oxford United	0-1		10150	1		3	4		6				5					2		7	8	9	10	11				
40		12	Watford	1-5	Mackin	7917	1		3	4		6			12	5					2		7	8	9	10	11				
41		13	Bury	0-1		7622	1	2	3	4		6				5							7	8	9	10	11				
42		16	WATFORD	1-1	Mackin	6732	1	11	3	4	6					5					2		7	8	9	10					1
43		20	Bournemouth	2-0	Fairbrother, Brown	6148	1	11	3	4	6					5					2		7	8	9	10	12				
44		23	PETERBOROUGH UTD.	3-1	Weaver 2, Fairbrother	8934	1	11	3	4	6					5					2		7	8	9	10					
45		27	COLCHESTER UNITED	2-2	Flowers, Byrne	6859	1	11	3	4	6	12				5					2		7	8	9	10					
46	May	4	Peterborough United	0-4		6658	1	2	3	4	6					5							7	8	9	10	11				
			Apps				39	39	24	32	40	37	8	27	16	37	17	40	18	12	24	6	23	22	16	14	16	6	1	1	1
			Goals					6			2	2	2	12	7		2	2	1		4		5	3	5	4					

One own goal

F.A. Cup

	Date		Opponent	Score		Att	Harvey BR	Mackin J	Walker DCA	Kurila J	Flowers R	Kiernan J	Best WJB	Martin D			Hall JL	Faulkes BK	Felton GM		Roberts IG
R1	Dec	9	Bournemouth	0-2		4998	1	11	3	4	5	12	8	7			10	6	2		9

F.L. Cup

	Date		Opponent	Score	Scorers	Att	Harvey BR	Mackin J		Kurila J	Flowers R	Kiernan J		Martin D	Large F	Carr WG	Hall JL	Faulkes BK	Felton GM	Lines B
R1	Aug	23	Peterborough Utd.	3-2	Kiernan, Martin, Large	8157	1	2		4		6		8	9	5	10	3	7	11
R2	Sep	13	ASTON VILLA	3-1	Mackin, Large, Hall	11832	1	2		4		6		8	9	5	10	3	7	11
R3	Oct	11	MILLWALL	0-0		12282	1	2		4	5	6		8	9	10	11	3	7	
rep		16	Millwall	1-5	Best	10167	1	11	3	4	5	6	7	8	9		10		2	

		P	W	D	L	F	A	W	D	L	F	A	Pts
1	Oxford United	46	18	3	2	49	20	4	10	9	20	27	57
2	Bury	46	19	3	1	64	24	5	5	13	27	42	56
3	Shrewsbury Town	46	14	6	3	42	17	6	9	8	19	32	55
4	Torquay United	46	15	6	2	40	17	6	5	12	20	39	53
5	Reading	46	15	5	3	43	17	6	4	13	27	43	51
6	Watford	46	15	3	5	50	20	6	5	12	15	30	50
7	Walsall	46	12	7	4	47	22	7	5	11	27	39	50
8	Barrow	46	14	6	3	43	13	7	2	14	22	41	50
9	Peterborough Utd.	46	14	4	5	46	23	6	6	11	33	44	50
10	Swindon Town	46	13	8	2	51	16	3	9	11	23	35	49
11	Brighton & Hove A.	46	11	8	4	31	14	5	8	10	26	41	48
12	Gillingham	46	13	6	4	35	19	5	6	12	24	44	48
13	Bournemouth	46	13	7	3	39	17	3	8	12	17	34	47
14	Stockport County	46	16	5	2	49	22	3	4	16	21	53	47
15	Southport	46	13	6	4	35	22	4	6	13	30	43	46
16	Bristol Rovers	46	14	3	6	42	25	3	6	14	30	53	43
17	Oldham Athletic	46	11	3	9	37	32	7	4	12	23	33	43
18	NORTHAMPTON TOWN	46	10	8	5	40	25	4	5	14	18	47	41
19	Orient	46	10	6	7	27	24	2	11	10	19	38	41
20	Tranmere Rovers	46	10	7	6	39	28	4	5	14	23	46	40
21	Mansfield Town	46	8	7	8	32	31	4	6	13	19	36	37
22	Grimsby Town	46	10	7	6	33	21	4	2	17	19	48	37
23	Colchester United	46	6	8	9	29	40	3	7	13	21	47	33
24	Scunthorpe United	46	8	9	6	36	34	2	3	18	20	53	32

1967/68 SEASON
Back: Carr, Kiernan, Clarke, Harvey, Kurila, Martin
Middle: Faulkes, Walker, Perryman, Mackin, Jordan
Front: Payne(Trainer), Felton, Large, Best, Bowen(Manager), Lines, Hall, Price, Mills(Asst. Trainer)

1968/69 SEASON
Back: Flowers(Player/man), Roberts, Clarke, Mackin, Barron, Byrne, Brown, Rankmore, Gordon(Train)
Front: Fairbrother, Faulkes, Weaver, Kiernan, Felton, Walker, Lines, Knox, Fairfax

1968/69 — 21st in Division 3: Relegated

Player columns (left to right): Morritt GR · Fairfax RJ · Walker DCA · Clarke JL · Rankmore FEJ · Flowers R · Weaver E · Byrne J · Fairbrother J · Brown DJ · Knox T · Felton GM · Roberts JG · Lines B · Neal PG · Mackin J · Kiernan J · Faulkes BK · Hatton RJ · Townsend NR · Hawkins PM · Barron RW · Skeet SC

#	Date	Opponent	Score	Scorers	Att	Mrt	Fax	Wlk	Clk	Rnk	Flo	Wvr	Byr	Fbr	Brn	Knx	Flt	Rob	Lns	Nel	Mck	Krn	Flk	Hat	Twn	Hwk	Brr	Skt
1	Aug 16	Reading	0-1		7515	1	2	3	4	5	6	7	8	9	10	11												
2	27	STOCKPORT COUNTY	1-1	one og	9622	1	2	3	4	5	6		8		10	11	7	9										
3	31	Walsall	1-0	Lines	7768	1	2	3	4	5			8	10			7	9	11		6							
4	Sep 7	BOURNEMOUTH	1-3	Fairbrother	7812	1	2	3		5	6		8	9		11	7	4	10									
5	10	WATFORD	2-0	Roberts 2	6824	1	2	3		5	6	7	8	9			12	10	11	4								
6	14	Crewe Alexandra	2-2	Flowers, Fairbrother	5386	1	2	3		5	6	7	8	9					11	4	10							
7	17	BRISTOL ROVERS	2-2	Fairbrother, Lines	8002	1	2	3		5	6	7	8	9			12		11	4	10							
8	21	HARTLEPOOL	0-0		6749	1	2	3		5	6		8	9				10	11			7	4					
9	28	Plymouth Argyle	1-0	Lines	10505	1	2		4		6	7	8	9				5	11		10				3			
10	Oct 5	ROTHERHAM UNITED	1-0	Fairbrother	8602	1	2		4		6	7	8	9				5	11		10				3			
11	7	Stockport County	0-1		7979	1	2	3	4		6	7	8	9				5	11		10							
12	19	TRANMERE ROVERS	2-1	Hatton 2	7359	1	3			5	6	7	8	10				4						2	9			
13	26	Luton Town	1-2	Fairbrother	17818	1	3			5	6	7	8	10				4					11	2	9			
14	Nov 2	TORQUAY UNITED	1-1	Fairbrother	7279	1	3			5	6	7	8	10			11	4						2	9			
15	5	GILLINGHAM	0-1		5545	1	3			5	6	7		10			11	4	8					2	9			
16	9	Mansfield Town	2-0	Fairbrother, Byrne	4635	1	3			5		7	8	12				10	11		6			2	9	4		
17	23	Brighton & Hove Albion	1-1	Rankmore	6813	1	2			5	4	11	10	7				8					3	9	6			
18	26	SWINDON TOWN	2-6	Roberts, Hatton	6827	1	3			5	6	7				12		10	11				8	2	9	4		
19	30	BARNSLEY	3-1	Rankmore, Flowers, Fairbrother	6195	1	3			5	6		7	8	10				11				4	2	9			
20	Dec 9	Orient	0-0		3240	1				5			7	8	12			6	11			10		2	9			
21	14	ORIENT	4-1	Walker, Rankmore, Fairbrother, Felton	5405	1	2	3		5				8			7	10	11		6				9	4	12	
22	20	Tranmere Rovers	1-2	Rankmore	4502	1	2	3		5				8			7	10	11		6				9	4		
23	28	LUTON TOWN	0-2		15161	1	2	3		5				8			7	10			6				9	4	11	
24	Jan 11	Torquay United	0-2		7570	1	2	3	4	5				8		11		6		7	10				9			
25	18	MANSFIELD TOWN	0-0		5840	1	2	3	4	5		7		8	12	11		10			6				9			
26	21	Rotherham United	1-0	Weaver	8483	1	2	3	4	5		7		8		11		10			6				9			
27	25	Gillingham	0-2		4532	1	2	3	4	5		7		8		11		10			6				9			
28	28	BARROW	4-0	Weaver, Brown, Hatton, Hawkins	5375	1	2	3	4	5		7			10				11	6	12			9		8		
29	Feb 22	OLDHAM ATHLETIC	1-1	Hatton	5419	1		3	4	5		7		8		11			12	6	2			9		8		
30	25	BRIGHTON & HOVE ALB	1-1	Weaver	4554	1		3	4	5		7		8				10	11	6	2				9	12		
31	Mar 1	Swindon Town	0-1		17281	1		3	4	5		7		12	8			10	11	6				2	9			
32	3	Barrow	2-0	Brown, Hatton	2919	1	2	3	4					11	8		7	5		6		10		9	12			
33	8	READING	4-2	Fairbrother 3, Roberts	6072		2	3	4					11	8		7	5		6		10		9			1	
34	11	SOUTHPORT	1-0	Neal	5534		2	3	4					11	8		7	5		6		10		9			1	
35	14	Watford	0-3		16549		2	3	4					11	8		7	5		6	12	10		9			1	
36	22	WALSALL	3-1	Brown, Roberts, Neal	5763		2	3	4						8		7	9		6	11	10		12	5		1	
37	26	Southport	0-2		3248		2	3	4						8		7	9		6	11	10		12	5		1	
38	29	Bournemouth	2-3	Neal, Hatton	5089			3	4						8		7	10		6	2	11		9	5		1	
39	Apr 4	Bristol Rovers	1-2	Weaver	9424			3	2	5	11				8		7	10		6				9	4		1	
40	5	PLYMOUTH ARGYLE	1-1	Roberts	6306			3	2	5	12				8		7	9		6		10			4	11	1	
41	8	SHREWSBURY TOWN	3-4	Rankmore, Roberts, Neal	5521			3	2	5	6					12	11	10		8	7			9	4			1
42	11	Hartlepool	0-3		3729			3	2	5	6					11	7	10		8				9	4		1	
43	16	Shrewsbury Town	0-1		6770			3	2	5	6					11	7	10		8				9	4		1	
44	19	CREWE ALEXANDRA	0-1		4406			3	2							11	7	5		6	12	10		9	4		1	
45	25	Barnsley	1-2	Fairbrother	7640	1	3		2				6	8	10		7	5	11		12			9	4			
46	29	Oldham Athletic	1-1	one og	2073	1	3		2				6	8	11		7	5			10			9	12	4		

	Mrt	Fax	Wlk	Clk	Rnk	Flo	Wvr	Byr	Fbr	Brn	Knx	Flt	Rob	Lns	Nel	Mck	Krn	Flk	Hat	Twn	Hwk	Brr	Skt
Apps	34	43	26	29	33	22	24	18	32	24	14	24	38	22	21	17	21	12	33	20	7	11	1
Goals			1		5	2	4	1	13	3		1	7	3	4				7		1		

Two own goals

F.A. Cup

	Date	Opponent	Score	Scorers	Att	Mrt	Fax	Wlk	Clk	Rnk	Flo	Wvr	Byr	Fbr	Brn	Knx	Flt	Rob	Lns	Nel	Mck	Krn	Flk	Hat	Twn	Hwk	Brr	Skt
R1	Nov 16	MARGATE	3-1	Fairbrother, Roberts 2	7672	1	3			5		7	6	8			11	10				4		2	9			
R2	Dec 7	Brighton & Hove Alb.	2-1	Hatton, Townsend	8839	1	3			5	4		7	12				10	11	8				2	9	6		
R3	Jan 4	Bolton Wanderers	1-2	Knox	12632	1	2	3	4	5				8		11		6		7	10				9			

F.L. Cup

	Date	Opponent	Score	Scorers	Att	Mrt	Fax	Wlk	Clk	Rnk	Flo	Wvr	Byr	Fbr	Brn	Knx	Flt	Rob	Lns	Nel	Mck	Krn	Flk	Hat	Twn	Hwk	Brr	Skt
R1	Aug 14	Crewe Alexandra	1-1	Brown	5105		2	3	4	5	6	7	8	9	10	11											1	
rep	21	Crewe Alexandra	0-1		5502		2	3	4	5		7	8	9	10	11		6	12								1	

Both games at Crewe.

		P	W	D	L	F	A	W	D	L	F	A	Pts
1	Watford	46	16	5	2	35	7	11	5	7	39	27	64
2	Swindon Town	46	18	4	1	38	7	9	6	8	33	28	64
3	Luton Town	46	20	3	0	57	14	5	8	10	17	24	61
4	Bournemouth	46	16	2	5	41	17	5	7	11	19	28	51
5	Plymouth Argyle	46	10	8	5	34	25	7	7	9	19	24	49
6	Torquay United	46	13	4	6	35	18	5	8	10	19	28	48
7	Tranmere Rovers	46	12	3	8	36	31	7	7	9	34	37	48
8	Southport	46	14	8	1	52	20	3	5	15	19	44	47
9	Stockport County	46	14	5	4	49	25	2	9	12	18	43	46
10	Barnsley	46	13	6	4	37	21	3	8	12	21	42	46
11	Rotherham United	46	12	6	5	40	21	4	7	12	16	29	45
12	Brighton & Hove A.	46	12	7	4	49	21	4	6	13	23	44	45
13	Walsall	46	10	9	4	34	18	4	7	12	16	31	44
14	Reading	46	13	3	7	41	25	2	10	11	26	41	43
15	Mansfield Town	46	14	5	4	37	18	2	6	15	21	44	43
16	Bristol Rovers	46	12	6	5	41	27	4	5	14	22	44	43
17	Shrewsbury Town	46	11	8	4	28	17	5	3	15	23	50	43
18	Orient	46	10	8	5	31	19	4	6	13	20	39	42
19	Barrow	46	11	6	6	30	23	6	2	15	26	52	42
20	Gillingham	46	10	10	3	35	20	3	5	15	19	43	41
21	NORTHAMPTON TOWN	46	9	8	6	37	30	5	4	14	17	31	40
22	Hartlepool	46	6	12	5	25	29	4	7	12	15	41	39
23	Crewe Alexandra	46	11	4	8	40	31	2	5	16	12	45	35
24	Oldham Athletic	46	9	6	8	33	27	4	3	16	17	56	35

1969/70 14th in Division 4

#	Date	Opponent	Score	Scorers	Att	Book K	Brookes E	Clarke JL	Fagan B	Fairbrother J	Fairfax RJ	Felton GM	Hawkins PM	Kiernan J	Knight BM	Large F	Lines B	Mornitt GR	McNeil R	McPartland D	Neal PG	Rankmore FEJ	Ross WE	Townsend NR	Weaver E
1	Aug 9	Crewe Alexandra	0-2		3813		3	4		9	2	7	8	6			12	1	10			5			11
2	23	Port Vale	1-4	Felton	4809		3	4		10	2	7		6	9	11		1			12	5			8
3	26	OLDHAM ATHLETIC	0-0		6357		3			10	2	7		6	9	12				1	4	5	8		11
4	30	LINCOLN CITY	1-1	Neal	6026		3			10	2	7		6	9	12				1	4	5	8		11
5	Sep 6	Hartlepool	1-1	Fairbrother	3090		3	6		10	2	7			9					1	4	5	8		7
6	13	DARLINGTON	1-1	Hawkins	4922		3	6		10	2	12	11		9					1	4	5	8		7
7	17	Peterborough United	0-1		8557		3	6		9	2	10	11							1	4	5	8		7
8	20	Swansea Town	2-3	Hawkins, Townsend	6660		3	6		7		10	11		9					1	4	5	8	2	
9	27	NEWPORT COUNTY	4-1	Fairbrother, Felton, Large 2	4665		3	2		10		7	11			9		1			4	5	8	6	
10	30	NOTTS COUNTY	3-1	Kiernan, Large, Rankmore	6609		3	2		10		7		4		9		1				5	8	6	11
11	Oct 4	Bradford Park Avenue	2-1	Fairbrother, Large	2555		3	6		10		7		4	2	9		1				5	8		11
12	8	Workington	0-2		1738		3	6		10		7		4	2	9		1				5	8		11
13	11	WREXHAM	0-1		6994			2		10		7	12	6	3	9		1				5	8	4	11
14	18	Aldershot	2-5	Felton, Rankmore	5747			2		10		7	9	6	3			1			11	5	8	4	
15	25	SOUTHEND UNITED	2-0	Felton, Rankmore	5154	1	3	4	11	10	2	7		6		9						5	8		
16	28	WORKINGTON	3-0	Fairbrother, Large 2	6243	1	3	4	11	10	2	7		6		9						5	8		
17	Nov 1	York City	1-1	Fairbrother	4808	1	3	4	11	10	2	7		6		9						5	8		
18	8	CHESTER	0-1		5659	1	3	4	11	10	2	7		6		9						5	8		12
19	22	BRENTFORD	1-1	Fairbrother	5315	1		4	6	10	2	7			8	9						5	11		3
20	25	COLCHESTER UNITED	1-1	Kiernan	3256	1		4	6	10	2	7	9	8							12	5	11		3
21	Dec 13	Darlington	2-2	Fairbrother 2	2063	1	3	4		10	2	7	11	6		9						5	8		
22	20	HARTLEPOOL	0-1		2979	1	3	4		10	2	7		6		9			11			5	8		
23	26	PORT VALE	2-0	Rankmore 2	7522	1	3	4		10	2	7		6		9			11			5	8		
24	27	Lincoln City	0-0		7866	1	3	4		10	2	7		6		9			11			5	8		
25	Jan 17	Newport County	2-0	Fairbrother 2	2280	1	3	4		10	2	7		6		9			11			5	8		
26	31	BRADFORD PARK AVE.	3-0	Fairfax, McNeil, Rankmore	12972	1	3	4		10	2	7		6		9			11			5	8		
27	Feb 18	SCUNTHORPE UNITED	2-1	Fairbrother, Large	3635	1	3	4		10	2	7		6		9			11			5	8		
28	21	Chester	1-2	Ross	3782	1	3	4		10	2	7		6		9			11			5	8		
29	23	CREWE ALEXANDRA	1-2	Rankmore	5315	1	3	4		10	2	7		6		9			11			5	8		
30	28	ALDERSHOT	4-0	Fairbrother, Large, Ross 2	4833	1	3	4		10	2	7		6	12	9	11					5	8		
31	Mar 2	EXETER CITY	2-0	Felton, Large	4974	1	3	4		10	2	7		6		9	11					5	8		
32	7	Brentford	0-1		7292	1	3	4		10	2	7		6	12		11		9			5	8		
33	9	Chesterfield	1-2	McNeil	9624	1	3	4		10	2	7		6	8		11		9			5			
34	14	GRIMSBY TOWN	3-1	Fairbrother, Kiernan, McNeil	4537	1	3	4		10	2	7		6	8	9			11			5			
35	17	Scunthorpe United	0-1		3090	1	3	4		10	2	7		6	8	9			11			5	12		
36	21	Exeter City	0-1		4981	1	3	4		10	2	7		6		9			11			5	8		
37	27	Southend United	2-2	Fairbrother 2	6359	1	3	4		10	2	7		6	8	9			11			5	12		
38	28	CHESTERFIELD	0-1		5740	1	3	4		10	2	7		6	8	9	11				12	5	7		
39	31	YORK CITY	2-2	Brookes, Fairbrother	4128	1	3	4		10	2	7		6		9			11			5	8		
40	Apr 4	Oldham Athletic	2-0	Fairbrother 2	5774	1	3	4		10	2	7		6		9			11			5		8	
41	6	Colchester United	3-0	McNeil 3	3776	1	3	4		10	2	7		6	12	9			11			5		8	
42	10	SWANSEA TOWN	4-1	Fairbrother 2, Felton, Large	4104	1	3	4		10	2	7		6		9	12		11			5		8	
43	14	PETERBOROUGH UTD.	2-2	Fairbrother 2	6/32	1	3	4		10	2	7		6		9	12				11	5		8	
44	18	Grimsby Town	1-0	Fairbrother	3445	1	3	4		10	2	7		6		9	11					5		8	12
45	24	Notts County	0-2		2456	1	3	4		10	2	7		6		9					12	5		8	11
46	27	Wrexham	0-3		9965	1	3	4		10	2	7		6		9					11	5		8	
		Apps				32	42	44	6	46	39	44	11	41	12	40	12	8	19	6	13	45	35	13	16
		Goals					1			23	1	6	2	3		10			6		1	7	3	1	

F.A. Cup

Rd	Date	Opponent	Score	Scorers	Att	Book K	Brookes E	Clarke JL	Fagan B	Fairbrother J	Fairfax RJ	Felton GM	Hawkins PM	Kiernan J	Knight BM	Large F	Lines B	Mornitt GR	McNeil R	McPartland D	Neal PG	Rankmore FEJ	Ross WE	Townsend NR	Weaver E
R1	Nov 15	WEYMOUTH	0-0		5005	1	12	4	6	10	2	7				9	11					5	8		3
rep	19	Weymouth	3-1	Rankmore 2, Fairbrother	4500	1	12	4	6	10	2	7		8		9						5	11		3
R2	Dec 6	EXETER CITY	1-1	Neal	5227	1	3	4		10	2	7		6	11	9					12	5			8
rep	10	Exeter City	0-0		8930	1	3	4		10	2	7		6		9					12	5	8		11
rep2	15	Exeter City	2-1	Large, McNeil	2494	1	3	4		10	2	7		6		9			11		12	5	8		
R3	Jan 12	Brentwood	1-0	Fairbrother	5320	1	3	4		10	2	7		6		9			11			5	8		
R4	24	Tranmere Rovers	0-0		7590	1	3	4		10	2	7		6		9			11			5	8		
rep	27	TRANMERE ROVERS	2-1	Rankmore, Felton	16142	1	3	4		10	2	7		6		9			11			5	8		
R5	Feb 7	MANCHESTER UTD.	2-8	Large, McNeil	21771	1	3	4		10	2	7		6		9			11			5	8		

R2 replay a.e.t. R2 second replay at Swindon.

F.L. Cup

Rd	Date	Opponent	Score	Scorers	Att	Book K	Brookes E	Clarke JL	Fagan B	Fairbrother J	Fairfax RJ	Felton GM	Hawkins PM	Kiernan J	Knight BM	Large F	Lines B	Mornitt GR	McNeil R	McPartland D	Neal PG	Rankmore FEJ	Ross WE	Townsend NR	Weaver E
R1	Aug 13	Oxford United	0-2		7158		3			9	2	7	12	6			11	1	10		4	5			8

	P	W	D	L	F	A	W	D	L	F	A	Pts
1 Chesterfield	46	19	1	3	55	12	8	9	6	22	20	64
2 Wrexham	46	17	6	0	56	16	9	3	11	28	33	61
3 Swansea Town	46	14	8	1	43	14	7	10	6	23	31	60
4 Port Vale	46	13	9	1	39	10	7	10	6	22	23	59
5 Brentford	46	14	8	1	36	11	6	8	9	22	28	56
6 Aldershot	46	16	5	2	52	22	4	8	11	26	43	53
7 Notts County	46	14	4	5	44	21	8	4	11	29	41	52
8 Lincoln City	46	11	8	4	38	20	6	8	9	28	32	50
9 Peterborough Utd.	46	13	8	2	51	21	4	6	13	26	48	48
10 Colchester United	46	14	5	4	38	22	3	9	11	26	41	48
11 Chester	46	14	3	6	39	23	7	3	13	19	43	48
12 Scunthorpe United	46	11	6	6	34	23	7	4	12	33	42	46
13 York City	46	14	7	2	38	16	2	7	14	17	46	46
14 NORTHAMPTON TOWN	46	11	7	5	41	19	5	5	13	23	36	44
15 Crewe Alexandra	46	12	6	5	37	18	4	6	13	14	33	44
16 Grimsby Town	46	9	9	5	33	24	5	6	12	21	34	43
17 Southend United	46	12	8	3	40	28	3	2	18	19	57	40
18 Exeter City	46	13	5	5	48	20	1	6	16	9	39	39
19 Oldham Athletic	46	13	4	6	48	28	2	9	12	15	37	39
20 Workington	46	9	9	5	31	21	3	5	15	15	43	38
21 Newport County	46	12	3	8	39	24	1	8	14	14	50	37
22 Darlington	46	8	7	8	31	27	5	3	15	22	46	36
23 Hartlepool	46	7	7	9	31	30	3	3	17	11	52	30
24 Bradford Park Ave.	46	6	5	12	23	32	0	6	17	18	64	23

1969/70 SEASON
Back: Felton, McNeil, Clarke, Large, Knibb, Book, Townsend, Brookes, Neal, Fairbrother
Front: Fairfax, Kiernan, East, Rankmore, McGleish, Hawkins, Ross

1970/71 SEASON
Back: Hawkins, Brookes, Clarke, Book, Fairbrother, Large, Kiernan
Front: East, Gould, Rankmore, Fairfax, McNeil

1970/71   7th in Division 4

No	Date	Opponent	Score	Scorers	Att	Book K	Fairfax RJ	Brookes E	Clarke JL	Rankmore FEJ	Kiernan J	McNeil R	East KMG	Large F	Gould TR	Fairbrother J	Felton GM	Neal PG	Ross WE	Hawkins PM	McGleish JJ	Townsend NR	Buchanan J	Heslop B	Oman AJ	Hill DR
1	Aug 15	Newport County	1-0	Rankmore	4518	1	2	3	4	5	6	11	8	9	10	7										
2	22	CAMBRIDGE UNITED	2-1	East, Neal	7901	1	2	3	4	5	6		8	9	10	7		11								
3	29	Colchester United	1-1	East	5220	1	2	3	4	5	6	11	8	9	10	7										
4	Sep 1	SOUTHPORT	2-1	Rankmore, East	6264	1	2	3	4	5	6	11	8	9	10	7										
5	5	YORK CITY	3-2	East, Large, Felton	7038	1	2	3	4	5	6	11	8	9	10	7			12							
6	12	Grimsby Town	2-0	Large, Fairbrother	4760	1	2	3	4	5	6	11	8	9	10	7										
7	19	BARROW	1-0	Felton	6509	1	2	3	4	5	6	11	8	9	10	7			12							
8	22	STOCKPORT COUNTY	1-1	Fairbrother	7873	1	2	3	4	5	6	11	8	9	10	7										
9	25	Southend United	0-1		9623	1	2	3	4	5	6	11	8		10		9	7	12							
10	Oct 3	BRENTFORD	1-0	Ross	6282	1	2	3	4	5	6	12	8	9	11	7			10							
11	10	Workington	0-2		2564	1	2	3	4	5	6	7	8	9		11		10	12							
12	17	NEWPORT COUNTY	1-0	McNeil	6171	1	2	3	4	5	6	7	8	9	10	11										
13	20	CHESTER	3-1	East, Large, Fairbrother	6152	1	2	3	4	5	6	7	8	9	10	11										
14	24	Darlington	0-0		2815	1	2	3	4	5	6	7	8	9	10	11										
15	31	HARTLEPOOL	2-0	McNeil, Neal	6049	1	2	3	4	5	6	7		9	10			8			11	12				
16	Nov 7	Notts County	0-1		21012	1	2	3	4	5	6	11	8	9	10	7										
17	10	PETERBOROUGH UTD.	2-0	McNeil 2	8190	1	2	3	4	5	6	11	8	9	10	7	12									
18	14	CREWE ALEXANDRA	1-1	Rankmore	5963	1	2	3	4	5	6	11	8	9	10	7	12									
19	18	Lincoln City	3-1	Kiernan, McNeil, Large	3689	1	2	3	4	5	6	11		9	10	8										
20	28	Scunthorpe United	2-2	Large 2	3463	1	2	3	4		6	11	8	9		7						5	12			
21	Dec 5	OLDHAM ATHLETIC	1-3	McNeil	6487	1	2	3	4	5	6	11	8	9	10				7							
22	12	Stockport County	1-1	Fairbrother	1846	1	2	3	4	5	6	11		9	10			8	7							
23	19	Cambridge United	2-0	Large, Felton	4814	1	2	3	4	5	6	10		9		11	7	8								
24	26	ALDERSHOT	2-0	East, Felton	6354	1	2	3	4	5	6	11		9	10	7	8									
25	Jan 9	LINCOLN CITY	2-1	Large, Fairbrother	5957	1	2	3	4	5	6	7		9	10	11	8									
26	16	Chester	2-2	McNeil, Fairbrother	4031	1	2	3	4	5	6	7		9	10	11	8									
27	23	Bournemouth	2-4	McNeil, Large	8763	1	2	3	4		6	7		9	10	11	8					5				
28	30	SCUNTHORPE UNITED	1-0	Large	4607	1	2	3	4		6	7		9	10	11	8					5				
29	Feb 6	Oldham Athletic	1-1	Large	12806	1		3	4		6	7		9	10	11	8	2				5				
30	9	Exeter City	1-1	Fairbrother	5016	1		3	4		6	7		9	10	11	8	2				5				
31	13	BOURNEMOUTH	2-3	Fairbrother 2	8854	1		3	4		6	7		9	10	11	8	2				5				
32	20	Peterborough United	0-1		8066	1	2	3	4		6	7		9	10	11	8					5				
33	27	Hartlepool	2-2	Fairbrother, Ross	1288	1		2	4		6	8		9	10	11			7			5		3		
34	Mar 5	DARLINGTON	2-0	East, Large	6040	1	2	3	4		6	7	9		10	11		8				5				
35	13	Crewe Alexandra	0-3		3242	1		3	4		6	7		9	10	11	8	2				5				
36	16	EXETER CITY	2-2	Fairbrother 2	5724	1		3	4		6	7		9	10	11	8	2				5				
37	20	NOTTS COUNTY	1-1	Large	11923	1			4			7	12	9	10	11	8	2	6			5		3		
38	27	York City	1-4	Fairbrother	7393	1			4		6	7	12	9	10	11	8	2				5		3		
39	Apr 3	COLCHESTER UNITED	2-1	McNeil 2	7909	1		4			6	7		9	10	11	8	2						3		
40	9	Brentford	0-3		10058	1		4			6	7		9	10	11	8	2						3		
41	10	Aldershot	1-1	Fairfax	4461	1	1	6				7		5	10	11	12	2	8	9				3		
42	13	GRIMSBY TOWN	0-4		6538	1	2		4		6	7		9	10	11	8					5		3		
43	17	WORKINGTON	5-0	McNeil, Large, Gould, Fairbrother 2	3337	1			4		6	7		9	10	11	8	2				5		3		
44	24	Barrow	1-2	McNeil	1466	1			4		6	8		9	10	11	7	2	12			5		3		
45	26	Southport	1-2	McNeil	1550	1			4			12	7		10			2	6	9	8	5	11	3		
46	May 1	SOUTHEND UNITED	0-2		3713				4				8	10				2		11	7	5	9	3	6	1
Apps						45	34	38	42	25	43	44	29	41	35	42	27	18	18	6	3	15	3	10	2	1
Goals							1			3	1	13	7	14	1	15	4	2	2							

F.A. Cup

R	Date	Opponent	Score	Scorers	Att	Book K	Fairfax RJ	Brookes E	Clarke JL	Rankmore FEJ	Kiernan J	McNeil R	East KMG	Large F	Gould TR	Fairbrother J	Felton GM	Neal PG
R1	Nov 21	Hereford United	2-2	McNeil, Fairbrother	10401	1	2	3	4	5	6	11		9	10	7		8
rep	24	HEREFORD UNITED	1-2	Rankmore	10641	1	2	3	4	5	6	11		9	10	7	12	8

F.L. Cup

R	Date	Opponent	Score	Scorers	Att	Book K	Fairfax RJ	Brookes E	Clarke JL	Rankmore FEJ	Kiernan J	McNeil R	East KMG	Large F	Gould TR	Fairbrother J	Felton GM	Neal PG	Ross WE
R1	Aug 19	Scunthorpe United	3-2	Brookes, East, Fairbrother	4470	1	2	3	4	5	6		8	9	10			11	7
R2	Sep 9	York City	0-0		5265	1	2	3	4	5	6	11	8	9	10	7			
rep	15	YORK CITY	1-1	Brookes	7247	1	2	3	4	5	6	11	8	9	10	7			12
rep2	28	York City	2-1	East, Fairbrother	2561	1	2	3	4	5	6	12	8	9	11	7		10	
R3	Oct 7	ASTON VILLA	1-1	Large	15072	1	2	3	4	5	6	7	8	9		11		10	
rep	13	Aston Villa	0-3		25822	1		3	4	5	6	7	8	9		11	2	10	

R2 replay a.e.t. R2 replay 2 at Villa Park.

		P	W	D	L	F	A	W	D	L	F	A	Pts
1	Notts County	46	19	4	0	59	12	11	5	7	30	24	69
2	Bournemouth	46	16	5	2	51	15	8	7	8	30	31	60
3	Oldham Athletic	46	14	6	3	57	29	10	5	8	31	34	59
4	York City	46	16	6	1	45	14	7	4	12	33	40	56
5	Chester	46	17	2	4	42	18	7	5	11	27	37	55
6	Colchester United	46	14	6	3	44	19	7	6	10	26	35	54
7	NORTHAMPTON TOWN	46	15	4	4	39	24	4	9	10	24	35	51
8	Southport	46	15	2	6	42	24	6	4	13	21	33	48
9	Exeter City	46	12	7	4	40	23	5	7	11	27	45	48
10	Workington	46	13	7	3	20	13	5	5	13	20	36	48
11	Stockport County	46	12	8	3	28	17	4	6	13	21	48	46
12	Darlington	46	15	3	5	42	22	2	8	13	16	35	45
13	Aldershot	46	8	10	5	32	23	6	7	10	34	48	45
14	Brentford	46	13	3	7	45	27	5	5	13	21	35	44
15	Crewe Alexandra	46	13	1	9	49	35	5	7	11	26	41	44
16	Peterborough Utd.	46	14	3	6	46	23	4	4	15	24	48	43
17	Scunthorpe United	46	9	7	7	36	23	6	6	11	20	38	43
18	Southend United	46	8	11	4	32	24	6	4	13	21	42	43
19	Grimsby Town	46	13	4	6	37	26	5	3	15	20	45	43
20	Cambridge United	46	9	9	5	31	27	6	4	13	20	39	43
21	Lincoln City	46	11	4	8	45	33	2	9	12	25	38	39
22	Newport County	46	8	3	12	32	36	2	5	16	23	49	28
23	Hartlepool	46	6	10	7	28	27	2	2	19	6	47	28
24	Barrow	46	5	5	13	25	38	2	3	18	26	52	22

1971/72   21st in Division 4

Player columns (left to right): Starling AW | Neal PG | Folds RJ | Clarke JL | Heslop B | Gould TR | Kiernan J | McNeil R | Felton GM | Large F | Fairbrother J | Hold ID | Hawkins PM | Buchanan J | Ross WE | Chatterley LC | Bailey RR | Bukowski DJ | Tucker WB | Oman AJ | Townsend NR | Rioch NG | Book K

#	Date	Opponent	Res	Scorers	Att	Sta	Nea	Fol	Cla	Hes	Gou	Kie	McN	Fel	Lar	Fai	Hol	Haw	Buc	Ros	Cha	Bai	Buk	Tuc	Oma	Tow	Rio	Boo
1	Aug 14	Barrow	1-0	Hawkins	2690	1	2	3		4	10	6		7	5	9		11	8									
2	21	Cambridge United	1-1	Hold	5638	1	2	3		4	8	6	10	7	5	12	11		9									
3	28	EXETER CITY	1-1	McNeil	5926	1	2	3		4	9	6	8	7	5		10	11										
4	30	Southport	0-4		4370	1	2	3	9	4		6	8	7	5			11			10							
5	Sep 4	Newport County	1-1	McNeil	4146	1	2	3	6	4	12	11	8	7	9			10			5							
6	10	STOCKPORT COUNTY	2-0	McNeil 2	5851	1	2	3	6	4		11	7	9	10				8		5							
7	17	Scunthorpe United	0-0		5440	1	2	3	4	6			8	10	9			11		7	5							
8	25	COLCHESTER UNITED	1-1	Hawkins	5800	1	2	3	4	6		11	9	7	8			10	12		5							
9	29	Chester	2-3	Large, McNeil	3454	1	2	3	6	4			8	10	9			11	7		5							
10	Oct 2	Brentford	1-6	McNeil	11004	1	2	3	6	4	8	11		5			10	9	7		5							
11	9	READING	5-0	Hawkins, McNeil (p), Large, Buchanan 2	5255	1	2	3	4	6			8	10	9			11	7		5							
12	15	BARROW	2-0	Buchanan, McNeil	6182		2	3	4	7		6		10	9			11	8		5							1
13	19	ALDERSHOT	2-3	Large, Neal	5881	1	2	3	4	7		6		10	9			11	8		5							
14	22	Doncaster Rovers	1-1	Large	5988	1	6	3	4	5	2			10	9			8	11	7		4						
15	30	GRIMSBY TOWN	3-0	Large, Hold, Buchanan	6220	1	10	3		4	6	2		9	8		11	12		7	5							
16	Nov 6	Lincoln City	0-2		6529	1	8	3	5	6	2			10	9		11	12		7	4							
17	12	CREWE ALEXANDRA	4-1	McNeil, Large 2, Buchanan	5299	1	10	3	4		2		11	7	9				8		5			6				
18	27	Bury	2-4	McNeil, Large	2895	1	8	3	5	6	2	10		7	9				11		4				12			
19	Dec 4	HARTLEPOOL	2-1	McNeil 2	4507	1	8			4		6	10	7	9		12	11			6					3	2	
20	18	NEWPORT COUNTY	1-1	McNeil	4151	1	4			5			8	7	9		10	11			6					2	3	
21	27	Gillingham	1-4	Gould	11795	1	8			4	2	6		7	10	9			11		5					3		
22	Jan 1	SCUNTHORPE UNITED	0-2		3929	1	2			3	7	8	10	12				9	11		6					5		
23	8	Exeter City	3-1	Hold 2, McNeil	4485	1	2	3	4	7		8	11		9		10				6					5		
24	15	WORKINGTON	1-2	Gould	3389	1		3	4	7	2	8		12	10		9	11			6					5		
25	22	CHESTER	4-2	Chatterley, Large 3	3161	1		2	4	3	7	10		11	9		8				6	5						
26	29	Aldershot	2-0	Large.Felton	2471	1		3	4	7	2			11	9		8				6		5		10			
27	Feb 5	PETERBOROUGH UTD.	1-1	Large	5186	1	4	2	5	3		8	10	11	9		7	12			6							
28	12	DONCASTER ROVERS	1-1	Felton	3565	1	5	3	4	7	2		10	11	9		8	12					6					
29	19	Grimsby Town	2-4	Chatterley (p), Large	10035	1	4	12	10	5	2	6		11	9		7				3		8					
30	26	LINCOLN CITY	2-3	Large, Felton	4970	1	4		10	3	2	6		11	9		7		8				12			5		
31	Mar 4	Crewe Alexandra	1-0	Hold	1552	1	4	3	10		2	6		11	9		7		8							5		
32	11	Reading	1-2	Large	4078	1	4	3	10		2	6		11	9		7		8							5		
33	15	Workington	0-2		2130	1	4	3	10		2	6		11			7		8							5	9	
34	18	CAMBRIDGE UNITED	1-2	Large	3781	1	8	3	4	10	2			7	9		12	11								5	6	
35	20	Darlington	2-5	Hold, Rioch (p)	2055	1	4	3	10	6	2			11	8		7						5				9	
36	24	Stockport County	1-3	Rioch	2262	1	10		4	11	2	6		9			12	7							3	5	8	
37	31	Colchester United	0-2		5375	1	11			8	2	6		10			9	7							3	5	4	
38	Apr 1	GILLINGHAM	6-1	Hawkins 2, Large 2, Rioch 2 (1 p)	2625	1	7		4	6	2	10			9			11	12						3	5	8	
39	3	Brentford	0-0		5314	1	7		4	6	2	10			9			11							3	5	8	
40	8	Peterborough United	0-1		5484	1	4		2	5	6	9		12	8			10							3	11	7	
41	11	SOUTHEND UNITED	1-1	Gould	3604	1			2	6	4	10		7	9		8	11							3	5		
42	15	BURY	2-2	Felton, Hold	3175	1			2	6	4	8		7	9		10	11							3	5		
43	17	Southend United	1-4	Felton	13642	1	11		4	12	6	8		7	9	6	10								3	5		
44	22	Hartlepool	0-2		6907	1	11		2		4	8		7	9		10		12						3	6	5	
45	25	SOUTHPORT	0-0		2747	1	11		2	3	4	8		7	9		10									6	5	
46	29	DARLINGTON	1-2	Hawkins	2658	1	11		2		4	8		7	9		12	10							3	6	5	
				Apps		45	41	30	40	40	35	38	22	27	44	4	24	25	28	4	23	1	7	1	13	19	14	1
				Goals			1				3		14	5	19		7	6	5		2						4	

F.A. Cup

	Date	Opponent	Res	Scorers	Att	Sta	Nea	Fol	Cla	Hes	Gou	Kie	McN	Fel	Lar	Fai	Hol	Haw	Buc	Ros	Cha	Bai	Buk	Tuc	Oma	Tow	Rio	Boo
R1	Nov 20	BASINGSTOKE T	5-1	McNeil 2, Large, Buchanan 2	3400	1	8	3	4	6	2	10	7		9			12	11		5							
R2	Dec 11	Hereford United	0-0		9519	1	8		4	6	10		7		9			11			5				2	3		
rep	14	HEREFORD UNITED	2-2	Large, Hawkins	9099	1	2			6		8	7	12	9		10	11			5				4	3		
rep2	20	Hereford United			8331	1	8		4	2		6	7	12	9		10	11			5					3		

Both R2 replays a.e.t. Second replay at West Bromwich.

F.L. Cup

	Date	Opponent	Res	Scorers	Att	Sta	Nea	Fol	Cla	Hes	Gou	Kie	McN	Fel	Lar	Fai	Hol	Haw	Buc
R1	Aug 18	Watford	0-2		7663	1	2	3		4	10	6		7	5	9		11	8

		P	W	D	L	F	A	W	D	L	F	A	Pts
1	Grimsby Town	46	18	3	2	61	26	10	4	9	27	30	63
2	Southend United	46	18	2	3	56	26	6	10	7	25	29	60
3	Brentford	46	16	2	5	52	21	8	9	6	24	23	59
4	Scunthorpe United	46	13	8	2	34	15	9	5	9	22	22	57
5	Lincoln City	46	17	5	1	46	15	4	9	10	31	44	56
6	Workington	46	12	9	2	34	7	4	10	9	16	27	51
7	Southport	46	15	5	3	48	21	3	9	11	18	25	50
8	Peterborough Utd.	46	14	6	3	51	24	3	10	10	31	40	50
9	Bury	46	16	4	3	55	22	3	8	12	18	37	50
10	Cambridge United	46	11	8	4	38	22	6	6	11	24	38	48
11	Colchester United	46	13	6	4	38	23	6	4	13	32	46	48
12	Doncaster Rovers	46	11	8	4	35	24	5	6	12	21	39	46
13	Gillingham	46	11	5	7	33	24	5	8	10	28	43	45
14	Newport County	46	13	5	5	34	20	5	3	15	26	52	44
15	Exeter City	46	11	5	7	40	30	5	6	12	21	38	43
16	Reading	46	14	3	6	37	26	3	5	15	19	50	42
17	Aldershot	46	5	13	5	27	20	4	9	10	21	34	40
18	Hartlepool	46	14	2	7	39	25	3	4	16	19	44	40
19	Darlington	46	9	5	9	37	24	5	2	16	27	58	39
20	Chester	46	10	11	2	34	16	0	7	16	13	40	38
21	NORTHAMPTON TOWN	46	8	9	6	43	27	4	4	15	23	52	37
22	Barrow	46	8	8	7	23	26	5	3	15	17	45	37
23	Stockport County	46	7	10	6	33	32	2	4	17	22	55	32
24	Crewe Alexandra	46	9	4	10	27	25	1	5	17	16	44	29

1972/73 — 23rd in Division 4

No.	Date	Opponent	Score	Scorers	Att	Starling AW	Clarke JL	Burt JHL	Baxter WA	Robertson SJ	Bruck DJ	Felton GM	Buchanan J	Large F	Neal PG	Hold JD	Tucker WB	Gould TR	Oman AJ	McGleish JJ	Stratford P	Roberts JT	Rogers E	Hunt RR	Hawkins PM	Riddick GG	Gregory JC	Bukowski DI	Buck AR	Park RC	Hurrell WT
1	Aug 12	Mansfield Town	0-1		4303	1	2	3	4	5	6	7	8	9	10	11															
2	25	Gillingham	3-1	Neal 2, Buchanan	3544	1		3	5	6	4	7	11		8	10	2	9													
3	28	Peterborough United	2-1	Hold, Felton	3628	1		3	4	5	6	7	8		11	10	2	9													
4	Sep 1	CHESTER	1-0	Gould	5008	1		3	4	5	6	7	8	12	11	10	2	9													
5	9	Bradford City	1-2	Buchanan	2427	1		3	4	5	6		11	9	8	10	2	7													
6	16	READING	1-1	Neal	3752	1		2	5	4	6	7	8	12	10	11		9	3												
7	19	Bury	2-2	Buchanan, Neal	2272	1		3	4	5	6		11	8	10		2	9		7	12										
8	22	Colchester United	2-2	Neal, Robertson	3543	1		3	4	5	6	7	11		8	10	2	9													
9	26	NEWPORT COUNTY	0-1		4014	1		3	4	5	6	7	11	9	10		2	8													
10	30	CAMBRIDGE UNITED	2-2	Neal 2	3439	1		3	4	5	6	8	11		9	10	2		7												
11	Oct 6	Doncaster Rovers	0-3		2489	1			3	5	4	6		11	10	9	8	2	7												
12	11	Lincoln City	1-1	Neal	6198	1	6		5	4	2		8	11	10	9		7	3												
13	14	BARNSLEY	2-2	Baxter (p), Gould	3013	1	6	12	5	4	2			11	10	9		8	7	3											
14	21	Hereford United	0-2		7202	1	3		4	5	2	7			9	10	12	6	8			11									
15	24	WORKINGTON	1-0	Hold	2897	1		12	4	5			7	8		9	10	2	6	3		11									
16	28	CREWE ALEXANDRA	1-0	Stratford	3041	1	6	12	5			7	4		9	10	2	8	3			11									
17	Nov 4	Newport County	0-1		4829	1	4		5			9	6		7	10	2	8	3			11									
18	11	BURY	0-1		2654	1	4	12	5			10	11	6		8	9	2	7	3											
19	25	EXETER CITY	1-2	Oman	2263	1	6		5	4	2	9	7		8	10			3			11									
20	Dec 9	Cambridge United	1-3	Rogers	3539		6	3	5	4	2	7	10		12						1	8	9	11							
21	15	SOUTHPORT	0-1		2407		6	3	5	4	2	9			8						1	7	11		10						
22	23	Torquay United	1-2	Hunt	2788		6		4	5	2	10			8		12	3			1	7	11		9						
23	26	COLCHESTER UNITED	4-0	Baxter (p), Riddick, Hunt 2	3298		6		5	4	2	9			8		12	3			1	7	11		10						
24	29	Stockport County	0-0		3496		6		5			9			8			2	3					11	7	10					
25	Jan 6	GILLINGHAM	2-1	Felton, Neil	2452		6		4	5		10			9			2	3	8	1				11	7					
26	13	Workington	0-3		1444		6		4	5		8			10		12	2	3	11	1				9	7					
27	17	Aldershot	0-3		3080		6	2	4	5		10	9					11		8	1				7	3					
28	27	BRADFORD CITY	1-2	Baxter (p)	2468		6		4	5			10			7		9	2	3						8	12	11			
29	Feb 3	LINCOLN CITY	0-0		2381	1	6		4	5		7					10	2	3							9		5	11	8	
30	10	Reading	0-3		5443	1	6		4	5		7					10	2	3							8			9	11	
31	13	STOCKPORT COUNTY	1-1	Buck	1180	1	6		4	5		7				10		2	3							9			11	8	
32	16	MANSFIELD TOWN	1-0	Buchanan	2288	1	6		4	5		7	12		11			2	3							9			10	8	
33	23	Southport	2-1	Buck, Robertson	3262	1	6		4	5		7			11			2	3							9			10	8	
34	Mar 2	DONCASTER ROVERS	0-2		4509	1	6		4	5		7	12		11			2	3							9			10	8	
35	5	Hartlepool	0-2		3822	1	6		4	5		9	12		8			2	3							10			11	7	
36	10	Barnsley	0-2		2244	1	6		4			7	10		8			2	3								11		9	6	
37	17	HEREFORD UNITED	0-4		4489	1	5						12		7			9	2							10	8	11		6	
38	20	DARLINGTON	2-2	Baxter, Buck	1867	1	6		4				12		8			2	3	11						9	5		10	7	
39	24	Crewe Alexandra	0-1		1577	1			4				6		8		12	2	3							9	5	11	10	7	
40	28	Chester	0-3		1469	1			4			7						2	3	9						11	10	5	8		
41	31	Exeter City	1-4	Riddick	3137				5		3					11		8	2		6	1			9	7			4	12	10
42	Apr 7	ALDERSHOT	0-2		1877			3		2						10	12	6	4	8		1				11	9			7	5
43	14	Darlington	0-0		1937			12					3	8				9	2	4		1				11	6		10	7	5
44	21	HARTLEPOOL	3-1	Dawes (og), Hold, Hawkins	1478			3					2	8				9	6	4		1				11			10	7	5
45	23	TORQUAY UNITED	0-2		1982								2	8	12			9	6	4	3	1				11			10	7	5
46	28	PETERBOROUGH UTD.	1-3	Hold	2411	1							2	8				9	6	4	3					11			10	7	5
		Apps				33	27	21	41	31	26	36	30	11	38	20	30	35	30	5	9	13	4	5	11	20	9	6	15	18	5
		Goals							4	2		2	4		9	4		2	1		1		1	3	1	2			3		

One own goal

F.A. Cup

	Date	Opponent	Score		Att	Starling AW	Clarke JL	Burt JHL	Baxter WA	Robertson SJ	Bruck DJ	Felton GM	Buchanan J	Large F	Neal PG	Hold JD	Tucker WB	Gould TR	Oman AJ	McGleish JJ	Stratford P	Roberts JT
R1	Nov 16	Peterborough Utd.	0-1		7815	1	4			5	6	10	11		9	8		2			3	7

F.L. Cup

	Date	Opponent	Score		Att	Starling AW	Clarke JL	Burt JHL	Baxter WA	Robertson SJ	Bruck DJ	Felton GM	Buchanan J	Large F	Neal PG	Hold JD
R1	Aug 16	CHARLTON ATHLETIC	0-3		4282	1	2	3	4	5	6	7		9	8	10

Played at no. 11: Parker

		P	W	D	L	F	A	W	D	L	F	A	Pts
1	Southport	46	17	4	2	40	19	9	6	8	31	29	62
2	Hereford United	46	18	4	1	39	12	5	8	10	17	26	58
3	Cambridge United	46	15	6	2	40	23	5	11	7	27	34	57
4	Aldershot	46	14	6	3	33	14	8	6	9	27	24	56
5	Newport County	46	14	6	3	37	18	8	6	9	27	26	56
6	Mansfield Town	46	15	7	1	52	17	5	7	11	26	34	54
7	Reading	46	14	7	2	33	7	3	11	9	18	31	52
8	Exeter City	46	13	8	2	40	18	5	6	12	17	33	50
9	Gillingham	46	15	4	4	44	20	4	7	12	19	38	49
10	Lincoln City	46	12	7	4	38	27	4	9	10	26	30	48
11	Stockport County	46	14	7	2	38	18	4	5	14	15	35	48
12	Bury	46	11	7	5	37	19	3	11	9	21	32	46
13	Workington	46	15	7	1	44	20	2	5	16	15	41	46
14	Barnsley	46	9	8	6	32	24	5	8	10	26	36	44
15	Chester	46	11	6	6	40	19	3	9	11	21	33	43
16	Bradford City	46	12	6	5	42	25	4	5	14	19	40	43
17	Doncaster Rovers	46	10	8	5	28	19	5	4	14	21	39	42
18	Torquay United	46	8	10	5	23	17	4	7	12	21	30	41
19	Peterborough Utd.	46	10	8	5	42	29	4	5	14	29	47	41
20	Hartlepool	46	8	10	5	17	15	4	7	12	17	34	41
21	Crewe Alexandra	46	7	8	8	18	23	2	10	11	20	38	36
22	Colchester United	46	8	8	7	36	28	2	3	18	12	48	31
23	NORTHAMPTON TOWN	46	7	6	10	24	30	3	5	15	16	43	31
24	Darlington	46	5	9	9	28	41	2	6	15	14	44	29

1972/73 SEASON
Back: Buchanan, Robertson, Starling, Roberts, Neal, Hold
Middle: McCormick(Trainer), Large, Clarke, Parker, Baxter, Burt, Gregory
Front: Bruck, Felton, Bray, Gould, McGleish, Tucker, Hawkins, Oman

1973/74 SEASON
Back: Buck, Neal, Raynor, Starling, Gregory, Hurrell, Clarke
Middle: Riddick, Park, Bruck, Robertson, Oman, Felton   Front: Stratford, Buchanan

1973/74   5th in Division 4

#		Date	Opponent	Score	Scorers	Att	Starling AW	Bruck DJ	Oman AJ	Gregory JC	Riddick GG	Robertson SJ	Felton GM	Neal PG	Buchanan J	Park RC	Stratford P	Clarke IL	Hawkins PM	Buck AR	Best WJB	Carlton DG	Tucker WB	Watts D	Krzywicki RL	Christie DHM	Wainwright RK	John M
1	Aug	25	ROTHERHAM UNITED	3-1	Robertson, Felton, Neal	4098	1	2	3	4	5	6	7	8	9	10	11	12										
2	Sep	1	Mansfield Town	0-2		3109	1	2	3	6	4	5		8	9	10	7	12	11									
3		7	COLCHESTER UNITED	0-0		4916	1	2	3	6	4	5	7	8	9	10	11					12						
4		11	NEWPORT COUNTY	1-0	Buchanan	4061	1	2	3	6	4	5	7	8	9	12	11	10										
5		14	Stockport County	2-2	Stratford, Riddick	3552	1	2	3	6	4	5	7	8	9		11	10										
6		18	Swansea City	1-1	Robertson	1301	1	2	3	6	4	5	7	8	9		11	10										
7		21	SCUNTHORPE UNITED	2-0	Stratford 2	5049	1	2	3	6	4	5	7	8	9		11	10										
8		29	Workington	0-1		970	1	2	3	6	4	5	7	8	9		11	10				12						
9	Oct	2	SWANSEA CITY	2-0	Buchanan, Robertson	5287	1	2	3	6		5	7	8	9	12	11	10				4						
10		5	TORQUAY UNITED	0-0		6640	1	2	3	6		5	7	8	9		11	4				10						
11		13	Bradford City	1-1	Stratford	3343	1	2	3	6		5	12	8	9		11	4				10	7					
12		20	EXETER CITY	1-2	Stratford	4923	1	2	3	6		5	7	8	9		11					10	4					
13		23	Newport County	1-3	Neal (p)	3592	1	2	3	6		5	9	8			11	4				10	7	12				
14		27	Bury	1-3	Stratford	4360	1	3		6			9	8	7		11	5				10	4	2	12			
15	Nov	3	HARTLEPOOL	1-0	Stratford	3715	1			3		5	7	4	9		11	6				10	8	2				
16		10	Darlington	3-2	Neal, Buchanan, Best	2063	1			6		5	7	8	9		11	3				10	4	2				
17		13	BARNSLEY	2-1	Oman, Clarke	4299	1		3	6		5	7		9		11	4			8	10	2					
18		17	Peterborough United	0-3		10351	1		3	6		5	7	8	12		11	9			10	4	2					
19	Dec	8	LINCOLN CITY	1-0	Best	3464	1			3		5	7	4	6		11	12			8	10	2		9			
20		22	WORKINGTON	1-0	Krzywicki	4038	1			6		5	7	3	4		11	10			8		2		9			
21		26	Gillingham	1-3	Felton	11313	1			6		5	7	3	4		11	10			8		2		9			
22		29	Colchester United	0-1		5042	1			6		5	7	3	4			11			8	10	2		9			
23	Jan	1	MANSFIELD TOWN	2-0	Neal (p), Krzywicki	6231	1			6		5	7	3	4		11	10			8		2		9			
24		5	Hartlepool	0-1		2078	1	4		6				3		12	11	10		9	8		2		7			
25		12	STOCKPORT COUNTY	2-0	Krzywicki, Stratford	3396	1			6		5	7	4			11	3			8	10	2		9			
26		20	Rotherham United	2-1	Buchanan 2	4609	1			6		5	7	3	12		11	4			8	10	2		9			
27		27	READING	3-3	Best 2, Stratford	7599	1			6			7	3	4		9	5			8	10	2			11		
28	Feb	2	BRENTFORD	0-0		4130	1			6		5	7	3	9		11	4			8	10	2			12		
29		10	Scunthorpe United	2-1	Buchanan, Stratford	3603	1			6		5	7	3	9		11	4			8	10	2					
30		17	BRADFORD CITY	3-0	Buchanan, Neal, Robertson	8146	1		12	6		5	7	3	9		11	4			8	10	2					
31		24	Torquay United	0-1		4186	1			6		5	7	3	9		11	4			8	10	2				12	
32	Mar	3	GILLINGHAM	0-0		8583	1			6		5	7	3	9		11	4			8	10	2					
33		9	BURY	3-1	Best, Buchanan 2	4884	1			6		5	7	3	9		11	4			8	10	2					
34		16	Exeter City	1-1	Felton	4052	1		12	5			7	3	6		11	4			8	10	2					9
35		18	Brentford	1-3	John	3686	1		3	5			7	4	6		11				8	10	2					9
36		24	DARLINGTON	5-0	John, Best, Neal (p), Stratford 2	5416	1		12	5			7	6	4		11	3			8	10	2					9
37		26	CHESTER	3-3	Neal (p), Buchanan, John	5969	1			5			7	6	4		11	3			8	10	2					9
38	Apr	3	Reading	2-1	Buchanan 2	7055	1		12	5			7	6	4		11	3			8	10	2					9
39		6	Barnsley	2-0	Neal, John	3646	1			5			7	6	4		11	3			8	10	2					9
40		13	PETERBOROUGH UTD.	0-1		11378	1			3			7	5	4		11	6			8	10	2					9
41		15	CREWE ALEXANDRA	1-1	Neal	5389	1			6			7	5	4		9	3			8	10	2					11
42		16	Crewe Alexandra	2-0	Stratford 2	1498	1			5			7	6	4		9	3			8	10	2					11
43		20	Lincoln City	1-1	Felton	2530	1		12	5			7	6	4		9	3			8	10	2					11
44		23	Doncaster Rovers	1-2	Stratford	1561	1		3	5			7	6	4		9				8	10	2				12	11
45		27	DONCASTER ROVERS	3-1	Buchanan, Best, Felton	3137	1			5			7	6	4		9	3			8	10	2					11
46	May	1	Chester	0-0		1928	1			5			7	6	4		9	3			8	10	2					11
					Apps		46	15	22	46	8	31	44	46	42	6	45	42	1	2	39	32	34	1	8	3	1	13
					Goals				1		1	4	5	9	13		15	1			7				3			4

F.A. Cup

		Date	Opponent	Score	Scorers	Att	Starling AW	Bruck DJ	Oman AJ	Gregory JC	Riddick GG	Robertson SJ	Felton GM	Neal PG	Buchanan J	Park RC	Stratford P	Clarke IL	Hawkins PM	Buck AR	Best WJB	Carlton DG	Tucker WB
R1	Nov	24	Banbury United	0-0		4800	1		3	6		5	7		9		11	4			8	10	2
rep		29	Banbury United	3-2	Felton, Robertson, Best	2995	1		3	6		5	7		9		11	4			8	10	2
R2	Dec	15	BRISTOL ROVERS	1-2	Buchanan	6181	1			6		5	7	3	4		11	10		8	9		2

F.L. Cup

		Date	Opponent	Score	Scorers	Att	Starling AW	Bruck DJ	Oman AJ	Gregory JC	Riddick GG	Robertson SJ	Felton GM	Neal PG	Buchanan J	Park RC	Stratford P	Clarke IL
R1	Aug	28	Grimsby Town	1-2	Buchanan	7829	1	2	3	6	4	5	7	8	9	10	11	12

		P	W	D	L	F	A	W	D	L	F	A	Pts
1	Peterborough Utd.	46	19	4	0	49	10	8	7	8	26	28	65
2	Gillingham	46	16	5	2	51	16	9	7	7	39	33	62
3	Colchester United	46	16	5	2	46	14	8	7	8	27	22	60
4	Bury	46	18	3	2	51	14	6	8	9	30	35	59
5	NORTHAMPTON TOWN	46	14	7	2	39	14	6	6	11	24	34	53
6	Reading	46	11	9	3	37	13	5	10	8	21	24	51
7	Chester	46	13	6	4	31	19	4	9	10	23	36	49
8	Bradford City	46	14	7	2	45	20	3	7	13	13	32	48
9	Newport County	46	13	6	4	39	23	3	8	12	17	42	45
10	Exeter City	45	12	5	6	37	20	6	3	13	21	35	44
11	Hartlepool	46	11	4	8	29	16	5	8	10	19	31	44
12	Lincoln City	46	10	8	5	40	30	6	4	13	23	37	44
13	Barnsley	46	15	5	3	42	18	2	5	16	16	48	44
14	Swansea City	46	11	6	6	28	15	5	5	13	17	31	43
15	Rotherham United	46	10	9	4	33	22	5	4	14	23	36	43
16	Torquay United	46	11	7	5	37	23	2	10	11	15	34	43
17	Mansfield Town	46	13	8	2	47	24	0	9	14	15	45	43
18	Scunthorpe United	45	12	7	3	33	17	2	5	16	14	47	42
19	Brentford	46	9	7	7	31	20	3	9	11	17	30	40
20	Darlington	46	9	8	6	29	24	4	5	14	11	38	39
21	Crewe Alexandra	46	11	5	7	28	30	3	5	15	15	41	38
22	Doncaster Rovers	46	10	7	6	32	22	2	4	17	15	58	35
23	Workington	46	10	8	5	33	26	1	5	17	10	48	35
24	Stockport County	46	4	12	7	22	25	3	8	12	22	44	34

1974/75 16th in Division 4

	Date		Opponent	Score	Scorers	Att	Anderson GL	Best WJB	Buchanan J	Carlton DG	Cegielski W	Christie DHM	Clarke JL	Farrington JR	Felton GM	Garnham SE	Gregory JC	Hall IL	John M	Kilkelly TF	Mabee GL	Moore J	Neal PG	Oman AJ	Robertson SJ	Starling AW	Stratford P	Tucker WB	Tumbridge RA	Wainwright RK
1	Aug	17	Brentford	0-1		5147	8	11					3		7		6				12			4	5		1	9	2	10
2		24	BRADFORD CITY	1-2	Best	4408	8	11					3		7		6				12			4	5		1	9	2	10
3		31	Reading	2-3	Wagstaff (og), Stratford	5464	8	4		10			3		7								6	9		5	1	1	2	12
4	Sep	6	DARLINGTON	3-0	Mabee, Stratford, Carlton	4003	8	4		10					7		5				9	6	3				1	11	2	
5		14	Lincoln City	2-2	Neal 2 (1p)	3113	8	4		10					7		5				9	6	3				1	11	2	12
6		21	SHREWSBURY TOWN	3-3	Stratford, Best, Carlton	4001	8	4		10					7		5				9	6	3				1	11	2	12
7		24	DONCASTER ROVERS	2-0	Mabee, Buchanan	4269	8	4		10					7		5				9	6	3				1	11	2	
8		28	Torquay United	1-0	Wainwright	3004	8	4		10		12			7		5				9	6	3				1	11	2	7
9	Oct	1	WORKINGTON	3-0	Stratford 3	4783	8	4		10		12	3		7		5				9	6	5				1	11	2	7
10		5	Rotherham United	3-1	Mabee 2, Carlton	4934	3	4		10		12			8						9	6	5				1	11	2	7
11		11	STOCKPORT COUNTY	4-1	Stratford, Buchanan, John, Mabee	5846	3	4		10					1		8	6	9	5								11	2	7
12		18	Newport County	1-2	Stratford	2149	3			10				7			4	8	12	9	5						1	11	2	6
13		21	Rochdale	2-2	Wainwright, Mabee	1379	8			4				7			5		3	9	6						1	10	2	11
14		26	SWANSEA CITY	5-1	Stratford, Mabee 2, Farrington, Wainwright	5096	6			4				7	12		3	8		9	5						1	11	2	10
15		28	Mansfield Town	0-3		5310	3			6				7			4	8		9	5						1	10	2	11
16	Nov	1	Cambridge United	4-3	Mabee 2, Carlton, Stratford	3589	8			6				7			5		12	9	4				3		1	10	2	11
17		5	ROCHDALE	0-1		5695	8			6				7			4		12	9					3	5	1	11	2	10
18		9	CHESTER	2-0	Tucker (p), Wainwright	5240	8							7			4		6	9					3	5	1	11	2	10
19		15	Southport	0-0		1851	8			6				7			4		10	9					3	5	1	11	2	12
20		29	CREWE ALEXANDRA	3-0	Mabee 2, Stratford	5037	8			12				7			4		6	9					3	5	1	11	2	10
21	Dec	7	Exeter City	2-2	Wainwright, Best	3497	8			6				7			4			9					3	5	1	11	2	10
22		21	Barnsley	1-5	Stratford	2666	8			6				7	11		4		10						3	5	1	9	2	12
23		26	LINCOLN CITY	1-0	Stratford	7275	8			6				7			4			9					3	5	1	11	2	10
24	Jan	1	Hartlepool	0-2		5178	8			6				7			4		12	9					3	5	1	11	2	10
25		4	BRENTFORD	0-0		4735	8			6				7			4			9					3	5	1	11	2	10
26		11	EXETER CITY	1-1	Best	4104	8			6				7	11		4		12	9					3	5	1		2	10
27		18	Crewe Alexandra	1-3	Mabee	1859	8			6				7	11		4			9					3	5	1		2	10
28	Feb	1	Chester	1-4	Hall	5209	8							7			4	10	12						3	5	1	11	2	6
29		8	CAMBRIDGE UNITED	1-2	Farrington	4126	8							7			4	9	12		10				3	5	1	11	2	6
30		11	SCUNTHORPE UNITED	3-0	Robertson, Hall 2	3079	8			10				7			4	9	6						3	5	1	11	2	12
31		15	Scunthorpe United	1-2	Best	1975	8			6			12	7			4	9	10						3	5	1	11	2	
32		22	SOUTHPORT	1-1	Hall	3320	8			6				7			4	9	12						3	5	1	11	2	
33		28	READING	0-3		3039	2			6			10	7			4				8		9			5	1	11		3
34	Mar	8	Doncaster Rovers	0-2		5319	8			6			10	7			4		9							5	1	11	2	3
35		22	Darlington	0-2		1582	11	8		6	5	10		7			4										1	9	2	3
36		25	MANSFIELD TOWN	0-2		3846	10	8				6		7			4				9				5	1	11	2	3
37		28	BARNSLEY	2-1	Best, Farrington	2594	10	8			6			7			4				9				5	1	11	2	3
38		31	Shrewsbury Town	0-6		4315	10	8			6			7			4		12		9				5	1	11	2	3
39	Apr	1	HARTLEPOOL	3-0	John 2, Best	2758	2	8			6	10		7			4		9						5	1	11		3
40		5	Swansea City	0-1		1591	2	8			6	10		7			4		9						5	1	11	3	12
41		9	Workington	2-2	Stratford, Best	1455	2	8			6	10		7			4		9						3	5	1	11	
42		12	ROTHERHAM UNITED	1-1	Gregory (p)	3714	2	8			6	10		7			4		9						3	5	1	11	
43		15	TORQUAY UNITED	1-1	Oman	2658	2	8			6	10		7			4		9						3	5	1	11	
44		18	Stockport County	0-1		1978	2	8			6	10		7					9						3	5	1	11	12
45		23	Bradford City	1-2	John	1697	2	8		6		10		7			4		9							5	1	11	3
46		25	NEWPORT COUNTY	3-2	Stratford, Carlton, Best	2482		8		6	5	10					4		9		12					1	11	2	3	7
					Apps		11	46	11	32	11	14	6	34	11	1	41	5	28	4	32	14	10	21	31	45	44	38	11	31
					Goals			9	2	5				3			1	4	4		13		2	1	1		15	1		5

One own goal

F.A. Cup

	Date		Opponent	Score	Scorers	Att	Anderson GL	Best WJB	Buchanan J	Carlton DG	Cegielski W	Christie DHM	Clarke JL	Farrington JR	Felton GM	Garnham SE	Gregory JC	Hall IL	John M	Kilkelly TF	Mabee GL	Moore J	Neal PG	Oman AJ	Robertson SJ	Starling AW	Stratford P	Tucker WB	Tumbridge RA	Wainwright RK
R1	Nov	23	Torquay United	1-0	Gregory	2659	8							12			7		6		4			9		3	5	1	11	2	10
R2	Dec	14	Rotherham United	1-2	Stratford	4741	8			6				12			7		4		9				3	5	1	11	2	10

F.L. Cup

	Date		Opponent	Score	Scorers	Att	Anderson GL	Best WJB	Buchanan J	Carlton DG	Cegielski W	Christie DHM	Clarke JL	Farrington JR	Felton GM	Garnham SE	Gregory JC	Hall IL	John M	Kilkelly TF	Mabee GL	Moore J	Neal PG	Oman AJ	Robertson SJ	Starling AW	Stratford P	Tucker WB	Tumbridge RA	Wainwright RK
R1	Aug	20	PORT VALE	1-0	Robertson	5688	8	11					3		7		6				12			4	5		1	9	2	10
R2	Sep	10	BLACKBURN ROVERS	2-2	Neal, 1 og	5706	8	4		10					7		5				9	6	3				1	11	2	
rep		18	Blackburn Rovers	0-1		8566	8	4		10					7		5				9	6	3				1	11	2	

		P	W	D	L	F	A	W	D	L	F	A	Pts
1	Mansfield Town	46	17	6	0	55	15	11	6	6	35	25	68
2	Shrewsbury Town	46	16	3	4	46	18	10	7	6	34	25	62
3	Rotherham United	46	13	7	3	40	19	9	8	6	31	22	59
4	Chester	46	17	5	1	48	9	6	6	11	16	29	57
5	Lincoln City	46	14	8	1	47	14	7	7	9	32	34	57
6	Cambridge United	46	15	5	3	43	16	5	9	9	19	28	54
7	Reading	46	13	6	4	38	20	8	4	11	25	27	52
8	Brentford	46	15	6	2	38	14	3	7	13	15	31	49
9	Exeter City	46	14	3	6	33	24	5	8	10	27	39	49
10	Bradford City	46	10	5	8	32	21	7	8	8	24	30	47
11	Southport	46	13	7	3	36	19	2	10	11	20	37	47
12	Newport County	46	13	5	5	43	30	6	4	13	25	45	47
13	Hartlepool	46	13	6	4	40	24	3	5	15	12	38	43
14	Torquay United	46	10	7	6	30	25	4	7	12	16	36	42
15	Barnsley	46	10	7	6	34	24	5	4	14	28	41	41
16	NORTHAMPTON TOWN	46	12	6	5	43	22	3	5	15	24	51	41
17	Doncaster Rovers	46	10	9	4	41	29	4	3	16	24	50	40
18	Crewe Alexandra	46	9	9	5	22	16	2	9	12	12	31	40
19	Rochdale	46	9	9	5	35	22	4	4	15	24	53	39
20	Stockport County	46	10	8	5	26	27	2	6	15	17	43	38
21	Darlington	46	11	4	8	38	27	2	6	15	16	40	36
22	Swansea City	46	9	4	10	25	31	6	2	15	21	42	36
23	Workington	46	7	5	11	23	29	3	6	14	13	37	31
24	Scunthorpe United	46	7	8	8	27	29	0	7	16	14	49	29

1974/75 SEASON
Top: Best, Tucker, Jarram, Christie, Buchanan, Felton, Mabee, Stratford, Liddle, Clarke,
Bottom: Carlton, Starling, Hurrell, Neal, Moore, Robertson, Gregory, Wainwright

1975/76
Back: Anderson, Clarke, Robertson, Hall, Gregory, Parton, Starling,
Wainwright, McNichol, Cariton, Oman,
Front: Farrington, Stratford, Tucker, Best, Christie, Mabee, McGowan, Liddle

1975/76   2nd in Division 4: Promoted

#	Date		Opponent	Score	Scorers	Att	Anderson GL	Best WJB	Carlton DG	Christie DHM	Davids NG	Farrington JR	Felton GM	Gregory JC	Hall IL	Mabee GL	Martin D	Mayes AK	McGowan A	Parton JI	Robertson SI	Starling AW	Stratford P	Tucker WB	Phillips SE
1	Aug	16	Huddersfield Town	1-1	Tucker	3595	3	8	4	10		7		6	9	12				1	5			11	2
2		22	Stockport County	3-1	Hall 2, Farrington	2932	3	8	7	10		4		6	9					1	5			11	2
3		30	Barnsley	1-3	Hall	3649	3	8	4	10		7		6	9				12	1	5			11	2
4	Sep	5	BRADFORD CITY	4-2	Christie, Gregory, Robertson, McGowan	3675		2		8	4	7		6	9				10		5	1		11	3
5		13	Darlington	1-0	Gregory	3788		2	12	8	4	7		6	9				10		5	1		11	3
6		19	SWANSEA CITY	0-0		5428		2		8	4	7		6	9				10		5	1		11	3
7		23	WORKINGTON	2-1	Stratford, Best	4677		2	12	8	6	7		4	9				10		5	1		11	3
8		27	Torquay United	1-0	Best	2087		8	4		2	7		3	9				10		5	1		11	6
9	Oct	3	DONCASTER ROVERS	2-1	Hall, Stratford	6155		2		8	12	4		6	9				10		5	1		11	3
10		10	Tranmere Rovers	0-2		4808		2		8		4		6	9				10		5	1		11	3
11		18	LINCOLN CITY	1-0	Stratford	6566		2	4			7	12	6	9				10		5	1	8	11	3
12		21	BRENTFORD	3-1	Farrington, Best 2	6225		8				4	7	2	9				10		5	1	6	11	3
13		25	Scunthorpe United	2-0	Stratford 2	2112		4	6			7	12	2	9				8		5	1	10	11	3
14	Nov	1	WATFORD	3-0	Hall, Felton, Phillips	6656		4	6			7		2	9				8		5	1	10	11	3
15		3	Rochdale	2-0	Robertson, Stratford	2995		4	6			7		2	9				8		5	1	10	11	3
16		8	Cambridge United	1-0	Hall	5560		4	6			7		2	9				8		5	1	10	11	3
17		15	SOUTHPORT	1-0	Farrington	6089		4	6	12		7		2	9				8		5	1	10	11	3
18		29	Bournemouth	0-0		5891		4	6			7		2	9		11		8		5	1	10		3
19	Dec	6	CREWE ALEXANDRA	2-1	Hall, McGowan	5705		4	6			7		2	9		11		8		5	1	10		3
20		13	Exeter City	0-0		3394		4	6			7		2	9		11		8		5	1	10		3
21		20	EXETER CITY	3-1	Hall 2, Phillips	5212		4	6			7		2	9		11		8		5	1	10		3
22		26	Hartlepool	0-3		5077		4	6			11		2	7		9				5	1	8		3
23		27	NEWPORT COUNTY	3-0	Phillips, Robertson, Hall	8448		4	6	12		7		2	9		11		8		5	1	10		3
24	Jan	3	Reading	0-1		10360		4	6			7		2	9		11		8		5	1	10		3
25		10	BARNSLEY	5-0	Carlton, Robertson, Hall 2, Best	6132		4	6			7		2	9			8			5	1	10	11	3
26		16	Swansea City	1-1	Mayes	3656		4	6	12		7			9		2	8			5	1	10	11	3
27		24	DARLINGTON	3-2	Robertson, Hall 2	5135		4	12			7		6	9		2	8			5	1	10	11	3
28		31	Brentford	1-2	Hall	4114		4	6			7		2	9			8	12		5	1	10	11	3
29	Feb	7	ROCHDALE	1-1	Stratford	5393		4	6					2	9		7	8			5	1	10	11	3
30		14	CAMBRIDGE UNITED	4-2	Smith (og), Mayes 2, Robertson	5969		4	6			7		2			9	8	12		5	1	10	11	3
31		21	Southport	1-0	Farrington	1332		4	6			7		2			9	8	12		5	1	10	11	3
32		25	Workington	0-1		1135		4	6	12		7		2	9		8	11			5	1	10		3
33		27	SCUNTHORPE UNITED	2-1	Mayes, Martin (p)	6804		4	6			7		2	9		12	8	10		5	1		11	3
34	Mar	6	Watford	1-0	Hall	7389		4				7		2	9		6	8	10		5	1		11	3
35		9	Doncaster Rovers	4-0	Stratford 2, McGowan, Phillips	8737			12	6		7		2	9		4		10		5	1	8	11	3
36		12	TRANMERE ROVERS	1-1	Phillips	8247			12	6		7		2	9		4		10		5	1	8	11	3
37		17	Lincoln City	1-3	Stratford	13880		4				7		2	9		6		8		5	1	10	11	3
38		20	BOURNEMOUTH	6-0	Hall 3, Best 2, Stratford	6780		4		12		7		2	9		6		10		5	1	8	11	3
39		27	Crewe Alexandra	1-0	Best	2865		4	11	7				2	9		6				5	1	10		3
40	Apr	3	HUDDERSFIELD T	1-1	Phillips	7218		4	11	7				2	9		6				5	1	10		3
41		6	TORQUAY UNITED	2-2	Phillips, Gregory	6263		4	6	11		12		2	9		5				7	1	10		3
42		10	Bradford City	2-1	Hall 2	3175		4	6			7		2	9		5					1	10	11	3
43		15	READING	4-1	McGowan, Stratford 2, Martin	9584		4				6	7	2	9		5		10			1	8	11	3
44		17	HARTLEPOOL	5-2	Starling (p), Martin 3 (1p), Robertson	7555		4				12	7	2	9		6		10		5	1	8	11	3
45		20	Newport County	1-1	Martin (p)	1718		4					7	2	9		6		10		5	1	8	11	3
46		23	Stockport County	4-0	Stratford 3, Martin	7680		4					7	2	9		6		10		5	1	8	11	3
					Apps		3	44	34	19	9	38	10	45	43	1	29	10	42	3	44	43	30	46	34
					Goals			8	1	1		4	1	3	21		7	4	4		7	1	16	1	7

one own goal

F.A. Cup

Round	Date	Opponent	Score	Att	Best	Carlton	Christie	Farrington	Felton	Gregory	Hall	McGowan	Robertson	Starling	Phillips
R1	Nov 22	Brentford	0-2	6640	4	6	10	11	7	2	9	8	5	1	3

F.L. Cup

Round	Date	Opponent	Score	Att	Anderson	Best	Carlton	Christie	Farrington	Gregory	Hall	Mabee	Parton	Robertson	Tucker	Phillips
R1/1	Aug 19	Watford	0-2	3368	3	8		10	4	6	9	7	1	5	11	2
R1/2	Aug 27	WATFORD	1-1 Hall	4255	3	8	4	10	7	6	9		1	5	11	2

	Team	P	W	D	L	F	A	W	D	L	F	A	Pts
1	Lincoln City	46	21	2	0	71	15	11	8	4	40	24	74
2	NORTHAMPTON TOWN	46	18	5	0	62	20	11	5	7	25	20	68
3	Reading	46	19	3	1	42	9	5	9	9	28	42	60
4	Tranmere Rovers	46	18	3	2	61	16	6	7	10	28	39	58
5	Huddersfield Town	46	11	6	6	28	17	10	8	5	28	24	56
6	Bournemouth	46	15	5	3	39	16	5	7	11	18	32	52
7	Exeter City	46	13	7	3	37	17	5	7	11	19	30	50
8	Watford	46	16	4	3	38	18	6	2	15	24	44	50
9	Torquay United	46	12	6	5	31	24	6	8	9	24	39	50
10	Doncaster Rovers	46	10	6	7	42	31	9	5	9	33	38	49
11	Swansea City	46	14	8	1	51	21	2	7	14	15	36	47
12	Barnsley	46	12	8	3	34	16	2	8	13	18	32	44
13	Cambridge United	46	7	10	6	36	28	7	5	11	22	34	43
14	Hartlepool	46	10	6	7	37	29	6	4	13	25	49	42
15	Rochdale	46	7	11	5	27	23	5	7	11	13	42	42
16	Crewe Alexandra	46	10	7	6	36	21	3	8	12	22	36	41
17	Bradford City	46	9	7	7	35	26	3	10	10	28	39	41
18	Brentford	46	12	7	4	37	18	2	6	15	19	42	41
19	Scunthorpe United	46	11	3	9	31	24	3	7	13	19	35	38
20	Darlington	46	11	7	5	30	14	3	3	17	18	43	38
21	Stockport County	46	8	7	8	23	23	5	5	13	20	53	38
22	Newport County	46	8	8	3	35	33	5	2	16	22	57	35
23	Southport	46	6	6	11	27	31	2	4	17	14	46	26
24	Workington	46	5	4	14	19	43	2	3	18	11	44	21

1976/77   22nd in Division 3: Relegated

No	Date	Opponent	Score	Scorers	Att	Bowen KB	Bowker K	Carlton DG	Christie DHM	Bryant SP	Farrington JR	Best WJB	Gregory JC	Gilligan JJ	Hall IL	Haywood RJ	Malcolm AA	Martin D	McGowan A	Owen R	Phillips SE	Parton JJ	Robertson SJ	Reilly GG	Starling AW	Stratford P	Ross I	Tucker WB	Ward RA	Williams KD
1	Aug 21	Chesterfield	0-0		4052				7		12	4	2		9			6	10		8			5	1	11		3		
2	25	Sheffield Wednesday	1-2	Christie	11684			7	10		12	4	2					9	6		8			5	1	11		3		
3	28	LINCOLN CITY	1-0	Christie	6350			7	10		12	4	2					9	6		8			5	1	11		3		
4	Sep 4	Gillingham	1-1	Hall	5375			6	7			4	2		9			11	8					5	1	10		3		
5	11	READING	1-2	Robertson	6176			7	8		12	4	2		9			6	10					5	1	11		3		
6	18	Shrewsbury Town	0-3		4191			6	7			4	2		9			11	8					5	1	10		3		
7	25	WALSALL	0-1		5656			7	8			4	2		9			11	6				12	5	1	10		3		
8	Oct 1	WREXHAM	0-2		5114				11		7	4	2						8		6			5	1	9		3		
9	8	Port Vale	1-2	Phillips	3962	12			11		7	4	2			10			8		6			5	1	9		3		
10	15	PORTSMOUTH	3-1	Hall, Robertson, Reilly	4805				11		7	4	2			10			8		6			5	1	9		3		
11	23	Swindon Town	1-5	McGowan	7483				11		7	4	2			10			8		6			5	1	9		3		
12	26	York City	4-1	Christie 2, Farrington, Stratford	2634				11		7	4	2			10			12		8			6	1	9		3		
13	30	BRIGHTON & HOVE ALB	0-2		7782				10		7	4	2						8	9	6			5	1	11		3		
14	Nov 2	PETERBOROUGH UTD.	2-2	Stratford, og	7483				11		7		2					4	8	10	6		12	5	1	9		3		
15	6	Preston North End	0-3		7306				11		7		2					4	8	10	6		12	5	1	9		3		
16	13	OXFORD UNITED	1-0	Robertson	7021				11				2	9				4	8	6		1	5	3		10		7		
17	27	Chester	1-2	Phillips	3917				9		12	5	2				3	8	10		6	1		4		11		7		
18	Dec 18	Crystal Palace	1-1	McGowan	11032				7	3		4	2		9			6	8		10			5	1	11				
19	27	ROTHERHAM UNITED	1-4	Gregory	6963		9		7	3	12	4	2					11	8		6			5	1	10				
20	Jan 1	PRESTON NORTH END	0-1		5024		9		11	3	7	4	2						8					5	1	10	6			
21	3	Brighton & Hove Albion	0-2		22517		9		12	3	11		2						8		6		4	5	1	10	7			
22	7	TRANMERE ROVERS	3-4	Best, Martin, Stratford	4267				12	3	11	6	2					9	8				4	5	1	10		7		
23	15	SHEFFIELD WEDNESDAY	0-2		5828		9		12	3	7	6	4					10	8					5	1	11		2		
24	22	CHESTERFIELD	2-1	Best, Gilligan	3911					3	7	8	4	10				9					6	5	1	11		2		
25	29	Grimsby Town	1-0	Farrington	3909				12	3	7	6	4	10				9	8					5	1	11		2		
26	Feb 5	Lincoln City	4-5	Best 3, Robertson	5869				12	3	7	6	4	10				9	8					5	1	11		2		
27	12	GILLINGHAM	1-2	Farrington	4391				12	3	7	6	4	8				9					11	5	1	10		2		
28	15	Bury	1-1	Farrington	3809				8	3	7	6	4					9					11	5	1	10		2		
29	19	Reading	4-2	Christie, McGowan 2, Stratford	5051				8	3	7	6	4		10			9	12					5		11		2	1	
30	26	SHREWSBURY TOWN	5-3	Best 2, Gregory, Martin, Stratford	5112				11	3	7	6	4					9	12					5		10		2	1	8
31	Mar 5	Walsall	3-0	Martin, Stratford 2	4806				11	3	7	6	4					9						5		10		2	1	8
32	8	MANSFIELD TOWN	0-1		7283				11	3	7	6	4					9	12					5		10		2	1	8
33	12	Wrexham	1-3	Best	6775				11	3	7	6	4			12		9						5		10		2	1	8
34	15	CRYSTAL PALACE	3-0	Gregory, Haywood, Stratford	6253				11	3	7	6	4			9			12					5		10		2	1	8
35	19	PORT VALE	3-0	Best, Stratford 2	5808				11	3	7	6	4			9								5		10		2	1	8
36	26	Portsmouth	1-2	Stratford	9195				11	3	7		4			9					6			5		10		2	1	8
37	Apr 1	SWINDON TOWN	1-1	Best	5609				11		7	6	4			9	3		12			1		5		10		2		8
38	9	BURY	3-0	Best, Stratford, og	5262				11	3	7	6	4			9			12			1		5		10		2		8
39	11	Rotherham United	0-2		7286				11	3	7	6	4			9			12			1		5		10		2		8
40	12	Peterborough United	1-3	Gregory	8944				11	3	7		4			9			6	12		1		5	10			2		8
41	16	YORK CITY	3-0	Best, Reilly, Williams	5427				11	3	7		4			12		9				1		5	10			2		8
42	19	GRIMSBY TOWN	0-0		5699				10	3	7	6	4			11		2	12			1		5	9					8
43	23	Oxford United	0-1		5075				11	3	7	6	4					2	12			1		5	9	10				8
44	29	CHESTER	0-0		5015				10	3	7	6	4			9		2				1		5		11				8
45	May 2	Tranmere Rovers	1-2	Haywood	2030				12	3	7	6	4			9		2	10			1		5		11				8
46	7	Mansfield Town	0-3		11314				12	3	7	6	4			9		2	10			1		5	12	11				8
		Apps				1	4	6	44	28	41	40	46	5	11	13	2	38	31	5	17	12	41	22	26	42	2	37	8	17
		Goals							5		4	12	4	1		2		2	3				4	2		4		2		1

Two own goals

F.A. Cup

No	Date	Opponent	Score		Att	Christie DHM	Farrington JR	Best WJB	Gregory JC	Haywood RJ	McGowan A	Phillips SE	Parton JJ	Robertson SJ	Reilly GG	Starling AW	Stratford P	Tucker WB
R1	Nov 20	Leatherhead	0-2		3550	7	12	4	2	10	8	6	1		5	9	11	3

F.L. Cup

No	Date	Opponent	Score	Scorers	Att	Christie DHM	Farrington JR	Best WJB	Gregory JC	Hall IL	Martin D	McGowan A	Phillips SE	Reilly GG	Starling AW	Stratford P	Tucker WB
R1/1	Aug 14	Swindon Town	2-3	Christie, Gregory	6353	7	12	4	2	9	6	8	10	5	1	11	3
R1/2	18	SWINDON TOWN	2-0	Martin, Stratford	7037	7		4	2	9	6	8	10	5	1	11	3
R2	31	HUDDERSFIELD T	0-1		6641	7	12	4	2	9	6	8	11	5	1	11	3

1976/77 SEASON
Back: Petts(Trainer), McCormick(Gymnast), Hall, Liddle, Gregory, Parton, Starling,
Robertson, Carlton, Martin, Farrington, Crerand(Manager)
Front: Graham, Bradley, Phillips, Tucker, Best, McGowan, Stratford, Christie, Cullinane

1977/78 SEASON
Back: Robertson, Reilly, Best, Hall, Parton, Martin, Farrington, Bryant, Petts(Manager)
Front: Christie, Tucker, McGowan, Williams, Liddle

1977/78   10th in Division 4

No	Date	Opponent	Score	Scorers	Att	Best WJB	Bryant SP	Christie DHM	Farrington JR	Garnham SE	Hall JL	Haywood RJ	Geldmintis AJ	Liddle DN	Litt SE	Jayes CG	Martin D	Mead PS	McGowan A	Parton JJ	Poppy APC	Reilly GG	Robertson SJ	Stratford P	Tucker WB	Williams KD	Wassall KD	Lyon DG
1	Aug 20	Brentford	0-3		5492		3	12	7	1		10		4			11		6			9	5		2	8		
2	22	Southend United	0-0		3693	6	3	11	7	1		10		4								9	5		2	8		
3	27	Halifax Town	1-0	Bryant	1869	6	3	11	7	1		10		4					12			9	5		2	8		
4	Sep 3	TORQUAY UNITED	1-0	Christie	3889	6	3	11	7	1				4					10			9	5		2	8		
5	9	Southport	1-3	Robertson	2677	6		11	7	1				4			3		10			9	5		2	8		
6	13	STOCKPORT COUNTY	2-1	Farrington, Reilly	3880	6		12	7	1				4			10	3	11			9	5		2	8		
7	17	HARTLEPOOL UNITED	5-3	Martin, Reilly 3, Robertson	3499		6	12	7	1				4			10	3	11			9	5		2	8		
8	24	Wimbledon	0-2		3236	12	6		7	1				4	5		10	3	11			9			2	8		
9	27	HUDDERSFIELD T	3-1	Best, Reilly 2	3942	8	6	11	7	1				4			10	2				9	5		3			
10	Oct 1	Scunthorpe United	2-2	Martin 2	2711	10	6	11	7	1					5		9	2				8	4		3	12		
11	4	Darlington	0-2		1729	10	6	11	7	1			12		5		9	2				8			3	4		
12	8	READING	0-2		3861	10	6	11	7	1					5		9	2		1		8	4		3	12		
13	11	ROCHDALE	3-1	Christie 2, Reilly	2965	8	6	11	7						5			2	10	1		9	4		3			
14	14	Crewe Alexandra	2-3	Best, Christie	2807	8	6	11	7						5			2	10	1		9	4		3		12	
15	22	BOURNEMOUTH	1-0	Reilly	3479	8	6	11	7						5			2	10	1		9	4		3		12	
16	29	Rochdale	1-1	Farrington	1198		6	11	7						5			2	10	1		9			3			4
17	Nov 5	NEWPORT COUNTY	2-4	Christie, Martin	3568		6	11	7						5		8	2	10	1		9			3			4
18	12	Doncaster Rovers	2-4	Hall, McGowan	2688		6	11	7		8				5	1		2	10			9			3			4
19	19	BARNSLEY	1-1	Reilly	3131		3	11			9			4	6		7		8	1		10	5		2			
20	Dec 3	Swansea City	4-2	Christie, Farrington, Liddle, Reilly	4735		3	11	7					4	6	1	8					10	5		2	12		9
21	10	YORK CITY	1-1	Martin	3108		3	11	7					4	5		6	12		1		10			2	8		9
22	26	Watford	0-3		15056		3	11						4	6	1	8	7				9	5		2	10		
23	27	GRIMSBY TOWN	2-1	Martin, Tucker	3518		6	7	8						4	1	12	3				10	5	9	2	11		
24	31	ALDERSHOT	1-1	Farrington	3598	9	6	11	7						4	1	12	3				10	5		2	8		
25	Jan 2	Newport County	3-5	Farrington, Reilly 2	7160	4	3	11	7						6	1	12					10	5	9	2	8		
26	14	BRENTFORD	2-2	Reilly 2	4050	6	10	11	7					4	5	1	12	3				9			2	8		
27	28	Torquay United	1-2	Reilly	2443	4	9	8	10						12	1		3	7			11	6		2	5		
28	Feb 4	SOUTHPORT	1-0	Mead	2374	4	6	11	7			10				1		3				9	5		2	8		
29	25	SCUNTHORPE UNITED	1-2	Christie	2952	4		11	7		8		2	12		1		3	10			9	5		6			
30	28	WIMBLEDON	0-3		2643	4		11	7		8		2	3		1	12		10		6	9						5
31	Mar 4	Reading	0-0		4321	4		11	7		8		2	6		1	12	3	10			9	5					
32	6	Stockport County	2-1	Liddle, Reilly	3358	6	4	12	7	11	8		2	6		1		3	9			10	5					
33	11	CREWE ALEXANDRA	0-0		2842	6	12	11	7	9			2	4		1		3	8			10	5					
34	14	HALIFAX TOWN	1-2	Farrington	2278	4	6	11	7	9			2	8		1	12	3				10	5					
35	17	Bournemouth	1-1	McGowan	2221	4	6	11	7	9			2	8		1		3	12			10	5					
36	21	SOUTHEND UNITED	0-0		2431	4	6	11	7				2	8		1		3	10			9	5					
37	25	Grimsby Town	1-0	McGowan	5077	4	6	11	7				2	8		1	12	3	10			9	5					
38	28	WATFORD	0-2		8041	4	6	11	7				2	8			12	3	10	1		9	5					
39	Apr 1	Aldershot	1-2	Martin	3353	4	6	12	7				2	11			9	3	10	1			5			8		
40	4	Huddersfield Town	1-0	Bryant	3488	4	6		7				2			1	10	3	9				5			8	11	
41	8	DONCASTER ROVERS	0-0		2793	4	6		7				2					3	9			10	5			8	11	
42	11	Hartlepool United	2-0	McGowan 2	2844	4	6	11	7				2					3	9			10	5			8		
43	15	Barnsley	3-2	Farrington, Christie, Reilly	3434	4	6	11	7				2					3	9			10	5			8		
44	22	SWANSEA CITY	3-1	Christie, Reilly, Robertson	4865	4	6	11	7				2					3	9			10	5			8	12	
45	25	DARLINGTON	2-2	McGowan, Reilly	3181		6	11	7				2	4				3	9			10	5			8		
46	29	York City	3-0	Reilly 2, Williams	1389		6	11	7				2	4				3	9			10	5			8	12	
				Apps		34	41	43	44	11	10	3	18	27	20	25	25	38	32	10	1	44	38	2	28	28	7	6
				Goals		2	2	9	7		1			2			7	1	6			21	3		1	1		

F.A. Cup

No	Date	Opponent	Score	Scorers	Att	Best	Bryant	Christie	Farrington	Garnham	Hall	Haywood	Geldmintis	Liddle	Litt	Jayes	Martin	Mead	McGowan	Parton	Poppy	Reilly	Robertson	Stratford	Tucker	Williams	Wassall	Lyon
R1	Nov 26	Tooting & Mitcham	2-1	Christie, Martin	3513		3	11	7		9			4	6	1	8					10	5		2			
R2	Dec 17	ENFIELD	0-2		5249	10	3	11	7					4	6	1	8					9	5		2	12		

F.L. Cup

No	Date	Opponent	Score	Scorers	Att	Best	Bryant	Christie	Farrington	Garnham	Hall	Haywood	Geldmintis	Liddle	Litt	Jayes	Martin	Mead	McGowan	Parton	Poppy	Reilly	Robertson	Stratford	Tucker	Williams	Wassall	Lyon
R1/1	Aug 13	Southend United	3-2	Farrington, Reilly, Williams	4654	6	3		7			10		4			11			1		9	5		2	8		
R1/2	16	SOUTHEND UNITED	2-1	Best, Martin	4395	6	3	12	7					4			11		10	1		9	5		2	8		
R2	30	Ipswich Town	0-5		15443	6	3	11	7	1				4			10		12			9	5		2	8		

		P	W	D	L	F	A	W	D	L	F	A	Pts
1	Watford	46	18	4	1	44	14	12	7	4	41	24	71
2	Southend United	46	15	5	3	46	18	10	5	8	20	21	60
3	Swansea City	46	16	5	2	54	17	7	5	11	33	30	56
4	Brentford	46	15	6	2	50	17	6	8	9	36	37	56
5	Aldershot	46	15	8	0	45	16	4	8	11	22	31	54
6	Grimsby Town	46	14	6	3	30	15	7	5	11	27	36	53
7	Barnsley	46	15	4	4	44	20	3	10	10	17	29	50
8	Reading	46	12	7	4	33	23	6	7	10	22	29	50
9	Torquay United	46	12	6	5	43	25	4	9	10	14	31	47
10	NORTHAMPTON TOWN	46	9	8	6	32	30	8	5	10	31	38	47
11	Huddersfield Town	46	13	5	5	41	21	2	10	11	22	34	45
12	Doncaster Rovers	46	11	8	4	37	26	3	9	11	15	39	45
13	Wimbledon	46	8	11	4	39	26	6	5	12	27	41	44
14	Scunthorpe United	46	12	6	5	31	14	2	10	11	19	41	44
15	Crewe Alexandra	46	11	8	4	34	25	4	6	13	16	44	44
16	Newport County	46	14	6	3	43	22	2	5	16	22	51	43
17	Bournemouth	46	12	6	5	28	20	2	9	12	13	31	43
18	Stockport County	46	14	4	5	41	19	2	6	15	15	37	42
19	Darlington	46	10	8	5	31	22	5	4	14	21	37	42
20	Halifax Town	46	7	10	6	28	23	3	11	9	24	39	41
21	Hartlepool United	46	12	4	7	34	29	3	3	17	17	55	37
22	York City	46	8	7	8	27	31	4	5	14	23	38	36
23	Southport	46	5	13	5	30	32	1	6	16	22	44	31
24	Rochdale	46	8	6	9	29	28	0	2	21	14	57	24

1978/79 19th in Division 4

#	Date	Opponent	Score	Scorers	Att	Ashenden RH	Bowen KB	Bryant SP	Cordice NA	Christie DHM	Farrington JR	Froggatt JL	Geidmintis AJ	Jayes CG	Liddle DN	Matthews PW	Mead PS	McCaffrey J	Reilly GG	Robertson SJ	Perkins GS	Saunders PB	Poole AJ	Waldock DH	Walker RP	Wassall KD	Woollett AH	Williams KD
1	Aug 19	Torquay United	1-0	Liddle	3125			6		11	7		2	1	10		3		9							5	4	8
2	23	HARTLEPOOL UNITED	1-1	Farrington	4288			6		11	7		2	1	10		3		9						12	5	4	8
3	26	Wimbledon	1-4	Reilly	2644			12	10	11	7			1	6		3		9	5					2		4	8
4	Sep 2	BRADFORD CITY	1-0	Cordice	3320			6	10	11	7		2				3		9	5							4	8
5	9	York City	0-1		2443			6	12	11	7	9	2	1			3		10	5							4	8
6	12	DARLINGTON	4-1	Christie, Froggatt 2, Reilly	3443			6	12	11	7	9	2	1					10	5					3		4	8
7	15	SCUNTHORPE UNITED	1-0	Bryant	3859			6		11	7	10	2	1					9	5					3		4	8
8	23	Huddersfield Town	0-1		3320			6		11	7	9	2				12		10	5			1		3		4	8
9	26	Port Vale	2-2	Farrington, Froggatt	3245			6		11	7	9	2				3		10	5			1				4	8
10	30	DONCASTER ROVERS	3-0	Mead, Robertson, Christie	3011			6	12	11	7	9	2				3		10	5			1				4	8
11	Oct 7	Barnsley	1-1	Farrington	10336			6		11	7	9	2				3			5			1			10	4	8
12	14	READING	2-2	Farrington, Mead	4694			6		11	7	9	2	1			3		5			12				10	4	8
13	17	Grimsby Town	3-4	Christie, Froggatt, Bryant	5777			6		11	7	9	2	1			3		5			10					4	8
14	21	STOCKPORT COUNTY	2-2	Froggatt, Mead	3867			6	12	11	7	9	2	1			3		10			5					4	8
15	28	Wigan Athletic	0-2		6264			6		11	7	9	2	1			3		10	5		4			12		4	8
16	Nov 4	NEWPORT COUNTY	3-1	Froggatt, Farrington, Reilly	3065	12		6			7	9	2	1			3		10	5						11	4	8
17	11	Bradford City	0-3		3361			6			7	9	2	1			3		10	5		12				11	4	8
18	18	WIMBLEDON	1-1	Geidmintis (p)	3625			6	9		7		10	2			3			5			1			11	4	8
19	Dec 2	PORTSMOUTH	0-2		3592	6			9		7		10	2	1		3		4	5					12	11		8
20	9	Hereford United	3-4	Froggatt, Farrington, Reilly	2879	6	12			7	9	4	1			3		10	5						2	11		8
21	26	ALDERSHOT	2-3	Reilly, McCaffrey	3325			6			7	9	4	1			3	11	10	5					2	12		8
22	30	HALIFAX TOWN	2-1	Reilly, McCaffrey	2208		12	6			7	9	4	1			3	11	10	5					2			8
23	Feb 10	Doncaster Rovers	0-2		1922			6			7	9	4	1			3	11	10	5					2			8
24	21	Bournemouth	0-0		3990			6			7	9	2	1			3	11	10	5							4	8
25	24	Reading	1-5	Reilly	6933			6	10		7	9	2	1			3	11	4	5		12						8
26	Mar 2	Stockport County	1-2	Reilly	2929			6			7	9	2				3	11	10	5		4	1			12		8
27	6	HUDDERSFIELD T	2-3	Reilly 2	1823			6			7	9	2				3	11	10	5		4	1			12		8
28	10	WIGAN ATHLETIC	2-4	Froggatt, Bryant	2275	12		6			7	9	2	1			3	11	10	5		8					4	
29	13	PORT VALE	1-0	Farrington	1572	12		3			7	9	2					11	10	5		6	1				4	8
30	16	Newport County	1-2	Robertson	3018	12		3			7	9	2					11	10	5		6	1				4	8
31	20	Scunthorpe United	3-0	Reilly 3	1868						7	9	2	1				11	10	5		6	1				4	8
32	24	TORQUAY UNITED	1-2	Robertson	2194						7	9	2	1				11	10	5		6	1				4	8
33	31	ROCHDALE	1-0	Robertson	1653							6	11	2	1	8	3	9	10	5		4						7
34	Apr 3	YORK CITY	1-0	Froggatt	1628							6	11	2	1	8	3	9	10	5		4						7
35	7	Portsmouth	0-1		8166	12						6	11	2	1	8	3	9	10	5		4						7
36	10	Crewe Alexandra	4-2	Robertson, Farrington, Froggatt, Williams	1291	12						6	11	2	1	8	3	9	10	5		4	1					7
37	14	Aldershot	0-2		4438							6	11	2	1	8	3		10	5		4					9	7
38	16	BOURNEMOUTH	4-2	Reilly 3, Froggatt	2253	12						6	11	2	1	8	3	9	10	5		4						7
39	17	CREWE ALEXANDRA	3-1	Reilly 2, Froggatt	2570	12						6	11	2	1	8	3	9	10	5		4						7
40	21	Halifax Town	2-2	McCaffrey, Froggatt	1172							6	11	2	1	8	3	9	10	5		4						7
41	24	GRIMSBY TOWN	1-2	Williams	3019							6	11	2	1	8	3	9	10	5		4						7
42	26	BARNSLEY	0-1		3305	12						6	11	2		8	3	9	10	5		4	1					7
43	28	HEREFORD UNITED	2-1	Robertson, McCaffrey	2001	8						6	11	2		12	3	9		5		4	1		10			7
44	May 5	Rochdale	1-4	Reilly	1751	8						6	11	4		7		9	10			5	1	3	2			
45	14	Darlington	0-0		1333		10					6	11	2		8		9	4			5	1	3				7
46	17	Hartlepool United	0-2		1769		10					6	11	2		8		9	4		12	3	1	5				7
				Apps		13	5	28	8	15	46	42	45	29	4	13	39	25	43	38	1	27	17	3	13	13	23	44
				Goals				3	1	3	8	13	1		1		3	4	19	6								2

F.A. Cup

R	Date	Opponent	Score	Scorers	Att	Ashenden RH	Bowen KB	Bryant SP	Cordice NA	Christie DHM	Farrington JR	Froggatt JL	Geidmintis AJ	Jayes CG	Liddle DN	Matthews PW	Mead PS	McCaffrey J	Reilly GG	Robertson SJ	Perkins GS	Saunders PB	Poole AJ	Waldock DH	Walker RP	Wassall KD	Woollett AH	Williams KD
R1	Nov 25	Portsmouth	0-2		13338				12		7	9	2	1			3		10	5		6				11	4	8

F.L. Cup

R	Date	Opponent	Score	Scorers	Att	Ashenden RH	Bowen KB	Bryant SP	Cordice NA	Christie DHM	Farrington JR	Froggatt JL	Geidmintis AJ	Jayes CG	Liddle DN	Matthews PW	Mead PS	McCaffrey J	Reilly GG	Robertson SJ	Perkins GS	Saunders PB	Poole AJ	Waldock DH	Walker RP	Wassall KD	Woollett AH	Williams KD
R1/1	Aug 12	Cambridge United	2-2	Farrington, Reilly	4043			6		11	7		2	1	10		3		9	5							4	8
R1/2	16	CAMBRIDGE UNITED	2-1	Reilly, Christie	4721			6		11	7		2	1	10		3		9	5					12		4	8
R2/1	30	HEREFORD UNITED	0-0		3991			6		11	7		2	1			3		9	5		10			12		4	8
R2/2	Sep 6	Hereford United	1-0	Reilly	4205	12		6	10	11	7		4	1			3		9	5					2			8
R3	Oct 4	STOKE CITY	1-3	Reilly	11235			6	10	11	7		2				3		9	5			1			12	4	8

		P	W	D	L	F	A	W	D	L	F	A	Pts
1	Reading	46	19	3	1	49	8	7	10	6	27	27	65
2	Grimsby Town	46	15	5	3	51	23	11	4	8	31	26	61
3	Wimbledon	46	18	3	2	50	20	7	8	8	28	26	61
4	Barnsley	46	15	5	3	47	23	9	8	6	26	19	61
5	Aldershot	46	16	5	2	38	14	4	12	7	25	33	57
6	Wigan Athletic	46	14	5	4	40	24	7	8	8	23	24	55
7	Portsmouth	46	13	7	3	35	12	7	5	11	27	36	52
8	Newport County	46	12	5	6	39	28	9	5	9	27	27	52
9	Huddersfield Town	46	13	8	2	32	15	5	3	15	25	38	47
10	York City	46	11	6	6	33	24	7	5	11	18	31	47
11	Torquay United	46	14	4	5	38	24	5	4	14	20	41	46
12	Scunthorpe United	46	12	3	8	33	30	5	8	10	21	30	45
13	Hartlepool United	46	7	12	4	35	28	6	6	11	22	38	44
14	Hereford United	46	12	8	3	35	18	3	5	15	18	35	43
15	Bradford City	46	11	5	7	38	26	6	4	13	24	42	43
16	Port Vale	46	8	10	5	29	28	6	4	13	28	42	42
17	Stockport County	46	11	5	7	33	21	3	7	13	25	39	40
18	Bournemouth	46	11	6	6	34	19	3	5	15	13	29	39
19	NORTHAMPTON TOWN	46	12	4	7	40	30	3	5	14	25	44	39
20	Rochdale	46	11	4	8	25	26	4	5	14	22	38	39
21	Darlington	46	8	8	7	25	21	3	7	13	24	45	37
22	Doncaster Rovers	46	8	8	7	25	22	5	3	15	25	51	37
23	Halifax Town	46	7	5	11	24	32	2	3	18	15	40	26
24	Crewe Alexandra	46	3	7	13	24	41	3	7	13	19	49	26

1978/79 SEASON Back: Christie, Saunders, Mead, Williams
Middle: Keen, McNichol, Cordice, Jayes, Poole, Bryant, Farrington, Walker(Coach)
Front: Reilly, Liddle, Woollett, Robertson, Wassall, Walker

1979/80 SEASON (Right to Left) Farrington, Perkins, McCaffrey, Ashenden, Taylor, Denyer, Williams, Walker, Saunders, Sargent, Waldock, Ward, Poole, Jayes, Byatt, Reilly, McNichol

1979/80   13th in Division 4

#	Date	Opponent	Score	Scorers	Att	Poole AJ	Byatt DJ	Reilly GG	Farmer KJ	Taylor A	Ward SC	Denyer PR	Ashenden RH	McCaffrey J	Bowen KB	Sargent GS	Waldock DH	Jayes CG	Walker RP	Saunders PB	Farrington JR	Townsend RN	Sandercock PJ	O'Donoghue MG	Sandy AVC	Williams KD	Gage WAJ	Leonard GE	Ingram GP	Heeley DM	Muir M
1	Aug 18	Doncaster Rovers	1-2	McCaffrey	4402	1	2	4	5	3	6	7	9	11	8	10	12														
2	22	BRADFORD CITY	1-2	Denyer	2555		2	9	5	3	6	7		11	8	10	4	1													
3	25	WALSALL	1-2	Bowen	3136			10	5	3	6	7	12	11	9	8	4	1	2												
4	Sep 1	Torquay United	2-2	Denyer, Ward	2825			9	4		6	7		11	10	8	5	1	2	3											
5	7	HALIFAX TOWN	0-0		2759			10	4		6	7		9	11	8	5	1	2	3											
6	15	Port Vale	0-5		2847		3	10	4		6	7	12	11	8	5		1	2		9										
7	18	Newport County	1-2	Waldock	3185			4		3	6	7	12	11	9	10	5	1	2		8										
8	22	PETERBOROUGH UTD.	1-0	Bowen	3680			4	12		6	7	3	11	10	9	5	1	2		8										
9	29	Crewe Alexandra	1-2	Waldock	1909	1		4	12		6	7		11	10	9	5		2		8		3								
10	Oct 2	NEWPORT COUNTY	3-2	Waldock, McCaffrey, Reilly	2346			5	12		6	7		9		10	4	1	2		11	8	3								
11	6	TRANMERE ROVERS	2-1	Reilly, Sargent	2324			9	6		4	7				10	5	1	2		11	8	3								
12	10	Bradford City	1-3	Reilly	4534		12	11	6		4	9				10	5	1	2	8	7		3								
13	13	Aldershot	0-2		3799		11	10	12		4	9				8	5	1	2		6	7	3								
14	20	HEREFORD UNITED	2-0	Farmer 2	2319		6	9	11			4				10	5	1	2		7	8	3								
15	23	HUDDERSFIELD T	4-2	Sargent, Farrington, Farmer 2	3210		4	10	11			7				9	5	1	2		6	8	3								
16	26	Rochdale	2-3	Farmer, Byatt	1468		4	10	11			7		12		9	5	1	2		6	8	3								
17	Nov 3	DONCASTER ROVERS	1-0	Sandercock	3427	1	4	9	11			7				10	5		2		6	8	3								
18	6	Huddersfield Town	0-5		6552	1	4	10	11		12	8				9	5		2	7	6		3								
19	10	Darlington	0-0		1559	1	4		11			8				9	5		2	7	6		3	10							
20	17	HARTLEPOOL UNITED	2-1	O'Donoghue, Farrington	2251	1	4		9			7		10		8	5		2		6		3	11							
21	Dec 1	Wigan Athletic	0-0		6158	1	4	10				7		11			5		2	8	6		3	9	12						
22	8	SCUNTHORPE UNITED	0-0		2120	1	4	10				7		11			5		2	8	6		3	9							
23	21	Bournemouth	2-2	Denyer 2	2335	1	4	10				7		11	9		5		2				3		6	8					
24	26	STOCKPORT COUNTY	2-0	Bowen 2	3054	1	4	10				7		11	9				2				3		6	8		5			
25	29	Portsmouth	1-6	Bowen	15579	1	4	10				7		11	9	12			2				3		6	8		5			
26	Jan 5	YORK CITY	2-0	Ward, Farmer	2095	1	4	10			8	7		11	9		5		2				3		6						
27	26	Walsall	1-5	Bowen	5646	1	4	9			6	7		11	10	12	5		2				3		8						
28	Feb 2	PORT VALE	3-1	Sargent, Gage, Bowen	1946	1	4				6	7		11	10	9			2				3		8		5				
29	9	Peterborough United	0-0		4960	1	4	8		12	9	7		11					2		6		3		10		5				
30	13	Lincoln City	0-0		3652	1	4	10				7		9		11			2		6		3		8		5				
31	16	CREWE ALEXANDRA	1-0	Saunders	1852	1	4	10				7		9		11			2	12	6		3		8		5				
32	23	ALDERSHOT	2-1	Farrington, Denyer	2592	1	4					7		9	10	11			2		6		3		8		5				
33	Mar 1	Hereford United	1-0	Bowen	2299	1	4					7		9	10	11			2		6		3		8		5				
34	4	Halifax Town	1-2	Byatt	1377	1	4					7		9	10	11			2		6		3		8		5				
35	8	ROCHDALE	0-0		2370	1	4					7		9	10	11			2		6		3		8		5				
36	14	Tranmere Rovers	1-1	Bowen	1500	1	4	11				7		9	10				2	8	6		3				5				
37	18	TORQUAY UNITED	3-0	Byatt, Bowen, Ingram	2659	1	4					6			10	8			2				3		7		5		11	9	
38	22	DARLINGTON	2-0	Bowen, Ingram	3209	1	4					6			10	8			2				3		7		5		11	9	
39	29	Hartlepool United	1-2	Ingram	1995	1	4					6			10	8			2				3		7		5		11	9	
40	Apr 4	Stockport County	0-2		2499	1						6			10	8	4		2				3		7		5		11	9	
41	7	LINCOLN CITY	0-0		3371	1	4	10				6				8			2				3		7		5		11	9	
42	8	BOURNEMOUTH	0-1		3175	1	4					6				8			2	10		12	3		7		5		11	9	
43	12	York City	2-1	Ingram, Sandercock	2161	1		9				6		7		8	4		2	12		10	3				5		11		
44	19	WIGAN ATHLETIC	1-1	Sargent	2378	1						7		9		8			2	4		6	3		10		5		11		
45	25	Scunthorpe United	0-3		1810	1		10				6				7			2	4			3		8		5		11	9	12
46	May 3	PORTSMOUTH	0-2		10713	1	4	11				6							2				3		8		5		10	9	
			Apps			32	33	18	34	4	15	46	5	32	24	40	28	14	38	12	29	13	38	4	22	3	21	1	10	8	1
			Goals				3	3	6		2	5		2	11	4	3			1	3		2	1			1		4		

F.A. Cup

#	Date	Opponent	Score	Scorers	Att	Poole AJ	Byatt DJ	Reilly GG	Farmer KJ	Taylor A	Ward SC	Denyer PR	Ashenden RH	McCaffrey J	Bowen KB	Sargent GS	Waldock DH	Jayes CG	Walker RP	Saunders PB	Farrington JR	Townsend RN	Sandercock PJ
R1	Nov 24	Hereford United	0-1		3384	1		4	9			7		12	10	8	5		2		6	11	3

F.L. Cup

#	Date	Opponent	Score	Scorers	Att	Poole AJ	Byatt DJ	Reilly GG	Farmer KJ	Taylor A	Ward SC	Denyer PR	Ashenden RH	McCaffrey J	Bowen KB	Sargent GS	Waldock DH	Jayes CG	Walker RP	Saunders PB	Farrington JR	Townsend RN	Sandercock PJ
R1/1	Aug 13	MILLWALL	2-1	Reilly 2	3559	1	2	9	5	3		7	12	11	8	10				6	4		
R1/2	15	Millwall	2-2	McCaffrey, Bowen	4218	1	2	4	5	3	6	7		9	11	8	10						
R2/1	28	OLDHAM ATHLETIC	3-0	Reilly 2, Ward	3053			10	4		6	7		11	9	8	5	1	2		3		
R2/2	Sep 5	Oldham Athletic	1-3	Denyer	4850			10	4	12	6	7		9	11	8	5	1	2		3		
R3	27	BRIGHTON & HOVE ALB.	0-1		7105	1		4	12		6	7	3	11	9	10	5		2		8		

	P	W	D	L	F	A	W	D	L	F	A	Pts
1 Huddersfield Town	46	16	5	2	61	18	11	7	5	40	30	66
2 Walsall	46	12	9	2	43	23	11	9	3	32	24	64
3 Newport County	46	16	5	2	47	22	11	2	10	36	28	61
4 Portsmouth	46	15	5	3	62	23	9	7	7	29	26	60
5 Bradford City	46	14	6	3	44	14	10	6	7	33	36	60
6 Wigan Athletic	46	13	5	5	42	26	8	8	7	34	35	55
7 Lincoln City	46	14	8	1	43	12	4	9	10	21	30	53
8 Peterborough Utd.	46	14	3	6	39	22	7	7	9	19	25	52
9 Torquay United	46	13	7	3	47	25	2	10	11	23	44	47
10 Aldershot	46	10	7	6	35	23	6	6	11	27	30	45
11 Bournemouth	46	8	9	6	32	25	5	9	9	20	26	44
12 Doncaster Rovers	46	11	6	6	37	27	4	8	11	25	36	44
13 NORTHAMPTON TOWN	46	14	5	4	33	16	2	7	14	18	50	44
14 Scunthorpe United	46	11	9	3	37	23	3	6	14	21	52	43
15 Tranmere Rovers	46	10	4	9	32	24	4	9	10	18	32	41
16 Stockport County	46	9	7	7	30	31	5	5	13	18	41	40
17 York City	46	9	6	8	35	34	5	5	13	30	48	39
18 Halifax Town	46	11	9	3	29	20	2	4	17	17	52	39
19 Hartlepool United	46	10	7	6	36	28	4	3	16	23	36	38
20 Port Vale	46	8	6	9	34	24	4	6	13	22	46	36
21 Hereford United	46	8	7	8	22	21	3	7	13	16	31	36
22 Darlington	46	7	11	5	33	26	2	6	15	17	48	35
23 Crewe Alexandra	46	10	6	7	25	27	1	7	15	10	41	35
24 Rochdale	46	6	7	10	20	28	1	6	16	13	51	27

1980/81   10th in Division 4

#		Date	Opponent	Score	Scorers	Att	Poole AJ	Walker RP	Sandercock PI	Byatt DJ	Gage WAJ	Heeley DM	Denyer PR	Sargent GS	Phillips SE	Bowen KB	Farmer KJ	Saunders PB	Sandy AVC	Williams KD	Carlton DG	Saxby GP	Waldock DH	Cooke PC	Leonard GE
1	Aug	16	Darlington	0-1		1763	1	2	3	4	5	6	7	8	10	11	9	12							
2		23	Bournemouth	0-0		2875	1			4	5	6	2		9	10	11	3	7	8					
3	Sep	6	Hartlepool United	3-2	Bowen, Farmer, Phillips	2435	1			4	5	6	2		9	10	11	3	7	8					
4		13	DONCASTER ROVERS	0-2		2280	1			4	5	6	2		9	10	11	3	12	8	7				
5		17	Bradford City	1-3	Phillips	2765	1		4		5	6	2		9	10	11	3		8	7				
6		19	YORK CITY	2-0	Phillips, Saxby	1843	1		4		5	6	2		9		11	3	10	8	7	12			
7		23	SOUTHEND UNITED	2-0	Carlton, Phillips	2337	1		4		5		2		9		11	3	10	8	7	6			
8		27	Hereford United	1-4	Phillips (p)	2693	1		4		5	6	2		9	10	12	3	8		7	11			
9		30	BRADFORD CITY	0-1		2293	1		4		5	11	2		9	10	12	3		8	7	6			
10	Oct	3	STOCKPORT COUNTY	0-1		1902	1		4		5	6	2	10	9		11			8	7	12	3		
11		7	Bury	2-1	Denyer, Waldock	1779	1		4		5	6	8	10	9		11		12		7	2	3		
12		11	Scunthorpe United	2-0	Phillips 2	2650	1		4		5	6	8		9		11			10	7	2	3		
13		17	CREWE ALEXANDRA	4-1	Phillips 2, Farmer 2	2179	1		4		5	6	8		9		11	3		10	7	2			
14		21	ALDERSHOT	2-0	Gage, Heeley	3194	1		3		5	7	10		9		11		12		8	2	4		6
15		25	Lincoln City	0-8		4060	1				5	6	8		9		11	3	10		7	2	4	12	
16		27	Mansfield Town	0-2		3560	1		3		5	6	8		9		11			10	7	2	4		
17		31	HALIFAX TOWN	2-1	Phillips 2	2226	1		3		5	6	8		9		11			10	7	2	4		
18	Nov	4	BURY	5-3	Denyer 3 (1p), Saunders 2	2229	1		3	5			8		9		11	12	6	10	7	2	4		
19		8	Wimbledon	0-1		2029	1		3	5			8		9	11			6	10	7	2	4		
20		12	Wigan Athletic	0-3		3375	1		3	5			12	8	9				6	11	7	2	4		
21		15	DARLINGTON	2-2	Denyer, Phillips	1656	1		3	5	7	11	8		9				6	10		2	4		
22		29	TRANMERE ROVERS	3-1	Phillips 2, Sandy	1487	1		3		12	11	5		9	7	10		6	2	8		4		
23	Dec	6	Torquay United	3-3	Bowen 2, Williams	1975	1		3		5	11	10		9	7			6	2	8		4		
24		20	ROCHDALE	3-2	Phillips, Denyer, Bowen	1705	1		3	5		11	6		9	10			8	2	7	12	4		
25		26	Peterborough United	0-3		6265	1		3	5			10		9	7			6	11	8	2	4		
26		27	PORT VALE	5-1	Farmer, Bowen 2, Sandercock, Denyer	2978	1		3	5			6		9	10	11		8	7			4	2	
27	Jan	3	Aldershot	0-0		2992	1		3	5			6		9	10	11		2	8	7		4		
28		10	MANSFIELD TOWN	0-1		2985	1		3	5			8		9	10	11		2	6	7	12	4		
29		16	Tranmere Rovers	2-3	Bramhall (og), Bowen	1246	1		3	5		11	8		9	10	12		6	2	7		4		
30		23	Southend United	0-0		6191	1		3	5		11	2		9	10	4		8	6	7	12			
31		31	BOURNEMOUTH	0-1		2140	1		3			11	2		9	10	4		8	6	7	12	5		
32	Feb	3	WIGAN ATHLETIC	1-1	Farmer	1708	1		3				11		9	10	4		12	8	6	7	2	5	
33		6	Doncaster Rovers	1-1	Bowen	5680	1		3				11		9	10	4	5	8	6	7	2			
34		14	HARTLEPOOL UNITED	3-1	Bowen 2, Denyer	2032	1		3		12	7	11		9	10	4	5	8	6		2			
35	Mar	6	Stockport County	2-1	Phillips, Cooke	1945	1		3			12	6		9		4	5	10	8	7	2		11	
36		13	SCUNTHORPE UNITED	3-3	Denyer 3 (1p)	2046	1		3				6		9	10	4	5	8		7	2		11	
37		21	Crewe Alexandra	1-3	Williams	2120	1					12	6		9	10	4	5	11	3	7	2		8	
38		28	LINCOLN CITY	1-1	Heeley	2424	1				3	11	6		9	10	4	5	2	8	7				
39	Apr	4	Halifax Town	1-0	Phillips	1996	1				3	11	6		9	10	4	5	12	8	7	2			
40		11	WIMBLEDON	1-1	Bowen	2121	1				3	11	6		9	10	4	5		8	7	2			
41		14	HEREFORD UNITED	0-0		1380	1				5	9	11			10	4	3	8	6	7	2			
42		18	Port Vale	1-1	Farmer	2371	1				5	11	8		9	10	4	3	6		7	2			
43		21	PETERBOROUGH UTD.	2-2	Denyer, Phillips	3800	1				3	11	6		9	10	4	5		8	7	2			
44	May	1	TORQUAY UNITED	1-0	Bowen	1562	1				3	11	6		9	10	4	5	7	8		2			
45		3	Rochdale	1-0	Denyer	1474	1			4		11	6		9	10		5	7	8		3	2		
46		5	York City	2-1	Bowen, Phillips	1167	1			3		11			9	10	4	5	6	8	7	2	12		
			Apps				46	2	31	14	31	36	45	3	45	32	39	28	36	39	39	34	23	5	1
			Goals						1		1	2	13		19	13	6	2	1	2	1	1	1	1	

F.A. Cup

	Date	Opponent	Score	Scorers	Att	Poole AJ	Sandercock PI	Byatt DJ	Gage WAJ	Heeley DM	Denyer PR	Phillips SE	Bowen KB	Sandy AVC	Williams KD	Saxby GP	Waldock DH
R1	Nov 22	PETERBOROUGH UTD.	1-4	Phillips	5542	1	3	12	5	11	10	9	7	6	8	2	4

F.L. Cup

	Date	Opponent	Score	Scorers	Att	Poole AJ	Walker RP	Sandercock PI	Byatt DJ	Gage WAJ	Heeley DM	Denyer PR	Sargent GS	Phillips SE	Bowen KB	Farmer KJ	Saunders PB	Williams KD	Saxby GP	Waldock DH
R1/1	Aug 8	READING	0-2		3294	1	2	3	4				7	9	10	11	12	8	6	5
R1/2	13	Reading	3-2	Denyer, Phillips 2	4357	1	2	3	4	5	6	7	8	10	11	9				

		P	W	D	L	F	A	W	D	L	F	A	Pts
1	Southend United	46	19	4	0	47	6	11	3	9	32	25	67
2	Lincoln City	46	15	7	1	44	11	10	8	5	22	14	65
3	Doncaster Rovers	46	15	4	4	36	20	7	8	8	23	29	56
4	Wimbledon	46	15	4	4	42	17	8	5	10	22	29	55
5	Peterborough Utd.	46	11	8	4	37	21	6	10	7	31	33	52
6	Aldershot	46	12	9	2	28	11	6	5	12	15	30	50
7	Mansfield Town	46	13	5	5	38	15	7	4	12	22	29	49
8	Darlington	46	13	6	4	43	23	6	5	12	22	36	49
9	Hartlepool United	46	14	3	6	42	22	6	6	11	22	39	49
10	NORTHAMPTON TOWN	46	11	7	5	42	26	7	6	10	23	41	49
11	Wigan Athletic	46	13	4	6	29	10	5	7	11	22	39	47
12	Bury	46	10	8	5	38	21	7	3	13	32	41	45
13	Bournemouth	46	9	8	6	30	21	7	5	11	17	27	45
14	Bradford City	46	9	9	5	30	24	5	7	11	23	36	44
15	Rochdale	46	11	6	6	33	25	3	9	11	27	45	43
16	Scunthorpe United	46	8	13	4	40	31	3	8	12	20	38	42
17	Torquay United	46	13	2	8	38	26	5	3	15	17	37	41
18	Crewe Alexandra	46	10	7	6	28	20	3	7	13	20	41	40
19	Port Vale	46	10	8	5	40	23	2	7	14	17	47	39
20	Stockport County	46	10	5	8	29	25	6	2	15	15	32	39
21	Tranmere Rovers	46	12	5	6	41	24	1	5	17	18	49	36
22	Hereford United	46	8	8	7	29	20	3	5	15	9	42	35
23	Halifax Town	46	9	3	11	28	32	2	9	12	16	39	34
24	York City	46	10	2	11	31	23	2	7	14	16	43	33

1980/81 SEASON   Back: Williams, Heeley, Denyer, Saxby, Saunders, Sargent
Middle: Byatt, Gage, Bowen, Overton, Poole, Farmer, Cooke, Sandercock
Front: Harvey(Trainer), Walker, Sandy, Leonard, Corcoran, Waldock, Walker(Manager)

1981/82 SEASON
Back: Walker(Trainer coach), Leonard, Cooke, Alexander, Poole, Farmer, Gage, Bowen, Carlton
Middle: Coffill, Saunders, Denyer, Phillips, Saxby, Waldock
Front: Wall, Spence, Heeley, Sandy, Taylor, Tarbuck

1981/82   22nd in Division 4

#		Date	Opponent	Score	Scorers	Att	Poole AJ	Brady PJ	Saunders PB	Farmer KJ	Denyer PR	Coffill PT	Carlton DG	Heeley DM	Phillips SE	Bowen KB	Alexander JE	Sandy AVC	Gage WAJ	Saxby GP	Taylor Andy	Buchanan J	Russell R	Mahoney AJ	Perrin SC	Kruse PK	Massey S	Bryant SP	Muir M	Belfon F
1	Aug 29		SCUNTHORPE UNITED	1-1	Heeley	2064	1	2	3	4	5	6	7	8	9	10	11	12												
2	Sep 4		York City	1-2	Phillips	2086	1	2		4	3	6	7	8	9	10	11	12	5											
3		12	HULL CITY	1-1	Denyer (p)	1938	1	2		4	3	6	7		9	10	11		8	5	12									
4		19	Wigan Athletic	1-3	Denyer	3996	1	2	12	4	7	6	3		9		11		8	5	10									
5		21	Mansfield Town	1-4	Brady	2612	1	2	3	4		6	7	8	9		11		10	5										
6		26	HEREFORD UNITED	2-3	Phillips 2	1552	1	2	12		7	6	3	10	9		11		8	5				4						
7		29	STOCKPORT COUNTY	0-0		1865	1		4		7	6		12	10		11	8	5	3	2				9					
8	Oct 2		Colchester United	1-5	Denyer (p)	2760	1		4		7	6	3		9		11	10	5		2				8					
9		10	Bournemouth	1-1	Denyer	5241	1		4		5	6	3	7		10		11	8		12	2			9					
10		13	BLACKPOOL	0-1		2376	1		4		5	7	3	6	9		11	10			2	8			12					
11		17	BRADFORD CITY	0-2		2053	1	11	12		5		3	7	10				8	4	6	2			9					
12		21	Torquay United	2-2	Heeley, Sandy	2526	1	5				6		7	3		11	8		4	3	2		6	9					
13		24	TRANMERE ROVERS	3-2	Buchanan 2, Bramhall (og)	1722	1	8			5			3	7	10			12	4	6	2			9		11			
14		31	Bury	1-7	Phillips (p)	3375	1	5				12	7	6	9				8	4	3	2			10		11			
15	Nov 3		SHEFFIELD UNITED	1-2	Phillips	4168	1	4	9			6	8		10					5	3	2		7			11			
16		8	CREWE ALEXANDRA	3-0	Phillips, Saxby, Brady	2794	1	5	7			9	8		10			12		4	3	2		6			11			
17		14	Hartlepool United	1-3	Phillips	1641	1	5	6				8		10				9	4	3	2		7			11			
18		28	Peterborough United	0-1		5293	1	4	9						7		11		6	5	3	2		8						
19	Dec 5		DARLINGTON	0-1		1669	1	4	9							8	10		6	5	3	2		7	11					
20	Jan 23		Scunthorpe United	1-2	Perrin	1439	1	4	6				12		7	11	8		10	5	3	2			9					
21		30	WIGAN ATHLETIC	2-3	Denyer, Perrin	2418	1	5			7		2		9		11	6	4	3		8			10					
22	Feb 2		PORT VALE	3-5	Alexander, Phillips, Saxby	1644	1	4			6		2	11	10	7			5	3		8			9					
23		6	Hull City	1-0	Alexander	3627	1	4	3		7		2	6	9	11	12		5			8			10					
24		9	MANSFIELD TOWN	1-1	Denyer	1945	1	4	3		7		2	11	9	6			5			8			10					
25		14	COLCHESTER UNITED	1-2	Coffill	3102	1		3		6	7	2		9	11	8		5	4					10					
26		17	Blackpool	0-1		2231	1		3		11	7	8		9	10	6		5		2					4				
27		20	Hereford United	1-2	Phillips	2229	1		3		11	6	2	7	9		12		4			8			10	5				
28		23	Aldershot	1-2	Phillips (p)	1171	1		3	8			6	2	7	9	11		4			10				5				
29		27	BOURNEMOUTH	1-0	Gage	2125	1	2	3		6			10				9	4	8		11				5	7			
30	Mar 2		ROCHDALE	2-1	Massey, Gage	1916	1	2	3		8			12	10			6	4	11		7				5	9			
31		7	Bradford City	1-2	Perrin	4836	1	2	3		6	8	11					12	4	7					9	5	10			
32		9	TORQUAY UNITED	2-0	Massey, Alexander	1599	1	2	3		6						11	8	4	7					9	5	10			
33		13	Tranmere Rovers	2-0	Perrin, Saxby	1198	1	2	3		6							9	4	7		8			10	5	11			
34		16	Sheffield United	3-7	Massey 2 (1p), Perrin	15716	1	2	3		6				12			8	4	7		9			11	5	10			
35		20	BURY	1-0	Bradley (og)	2109	1	2			6	3	9					12	4	7		8			10	5	11			
36		23	YORK CITY	5-0	Buchanan 2, Czuczman (og), Perrin, Aitkin	2452	1	2			6	3						9	4	7		8			10	5	11			
37		27	Crewe Alexandra	2-2	Saxby 2	1801	1	2			6	3						4	8	7					10	5	11	9		
38	Apr 3		HARTLEPOOL UNITED	2-1	Saxby, Coffill	1890	1		2		6	3	11					12	4	7		8				5	10	9		
39		10	ALDERSHOT	0-0		2365	1		2		6	3						12	4	7		8			11	5	10	9		
40		12	Port Vale	0-1		3014	1	5			6	7	2					9	4	11		8					10	3		
41		17	Darlington	0-3		1729	1				6	3						11	4	7		8				5	10	9		
42		20	HALIFAX TOWN	0-1		1935	1	2	5		6	3						10	4	7		8					11	9	12	
43		24	PETERBOROUGH UTD.	1-0	Saxby	4975	1	2			6	3	11					4	7	8					9		10	5		
44		30	Stockport County	0-0		1658	1				6	2						3	4	7	8				11	5	10	9		
45	May 4		Halifax Town	1-2	Sandy	1730	1	12			7	2	6					10	4	9	8				5	11	3			
46		15	Rochdale	3-5	Heeley, Massey (p), Sandy	1056	1				7		6					10	4		2				9	5	11	3		8
				Apps			46	39	24	4	22	36	37	26	30	3	22	39	43	34	17	34	1	6	18	18	18	10	1	1
				Goals				2			5	2		3	10			4	3	2	7		4		6		5			

Four own goals

F.A. Cup

	Date	Opponent	Score	Scorers	Att	Poole AJ	Brady PJ	Saunders PB	Farmer KJ	Denyer PR	Coffill PT	Carlton DG	Heeley DM	Phillips SE	Bowen KB	Alexander JE	Sandy AVC	Gage WAJ	Saxby GP	Taylor Andy	Buchanan J	Russell R	Mahoney AJ	Perrin SC
R1	Nov 20	Weymouth	0-0		2600	1	5	6					8	9	10			12	4	3	2		7	11
rep	24	WEYMOUTH	6-2	Carlton, Phillips, Sandy, Gage 2, Mahoney	2613	1	4						7	9	10			6	5	3	2	8		11
R2	Dec 15	Bristol City	0-3		2901	1	2	4			6			8	10		12	9	5	3			7	11

F.L. Cup (The Milk Cup)

	Date	Opponent	Score	Scorers	Att	Poole AJ	Brady PJ	Saunders PB	Farmer KJ	Denyer PR	Coffill PT	Carlton DG	Heeley DM	Phillips SE	Bowen KB	Alexander JE	Sandy AVC	Gage WAJ	Saxby GP	Taylor Andy	Buchanan J	Mahoney AJ
R1/1	Sep 1	HARTLEPOOL UTD.	2-0	Denyer, Alexander	1480	1	2		4	3	6	7	8	9	10	11		5				
R1/2	16	Hartlepool United	1-2	Denyer	1975	1	2		4	3	6	7	10	9	11			8	5			
R2/1	Oct 6	BRISTOL ROVERS	2-1	Phillips, Sandy	4476	1	4			7	6	3	8	10		11	9	5			2	
R2/2	27	Bristol Rovers	3-1	Heeley, Saxby, Mahoney	3543	1	5			10	7	8	9			6	4	3	2			11
R3	Nov 11	Manchester City	1-3	Mahoney	21139	1	5	7			9	8		10		12	6	4	3	2		11

1982/83   15th in Division 4

#	Date	Opponent	Score	Scorers	Att	Freeman N	Brady PI	Phillips IA	Gage WAJ	Burrows AM	Coffill PT	Denyer PR	Saunders PB	Heeley DM	Perrin SC	Syrett DK	Saxby GP	Massey S	Buchanan J	Kendall MI	Belfon F	Tucker WB	Buchanan D	Key RM	Sandy AVC	Muir M	Patching M	Gleasure PF	Beavon DG	Jeffrey WG
1	Aug 28	Wimbledon	1-1	Syrett	1703	1	2	3	4	5		7	8	9	6	11	10	12												
2	Sep 4	YORK CITY	1-1	Massey	2257	1	2	3	4	5			11	7	6		9	8	10											
3		7 CHESTER	1-1	Saxby	2171	1	2	3	4	5			11	7	6		9	8	10	12										
4		11 Hartlepool United	1-2	Gage	947	1	2	3	4	5			11	7	6		9	8	10	1										
5		19 BRISTOL CITY	7-1	Syrett 4, Massey 2, Denyer	2967	1	2	3	4	5		12		7	6		9	8	10	11										
6		21 BURY	0-3		2792	1	2	3	4	5		12		7	6		9	8	10	11										
7		24 Stockport County	1-0	Massey	1621	1	2	3	4	5	6	8	7					10	11											
8		28 SWINDON TOWN	0-1		2706	1	2	3	4	5	6	8	7				9	12	10	11										
9	Oct 2	ALDERSHOT	1-1	Massey	1706	1		3	4	5	6	12	7				9	2	10	8		11								
10		10 TRANMERE ROVERS	1-0	Massey	2433	1	12	3		4	6	7	5			10		9	11	8		2								
11		16 Torquay United	1-3	Wilson (og)	2015	1	5	3		4	12	7	6	9	11			10	8			2								
12		19 COLCHESTER UNITED	2-1	Denyer, Burrows	1955	1		3	5	4	12	7	6	9	11			10	8			2								
13		23 Hull City	0-4		4317	1		3	5	4		7	6	9		12		10	8			2	11							
14		30 PETERBOROUGH UTD.	0-0		3284	1		3		5		9	4	6		10	7		8			2	11							
15	Nov 2	Rochdale	0-2		1019	1		3		4		7	5	6		10	11		8			2	9							
16		6 Scunthorpe United	1-5	Massey	3412			3		5		7	4	6		9	10	11	8			2	12	1						
17		13 BLACKPOOL	2-1	Denyer 2	1893			3	9	5		7	4	6			10	11	8			2	12	1						
18		28 DARLINGTON	3-3	Massey 2 (1p), Burrows	2599	1		3	4	5	6	11					7	10	8			2			9					
19	Dec 18	Hereford United	1-1	Massey	1679	1		3	4	5	6	11		7				10	8		12	2			9					
20		27 CREWE ALEXANDRA	4-0	Burrows, Massey, Saxby, Belfon	7494	1		3	4	5	7	10					6	11	8		12	2			9					
21		28 Mansfield Town	0-2		2843	1		3	4	5	6	11					7	10	8		12	2			9					
22	Jan 1	PORT VALE	2-2	Massey, Syrett	3618	1		3	4	5	7					11	6	10	8			2			9					
23		3 Bury	1-1	Syrett	3398	1		5	4	3	6			12		10	7	9	8			2			11					
24		15 WIMBLEDON	2-2	Brady, Saunders	2290	1	5	3	4		6		7			9	11	11				2			8					
25		22 Bristol City	3-1	Phillips, Syrett, Massey	4874	1	5	3	4				7			10		11				2				9	8			
26		29 HARTLEPOOL UNITED	3-1	Syrett 2, Massey	2181			3	4	5	6		7			11		10	12	1		2				9	8			
27	Feb 1	Halifax Town	0-2		1927			3	4	5	6	12	7			10		11	9	1		2					8			
28		5 STOCKPORT COUNTY	2-3	Patching, Burrows	1982			3	4	5	6		9			11		10	8	1	12	2					7			
29		12 Aldershot	0-3		1761				4	5	6	12	3			10		11	8	1	9	2					7			
30		19 Tranmere Rovers	1-2	Syrett	1466			3	4	5	6		9			10		11	8	1		2					7			
31		26 TORQUAY UNITED	2-0	Saxby, Massey	1817			3	4	5	6	7	9			10	8	11	12	1		2								
32	Mar 1	Colchester United	1-3	Massey	2501			3	4	5	6	8	10			9	7	11		1		2								
33		5 HULL CITY	1-2	Gage	2879			3	4	5	6	7	10			9	8	11		1		2					12			
34		12 Peterborough United	0-2		3778			3	4			12	5			11	6	10	7	1		2			8	9				
35		15 York City	2-5	Massey (p), Tucker	2802			3	4	5	6		9			10	8	11	7	1		2								
36		20 SCUNTHORPE UNITED	2-1	Gage, Sandy	2634			3	4	5	6	12				9	11	10	7			2			8			1		
37		26 Blackpool	0-0		2054				4	5	6	11	8			9	3	10				2						1	7	
38	Apr 2	MANSFIELD TOWN	1-2	Saunders	1988				4	5	6	11	8			10	2					3			12			1	9	7
39		4 Crewe Alexandra	0-1		2197			3	4	5	6		8			9		10	11			2						1		7
40		10 HALIFAX TOWN	3-1	Buchanan 2, Jeffrey	2208			3	5	4	7			12		10		11	9			2				6		1		8
41		16 Chester	1-2	Tucker	1267			3	5	4	7	12		6		10		11	9			2						1		8
42		19 ROCHDALE	1-1	Tucker (p)	1728			3	4	5				6		10	8	11	9			2			12			1		7
43		23 HEREFORD UNITED	2-1	Sandy, Massey	2071			3	4	5		12		6		10		11	8			2			9			1		7
44		30 Darlington	0-2		1042			3	4	5	12			6		11		10	8			2			9			1		7
45	May 8	Swindon Town	5-1	Massey 2, Denyer, Jeffrey, Syrett	3554			3		5	11	8	4	6		9		10				2						1		7
46		14 Port Vale	2-1	Coffill, Tucker (p)	6761				3	5	11	8	4	6		9		10				2						1		7

| | | | | | Apps | 22 | 12 | 42 | 40 | 43 | 33 | 34 | 34 | 22 | 4 | 38 | 28 | 42 | 35 | 11 | 6 | 37 | 5 | 2 | 7 | 11 | 6 | 11 | 2 | 9 |
| | | | | | Goals | | 1 | 1 | 3 | 4 | 1 | 5 | 2 | | | 12 | 3 | 20 | 2 | | 1 | 4 | | | 2 | | 1 | | | 1 |

Two own goals

F.A. Cup

R	Date	Opponent	Score	Scorers	Att	Fre	Bra	Phi	Gag	Bur	Cof	Den	Sau	Hee	Per	Syr	Sax	Mas	BuJ	Ken	Bel	Tuc	BuD	Key	San	Mui
R1	Nov 20	WIMBLEDON	2-2	Burrows, Denyer	2832	1	2	3	4	5	12	10	9	6			7	11	8							
rep	23	Wimbledon	2-0	Coffill 2	2097	1	2	3	4	5	9	10		6			7	11	8							
R2	Dec 11	Gillingham	1-1	Saxby	4054	1	2	3	4	5	6	11					7	10	8						9	
rep	14	GILLINGHAM	3-2	Massey, Belfon 2	4290	1	2	3	4	5	6	10					7	11	8	12					9	
R3	Jan 8	ASTON VILLA	0-1		14529	1		3	4	5	6			11			9	7	10	8		2				12

F.L. Cup (The Milk Cup)

R	Date	Opponent	Score	Scorers	Att	Fre	Bra	Phi	Gag	Bur	Cof	Den	Sau	Hee	Per	Syr	Sax	Mas	BuJ	Ken	Bel	Tuc	BuD	Key	San	Mui
R1/1	Aug 31	Millwall	2-0	Syrett, Saxby	2947	1	2	3	4	5			11	7	6		9	8	10							
R1/2	Sep 14	MILLWALL	2-2	Massey 2	2855		2	3	4		12	11	7	6			9	8	10	5	1					
R2/1	Oct 5	BLACKPOOL	1-1	Massey	2490	1		3	4	5	6	9	8	11	12		2	10	7							
R2/2	26	Blackpool	1-2	Syrett	3219	1	4	3		5	12	2	8	6		9		10	7						11	

R2/2 a.e.t.

Football League Trophy

R	Date	Opponent	Score	Scorers	Att	Fre	Bra	Phi	Gag	Bur	Cof	Den	Sau	Hee	Per	Syr	Sax	Mas	BuJ	Ken
R1	Aug 14	Norwich City	0-3		1801		4	3		5	7	8	9	6			10	2	11	12	1
R1	16	Mansfield Town	2-1	Syrett, Massey	1485		2	3	4			5	6	8	9	7	10	11	1	
R1	21	Peterborough United	2-5	Denyer, Syrett	2192		2	3	5	12		14	4	8	10	11	7	9	6	1

1982/83 SEASON Back: Syrett, Muir, Denyer, Massey, Buchanan
Middle: Coffill, Burrows, Brady, Kendall, Gage, Wall, Walker(Manager)
Front: Sandy, Saunders, Phillips(Captain), Saxby, Brough

1983/84 SEASON
Back: Norman(Train.), Phillips, Burrows, Syrett, Gage, Kendall, Gleasure, Forster, Lewis, Walker(Man.)
Front: Hayes, Tucker, O'Neill, Jeffrey, Belfon, Mundee, Austin

1983/84   18th in Division 4

#	Date		Opponent	Score	Scorers	Att	Gleasure PF	Tucker WB	Forster MG	Gage WAJ	Lewis R	Burrows AM	O'Neill T	Jeffrey WG	Syrett DK	Belfon F	Hayes AWP	Austin TW	Mundee BG	Muir M	Brough NK	Martinez E	Mann AG	Brown SF
1	Aug	27	Chester City	1-1	Belfon	1707	1	2	3	4	5	6	7	8	9	10	11	12						
2	Sep	3	DARLINGTON	2-0	O'Neill, Austin	2009	1	2	3	4	5	6	7	8		10	11	9						
3		6	TRANMERE ROVERS	0-0		2326	1	2	3	4	5	6	8	7	12	10	11	9						
4		10	Blackpool	3-2	Gage, Belfon, Austin	3216	1	2	3	4	5	6	8	7		10	11	9	12					
5		18	STOCKPORT COUNTY	0-0		3189	1	3	2	4	5	6	8	7	9	10	12			11				
6		24	Rochdale	1-1	O'Neill	1402	1	3	2	4	5	6	8	7	9	10	11							
7		27	Halifax Town	2-2	Jeffrey, Syrett	1519	1	3	2		5	6	8	7	9	10			11	4				
8	Oct	1	CHESTERFIELD	1-1	Belfon	2733	1	3	2		5	6	8	7	4	10	11	9						
9		9	READING	2-2	Gage, Austin	3825	1	8	2		4	5	6		7	10	11	9	3					
10		15	Colchester United	2-2	Austin, O'Neill	1964	1	3	2	4	5	6	8	7		9	12	11	10					
11		18	TORQUAY UNITED	2-1	Hayes, Tucker	2573	1	3	2	4	5	6	8	7		10	11	9	12					
12		22	Crewe Alexandra	2-3	Jeffrey, Gage	2107	1	3	2	4	5	6	8	7		9	10	11						
13		29	YORK CITY	1-2	Belfon	2956	1	3	2	4	5	6	8	7		9	10	11	12					
14	Nov	1	Aldershot	0-1		1711	1	11	2	4	5	6	8	7		10	12	9	3					
15		5	SWINDON TOWN	2-0	Austin 2	2354	1		2	4	5	6	8	7		10	11	9	3			12		
16		12	Hereford United	0-0		3007	1		2	4	5	6	8	7		10	11	9	3					
17		26	Wrexham	1-0	Austin	1234	1		2	4	5	6	8	7		10	11	9	3		12			
18	Dec	3	BRISTOL CITY	1-0	Belfon	2823	1		2	4	5	6	8	7		10	11	9	3		12			
19		18	MANSFIELD TOWN	2-1	Austin, Lewis	2628	1		2	4	5	6	8	7		10	11	9	3					
20		26	Doncaster Rovers	0-1		3827	1		2	4	5	6	8	7		10	11	9	3		12			
21		27	PETERBOROUGH UTD.	2-1	Jeffrey, Hayes	6464	1		2	4	5	6	8	7		10	11	9	3		12			
22		31	Hartlepool United	0-2		1706	1	8	2	4	5	6			7	10	11	9	3		12			
23	Jan	2	BURY	1-0	O'Neill	2525	1		2	4	5	6	8	7		10	11	9	3					
24		14	CHESTER CITY	2-1	Lewis, Belfon	2198	1		2	4	5	6	8	7		10	11	9	3		12			
25		20	Stockport County	0-1		1846	1	2		4	5	6	8	7		10	11	9	3					
26	Feb	4	Chesterfield	1-2	Hayes	3250	1	10	2	4	5	6	8	7			11	9	3		12			
27		11	ROCHDALE	1-1	Hayes	2022	1	2		4	5	6	8	7		10	11	9	3		12			
28		14	ALDERSHOT	1-4	Belfon	1573	1	2	12	4			5	7	6		11	9	3	8				
29		18	York City	0-3		3941	1	9	2	4	5	6	8	7		10	11		3					
30		25	CREWE ALEXANDRA	2-0	Gage, Hayes	1696	1		2	4	5	6	8	7			10	9	3			11		
31		28	Darlington	3-5	Hayes 2, Martinez	1278	1	4	2		5	6	8	7		12	10	9	3			11		
32	Mar	3	Torquay United	1-2	Martinez	2042	1	4	2		5	6	8	7			10	9	3	12		11		
33		6	Swindon Town	0-0		2798	1		2	4	5	6	8	7			10	9	3			11		
34		10	HEREFORD UNITED	0-3		1592	1		2	4	5	6	8	7			10	9	3	12		11		
35		17	Reading	0-3		3695	1		2	4	5		8	7		12	10	9	3	6		11		
36		20	BLACKPOOL	1-5	O'Neill	1337	1		2	4	5	6	8	7		12	10	9	3			11		
37		24	COLCHESTER UNITED	3-1	Austin, Gage, Belfon	1499	1		2	4	3	5	8	7		10	6	9				11		
38		30	Tranmere Rovers	0-1		1829	1			4	5	6	8	7		2	10	9	3			11		
39	Apr	7	HALIFAX TOWN	1-1	Hayes	1356	1	12	3	4	2	5	8	7		10	6	9				11		
40		10	HARTLEPOOL UNITED	1-1	Hayes	1109	1		3	4	2	5	8	7		10	6	9		12		11		
41		14	Bristol City	1-4	O'Neill (p)	6655	1		3	4	2	5	8	7		12	6	10	9			11		
42		21	DONCASTER ROVERS	1-4	Lewis	1912	1	6		4	2	5	8	7		12	9	10	3			11		
43		24	Peterborough United	0-6		3481	1	11	2	4	6	5	8				7	10	3			9		
44		28	WREXHAM	3-3	Belfon, Gage, Austin	1189	1	11	3	4	6	5	8	12		10		9	2		7			
45	May	5	Bury	2-1	Mundee, Lewis	1096	1		3		2	5	8	4		10		9	6		7		11	
46		12	Mansfield Town	1-3	Jeffrey	2143	1		3		2	5		4		10	8	9	6		7		11	12
			Apps				46	26	42	40	45	45	43	45	6	40	43	43	36	15	5	12	2	1
			Goals					1		6	4		6	4	1	9	9	10	1			2		

F.A. Cup

	Date		Opponent	Score	Scorers	Att	Gleasure PF	Tucker WB	Forster MG	Gage WAJ	Lewis R	Burrows AM	O'Neill T	Jeffrey WG	Syrett DK	Belfon F	Hayes AWP	Austin TW	Mundee BG	Muir M	Brough NK	Martinez E	Mann AG	Brown SF
R1	Nov	19	WATERLOOVILLE	1-1	Gage	2627	1	3	2	4	5	6	8	7		10	11	9				12		
rep		23	Waterlooville	1-1	Austin	3500	1		2	4	5	6	8	7		10	11	9	3			12		
rep2		28	WATERLOOVILLE	2-0	O'Neill, Mundee	3534	1		2	4	5	6	8	7			11	9	3	10				
R2	Dec	10	TELFORD UNITED	1-1	Austin	3903	1		2	4	5	6	8	7		10	11	9	3			12		
rep		14	Telford United	2-3	Jeffrey, Muir	3320	1		2	4	5	6	8	7		10	11	9	3			12		

F.L. Cup (The Milk Cup)

	Date		Opponent	Score	Scorers	Att	Gleasure PF	Tucker WB	Forster MG	Gage WAJ	Lewis R	Burrows AM	O'Neill T	Jeffrey WG	Syrett DK	Belfon F	Hayes AWP	Austin TW	Mundee BG
R1/1	Aug	29	Millwall	0-3		4158	1	2		4	5	6	8	7	9	10	11	12	
R1/2	Sep	13	MILLWALL	1-2	Gage	2313	1	3	2	4	5	6	8	7		10	11	9	12

Played in R1/1: IA Phillips (at 3).

Associate Members' Cup

	Date		Opponent	Score	Scorers	Att	Gleasure PF	Tucker WB	Forster MG	Gage WAJ	Lewis R	Burrows AM	O'Neill T	Jeffrey WG	Syrett DK	Belfon F	Hayes AWP	Austin TW	Mundee BG
R1	Feb	21	Walsall	1-3	Austin	3190	1		2	4	5	6	8	7		10	11	9	3

1984/85   23rd in Division 4

No	Date	Opponent	Score	Scorers	Att	Gleasure PF	Cavener P	Mundee BG	Barnes MF	Gage WAl	Brough NK	Train R	Shirtliff PR	Lee TC	Bancroft PA	Hayes AWP	Benjamin IT	Lewis R	Belfon F	Scott GS	Mann AG	Poole K	Perry MA	Hutchinson CM	Brown SF	Donald WR	Thompson KA	Bushell MJ
1	Aug 25	Exeter City	0-5		3166	1	2	3	4	5	6	7	8	9	10	11	12											
2	Sep 1	CHESTERFIELD	1-3	Hayes (p)	2554	1	2	3	5		12	8	7	10	9	11	6	4										
3	8	Darlington	0-4		1110	1	2	3		4	6	7	12	10		11	8	5	9									
4	15	HALIFAX TOWN	0-1		1437	1	9	3	5	4		6	8	10		11	7	2	12									
5	18	ROCHDALE	0-0		1653	1	2	3		4		6		9	10	11	8	5	7									
6	22	Chester City	0-1		1845	1	9	3		4		6		10	8	11	7	2	12	5								
7	29	COLCHESTER UNITED	1-3	Hayes	1595	1	9	3		4		6			8	11	7	2	10	5								
8	Oct 1	Port Vale	3-0	Belfon, Cavener, Hayes	3235	1	7	3		4		6	8		10	11		2	9	5								
9	6	SCUNTHORPE UNITED	0-2		1813	1	2	3		4		6	8		10	11		2	9	5	12							
10	13	Southend United	1-2	Belfon	2265	1	2		5	4		6		7	10	11	12	3	9		8							
11	16	Wrexham	3-0	Benjamin 2, Gage	1748	1	2		5	4		6		7		11	10	3	9		8							
12	20	ALDERSHOT	4-0	Benjamin 3, Gage	1864	1	2		5	4		6		7	9	11	3	10			8							
13	27	Blackpool	1-2	Mann	3577	1	2		5	4		6			9	11	3	10	7		8							
14	Nov 3	BURY	0-1		2240	1	2		5	4		6		7	9	11	3	10			8							
15	6	Crewe Alexandra	2-3	Belfon, Benjamin	2154	1	2		5	4		6		7		11	10	3	9	12	8							
16	10	SWINDON TOWN	4-0	Benjamin, Gage, Hayes 2 (1p)	2274	1	2		5	4		6		7		11	10	3	9		8		1					
17	23	Tranmere Rovers	2-1	Belfon, Benjamin	1899	1		3	5	4		6		7		11	10	2	9		8		1					
18	Dec 1	HEREFORD UNITED	0-3		2523			3		4	12	6	2	8		11	10	5	9		7		1					
19	15	Hartlepool United	0-0		2207	1		3	5			6		7		11	10	2	9	4	8							
20	22	Mansfield Town	0-2		1783	1	9	12	5	4		7	8			11	10	2		3	6							
21	26	PETERBOROUGH UTD.	0-3		4350	1	9	3	5	4		6		7		11	2				8			10				
22	29	TORQUAY UNITED	3-1	Cavener 3 (1p)	1496	1	9		5	4		7	2	8		11	3				6			10				
23	Jan 1	Stockport County	2-4	Benjamin, Lewis	1726	1	11		5	4		6	2	7			10	3	9		8							
24	5	EXETER CITY	5-2	Benjamin 3, Cavener 2 (1p)	1475	1	11	3		4		7	2	8			10		12	5	6				9			
25	12	Chesterfield	1-2	Cavener (p)	3759	1	11	3		4		7	2	8			10		9	5	6							
26	Feb 1	Colchester United	1-4	Mundee	2314	1	11	3		4		6		7			10	2	9	5	8							
27	16	Rochdale	0-3		1228	1	11	3	5	4		6		7			10	2	9		8							
28	23	Bury	1-3	Barnes	2938	1	9	3	5	4		8			12	11	2	10	7	6								
29	26	Halifax Town	0-1		1009	1	11	3		4		6	2		9	10		5		7	8				12			
30	Mar 2	BLACKPOOL	0-1		1860	1	9	3		4		7	2			11		5	10		8		12		6			
31	5	WREXHAM	0-4		1223	1	11	3		12		6	2	7		10		5		9	4				8			
32	9	Aldershot	0-0		1955	1		3		4	12	6	2	7		10			5	9	8				11			
33	17	SOUTHEND UNITED	1-2	Belfon	1702	1		3		4	12	6	2	7		10			5	9	8				11			
34	19	CHESTER CITY	0-2		942	1		3		4		6	2			11	10	5	9		8							
35	22	Scunthorpe United	1-2	Benjamin	2024	1		3		4		6	2			11	10	5	9		8				7			
36	30	CREWE ALEXANDRA	1-3	Benjamin	1264	1		3		4		6	2				10	5		12	7				11	8	9	
37	Apr 2	Peterborough United	0-0		2482	1		3		4		6	2				10	5			7				11	8	9	
38	9	STOCKPORT COUNTY	4-0	Benjamin, Brown, Donald, Mann	1426	1		3		4		6					10	5			7				11	8	9	2
39	13	Swindon Town	0-2		3642	1		3		4		6	2				10	5			7				11	8	9	
40	15	HARTLEPOOL UNITED	2-0	Donald, Mundee	1181	1		3		4		6	2				10	5			7				11	8	9	
41	17	Port Vale	1-0	Gage	1311	1		3		4		6	2				10	5			7				11	8	9	
42	20	TRANMERE ROVERS	2-0	Benjamin, Brown	1581	1		3		4		8	2				10	5			6				9	7	11	
43	23	DARLINGTON	2-1	Benjamin, Thompson	1838	1		3		4		6	2				10	5			7				11	8	9	
44	27	Hereford United	1-1	Brown	3266	1				4		6	2		3		10	5			8				11	7	9	
45	30	MANSFIELD TOWN	1-0	Train	2350	1				4		6	2		3		10	5		12	7				11	8	9	
46	May 6	Torquay United	2-0	Benjamin, Lewis	1181	1		3		4		6	2				10	5	9		7				11	8		
		Apps				43	28	33	19	43	7	46	29	24	16	20	44	44	31	17	38	3	4	2	14	11	10	1
		Goals					7	2	1	4		1				5	18	2	5		2				3	2	1	

F.A. Cup

Rd	Date	Opponent	Score	Scorers	Att	Gleasure	Cavener	Mundee	Barnes	Gage	Brough	Train	Shirtliff	Lee	Bancroft	Hayes	Benjamin	Lewis	Belfon	Scott	Mann	Poole	Perry	Hutchinson	Brown	Donald	Thompson	Bushell
R1	Nov 17	V.S. RUGBY	2-2	Train, Lee	4815	1	2		5	4		6		8		11	10	3	9	12	7							
rep	21	V.S. Rugby	1-0	Gage	3561	1		3	5	4		6		8		11	10	2	9		7							
R2	Dec 8	Brentford	2-2	Train, Lee	4449	1		3	5			6		7		11	10	2	9	4	8							
rep	17	BRENTFORD	0-2		3610	1		3	5	12		6		7		11	10	2	9	4	8							

F.L. Cup (The Milk Cup)

Rd	Date	Opponent	Score	Scorers	Att	Gleasure	Cavener	Mundee	Barnes	Gage	Brough	Train	Shirtliff	Lee	Bancroft	Hayes	Benjamin	Lewis	Belfon	Scott	Mann	Poole	Perry	Hutchinson	Brown	Donald	Thompson	Bushell
R1/1	Aug 27	Crystal Palace	0-1		3752	1	2	3	5	4		8	7	10	9	11	6											
R1/2	Sep 4	CRYSTAL PALACE	0-0		2979	1	7	3	5	4		6		9		11	8	2	10									

A.M.C. (Freight Rover Trophy)

Rd	Date	Opponent	Score	Scorers	Att	Gleasure	Cavener	Mundee	Barnes	Gage	Brough	Train	Shirtliff	Lee	Bancroft	Hayes	Benjamin	Lewis	Belfon	Scott	Mann	Poole	Perry	Hutchinson	Brown	Donald	Thompson	Bushell
R1/1	Jan 29	Port Vale	1-1	Benjamin	1385	1	11	3		4		6		7			10	2	9	5	8							
R1/2	Feb 5	PORT VALE	1-2	Belfon	1407	1		3		4	8	6		7		12	10	2	9	5					11			

R1/2 a.e.t.

1984/85 SEASON
Back: Bancroft, Lewis, Brough, Gage, Gleasure, Barnes, Benjamin, Lee
Front: Norman (Coach), Hayes, Shirtliff, Mundee, Barton (Manager),
Train, Cavener, Belfon, Walker (Re./Youth Man.)

1985/86 SEASON
Back: Bushell, Chard, Hill, Mundee, Nohilly, Cavener,
Middle: Walker (Coach), Benjamin, Lewis, Gleasure, Dawes, Brown, Casey (Physio)
Front: Schiavi, Reed, Morley, Carr (Manager), Mann, Donald, Curtis

1985/86   8th in Division 4

						Gleasure PF	Curtis PAE	Mundee BG	Dawes IM	Lewis R	Hill RW	Mann AG	Benjamin IT	Reed G	Morley TW	Cavener P	Chard PJ	Schiavi MA	Donald WR	Nebbeling GM	McPherson KA	Friar JP	Sugrue PA	Hamill SP	Garner TJ
1	Aug	17	Burnley	2-3	Morley, Reed	4279	1	2	3	4	5	6	7	8	9	10	11									
2		26	Exeter City	2-1	Morley, Benjamin	2392	1	2	3		5	6	7	8	9	10	11	4								
3		31	MANSFIELD TOWN	1-0	Cavener (p)	2739	1	2	3	12	5	6	7	8	9	10	11	4								
4	Sep	6	Swindon Town	2-3	Hill, Cavener (p)	4102	1	2	3		5	6	7	8	9	10	11	4								
5		10	PRESTON NORTH END	6-0	Benjamin 2, Hill 3, Morley	2171	1	2	3			6	7	8	9	4	10	11	5	12						
6		14	CREWE ALEXANDRA	0-1		2654	1	2	3			5	7	8	9	4	10	11	6	12						
7		18	Hartlepool United	1-2	Benjamin	2200	1	2	3			5	6	12	8	9	10	11	4	7						
8		21	STOCKPORT COUNTY	3-1	Benjamin, Hill, Morley	1954	1	2	3			5	6	12	8	9	10	11	4	7						
9		28	Rochdale	2-3	Hill, Benjamin	1954	1	2	3			5	6	12	8	9	10	11	4	7						
10	Oct	1	WREXHAM	1-2	Hill	2234	1	2	3			5	6	12	8	9	10	11	4	7						
11		5	HEREFORD UNITED	1-3	Chard	1998	1	2	3	12	5	6	7	8	9	10		4	11							
12		12	Peterborough United	5-0	Chard, Mann 2, Cavener, Benjamin	3901	1	2	3			5	6	11	8	9	10	12	4		7					
13		19	Torquay United	1-1	Chard	1186	1	2	3	6	5		11	8		10	9	4		7						
14		22	CHESTER CITY	2-2	Morley, Benjamin	2323	1	2	3	6	5		11	8		10	9	4	12	7						
15		26	Colchester United	2-0	Chard, Mann	2872	1		3		5	9	11	8	2	10	12	4		7	6					
16	Nov	2	SCUNTHORPE UNITED	2-2	Benjamin, Cavener (p)	2343	1		3		5	7	9	11	2	10	12	6		8	4					
17		5	TRANMERE ROVERS	2-2	Donald, Benjamin	2005	1		3		5	9		8	2	10	7	4		11	6					
18		9	Aldershot	0-1		1556	1		3		5	9	11	8	2	10	12	4		7	6					
19		23	HALIFAX TOWN	4-0	Chard(p), Benjamin, Morley, Schiavi	1514	1		3		5	9		8	2	10		4	11	7	6					
20		30	Cambridge United	5-2	Benjamin 3 (1p), Schiavi, Morley	2235	1		3		5	9	12	8	2	10		4	11	7	6					
21	Dec	6	Southend United	4-0	Schiavi, Curtis, Benjamin 2	2527	1	2	3		5	9	4	8		10			11	7	6					
22		14	PORT VALE	2-2	Morley, Chard	3259	1	2	3		5	9		8		10		4	11	7	6					
23		21	Preston North End	1-1	Hill	2570	1		3		5	11		8	2	10		4	9	7	6					
24	Jan	11	Mansfield Town	0-1		3836	1		3		5	11		8	2	10		4	9	7	6					
25		18	BURNLEY	2-0	Morley, Hill	3095	1		3		5	11		8	2	10		4	9	7	6					
26		25	Crewe Alexandra	1-0	Morley	1856	1		3		5		11	8	2	10		4	9	7		6				
27	Feb	1	SWINDON TOWN	0-1		4449	1		3		5	11		8	2	10		4	9	7		6				
28		5	Chester City	3-2	Hill, Schiavi, Morley	3332	1		3		5	11	7	8	2	10		4	9			6				
29		21	Stockport County	0-1		2011	1		3		5	11	7	8	2	10		4	9			6				
30	Mar	1	ROCHDALE	1-0	Benjamin	2146	1	2	3		5	9	11	8		10		4		7		6				
31		4	Wrexham	0-1		1433	1	2	3		5		11	8		10		4	9	7		6				
32		8	Hereford United	0-3		2478	1	2			5		11	8		10		4	9	7		6	3			
33		11	HARTLEPOOL UNITED	3-0	Benjamin 2, Hill	1815	1				5	11	7	8		10		2	9	4		6	3			
34		15	PETERBOROUGH UTD.	2-2	Morley, Hill	3332	1				4	11	7	8	12	10		2	9	6		5	3			
35		18	Scunthorpe United	0-1		1355	1	2			5	11		8		10		9	7	4		6	3	12		
36		22	COLCHESTER UNITED	1-0	Donald	2035	1				4	11		9	2	10		5	8	7		6	3	12		
37		29	Orient	1-0	Benjamin	2920	1				5	11		8	2	10		9	7	4		6	3			
38		31	SOUTHEND UNITED	0-0		3527	1				5	11	12	8	2	10		9	7	4		6	3			
39	Apr	4	Tranmere Rovers	3-1	Hamill, Benjamin, Sugrue	1103	1	2				11		8	5	10			9	4		6	3	12	7	
40		8	EXETER CITY	2-2	Donald, Hill	2213	1	2				11		9	4	10			8	6		5	3	12	7	
41		12	Aldershot	2-3	Sugrue, Chard (p)	2049	1	2				11	12	8	5	10		3	9			6		4	7	
42		15	ORIENT	2-3	Morley, Hill	1731	1				5	11		8	2	10		9	7	4		6	3	12		
43		18	Halifax Town	0-2		1105	1	2			5	11		8		10		9	7	4		6	3	12		
44		26	CAMBRIDGE UNITED	0-2		2100	1	2			5	11	7	8	12			10		4		6	3	9		
45		29	TORQUAY UNITED	5-1	Hill 3 (1p), Schiavi, Compton (og)	1167		2			5	11	7	8	9				10	4		6	3			1
46	May	3	Port Vale	0-0		3873		2			5	11	7	8	9			6	10	4			3			1

	Apps	44	27	31	5	43	41	32	46	36	43	17	41	34	32	11	20	14	8	3	2
	Goals		1				17	3	21	1	13	4	7	5	3				2	1	

One own goal

F.A. Cup

| R1 | Nov | 16 | Gillingham | 0-3 | | 3991 | 1 | 2 | 3 | | 5 | 9 | | 8 | 6 | 10 | 11 | 4 | | 7 | | | | | | |

F.L. Cup (The Milk Cup)

R1/1	Aug	21	Peterborough Utd.	0-0		3117	1	2	3		5	6	7	8	9	10	11	4								
R1/2	Sep	3	PETERBOROUGH UNITED	2-0	Cavener, Chard	2446	1	2	3	9	5	6	7	8		10	11	4	12							
R2/1		25	Oxford United	1-2	Benjamin	5664	1	2	3		5	6		8	9	10	11	4	7							
R2/2	Oct	8	OXFORD UNITED	0-2		5076	1	2	3		5	6	11	8	9	10	12	4		7						

A.M.C. (Freight Rover Trophy)

R1	Jan	21	COLCHESTER UNITED	2-1	Benjamin, Schiavi	1958	1		3		4	8	12	9	2	10		6	11	7	5					
R1	Mar	13	Southend United	3-1	Hill, Benjamin 2	683	1				5	11	7	8	12	10		2	9	4		6	3			
QF		27	Bristol City	2-3	Hill, Hamill	3038	1				5	11		8	2	10		6	9	4			3	12	7	

1986/87 — Champions of Division 4

No	Date		Opponent	Score	Scorers	Att	Gleasure PF	Reed G	Chard PJ	Donald WR	Coy RA	McPherson KA	McGoldrick EJP	Gilbert DJ	Benjamin IT	Morley TW	Hill RW	Schiavi MA	Mann AG	Wilcox R	Germon FAJ	Millar J	McMenemy PC	Logan D	Henry CA	Bunce PE
1	Aug	23	Scunthorpe United	2-2	Hill, Reed	2302	1	2	3	4	5	6	7	9	8	10	11	12								
2		31	TORQUAY UNITED	1-0	Benjamin	3558	1	2	3	4	5	6	7	9	8	10	11									
3	Sep	6	Rochdale	2-1	Benjamin, Chard	1606	1	2	3	4	5	6	7	9	8	10	11									
4		14	PETERBOROUGH UTD.	2-1	Morley, Chard (p)	5517	1	2	3	4	5	6	7	9	8	10	11									
5		17	TRANMERE ROVERS	2-0	McGoldrick, Hill	3873	1	2	3	4	5	6	7	9	8	10	11									
6		20	Swansea City	1-2	Chard	6902	1	2	3	4	5	6	7	9	8	10	11		12							
7		27	WOLVERHAMPTON W.	2-1	Morley, Hill	5713	1	2	3	4	5	6	7	9	8	10	11			12						
8		30	Halifax Town	6-3	Donald, Hill 3 (1p), Benjamin, Chard	1034	1	2	3	4	5	6	7	9	8	10	11									
9	Oct	4	ALDERSHOT	4-2	Hill 2, Morley, Chard	4304	1	2	3	4	5	6	7	9	8	10	11									
10		17	Cambridge United	3-2	McPherson, Chard (p), Morley	6283	1	2	3	4		6	7	9	8	10	11			5						
11		22	BURNLEY	4-2	Morley 2, Benjamin, Hill	5718	1	2	3	4		6	7	9	8	10	11			5						
12		25	HEREFORD UNITED	3-2	Morley, Benjamin, Hill	5336	1	2	3	4		6	7	9	8	10	11			5						
13		27	Stockport County	3-0	Hill 2, Morley	1729	1	2	3	4		6	7	9	8	10	11			5						
14	Nov	1	Hartlepool United	3-3	Chard (p), Hill 2	1657	1	2	3	4		6		9	8	10	11		7	5						
15		4	Orient	1-0	Benjamin	3496	1	2	3	4	7	6		9	8	10	11			5						
16		8	PRESTON NORTH END	3-1	Benjamin, McPherson, Hill	6537	1	2	3	4		6	12	9	8	10	11			5		7				
17		28	Crewe Alexandra	5-0	Benjamin, McPherson, Hill 3	2331	1	2				6	7	9	8	10	11		4	5	3					
18	Dec	2	EXETER CITY	4-0	Morley, McGoldrick, Hill 2	6639	1	2				6	7	9	8	10	11		4	5	3					
19		13	WREXHAM	2-2	Wilcox, Benjamin	6070	1	2		4		6	7	9	8	10	11			5	3					
20		21	LINCOLN CITY	3-1	Gilbert (p), McGoldrick, Benjamin	7063	1		2	4		6	7	9	8	10	11			5	3					
21		26	Southend United	4-0	Hill 2, Benjamin, Donald	8541	1		2	4	12	6		9	8	10	11		7	5	3					
22		28	CARDIFF CITY	4-1	Benjamin, Gilbert (p), Morley, Hill	11138	1		2	4		6	7	9	8	10	11			5	3					
23	Jan	1	COLCHESTER UNITED	3-2	Benjamin, Gilbert, Morley (p)	8215	1		2	4		6	7	9	8	10	11			5	3					
24		3	Exeter City	1-1	Hill	4331	1		2	4		6	7	9	8	10	11			5	3					
25		24	ROCHDALE	5-0	McMenemy 2, Chard, McGoldrick, Hill	5484	1	2	9	4		6	7		8		11			5			3	10		
26		31	Peterborough United	1-0	Benjamin	7911	1	2	3	4		6	7	9	8		11			5				10		
27	Feb	6	Tranmere Rovers	1-1	Hill	2583	1	2	3	4		6	7	9	8		11			5				10		
28		14	SWANSEA CITY	0-1		8288	1	2	3	4		6	7	9	8		11			5				10		
29		21	Wolverhampton Wan.	1-1	Chard	9991	1	2	10	4		6	12	9	8		11		7	5				3		
30		24	Torquay United	1-0	Donald	1780	1	2	10	4		6		9	8		11		7	5				3		
31		27	HALIFAX TOWN	1-0	Benjamin	6351	1	2	10	4	12	6	7	9	8		11			5				3		
32	Mar	4	HARTLEPOOL UNITED	1-1	Benjamin	5470	1	10		4	2	6	7	9	8		11			5				3		
33		11	SCUNTHORPE UNITED	1-0	Morley	5352	1	2				6	7	9	8	10	11		4	5				3		
34		14	CAMBRIDGE UNITED	3-0	Gilbert 2 (2p), Hill	6201	1	2	4			6		9	8	10	11			5				3	7	
35		17	Burnley	1-2	Henry	2691	1	2	4			6		9	8	10	11			5				3	7	
36		21	STOCKPORT COUNTY	2-1	Chard 2	5466	1	2	11	4		6	12	9	8	10				5				3	7	
37	Apr	3	Preston North End	0-1		16556	1	2	3	4		6	7	9	8		11			5					10	
38		8	Hereford United	2-3	Chard, Morley	2758	1	2	9	4		6	12	7	8	10	11			5				3		
39		12	ORIENT	2-0	Gilbert, McPherson	6711	1	2	3	4		6	7	9	8	10	11			5				3		
40		17	Colchester United	1-3	Logan	3676	1	2	12	4		6	7	9	8	10	11			5				3		
41		20	SOUTHEND UNITED	2-1	Hill, McPherson	7383	1		2	4		6	7	9	8	10	11			5				3		
42		26	Lincoln City	1-3	McGoldrick	4012	1	12	2	4		6	7	9	8	10	11			5				3		
43		29	CREWE ALEXANDRA	2-1	Gilbert (p), Hill	8890	1		2	4	5	6	7	9	8	10	11							3		
44	May	4	Cardiff City	1-1	Benjamin	2682	1		2	4	5	6	7	9	8	10	11							3		
45		6	Aldershot	3-3	Gilbert, Benjamin, Morley	3377	1	2	3	4	5	6	7	9	8	10	11									12
46		9	Wrexham	3-1	Bunce, Morley 2	2709	1		3	4	2	6		9	8	10	11			5						7
			Apps				46	37	40	41	17	46	39	45	46	37	45	1	8	35	9	1	4	15	4	2
			Goals					1	12	3		5	5	8	18	16	29			1			2	1	1	1

F.A. Cup

No	Date		Opponent	Score	Scorers	Att	Gleasure PF	Reed G	Chard PJ	Donald WR	Coy RA	McPherson KA	McGoldrick EJP	Gilbert DJ	Benjamin IT	Morley TW	Hill RW	Schiavi MA	Mann AG	Wilcox R	Germon FAJ	Millar J	McMenemy PC
R1	Nov	16	PETERBOROUGH UTD.	3-0	McGoldrick, Gilbert, Benjamin	9114	1	2				6	7	9	8	10	11		4	5	3		
R2	Dec	5	Southend United	4-4	Donald, Benjamin, Hill 2	7412	1	2	10	4		6	7	9	8		11			5	3		
rep		10	SOUTHEND UNITED	3-2	Gilbert 2, Benjamin	10603	1	2	3	4		6	7	9	8	10	11			5			
R3	Jan	21	Newcastle United	1-2	Hill	23177	1	2	9	4		6	7		8	10	11		12	5			3

Played in R2: Gorman (at 12)

F.L. Cup (Littlewoods Cup)

No	Date		Opponent	Score	Scorers	Att	Gleasure PF	Reed G	Chard PJ	Donald WR	Coy RA	McPherson KA	McGoldrick EJP	Gilbert DJ	Benjamin IT	Morley TW	Hill RW	Schiavi MA	Mann AG
R1/1	Aug	25	Gillingham	0-1		2945	1	2	3		5	6	7	8	9	10	11		4
R1/2	Sep	3	GILLINGHAM	2-2	Coy, Benjamin	2727	1	2	3	4	5	6	7	9	8	10	11		

A.M.C. (Freight Rover Trophy)

No	Date		Opponent	Score	Scorers	Att	Gleasure PF	Reed G	Chard PJ	Donald WR	Coy RA	McPherson KA	McGoldrick EJP	Gilbert DJ	Benjamin IT	Morley TW	Hill RW	Schiavi MA	Mann AG	Wilcox R	Germon FAJ
PR	Dec	16	Gillingham	0-1		2046	1			4	2	6	7	9	8	10	11		12	5	3
PR	Jan	5	NOTTS COUNTY	3-0	Gilbert, Hill, Mann	3500	1	2				6	7	9	8	10	11		4	5	3
R1		26	Fulham	2-3	Chard, Benjamin	2080	1	10	2	4		6	7	9	8		11		12	5	3

Played v. Gillingham: Gorman (at 14). In R1, GP Donegal (at 14).

1986/87 SEASON   Back: Donegal, Bushell, Coy, Schiavi, Hill
Middle: Walker(Asst. Man), Benjamin, Reed, Gleasure, Wilcox, McPherson, Casey(Phsio)
Front: Curtis, Gilbert, Morley, Carr(Manager), Chard, Donald, Mann

1987/88 SEASON   Back: McGoldrick, Logan, Coy, Senior, Wilcox, Longhurst
Middle: Casey(Physio), Wilcox, Benjamin, Gleasure, Donegal, Harris, McPherson, Walker
Front: Gilbert, Donald, Chard, Carr(Man), Morley, Bunce, Mann

1987/88   6th in Division 3

#	Mon	Date	Opponent	Score	Scorers	Att	Gleasure PF	Reed G	Logan D	Donald WR	Wilcox R	McPherson KA	Longhurst DJ	Benjamin IT	Morley TW	Chard PJ	Gilbert DJ	Senior S	McGoldrick EJP	Mann AG	Bunce PE	Culpin P	Singleton MD	Donegal GP	Sandeman BR	O'Donnell C	Williams B	Adcock AC	Wilson PA	Slack TC	Carter LR
1	Aug	15	Chester City	5-0	Morley, Chard, Wilcox, Longhurst, Gilbert	3453	1	2	3	4	5	6	7	8	10	11	9	12	14												
2		29	Walsall	0-1		5993	1	2	3	4	5	6	7	8	10	11	9	12	14												
3		31	BRIGHTON & HOVE ALB	1-1	Morley	7934	1	2	3	4	5	6	7	8	10		9		11												
4	Sep	5	Doncaster Rovers	2-0	Morley, Longhurst	1869	1	2	3	4	5	6	7	8	10		9		11												
5		9	BRENTFORD	2-1	Gilbert, Longhurst	5748	1	2	3	4	5	6	7	8	10	12	9		11												
6		12	NOTTS COUNTY	0-1		6023	1	2	3		5	6		8	10	4	9		11		7	12									
7		15	Preston North End	0-0		5179	1	2	3		5	6		8	10	4	9		11		7										
8		19	Bristol Rovers	2-0	Morley, Chard	3668	1	2	3		5	6		8	10	4	9		11		7										
9		26	PORT VALE	1-0	Chard	5072	1	2	3	12	5	6		8	10	4	9		11		7										
10		29	Southend United	1-1	Morley	3506	1	2	3		5	6		8	10	4	9	12	11		7										
11	Oct	3	BRISTOL CITY	3-0	Chard 2, Bunce	6234	1	2	3		5	6		8	10	4	9		11		7										
12		11	Rotherham United	2-2	Culpin, Morley	5173	1	2	3	4	5	6		12	10	11	9		7			8									
13		17	CHESTERFIELD	4-0	Morley, Culpin 2, Benjamin	5073	1	2	3	4	5	6		11	10		9		7			8									
14		20	Mansfield Town	1-3	Culpin	3646	1	2	3	4	5	6		11	10		9		7			8									
15		24	GRIMSBY TOWN	2-1	Gilbert (p), Culpin	5388	1	2	3	4	5	6		12	10	11	9		7			8									
16		31	Aldershot	4-4	Culpin, Roberts (og), Morley, Longhurst	3358	1	2		4	5	6	11		10	3	9		7			8									
17	Nov	4	YORK CITY	0-0		4950	1	2		4	5	6	11		10	3	9		7	12		8									
18		7	Fulham	0-0		6733	1	2		4	5	6	11		10	3	9		7			8									
19		21	GILLINGHAM	2-1	Morley, Wilcox	5151	1	2	12	4	5	6	11		10	3			9			8									
20		28	Blackpool	1-3	Longhurst	3593	1	2	12	4	5	6	11		10	3			9		14	8									
21	Dec	12	SUNDERLAND	0-2		7279	1	2	3	4	5	6	14		10	11			9		7	8	12								
22		19	Wigan Athletic	2-2	Donald, Singleton	2692	1		3	4	5	6	11		10	2			9		12	8	7								
23		26	Port Vale	1-1	Singleton	4446	1		3	4	5	6	11		10	2			9		12	8	7								
24		28	BURY	0-0		6067	1		3	4	5	6	11		10	2			9			8	7	12							
25	Jan	1	WALSALL	2-2	Chard, Donegal	6034	1		3	4	5	6	11		10	2			9			8	7	14							
26		2	Notts County	1-3	Morley (p)	8153	1	12	3	4	5	6	11		10	2			9			8	7								
27		9	Brentford	1-0	Chard	6025	1	2	3	4	5	6	11		10		9					8	7	12							
28		16	BRISTOL ROVERS	2-1	Gilbert, Donald	4473	1			4	5		11				9					8	7		12		2	3			
29		27	PRESTON NORTH END	0-1		5052	1			4	5	6	11			2			9			8	7				12	10	3		
30		30	WIGAN ATHLETIC	1-1	Adcock	4825	1			4	5	6				2			9			8	7				11	10	3		
31	Feb	6	DONCASTER ROVERS	1-0	Adcock	4381	1	2		4	5	6	11						9			8	7				12	10	3		
32		13	Bury	0-0		2172	1	2		4	5		11	8					9				7					10	3	6	
33		20	CHESTER CITY	2-0	Adcock, Slack	4285	1	2		4	5		11	8					9				7					10	3	6	
34		27	Bristol City	2-2	Adcock, Chard	8578	1	2		4	5		11	8					9				7					10	3	6	
35	Mar	2	SOUTHEND UNITED	4-0	McGoldrick, Longhurst, Wilcox, Adcock	4249	1			4	5		11	8					9			2	7					10	3	6	
36		5	Chesterfield	2-0	McGoldrick, Gilbert	2400	1			4	5		11	8					9			2	7					10	3	6	
37		11	ROTHERHAM UNITED	0-0		5432	1			4	5		11	8					9			2	7					10	3	6	
38		19	ALDERSHOT	1-1	Adcock	4322	1	2			5		11				4	9				4	7					10	3	6	
39		26	Grimsby Town	2-2	Singleton, Culpin	3406	1	12		4	5		11						9			2	7	8			14	10	3	6	
40	Apr	2	FULHAM	3-2	Adcock, Stannard (og), Culpin	6211	1	12		4	5	6	11						9			2	7	8				10	3		
41		4	Gillingham	2-1	Culpin, Adcock	4131	1			4	5	6	11						9			2	7	8			12	10	3		
42		10	MANSFIELD TOWN	2-0	Wilcox, Kenworthy (og)	6917	1			4	5	6	11						9			2	7	8				10	3	6	
43		15	Brighton & Hove Albion	0-3		14455	1	12		4	5		11						9			2	7	8			14	10	3	6	
44		23	York City	2-2	Culpin, Wilson	2048	1			4	5		11						9			2	7	8				10	3	6	14
45		30	BLACKPOOL	3-3	Longhurst, Gilbert, Adcock	5730	1			4	5		11						9			2	7	8				10	3	6	
46	May	2	Sunderland	1-3	Adcock	29454	1			4	5								9			2	7	8				10	3	6	
						Apps	46	31	26	40	46	32	35	14	27	34	41	4	46	1	10	20	29	11	2	1	4	18	15	13	1
						Goals				2	4		7	1	10	8	6		2		1	10	3	1				10	1	1	

Three own goals

F.A. Cup

	Date		Opponent	Score	Scorers	Att	Gleasure	Reed	Logan	Donald	Wilcox	McPherson	Longhurst	Benjamin	Morley	Chard	Gilbert	Senior	McGoldrick	Mann	Bunce	Culpin	Singleton
R1	Nov	14	NEWPORT COUNTY	2-1	Morley, Chard	4581	1	2		4	5	6	11		10	3			9	12		8	7
R2	Dec	5	BRIGHTON & HOVE ALB.	1-2	Morley	6444	1	2	12	4	5	6	11		10	3			9		14	8	7

F.L. Cup (Littlewoods Cup)

	Date		Opponent	Score	Scorers	Att	Gleasure	Reed	Logan	Donald	Wilcox	McPherson	Longhurst	Benjamin	Morley	Chard	Gilbert	Senior	McGoldrick	Mann	Bunce	Culpin	Singleton	Donegal
R1/1	Aug	17	Port Vale	1-0	Longhurst	3398	1	2		4	5	6	7	8	10	11	9	3						
R1/2	Sep	2	PORT VALE	4-0	McPherson, Morley 3	4748	1	2	3	4	5	6	7	8	10		9		11					
R2/1		22	Ipswich Town	1-1	Gilbert	5645	1	2	3		5	6	7	8	10	4	9		11		12			
R2/2	Oct	7	IPSWICH TOWN	2-4	Morley, Donegal		1	2	3		5	6		8	10	4	9	12	11		7			14

R2/2 a.e.t.   Played in R2/1: C Scott (at 14).

A.M.C. (Sherpa Van Trophy)

	Date		Opponent	Score	Scorers	Att	Gleasure	Reed	Logan	Donald	Wilcox	McPherson	Longhurst	Benjamin	Morley	Chard	Gilbert	Senior	McGoldrick	Mann	Bunce	Culpin	Singleton
PR	Oct	13	NOTTS COUNTY	0-1		2351	1	2	3	4	5	6	7		10				8			11	9
PR		28	BRENTFORD	1-0	Longhurst	3076	1	2		4	5	6	11		10	3			9			7	8

1988/89   20th in Division 3

#		Date	Opponent	Score	Scorers	Att	Gleasure PF	Reed G	Thomas DR	Donald WR	McGoldrick EJP	McPherson KA	Singleton MD	Longhurst DJ	Gilbert DJ	Adcock AC	Donegal GP	Wilson PA	Sandeman BR	Flexney P	Culpin P	Garwood J	Preece AP	Cobb GE	Johnson I	Blair A	Berry SA	Williams, Wayne	Anderson DE	Bodley MJ	Quow TS	Collins D	Wilcox R	Craig AH
1	Aug	27	Mansfield Town	1-1	Donegal	4042	1	2	3	4	5	6	7	8	9	10	11	14	12															
2	Sep	3	BRENTFORD	1-0	Wilson	4488	1	5	3	4	2		7		9	10	11	8			6	12												
3		10	Notts County	1-0	Culpin	6340	1	6	3	4	2		7		9	10				5	8	11												
4		17	CHESTERFIELD	3-0	Adcock 3	4520	1	6	3	4	2		7		9	10				5	8	11												
5		20	Sheffield United	0-4		11904	1	6	3	4	2		7		9	10	14	12		5	8	11												
6		24	BRISTOL ROVERS	1-2	Adcock	3886	1	6	3	4	2		7		9	10		12		5	8	11												
7	Oct	1	ALDERSHOT	6-0	Culpin 3, Gilbert, Adcock	3477	1		3	4	2	6	7		9	10		12		5	8	11												
8		4	Blackpool	1-3	Gilbert	3034	1		3	4	2	6	7	12	9	10		11	14	5	8													
9		8	HUDDERSFIELD T	1-3	Singleton	3975	1		3	4	2	6	7		9	10	8	11	14	5		12												
10		15	Swansea City	0-1		4583	1	5	3	4	2	6	7		9	10	8	12	14			11												
11		22	BRISTOL CITY	1-3	McGoldrick	3668	1	8	3	4	2	6	7		9	10		14	11	5								12						
12		25	Fulham	2-3	Sandeman, Adcock	4644	1		3	4	2	6			9	10	11		7		8					5								
13		29	READING	1-3	McGoldrick	4355	1		3	4	2	6			9	10		12		5	8						7	11						
14	Nov	5	Wigan Athletic	3-1	Berry, Adcock, Culpin	2472	1		3	4	2	6			9	10		11		5	8						12	7						
15		8	PORT VALE	1-3	Culpin	3796	1		3	4		6			9	10	11	7		5	8							2						
16		12	Cardiff City	0-1		3342	1		3	4	2	6			9	10		11	14		8						12	7	5					
17		26	Bolton Wanderers	1-2	Culpin	4446	1		3	4	11	6			9	10				5	8						7	2						
18	Dec	4	WOLVERHAMPTON W.	3-1	Williams, Thomas, Adcock	6907	1		3	4	5	6			9	10	11				8						7	2						
19		18	GILLINGHAM	1-2	Gilbert	3829	1		3	4	5	6			9	10	12	11	7		8				14			2						
20		26	Southend United	1-2	Adcock	5034	1		3		5	6			9	10	12	7	4		8							2	11					
21		31	Chester City	1-2	Culpin	2741	1		3	4	5	6			9	10		7			8							2	11					
22	Jan	2	PRESTON NORTH END	1-0	Thomas	4219	1		3	4	5	6			9	10		7			8							2	11					
23		7	BURY	2-0	Culpin, Sandeman	3463	1		3	4	5	6			9	10		7	12		8							2	11					
24		14	Brentford	0-2		6043	1		3	4		6			9	10		7	12		8						11	2		5	14			
25		21	NOTTS COUNTY	1-3	Adcock	3704	1			4		6			9	10		3			8						11	2	12	5	7			
26		28	Chesterfield	1-1	Craig	3920	1			4		6				10		3	12		8						11	2		5	9			7
27	Feb	4	Aldershot	1-5	Wignall (og)	2244	1			4		6		8		10		3	12								11	2		5	9	14		7
28		11	BLACKPOOL	4-2	Gilbert 2 (1p), Adcock, Berry	3303	1					6			9	10		3	4		8						11	2		5	7			
29		18	Huddersfield Town	2-1	Gilbert (p), Culpin	5802	1					6			9	10		3	4		8						11	2		5	7			
30		25	SWANSEA CITY	1-0	Thomas	3900	1			4		6			9	10		3			8						11	2		5	7			
31		28	FULHAM	2-1	Gilbert, Thomas	3948	1			4		6			9	10		3			8						11	2		5	7			
32	Mar	4	Bristol City	1-3	Walsh (og)	7197	1			4		6			9	10		3	14	12							11	2		5	7	8		
33		11	WIGAN ATHLETIC	1-1	Adcock	3443	1			4		6			9	10		3	5	12							11	2			7	8		
34		15	Reading	1-1	McPherson	3746	1		4	5		6			9	10		3			8						11	2			7			
35		18	MANSFIELD TOWN	2-1	Thomas, Donald	2821	1		4	5		6			9	10		3			8						11	2			7	12		
36		25	Preston North End	2-3	Thomas, Adcock	9138	1		4	5		6				10		3									11	2		8	7		9	
37		27	SOUTHEND UNITED	2-2	Adcock, Culpin	3707	1		4	5		6				10		3	14	12							11	2		8	7		9	
38	Apr	1	Gillingham	0-1		3447	1		4	5		6				10		3	12	7							11	2		8		14	9	
39		4	Bury	1-0	Quow	1965	1		4	5		6				10					8						11	2		3	7		9	
40		8	CHESTER CITY	0-2		2845	1		4	5		6				10					8						11	2		3	7	12	9	
41		15	SHEFFIELD UNITED	1-2	McPherson	5030	1		4	5		6				10			14	12							11	2		3	7	8	9	
42		22	Bristol Rovers	1-1	Adcock	5568	1		4	5		6				10	11		12								8	2		3	7		9	
43		29	CARDIFF CITY	3-0	Thomas 2, Berry	3194	1		4	5		6				10	11				8						7	2		3			9	
44	May	1	Port Vale	2-1	Culpin, Thomas	6604	1		4	5		6				10	11				8						7	2		3			9	
45		6	Wolverhampton Wan.	2-3	Wilcox, Donegal	15259	1		4	5		6				10	12	11	14		8						7	2		3			9	
46		13	BOLTON WANDERERS	2-3	Adcock, Culpin	3655	1		4	5		6				10		11			8						7	2		3			9	

| Apps | | | | | | | 46 | 8 | 43 | 37 | 22 | 41 | 11 | 2 | 34 | 46 | 9 | 39 | 22 | 12 | 39 | 6 | 1 | 1 | 3 | 3 | 34 | 26 | 5 | 20 | 18 | 8 | 11 | 2 |
| Goals | | | | | | | | | 9 | 1 | 2 | 2 | 1 | | 7 | 17 | 2 | 1 | 2 | | 13 | | | | | | 3 | 1 | | | 1 | | 1 | 1 |

Two own goals

F.A. Cup

		Date	Opponent	Score	Scorers	Att	G	Re	Th	Do	Mg	Mp	Si	Lo	Gi	Ad	Dg	Wi	Sa	Fl	Cu	Ga	Pr	Cb	Jo	Bl	Be	Wm	An	Bo	Qu	Co	Wc	Cr
R1	Nov	19	Swansea City	1-3	Berry	4521	1		3	12	2	6			9	10	14	4	7	5	8						11							

F.L. Cup (Littlewoods Cup)

		Date	Opponent	Score	Scorers	Att	G	Re	Th	Do	Mg	Mp	Si	Lo	Gi	Ad	Dg	Wi	Sa	Fl	Cu	Ga	Pr	Cb	Jo	Bl	Be	Wm	An	Bo	Qu	Co	Wc	Cr
R1/1	Aug	30	Colchester Utd.	0-0		1678	1	5	3	4	2		7		9	10	11				6	8												
R1/2	Sep	6	COLCHESTER UTD.	5-0	Singleton, Gilbert (p), Adcock 2, Culpin	3953	1	5	3	4	2		7		9	10		11			6	8												
R2/1		27	CHARLTON ATHLETIC	1-1	Culpin	5290	1	6	3	4	2		7		9	10				5	8	11												
R2/2	Oct	11	Charlton Athletic	1-2	Wilson	2782	1		3	4	2	6	7		9	10	11	8	5				12											

Played in R1/2: TC Slack (12)

A.M.C. (Sherpa Van Trophy)

		Date	Opponent	Score	Scorers	Att	G	Re	Th	Do	Mg	Mp	Si	Lo	Gi	Ad	Dg	Wi	Sa	Fl	Cu	Ga	Pr	Cb	Jo	Bl	Be	Wm	An	Bo	Qu	Co	Wc	Cr
PR	Nov	22	CAMBRIDGE UNITED	1-1	McGoldrick	1806	1		3	4	7	6			9	10				5	8						11	2						
PR	Dec	21	Peterborough Utd.	2-0	Adcock, Culpin	1754	1		3	4	5	6			9	10		12			8					2	7		11					
R1	Jan	17	SOUTHEND UNITED	2-1	Berry, 1 og	2539	1			4		6			9	10	12	3	7		8						11	2		5				
R2	Feb	21	Wolverhampton Wand.	1-3	1 og	16815	1		7			6			9	10		3	4		8					14	11	2		5			12	

R1 and R2 games a.e.t.

1988/89 SEASON
Back: Culpin, Reed, Adcock, Slack, McGoldrick, Wilson
Middle: Holmes(Youth Team), Casey(Phsio), Johnson, McPherson, Gleasure, Sylvester,
Donegal, Wilcox, Walker(Asst. Man), Knight(Res. Man)
Front: Thomas, Longhurst, Sandeman, Carr(Man), Singleton, Gilbert, Donald

1989/90 SEASON
Back: Wilson, Williams, Tarry, Gleasure, Sandeman, Culpin, Berry
Middle: Knight(Res. Man), McPherson, Donegal, Collins, Johnson, Brown, Casey(Phsio), Walker(Coach)
Front: Thorpe, Singleton, Adcock, Carr(Man), Wilcox, Donald, Quow

1989/90   22nd in Division 3: Relegated

No	Date	Opponent	Score	Scorers	Att	Gleasure PF	Williams Wayne	Wilson PA	Thomas DR	Wilcox R	McPherson KA	Quow TS	Culpin P	Donald WR	Adcock AC	Berry SA	Sandeman BR	Collins D	Scope DF	Donegal GP	Brown SF	Barnes DO	Gernon FAJ	Chard PJ	Singleton MD	McPhillips T	Terry SG	Leburn CW	Thorpe A	Johnson DD	Bell M
1	Aug 19	Walsall	0-1		5020	1	2	3	4	5	6	7	8	9	10	11	12	14													
2	26	Swansea City	1-1	Collins	3637	1		3	4	5	6	7		9	10	11	2	8													
3	Sep 2	BRISTOL CITY	2-0	Thomas, Adcock (p)	4088	1		3	4	5	6	7		9	10	11	2	8													
4	9	Wigan Athletic	0-0		2289	1		3	4	5	6	7	12	9	10	11	2	8													
5	16	SHREWSBURY TOWN	2-1	Collins, Adcock (p)	3084	1	12	3	4	5	6	7		9	10	11	2	8													
6	23	Crewe Alexandra	1-2	Collins	3165	1		3	4	5	6	7	12		10	11	2	8	9												
7	26	Cardiff City	3-2	Quow, Adcock, Thomas	2801	1	9	3	4	5	6	7			10	11	2	8	12												
8	30	BURY	0-1		3486	1	2	3	4	5	6	7	12	14	10	11		8	9												
9	Oct 7	PRESTON NORTH END	1-2	Collins	3039	1	2	3	4	5	6	7		9		11		8		10	12										
10	14	Birmingham City	0-4		8731	1		3	4	5	6	2		9		7		8	12		11	10									
11	17	BLACKPOOL	4-2	Donald, Wilcox, Barnes, Collins	3098	1		3	4	5	6	2		8		7	12	9			11	10									
12	21	Bristol Rovers	2-4	Brown, Barnes (p)	4920	1			4	5	6	2		8		7	12	9			11	10	3								
13	28	NOTTS COUNTY	0-0		3734	1			4	5	6	8				7		9			11	10	3	2							
14	31	Fulham	1-1	Barnes (p)	3518	1			4	5	6	8		12		7	14	9			11	10									
15	Nov 4	ROTHERHAM UNITED	1-2	Barnes (p)	3598	1			4	5	6	8		11		7	14	9				10	3	2	12						
16	11	Huddersfield Town	2-2	Gernon, barnes	4973	1			4	5	6	12		11		7	8	9				10	3	2	14						
17	25	BRENTFORD	0-2		3165	1			4	5	6	11		14		7	8	9				10	3	2		12					
18	Dec 2	Bolton Wanderers	3-0	Barnes 2, Donald	5501	1		3	4	5	6			8		7		9			11	10		2	12						
19	17	READING	2-1	Barnes, Collins	3025	1			4	5	6	12				7		9			11	10	3	2	8						
20	26	Leyton Orient	1-1	Barnes	4784	1			4	5	6	12				7		9			11	10	3	2	8						
21	30	Mansfield Town	2-1	Berry, Barnes	3210	1			4	5	6	12				7		9			11	10	3	2	8						
22	Jan 1	CHESTER CITY	1-0	Berry	3823	1			4	5	6	8				7		9			11	10	3	2							
23	13	SWANSEA CITY	1-1	Barnes	3944	1			4	5	6	8		14		7		9			11	10	3	2	12						
24	Feb 17	BOLTON WANDERERS	0-2		3432	1		3	4	5	6	8				7	2	9	12			10				11					
25	20	WALSALL	1-1	Collins	2617	1		3	4	5	6	8				7	2	9			11	10									
26	25	Brentford	2-3	Thomas, Collins	6391	1		3	4	5	6	8				7	2	9			11	10									
27	Mar 3	TRANMERE ROVERS	0-4		3147	1		3		5	6	8		14		7	4	9			12	10		2					11		
28	6	Bury	0-1		2327	1		12	4	5	6			8		7	11	9				10	3	2							
29	10	CARDIFF CITY	1-1	Barnes (p)	2574	1		3	4	5	6			11		7	8	9	12			10		2							
30	13	WIGAN ATHLETIC	1-1	Chard	2172	1		3	9	5	6			8		7	11					10		2			4				
31	17	Preston North End	0-0		5686	1		3	9	5	6			8		7	2					10					4		11		
32	20	BIRMINGHAM CITY	2-2	Terry, Wilcox	4346	1		3	9	5	6					7	2				12	10			8		4		11		
33	24	Blackpool	0-1		3296	1				5	6			8		7	2				12	10	3				4	9	11		
34	27	Bristol City	1-3	Barnes	11965	1		3		5	6	12		8		7						10		2			4	9	11		
35	31	BRISTOL ROVERS	1-2	Thorpe	3774	1		3		5	6					7	12	8				10		2			4	9	11		
36	Apr 3	Shrewsbury Town	0-2		2314	1	2	3		5	6			6		7		8			14	10					4	9	11	12	
37	7	FULHAM	2-2	Sandeman, Thorpe	2882	1	2	3		5						7	6	8			9	10					4		11		
38	10	Notts County	2-3	Terry, Barnes	5396	1	2			5	6					7	9					10	3		8		4		11		
39	14	Chester City	1-0	Barnes	2242	1	2	3		5	6	8				7						10		9			4		11		
40	16	LEYTON ORIENT	0-1		3215	1	2	3		5	6	8				7	14	12				10		9			4		11		
41	21	Reading	2-3	Barnes (p), McPherson	3140	1				5	6	8				7	12	11				10		2			4	9		3	14
42	24	MANSFIELD TOWN	1-2	Wilcox	2119	1	2			5	6			9		7						10			8		4		11	3	7
43	28	HUDDERSFIELD T	1-0	Barnes	2388	1	2			5	6					7						10			8		4	9	11	3	7
44	30	CREWE ALEXANDRA	3-1	Barnes (p), Chard, Thorpe	2622	1	2			5	6					7						10		9			4	8	11	3	7
45	May 2	Tranmere Rovers	0-0		5363	1	2			5	6			12			14					10			8		4	9	11	3	7
46	5	Rotherham United	0-2		3420	1	2			5	6								12		14	10			8		4	9	11	3	7
		Apps				46	15	27	31	46	43	30	4	27	8	41	29	35	7	1	21	37	12	29	10	1	17	9	13	7	6
		Goals							3	3	1	1		2	3	2	1	8			1	18	1	2			2		3		

F.A. Cup

Rd	Date	Opponent	Score	Scorers	Att	Gleasure PF	Williams Wayne	Wilson PA	Thomas DR	Wilcox R	McPherson KA	Quow TS	Culpin P	Donald WR	Adcock AC	Berry SA	Sandeman BR	Collins D	Scope DF	Donegal GP	Brown SF	Barnes DO	Gernon FAJ	Chard PJ	Singleton MD	McPhillips T
R1	Nov 18	Kettering Town	1-0	Thomas	6100	1			4	5	6	8				7	11	9				10	3	2		
R2	Dec 9	AYLESBURY UNITED	0-0		6098	1		3	4	5	6			8		7		9			11	10		2		
rep	13	Aylesbury United	1-0	Barnes	4895	1		11	4	5	6			8		7	9					10	3	2	12	14
R3	Jan 6	COVENTRY CITY	1-0	Berry	14529	1			4	5	6	8				7		9			11	10	3	2		
R4	27	Rochdale	0-3		9048	1		3	4	5	6	8		14		7		9			11	10		2	12	

F.L. Cup (Littlewoods Cup)

Rd	Date	Opponent	Score	Scorers	Att	Gleasure PF	Williams Wayne	Wilson PA	Thomas DR	Wilcox R	McPherson KA	Quow TS	Culpin P	Donald WR	Adcock AC	Berry SA	Sandeman BR	Collins D
R1/1	Aug 22	Mansfield Town	1-1	Adcock	3095	1	2	3	4	5	6	7	8	9	10	11	12	14
R1/2	Sep 5	MANSFIELD TOWN	0-2		3963	1	12	3	4	5	6	7	14	9	10	11	2	8

A.M.C. (Leyland DAF Cup)

Rd	Date	Opponent	Score	Scorers	Att	Gleasure PF	Williams Wayne	Wilson PA	Thomas DR	Wilcox R	McPherson KA	Berry SA	Sandeman BR	Collins D	Scope DF	Barnes DO	Gernon FAJ	Chard PJ	Singleton MD	McPhillips T	Donald WR
PR	Nov 7	Colchester Utd.	3-0	Collins, Barnes, Chard	1780	1			4	5	6	7	9	12	11	10	3	2	8		
PR	28	MAIDSTONE UNITED	2-4	Wilcox, Gernon	1665	1	2	11	4	5	6	7	8	12		10	3	9		14	
R1	Jan 17	Southend United	1-2	Collins	1346	1		12	4	5	6	7	2	9		10	3		8		11

1990/91   10th in Division 4

Player columns (left to right): Adcock AC · Angus TN · Beavon MS · Berry SA · Barnes DO · Brown SF · Bell M · Beresford M · Chard PJ · Collins D · Campbell GR · Evans GI · Fee GP · Gleasure PF · Gernon FAJ · Johnson DD · Hitchcock KJ · Scully PJ · Sandeman BR · Scope DF · Terry SG · Thorpe A · Wilson PA · Wilkin K · Williams Wayne · Quow TS · Wood D

#	Date	Opponent	Res	Scorers	Att	Adck	Angs	Beav	Berr	Barn	Brwn	Bell	Bres	Chrd	Coll	Camp	Evan	Fee	Glea	Gern	John	Hitc	Scul	Sand	Scop	Terr	Thor	Wils	Wilk	Will	Quow	Wood
1	Aug 25	Hereford United	2-1	Wilkin, Barnes	3187			7	9	10	11			2					1				5			4	12	3	8			6
2	Sep 1	Maidstone United	3-1	Wilson, Wood, Thorpe	2049			7	9	10	11			2					1				5			4	12	3	8			6
3	8	BLACKPOOL	1-0	Barnes	4544		6	7	9	10	11			2					1				5	12		4	14	3	8			
4	14	Aldershot	3-3	Wilkin, Barnes, Beavon	2741		6	7	9	10	11			2					1				5	14		4	12	3	8			
5	18	Scarborough	1-2	Barnes (p)	1525		6	7	9	10	11			2					1				5	14		4	12	3	8			
6	22	PETERBOROUGH UTD.	1-2	Barnes	5549		6	7	9	10	11	14		2					1				5			4	12	3	8			
7	29	HALIFAX TOWN	1-0	Collins	2977		6	7	12	10	11	9	1	2	14								5			4		3	8			
8	Oct 2	Burnley	0-3		6273		6	7	11	10		9	1	2	8						14		5			4		3		12		
9	6	Chesterfield	0-0		3826		6	7	11	10	14	9	1	2	8								5			4		3		12		
10	13	STOCKPORT COUNTY	1-0	Chard	3927		6	7	9	10	11	12	1	2	8	14							5			4		3				
11	19	WALSALL	5-0	Barnes, Terry, Campbell 2, Chard	4055		6	7		10	11	9	1	2	8								5			4	12	3				
12	23	Darlington	1-1	Barnes	4882		6	7	12	10		9	1	2	8						11		5			4	14	3				
13	27	Lincoln City	1-3	Terry	3352		6	7		10		9	1	2	8						11		5			4	12	3				
14	Nov 3	HARTLEPOOL UNITED	3-2	Wilson 2, Beavon	3342		6	7	12	10		9	1	2	14	8					11					4		3		5		
15	9	WREXHAM	1-0	Barnes	3855			7	14	10	11		1	2	12	8							5			4	9	3		6		
16	24	York City	1-0	Barnes	2202		6	7		10	11		1	2		8					12		5			4	9	3				
17	Dec 1	ROCHDALE	3-2	Chard 2, Beavon (p)	3809		6	7		10	11		1	2	12	8	5				14					4	10	3				
18	15	Carlisle United	1-4	Campbell	2872		6	7	9		11		1	2		8			5		12				14	4	10	3				
19	21	CARDIFF CITY	0-0		3033		6	7		10	11	9	1	2		8			5						12	4		3				
20	29	Gillingham	0-0		4969		6	7		10	11	12		2		8	9		5			1				4		3				
21	Jan 1	DONCASTER ROVERS	0-0		5270		6	7	14	10	11	8		2			9		5	3		1			12	4						
22	12	MAIDSTONE UNITED	2-0	Adcock, Barnes	3710	9	6	7		10	11	8		2					5	3		1			12	4						
23	19	HEREFORD UNITED	3-0	Chard, Beavon (p), Angus	3577	9	6	7		10	11	8		2								1			5	4	12	3				
24	26	ALDERSHOT	2-1	Adcock, Beavon (p)	3800	9	6	7		10	11	12		2								1			5	4	8	3				
25	Feb 1	SCARBOROUGH	0-2		4058	9	6	7	12	10	11	8		2								1		14	5	4		3				
26	5	Peterborough United	0-1		5952	9	6	7		10	11	8		2								1		12		4	14	3		5		
27	15	YORK CITY	2-1	Angus, Barnes	2685	9	6	7		10	11	8		2								1				4	12	3		5		
28	23	Wrexham	2-0	Terry, Barnes	1790	9	6			10	11	8		2							14	1				4	12	3		5	7	
29	Mar 2	Rochdale	1-1	Beavon (p)	1890	9	6	7		10	11	8		2							14	1				4	12	3		5		
30	5	Scunthorpe United	0-3		2852	9	6	7		10	11	8		2		14					5	1				4		3			12	
31	9	CARLISLE UNITED	1-1	Campbell	3216		6	7	10		11	8		2		9					14	1				4		3		5	12	
32	12	BURNLEY	0-0		3710		6	7		10	11			2		9					14	1				4	8	3		5	12	
33	15	Halifax Town	1-2	Brown	1347		6	7		10	11			2		9					14	1				4	8	3		5	12	
34	23	CHESTERFIELD	2-0	Chard, Beavon (p)	3379	9	6	7		10	11			2		8					5	1				4		3		5		
35	26	Torquay United	0-0		2745	9	6	7		10	11			2		8						1				4		3		5		
36	30	SCUNTHORPE UNITED	2-1	Terry, Beavon (p)	3728	9	6	7		10	11			2		8					12	1				4		3		5		
37	Apr 1	Cardiff City	0-1		4805	9	6	7	14	10	11			2		8			1		12					4		3		5		
38	6	GILLINGHAM	2-1	Berry, Chard	2993	10	6	7	9		11	8		2		14			1		12					4		3		5		
39	9	Stockport County	0-2		3707	14	6	7			11	10		2		8			1		12					4	9	3		5		
40	13	Doncaster Rovers	1-2	Beavon	2939		6	7	11	12	5	10		2		8			1		14					4	9	3				
41	16	TORQUAY UNITED	1-4	Adcock	2678	9	6	7	11	10	12			2					1	5						4	8	3				
42	20	Walsall	3-3	Barnes, Beavon, Terry	3345		6	7	11	10				2					1		12					4	7	3		10		
43	27	DARLINGTON	0-3		4884	9	6	7	8	10	11			2					1		14					4	5	3		12		
44	30	LINCOLN CITY	1-1	Berry	2544	9	6		8	10		14				12			1	5	11					4		3		2	7	
45	May 7	Blackpool	1-2	Terry	7298	9	6		8	10	11	14				12			1	5						4		3		2	7	
46	11	Hartlepool United	1-3	Brown	6957	9	6			10	11	8		7					1		12					4	14	3		2	5	
				Apps		21	42	41	27	43	40	28	13	43	8	25	2	1	16	8	25	17	15	5	7	46	27	44	9	14	13	2
				Goals		3	2	10	2	13	2			7	1	4										6	1	3	2			1

F.A. Cup

Rnd	Date	Opponent	Res	Scorers	Att	Adck	Angs	Beav	Berr	Barn	Brwn	Bell	Bres	Chrd	Coll	Camp	Evan	Fee	Glea	Gern	John	Hitc	Scul	Sand	Scop	Terr	Thor	Wils	Wilk	Will	Quow	Wood
R1	Nov 17	Littlehampton	4-0	Beavon, Barnes 2, Campbell	3800			7	12	10	11			2	14	8			1	5						4	9	3		6		
R2	Dec 8	Barnet	0-0		5022			7		10	11			2	9	8	5		1		6				12	4		3				
rep	12	BARNET	0-1		5387	14		7		10	11			2		8	5		1		6				12	4	9	3				

F.L. Cup (Rumbelows League Cup)

Rnd	Date	Opponent	Res	Scorers	Att	Adck	Angs	Beav	Berr	Barn	Brwn	Bell	Bres	Chrd	Coll	Camp	Evan	Fee	Glea	Gern	John	Hitc	Scul	Sand	Scop	Terr	Thor	Wils	Wilk	Will	Quow	Wood
R1/1	Aug 29	Brighton & Hove Albion	2-0	Wilkin 2	3834			7	9	10	11			2		12			1							4	14	3	8	5		6
R1/2	Sep 4	BRIGHTON & HOVE ALB.	1-1	Brown	4760		6	7	9	10	11			2					1							4	12	3	8	5		
R2/1	25	SHEFFIELD UNITED	0-1		6910		6	7		10	11	9		2	12				1						14	4		3	8	5		
R2/2	Oct 10	Sheffield United	1-2	Barnes	8679		6	7	10	9	11	12		2	8				1						14	4		3		5		

A.M.C. (Leyland DAF Cup)

Rnd	Date	Opponent	Res	Scorers	Att	Adck	Angs	Beav	Berr	Barn	Brwn	Bell	Bres	Chrd	Coll	Camp	Evan	Fee	Glea	Gern	John	Hitc	Scul	Sand	Scop	Terr	Thor	Wils	Wilk	Will	Quow	Wood
PR	Nov 7	Stoke City	1-1	Beavon	4339			7	12	10	11		1	2	14	8							5			4	9	3		6		
PR	27	MANSFIELD TOWN	1-2	Beavon	2186		6	7	5		11		1	2	12	8					14				10	4	9	3				
R1	Feb 19	Torquay United	0-2		2112		6			10	11	8		2								1			12	4	9	3		5	7	

1990/91 SEASON
Back: Sandeman, Wilson, Bell, Tarry, Berry, Williams, Capone, Wilkin, Hall
Middle: Casey(Phsio), Johnson, Wood, Carr, Angus, Gleasure, Watts, Gernon, Terry,
Collins, Campbell, Brown, Carney(Youth Team)
Front: Foley(Man), Singleton, Beavon, Thorpe, Quow, Chard, Scope, Barnes, Kiernan(Coach)

1991/92 SEASON
Back: Bell, Scope, Parker, Burnham, Campbell, Wilkin, Adcock, Wilson
Middle, Casey(Physio), Johnson, Terry, Angus, Gleasure, Brown, Wood, Gernon, Best(Youth coach)
Front: Foley(Man), Quow, Beavon, Chard, Thorpe, Barnes, Kiernan(Coach)

1991/92   16th in Division 4

#		Date	Opponent	Result	Scorers	Att	Aldridge MI	Angus TN	Adcock AC	Bulzis RRB	Beresford M	Brown SF	Burnham IJ	Benton J	Bell M	Barnes DO	Beavon MS	Chard PJ	Campbell GR	Colkin L	Edwards DS	Farrell SP	Gernon FAJ	Johnson DD	Kiernan DJ	McClean CA	Parker S	Parsons MC	Quow TS	Richardson B	Scope DF	Terry SG	Thorpe A	Wilson PA
1	Aug	17	Halifax Town	1-0	Chard	1834		5	9		1	6	7		10			2	12				11						8			4		3
2		30	Wrexham	2-2	Angus, Thorpe	2196		5			1	6	7		10			2	9				3						8			4	11	
3	Sep	3	DONCASTER ROVERS	3-1	Ormsby (og), Thorpe, Brown	2742		5			1	6	7		10			2					3	12					8			4	11	9
4		7	BARNET	1-1	Barnes	4344		5			1	6	7		10	12		2					9						8			4	11	3
5		14	Rochdale	0-1		2631		5			1	6	7		10	12		2					9	14					8			4	11	3
6		17	Crewe Alexandra	1-1	Farrell (p)	3597		5			1	6	14		10			2				7	9	12					8			4	11	3
7		21	CARLISLE UNITED	2-2	Wilson, Barnes	2657		5			1	6	12		11	10		2				7	9						8		14	4		3
8	Oct	5	BLACKPOOL	1-1	Barnes	3318					1	6	5	12	10			2				7	9	14					8		11	4		3
9		12	Scarborough	1-2	Adcock	2023		5	7		1	6			11	10		2	12				9	8								4		3
10		15	CHESTERFIELD	1-1	Adcock	2430		5	11		1	6	3			10	8	2	7				9									4		12
11		19	SCUNTHORPE UNITED	0-1		2583		5	11		1	6			10		7	2					9						8		12	4		3
12		26	Gillingham	1-3	Campbell	2543		5	11		1	6	14	12			7	2	10				9						8			4		3
13	Nov	2	Rotherham United	0-1		3146		5	11		1	14	12				7	2	10				9						8			4		3
14		5	MANSFIELD TOWN	1-2	Adcock	2181		5	11		1	12	6	14			7	2	10				9						8			4		3
15		9	LINCOLN CITY	1-0	Adcock	2575		5	11		1	4	6				7	2					9	12		10			8					3
16		23	Cardiff City	2-3	Burnham 2	2922		5	11			14	6		10		8	2	7				4	3		9			12	1				
17		30	BURNLEY	1-2	Campbell	4020		5	11				6		10		8	2	7				4	3		9			12	1				14
18	Dec	7	SCARBOROUGH	3-2	Barnes, Adcock, Bell	1815		5	11				6		10	12	8	2	7					14		9			4	1		3		
19		21	Chesterfield	2-1	McClean, Terry	3048		5	11				6		10		8	2	7				12		14	9			4	1		3		
20		26	HALIFAX TOWN	4-0	Adcock 2, Chard, Barnes	3147		5	11				6		10		8	2	7				12			9			4	1		3		
21		28	WREXHAM	1-1	Angus	3209		5	11				6		10		8	2	7				12			9			4	1		3		
22	Jan	1	Doncaster Rovers	3-0	Chard, Campbell, Scope	1973		5					6	12			8	2	7				11		10	9			4	1	14	3		
23		11	YORK CITY	2-2	Terry, Barnes	3361		5					6		10	9	8	2	7				11						4	1	12	3		
24		18	Maidstone United	1-1	Terry	1364		5					6		10		8	2	7				14	12		11			4	1		3	9	
25		28	Walsall	2-1	Beavon 2	2399		5					6		10		8	2	7				12			11			4	1		3	9	
26	Feb	8	GILLINGHAM	0-0		3183		5					6		9		8		7				2		10	11			4	1		3		
27		11	Burnley	0-5		8760		5					6		9		8		7				2	10	12	11			4	1		3		
28		15	WALSALL	0-1		2480		5					6				8		7	12	9		2	10	14	11	4			1		3		
29		22	York City	0-0		2065		5					6	12	10		8		7				2	4		11				1		3	9	
30		29	HEREFORD UNITED	0-1		2430		5					6		10		8		7			11		12	14			2		1		3	9	
31	Mar	3	MAIDSTONE UNITED	1-0	Brown	1784		5				6			10		8		7		4	11						2		1		3	9	
32		10	Mansfield Town	0-2		2854		5				6			10		8		7		4		9			11		2		1		3		
33		14	ROTHERHAM UNITED	1-2	Brown	2561		5				6			10		8	12	7		4		9	3		11		2	14	1		3		
34		21	Lincoln City	2-1	Bell, Beavon (p)	2486		5				6			10		8	12	7		4		9			11		2		1		3		
35		28	CARDIFF CITY	0-0		2678		5				6			10		8		7		4		9			11		2		1		3	12	
36		31	ROCHDALE	2-2	McClean 2	2010		5				6			10		8		7				9			11		2		1		3	4	
37	Apr	4	Barnet	0-3		2816	12	5	14			6			10		8		7			11				9	4	2		1		3		
38		11	CREWE ALEXANDRA	0-1		3300		5	12			6		4	10		8		7			11				9		2		1		3		
39		14	Scunthorpe United	0-3		2286	14		11			6		12	10		8		7		5					9	4	2		1		3		
40		18	Carlisle United	1-2	Benton	1935	12		14			6		5	10		8		7			3	11			9		2		1		4		
41		25	Blackpool	0-1		5915	10					6		5			8		7			11				9	4	2		1		3		
42		28	Hereford United	2-1	Bell 2	1294						6		5	10		8		7			11				9	4	2		1		3		
			Apps				5	37	14	4	15	35	40	5	30	18	33	29	22	3	7	4	28	15	9	19	6	13	27	27	5	37	12	16
			Goals					2	7			3	2	1	4	6	3	3	3			1				3					1	3	2	1

Played in game 13: D Wood (at 6). In game 41: CL Adams (12).

One own goal

F.A. Cup

		Date	Opponent	Result	Scorers	Att	Aldridge MI	Angus TN	Adcock AC	Bulzis RRB	Beresford M	Brown SF	Burnham IJ	Benton J	Bell M	Barnes DO	Beavon MS	Chard PJ	Campbell GR	Colkin L	Edwards DS	Farrell SP	Gernon FAJ	Johnson DD	Kiernan DJ	McClean CA	Parker S	Parsons MC	Quow TS	Richardson B	Scope DF	Terry SG	Thorpe A	Wilson PA
R1	Nov	16	Crawley Town	2-4	Adcock, Chard	3370		4	11			7	6		10			2	14				12			9			8	1		5		3

F.L. Cup (Rumbelows League Cup)

		Date	Opponent	Result	Scorers	Att	Aldridge MI	Angus TN	Adcock AC	Bulzis RRB	Beresford M	Brown SF	Burnham IJ	Benton J	Bell M	Barnes DO	Beavon MS	Chard PJ	Campbell GR	Colkin L	Edwards DS	Farrell SP	Gernon FAJ	Johnson DD	Kiernan DJ	McClean CA	Parker S	Parsons MC	Quow TS	Richardson B	Scope DF	Terry SG	Thorpe A	Wilson PA
R1/1	Aug	20	Leyton Orient	0-5		2954		5	9			6	7		10			2	12				11	14					8			4		3
R1/2	Sep	10	LEYTON ORIENT	2-0	Barnes 2	1437		5			1	6	7		10			2			9								8	1		4	11	3

Played in R1/1: PF Gleasure (at 1)

A.M.C. (Autoglass Trophy)

		Date	Opponent	Result	Scorers	Att	Aldridge MI	Angus TN	Adcock AC	Bulzis RRB	Beresford M	Brown SF	Burnham IJ	Benton J	Bell M	Barnes DO	Beavon MS	Chard PJ	Campbell GR	Colkin L	Edwards DS	Farrell SP	Gernon FAJ	Johnson DD	Kiernan DJ	McClean CA	Parker S	Parsons MC	Quow TS	Richardson B	Scope DF	Terry SG	Thorpe A	Wilson PA
PR	Nov	20	Reading	2-0	Adcock, McClean	1151		5	11			6			10		8	2	7				4	3		9			12	1				
PR	Dec	3	LEYTON ORIENT	1-2	Chard	1193		5	11			6		12	10		8	2	7					3		9			4	1				14
R1	Jan	14	Barnet	2-3	Thorpe 2	1422		5				6		14	10		8	7					11	12				2	4	1		3	9	

1992/93 20th in Division 3 (Formerly Division 4)

#	Date		Opponent	Score	Scorers	Att	Richardson B	Parker S	Burnham JJ	Beavon MS	Angus TN	Terry SG	Bell M	Lamb PD	Scott MJ	Brown SF	Wilkin K	Chard PJ	Parsons MC	Colkin L	Aldridge MJ	Benton J	Curtis PAE	Harmon DJ	McParland IJ	Young SR	Tisdale PR	Gavin PJ	Holmes MA	Gillard KJ	Hawke WR	Fox MC
1	Aug	15	Gillingham	3-2	Brown, Scott, Chard	3869	1	2	3	4	5	6	7	8	9	10	11	12														
2		28	Crewe Alexandra	2-3	Brown, Terry	3608	1		3	4	5	6	7	8	9	10	11	12	2													
3	Sep	1	Cardiff City	1-2	Brown	7494	1		3	4	5	6	7		9	10	11	12	2	8												
4		6	HEREFORD UNITED	1-1	Beavon (p)	2668	1			12	4	5	6	7	9	10	11	3	2	8												
5		12	SCUNTHORPE UNITED	1-0	Wilkin	1961	1	9	7	4	5	6	12			10	11	3	2	8												
6		15	Barnet	0-3		2885	1	9	7	4	5	6	12		14	10	11	3	2	8												
7		19	Torquay United	0-1		2393	1	9	7	4	5	6	12		14	10	11	3	2	8												
8		26	HALIFAX TOWN	2-5	Wilkin, Brown	2021	1		7	4	5	6	12	14	9	10	11	3	2		8											
9	Oct	3	LINCOLN CITY	0-2		1929	1		7	4	5	6	8		12	10	11	3			9		2									
10		10	Scarborough	2-4	Terry, Aldridge	1539	1		7	4	5	6	8			10	11	3		12	9	14	2									
11		13	CHESTERFIELD	0-1		1922	1		7	4	5	6	8		14	10	11			3	9	12	2									
12		17	DONCASTER ROVERS	0-1		2138	1		7	4	5	6	11		12	10	8			3	9		2									
13		24	Wrexham	1-0	Bell	3095	1		7		5	6	11			10	8	12		3			2	4	9							
14		31	SHREWSBURY TOWN	0-0		2730	1		7	12	5	6				10	8	11		3			2	4	9							
15	Nov	3	DARLINGTON	1-2	Wilkin	1991	1		7		5	6				10	8	11		3			2	4	9							
16		21	YORK CITY	4-3	Angus, Curtis, Terry, Chard	2812	1		7	3	5	6	9			10	8	11					2	4								
17		28	Carlisle United	0-2		3607	1		7	3	5	6	9			10	8	11				12	2	4								
18	Dec	12	Bury	3-3	McParland, Terry, Bell	1954	1		7	3	5	6	12			10	8					9	2	4	11							
19		26	COLCHESTER UNITED	1-0	McParland	4962	1		7		5	6	9			10	8	3					2	4	11							
20		28	Walsall	0-2		5080	1		7		5	6	9			10	8	3					2	4	11							
21	Jan	8	BARNET	1-1	Wilkin	4253	1		7		5	6	9			10	8	3	2					4	11							
22		16	Halifax Town	2-2	Hammon, McParland	1323	1		7		5	6	9		12	10	8		2				3	4	11							
23		23	TORQUAY UNITED	0-1		3082	1		7		5	6	9		8	10	12		2				3	4	11							
24		26	CREWE ALEXANDRA	0-2		2510	1		7	14	5	6	9		8	10	12		2				3	4	11							
25		30	Chesterfield	3-1	Chard, Terry, Scott	3031	1		7	2	5	6	9		8		11	10					3	4								
26	Feb	6	GILLINGHAM	2-2	Brown, Bell	3812	1		12		5	6	9		8	10	11	2					3	4		7						
27		13	Hereford United	2-3	Young, Chard	2358	1		7		5	6	9		3	10	14	12					2	4	11	8						
28		19	CARDIFF CITY	1-2	Brown (p)	4522	1		7		5	6	9			10	12	3					2	14	4	11	8					
29		27	SCARBOROUGH	1-3	Bell	2455	1		7		5	6	9			10	12		3				2	14		11	8	4				
30	Mar	6	Lincoln City	0-2		3328	1		14	7	5	6	9			10	12						2			11	8	4	3			
31		9	Rochdale	3-0	Chard, Brown, Young	1446	1			7	5	6	9			10		2								11	8	4	3			
32		20	Darlington	1-3	Bell	2106	1		7			6	11				12	5	3				2					9	8	4	10	
33		23	CARLISLE UNITED	2-0	Gavin, Angus	2561	1		4		5	6	11				7	2						12				9	8	3	10	
34		26	York City	1-2	Gavin	3334	1				5	6	11			4	7	2						12				9	8	3	10	
35		30	Scunthorpe United	0-5		2307	1			14	5	6	11			4	7	2						10				9	8	3		12
36	Apr	2	ROCHDALE	1-0	Brown	3037	1				5	6	11			10	7	2					4					9	3	8		
37		6	BURY	1-0	Hawke	2878	1					6	11			10	7	5	2				4					9	3	8		
38		12	WALSALL	0-0		4177	1					6	11			10	7	5	2		12		4					9	3	8		
39		20	Colchester United	0-2		3519	1					6	11			10	7	5	2		12		4					9	3	8		
40		24	Doncaster Rovers	2-2	Brown, Aldridge	2111	1					12	6			10	7	5	2	11	8		4					9	3			
41		27	WREXHAM	0-2		7504	1		3			6	11			10	7	5	2		8		4					9				
42	May	8	Shrewsbury Town	3-2	Chard, Gavin 2	7278	1				7	5	6		11		8	10	2	3	9		4					12				

| | | | | Apps | | | 42 | 4 | 31 | 24 | 37 | 42 | 39 | 3 | 17 | 38 | 41 | 34 | 19 | 13 | 9 | 5 | 22 | 25 | 11 | 8 | 5 | 14 | 6 | 9 | 7 | 1 |
| | | | | Goals | | | | | 1 | 2 | 5 | 5 | | 2 | 9 | 4 | 6 | | 2 | | | | 1 | 1 | 3 | 2 | | 4 | | | 1 | |

F.A. Cup

	Date		Opponent	Score	Scorers	Att	Richardson B	Burnham JJ	Beavon MS	Angus TN	Terry SG	Bell M	Scott MJ	Brown SF	Wilkin K	Chard PJ	Parsons MC	Curtis PAE	Harmon DJ	McParland IJ
R1	Nov	14	FULHAM	3-1	Terry, Brown, Wilkins	4823	1	7	3	5	6	9		10	8	11		2	4	
R2	Dec	6	Bath City	2-2	Brown, Chard	3626	1	7	3	5	6	9		10	8	12		2	4	11
rep		15	BATH CITY	3-0	Bell, Wilkins, McParland	4106	1	7	3	5	6	9		10	8	4		2		11
R3	Jan	12	ROTHERHAM UNITED	0-1		7256	1			5	6	9	12	10	8		2	3	4	11

F.L. Cup (Coca Cola Cup)

	Date		Opponent	Score		Att	Richardson B	Parker S	Burnham JJ	Beavon MS	Angus TN	Terry SG	Bell M	Lamb PD	Scott MJ	Brown SF	Wilkin K	Chard PJ	Parsons MC	Colkin L	Aldridge MJ
R1/1	Aug	18	Gillingham	1-2	1 og	2245	1	2	3	4	5	6	7	8	9	10	11	12			
R1/2	Sep	9	GILLINGHAM	0-2		2390	1		12	4	5	6	7		9	10	11	3	2	8	14

A.M.C. (Autoglass Trophy)

	Date		Opponent	Score	Scorers	Att	Richardson B	Burnham JJ	Beavon MS	Angus TN	Terry SG	Bell M	Scott MJ	Brown SF	Wilkin K	Chard PJ	Parsons MC	Aldridge MJ	Curtis PAE	Harmon DJ	McParland IJ
R1	Dec	1	Colchester United	2-1	Beavon, Brown	1454	1	7	3	5	6	9		10	8			12	2	4	11
R1		9	BARNET	2-1	Scott, McParland	1591	1	7	3	5	6	12	14	10	8			9	2	4	11
R2	Jan	19	HEREFORD UNITED	4-0	Bell, Scott, McParland 2	1962	1	7	12	5	6	9	8	10	14		2		3	4	11
QF	Feb	2	Port Vale	2-4	Scott, Chard	4834	1	7	2	5	6	9	8		11	10	12		3	4	

1992/93 SEASON
Back: Aldridge, Stackman, Stancombe, Wareing, Preston, Reed, Tero
2nd Row: Curtis(Youth Team Coach), Parsons, Adams, Angus, Richardson, Brown,
Bell, Parker, Knigh(Res Train), Lewis(foot. comm. off.)
3rd Row: Colkin, Burnham, Beavon, Chard, Wilkin, Terry, Scott
Front: Scott, Bulgis, Lamb, Knight, Willoughby, Justin, Benton

1993/94 SEASON
Back: Colkin, Burnham, Aldridge, Parsons
Middle: Casey(Phsio), Wilkin, Terry, Richardson, Sherwood, Chard, Gillard, Curtis(Youth Team Man)
Front: Gilzean, Fleming, Brown, Barnwell(Man), Williams, Bell, Harmon

Player columns (left to right): Richardson B · Parsons MC · Gillard KJ · Phillips LM · Terry SG · Wood D · Fleming TM · Wilkin K · Gilzean IR · Brown SF · Bell M · Chard PJ · Colkin L · Aldridge MJ · Harmon DJ · Francis SR · Burnham JJ · Sherwood S · Preston RJ · Hyslop CT · Sampson I · Patmore WJ · Harrison GM · Gallacher B · Elad DE · Warburton R · Fitzpatrick PJ · Cornwell JA

#	Date	Opponent	Res	Scorers	Att	Ric	Par	Gll	Phi	Ter	Woo	Fle	Wil	Glz	Bro	Bel	Cha	Col	Ald	Har	Fra	Bur	She	Pre	Hys	Sam	Pat	Hrr	Gal	Ela	War	Fit	Cor
1	Aug 14	Bury	0-0		2540	1	2	3	4	5	6	7	8	9	10	11				12													
2	28	Colchester United	2-3	Brown, Gilzean	2874	1	2	3	4	5		7		9	10	11	6	8															
3	31	Crewe Alexandra	1-3	Gilzean	3155	1	2	3	4	5		7		9	10	11	6	8				12											
4	Sep 4	WALSALL	0-1		3278		2	3	4	5		7		9	10	11	6	8			12			1									
5	11	Hereford United	1-1	Gilzean	2260		2		4	5		7		9	10	11	6	8		12			3			1							
6	18	WIGAN ATHLETIC	0-2		2281		2	12	4	5		7		9	10	11	6	8					3			1							
7	25	Lincoln City	3-4	Aldridge, Brown, Harmon	2705		2		4	5			12	9	10	11	6		8	7			3			1							
8	Oct 2	DARLINGTON	1-0	Aldridge	2268		2	3	4	5				9	10	11	6		8	7			12			1							
9	9	WYCOMBE WANDERERS	1-1	Aldridge	5414		2	3	4	5				9	10	11	6		8	7						1							
10	12	MANSFIELD TOWN	5-1	Gilzean, Harmon, Terry, Brown 2	2842		2	3	4	5				9	10	11	6		8	7			12			1							
11	16	Scunthorpe United	0-7		2814		2	3	4	5			12	9	10	11	6		8	7						1							
12	23	CARLISLE UNITED	1-1	Aldridge	2886	1	2	3	4	5			12	9	10	11	6		8	7													
13	30	Doncaster Rovers	1-2	Gilzean	2227	1	2		4	5			12	9	10	11		3	8	7			6										
14	Nov 2	Torquay United	0-2		2704	1	2		4	5		7		9	10	11	6	3		12			8										
15	6	SHREWSBURY TOWN	0-3		2639	1			4	5			12	9	10	11	6		7	8			3			2							
16	20	Chester City	0-1		2650		2	3	4	5				9		11	6		12	8	7				10	1							
17	27	CHESTERFIELD	2-2	Gilzean, Aldridge	1866		2	3	4	5				9		11	6		7	8					10	1							
18	Dec 11	Mansfield Town	0-1		2491		2		4	5					10	11	7			8					1	3	6	9					
19	18	BURY	0-1		2369		2		4	5					10	11	7	14	12						1	3	6	9	8				
20	27	Gillingham	0-1		4573				4	5		7			10		2	11	12						1	3	6	9	8				
21	Jan 1	Rochdale	2-6	Gilzean, Harmon	2453		2		4	5			7	12	10			11	8	14					1	3	6	9					
22	3	CREWE ALEXANDRA	2-2	Gilzean, Colkin	3404				4	5				9	10			11	8	2					1	3	6						
23	8	Scarborough	1-2	Gilzean	1703	1				5		4	7	9	10	12		11	8	2						3	6						
24	22	Wycombe Wanderers	0-1		6737	1			4	5		2	7	9	10	11		12	8							3	6		14				
25	29	DONCASTER ROVERS	0-0		2900	1			4	5		2	7	9	10	11			8							6			3	12			
26	Feb 5	Carlisle United	1-0	Chard	4535	1						2	7	12	10	11	6		4							3	9				8	5	
27	12	SCARBOROUGH	3-2	Harmon, Fitzpatrick, Gilzean	2974	1		3				2	7	9		11	6		4							3	9				8	5	10
28	19	COLCHESTER UNITED	1-1	Wilkin	3205	1		3				2	7	9		11	6		4								12				8	5	10
29	26	Walsall	3-1	Harmon, Wilkin, Patmore	4553	1					6	2	7	12		11	3		4								9				8	5	10
30	Mar 5	HEREFORD UNITED	0-1		5394	1					6	2	7	12		11			4		3						9				8	5	10
31	8	SCUNTHORPE UNITED	4-0	Harmon, Fleming (p), Aldridge, Wilkin	3192	1					6	2	7	9		11			12	4	3										8	5	10
32	12	Wigan Athletic	1-1	Cornwell	1855	1					6	2	7	9		11			8	4	3											12	10
33	15	PRESTON NORTH END	2-0	Fensome (og), Aldridge	3845	1					6	2	7	9		11			8	4	3											5	10
34	19	LINCOLN CITY	0-0		3868	1					6	2	7	9		11			8	4	3						12					5	10
35	26	Darlington	1-0	Warburton	3226	1					6	2	7	9		11	12		8	4	3											5	10
36	Apr 2	GILLINGHAM	1-2	Patmore	4628	1					6	2	7	9		11	12		8	4	3						14					5	10
37	4	Preston North End	1-1	Harmon	7517	1					6	2	7			11	3		8	4							9					5	10
38	9	ROCHDALE	1-2	Aldridge	3330	1					6	2	7			11	3		8	4							9					5	10
39	16	TORQUAY UNITED	0-1		3519	1					6	2	7			11	8		12	4							9		3			5	10
40	23	Shrewsbury Town	1-2	Wilkin	6512	1					6	2	7			11	8	9		4							12		3	14		5	10
41	30	CHESTER CITY	1-0	Wilkin	6432	1			10	6		2	7			11		9		4							12		3	8	5		
42	May 7	Chesterfield	0-4		5285	1			10	6		2	7				12	9		4							11		3	8	5		

Played in game 14: HS Stackman (at 14).

	Ric	Par	Gll	Phi	Ter	Woo	Fle	Wil	Glz	Bro	Bel	Cha	Col	Ald	Har	Fra	Bur	She	Pre	Hys	Sam	Pat	Hrr	Gal	Ela	War	Fit	Cor
Apps	27	19	14	26	39	1	31	24	33	24	38	28	20	28	31	1	17	16	1	8	8	17	2	5	10	17	2	13
Goals					1		1	5	10	4		1	1	8	7							2				1	1	1

One own goal

F.A. Cup

Rd	Date	Opponent	Res	Scorers	Att	Ric	Par	Gll	Phi	Ter	Woo	Fle	Wil	Glz	Bro	Bel	Cha	Col	Ald	Har	Fra	Bur	She	Pre	Hys	Sam	Pat
R1	Nov 13	BROMSGROVE ROVERS	1-2	Aldridge	3382		2	3	4	5			12	9		11	6		8	7					10	1	

F.L. Cup (Coca Cola Cup)

Rd	Date	Opponent	Res	Att	Ric	Par	Gll	Phi	Ter	Woo	Fle	Wil	Glz	Bro	Bel	Cha	Col	Ald	Har	Fra	Bur	She	Pre	Hys	Sam
R1/1	Aug 18	Reading	0-3	3283	1	2	3	4	5	6	7		9	10	11			12	8	14					
R1/2	Sep 7	READING	0-2	1631		2		4	5		7		9	10	11	6	8		12			3			1

A.M.C. (Autoglass Trophy)

Rd	Date	Opponent	Res	Scorers	Att	Ric	Par	Gll	Phi	Ter	Woo	Fle	Wil	Glz	Bro	Bel	Cha	Col	Ald	Har	Fra	Bur	She	Pre	Hys	Sam
R1	Oct 19	Walsall	0-0		1897	1	2	3	4	5				9	10	11	6		8	7						
R1	Nov 9	HEREFORD UNITED	1-1	Aldridge	1062			3	4	5			12	9	10	11	6		8	7				1	2	
R2	Dec 1	Reading	1-4	Aldridge	1811		2	3	4	5				9	10	11	6		8			7	1			

1994/95   17th in Division 3

League (Division 3)

#	Date	Opponent	Score	Scorers	Att	Stewart WI	Pascoe J	Curtis R	Norton DW	Warburton R	Sampson I	Harmon DJ	Trott DD	Grayson N	Bell M	Wilkin K	Colkin L	Aldridge MJ	Robinson P	Williams GJ	Ovendale MJ	Skelly RB	Cahill OF	Turner GM	Harrison GM	Brown IO	Patmore WJ	Hughes DJ	Burns C	Smith NL	Thompson GL	Martin, Dave	Daniels SC	Woodman AJ	O'Shea DE
1	Aug 20	Doncaster Rovers	0-1		2154	1	2	3	4	5	6	7		9	10	11	14	12																	
2	27	Scunthorpe United	1-1	Trott	2499	1	2			4	5	6	7	9	12	11	10	3																	
3	30	Torquay United	1-2	Sampson	3619	1	2	6	8	5	4	7		9	10	11		3	12																
4	Sep 3	Walsall	1-1	Trott	4249	1		6	2	5	4	7		9	10	11		3	12	8															
5	10	ROCHDALE	1-2	Trott	2887	1			2	5	4	7		9	10	11	8	3		6															
6	13	HARTLEPOOL UNITED	1-1	Aldridge	2466	1	8		2	5	4	7		9	10	11		3	12	6															
7	17	Mansfield Town	1-1	Aldridge	2557	1		6	2	5	4	7	9			11		3	10	8															
8	24	CARLISLE UNITED	2-1	Aldridge, Bell	3508	1		6	2	5	4	7	9			11		3	10	8															
9	Oct 1	Lincoln City	2-2	Harmon, Warburton	3248	1		6	2	5	4	7	9			11		3	10	8															
10	8	Exeter City	0-0		3015	1		6	2	5	4	7	9			11		3		8	10														
11	11	MANSFIELD TOWN	0-1		4993	1		6	2	5	4	7	9		14	11		3	12	8	10														
12	15	BARNET	1-1	Aldridge	7461	1	2			5	4	7	9		12	11		3	10	6	8														
13	22	WIGAN ATHLETIC	1-0	Grayson	6379	1	2	6		5	4	7		9			3	10	11	8			12												
14	29	Scarborough	0-0		1468	1	2			5	4	7	9	8			11	12	10	6		3													
15	Nov 5	FULHAM	1-0		7366	1	2			12	5	4	7	8			3	9	10	6			11												
16	19	Preston North End	0-2		7043	1	14			2	5	4	7	9		11		3	8	10	6	1	12												
17	26	HEREFORD UNITED	1-3	Cahill	5148	1				2	5	4	7	9	12			8	10	6		3	11												
18	Dec 10	DONCASTER ROVERS	0-0		4463	1	3			2	5	4	7	9	8			12		6			11		10											
19	16	SCUNTHORPE UNITED	0-1		3841	1	12			2	5	4	7	9	3	14		8		6			11		10											
20	26	Colchester United	1-0	Harmon (p)	5064	1	12	5	2			4	7	9				3		11						8	14									
21	27	CHESTERFIELD	2-3	Brown, Harmon (p)	6329	1	2	5	6			4	7	9				3		11					14	8	12									
22	31	Darlington	1-4	Grayson	2247	1		6	2	5	4			10				3	12	11					7	8	9									
23	Jan 7	Wigan Athletic	1-2	Colkin	1911	1	12	6	2	5	4			11			10	9			3				7	8										
24	14	GILLINGHAM	2-0	Harmon (p), Trott	5529	1				2	5	4	7	12	11		6	9								8			3		10					
25	28	SCARBOROUGH	0-3		5737	1				2	5	4	7	9	11											8	12	3	10	6						
26	Feb 4	Hereford United	1-2	Grayson	2443				2	5	6	14	9	10					1						11	8		12	7	4			3			
27	11	PRESTON NORTH END	2-1	Burns, Smith	5197				2	5	4	6		11					7					1		8		10	3	9						
28	14	Fulham	4-4	Aldridge 2, Brown, Grayson	3423				2	5	4	12		11					7					1		8		10	3	9	6					
29	18	Gillingham	1-3	Thompson	4072	1			2	5	4	12		11					7							10	8		3	9	6					
30	25	LINCOLN CITY	3-1	Brown (og), Grayson, Aldridge	4821				2	5	4	10		11					7			1				12	8		3	9	6					
31	Mar 4	Carlisle United	1-2	Martin	6744	13			2	5	4	12		11			3	7		14	1					8		10		9	6					
32	7	BURY	0-5		4208	1			2	5	4	12		11			3	7					14			8		10		9	6					
33	11	Rochdale	0-0		1894				2	5	4			11			12	14					7			8		3	10	9	6		1			
34	18	TORQUAY UNITED	2-0	Grayson, Brown	3957				2	5	4			11			12	7								8		3	10	9	6		7	1		
35	25	WALSALL	2-2	Grayson, Warburton	6282				2	5	4	14		11			6			12						8		3	10	9		7	1			
36	Apr 1	Hartlepool United	1-1	Thompson	2113				2	5	4			11			12							10		8		3	10	9		7	1		6
37	8	DARLINGTON	2-1	Thompson, Grayson	4496				2	5	4			11			7							12		8		3	10	9		12	1		6
38	15	Chesterfield	0-3		4884		5		2					11			7									8		3	10	9			1		6
39	17	COLCHESTER UNITED	1-1	Brown	5011				12	5	4			11			7									8		3	10	9		2	1		6
40	22	Bury	0-5		2921					5	4	10	9	11			7									8		3	12			2	1		6
41	29	Barnet	3-2	Burns, Thompson, Warburton	2796				2	5	4			11			7	14								8		3	10	9		12	1		6
42	May 6	EXETER CITY	2-1	O'Shea, Sampson	6734				2	5	4			11			12							7		8		3	10	9		14	1		6
		Apps				27	15	13	38	39	42	33	22	38	12	4	33	27	14	15	6	3	8	4	5	23	4	13	17	6	15	7	8	10	7
		Goals								3	2	4	4	8	1		1	7					1			4			2	1	4	1			1

Played in game 20: BR Sedgemore (6). In game 20,21: AJ Flounders (10).
In games 1 and 2: R Byrne (8). In game 5: B McNamara (12).

One own goal

F.A. Cup

#	Date	Opponent	Score	Att	Stewart WI	Pascoe J	Curtis R	Norton DW	Warburton R	Sampson I	Harmon DJ	Trott DD	Grayson N	Bell M	Wilkin K	Colkin L	Aldridge MJ	Robinson P	Williams GJ	Ovendale MJ
R1	Nov 12	Peterborough Utd.	0-4	8739	1	2			11	5	4	7	9	8			3	12	10	6

F.L. Cup (Coca Cola Cup)

#	Date	Opponent	Score	Att	Stewart WI	Pascoe J	Curtis R	Norton DW	Warburton R	Sampson I	Harmon DJ	Trott DD	Grayson N	Bell M	Wilkin K	Colkin L	Aldridge MJ	Robinson P	Williams GJ
R1/1	Aug 16	Bournemouth	0-2	2587	1	2	3	4	5	6	7		9	10	11	12			
R1/2	Sep 6	BOURNEMOUTH	0-1	3249	1		6	2	5	4	7		9	10	12		3	11	8

Played in R1/1: R Byrne (8).

A.M.C. (Auto Windscreen Shield)

#	Date	Opponent	Score	Scorers	Att	Stewart WI	Pascoe J	Curtis R	Norton DW	Warburton R	Sampson I	Harmon DJ	Trott DD	Grayson N	Bell M	Wilkin K	Colkin L	Aldridge MJ	Robinson P	Williams GJ	Ovendale MJ	Skelly RB	Cahill OF	Turner GM	Harrison GM	Brown IO	Patmore WJ
R1	Oct 18	Cambridge United	3-1	Warburton, Grayson, Aldridge	1497		2	6		5	4	7			11		14	10			8	1	3	12			
R1	Nov 1	BARNET	3-1	Harmon, Grayson, Aldridge	2618		2			5	4	7			8		3	9	10	6	1		12	11			
R2	29	SWANSEA CITY	0-1		2706	1		14	2	5	4	7	9	8			10	6		3	11		12				

Played in first game: B McNamara (9).

1994/95 SEASON
Back: Colkin, Pascoe, Wilkin, Curtis, Stackman, Skelly
Middle: Casey(Physio), Byrne, Turner, Trott, Stewart, Sampson, Middlemass,
Preston, Curtis(Youth team coach)
Front: Morris (Asst. Man), Harrison, Grayson, Warburton, Bell, Harmon, Barnwell(Manager)

1995/96 SEASON   Back: Warner, Aldridge, Cahill, White, Hughes, Lee
Middle: Casey(Physio),Beckford,Peer,Woodman,Burns,Turley,Sampson,Thompson,Curtis(Youth Coach)
Front: Williams, Grayson, Warburton, Atkins(Man), O'Shea, Colkin, Norton

1995/96 11th in Division 3

Player columns (left to right): Aldridge M, Armstrong G, Burns C, Cahill O, Colkin L, Doherty N, Gibb A, Grayson N, Hughes D, Hunter R, Lee C, Maddison L, Mountfield D, Norton D, O'Shea D, Peer D, Sampson I, Scott R, Smith A, Taylor Steve, Thompson, Turley W, Warburton R, White J, Williams G, Woodman A, Worboys G

#		Date / Opponent	Res	Scorers	Att	Ald	Arm	Bur	Cah	Col	Doh	Gib	Gra	Hug	Hun	Lee	Mad	Mou	Nor	OSh	Pee	Sam	Sco	Smi	Tay	Tho	Tur	War	Whi	Wil	Woo	Wor
1	12	Aug BURY	4-1	Grayson(3), Burns(p)	4487			10		11			9	3	12				2	4	7	6						14	5	8	1	
2	19	Cardiff City	1-0	Peer	7872			10		11			9		14				2	4	7	6	3						5	12	8	1
3	26	MANSFIELD TOWN	3-3	White, Burns(2,1p)	4797			10		11				14					2	4	7	6	3			8		5	9	12	1
4	29	Hartlepool United	1-2	Thompson	2390			10		11			8	3	12				2	4	7	6				14		5	9	8	1
5	2	Sep Rochdale	2-1	Burns, White	2193			10		11				3	12				2	4	7	6				14		5	9	8	1
6	9	EXETER CITY	0-0		5625			10		11			14	3					2	4	7	6				12		5	9	8	1
7	12	LEYTON ORIENT	1-2	Williams	5072			10		11			4	3					2		7	6				14		5	9	8	1
8	16	Doncaster Rovers	0-1		2353			10		12			8	3					2	4	7	6				14		5	9	11	1
9	23	Torquay United	0-3		2314			10		11	7		8	3					2	4	14	6				12		5	9		1
10	30	FULHAM	2-0	Grayson, White	5778			10		14	7		11			15	3		2	12	4	6				8		5	9		1
11	7	Oct Scunthorpe United	0-0		2455			10			7		11				3	6	2		4					8		5	9	12	1
12	14	CAMBRIDGE UNITED	3-0	Grayson, Burns, Colkin	6301			10		14	7		11				3	6	2		4	15				8		5	9	12	1
13	21	Colchester United	0-1		3823			10	9		7		11			15	3	6	2		4	8						5	12	14	1
14	28	BARNET	0-2		5376			10	14		7		11				3	6	2		4	12		8				5	9	15	1
15	31	PRESTON NORTH END	1-2	Gibb	4695			10		11	7		8		12		3		2		4	6			15			5	14	9	1
16	6	Nov Gillingham	0-0		7207			10		11	7		8		14		3		2	9	4	6						5	15	12	1
17	18	WIGAN ATHLETIC	0-0		4102					11	7		10			12	3		2	6	4							5	9	8	1
18	25	Lincoln City	0-1		3287					12			10			7	3		2	6	4		11					5	9	8	1
19	9	Dec TORQUAY UNITED	1-1	White	3656			10	7	12					8		3		2	6	4		11					14	5	9	1
20	16	Fulham	3-1	Thompson, White(2)	3421					4					12	14	3		2	6	9		7			11	1	5	10	8	
21	23	Scarborough Unite	1-2	White	1404			12		4			14				3		2	6	9		7			11		5	10	8	1
22	26	HEREFORD UNITED	1-1	White	6222			9		12			8		4		3		2	6			7			11		5	10	14	1
23	6	Jan Darlington Rovers	2-1	White(2)	1943	11	7						8		4		3		2	6	9					12		5	10	14	1
24	13	CARDIFF CITY	1-0	Armstrong	4454	11	14	15					8		4		3		2	6	12					9		5	10	7	1
25	20	Bury	1-0	White	3074			11					8		4		3			6	7	2				9		5	10	12	1
26	30	PLYMOUTH ARGYLE	1-0	Sampson	3911	7		11					8		4		3		12	6		2				9	1	5	10		14
27	3	Feb Mansfield Town	0-0		2981	7		12					8		4		3		11	6	14	2				5		10		1	9
28	10	DARLINGTON ROVERS	1-1	White	4926			7				15	8		4		3		11	6	14	2				9		5	10	1	12
29	17	Leyton Orient	0-2		4444			7			14	12	8		4		3		2	6	11					5		10	15	1	9
30	19	ROCHDALE	2-1	Warburton, Warboys	3090			11			14	7	8		4		3		2	6	12					9		5	10	1	15
31	24	DONCASTER ROVERS	3-3	Sampson, Doherty, White(p)	4738			11			7	14	12		4				2	6	8	3				9		5	10	1	15
32	27	Exeter City	2-1	Warburton, Grayson	2663			11			8		12		3				2	6	4					9		5	10	1	
33	2	Mar Hereford United	0-1		2822			11			8		12		3				2	6	4	7				9		5	10	1	15
34	9	SCARBOROUGH	2-0	White, Sampson	4621			11					3		4				2	6	8	5				9			10	7	1
35	16	Plymouth Argyle	0-1		7001			11			12	15	3		4				2	6	8	5				9			10	7	14
36	20	HARTLEPOOL UNITED	0-0		3537			11			14	15	3		8				2	6		4				12		5	10	7	1
37	23	CHESTER CITY	1-0	Burns	4810			11			14	3	8						2	6	4					9		5	10	7	12
38	30	SCUNTHORPE UNITED	1-2	Grayson	4290			11			14	3	8						2	6	4	15				9		5	10	7	12
39	2	Apr Cambridge United	1-0	White	3631			11				8	3						2		4	6				12		5	10	7	9
40	6	Barnet	0-2		3315			11			15	12	3		8				2		4	6				9		5	10	7	14
41	8	COLCHESTER UNITED	2-1	Grayson, Gibb	5021			11			14	15	3		8	12				6	4	2				9		5	10	7	
42	13	Preston North End	3-0	Grayson(3)	11774			4					3		11				2	6	8	9						5	10	7	
43	20	GILLINGHAM	1-1	Burns	7427			4				14	3		11				2	6	8	9				12		5	10	7	
44	23	Chester	0-1		1674			4		15		14	3		11				2	6	8	9				12		5	10	7	
45	27	LINCOLN CITY	1-1	Warburton	5166			4		8		14	3		4				12	6		9						5	10	7	
46	4	May Wigan Athletic	2-1	Sampson, White	2390			10			13			3			11	2	2	6	8	9						5	12	7	1
		Apps				4	43	3	24	9	23	42	8	34	5	21	4	44	38	42	33	5	2	2	34	2	44	45	35	44	13
		Goals					1	7		1	1	2	11								1	4				2		3	16	1		1

Played in game 7: D Beckford (12). In game 32: M Taylor (7).

F.A. Cup

	Date / Opponent	Res	Scorers	Att	Bur	Col	Gib	Hun	Mad	Nor	OSh	Pee	Sco	Tho	Whi	Wil	Woo	Wor
11	Nov HAYES	1-0	Warburton	5389	10	12	8	11	7	3	2	6	4		5	9	1	
2	Dec Oxford United	0-2		6348	10	15	11	8	12	3	2	6	4		5	9	7	1

Played in game 2: D Beckford (14).

League Cup

	Date / Opponent	Res	Scorers	Att	Bur	Col	Gra	Nor	OSh	Pee	Sam	Smi	Tho	Whi	Wil	Woo	Wor
15	Aug West Bromwich Albion	1-1	Colkin	6489	10	11	9	2	4	7	6	3	12	5	8	1	
22	WEST BROMWICH ALBION	2-4	Burns(p), Peer	7083	10	11	9	2	4	7	6	3	12	5	14	8	1

A.W.S.

	Date / Opponent	Res	Scorers	Att	Ald	Bur	Col	Gib	Hug	Hun	Mad	Nor	OSh	Pee	Sam	Tur	War	Whi	Wil	Woo	Wor
16	Oct Peterborough Utd	0-0		3045		10	11	7			3	2	8			4	6	5	9	1	
8	Nov PLYMOUTH ARGYLE	1-0	Burns	2109	14	10	11	7				3	8	2	12	4	6	5	9	8	1
28	Cardiff City	2-1	Hunter, Grayson	1450	12	10	7			10		2	7	3		6	4	11	5	9	8	1
9	Jan Hereford United	0-1		2909		10	7			8		2	6	4	9	3		14	5	11	12	1

Played in game 1: D Beckford (12) and 3: (14).

1996/97 4th promoted in Division 3

#	Dt	Match	Res	Scorers	Att	Burns C	Clarkson I	Colkin L	Cooper M	Frain J	Gayle J	Gibb A	Grayson N	Hunter R	Kirby R	Lee C	Lyne N	Maddison L	Martin D	O'Shea D	Parrish S	Peer D	Rennie D	Rush M	Sampson I	Smart A	Stant P	Turley W	White J	Woodman A	Warner M	Warburton R
1	17	Aug Wigan Athletic	1-2	Cooper	2499	7	2		9			15	10	11				14		3	6		8	5	4				12	1		
2	24	MANSFIELD town	3-0	Rennie, Hunter, Cooper	4162	7	2		9					11		12				3	4	14	8	6	5				10	1		
3	28	TORQUAY UNITED	1-1	Rennie	4123	7	2	14	9			12	11	8				15		3	4		10	6	5					1		
4	31	Scarborough	1-1	Lee	2520	7	2		9				11	12		4		15		3			8	6	5				10	1	14	
5	7	Sep Barnet	1-1	Lee	2982		2		9			12	7	11		8				3	4		10	6	5				14	1		
6	10	LEYTON ORIENT	0-1		3994	9	2					14	3	11	7					4	8	15		6	5				10	1		
7	14	CAMBRIDGE UNITED	1-2	Rennie	4584	8	2	12				7		11		15				3	5	14	6		4	9			10	1		
8	21	Cardiff City	2-2	Cooper, Hunter(p)	4124		2	14	9			12		11						3	5	8	7	6	4				10	1		
9	28	BRIGHTON	3-0	Hunter(p), Lee, Gibb	4402		2		9			7	12	11		8				3	5		10		4				15	1	14	
10	1	Oct Chester City	1-2	Grayson	1791		2		9			7	12	11		8				3	5		10		4				14	1		
11	5	FULHAM	0-1		6171		2		9			7	12	11		8				3	5		10	14	6				15	1		
12	12	Exeter City	1-0	Lee	3002		2	14	9				8					3		11	10	7		6	4				12	1		5
13	15	Scunthorpe United	1-2	Sampson	2079		2		9						14	8		3		11	10	7		6	4				12	1		5
14	19	COLCHESTER UNITED	2-1	Parrish, Grayson	4119		2		9				12	8				14		3	11	7		6	4				10	1		5
15	26	DARLINGTON	3-1	Grayson, Warburton, Parrish	4123		2		9				10	15				14		3	11	7		6	4				8	1	12	5
16	29	Hartlepool United	2-0	Grayson, Parrish	1254		2		9				10					14		3	11	7		6	8	4				1	12	5
17	2	Nov Swansea City	0-1		3335		2		9				10	14				15		3	11	7		6	8	4			12	1		5
18	9	CARLISLE UNITED	1-1	Parrish	4682		2						10	9		12				3	11	7	5	8	4				14	1		6
19	19	Doncaster Rovers	2-1	Warburton, Rush	1030		2		9				10	6		12				3	11	7	15	8	4				14	1		5
20	23	ROCHDALE	2-2	Hunter, White	3836		2	15					10	6						3	11	7	12	8	4		9		14	1		5
21	30	Darlington	1-3	Cooper	2266		2		9				10	6					12	3	11	7			4		14			1	15	5
22	3	Dec HULL CITY	2-1	Stant 2(1p)	3519		2		9				12						8	3	11	7		6			10			1	11	5
23	14	Lincoln City	1-1	Rennie	2702		2		9				8	12					4	3	11	7	14	6			10			1		5
24	20	HEREFORD	1-0	Grayson	4238		2		9				12	15					4	3	11	7	14	6	8		10			1		5
25	28	Leyton Orient	1-2	Grayson	4492		2		9				8	12					4	3	11	7		6			10		14	1		5
26	28	BARNET	2-0	Sampson, Cooper	5060		2		9				8	12					3		11	7		6	4		10			1		5
27	1	Jan CARDIFF CITY	4-0	Warburton, (og), Cooper, Grayson	4416		2		9				8	12					14	3	6	11	7				10		15	1		5
28	18	CHESTER CITY	5-1	Rush, Cooper, Grayson, Sampson, Warburton	4434		2		9				8						3		11	7	12	6	10		4		14	1		5
29	25	HARTLEPOOL	3-0	Grayson(3)	5093		2		9	7			8	14					3		11		12	6	10		4		15	1		5
30	1	Feb Carlisle	1-2	Lee	5271		2		9	7			8	15						3	11		12	6	4					1		5
31	8	SWANSEA CITY	1-2	Lee	6178		2		9	11			8						15	3	7		12	14	6		10		14	1		5
32	15	Rochdale	1-1		1988		12	10	9	6				2				7		11	15	3	8	4					14			5
33	22	DONCASTER ROVERS	2-0	Cooper, Grayson	4577		2		9	8	14	7	10	15				11		3				6	4						12	5
34	1	Mar Hull City	1-1	(og)	3495		2		9	14	12	10	8						3	11		7		6	4							5
35	4	Brighton	1-2	Peer	4943		2		9	15		10	8						3	11		7	12	6	4						14	5
36	8	Hereford	2-1	Parrish, Peer	8043		2		9	14	15	10	8	11					3		7	12	6		4			1				5
37	15	LINCOLN CITY	1-1	Hunter(p)	5266		2	15	9				8	11					3	14	7			6	4				10	1	12	5
38	22	Mansfield Town	0-1		2596		2	3	9				8	11							7	10	6		4				12	1		5
39	29	WIGAN ATHLETIC	0-1		5914		2	12	3	9	14	8	11								7			6	4				10	1		5
40	31	Torquay United	2-1	Parrish, Sampson	2336		2			3	9		8	11		12			14		7			6	4				10	1		5
41	5	Apr SCARBOROUGH	1-0	Hunter(p)	4854		2	10	3	9	14	8		11						15	7	12		6	4					1		5
42	8	Cambridge City	0-0		4412		2	14	3	9			11	8							12	7		6			10			1		5
43	12	Fulham	1-0	White	11419		2	8	3	9			8	11					14		12	7		6			10			1		5
44	19	EXETER CITY	4-1	Parrish, Cooper(2), Gayle	6400		2	7	3	9			10								12	11		6	4				9	1		5
45	26	Colchester United	0-0		5956		2	8	7	9	14	12	11						3					6	4				10	1		5
46	3	May SCUNTHORPE UNITED	1-0	Parrish	6828		2	10	3	9	12	8	11								7	14	6							1		5

| | | | | | Apps | 6 | 45 | 6 | 41 | 13 | 13 | 18 | 40 | 36 | 1 | 29 | 1 | 34 | 12 | 35 | 39 | 21 | 43 | 14 | 43 | 1 | 5 | 1 | 32 | 45 | 9 | 35 |
| | | | | | Goals | | | 10 | 1 | 1 | 12 | 6 | | 7 | | | | | | 8 | 1 | 4 | 3 | 4 | | 2 | | | 2 | | | 4 |

Played in game 6: Thompson(12) Two own goals

F.A. Cup

						Burns C	Clarkson I	Colkin L	Cooper M	Frain J	Gayle J	Gibb A	Grayson N	Hunter R	Kirby R	Lee C	Lyne N	Maddison L	Martin D	O'Shea D	Parrish S	Peer D	Rennie D	Rush M	Sampson I	Smart A	Stant P	Turley W	White J	Woodman A	Warner M	Warburton R
17	Nov WATFORD	0-1			7342		2	12	9				10	6				14		3	11	7			4				8	1	15	5

League Cup

20	Aug Cardiff City	0-1			2294	7	2	12	9			8	10	11						3	6	15		5	4				14	1		
3	Sep CARDIFF CITY	2-0	Lee(2)		3567		2	12	9			7	3	11		8		15		4	10			6	5				14	1		
18	Stoke City	0-1			6093		2	14				12	7	11						3	4	9	8	6					10	1		
24	STOKE CITY	1-2	(og)		5088		2	11	9				15	10						3	5	8	14	6	4				12	1		

A.W.S.

4	Feb LUTON TOWN	1-0	Rush		4201		2	15		7			8			9			3	12		14	6	10	4					1	11	5
11	Plymouth Argyle	2-0	Martin, Gayle		1499		2			3	9		8						6	11	7				4				10	1		5
18	Colchester	1-2	Martin		3975		2	12		11	9		4	10					3	7			8		6				14	1		5

Play-offs

11	May Cardiff	1-0	Parrish		11369		2	10	3	9			8	11					12		7	14	6		4					1		5
14	CARDIFF	3-2	Sampson, Warburton, Gayle		7302		2			3	9	12	8	11					15		7	14	6						10	1		5
24	Swansea	1-0	Frain		46804		2			3	9		8	11					10		7	12	6						14	1		5

1996/97 SEASON

Back: Casey(Physio), Frain, Rennie, Colkin, Maddison, Lee, Devito, White, Godden(Goalkeeper Coach)

Middle: Curtis(Youth Team), Warner, Cooper, Peer, Gayle, Turley, Woodman, Sampson, Martin, Parrish, Clarkson, Broadhurst(Coach/Scout)

Front: Atkins(Manager), Gibb, Hunter, Grayson, Warburton, O'Shea, Boxford, Thompson(Res. Coach)

ADVANCED SUBSCRIBERS

Dustine Grande, Kingsthorpe

Georgia Grande, Kingsthorpe

Geoff Best, Upton

Pete Norton, Northamtpon

Dave Waldren, Northampton

John Harley, Earl Shilton

Keith Rimmington, Northampton

Richard Rimmington, Salisbury

Rowland Jordan

Graham & Andrew Onley

John Wallington, Kislingbury

Patrick McNeela, Wellingborough

Tommy O'Reilly, Anthony O'Reilly

Ian Cooper, Saudi Arabia

Scott Hayman, Abington, Northampton

Eric Fisher

Robert Spick, Duston, Northampton

Tony Wilson

Colin Eldred, Pitsford

Jackie Warner, Northampton

Matt Facer, Northampton

John Tigges, Piddington, Northants

Heath Osborn, Lakeside, California

Ian Stewart, West Hunsbury

Dave Drage, Birmingham

John White

The Smith Family, Moulton

Mark Herbert, Roselands, Northampton

David West

Stephen Hollowell, Northampton

John Clayton, Rushden

Robert Cook, Rugby

Roger Averill, Earls Barton

Andrew J. Charter

Abraham Anstruther

Bob Murray, Northampton

Iain Paterson, Wootton

M.J. Brown, Northampton

Russell Bott, Broughton Astley

Mary Bott, Rugby

Glen Powell, Northampton

Liam James Taylor

Mark Crane, Horsham, Sussex

Jim Powell, Eastbourne

R.Sturgen, Rushden

Steven York, Kingsthorpe, Northampton

Benjamin Markland, Ecton Brook

Michael Norris, Highlands, Northampton

David Norris, Highlands, Northampton

Graham Wills, Daventry

David Nikel, West Haddon

Alexander Pinfold, Northampton

Peter Watson, Wellingborough

Mark Howes, Northampton

Richard Green, Pattishall, Northants

Michael Green, Newtown, Powys

Andy Roberts

Janet York, NTFC

Nick Ancel, NTFC

Philip Edward Curtis, Northampton

Robert Dunkley, Harpenden, Hertfordshire

Gavin Morgan, Byfield, Northants

Steven Walsh, Parklands, Northampton

Trevor Liddle, Hemel Hempstead

Colin Wood, Northampton

Clive Stock, Wimborne, Dorset

Ray and Deryth Clements

Barry Stonhill, Northampton

Gerald Pitt, Northampton

Eric Dix, Northampton

Neil Dix, Northampton

Eyre Family, Earls Barton

Alan Frampton

John Frampton

Ben & Amy Rodhouse

Graham Rodhouse, Veldhoven, Holland

Jason Rodhouse, Daventry, Northants

Emma Tack, Parklands, Northampton

Peter Isham, Buckingham

Richard Eason, Moulton, Northampton

Stephen Goddard, Staverton Daventry

Richard Greenwood, Daventry, Northants

McGlasham Family, Great Billing

Dave Thompson, Corby

D.G. Church, Lincoln

David Mead

Clive Reece

Bob Russell, Draughton Village

David Kerr, Northampton

Robert Stamp, Moulton

Paul Richardson, Geddington

John Watson, Duston, Northampton

Barry & Liz. Taylor, Stanwick

Katrina Wells, Leighton Buzzard

Tony Ingram, Spinney Hill

Dale McCann, Rothwell

Simon Oliver, Duston, Northampton

Ann & Ivor Skeats, Haversham

D.J. Miller, Northampton

Les Hawkins, Brixworth, Northampton

Derrick Pegg, Jenny Lea

Gavin Jones

Mike Taylor, Weston Favell

Nigel Steele

Andrew Dearn, Wellingborough

Adam Roy Johnson, Duston

Roger Sawford, Abington, Northampton

Jamie McDonald, East Hunsbury

Miss. Lynn (Griffin) Kennedy

Edwin Lane, Kieran Lane

Chris, Jessica, Abbey, Smith

S.J. Bence, Raunds

John Cosford, Bramcote, Nottingham

Simon Halls, Lordswood, Kent

ADVANCED SUBSCRIBERS

John & Dianne Ward

Derek Gray, Kettering

Chris Gedge, Old Stratford

Ralph, Rory, Sadie

Alan Ringrose, East Kilbride

A.M. George, Rushden

Alan Watson, Rushden

Graeme Andrew Scott, Irchester

Martyn Dearden, Midhurst, Sussex

John Humphrey, Roade

Rob Duncan, Leamington Spa

Trevor Lugg, Kingsthorpe

R.M. Harris, The Headlands

Ian Warren, Derby

Robert Osborne, Abingdon, Oxon

Stephen R. Haynes, Northampton

Steve Albert, Delapre, Northampton

John Wright, Sunnybank, Australia

John Hunt, Cogenhoe

Kevin Gamble, Kingsthorpe

James Frampton

Chris Jackson, Christmas 1997

John, Sylvia, Carl - Duston

Graham Beesley

Brian, Mark Roberts - Chelmsford

Peter Stuart, Robertson

John Rowe, Northampton

Glenys, Derrick Holden, Northampton

Sandra Green, Northampton

Rod Kilsby, Taunton, Somerset

Keith Onley

Paul James Gibbs

Raymond Shaw

G.T. Allman

Peter Cogle, Aberdeen

Graham Spackman

David Keats, Thornton Heath

Steve Emms, Evesham

Dave Parine, Warlingham

Keith Coburn

John Motson

George Painter, Castle Cary

B.H. Standish, Banbury

David Jowett

Martin Cripps, Sussex

Moira and Frederick Furness

Derek Hyde

Gordon Macey (Q.P.R.Historian)

John Stephen Holbrook

Ray Bickel

K.J. Bond, Swindon

Jonny Stokkeland, Kvinesdal, Norway

A.H. Atkins, Ontario, Canada

Phil Hollow

Duncan Watt, Sleaford

Phil Newport, Sutton Coldfield

David J. Godfrey

Diarmuid Murphy

Paul Johnson, Birmingham City

Philip H. Whitehead

Dave Windross, York City

S.J. Hester

John Coyle

Dave McPherson, Colchester

Geoffrey Wright

Alan Pennington, Stoke City

Michael Campbell, Kingsbury

Stewart Davidson, Paisley

Richard Wells

A. & J.A. Waterman

Chris Marsh, Chesterfield

Colin Cameron, Sidcup, Kent

Peter Pickup Programmes, Pudsey

Brian Tabner

Philip Pike

David Woods (Bristol Babe)

David and Matthew Fleckney

Jonathan Hall

Richard Lane, Norwell, Notts.

Roger Wash, Newmarket

Örjan Hansson

John R. Orton

Terry Frost

Peter Buckley

Peter Baxter

Alan Hindley

Christer Svensson

Richard Stocken

A.N.Other

Michael John Griffin

Richard Shore

Mick McConkey, Luton, Beds

Trond Isaksen, Norway

B. Park, London

I. Strömberg, V Frölunda, Sweden

Robert M. Smith

D. and G. Phillips

John Rawnsley

Stephen Kieran Byrne

Fred Lee, Plymouth Argyle

Martin Simons, Belgium

Raymond Koerhuis, Netherlands

Terry Luckett, Welwyn, Herts

Willy Østby, Norway

Bob Lilliman

J.Ringrose

S.Metcalfe

Arran and Nicholas Matthews

YORE PUBLICATIONS

We specialise in books normally of an historic nature, especially fully detailed and well illustrated Football League club histories (over twenty to date). Also those with a diverse appeal, such as the *'Rejected F.C.'* series (compendium histories of the former Football League and Scottish League clubs, each in three volumes), *'The Code War'* (The history of football in respect of its splitting into the three 'codes'), *'Theatre of Dreams - The History of Old Trafford'*, *'The Little Red Book of Chinese Football'* (A history of football in the area, plus the Author's football travels in China and Hong Kong), plus non-League football, notably the *'Gone But Not Forgotten'* series (each booklet issued every six months, covering the histories of former grounds and clubs).

We publish a free newsletter three times per year.
For your first copy please send a S.A.E. to:

YORE PUBLICATIONS,
12 The Furrows, Harefield, Middlesex, UB9 6AT